THE PAPERS OF

THOMAS JEFFERSON

JAMES P. McCLURE
GENERAL EDITOR

THE PAPERS OF

Thomas Jefferson

Volume 46
9 March to 5 July 1805

JAMES P. McCLURE, EDITOR

TOM DOWNEY, MARTHA J. KING, AND
W. BLAND WHITLEY, SENIOR EDITORS

JAMES ALEXANDER DUN, ANDREW J. B. FAGAL,
AND MERRY ELLEN SCOFIELD, ASSOCIATE EDITORS

CHRISTINA R. CARRICK, ASSISTANT EDITOR

LINNY SCHENCK, EDITORIAL ASSOCIATE

ALISON E. DOLBIER, RESEARCH ASSOCIATE

PRINCETON AND OXFORD
PRINCETON UNIVERSITY PRESS
2022

Published by Princeton University Press, 41 William Street,
Princeton, New Jersey 08540
In The United Kingdom:
Princeton University Press,
99 Banbury Road, Oxford OX2 6JX

ISBN 9780691230740

Library of Congress Number: 50-7486

This book has been composed in Monticello

Princeton University Press books are printed on
acid-free paper and meet the guidelines for permanence
and durability of the Committee on Production
Guidelines for Book Longevity of the
Council on Library Resources

Printed in the United States of America

DEDICATED TO THE MEMORY OF

ADOLPH S. OCHS

PUBLISHER OF THE NEW YORK TIMES

1896-1935

WHO BY THE EXAMPLE OF A RESPONSIBLE

PRESS ENLARGED AND FORTIFIED

THE JEFFERSONIAN CONCEPT

OF A FREE PRESS

ADVISORY COMMITTEE

CONSULTANTS

SUPPORTERS

THIS EDITION was made possible by an initial grant of $200,000 from the New York Times Company to Princeton University. Contributions from many foundations and individuals have sustained the endeavor since then. For their unprecedented generous support, we are also indebted to the Princeton University History Department and Christopher L. Eisgruber, president of the university. The Packard Humanities Institute (through Founding Fathers Papers, Inc.), the National Endowment for the Humanities, and the National Historical Publications and Records Commission have been crucial to progress on the edition. Support has come from the Florence Gould Foundation, the National Trust for the Humanities and the Cinco Hermanos Fund, the New York Times Company Foundation, the Dyson Foundation, the Andrew W. Mellon Foundation, and the Pew Charitable Trusts. Other contributors have been the Ford Foundation, the Lyn and Norman Lear Foundation, the Lucius N. Littauer Foundation, the Charlotte Palmer Phillips Foundation, the L. J. Skaggs and Mary C. Skaggs Foundation, the John Ben Snow Memorial Trust, Time, Inc., Robert C. Baron, B. Batmanghelidj, David K. E. Bruce, and James Russell Wiggins. Benefactions from a greatly expanded roster of dedicated individuals have underwritten the volumes: Sara and James Adler, Helen and Peter Bing, Diane and John Cooke, Judy and Carl Ferenbach III, Mary-Love and William Harman, Frederick P. and Mary Buford Hitz, Governor Thomas H. Kean, Ruth and Sidney Lapidus, Lisa and Willem Mesdag, Tim and Lisa Robertson, Ann and Andrew C. Rose, Sara Lee and Axel Schupf, the Sulzberger family through the Hillandale Foundation, Richard W. Thaler, Tad and Sue Thompson, the Wendt Family Charitable Foundation, and Susan and John O. Wynne. For their vision and extraordinary efforts to provide for this edition, we owe special thanks to John S. Dyson, Governor Kean, H. F. Lenfest and the Lenfest Foundation, Rebecca Rimel, and Jack Rosenthal.

FOREWORD

TIME PLAYED its tricks in 1805. Crucial events occurred far from Washington, but distance and limitations of communication meant that they were not known to Jefferson and others in his administration until months later. Meriwether Lewis and William Clark wrote from Fort Mandan in the first week of April, before setting out up the Missouri River after the winter layover. Jefferson did not receive their reports until mid-July. It would be more than a year after that, when they arrived in St. Louis in September 1806 on their return journey from the Pacific, before he heard directly from them again.

Similarly, occurrences in the Mediterranean in the spring would be known only later. In April, William Eaton coordinated an attack that included the U.S. Navy and marines and captured the port of Derna. Early in June, as Eaton prepared to advance the campaign against the city of Tripoli, Tobias Lear negotiated terms of peace with Pasha Yusuf Qaramanli and ended the war. No one in the United States knew anything of those extraordinary events until September.

Meanwhile the past came haunting, in the form of what Jefferson termed, in a letter to Albert Gallatin on 21 June, "the revival of antient slanders." During the winter Federalists in Massachusetts had brought up a long list of charges against Jefferson, among them that as governor of Virginia he "abandoned his post" when the British invaded the state early in 1781; that prior to his marriage in 1772, he had attempted to seduce Elizabeth Moore Walker, the wife of a friend; that he lacked religious faith; that he had sought to use government resources to facilitate Thomas Paine's return to the United States; that he wanted to build expensive dry docks and employ ineffective gunboats rather than enlarge the deepwater navy; that he had provided financial support to the unscrupulous journalist James Thomson Callender (see the letter of Isaac Story of 8 Feb. 1805 in the previous volume). Most of the accusations had been raised several years earlier by Callender. They gained reinforcement at the end of May when the Boston *Repertory* published a letter from a Virginian, Thomas Turner, in support of the charges. Jefferson took action in response to two of the allegations. To refute the claims regarding his conduct in 1781, he sent Gallatin a detailed recounting of the events. The assertions regarding Elizabeth Walker he strove to manage, not rebut, circulating among "particular friends" an admission "that when young & single I offered love to a handsome lady" (see his letter to Robert Smith, 1 July).

Other charges he ignored. They included one "of having taken to his bosom a '*sable damsel*'" (Vol. 45:472n). Although Jefferson did not acknowledge that allegation, his relationship with Sally Hemings did not go unnoticed: on 28 Mch. a writer using the name Antoine Vosse closed a brief letter attacking the president "With Compliments to Sally."

Jefferson also faced the immediate demands of the present. Increasingly reliant on short-term bank loans, he began in March to manage his personal finances on a regular basis. He did this by sitting down each month to note the amounts he could draw on and then determining which demands for payment he would be able to cover (see Notes on Personal Finance at 10 Mch., 15 Mch., two at 4 May, two at 4 June, and 5 July; we have not found one from April). These notes were for his own use, and while they have similarities, he did not fix on a standard form.

The Eighth Congress completed its work at the end of a long day on Sunday, 3 Mch., the evening before Jefferson's second inauguration. The first session of the Ninth Congress did not convene until late in the calendar year. The president went home to Monticello in mid-March, stayed there almost a month, and was back in Washington on 17 Apr. Even with Congress adjourned and no legislative activity, the chief magistrate had responsibilities to fulfill. He granted six pardons in response to petitions he received that spring for crimes committed in the federal district. One of the convictions was for assault, one for larceny, two for keeping disorderly houses; in one case a woman, Jane McGraw, was found guilty of violating the terms of her liquor license by selling a quantity of spirits of less than a pint. In another case a Black man, known only by his first name, Charles, had been illegally classified as a slave and as a result received a death sentence on a charge of breaking and entering a house with an intent to steal. Jefferson issued a pardon in the case and ordered "it's safe & speedy transmission to the marshal" (see Petition for Charles at 30 Mch.). The president also issued a pardon in a case of a violation of the revenue laws. In each instance, his action was in response to attestations of the person's good character, but more important were certifications by the federal judges and U.S. attorneys who tried the case that compassion was in order. Jefferson did not grant clemency before trial to Robert Ware Peacock, a prominent and well-connected attorney charged with passing bogus foreign bills of exchange. The judges and attorneys in the case "declare they can offer no circumstance justifying an immediate pardon," Jefferson wrote to John P. Van Ness on 12 Mch. He deemed that "to grant it in such a case would be not a mitigation of the severity of the law where it's letter does what it's spirit did not mean, & for which purpose the power of pardon is confided to the Executive, but it would be to suspend the intended operations of the law, and to leave the nation exposed to unrestrained wrong." Peacock took relief into his own hands, breaking out of jail and fleeing U.S. jurisdiction with his supportive wife, Eliza Green Peacock, who had written several appeals to the president on her husband's behalf.

In foreign affairs, Jefferson devoted time and attention to learning and thinking about the southern plains west of the Mississippi River, where the new territories of the United States met those controlled by Spain. From information sent by Dr. John Sibley, a U.S. Indian agent who lived at Natchitoches, Jefferson made long, detailed sets of notes on Native American tribes, Spanish and French colonial settlements, and geography. He wrote to William C. C. Claiborne, the governor of Orleans Territory, on 26 May in hopes that Claiborne could obtain permission from Spanish authorities for a U.S. exploration along the Red River. In the president's view, "as we have to settle a boundary with Spain to the Westward they cannot expect that we will go blindfold into the business. both parties ought to be free to make surveys of experiment preparatory to settlement, and each having a certain claim to the country must have equal right to procure the information necessary for elucidating their right." To James Bowdoin, who was about to embark from the United States as the new minister to Spain, Jefferson wrote on 27 Apr. that it was "our most earnest desire" to be "of a peaceable & friendly character," and "had Spain met us with the same dispositions, our idea was that her existence in this hemisphere & ours, should have rested on the same bottom; should have swam or sunk together." Unfortunately, however, "she has met our advances with jealousy, secret malice, and ill faith." Therefore "our patience under this unworthy return of disposition is now on it's last trial."

In June news came that the *Huntress*, a chartered ship carrying stores for the squadron in the Mediterranean, had been captured by a Spanish privateer. There was a prospect that the captors would destroy the papers identifying the ship as in the service of a neutral nation and have the vessel and its cargo declared a lawful prize in some West Indian port. Before that could happen, a British ship captured the *Huntress*, which would in time be released by a British admiralty court. Although the stores ship was ultimately recovered, the incident underscored the threat posed to American shipping by privateers operating from ports in the West Indies.

A statute "for the more effectual preservation of peace in the ports and harbors of the United States, and in the waters under their jurisdiction," which Jefferson had drafted and Congress passed at the end of the session just before adjournment, appeared to offer a means of giving American merchant vessels some protection against privateers. The act empowered federal, state, and local authorities to take action if anyone on a foreign warship in an American port or on its territorial waters committed a crime or breach of the peace. Early in July, Jefferson drew up a plan for regular offshore patrols by armed U.S. vessels.

In a decision of enormous potential importance for his private affairs, Jefferson resolved to find a replacement for Gabriel Lilly, his manager at Monticello. As Jefferson wrote to his son-in-law Thomas Mann Randolph, his friend Wilson Cary Nicholas, and his neighbor John Strode, all on 5 June, he thought that Lilly, although not well educated, was good at taking care of things during Jefferson's absences, and "obliged as I am to abandon every thing to him, it is all-important to have one who may be confided in." Yet he felt he must replace Lilly, who insisted that he needed a two-thirds increase in compensation, from £60 to £100 Virginia currency.

ACKNOWLEDGMENTS

Many individuals have given the Editors the benefit of their aid in the preparation of this volume, and we offer them our thanks. At Princeton, we are grateful to Michael D. Gordin, Judith Hanson, and Debora Macy in the Department of History; in the libraries, Anne E. Jarvis, Colleen M. Burlingham, Deborah T. Paparone, Elaine Russian, and Anuradha Vedantham; in the Office of the Dean of the Faculty, Associate Dean Karen B. Haskin; Tim Aultom, Steven Semenuk, and Angela Ward in the Office of the Vice President for Finance and Treasurer; Kristen Hubbard and Maureen Thompson-Siegel in the Office of Research and Project Administration; and Professor William C. Jordan for assistance with language translations. Jason Bush, Paul Hayslett, and Allan Orsnes of IDM skillfully provide technical support. Our collaborative partners at Princeton University Press have our deepest admiration and appreciation, including Christie Henry, Eric Crahan, and Lauren Lepow; we rely on the remarkable contributions of Carmina Alvarez-Gaffin, Meghan Kanabay, Dimitri Karetnikov, and Erin Suydam. We are grateful to Bob Bartleson of IPS and his colleagues, especially Carol Pierson, for carefully and consistently handling the composition of the volumes. At the University of Virginia Press, we are indebted to David Sewell and Patricia Searl. Research assistant Abbie Minard performed a variety of essential tasks. We owe much to the skill of Gretchen Oberfranc in reading each volume. We are indebted to Lucia C. Stanton for sharing her wisdom and knowledge and to Alfred L. Bush for assistance, particularly with our illustrations. For special assistance on this volume, we appreciate the help of Sabina Beauchard, formerly of the Massachusetts Historical Society; Mariam Touba, the New-York Historical Society; and, for illustrations, Tabitha Pryor Corradi and John McKee, Thomas Jefferson Foundation at Monticello; Dan Hinchen and Hannah Elder, Massachusetts Historical Society; Erin Beasley, Smithsonian National Portrait Gallery; Britt Bowen, Harvard Art Museums; Tricia Pyne and Alison Foley, Associated Archives at St. Mary's Seminary & University, Baltimore; Sr. Mada-Anne Gell, Georgetown Visitation Monastery; and Suzanne Krebsbach, independent scholar.

We wish to thank Darrell Meadows and Christopher Eck of the National Historical Publications and Records Commission; Jason Boffetti and Lydia Medici of the National Endowment for the Humanities; Julie Miller and her colleagues in the Manuscript Division of the Library of Congress; Peter Drummey, Anna Clutterbuck-Cook,

Elaine Heavey, and Nancy Heywood of the Massachusetts Historical Society; Anna Berkes and Endrina Tay in the library of the Thomas Jefferson Foundation at Monticello; Molly Kodner of the Missouri History Museum Library and Research Center; Brenda Gunn, Anne Causey, Christina Deane, and Regina Rush at the University of Virginia Library; Jay Gaidmore of Swem Library at the College of William and Mary; John Deal and Brent Tarter of the Library of Virginia; Paige Newman of the Virginia Historical Society; Charles M. Harris of the Papers of William Thornton; John C. Van Horne; the staffs of the American Philosophical Society, the Huntington Library, the Gilder Lehrman Institute of American History, the New-York Historical Society, and the American Antiquarian Society; and our friends and fellow editors at the Thomas Jefferson Retirement Series at Monticello, the Adams Papers at the Massachusetts Historical Society, the Papers of James Madison and the Papers of George Washington at the University of Virginia, the Papers of Benjamin Franklin at Yale University, and the James Monroe Papers at the University of Mary Washington.

EDITORIAL METHOD AND APPARATUS

1. RENDERING THE TEXT

Julian P. Boyd eloquently set forth a comprehensive editorial policy in Volume 1 of *The Papers of Thomas Jefferson*. Adopting what he described as a "middle course" for rendering eighteenth-century handwritten materials into print, Boyd set the standards for modern historical editing. His successors, Charles T. Cullen and John Catanzariti, reaffirmed Boyd's high standards. At the same time, they made changes in textual policy and editorial apparatus as they deemed appropriate. For Boyd's policy and subsequent modifications to it, readers are encouraged to consult Vol. 1:xxix-xxxviii; Vol. 22:vii-xi; and Vol. 24:vii-viii.

The revised, more literal textual method, which appeared for the first time in Volume 30, adheres to the following guidelines: <u>Abbreviations</u> will be retained as written. Where the meaning is sufficiently unclear to require editorial intervention, the expansion will be given in the explanatory annotation. <u>Capitalization</u> will follow the usage of the writer. Because the line between uppercase and lowercase letters can be a very fine and fluctuating one, when it is impossible to make an absolute determination of the author's intention, we will adopt modern usage. Jefferson rarely began his sentences with an uppercase letter, and we conform to his usage. <u>Punctuation</u> will be retained as written and double marks of punctuation, such as a period followed by a dash, will be allowed to stand. Misspellings or so-called slips of the pen will be allowed to stand or will be recorded in a subjoined textual note.

English translations or translation summaries will be supplied for foreign-language documents. In some instances, when documents are lengthy and not especially pertinent to Jefferson's concerns or if our edition's typography cannot adequately represent the script of a language, we will provide only a summary in English. In most cases we will print in full the text in its original language and also provide a full English translation. If a contemporary translation that Jefferson made or would have used is extant, we may print it in lieu of a modern translation. Our own translations are designed to provide a basic readable English text for the modern user rather than to preserve all aspects of the original diction and language.

2. *TEXTUAL DEVICES*

The following devices are employed throughout the work to clarify the presentation of the text.

[. . .] Text missing and not conjecturable.
[ ] Number or part of a number missing or illegible.
[roman] Conjectural reading for missing or illegible matter. A question mark follows when the reading is doubtful.
[*italic*] Editorial comment inserted in the text.
<*italic*> Matter deleted in the MS but restored in our text.

3. *DESCRIPTIVE SYMBOLS*

The following symbols are employed throughout the work to describe the various kinds of manuscript originals. When a series of versions is recorded, the first to be recorded is the version used for the printed text.

Dft draft (usually a composition or rough draft; later drafts, when identifiable as such, are designated "2d Dft," &c.)
Dupl duplicate
MS manuscript (arbitrarily applied to most documents other than letters)
N note, notes (memoranda, fragments, &c.)
PoC polygraph copy
PrC press copy
Quad quadruplicate
RC recipient's copy
SC stylograph copy
Tripl triplicate

All manuscripts of the above types are assumed to be in the hand of the author of the document to which the descriptive symbol pertains. If not, that fact is stated. On the other hand, the following types of manuscripts are assumed *not* to be in the hand of the author, and exceptions will be noted:

FC file copy (applied to all contemporary copies retained by the author or his agents)
Lb letterbook (ordinarily used with FC and Tr to denote texts copied into bound volumes)
Tr transcript (applied to all contemporary and later copies except file copies; period of transcription, unless clear by implication, will be given when known)

4. LOCATION SYMBOLS

The locations of documents printed in this edition from originals in private hands and from printed sources are recorded in self-explanatory form in the descriptive note following each document. The locations of documents printed from originals held by public and private institutions in the United States are recorded by means of the symbols used in the National Union Catalog in the Library of Congress; an explanation of how these symbols are formed is given in Vol. 1:xl. The symbols DLC and MHi by themselves stand for the collections of Jefferson Papers proper in these repositories; when texts are drawn from other collections held by these two institutions, the names of those collections will be added. Location symbols for documents held by institutions outside the United States are given in a subjoined list.

CSmH	The Huntington Library, San Marino, California
DLC	Library of Congress
G-Ar	Georgia State Department of Archives and History, Atlanta
ICN	Newberry Library, Chicago
LU-Ar	Louisiana State University, Department of Archives and Manuscripts, Baton Rouge
MB	Boston Public Library
MBU	Boston University Libraries' Howard Gotlieb Archival Research Center
MH	Harvard University Library, Cambridge, Massachusetts
MHi	Massachusetts Historical Society, Boston
MdHi	Maryland Historical Society, Baltimore
MeB	Bowdoin College Library, Brunswick, Maine
MnHi	Minnesota Historical Society, St. Paul
MoSHi	Missouri History Museum Library and Research Center, St. Louis
Ms-Ar	Mississippi Department of Archives and History, Jackson
NHi	New-York Historical Society, New York City
NN	New York Public Library
NNC	Columbia University Library, New York City
NNMus	Museum of the City of New York
NNPM	Pierpont Morgan Library, New York City
NcD-MC	Duke University, Medical Center, Durham
NhPoS	Strawbery Banke, Portsmouth, New Hampshire
NjGbS	Rowan University (formerly Glassboro State College), New Jersey

NjMoHP	Morristown National Historical Park, New Jersey
NjP	Princeton University, New Jersey
OClWHi	Western Reserve Historical Society, Cleveland, Ohio
PHi	Historical Society of Pennsylvania, Philadelphia
PPAmP	American Philosophical Society, Philadelphia
PPRF	Rosenbach Foundation, Philadelphia
RHi	Rhode Island Historical Society, Providence
RNR	Redwood Library and Athenaeum, Newport, Rhode Island
TxU	University of Texas, Austin
Vi	Library of Virginia, Richmond
ViU	University of Virginia, Charlottesville
ViW	College of William and Mary, Williamsburg, Virginia

5. *NATIONAL ARCHIVES DESIGNATIONS*

Documents in the National Archives have the location symbol DNA, with identifications of record groups and series as follows:

RG 15	Revolutionary War Pension and Bounty-Land Warrant Application Files	
RG 26	Records of the United States Coast Guard	
RG 29	Records of the Bureau of Census	
RG 42	Records of the Public Buildings and Public Parks of the National Capital	
	LRDLS	Letters Received and Drafts of Letters Sent
RG 45	Naval Records Collection of the Office of Naval Records and Library	
	LSG	Letters Sent Concerning the Building of Naval Gunboats
	LSO	Letters Sent to Officers
	LSP	Letters Sent to the President
	MLR	Misc. Letters Received
	MLS	Misc. Letters Sent
RG 46	Records of the United States Senate	
	LPPM	Legislative Proceedings, President's Messages
RG 53	Records of the Bureau of Public Debt	
	RES	Registers, Estimates, and Statements
RG 56	General Records of the Department of the Treasury	

RG 59	General Records of the Department of State	
	AOC	Acceptances and Orders for Commissions
	CD	Consular Dispatches
	DD	Diplomatic Dispatches
	DL	Domestic Letters
	GPR	General Pardon Records
	LAR	Letters of Application and Recommendation
	MCL	Miscellaneous Commissions and Lists
	MPTPC	Misc. Permanent and Temporary Presidential Commissions
	NL	Notes from Legations
	RD	Resignations and Declinations
	TP	Territorial Papers
RG 75	Records of the Bureau of Indian Affairs	
	LSIA	Letters Sent by the Secretary of War Relating to Indian Affairs
RG 84	Records of the Foreign Service Posts of the Department of State	
	CR	Consular Records
RG 93	War Department Collection of Revolutionary War Records	
RG 94	Records of the Adjutant General's Office	
RG 107	Records of the Office of the Secretary of War	
	LRMS	Letters Received by the Secretary of War, Main Series
	LSMA	Letters Sent by the Secretary of War Relating to Military Affairs
	LSP	Letters Sent to the President
	MLS	Misc. Letters Sent
	RLRMS	Register of Letters Received, Main Series
RG 217	Records of the Accounting Officers of the Department of the Treasury	
	MTA	Misc. Treasury Accounts
RG 233	Records of the United States House of Representatives	
	PM	President's Messages

6. OTHER SYMBOLS AND ABBREVIATIONS

The following symbols and abbreviations are commonly employed in the annotation throughout the work.

Second Series The topical series to be published as part of this edition, comprising those materials which are best suited to a topical rather than a chronological arrangement (see Vol. 1:xv-xvi)

TJ Thomas Jefferson

TJ Editorial Files Photoduplicates and other editorial materials in the office of The Papers of Thomas Jefferson, Princeton University Library

TJ Papers Jefferson Papers (applied to a collection of manuscripts when the precise location of an undated, misdated, or otherwise problematic document must be furnished, and always preceded by the symbol for the institutional repository; thus "DLC: TJ Papers, 4:628-9" represents a document in the Library of Congress, Jefferson Papers, volume 4, pages 628 and 629. Citations to volumes and folio numbers of the Jefferson Papers at the Library of Congress refer to the collection as it was arranged at the time the first microfilm edition was made in 1944-45. Access to the microfilm edition of the collection as it was rearranged under the Library's Presidential Papers Program is provided by the Index to the Thomas Jefferson Papers [Washington, D.C., 1976])

RG Record Group (used in designating the location of documents in the National Archives)

SJL Jefferson's "Summary Journal of Letters" written and received for the period 11 Nov. 1783 to 25 June 1826 (in DLC: TJ Papers). This register, kept in Jefferson's hand, has been checked against the TJ Editorial Files. It is to be assumed that all outgoing letters are recorded in SJL unless there is a note to the contrary. When the date of receipt of an incoming letter is recorded in SJL, it is incorporated in the notes. Information and discrepancies revealed in SJL but not found in the letter itself are also noted. Missing letters recorded in SJL are, where possible, accounted for in the notes to documents mentioning them or in related documents. A more detailed discussion of this register and its use in this edition appears in Vol. 6:vii-x

SJPL "Summary Journal of Public Letters," an incomplete list of letters and documents written by TJ from 16 Apr. 1784 to 31 Dec. 1793, with brief summaries, in an amanuensis's hand. This is supplemented by six pages in TJ's hand, compiled at a later date, listing private and confidential memorandums and notes as well as official reports and communications by and to him as Secretary of State, 11 Oct. 1789 to 31 Dec. 1793 (in DLC: TJ Papers, Epistolary Record, 514-59 and 209-11, respectively; see

Vol. 22:ix-x). Since nearly all documents in the amanuensis's list are registered in SJL, while few in TJ's list are so recorded, it is to be assumed that all references to SJPL are to the list in TJ's hand unless there is a statement to the contrary

V Ecu

f Florin

£ Pound sterling or livre, depending upon context (in doubtful cases, a clarifying note will be given)

s Shilling or sou (also expressed as /)

d Penny or denier

ᵗᵗ Livre Tournois

₰ Per (occasionally used for pro, pre)

7. *SHORT TITLES*

The following list includes short titles of works cited frequently in this edition. Since it is impossible to anticipate all the works to be cited in abbreviated form, the list is revised from volume to volume.

ANB John A. Garraty and Mark C. Carnes, eds., *American National Biography*, New York and Oxford, 1999, 24 vols.

Annals *Annals of the Congress of the United States: The Debates and Proceedings in the Congress of the United States . . . Compiled from Authentic Materials*, Washington, D.C., Gales & Seaton, 1834-56, 42 vols. All editions are undependable and pagination varies from one printing to another. The first two volumes of the set cited here have "Compiled . . . by Joseph Gales, Senior" on the title page and bear the caption "Gales & Seatons History" on verso and "of Debates in Congress" on recto pages. The remaining volumes bear the caption "History of Congress" on both recto and verso pages. Those using the first two volumes with the latter caption will need to employ the date of the debate or the indexes of debates and speakers.

APS American Philosophical Society

ASP *American State Papers: Documents, Legislative and Executive, of the Congress of the United States*, Washington, D.C., 1832-61, 38 vols.

Bear, *Family Letters* Edwin M. Betts and James A. Bear, Jr., eds., *Family Letters of Thomas Jefferson*, Columbia, Mo., 1966

Betts, *Farm Book* Edwin M. Betts, ed., *Thomas Jefferson's Farm Book*, Princeton, 1953

Betts, *Garden Book* Edwin M. Betts, ed., *Thomas Jefferson's Garden Book, 1766-1824*, Philadelphia, 1944

Biog. Dir. Cong. *Biographical Directory of the United States Congress, 1774-1989*, Washington, D.C., 1989

Brigham, *American Newspapers* Clarence S. Brigham, *History and Bibliography of American Newspapers, 1690-1820*, Worcester, Mass., 1947, 2 vols.

Bush, *Life Portraits* Alfred L. Bush, *The Life Portraits of Thomas Jefferson*, rev. ed., Charlottesville, 1987

DAB Allen Johnson and Dumas Malone, eds., *Dictionary of American Biography*, New York, 1928-36, 20 vols.

DHSC Maeva Marcus and others, eds., *The Documentary History of the Supreme Court of the United States, 1789-1800*, New York, 1985-2007, 8 vols.

Dictionnaire *Dictionnaire de biographie française*, Paris, 1933- , 19 vols.

DNB H. C. G. Matthew and Brian Harrison, eds., *Oxford Dictionary of National Biography, In Association with The British Academy, From the Earliest Times to the Year 2000*, Oxford, 2004, 60 vols.

DSB Charles C. Gillispie, ed., *Dictionary of Scientific Biography*, New York, 1970-80, 16 vols.

DVB John T. Kneebone and others, eds., *Dictionary of Virginia Biography*, Richmond, 1998- , 3 vols.

EG Dickinson W. Adams and Ruth W. Lester, eds., *Jefferson's Extracts from the Gospels*, Princeton, 1983, *The Papers of Thomas Jefferson*, Second Series

Ford Paul Leicester Ford, ed., *The Writings of Thomas Jefferson*, Letterpress Edition, New York, 1892-99, 10 vols.

Gallatin, *Papers* Carl E. Prince and Helene E. Fineman, eds., *The Papers of Albert Gallatin*, microfilm edition in 46 reels, Philadelphia, 1969, and Supplement, Barbara B. Oberg, ed., reels 47-51, Wilmington, Del., 1985

HAW Henry A. Washington, ed., *The Writings of Thomas Jefferson*, New York, 1853-54, 9 vols.

Heitman, *Dictionary* Francis B. Heitman, comp., *Historical Register and Dictionary of the United States Army*, Washington, D.C., 1903, 2 vols.

Heitman, *Register* Francis B. Heitman, *Historical Register of Officers of the Continental Army during the War of the Revolution, April, 1775, to December, 1793*, new ed., Washington, D.C., 1914

Jackson, *Lewis and Clark* Donald Jackson, ed., *Letters of the Lewis and Clark Expedition, with Related Documents, 1783-1854*, 2d ed., Urbana, Ill., 1978

JEP *Journal of the Executive Proceedings of the Senate of the United States . . . to the Termination of the Nineteenth Congress*, Washington, D.C., 1828, 3 vols.

JHR *Journal of the House of Representatives of the United States*, Washington, D.C., 1826, 9 vols.

JS *Journal of the Senate of the United States*, Washington, D.C., 1820-21, 5 vols.

L & B Andrew A. Lipscomb and Albert E. Bergh, eds., *The Writings of Thomas Jefferson*, Washington, D.C., 1903-04, 20 vols.

Latrobe, *Correspondence* John C. Van Horne and Lee W. Formwalt, eds., *The Correspondence and Miscellaneous Papers of Benjamin Henry Latrobe*, New Haven, 1984-88, 3 vols.

LCB Douglas L. Wilson, ed., *Jefferson's Literary Commonplace Book*, Princeton, 1989, *The Papers of Thomas Jefferson*, Second Series

LECB David Thomas Konig and Michael P. Zuckert, eds., *Jefferson's Legal Commonplace Book*, Princeton, 2019, *The Papers of Thomas Jefferson*, Second Series

Leonard, *General Assembly* Cynthia Miller Leonard, comp., *The General Assembly of Virginia, July 30, 1619-January 11, 1978: A Bicentennial Register of Members*, Richmond, 1978

List of Patents *A List of Patents Granted by the United States from April 10, 1790, to December 31, 1836*, Washington, D.C., 1872

Madison, *Papers* William T. Hutchinson, Robert A. Rutland, J. C. A. Stagg, and others, eds., *The Papers of James Madison*, Chicago and Charlottesville, 1962- , 43 vols.

Sec. of State Ser., 1986- , 12 vols.

Pres. Ser., 1984-2020, 11 vols.

Ret. Ser., 2009- , 3 vols.

Malone, *Jefferson* Dumas Malone, *Jefferson and His Time*, Boston, 1948-81, 6 vols.

MB James A. Bear, Jr., and Lucia C. Stanton, eds., *Jefferson's Memorandum Books: Accounts, with Legal Records and Miscellany, 1767-1826*, Princeton, 1997, 2 vols., *The Papers of Thomas Jefferson*, Second Series

Miller, *Alexandria Artisans* T. Michael Miller, comp., *Artisans and Merchants of Alexandria, Virginia, 1780-1820*, Bowie, Md., 1991-92, 2 vols.

Miller, *Treaties* Hunter Miller, ed., *Treaties and Other International Acts of the United States of America*, Washington, D.C., 1931-48, 8 vols.

Monroe, *Papers* Daniel Preston and others, eds., *The Papers of James Monroe*, Westport, Conn., 2003- , 7 vols.

Moulton, *Journals of the Lewis & Clark Expedition* Gary E. Moulton, ed., *Journals of the Lewis & Clark Expedition*, Lincoln, Neb., 1983-2001, 13 vols.

NDBW Dudley W. Knox, ed., *Naval Documents Related to the United States Wars with the Barbary Powers*, Washington, D.C., 1939-44, 6 vols. and *Register of Officer Personnel and Ships' Data, 1801-1807*, Washington, D.C., 1945

Nichols, *Architectural Drawings* Frederick Doveton Nichols, *Thomas Jefferson's Architectural Drawings, Compiled and with Commentary and a Check List*, Charlottesville, 1978

Notes, ed. Peden Thomas Jefferson, *Notes on the State of Virginia*, ed. William Peden, Chapel Hill, 1955

OED J. A. Simpson and E. S. C. Weiner, eds., *The Oxford English Dictionary*, Oxford, 1989, 20 vols.

Peale, *Papers* Lillian B. Miller and others, eds., *The Selected Papers of Charles Willson Peale and His Family*, New Haven, 1983-2000, 5 vols. in 6

PW Wilbur S. Howell, ed., *Jefferson's Parliamentary Writings*, Princeton, 1988, *The Papers of Thomas Jefferson*, Second Series

RCHS *Records of the Columbia Historical Society*, 1895-1989

RS J. Jefferson Looney and others, eds., *The Papers of Thomas Jefferson: Retirement Series*, Princeton, 2004- , 17 vols.

Shaw-Shoemaker Ralph R. Shaw and Richard H. Shoemaker, comps., *American Bibliography: A Preliminary Checklist for 1801-1819*, New York, 1958-63, 22 vols.

Sowerby E. Millicent Sowerby, comp., *Catalogue of the Library of Thomas Jefferson*, Washington, D.C., 1952-59, 5 vols.

Stanton, *Free Some Day* Lucia Stanton, *Free Some Day: The African-American Families of Monticello*, Charlottesville, 2000

Stein, *Worlds* Susan R. Stein, *The Worlds of Thomas Jefferson at Monticello*, New York, 1993

Stets, *Postmasters* Robert J. Stets, *Postmasters & Postoffices of the United States 1782-1811*, Lake Oswego, Ore., 1994

Sturtevant, *Handbook* William C. Sturtevant, *Handbook of North American Indians*, Washington, D.C., 1978- , 15 vols.

Syrett, *Hamilton* Harold C. Syrett and others, eds., *The Papers of Alexander Hamilton*, New York, 1961-87, 27 vols.

Terr. Papers Clarence E. Carter and John Porter Bloom, eds., *The Territorial Papers of the United States*, Washington, D.C., 1934-75, 28 vols.

TJR Thomas Jefferson Randolph, ed., *Memoir, Correspondence, and Miscellanies, from the Papers of Thomas Jefferson*, Charlottesville, 1829, 4 vols.

Tulard, *Dictionnaire Napoléon* Jean Tulard, *Dictionnaire Napoléon*, Paris, 1987

Tyler, *New Handbook of Texas* Ron Tyler and others, eds., *The New Handbook of Texas*, Austin, 1996, 6 vols.

U.S. Statutes at Large Richard Peters, ed., *The Public Statutes at Large of the United States . . . 1789 to March 3, 1845*, Boston, 1855-56, 8 vols.

VMHB *Virginia Magazine of History and Biography*, 1893-

Washington, *Papers* W. W. Abbot, Dorothy Twohig, Philander D. Chase, Theodore J. Crackel, Edward C. Lengel, and others, eds., *The Papers of George Washington*, Charlottesville, 1983- , 68 vols.

Pres. Ser., 1987- , 20 vols.

Ret. Ser., 1998-99, 4 vols.

Rev. War Ser., 1985- , 28 vols.

WMQ *William and Mary Quarterly*, 1892-

CONTENTS

CONTENTS

APPENDICES

ILLUSTRATIONS

Following page 366

MEDALLION PORTRAIT BY GILBERT STUART

Gilbert Stuart painted three portraits of Jefferson, two in oil on canvas and a third one, illustrated here, on blue laid paper in mixed medium. Having been asked by the president in June 1805 to "sketch me in the Medallion form" (as Jefferson recalled to Henry Dearborn years later), Stuart executed Jefferson's profile as a grisaille, using neoclassical elements and gray tones to imitate sculpture. The technique was one that Stuart had never used before and one that he would not use again, but its success was evident. Family members considered the work to be one of the president's better portraits, and Jefferson himself wrote in 1815 that the profile was "deemed the best which has been taken of me." Several artists copied the portrait, including William Thornton and Charles Bird King. Another copy, the combined effort of William Russell Birch and engraver David Edwin, has graced this edition's title pages since Volume 1. Birch, an English enamel painter, saw the Stuart profile hanging in the President's House in October 1805 and asked permission to copy it. Jefferson approved of the result and suggested that it be engraved. Birch waited until he was sure that Stuart had no intention "to publish it himself" and then put his copy in the hands of Edwin, whose engraving abilities he judged "Superior in that line to myself." On 8 July 1812, Birch sent Jefferson a print of the 1809 engraving, writing that "I think it forms a butiful imitation of the Antiqua, and a strong Likeness of yourself Sir." That "strong Likeness" became the centerpiece for the title page of the *Papers*, designed by P. J. Conkwright for the Princeton University Press.

Jefferson gave Stuart $100 for the portrait, "probably the treble of what he would have asked." He received in return a drawing 18¾ inches by 18¾ inches that he described as having been completed in watercolor and crayon. In 1944, Fiske Kimball, director of the Philadelphia Museum of Art, argued that despite "Jefferson's careless allusions," the profile had, in fact, been created in oils. A decade later, Orland Campbell convinced the art world that Stuart had used an opaque watercolor (gouache). The Harvard Art Museums settled the debate in 2013 when a technical analysis determined that the artist had rendered the medallion portrait in an egg and oil mixture.

The Stuart profile passed from Martha Jefferson Randolph to her daughter Ellen Wayles Randolph Coolidge. It remained within the Coolidge family until 1960, when the portrait was presented to the Fogg Art Museum in the memory of Thomas Jefferson Newbold, a Jefferson descendant and Harvard graduate (Theodore E. Stebbins, Melissa Renn, Virginia Anderson, Kimberly Orcutt, and Ross Barrett, *American Paintings at Harvard*, 2 vols. [Cambridge, Mass., 2008], 1:450; Bush, *Life Portraits*, 61-3; Earle E. Coleman, "Princeton Printing before Conkwright," *Princeton University Library Chronicle*, 24 [1963], 141; Fiske Kimball, "The Life Portraits of Jefferson and Their Replicas," APS, *Proceedings*, 88 [1944], 521; RS, 5:221-2; 8:281; 10:71; 14:503, 504n; TJ to Stuart, 18 June).

Courtesy of Harvard Art Museums/Fogg Museum.

ILLUSTRATIONS

ARIADNE

This marble figure, sculpted by an unknown copyist, was given to Jefferson by James Bowdoin in 1805. It is a copy of the fountain statue acquired by Pope Julius II in 1512 for the Belvedere Courtyard of the Vatican Palace. Bowdoin viewed the original in Rome during an earlier European tour and in 1802 obtained the copy he presented to Jefferson. Bowdoin identified the reclining figure as Cleopatra, which was an accepted interpretation at the time but not the only one. The first argument against that identification appeared soon after the original statue was confiscated by Napoleon, along with other Vatican treasures, and exhibited at the Louvre. By the time it was returned to Rome in 1815, most scholars agreed that the figure was not the Egyptian queen succumbing to death from the bite of an asp, but the goddess Ariadne, abandoned by her lover Theseus as she slept. Jefferson's marble copy of Ariadne is 27 inches high by 37½ inches wide by 13½ inches deep, whereas the Vatican statue is larger than life.

The sculpture was placed on view in the entrance hall at Monticello, in front of the fireplace when it was not in use, and it remained there until Jefferson's estate was sold. On 21 July 1833, Ellen Randolph Coolidge wrote to Martha Jefferson Randolph that she had sold the last of her grandfather's art collection in hopes of providing some financial comfort for Martha. She had, though, held back the Ariadne and a few other pieces "because I thought it a pity to sacrifice them as the others were sacrificed." The sculpture stayed in the Coolidge family until 1928, when they loaned it to the Thomas Jefferson Foundation, which returned the sleeping goddess to the entrance hall. In 1993, T. Jefferson Coolidge, Jr., presented the statue as a gift to the foundation (Leonard Barkan, "The Beholder's Tale: Ancient Sculpture, Renaissance Narratives," *Representations*, 44 [1993], 138, 143, 156-7, 160-1n; Metropolitan Museum of Art, Art Institute of Chicago, and Fine Arts Museums of San Francisco, *The Vatican: Spirit and Art of Christian Rome* [New York, 1982], 180-1; Stein, *Worlds*, 69, 238; Susan E. Wegner, "Copies and Education: James Bowdoin's Painting Collection in the Life of Bowdoin College," in Bowdoin College Art Museum, *The Legacy of James Bowdoin III* [Brunswick, Me., 1994], 144, 167n; Ellen Wayles Randolph Coolidge to Martha Jefferson Randolph, 21 July 1833, in ViU: Ellen Wayles Randolph Coolidge Correspondence; James Bowdoin to TJ, 25 Mch. 1805).

Courtesy of the Thomas Jefferson Foundation at Monticello.

TRIPOLI

This detail of a 1798 British map shows the extent of Tripoli (part of what is now Libya), which stretched along the North African littoral between Tunis on the west and Egypt on the east. The city of Tripoli, on the coast to the west (left) of the large Gulf of Sidra, is across the Mediterranean Sea from Sicily. On the coast to the east of the gulf, opposite the Peloponnesian peninsula of Greece (labeled "Morea" on the map and part of the Ottoman Empire at the time), is the port of Derna. Directly by sea across the mouth of the gulf, the distance between Derna and the city of Tripoli is approximately 550 miles. In the spring of 1805, Ahmad Qaramanli, the disaffected brother of Tripoli's ruler, and U.S. envoy William Eaton led a military expedition overland from Egypt. Supported by ships, cannons, and a detachment of marines from the American squadron, their army of mercenary soldiers from North Africa and the eastern Mediterranean region captured Derna on 27 Apr. and held the city against counterattacks of troops sent by Pasha Yusuf Qaramanli. In early June, before Eaton and Ahmad Qaramanli could complete preparations for an attack on the Tripolitan capital, U.S. general consul Tobias Lear concluded a peace treaty with Yusuf Qaramanli. News of the taking of Derna and the peace agreement did not reach the United States until September. This detail is from James Rennell's map "shewing the Progress of Discovery & Improvement, in the Geography of North Africa," which depicts the African continent north of the equator and is approximately 15¾ inches by 27½ inches in size (ANB, "Eaton, William" and "Lear, Tobias"; Vol. 38:xlviii; Ahmad Qaramanli to TJ, 5 Aug.; Robert Smith to TJ, 7, 9 Sep. 1805).

Courtesy of the Library of Congress, Geography and Map Division.

ROUTE THROUGH NORTHERN VIRGINIA

These two manuscript pieces constitute a single survey of a route Jefferson traveled multiple times before and during his presidency. The survey was originally made by someone named John Triplett, probably the individual from Culpeper County, Virginia, who held the position of surveyor during the colonial era, or perhaps his son. Jefferson obtained Triplett's survey in 1792, and he shared a copy of it with Richard Fitzhugh in a letter of 26 Mch. 1805, which appears in this volume. Shown here is a copy in Jefferson's hand, originally one piece folded into six sections. The two sections showing the southwest end of the route (at left) are now detached from the other four sections (at right). The survey illustrates a southwesterly route from the ferry landing across the Potomac River from Georgetown (on the far right as shown) through parts of Fairfax, Prince William, and Fauquier Counties to Stevensburg, a settlement in Culpeper County (on the left). A table of distances at the Stevensburg end of the survey, demonstrating Jefferson's love of precision, indicates that the route measured 69¾ miles and 154 yards. Two straight lines, one connecting the ferry landing with Stevensburg and the other connecting the landing to Culpeper Courthouse, are marked as 56⅛ miles and 59⅝ miles, respectively. At the right end of the map as oriented here, Jefferson wrote a brief note on its provenance: "The road from the ferry landing opposite Georgetown to Stevensburg from actual survey by Capt John Triplett." The smaller piece is 4½ inches by 5 inches, the larger one 4½ inches by 10 inches. Also illustrated on the map is a different, straighter route of a portion of the main road. This course traveled through Ravensworth, a huge tract patented by William Fitzhugh, Richard Fitzhugh's great-grandfather, on a portion of which Fitzhugh lived.

The relatively better traveled and understood roads illustrated on this plat oversimplify Jefferson's strategy for making his way through northern Virginia. Jefferson placed a high priority on finding the best, fastest route to and from Washington, and his papers are filled with itineraries, surveys, and exchanged queries about the quality of roads. Jefferson had in the past used the main road through Ravensworth, but some alterations made by the Fitzhugh family rendered it, for a time at least, inconvenient. Hoping to avoid the main market road in 1804, Jefferson asked Richard Fitzhugh's brother Nicholas about a "better way through" Ravensworth and also if there was a road that would take him from Songster's Tavern (partway along the Ravensworth road) to the Red House Tavern (not marked but frequently on Jefferson's itineraries) while avoiding Centreville (Newgate on the map). Such discussions offer a sense of the experimentation required for a journey through the northern Virginia terrain, which featured steep hills, many streams, and a patchwork of indifferently maintained roads subject to inundations and the whims of individual landowners (Richard Beale Davis, ed., *William Fitzhugh and His Chesapeake World, 1676-1701: The Fitzhugh Letters and Other Documents* [Chapel Hill, 1963], 44, 177n, 191n, 373-4; VMHB, 7 [1900], 317-19; 8 [1901], 314-15; 36 [1928], 180-2; WMQ, 1st ser., 21 [1912], 119; MB, 1:525n; 2:832-5; undated manuscript itineraries and distances from Monticello to Georgetown, Thomas Jefferson Foundation; table of distances from Monticello to the Georgetown ferry, 28 Sep.-2 Oct. 1808, and itineraries from Monticello to the President's House, September 1807-June 1808, in DLC: TJ Papers, 233:41695-6; Vol. 24:154, 269, 368-9; Vol. 29:431-2, 529; Vol. 35:568-9; Vol. 37:384-6, 437, 533-4; Vol. 43:xlvi-xlvii, 90, 111, 125-6; TJ to Edmund Bacon, 12 Apr. 1808).

Courtesy of the Library of Congress.

PREBLE MEDAL

On 20 Feb. 1805, Jefferson forwarded to Congress Edward Preble's 18 Sep. 1804 letter to Robert Smith detailing the U.S. Navy's campaign against Tripoli between July and September the previous year. Jefferson believed that the "energy & judgement displayed by this excellent officer" could not "fail to give high satisfaction to Congress and their country." Congress agreed and passed a resolution on 3 Mch. that gave thanks to Preble and the men under his command. This resolution also requested that the president "cause a gold medal to be struck, emblematical of the attacks on the town, batteries and naval force of Tripoli, by the squadron under Commodore Preble's command, and to present it to Commodore Preble, in such manner as in his opinion will be most honourable to him."

Philadelphia die-sinker and medalist John Reich wrote to Jefferson that May, soliciting the opportunity to execute the work. Jefferson had a high regard for Reich's skill, as he had previously engraved medals celebrating Jefferson's inauguration and for presentation to Native American nations. While Preble was in Philadelphia in March, he sat for a profile drawing by Rembrandt Peale, which later became the basis for Reich's work. Jefferson reviewed this drawing and found that the initial design of four inches in diameter was too large, both as a matter of custom and as a practical consideration of minting. Robert Smith subsequently requested that the navy agent at Philadelphia, who oversaw Reich's work, reduce the medal's size. Smith also provided the navy agent with authorization to use the machinery at the U.S. Mint to strike the medal.

The medal was completed by the spring of 1806 and sent by Smith to Preble in May. At this point, Reich entered into a dispute with the Navy Department over his compensation. After reviewing his complaint, Jefferson wrote to Reich recounting the prices agreed upon in the 1780s with French engravers of the medals of various heroes of the American Revolution. Jefferson recommended that Reich receive the same amount as Pierre Simon Benjamin Duvivier, who had made a three-inch medal of George Washington. He hoped that Reich would "be sensible that we are not setting an arbitrary value on your time or talents, but allowing them the just measure ascribed to others."

After receiving the medal, Preble asked Smith to "communicate to the President of the United States that I accept with gratitude this honorable testimony of the approbation of my country, and I pray you to be assured that I feel truly sensible of the very handsome and obliging manner in which it has been presented." Following the production of the gold medal, there was a delay at the U.S. Mint in producing additional impressions in bronze due to the demand for coinage, but this production issue was resolved by late 1807. In circular letters dated 15, 23, and 24 Dec. 1807, Smith forwarded copies of the medal to former president John Adams and the governors of the states and federal territories. It is therefore likely that Jefferson obtained his copy of the medal at this time (U.S. Statutes at Large, 2:346-7; Christopher McKee, *Edward Preble: A Naval Biography, 1761-1807* [Annapolis, 1972], 314; George Henry Preble, "Correspondence Relating to the Preble Medal," *American Journal of Numismatics*, 6 [1871-72], 49-55; Stein, *Worlds*, 242-3; *National Intelligencer*, 2 July 1806; George Harrison to Smith, 17 June 1805, in DNA: RG 45, MLR; Smith to Preble, 17 May 1806, in same, LSO; circular letters in same, MLS; Vol. 9:241; Vol. 34:73n; Vol. 39:264-5; Vol. 45:550-1; Reich to TJ, 22 May 1805, 28 Apr., 24 May 1806; TJ to Smith, 21 June 1805; Smith to TJ, 23 June 1805, 26 June 1806; TJ to Reich, 27 June 1806).

The completed medal measures $2\frac{1}{2}$ inches in diameter. On the obverse side is a profile of Preble framed by the words "Edwardo Preble Duci Strenuo Comitia Americana": "The American Congress to Edward Preble, A Valiant Officer." On the reverse side is a depiction of the U.S. Navy bombarding Tripoli, framed by the inscription "Vindici Commercii Americani" with an exergue, "Ante Tripoli MDCCCIV": "To the Vindicator of American Commerce" and "Off Tripoli, 1804" (J. F. Loubat, *The Medallic History of the United States of America, 1776-1876*, 2 vols. [New York, 1878], 1:135).

Collection of the Massachusetts Historical Society.

THOMAS JEFFERSON BY GILBERT STUART

When Jefferson sat for Gilbert Stuart a second time in 1805, the artist produced one of the most popular and widely replicated likenesses of the president. It became the prototype for many copies, engravings, prints, and ultimately government-issued stamps and currency. While the likeness was already circulating among Jefferson admirers during the latter part of his second term, it took the president 16 years and significant effort to obtain the portrait for his own home. It later passed to Jefferson's Randolph family and became known as the Edgehill portrait for its decades-long display at that house. Jefferson embraced the painting as a life portrait from his 1805 sitting, but debate remains about whether the painting Jefferson ultimately received was the original or a version made by Stuart years later.

Shortly before James Bowdoin left to assume his appointment as minister to Spain in 1805, he commissioned Stuart to paint original portraits of

Jefferson and Madison. Stuart, unsatisfied with the likeness created in Jefferson's 1800 sitting, requested that Jefferson sit again in Washington. Since the portrait that he sat and paid for in 1800 had not been delivered, Jefferson requested the original life painting from this sitting. He also requested that Stuart sketch him in medallion form, which he paid for on 18 June; the sitting for the life portrait occurred some time prior. He later recalled that Stuart had "begged permission to keep" the new life painting "until he could get an engraving from it" (RS, 14:503). By 1813, Jefferson had still not received the painting. When Philadelphia publisher Joseph Delaplaine requested a portrait to accompany a publication about distinguished Americans, Jefferson inquired about the undelivered portraits, but Stuart did not respond. In 1818, Jefferson charged Henry Dearborn, who lived in Boston, with pressing Stuart about them. Stuart first evaded the question and then insisted that he had painted the portrait for his own use and not under a commission. When he eventually admitted that he owed Jefferson a painting, he asked what size Jefferson would prefer. Jefferson, of course, wanted only the original life portrait: "I have no doubt that mr. Stuart's justice will think me entitled to the original, & not merely to a copy" (RS, 15:488). Jefferson received this bust-size painting in 1821.

While Jefferson presumed that he received the life painting, art historians have questioned the Edgehill's composition date. Stuart painted at least five versions based on that sitting, including the painting for Bowdoin, finished in 1807, a bust-length painting owned by Madison, which was probably finished in 1805 and delivered by 1806, a painting for a series of presidential portraits for George Gibbs, Jr., probably made some years later, and a version for John Doggett, a Boston framer and gilder. The last was destroyed by fire at the Library of Congress in 1851. Some art historians theorize that a version other than the Edgehill portrait might have been the life painting. Details found in replicas made at various points between 1805 and 1820 point to a different prototype, while the dimensions of the wood panels and developments in Stuart's style indicate that the painting was possibly composed in Boston at some later time and not in Washington in 1805. The portrait, which measures $26\frac{2}{5}$ inches by $21\frac{1}{8}$ inches, is painted in oil on a mahogany panel (Carrie Rebora Barratt and Ellen G. Miles, *Gilbert Stuart* [New Haven, 2004], 277-83; Bush, *Life Portraits*, 57-9; Linda J. Docherty, "Original Copies: Gilbert Stuart's Companion Portraits of Thomas Jefferson and James Madison," *American Art*, 22, no. 2 [2008], 85-97; David Meschutt, "Gilbert Stuart's Portraits of Thomas Jefferson," *American Art Journal*, 13 [1981], 3-9, 13, 15-16; Stein, *Worlds*, 139-41; RS, 6:148-9; 7:525-8; 13:345, 360; 14:504n; 15:338-9, 373, 439; MB, 2:1018, 1156; Vol. 31:xliv-xlv, 586, 587n; TJ to Stuart, 18 June 1805).

Courtesy of the Thomas Jefferson Foundation at Monticello and the National Portrait Gallery, Smithsonian Institution.

JOHN WAYLES EPPES

Jefferson's son-in-law and nephew by marriage, John Wayles Eppes, lost his wife Maria in April 1804 and did not remarry until April 1809. His career as a congressman and later senator from Virginia, spanning intermittently from 1803 until 1819, kept him in Washington for parts of each year when Congress was in session. A staunch political supporter and correspondent, he continued to advise Jefferson on everything from legislative matters to horse purchases. In 1805, Jefferson promised his ongoing concern for Eppes's young children, Maria and Francis—the "objects of my tenderest sollicitudes"—and reiterated his intention to leave his Bedford County lands to them. Jefferson had also planned for his daughter's family to reside near him and ordered initial leveling of lands at Pantops. However, after Maria's untimely death, Eppes became eager to settle near his parents at Eppington. He hoped to exchange the Bedford property for comparable value in land adjoining Pantops. Jefferson ordered the Poplar Forest lands to be surveyed and laid out in preparation for an eventual bequest to his grandchildren.

Depicted here likely between 1806 and 1808, Eppes was the subject of one of many miniature portraits executed by the amateur artist and French émigré Joseph Pierre Picot de Limoëlan de Clorivière (1768-1826). The son of a Breton nobleman who died on the guillotine, Clorivière served as an officer in the army of Louis XVI and joined the counterrevolution. In December 1800 he was a conspirator in the "infernal machine" plot to assassinate Napoleon and was sentenced to death. He escaped to Savannah with his sister and her husband. While traveling to administer affairs for his brother-in-law, Clorivière took up the paint brush and advertised likenesses "for medallions, rings, or pins" that he often sold for $25 each. Clorivière was in Washington for the February terms of the Supreme Court in 1807 and 1808. It was probably during this period, and before he entered the Catholic seminary in Baltimore in April 1808, that he painted the miniature of Eppes. Clorivière was ordained a priest in 1812 and for many years served a pastorate in Charleston before becoming director of the Visitation Monastery in Georgetown, D.C.

The watercolor-on-ivory miniature measured 2¼ inches by 1¾ inches in its original condition; it was later framed in a gold medallion. The artist's signature "Picot" appears in the lower right (Providence, R.I., *United States Chronicle*, 25 Aug. 1803; *Columbian Museum & Savannah Advertiser*, 7 Apr. and 19 Dec. 1804; *Daily National Intelligencer*, 18 Sep. 1822, 14 Oct. 1826; Stephen C. Worsley, "Joseph-Pierre Picot de Limoëlan de Clorivière: A Portrait Miniaturist Revisited" and Appendix A & B, *Journal of Early Southern Decorative Arts*, 28 [Winter 2002], 1-69; Anna Wells Rutledge, "A French Priest, Painter, and Architect in the United States: Joseph Pierre Picot de Limoelan de Cloriviere," *Gazette des Beaux-Arts*, 33 [1948], 159-76; RS, 1:337-8n; Vol. 43:534, 582-4; Vol. 44:97-8; TJ to Eppes, 25 Mch. and 27 May 1805).

Courtesy of the Thomas Jefferson Foundation at Monticello.

Volume 46

9 March to 5 July 1805

JEFFERSON CHRONOLOGY

1743 • 1826

1743	Born at Shadwell, 13 April (New Style).
1760	Entered the College of William and Mary.
1762	"quitted college."
1762-1767	Self-education and preparation for law.
1769-1774	Albemarle delegate to House of Burgesses.
1772	Married Martha Wayles Skelton, 1 Jan.
1775-1776	In Continental Congress.
1776	Drafted Declaration of Independence.
1776-1779	In Virginia House of Delegates.
1779	Submitted Bill for Establishing Religious Freedom.
1779-1781	Governor of Virginia.
1782	His wife died, 6 Sep.
1783-1784	In Continental Congress.
1784-1789	In France as Minister Plenipotentiary to negotiate commercial treaties and as Minister Plenipotentiary resident at Versailles.
1790-1793	Secretary of State of the United States.
1797-1801	Vice President of the United States.
1801-1809	President of the United States.
1814-1826	Established the University of Virginia.
1826	Died at Monticello, 4 July.

VOLUME 46

9 March to 5 July 1805

14 Mch.	Leaves Washington for Monticello, arriving 17 Mch.
27 Mch.	Jacob Crowninshield writes that he "can not accept the office" of secretary of the navy.
7 Apr.	Meriwether Lewis reports from Fort Mandan, sending specimens and William Clark's journal.
14 Apr.	Leaves Monticello for Washington, arriving 17 Apr.
27 Apr.	Writes to James Bowdoin that U.S. relations with Spain are at a crucial point; military force under the command of William Eaton captures Derna, east of Tripoli.
6 May	Agrees to purchase "2. Negro men," Isaac and Charles.
26 May	Asks William C. C. Claiborne to request passports from Spanish authorities for safe passage of Red River expedition.
4 June	Tobias Lear concludes peace treaty with Tripoli.
11 June	Learns that the supply ship *Huntress* has been captured by a privateer.
13 June	Names Robert Patterson to succeed Elias Boudinot as director of the Mint.
18 June	Pays $100 to Gilbert Stuart "for drawing my portrait."
21 June	Sends Albert Gallatin documents to refute accusations published in Boston *Repertory*.
4 July	Independence Day celebrated with a public reception at the President's House and militia units parading in review.

THE PAPERS OF
THOMAS JEFFERSON

From Mary Bond

George Town—Saturday Morning March 9th. 1805.

Mrs. Mary Bond, an unfortunate woman, left a widow, with four small Children, pleads great poverty, makes application most humbly, to Mr. Jefferson, President of the United States, for a little assistance, being this present time, without one single cent, and what is an addition to her distress'd situation, in a Strange Place, and without one friend, to render her the least service, although she solicits every comfort in life, furthermore wishes to incert, that with the help of a little money, will carry her into the Country, to her friends, whom she is in hopes, will do something for her, in her very unhappy situation.—

Concludes beging leave to subscribe herself Your Obent. Servant

MARY BOND

RC (MHi); endorsed by TJ as received 9 Mch. and so recorded in SJL, where TJ listed letters received on 9 Mch. under 8 Mch.

From William Dunbar

Natchez March 9th. 1805

I have the pleasure of transmitting you the Conclusion of the Journal of the geographical Survey and a continuation of the Journal of occurrences & remarks. I have been again disappointed in assistance the person who was to come to write for me having engaged himself as a School master. I hope not to be disappointed in the measures I have taken to go on with great promptitude in future, having yet considerably more than half of the 2d Journal to be copied. I venture to send you a few vegetable specimens, which I hope may arrive by the mail in sufficient good order to enable a practical botanist to decide upon their genus.

With high respect and attachment I have the honor to be

List of Vegetable Specimens

No. 1. an aquatic plant described October 22d 1804
2. found on the hill west of hot springs December 13th
3.
4. found on Do.
5. Golden rod
6. Herbe au Crocodile
7. fm. hill W. of hot springs
8. fm. do
9. fm. do
10 fm. do
11 }
12 } Grass seeds October 21st. 1804
13 }

FC (Lb in Ms-Ar: William Dunbar Papers); follows Dunbar to TJ, [2 Mch. 1805]; at head of text: "To the Same." Recorded in SJL as received 23 Apr.

From Levi Lincoln

DEAR SIR Worcester March the 9th 1805

In my endeavours to forget my friends at Washington, & to transfer and fix my attention to objects within the reach of my influence and agency nearer home, I fear you will think I have succeeded too well. This is the first letter I have directed to the seat of Govt since I left it. A few days, after my arrival at Worcester, where I met my family and friends, generally, in health & spirits, Genl. Hull informed me by letter, in answer to one I had written him on the subject of his appointment, that he had written to Genl. Varnum that the office would be agreeable to him, & of which he would advise you. I yesterday Recd. a letter from Hull in which he seems to express some solicitude, that the appointment had not taken place—

The snow, in which we have been literally buried alive the winter past, is fast dissolving. The weather is now warm & pleasant, and the farmers having crawled out, like the swallows, from their dreary shelters, have reassumed a standing on the suffice of the earth, which is still sealed from improvement. I had been longing for one of the old fashion massachusetts's winters; am now satisfied. The contrast between here & the federal city is great indeed. Experiencing another season like the past, will raise my prejudices, and unless *remunerated* by a *consequent abundant produce*, make me a believer in a more temperate climate. I already begin to think with you, *Sir*, that a degree of cold, which imprisons & benumbs into dormancy, or pinches into agony, is not indispensably necessary to man's happiness and comfort, either in this world, or the next. From the severity of the season our journey home was long and tedious. At New York I repeatedly saw T Paine. He, to me, still appears to be the man of surprising intellect. Since lengthy peices, which he, with the readiness and correctness of a school boy, repeated from his published & unpublished writings, would be universally admired, as unrivalled originals, were they not his. Will the mind of man, will civil society, never be exalted to discriminations of truth and justice? will the disquisitions of genius and bold independent reflections, never be tolerated or countenanced; never be reckoned among the resources of a free Govt.? Paine Told me he was preparing for the press an edition of his works in five Vol Oto. half of which, to comprice matter never before published, with a statement of the occasions & circumstances, under which they were written. He appeared delighted with the auspicious aspect of our public concerns, and the more, from believing he had had an agency in its production. I discouraged him from a journey he was then contemplating to Washington, so far as could be effected, by a strong statement of the difficulties we had encountered. The chilling scenes, of being dragged across the Susquehanna on a long ladder to mount us above the water which spread over the ice, and to prevent a descent under it; and of being upset in a brook at midnight, seemed to cool the Phylosopher's ardor for his proposed Journey—As the Federal papers have announced no new dangers to their religious & powerful patrons, by an individual whom they represent as mad, besoted, in his dotage, and dispicable, It is presumed the journey has not been made. At N York I met with some of the 3d party Gent. so called. They profess the fullest respect and friendship for the principles and character of the national administration; but great distrust of some of its reputed friends. They effect to think the public opinion will change in reference to some of the new york popular leaders. It is certain that the efforts of this party will not be wanting to produce such a change. With us, in Mass; such a party is known only in name. we have no middle feelings or pursuits; parties remain marked, as wholly federal, or wholly republican, on the old principles of distinction. All agree that there are no half way temporising measures. The leaders of the opposition will submit to no terms but of their own choic, & quietly, to no Govt. which they do not administer themselves. They betray no symptoms of despair, unless encreased bitterness, and exertion are exhibitions of these symptoms. They effect to beleive that a new state of things will take place from the bickerings & divisions of Republicans among themselves, or from a propensity to change which they say is the characteristic of individuals & parties, in free govts. They are making every possible exertion to preserve the federal character of Mass. in our next elections, as a circumstance necessary to keep alive the drooping hopes of their deluded followers. The struggle will be the warmest & the most severe, we have ever experienced. The malignity & violence of the opposition are invincible. Neither things high or low, good or great, present or to come, standing in their way, will be respected. They are making some base, outrageous, and, it is presumed, false charges against Judge Sullivan. These like similar falshoods recoiling on their authors, will eventual add to the weight of that folly & wickedness which is crushing them. I am not confident as to the event of the conflict, except as to the representatives, which I think must be republican. Many of our friends are sanguine that our triumps will be complete. Republicans are certainly acting with greater concert, spirit, & advantage than ever—Yet there are some, *unmade*, *half-made*, *double-made*, verbal professional republicans, who give us trouble, and on whom no dependence can, or ought to be placed—Report says J Chase is acquitted with great honor, and federal mathematicians are exultingly calculating the expence of the trial. Whatever may have been the event, & whatever has been the expence, It is beleived the trial will be of essential service to our country. Whatever may have been the opinions, convictions, or scruples, of the individuals who composed the court, facts & principles have an independent existence, & being investigated, are the proper subjects of future discussion—They will not change, halt, or accommodate, like the limping sentiments of frail man. On the 4th. of March, my feelings in spite of myself, carried me to Washington, and reassociated me on the joyous occasion, with the political objects of my esteem, confidence, & affection; But not hearing your communication, am waiting with impatience, great impatience, to see it.

I have the honor to be, Sir, with perfect esteem & friendship most respectfully your obedt Servt Levi Lincoln

RC (DLC); at foot of text: "The Presidt. of the US."; endorsed by TJ as received 21 Mch. and so recorded in SJL.

ICE: the winter of 1804-1805 was widely noted as being particularly harsh, especially in the wake of a significant blizzard that struck the mid-Atlantic region in late January. A thaw in February caused flooding and loosened ice floes in area rivers (*Boston Gazette*, 14 Jan.; Norwich *Connecticut Centinel*, 29 Jan.; Sag Harbor, N.Y., *Suffolk Gazette*, 4 Feb.; *New-York Gazette & General Advertiser*, 28 Jan. and 27 Feb.).

CHASE IS ACQUITTED: see Memorandum of Votes in Chase Impeachment Trial, at 1 Mch. Public reports of the acquittal were not printed in Worcester until four days after Lincoln wrote to TJ (Worcester *National Aegis*, 13 Mch.).

Receipt of Rosanna McKenney

1805 Dr Mr. Thomas Jefferson—President of the United States
to Rosy Mckenney

March
9 To 9. Dozen of clothes washed at 5/6 $6.60

EE

Rece'd the above in full ROSY MCKENNY

MS (MHi); endorsed by TJ: "Mc. kenney."

Rosanna McKenney worked as a launderer for TJ from at least March 1805 into July 1807. The census of 1820 listed her as the head of a household of four. She was then 45 years of age or older. In 1822, the city of Washington's first directory listed her as Rosanna M'Kenna, a widow living a few blocks from the President's House. Her receipts to TJ were written in a variety of hands, as was her signature, and the spelling of the signature varied (Judah Delano, *The Washington Directory: Showing the Name, Occupation, and Residence, of Each Head of a Family and Person in Business* [Washington, D.C., 1822], 58; U.S. Census Schedules, DNA: RG 29; receipts, 13 July 1805, 8 Jan., ca. 5 May, ca. 20 July, 31 Dec. 1806, 4 Apr., 30 July 1807, in MHi).

CLOTHES WASHED: TJ noted McKenney's payment in his financial record of 11 Mch. as "pd. extra washing 10. D." (MB, 2:1148). The addition of washing as a separate presidential expense in TJ's memoranda occurred no more than four times a year between 1801 and 1807. Often he listed only the cost of the service, but he occasionally named McKenney and, before her, Sally Houseman in 1803 and Biddy Boyle in 1804 and early 1805. Beginning in October 1807, the cost of washing done for the president was most commonly incorporated in his memoranda as a category in Étienne Lemaire's monthly table of household accounts (MB, 2:1100, 1118, 1137, 1152, 1212).

From Eliza Peacock

SIR March 9 1805

Since I had the honour to address your Excellency before, I have received the inclosed Letter from Walter Jones Esqr., which I take the Liberty of offering to your perusal.

your Obedient and very humble Servant ELIZA PEACOCK

RC (DNA: RG 59, GPR); at foot of text: "To the President of the United States"; endorsed by TJ as received 9 Mch. and so recorded in SJL, where TJ listed letters received on 9 Mch. under 8 Mch. Enclosure: Walter Jones, Jr., to Peacock, Alexandria, 4 Mch., acknowledging the receipt of her letter of 27 Feb.; Jones is aware of Robert Ware Peacock's situation and strongly sympathizes with Eliza Peacock's sufferings, but his official situation forbids his becoming, "on any occasion of the sort, a petitioner in the common form, to the President"; she may count on his "friendly dispositions" toward her, however, and he assures her that if her petition fails, "it must be the inevitable result of a strict & conscientious regard to public duty, overcoming the suggestions of the Truest philanthropy" (RC in same).

ADDRESS: Eliza Peacock to TJ, 6 Mch.

From William Pryce

VERY DR SIR, Wilmington March 9th. 1805

With this I send you a Copy of the History of the Life of our Blessed Saviour Jesus Christ &c. which I hope you will find, interesting and instructive, equal to your expectations.

you have no doubt learned the liberty I have taken of publishing your kind favor to me; for which I feel bound to offer no apology, Conscious that it would do honor to the Head and Heart, of any man on Earth.

with my sincere prayers for your prosperity in this life, and Felicity in the next, I remain your's Sincerity, WILLIAM PRYCE

RC (ViW: Tucker-Coleman Collection); at foot of text: "Thomas Jefferson Esqr."; endorsed by TJ as received 12 Mch. and so recorded in SJL. Enclosure: Ebenezer Thompson and William C. Price, *The History of Our Blessed Lord and Saviour Jesus Christ*, 2 vols. (Wilmington, Del., 1805; Sowerby, No. 1493).

PUBLISHING YOUR KIND FAVOR: an extract of TJ's letter of 15 Oct. 1803, subscribing to Pryce's work, was widely reprinted in newspapers in 1804. The extract was prefaced: "It would seem that these publishers, both of whom are federalists, the first a pious Episcopal Clergyman, the latter printer of a federal paper, do not believe the story of Mr. Jefferson's *infidelity*" (Trenton *True American*, 30 Apr. 1804; Georgia *Augusta Chronicle, and Gazette of the State*, 26 May 1804; Sag Harbor, N.Y., *Suffolk Gazette*, 4 June 1804; Vol. 41:532).

From Philippe Reibelt

MONSIEUR LE PRESIDENT! Baltimore le 9 Mars 1805

Il est de mon devoir, de Vous accuser sans retard la reception de votre Assignation de 138,24 Cs. et de Vous en presenter mes remercimens.

Votre Compte est certainement tres exact, exceptè, que la Continuation des Annales du Museè &c p. Landon (Tomes 3, 4. et 5) n'y est pas compris.

Je souhaite du fond de mon Coeur, que le Voyage, que Vous allez faire a votre retraite momentaneè philosophique a Monticello contribue autant a la Conservation de votre Santè, qu'un homme aussi attachè aux principes vraiment republicains doit le desirer—et je Vous prie de vouloir bien accepter Gracieusement l'expression des Sentimens intimement respectueux, qui doivent necessairement deriver d'une Source Si pure et invariable. REIBELT.

EDITORS' TRANSLATION

MISTER PRESIDENT! Baltimore, 9 Mch. 1805

It is my duty to acknowledge without delay your payment of $138.24 and to extend my thanks.

Your calculation is indeed accurate, except that it does not include the sequel to the *Annales du Musée* by Landon (volumes 3, 4, and 5).

From the depths of my heart I hope the brief reflective trip you are taking to your Monticello retreat will contribute as much to preserving your health as a man so attached to truly republican principles could wish. I ask you to be kind enough to accept the expression of the deeply respectful sentiments which necessarily come from a pure, unchanging source. REIBELT.

RC (DLC); above signature: "Le Depot Americ. General de Levrault, Schoell et Comp. Imprim. Libr. a Paris"; endorsed by TJ as received 12 Mch. and so recorded in SJL.

VOTRE ASSIGNATION: TJ to Reibelt, 7 Mch.

To Benjamin Waterhouse

TH: JEFFERSON TO
DOCTR. WATERHOUSE Washington Mar. 9. 05.

Legerat hujus Amor titulum nomenque libelli.
Bella mihi, video, bella parantur, ait.

So Ovid introduces his book Remediorum amoris. a lecture against tobacco was calculated to excite a similar alarm in a Virginian, & a cultivator of tobacco. however being a friend neither to it's culture nor consequences, I thank you for the pamphlet, and wish a succesful opposition to this organ of Virginia influence, as well as to every other injurious to our physical, moral or political well being. Accept my friendly & respectful salutations.

PoC (DLC).

TJ referred to OVID's poem "Cures for Love," the first lines of which, loosely translated, are "When Love read the title of this book, he said, I see it is war you declare against me" (Ovid, *Remedia Amoris*, 1.1-2).

A LECTURE AGAINST TOBACCO: see Waterhouse to TJ, 20 Feb.

From William Wood

WORTHY SIR: March 9th 1805 Washington Citty

I must take the liberty to Congratulate you on your Reelection to that Solemn & Important task as the Chief of So Great a Nation & I hope Sir that that God whse dominion is over all May be your Giude,

Counselor, & Kind preserver though I belive You have Some Enemies yet Sure I am, Many there are that Implore the divine hand to bless you—I should be Very happy to Enjoy a Short Interview With Your Excelency but understanding you were about to depart for a little season I take the liberty Sir to Impart My desire by a few lines I Shall depart Shortly from this place & I understand by the land law pasd the last of the Session the Reserves made by Genral Wayne in the Indian treaty Were deposd With your Excelency to dispose of. Now Sir if you would Condescend to Grant a Settlement for about Twenty Familys in the 12 Mile Sqare Reserve on the Miami of the lake by Complying With the Terms of Sale My Wishes Signifyd in My Adress to you in decembr last Would be fulfild & the Wishes of a Number of Your Well Wishers. an Answer would be thankfuly Recd by your Excelency Obedient Servnt WIM. WOOD

RC (DLC); endorsed by TJ as received 9 Mch. and so recorded in SJL, where TJ listed letters received on 9 Mch. under 8 Mch.

William Wood may have been the individual of that name who helped found and became the first pastor of a Baptist church in Mason County, Kentucky, in the 1780s. Wood's land speculation led to his exclusion from his congregation, and he appears to have shifted his attention to Ohio, although it is unclear if he ever settled there permanently (John H. Spencer, *A History of Kentucky Baptists*, 2 vols. [Cincinnati, 1885], 1:67-8; Cincinnati *Western Spy, and Hamilton Gazette*, 30 July and 8 Oct. 1800; Cincinnati *Liberty Hall*, 1 Jan. 1812; Washington, Ky., *Union*, 10 Sep. 1814).

LAND LAW: a reference to section 2 of the supplemental act "for the disposal of public lands in the Indiana territory," which was passed on 3 Mch. The section authorized the president to have a ceded area "lying north and west of the Indian boundary" surveyed, subdivided, and offered for sale (U.S. Statutes at Large, 2:343-4).

MY ADRESS TO YOU: Wood may have accompanied a petition and letter to TJ from Ohio residents seeking his appointment as a missionary to Native Americans in the region (see Edward Tiffin and others to TJ, [before 22 Oct. 1804], and James McPherson and Isaac Zane to TJ, 22 Oct. 1804).

To William Wood

SIR Washington Mar. 9. 05.

I have been so closely engaged through the day that it has been impossible till this moment to open your letter. the matter which is the subject of it belongs to the department of the treasury the Secretary of which alone can inform you of the terms & conditions on which the lands of the reserve can be disposed of. I must therefore refer you to him, and should any circumstance require it he will confer with me on the subject. Accept my respects & good wishes

TH: JEFFERSON

PoC (DLC); at foot of text: "Mr. William Wood"; endorsed by TJ.

To Thomas Appleton

SIR Washington Mar. 10. 05.

Your favor of Dec. 24. is recieved. Mr. Latrobe superintendant of the public buildings having occasion for a good carver in stone, I have recommended him to mr Mazzei whose acquaintance in Florence will enable him to procure one who may suit us; and I have undertaken to assure mr Latrobe that if he will make the necessary arrangements for money paiments respecting the workman, with you, & for sending him on, you will be so good as to see to that, leaving to mr Mazzei no other trouble than that of selecting & agreeing with the workman. will you be so good as to assist mr Latrobe herein according to his desires & further to contrive the inclosed letter to mr Mazzei so as that he may not be burthened with postage if possible. the newspapers it contains would occasion that to be high. Accept my salutations & respects. TH: JEFFERSON

PoC (DLC); at foot of text: "Mr. Thomas Appleton"; endorsed by TJ. Enclosure: TJ to Philip Mazzei, 10 Mch. Enclosed in TJ to Benjamin H. Latrobe, 10 Mch.

On 6 Mch., LATROBE wrote to Philip Mazzei on TJ's directive, to request Mazzei's assistance in engaging "a good Sculptor of Architectural decorations" for the public buildings of Washington, especially the Capitol. Latrobe informed him of the dimensions and materials for the project as well as the anticipated wages and the desired personal characteristics of the sculptor. He also asked Mazzei to inquire about Antonio Canova's interest in sculpting a seated figure of Liberty for the House of Representatives chamber (Margherita Marchione, ed., *Philip Mazzei: Selected Writings and Correspondence*, 3 vols. [Prato, Italy, 1983], 3:372-4).

From Aaron Burr

Sunday.— [10 Mch. 1805]

Mr Burr having just now been informed that Mr Jefferson proposes to leave the City this Day, presents respectful Compliments & Requests to know his determination, if any has been made, with Respect to Dr Browne; as it may materially influence the movements of that Gentleman—

RC (DNA: RG 59, AOC); partially dated; endorsed by TJ as a letter of 10 Mch. 1805 received that day and "Browne Joseph to be Secretary," and so recorded in SJL.

Burr wrote to TJ on 1 Mch. to recommend his brother-in-law Joseph BROWNE as an appointee. TJ received the letter, which has not been found, on 7 Mch., recording it in SJL with the notation "Doctr. Joseph Browne to be Secy. Louisa." "An Act further providing for the government of the district of Louisiana," approved on 3 Mch., made Louisiana District a territory effective 4 July 1805 (U.S. Statutes at Large, 2:331-2; John Archer to TJ, 6 Mch.).

From Therese Ceracchi

MONSIEUR Vienne en Autriche ce 10 Mars 1805.

Ayant sur moi le devoir amer de chercher du Secours ou seulement ma faible memoire puisse me donner une Luëur d'Esperance j'azarde ses Lignes pour s'il est possible faire rétentir jusque dans Vos Contrées heureuses les Clameurs de la Deplorable famille de Joseph Cerachi; Veuve avec 6 Enfans n'ayant plus puë exister ni subsister a Rome le Desespoir me suggera de revenir dans ma Patrie pour y chercher du secours ayant duë par necessité abandonner 5 de mes Enfans a Rome je me rendis avec le plus petit içi mais helas! je me trouvais en la plus grande partie echuë dans mes Esperances, si bien que bien des fois après avoir passée la Nuit dans les larmes le Jour je ne sais de quoi pourvoir aux premieres necessité; n'existant de ce que jusqu'ici des Ames Généreuses m'aye par si par là donnée! Dieu qu'elle plus que Cruelle situation de savoir mes 5 fils dans la Maison des Orphelins a Rome manquant de Linge d'habillemens n'ayant aucune Education abandonnée a toute la rigeueur de la plus cruelle misere car Rome étant ruiné par les Echecs reçu cette Maison ne peut pas seulement subvenir a donner la nourriture necessaire a ses petits Delaissés et ne pouvoir les secourir! étant absorbée sous le poids énorme de toutes les privations et que ma santé delabrés par les angoisses continuelle d'un Desespoir concentré ne m'offre que peut être bientôt la fin de mes malheurs cet a dire la Tombe! Mais avant d'y descendre mon triste Nom de Mere m'inpose de cependant reveiller l'humanité Genereuse pour les secourir a qui puis-je bien m'addresser étant isolé dans ce monde qu'a Vous Homme Illustre par Votre Grandeur d'ame et Actions Vertueuses a jamais mémorables; et surtout sachant combien Vous avéz daignéz protéger mon Defunt Epoux que par sentimens d'humanité Vous daigneréz a Vous interresser a Notre Sort deplorable et de chercher des moyens pour nous arracher du Gouffre de nos malheurs, mais pour subvenir a Votre Memoire permettéz de Vous faire resouvenir que comme Vous le savéz Cerachi avait été chargé de L'Execution d'un Monument National pour perpetuer l'heureuse fondation de la Republique Americaine. Il a fait tous ses modeles en terre Cuitte et cet Ouvrage ayant été suspèndu Cerachi ne fut point payé[1] de ses travaux. Ne pourriéz Vous pas sous ce prétexte[2] decider le Gouvernement des Etats Unis a m'accorder une indemnité;[3] ou bien si cela ne pourrait aller a tacher a la fin de faire entre tous les Ames si Genereuses de Vos Contrées et Connaissances une Collecte afin de pouvoir du moins Voir en abandonnant la Vie mes pauvres Orphelins a l'abris de l'Affreuse Indigence ou ils sont présente-ment. Espérant que Vous daignneréz lire ses expositions et que Votre Coeur en sera touché et que par une Gracieuse reponse Vous tacheréz de rappeller a la Vie une Veuve Eploré![4] Ah Dieu avec quelle impatience n'attens je point ce feuille heureux. En attendant je ne puis que me nommer avec le plus Profond respect

Votre tres humble Servante THÉRÉSE CERACCHI

P.S: Si Vous vouléz avoir la grace de m'honorer d'une reponse Addressé Votre Lettre A Mess. les freres Smittmer Banquier d'ici

EDITORS' TRANSLATION

SIR, Vienna, Austria, 10 Mch. 1805

Finding myself in bitter need of seeking help where my feeble memory alone can provide a ray of hope, I venture to write these lines so the laments of Joseph Cerrachi's pitiable family may be heard in your fortunate country. Widowed with six children, unable to survive or subsist in Rome, I was impelled by despair to return home to seek help. Forced to abandon five of my children in Rome, I returned here with the youngest but found my hopes largely dashed, alas. Often, after weeping all night, I do not know how to provide the basic necessities when morning comes. So far, I have survived solely on what generous souls give me here and there. God knows how cruel it is to know that my five sons in the Roman orphanage lack clothing, receive no education, and are abandoned to the rigors of the most dire poverty. Since Rome has been ruined by defeats, the orphanage cannot even provide the necessary food to the little abandoned children, and I cannot help them since I am buried under the enormous weight of all these deprivations. My health is weakened by the constant anguish of unremitting despair. Perhaps it will soon grant me the end of my misfortunes—the tomb! But before going to the grave, I am obliged by my sad name of Mother to awaken generous humanity to help my children. Alone in the world, to whom can I turn except to you, illustrious for your eternally memorable greatness of soul and nobility of action. Knowing, above all, how much you graciously helped my late husband, I am certain your humane feelings will take an interest in our deplorable fate and try to pull us from the abyss of our misfortunes. To refresh your memory, allow me to remind you that Ceracchi was entrusted, as you know, with creating a national monument to immortalize the propitious founding of the American republic. He made all his models in terra cotta. When the project was suspended, Ceracchi was not paid for his work. Could you not therefore persuade the United States government to award me an indemnity on those grounds? Or, if not, try to take up a collection among all your generous friends and neighbors so I might at least see my poor orphans sheltered from the desperate poverty in which they find themselves?

I hope you will be good enough to read this account, that it will touch your heart, and that you will seek to revive a grieving widow through your gracious response. Heaven knows how impatiently I await that happy letter. Meanwhile, I can only call myself, with the deepest respect,

Your very humble servant, THÉRÉSE CERACCHI

P.S. If you honor me with a reply, please send it to the Smittmer brothers, who are bankers here.

RC (DLC); at head of text: "A Monsieur Jefferson"; endorsed by TJ as received 22 Aug. and so recorded in SJL. Dupl (same); dated 29 Apr.; addressed: "A Monsieur Jefferson President des Etats Unis d'Amerique"; lacks postscript; endorsed by TJ as received 2 Nov. and so recorded in SJL.

CHERCHER DU SECOURS: for Therese Ceracchi's previous attempts to receive payment for her husband's work, see Vol. 39:39-46, 107-8, 203-5; Vol. 40:657-9; Vol. 43:19-22.

[1] Dupl: "Cerachi n'est aucune indemnité."

[2] Preceding three words omitted in Dupl.

[3] Dupl: "m'accorder un secours digne de la Nation Américaine."

[4] Remainder of text in Dupl: "J'ai l'honneur d'ete avec la plus haute Estime."

To William C. C. Claiborne

DEAR SIR Washington Mar. 10. 05.

Being in the moment of my departure for Monticello where I shall be one month, I take time barely to write you on the subject of La Fayette's lands. Congress have passed a law which requires that he shall take his grant in portions of not less than 1000. acres each. by your letter of Dec. 22. & the plan it seems that the vacant lands on both sides the Canal of Carondelet may amount to not more than 600. as. but I have no doubt of the right to locate this as one of the lots of 1000. acres. whatever it falls short will be his loss. I will therefore pray you to advise with mr Briggs (whose office now extends to the Orleans territory) as to the form of location, and to locate & have surveyed as he shall direct 'all the ungranted lands on both sides and including the Canal of Carondelet and between the City of N. Orleans & the Bayou St. Jean,[1] whether covered with water or uncovered,' for Monsr. de la Fayette, and to forward to me such certificate &c. as will enable me to issue a grant. I will pay any expence incurred in this. in your letter you mention 3. positions in which the residue of the land may be located, towit 1. the island of N. Orleans. 2 the Attacapas. 3. the red river. will you be so good as to explain the peculiar properties, advantages & disadvantages of these 3. cantons, & what the lands might now be worth in each of them. on reciept of this I will decide for the General should his own decision not be recieved in the mean time. Accept my friendly & respectful salutations.

TH: JEFFERSON

RC (RNR); at foot of text: "Govr. Claiborne." PoC (ViU); fragment.

PASSED A LAW: section 8 of the 2 Mch. act for ascertaining and adjusting land titles in Orleans Territory and Louisiana District stated that no location or survey of Lafayette's lands should contain less than 1,000 acres "nor include any improved lands or lots, salt spring or lead mine" (U.S. Statutes at Large, 2:329; Kentucky Members of the House of Representatives to TJ, 28 Feb.).

[1]TJ interlined the text from "and between" to here.

To Lafayette

MY DEAR FRIEND Washington Mar. 10. 1805.

Your letter of July 1. came to hand Oct. 24. and gave me the hope I should soon recieve your instructions as to the location of your lands in the territory of Orleans. nothing however has yet been recieved from you on that head. in the mean time by an act passed this last session of Congress you will be obliged to take it in parcels of not less than 1000. acres each. there are adjacent to the town of N. Orleans on both sides the Canal of Carondelet a body of ungranted lands, swampy, supposed to contain about 600. acres. the city it is thought will very soon extend itself along this canal to the Bayou St. Jean. for tho' the ground is chiefly covered with water, & overgrown with Cypress, yet a common ditch will drain & protect the whole. considering the great value that this will very soon be of, as town lots, I have this day written to Governor Claiborne to have it located & surveyed for you, and to send me the papers that I may sign a grant for it so as to place it out of danger. but we shall be obliged to let it count against you as 1000. acres. in the plat of the town & country round it now inclosed I have made a line with a lead pencil thus  to shew you it's exact limits. as to the residue, the governor sais there are three positions where it may be laid. 1. in the island of N. Orleans. 2. at the Attacapas which is the seacoast at the Chafalya or Western mouth of the Missipi, I presume sugar lands. 3. on the Red river a hilly & healthy country with low ground on the river of the richest quality in the world. I have desired him to explain to me the properties, advantages, & disadvantages of each canton, & the present value of lands in them. that whole country will be immediately filled with Americans. I hope daily to recieve your instructions and to learn your determination to come & live there. until you come it is impossible for me to say a word as to the opportunities which could be given you there of being useful to our country. present my profound respects to Madame de la fayette and accept yourself my affectionate salutations & constant respect. TH: JEFFERSON

PoC (facsimile in Swann Galleries Catalogue, Sale 2123, Lot 143, New York, 11 Oct. 2007); at foot of text: "M. de la Fayette." Enclosure not found.

To Benjamin H. Latrobe

DEAR SIR Washington Mar. 10. 05.

I now inclose you the letter for mr Appleton which covers one for mr Mazzei according to promise.

I have considered the case of mr Lenthall according to your letter of Feb. 29. 04. and to the statement you put into my hands the other day, and I approve of your allowing him three dollars & two thirds a day. pressed with business before my departure I can only add my salutations and assurances of respect TH: JEFFERSON

PoC (DLC); at foot of text: "Mr. Latrobe"; endorsed by TJ. Enclosures: TJ to Thomas Appleton, 10 Mch., and enclosure.

CASE OF MR LENTHALL: the wages approved for John Lenthall, as clerk of the works at the Capitol and the President's House, were equivalent to those of George Blagden, the contract superintendent of the stone work (Vol. 42:569).

Latrobe's STATEMENT has not been found.

To Bishop James Madison

DEAR SIR Washington Mar. 10. 05.

Mr. Mazzei desires me to send him an authenticated certificate of the death of Bellini, with the seal of the state. will you be so good as to get one for me, and further to say whether there will be any property remaining after his debts are paid, and of what value? Accept my affectionate salutations. TH: JEFFERSON

PoC (MHi); at foot of text: "Bishop Madison"; endorsed by TJ.

In a letter of 18 July 1804, TJ informed Philip Mazzei of the DEATH of Carlo Bellini a month earlier. Although there is no record of Mazzei requesting the death certificate from TJ, it was likely needed along with the power of attorney in the settlement of Bellini's estate as administered by John Bracken (RS, 3:375-82; Vol. 33:307n).

To Philip Mazzei

DEAR SIR Washington Mar. 10. 05.

Mr. Latrobe, superintendant of the public buildings having occasion for a stone carver, capable of carving the Capitel & frize of a Corinthian order. I have taken the liberty of addressing him to you to seek a proper character, he arranging with mr Appleton to recieve the person on your recommendation & to pay whatever monies may be necessary. we want a mere workman, but of real proficiency in his art; yet of no higher pretension. will you be so good as to give the aid desired?

Your letters of June 15. 25. July 19. had been recieved in due time, and three days ago came to hand that of Dec. 15. with copies of 1801. Sep. 28. and 1803. Feb. 15. not before recieved. no trial has been made of the earth for floating bricks. a factitious stone which floats in water & is fire proof was invented here about 3. years ago, but offering no utility, tho' extremely cheap, is considered as a matter of mere curiosity. I write this day to Bishop Madison for an authenticated certificate of Bellini's death, which shall be forwarded to you. I am of opinion he left no property. he had asked of me to accept & place at Monticello mrs Bellini's picture. but the administrator has never sent it to me. should it be sent me, I should think his wishes better answered by consigning it to any one of her friends in Italy whom you should designate to me. I have just taken up & sent off the trees & grapes recieved from yourself & mr Appleton. a sufficient number are alive of all the kinds to ensure their preservation, except the Smyrna, of which 1. only lived, and the Peach apricot of which 1. lives. the stones were planted but have not yet come up. I set out immediately for Monticello to have them planted and hope they will be big enough to welcome my return there 4. years hence. while there I shall see mr Carr, who I think by this time must have got through all the doublings of the law with the purchaser of Colle, & recieved his last paiment. the moment he puts it into my hand, the balance due on that sale shall be remitted you with the account. that will close every thing which was left in charge with me. as to your concerns with Webb, Nicholas, Randolph, Page, nothing more need ever be thought of them. they are closed in bankruptcy. but your house & lot in Richmond are becoming of some value. a person has taken possession & keeps the house in repair, on his own authority, & nobody being authorised to call him to account he bids defiance. if you thought proper to send a blank power of attorney, I would insert the name of some good person who should recover it from him. if it is neglected much longer you will be barred by the act of limitation.

The late presidential election was determined by 162. against 14. votes, and these will be with us in one year more. I send you my inaugural address. as that of 1801. was a declaration of principles, this of 1805. is an account of practice on these principles, a compte rendu, which the nature of the occasion obliged to be very summary. the head of Indians was a little extended with an ironical eye to the modern declaimers against philosophy. a piece lately published in a Boston paper presents so just and concise a summary of the proceedings of the administration the last 4. years that I cannot help sending it to you. I shall put it under cover to mr Appleton with a desire to prevent it's saddling you with postage. I salute you with constant & affectionate friendship & respect.

TH: JEFFERSON

RC (DLC); at foot of first page: "Mr. Mazzei"; endorsed by Mazzei. Enclosure: Second Inaugural Address (see Document XIII at 4 Mch.). Other enclosure not found. Enclosed in TJ to Thomas Appleton, 10 Mch.

TAKEN THE LIBERTY OF ADDRESSING HIM: TJ to Benjamin H. Latrobe, 10 Mch.; see also TJ to Appleton, 10 Mch.

FLOATING BRICKS: see Mazzei to TJ, 15 Dec. 1804.

MRS BELLINI'S PICTURE: in 1799, Carlo Bellini had offered TJ a portrait of his wife, Gaspara Farolfi Bellini, which TJ agreed to accept as a "testamentary donation" after Bellini's death (Vol. 31:85-6, 98-9).

PURCHASER OF COLLE: Kemp Catlett (Vol. 29:83n).

In 1784 when he left America, Mazzei gave power of attorney to John Blair and Edmund Randolph to transact all his Virginia business and placed his house and LOT IN RICHMOND under the trusteeship of Foster Webb. Mazzei suffered financial losses in 1788 as a result of Webb's conduct and had ongoing concerns about the handling of his properties. In 1811, TJ assumed power of attorney for Mazzei and used it to convey the Richmond property, which sold for $6,500 in May 1813 (conveyance from Mazzei to Thomas Taylor, 17 May 1813 [Tr in Henrico Co. Deed Book, 13:315-8; with 27 Sep. 1784 power of attorney to Randolph and Blair]; RS, 3:375-82; 10:250-2; Vol. 13:166-7).

From Wilson Cary Nicholas

DEAR SIR

Norfolk March 10. 1805

I was very much mortified on my return to this place to find the inclosed in my desk, in a letter written at the moment of my departure, I suppose in my hurry I had put it there instead of sending it to the post office. I beg you Sir, to pardon this seeming inattention to your request that your letter to Col. Newton shou'd be returned immediately. The business of my office is in such a train that it can now be closed in as short a time as it will ever be practicable to do it in. I will therefore, as soon as I obtain your permission, address a letter of resignation to the Secretary of the treasury. I will take the liberty to mention that I am anxious to have this by the 15th. of apl. but I will with pleasure make the time of my doing so, suit your perfect convenience. If you think proper to offer this place to Col. Newton, or to any other person in this town, it will be a great gratification to me, if you shou'd find that you can in any manner make me useful to you. Since the date of your letter upon this subject Col. Newton has been appointed President of the Virginia bank in Norfolk but I do not know that that wou'd in any manner influence his dicision. The spirit of hostility among the republicans in this place, as in other parts of the U.S. has unfortunately increased since I had the pleasure of addressing you last. I do not know how it is to end, but I fear in the destruction of the party and the misery of our country. the selfishness and intemperance of many of our politicians makes them deaf and blind to the most obvious interest of their country. Every article of provision, is excessively high and likely to remain so, and it is said that tobacco will sell at a better price than it has done. there have not been any arrivals at this port as late as those that have been announced in the North. the merchants are under great alarm lest there should be a truce hatched up between England and France.

I am with the greatest respect & esteem, Dear Sir, your much obliged & devoted hum. Serv.
W. C. NICHOLAS

RC (DLC); endorsed by TJ as received 25 Mch. and so recorded in SJL. Enclosure: TJ to Thomas Newton, 6 Dec. 1804.

YOUR REQUEST: TJ to Nicholas, 19 Dec. 1804.

Notes on Personal Finance

[10 Mch. 1805 and after]

1804			
Mar. 10.	in bank		532.025
	cash		175.
			707.025
	Hepburn	27.675	
	Maine	38.	
	Harrison	2.	
	Treasury	40	
	Langdon	16.	
	<*Jones & Howell*	*144.47*>	
	<*Daugherty*>		
	Ingle	8.105	

Jones & Kain	19.	
Marsh	50.[1]	
Patterson	4.875	
Rigden	8.50	
Smith	2.	
Stage	19.75	260.905

Eppes	100
Barnes groc.	
March	88.50[2]
Wardlaw	46.12
Webb	
Lenox	
Jones & Howell	144.47
Polkinhorn & Hall.	17.77
Carpenter	194.25

Aug. 1st. week. G. Jeff. for C. Peyton 201.

paimts. to W.S. since Oct. 1803.

1804.	Mar.	17.	J.B.	500	
	May	10	J.B.	500	
	July	9	Th:J	500	
	Aug.	10	J.B.	500	
	Oct.	6	Th:J	500	
	Nov.	10	Th:J	500	
1805.	Feb.	8	Th:J	500	
		12			8787.69
	Mar.	11	Th:J	500	
	May	4.	Th:J.	500	

MS (CSmH); entirely in TJ's hand; on verso of sheet addressed "President of the United States."

These notes comprise bills, for most of which TJ had relevant invoices in hand by the middle of March 1805, not 1804 as he mistakenly wrote at the head of the document. This is the first of a series of documents that he created for the management of his finances. Similar notes appear in this volume at 15 Mch., 4 May, 4 June, and 5 July. In each case, after accounting for his available financial reserves, TJ compiled a list of payments to be made. A set of payments recorded in his financial memoranda at 11 Mch. matched many of the expenses listed above, including those to Alexander HEPBURN for plants, the TREASURY Department as reimbursement for coal, Jones & KAIN for carriage repair, Edgar PATTERSON for a cage, the firm of Burnett & RIGDEN for watch mending, and someone named SMITH for a blanket. He recorded making the first installment on his bill to Mrs. John March the following day, when he also paid Joseph Dougherty $18.59, an amount he did not include in his notes above (MB, 2:1148; Statement of Account with Mrs. John March, 7 Mch.; Statement of Account with Henry Ingle, 8 Mch.; Receipt from Richard Harrison, [11 Mch.]; TJ to John Langdon, 11 Mch.; Joseph Dougherty to TJ, 22 Mch.).

Below those earlier payments, TJ listed some other expected transactions, which he completed at different times in May and June. The payment to John Wayles EPPES was for a horse, while that to William WARDLAW was for doctor's bills. TJ recorded paying James WEBB $50.50 for "mahogy. tables &c." on 6 June. Payment of $31.48 for venetian blinds made by Peter LENOX, an amount that TJ does not appear to have known when compiling these notes, occurred on 7 May. TJ paid the tailor's bill from Thomas CARPENTER in two installments, on 7 May and 6 June (MB, 2:1152-6; Statement of Account with Thomas Carpenter, at 24 Jan.; Statement of Account with Polkinhorn & Hall, 12 Mch.).

TJ likely added information about a note due to Craven PEYTON on 28 Apr., when he recorded the pending transaction in his financial memoranda, having received a letter the day before from George Jefferson informing him of the debt (MB, 2:1151; TJ to Peyton, 13 June).

On or after 4 May, TJ listed some payments he had made to William Short (W.S.), either through his account with John Barnes (J.B.) or from his own banking account. He would subsequently make another $500 payment on 14 June (TJ to Short, 14 June).

[1] Number interlined in place of "88.50."
[2] Number interlined in place of "[60.50]."

To Madame de Tessé

DEAR MADAM Washington Mar. 10. 05.

Your favors of April 10. & Aug. 17. were not recieved till autumn. that of Aug. 17. only the 1st. of November. immediately on reciept of the former I wrote to a friend in Philadelphia to make the enquiries you desired respecting the affairs of M. de Noailles. I inclose you his answer, on which much reliance may be placed. I detained this in expectation of sending it early in winter with another collection of plants & seeds which had been prepared for you. but early in December every harbour from this place Northwardly blocked up with ice, and through the severest winter we have known for 20. years kept closed till within a few days past, so that no vessel could get out. now that our port (Alexandria) is open I find not a single vessel bound for any port of France except the Mediterranean. were the packages sent thither they would cost you more for transportation than they are worth, & would besides be entirely after the season. indeed, for the same reason, the expence of transportation, I should be afraid to send you boxes to any port except Havre; & we know not when the blockade of that will cease. we are therefore compleatly defeated for this year in the new supply of plants; & must comfort ourselves with better hope for the next.—your letters brought me information, always welcome, of your health continuing well. the flattering testimonies I recieve of the good will of my fellow citizens would have been a source of great happiness to me, were they not more than countervailed by domestic afflictions. I have had the inexpressible misfortune to lose my younger daughter, who has left me two grandchildren, & my elder one has such poor health, that I have little confidence in her life. she has 6. children. determined as I am to retire at the end of 4. years, I know not if I shall have a family to retire to. I must learn philosophy from you, & seek in a family of plants, that occupation & delight which you have so fortunately found in them. it will be the greater with me as it will give me opportunities of communicating to you new objects of enjoiment. will you permit me to place here my great respect for M. de Tessé, and to tender to yourself my friendly salutations and assurances of high consideration Th: Jefferson

PoC (MoSHi: Jefferson Papers); at foot of text: "Madame de Tessé"; endorsed by TJ. Enclosure: William Jones to TJ, 1 Oct. 1804.

wrote to a friend: TJ to Jones, 10 Sep. 1804.

From Pierre Chouteau

Monsieur St Louis le onze mars 1805

Le courier que nous attendions samedi dernier n'etant point arrivé, ma derniere lettre du deux mars partira avec celle cy. Je vous ai prevenu par elle du malheureux evenement qui a detruit la majeure partie de ma fortune et qui m'a été d'autant plus sensible que je crois pouvoir sans injustice L'imputer à la vengeance d'une de mes Esclaves que je n'ai pourtant point a me reprocher d'avoir maltraité, elle est actuellement en prison et la premiere cour generale decidera de son sort, mais non de son innocence car quant il n'y auroit point de preuves suffisantes de son crime pour la condamner, je n'en suis pas moins certain qu'elle a allumé de ses propres mains les flammes qui ont devoré mes propriétés et celles que j'avois aux Etats Unis. Je n'entrerai dans aucun detail de ce que je vous ai marqué par ma derniere lettre esperant qu'elle Vous parviendra surement. Il vient d'arriver à St Louis un Ne La Lime interprete pour les nations sauvages au fort Dearborn à qui le chef de la nation Peoria, nomme Decoines, a remis les lettres et discours dont vous trouverez ci joint copie et dont il s'est chargé pour les nations de cette partie. Je lui ai fait sentir qu'il etoit de son devoir de cooperer de tout son pouvoir a maintenir l'union parmi toutes les nations plutot que de chercher a la troubler, La guerre entre Les Sauvages ne pouvant qu'etre desavantageuse aux Etats Unis, mais comme il n'est point sous ma direction je me suis borné a lui faire connoitre les intentions du Gouvernement et a lui donner les avis que j'ai cru les meilleurs pour entretenir la paix parmi les nations et empecher un rassemblement qui nous donneroit beaucoup d'inquietudes. Cette guerre qui semble se preparer avec tant d'acharnement et de si grands preparatifs contre Les Ozages est fomentée par des blancs qui reveillent et excitent parmi les nations une jalousie aveugle sur le choix que Mr Le Capne Lewis a fait par préférence de la Nation osage pour l'envoyer auprès du gouvernement. Le sauvage livré a lui même et sur de mecontenter Le Gouvernement americain dont il connoit le pouvoir ne se porteroit point a de telles demarches, s'il n'y etoit poussé par des esprits inquiets et Dangereux; Cette observation, Monsieur, me fait insister sur la nécessité, J'ose dire, que personne ne puisse S'introduire chez les Nations du District De la Louisiane, soit pour commercer, ou voyager, ou tel autre pretexte que ce Soit sans un permis de L'agence generale et je croirai de mon devoir de le refuser à toute personne dont le caractere, Les intentions, la prudence ne me seront pas parfaitement connues Les Nations du District de la Louisiane sont nombreuses, beaucoup d'entre elles ne sont nullement civilisées, aucuns etablissements du coté de L'Ouest ne peuvent ni les surveiller, ni les contenir, ces considerations doivent engager le gouvernement a ne negliger aucunes des precautions que la prudence exige dans nos rapports avec ces nations sauvages, Je crois devoir ajouter, Monsieur, que dans la supposition que le Gouvernement se reserve a lui seul le commerce avec ces Nations comme des lors il sera forcé d'employer beaucoup d'agens subalternes, le choix de ces agens, qui peuvent si facilement indisposer, prevenir ou egarer ces nations, doit etre remis a L'Agent general, Ces reflexions me sont dictées par le zele le plus pur pour les interets des Etats Unis et la tranquillité de ses citoyens et par la crainte que j'ai de voir ma bonne volonté, mes efforts et mon credit auprès des nations sauvages devenir pour ainsi dire inutiles par les fausses demarches et les propros inconsiderés et même seditieux des blancs qui commercent avec eux. Peutêtre me trompai je dans les remedes que J'indique mais je croirois manquer à la confiance dont vous m'honorez et ne pas remplir les devoirs de la place que j'occupe si je ne vous communiquois mes idées dont j'espere Vous sentirez la Solidité. Ces Nouvelles me confirment dans L'opinion que je vous ai deja temoigné que tous ces bruits de guerre des Nations contre Les Etats Unis etoient sans fondements et n'ont été occasionnés que par les mouvements que les sauvages se donnent pour operer une ligne générale contre Les Nations osages. J'employerai tous les moyens de persuasion pour detourner les differentes nations de se rendre au rassemblement proposé et j'espere avoir assez de credit auprés de plusieurs d'entre elles pour les en detourner mais si je ne peux parvenir a le dissoudre entierement J'en donnerai avis aux Osages en les engageant a faire les demarches necessaires pour ramener la paix et leur faire voir que le gouvernement veille sur eux. Si L'interprete que j'ai envoyé reconnoitre le rassemblement que l'on m'a dit exister près la riviere des Moens m'assure de son existence je compte alors retarder de quelque tems mon voyage chez les osages et aller de Suite moi même trouver les sacquias, ayowas et autres nations reunies pour les ramener a des dispositions pacifiques. Soyez persuadé, Monsieur, que je ne cesserai dans toute occasion de faire tous mes efforts pour meriter votre confiance a la qu'elle J'attache le plus grand prix.

J'ai l'honneur d'etre avec le plus profond respect Monsieur Votre très humble et très obeissant serviteur. PRE. CHOUTEAU

EDITORS' TRANSLATION

SIR, St. Louis, 11 Mch. 1805

The mail we expected last Saturday did not arrive, so my last letter, from 2 Mch., will go out with this one. In that letter, I informed you about the terrible event that destroyed most of my fortune. It affected me all the more because I think I can rightly attribute it to the revenge of one of my former slaves, even though I have no reason to believe I mistreated her. She is now in prison, and the court will decide her fate, although not her innocence. There is not sufficient proof of her crime to condemn her, but I am no less certain that she personally set the fire that destroyed my property and all my possessions in the United States. I will not elaborate on any details from my last letter, hoping it will reach you safely.

A certain Mr. Lalime, an interpreter for the native nations at Fort Dearborn, just arrived in St. Louis. Ducoigne, chief of the Peoria nation, entrusted the enclosed letters and speeches to him on behalf of the nations of that region. I let him know he had an obligation to cooperate fully in order to preserve unity among all the nations and not seek to disrupt it. A war among the natives could only be detrimental to the United States. Since Lalime is not under my orders, I limited myself to informing him of the government's intentions and giving him my best advice about how to foster peace among the nations and prevent a gathering that would cause us problems.

The war against the Osages, which these nations seem to be planning with such care and determination, is fomented by whites who awaken and excite blind jealousy among them over Captain Lewis's decision to send the Osage nation to meet with the government. Natives, left to themselves and certain of displeasing the American government whose power they are aware of, would not undertake such actions if they were not pushed by dangerous, agitated people. This observation, Sir, prompts me to stress how necessary it is that no one be allowed to present himself to the nations of Louisiana District, whether for commerce, travel, or any other purpose, without a permit from the War Department. I would consider it my duty to refuse a permit to anyone whose character, intentions, and judgment I could not vouch for. The nations of Louisiana are numerous, and many of them are not civilized. There are no institutions on the western side to watch over or control them. The government must not neglect any prudent precaution in our relations with these native nations. I feel obliged to add, Sir, that if the government reserves sole rights of commerce with these nations, it will immediately be forced to appoint many deputy agents. The choice of these agents, who could easily irritate these nations or lead them astray, would need to be entrusted to a general agent. These observations are prompted by the purest zeal for the interests of the United States and the peace of its citizens and by my fear of seeing my good will, efforts, and standing among the native nations jeopardized by missteps and injudicious or even seditious words by the whites who interact with them. I may be wrong about the measures I suggest, but I would feel I had betrayed the trust with which you honor me and the duties of my function if I did not communicate these ideas, which I hope you will share.

The latest news confirms the belief I already expressed to you that all the rumors about war between the Indian nations and the United States are without basis; they were caused by actions the natives undertook to ally themselves against the Osage nation. I will use all means of persuasion to deter the various nations from attending the proposed gathering, and I hope to have enough authority among several of them to be able to deflect them. If I cannot fully dissuade them, I will inform the Osages and urge them to undertake the necessary steps to restore peace, letting them know the government is watching them. If the interpreter I am sending confirms the existence of the gathering I have heard is taking place near the Des Moines river, I will postpone my trip to the Osages and to go straight to the Sacs, Iowas, and other assembled nations to bring them back to peaceful sentiments. Be assured, Sir, that I will not not stop trying in all circumstances to warrant your trust, which I cherish.

With the deepest respect, Sir, I have the honor of being your very humble and obedient servant.

PRE. CHOUTEAU

RC (DLC); at foot of text: "Mr Jefferson President des Etats Unis"; endorsed by TJ as received 27 Apr. and so recorded in SJL. Enclosures: messages from Jean Baptiste Ducoigne, recorded at Kaskaskia, 2 Mch., by Jean Lalime; in the first, Ducoigne addresses "Como Mon Frere" (Gomo) and asks why the young men of his nation injure Ducoigne's, when they only want to live in peace with the Potawatomis, Ottawas, and Ojibwas; he extends his hand in peace; in the second message, addressed to "Saquinack. Mon parent" (Siggenauk), Ducoigne asks him to visit with his wife, so that she can see her father, mother, and siblings and he can see Ducoigne's desire for peace; in the last two messages, addressed to Gomo, Ducoigne mentions an alliance to wage war on the Osages; he has joined the effort and invites other nations to do the same; he expects the alliance to gather in St. Louis ("Pain Cour") in four and a half months and to muster 3,000 warriors to defeat the Osages; Ducoigne acknowledges the weakness of his nation but thinks it good that nations unite against the Osages; signed "Macouaissa" (Tr in same, TJ Papers, 147:25702; in French; translation, in different order, printed in *Terr. Papers*, 13:103-4, from copies sent by James Bruff to James Wilkinson).

CHEF DE LA NATION PEORIA: Ducoigne led the Kaskaskia tribe, which along with the Peorias formed the two remnants of the Illinois nations. Jean Lalime, the interpreter who took down Ducoigne's messages, indicated that they were intended for a Potawatomi chief "Residing at the

Peoria," most likely Gomo, who led a village on Lake Peoria. The other leader was likely Siggenauk, a longtime war chief in what is now southern Wisconsin and northern Illinois who eventually settled near the Chicago River (Sturtevant, *Handbook*, 15:673; R. David Edmunds, *The Potawatomis: Keepers of the Fire* [Norman, Okla., 1978], 101-2, 111-12, 125-7, 172-3; R. David Edmunds, "Main Poc: Potawatomi Wabeno," *American Indian Quarterly*, 9 [1985], 263; Vol. 6:63-4n).

To Jacob Crowninshield

Washington Mar. 11. 05.

Th: Jefferson presents his friendly salutations to mr Crownenshield, and presuming on his kindness formerly experienced asks the favor of him to procure for him a kental of the best dumb-fish to be forwarded to Gibson & Jefferson at Richmond for Monticello. It is intended for use in August & September. Th:J. leaves Washington the day after tomorrow, and will be back about the middle of April. health & respect.

PoC (MHi); endorsed by TJ.

KINDNESS FORMERLY EXPERIENCED: see Crowninshield to TJ, 14 July 1804; TJ to Crowninshield, 21 July; Crowninshield to TJ, 5 Dec.

DUMB-FISH, or dunfish, refers to New England cod that is salted and dried in a manner that gives it a dun color (OED).

From William Darlington

MUCH RESPECTED SIR/ Westchester, Penna. March 11th. 1805

Knowing your predilection for all subjects which have any relation to, or influence over the welfare of man, I have presumed to obtrude the accompanying sheets upon your view—not in consequence of any thing important contained in them, but because a subject is touched upon which I conceive to have a much greater influence upon mankind, whether considered with respect to health, morals, or government, than they are generally aware of—And of which a philosophical knowledge, and judicious application of the principles, would in my opinion, tend much to promote the Happiness of the human race;—viz. the power of *Habit*. Another inducement to this intrusion upon your time and pursuits, although perhaps less pertinent, yet not less pleasing, is that I may declare with how much Respect and Esteem I am your sincere (tho' unknown)

Friend, W. DARLINGTON

RC (DLC); at foot of text: "Thos. Jefferson, P.U.S."; endorsed by TJ as received 21 Mch. and so recorded in SJL. FC (Lucius Wilmerding, Jr., Princeton,

1946); in Darlington's hand; at head of text: "copy." Enclosure: William Darlington, *A Dissertation on the Mutual Influence of Habits and Disease* (Philadelphia, 1804; Sowerby, No. 990).

Physician and botanist William Darlington (1782-1863) began his medical training with an apprenticeship under John Vaughan in Delaware, followed by a degree from the University of Pennsylvania in 1804. After a year at sea as a ship's surgeon, Darlington opened a medical practice in West Chester. He served in the War of 1812 and was then elected as a Republican to the Fourteenth, Sixteenth, and Seventeenth Congresses, where he advocated against the expansion of slavery into the territories. Although Darlington enjoyed a successful career in medicine, his botanical pursuits, nurtured in college by teacher Benjamin Smith Barton, were of more lasting interest. He established a natural history society in West Chester, was a member of more than 40 other literary and scientific organizations, and wrote books on regional plant life. Darlington also worked to preserve and publish the letters of major Pennsylvania botanists, including Humphry Marshall, John Bartram, and former classmate and friend William Baldwin. His accomplishments in the field of botany led to honorary degrees at Yale and Dickinson College, and in 1853, John Torrey named the California pitcher plant, or *Darlingtonia californica*, after him, one of two such honors (ANB; Washington Townsend, "Memorial of William Darlington, M.D.," *Historical Magazine*, 7 [Aug. 1863], 235, 237, 241; Charles Lanman, "Our Historical Writers: William Darlington, LL.D.," *Historical Magazine*, 3d ser., 1 [Jan. 1872], 33).

Receipt from Robert Harrison

[11 Mch. 1805]

Mr Th Jefferson Dr to Robt Harrison

1805

Feby To Repairing three penns $2.0

Recd Payment

ROB HARRISON

MS (MHi); undated; endorsed by TJ: "Harrison Robert pd. Mar. 05."

Under 11 Mch. in his financial memoranda, TJ recorded paying two dollars through Joseph Dougherty for REPAIRING pens for the polygraph. Harrison subsequently received payments on several other occasions for work on TJ's polygraphs (MB, 2:1148, 1159, 1165, 1168, 1170).

To John Hawkins of Kentucky

Washington Mar. 11. 05.

Th: Jefferson presents his compliments to mr Hawkins & his thanks for the trouble he has taken in proposing to him the purchase of the pair of elks: but having no inclosure for confining such animals, nor expecting to have one for several years, he is obliged to decline it.

PoC (MHi); endorsed by TJ.

PROPOSING TO HIM: Hawkins to TJ, 1 Mch.

To John Langdon

My dear Sir — Washington Mar. 11. 05.

Your favor of the 25th. is recieved as is one also from your nephew at Boston inclosing a bill of lading for the 3. casks of perry; which I doubt not will arrive in due time. permit me now to inclose the cost 16. D. in such bills as I can get, which I am in hopes can be passed with you. I am just setting out for Monticello where I propose to pass three or four weeks in order to recruit after the fatigues of our winter campaign. Accept my affectionate salutations and assurances of constant friendship

Th: Jefferson

RC (NhPoS: John Langdon Papers); at foot of text: "J. Langdon esq." PoC (MHi); endorsed by TJ. Notation in SJL: "16. D."

one also from your nephew: Joshua B. Langdon to TJ, 20 Feb.

To James Madison

James Wilkinson of Maryland, Governor of the territory of Louisiana from & after the 3d. of July next for the term of 3. years then next ensuing, unless sooner &c.

Joseph Browne of N. York, Secretary of do. from & after &c.

*Return Jonathan Meigs of Lousiana
*John B. C. Lucas of Pensylvania
Rufus Easton of New York
} to be judges of the court of the territory of Louisiana from & after &c.

George Duffield of Tennissee to be a judge of the Superior court of the territory of Orleans. [he lives at Greenville Greene county. Tennissee]

James Brown late of Kentucky, now of Orleans. Attorney of the US. for the district of Orleans

Henry Hill junr. of N. York Consul for the island of Cuba.

Edward Carrington of R. Island Consul at Canton.

James M. Henry of Virginia Agent at Jamaica.

Th: Jefferson
Mar. 11. 05.

* I am not sure these Christian names are right

John Thompson of Kentucky Register of the land office in the Western part of the territory of Orleans

John W. Gurley of Orleans Register &c. in the Eastern part of the territory of Orleans.

James Tremble of Tennissee Recorder of the territory of Louisiana.

TH: JEFFERSON
Mar. 11. 05.

PoC (DLC); likely two communications copied on same sheet; brackets in original; at foot of text: "Mr. Madison." Notation in SJL: "Deptmt. State appointmts."

Enclosing a number of recommendations, HENRY HILL wrote to Madison on 12 Jan. soliciting the consulship at Havana. Hill presented his "connexions already formed at Havana" and his "knowledge of the Spanish Character, language and trade" as qualifications for the job (RC in DNA: RG 59, LAR; endorsed by TJ: "Hill Henry junr. to be Consul at Havanna"). Robert Young, who had previously held the commission, resigned the consulship in a letter of 25 Jan. to Madison (RC in DNA: RG 59, RD; endorsed by TJ: "Young Robert resigns Consulship of Havanna").

In a letter of 23 Feb. to Madison, William Jones recommended EDWARD CARRINGTON as a commercial agent at Canton. "The jealous and monopolizing spirit of the European agents" and "importance of our trade to Canton" required, Jones contended, "the permanent residence of a public agent of respectability." Jones was assured by a letter he enclosed from two Americans in Canton that Carrington met these requirements (RC in DLC: TJ Papers, 147:25659-60, endorsed by TJ: "Carrington Edwd. (Providence) to be Consul at Canton"; Madison, *Papers, Sec. of State Ser.*, 9:62-4).

On 25 Mch., Madison wrote to JAMES M. HENRY, informing him of the president's desire that he replace William Savage as U.S. agent for distressed and impressed seamen in Jamaica. Henry declined the appointment (same, 171).

To James Mease

SIR Washington Mar. 11. 05.

I am indeed a most unpunctual correspondt. but it is not from unwillingness to attend to those who favor me with their letters, but from the pressure of calls not admitting delay. since the reciept of your favor of Nov. 20. I have not lost sight of the subject, but I meant to answer you by sending a model of the sharp, as well as square toed mouldboard. that required that I should be half a day with a workman which I could not spare till very lately. I now send you a small box containing 1. a square toed mouldboard. 2. a sharp do. 3. a block shewing the method of making it the principle is the same. there is also a printed leaf describing the method. most persons who have seen these models prefer the [sharp] one. it will be clear of the disadvantage of clogging in front when the earth is a little wet: but it will not run so steadily. the incumbent earth makes the square one move as steadily as a vessel [. . .][w]ater. it is scarcely necessary to hold it. Accept my salutations & assurances of great respect

TH: JEFFERSON

PoC (DLC); faint; at foot of text: "Dr. Maese"; endorsed by TJ.

YOUR FAVOR OF NOV. 20: that is, Mease to TJ, 19 Nov. 1804, which TJ endorsed and recorded in SJL as a letter of 20 Nov.

PRINTED LEAF: see TJ to Samuel Harrison Smith, 21 Feb.

To Robert Moore

Washington Mar. 11. 05

Th: Jefferson presents his salutations to Mr. Robert Moore & his acknolegements for the Jerusalem wheat he was so kind as to forward him from his relation in Ireland. he prays him to be the channel of communicating his thanks to that gentleman and his assurances that the talent shall not be hidden in a napkin. the good men of the world form a nation of their own, and when[1] promoting the well-being of others never ask of what country they are. he hopes the US. will shew themselves worthy of these kindnesses. he tenders to mr Moore his respects and best wishes.

PoC (ViW: Tucker-Coleman Collection); at foot of text: "Mr. Moore"; endorsed by TJ.

JERUSALEM WHEAT: see William Moore to TJ, 19 Nov. 1804, and Robert Moore to TJ, 28 Feb. 1805.

HIDDEN IN A NAPKIN: Luke 19:20.

[1] TJ here canceled "doing."

To James Oldham

SIR Washington Mar. 11. 05

I received in due time your letter of Feb. 4. and immediately sent to mr Andrews's to get the information you desired, but he was gone to New York. I waited supposing he might return and being just now on my departure for Monticello, I sent to his house again to-day, but he is not returned, nor expected under a month. any thing however can be done in his absence where they have the moulds: but new moulds can only be made by him. if you can wait a month he will be returned & so shall I. or if you will be content with the moulds cut for my work, they will execute them on your order. they will be the cheaper where no new mould is to be cut. Accept my best wishes

TH: JEFFERSON

RC (ViU); at foot of text: "Mr. Oldham." PoC (DLC); endorsed by TJ.

YOUR LETTER: Oldham's letter of 4 Feb. has not been found, but see Oldham to TJ, 5 Mch.

To William Short

Dear Sir Washington Mar. 11. 05.

Your favors of Feb. 14. & 26. are now before me, and answering first to the former, I inclose you a copy of the cypher as well as of the cyphered letter therein referred to.

I have examined the two statements of our account. the first is perfectly intelligible, & right in principle. I have not attempted to examine the calculations, being on the point of departure for Monticello, & not doubting their correctness. the second statement is unintelligible to me, except the earlier part of it. the rest perhaps I might make out if I had time, for a debrouillement of the sums & operations it presents. but I believe it would be a waste of time and supposing it correct & knowing, if it is not, that you will correct it, I have not hesitated to fix the balance as there stated, and to inclose you an obligation for it, as an evidence & security for the debt in case of the death of either. if we both live, it will be easily done. I inclose you the statements according to your request and a draught on the bank of the US. for 500. Dollars to be added to the credits on these statements. no endeavors shall be wanting on my part to expedite the discharge.

I am just setting out for Albemarle to see my sick daughter whose situation in point of health is such as to fill me with disquietude. I do not expect to get back to Washington till the middle of April. we shall not be without hope of your passing the autumnal months with us at Monticello. Accept my affectionate salutations and assurances of great esteem & respect Th: Jefferson

RC (DLC: Short Papers); endorsed by Short. Notation in SJL: "500. D." Enclosures not found, but see Short to TJ, 14 Feb.

debrouillement: an unraveling.
draught: see mb, 2:1147-8.

To John Strode

Dear Sir Washington Mar. 11. 05.

Nothing is so common as to see men value themselves most for what they know least about. in truth ignorance is always the parent of vanity. this accounts for my valuing myself on the invention of a mouldboard for a plough and venturing to submit it to your judgment. in a small box which went by my cart from hence two days ago I sent you two models, and the block to shew how they were made. I sent at the same time the Domestic Encyclopedia in which the principles of the mouldboard are explained. the book however is more worthy your acceptance for it's other valuable contents than for this article. I shall set out for Monticello the 13th. and go by the court houses for the sake of dryer road, & probably return that way so that I do not promise myself the pleasure of seeing you till July. Accept my friendly salutations & best wishes Th: Jefferson

PoC (DLC); at foot of text: "Mr. Strode"; endorsed by TJ.

DOMESTIC ENCYCLOPEDIA: see James Mease to TJ, 5 Dec. 1803.

To John Abernethie

Sir Washington Mar. 12. 05.

On the reciept of your letter of Dec. 1. I referred it to the Secretary of the Treasury for information, sending him the inclosed loan-office certificate. his answer is that if the certificate be genuine it might have been funded under the funding act, until it became barred by the act of limitation of Mar. 3. 1795. & that act having been further suspended till the 12th. of June 1799 in favor of creditors, it might have been recieved at any time before that date. but it is now barred, after having been kept open 22. years. the public security requires that accounts should be closed within a convenient time. 22. years would seem long enough for any body's convenience. the act of limitation moreover is not merely expedient, it is also just when claims have been kept back till witnesses are all dead, documents lost, and no fair means are left of investigating the debt. in the present case, the officers who were conversant in loan office certificates, who had marks by which they knew the genuine from the counterfiet are all dead, or disappeared. I mention these circumstances to justify the public functionaries from the supposition that injustice to individuals is intended by their act of limitations, & to shew that their object is to guard the public against injustice. I mention it too for your own satisfaction which is more likely to ensue from knowing the real motives, than if you imagined the refusal arbitrary & without proper motive. I inclose you the certificate, & tender you my salutations & respects Th: Jefferson

PoC (DLC); at foot of text: "Mr. Abernethie." Enclosure not found.

REFERRED IT TO THE SECRETARY: TJ to Gallatin, 17 Feb.

HIS ANSWER: Gallatin to TJ, printed at 19 Feb.

To Thomas Allen

SIR Washington Mar. 12. 05.

Being in the moment of my departure for Monticello to take a short respite after our winter campaign, I have barely time to acknolege the reciept of your favor, and to thank you for the friendly dispositions it manifests. the last thirty years are probably more pregnant of instruction to mankind than any equal period which history furnishes. our portion of it will certainly exhibit what will be most pleasing to the friends of man. for those who live under it certainly no government can be more eligible. those indeed who administer it go through a fiery ordeal, and need all the devotion of patriotism which inspired a Decius. his sacrifice was life. with us character must be offered on the altar of public good. a few malicious men, availing themselves of the licentiousness of the press are able to test by the severest trials the firmness of a public man. but the justice which our citizens have shewn themselves capable of exercising, and their discernment between facts & falsehood will hold up an encouragement to future functionaries, which our late experiment warrants. after so much misrepresentation, to see my countrymen coming over daily to a sense of the injustice of a certain party towards me, is peculiarly gratifying & will sweeten the latest hours of retirement & life. Accept my salutations & assurances of respect

TH: JEFFERSON

PoC (DLC); at foot of text: "the revd. mr Allen."

YOUR FAVOR: Allen to TJ, [before 4 Mch. 1805].

During a battle in the fourth century B.C., Roman consul DECIUS offered himself to the gods before riding alone into the ranks of the enemy. His act of devotion inspired the Romans to victory (Livy, *History of Rome*, 8.9).

To George Blake

SIR Washington Mar. 12. 05.

I inclose you an application for pardon from a person of the name of John Southack, who says he is now in Boston jail under sentence for forgery, having been confined there already 22. months and having still 14. to remain, & a sum to be paid. considering the judges who sit in a cause, & the Attorney who tries it as possessed of those circumstances which may decide whether any & what mitigation of sentence may be admitted in conformity with the objects of the constitution in confiding the power of pardon to the Executive, I have usually referred these applications to them & asked their opinion. will you be so good as to make this request of them in the present case, & at the same time to favor me with your own opinion. Accept my salutations & assurances of great respect

Th: Jefferson

PoC (DLC); at foot of text: "George Blake esq." Enclosure: John Southack to TJ, 6 Feb., recorded in SJL as received 6 Mch. and "Boston prison" but not found.

George Blake (1769-1841) was a Massachusetts lawyer and politician. After studying law in Worcester and Boston, he was admitted to the bar in 1794. He practiced law briefly in Newburyport before relocating to Boston permanently. He was married twice, and had a son by his second wife. In addition to his private legal practice, he was recognized early in his career for his public orations and addresses, including a memorial opposing the Jay Treaty in 1795. He was elected as a state representative for Suffolk County in 1801. The same year he was appointed as U.S. district attorney for Massachusetts, a position he held until 1829. Thereafter he continued to be active in state politics. In addition to his political activities, Blake was a Freemason and a director of the Boston branch of the Bank of the United States (*New England Historical and Genealogical Register*, 11 [1857], 181-82; *Boston Gazette*, 6 July 1795, 13 Aug. 1801; Haverhill, Mass., *Guardian of Freedom*, 16 July 1795; Boston *Independent Chronicle*, 14 May 1801; JEP, 1:400-4, 405; 3:219, 225, 400, 624, 646; *Boston Commercial Gazette*, 12 Mch. 1829; Boston *Columbian Centinel*, 12 Dec. 1829, 6 Apr. 1831, 7 Jan. 1832, 20 Feb. 1839; *Gloucester Democrat*, 15 Jan. 1836; *A Masonic Eulogy, on the Life of the Illustrious Brother George Washington* [Boston, 1800]; Boston *Daily Atlas*, 7 Oct. 1841; *Hingham Patriot*, 9 Oct. 1841).

In June 1803, a U.S. circuit court in Boston convicted merchant JOHN SOUTHACK of forging a check for $6,800 on the Bank of the United States. He was sentenced to three years at hard labor and payment of costs (Boston *Independent Chronicle*, 6 June 1803; Boston *Gazetteer*, 11 June 1803; Vol. 34:79n).

From Patrick Byrne

Sir

philadelphia 12 March 1805

your draft for *$20.75* came safe to hand being the amt. of my demand for books sent you & is full of all accts. with me—my pamphlets are numerous, as yet I have not been able to make a complete list of them, when I do I shall send you a catalogue,

I am Sir with the greatest respect yr. oblidgd & very hue Sert

Pat. Byrne

RC (MHi); at foot of text: "182 Market St."; endorsed by TJ as received 21 Mch. and so recorded in SJL.

YOUR DRAFT: see TJ to Byrne, 7 Mch.

From John Dawson

DEAR SIR, Fredericksburg March 12. 1805

I have heard that Genl. Hull will not act as the Governor of Michigan—shoud that be the case, and you deem me qualified to fill that office, I will attempt to discharge its duties to the utmost of my powers

With much respect Your friend J DAWSON

RC (DNA: RG 59, LAR); endorsed by TJ as received 23 Mch. and "to be Govr. Detroit" and so recorded in SJL.

To Henry Dearborn

TH: JEFFERSON TO GENL. DEARBORNE March. 12. 05.

I think the cases both of Caston and Hibbs are within the spirit of our promise, altho' they both happen to be out of the letter of it. they have substantially fulfilled the object of the government; and could such cases have been stated to us before hand we should have offered the reward. should you be of this opinion I should approve of giving them the reward as if they were within the letter of the proclamation. Affectionate salutations

RC (PHi: Daniel Parker Papers); endorsed by Dearborn. Not recorded in SJL.

Seth CASTON claimed a reward for apprehending John Sutton (alias of murderer Wiley Harpe) and James May (alias of counterfeiter Peter Alston), two members of an infamous gang of highway robbers led by Samuel Mason. In early 1804, a court in the Mississippi Territory tried and executed the two men after they double-crossed Mason by killing him and bringing in his severed head in an attempt to claim reward money offered by William C. C. Claiborne (Otto A. Rothert, *The Outlaws of Cave-in-Rock* [Cleveland, 1924], 252-65, 272; Alex C. Finley, *The History of Russellville and Logan County, Ky., Which Is to Some Extent a History of Western Kentucky*, Vol. 1, Book II [Russellville, Ky., 1879], 40; Caston to Dearborn, 5 May 1804, recorded in DNA: RG 107, RLRMS; Madison, *Papers, Sec. of State Ser.*, 5:224-5; 6:589-90).

Jeremiah HIBBS applied for a reward for his capture of Samuel McKune, a confessed murderer (Jeremiah Hibbs Petition in DNA: RG 107, LRMS; Hibbs to Dearborn, received 7 Feb. 1805, recorded in DNA: RG 107, RLRMS).

SPIRIT OF OUR PROMISE: beginning in July 1803, for the period of one year, the administration offered a $400 reward for the apprehension of criminals who preyed upon travelers on the Natchez road (Vol. 41:34n).

To John Gassaway

SIR Washington Mar. 12. 05.

I have recieved a letter, which I presume I may consider as coming from yourself, proposing that your son, of 4. years old only may recieve the appointment of a Midshipman. after acknoleging my sense of the kind disposition manifested in the name given him, it is my duty to observe that the earliest period at which midshipmen are recieved is about 10. years of age, when they have learned to read, write, and the first rudiments of arithmetic. until that period therefore nothing of this kind can be done. Accept my salutations and respects.

TH: JEFFERSON

PoC (DLC); at foot of text: "Colo. Gassaway"; endorsed by TJ.

RECIEVED A LETTER: Thomas Jefferson Gassaway to TJ, 4 Mch.

John Gassaway (1754-1820) of Annapolis served as a lieutenant and captain in Maryland regiments during the American Revolution. After the war he was appointed as the register of wills for Anne Arundel County. Though he entertained hopes of taking a position in the Provisional Army of 1798 and was noted by Alexander Hamilton for his "uprightness & attachment to Government," by 1801 he was recommended to TJ as "unchangeably attach'd to Republican principles" (DNA: RG 15; Washington, *Papers, Pres. Ser.*, 16:99-100; "Gassaway Bible Records," *Genealogy: A Weekly Journal of American Ancestry*, 6 [New York, 1916], 101-2; Washington, *Papers, Ret. Ser.*, 2:566; Syrett, *Hamilton*, 22:291; *Baltimore Patriot & Mercantile Advertiser*, 28 June 1820; Vol. 33:217-19).

To Joseph Hiester

SIR Washington Mar. 12. 05.

I have recieved your favor of the 4th. inst. and thank you for the friendly expressions it contains. I see your retirement from the public councils with sincere regret, having always considered your conduct there as disinterested, moderate and conscientious. you can still however be useful in promoting at home a spirit of sound republicanism, and in healing those schisms which seem to threaten the happiness of your state and the weight of it's energies in support of the general government. Accept my friendly salutations & assures of great esteem & respect TH: JEFFERSON

PoC (DLC); at foot of text: "Colo. Joseph Heister"; endorsed by TJ.

Statement of Account with Polkinhorn & Hall

Geo. Town Columa.

Mr. T. Jefferson P.U.S.

To Polkinhorn & Hall Dr.

1804		\$cts
Novr. 28th	two girth straps to a saddle	.37½
	buckle to a girth	.12½
Decbr. 8th	half rein to a bridle	.31
	Cow hide whip	.20
1805		
Januy 9	Stable halter with 2 reins	1.75
17	two girth straps to a saddle	.37½
22	Thong to a whip & repairg halter	.50
	silk lash to a whip	.12½
26	Strap to a circingle	.25
March 6th	Pair best girths 1\$ Circingle 1\$.	2.
10	New pad to a saddle 2\$ stuff 1 ditto $\frac{50}{100}$	2.50
	fixing loops for valiece	.37½
	two tuggs to a britchen, & loops	.87½
	tongue to a buckle & sewing in the same	.37½
	Cow hide whip	.20
	6 luggage straps 1 Inch wide 5 foot long @ $\frac{75}{100}$ pr pair	2.25
	6 ditto do. 1¼ In wide 5. foot 6 In long @ \$1 pr pr	3.
	4 smaller do.	1.
		\$16.58½
12th	A Circingle 1\$. whip lash 18½/100	1.18½
	Total	\$17.77

March 12th. 1805. Received payment in full to date.

Polkinhorn & Hall

RC (MHi); on verso: "Mr. Jefferson wth Polkinn & Hall"; endorsed by TJ: "Polkinhorn & Hall. 17.77 May 10. 05. pd by check on bk US."

Henry Polkinhorn was a saddler and harness maker from whose Alexandria firm TJ made purchases in 1801. After his partnership with Richard Andrews dissolved, Polkinhorn in November 1803 took two nephews into business, William Hall in Georgetown and Richard M. Hall in Baltimore. The Georgetown partnership of Polkinhorn & Hall dissolved by mutual consent on 1 Oct. 1805 (*Federal Gazette & Baltimore Daily Advertiser*, 5 Apr.

1802; *Washington Federalist*, 28 Nov. 1803; *National Intelligencer*, 9 Oct. 1805; Vol. 36:688, 689).

CIRCINGLE: surcingle. VALIECE: valise. BRITCHEN: breeching.

PAYMENT IN FULL: according to his financial memoranda, on 7 May TJ gave Polkinhorn & Hall an order on the Bank of the United States for $17.77 on "their acct. for sadlery" (MB, 2:1153).

From Philippe Reibelt

MONSIEUR LE PRESIDENT! Baltimore le [12] Mars 1805

J'avois en Europe sur le haut Rhin a une fabrique de porcelaine, de terre Anglaise et de fayance—detruite par la dernière Guerre de revolution—Un Moulin *d'email* de 6 pillons et de 8 paires de Meules a 2½ pieds de diàmétre, dont le Mechanisme *mouvant*—extremement simple, n'exigant qu'un emplacement de 30 pieds □ et tres peu de reparation (5 Gourdes par An)—applicable au reste a toute sorte de Moulin sans exception—n'etoit ni eau, ni vent, ni Vapeur, ni Cheval &c. en General d'aucune des maniéres connues—remplacant Cependant parfaitement les fonctions de l'eau sans en avoir les inconveniens.

J'en ai—en 1788—cedè le Secret au feu frere de l'Electeur de Bauden, avec lequel j'etois amicalement lié—Il a—d'apres cette Methode—construit tout près de Carlsruhe un Moulin, ou il appliqua au même Mechanisme Mouvant, de la même proportion—3 pairs de Meules ordinaires, une a còuper l'orge pour Sa brasserie, l'autre a faire de la farine pour Son Menage et ses fabriques, et la derniére pour presser des Graines huileuses.

Ce Moulin existoit encore lorsque je quittois les bords du Rhin, comme proprieté de son fils.

Çe Mechanisme mouvant couta au prince et à Moi environs 100 piastres.

Vous conviendroit il peut étre, d'en avoir un Semblable sur Votre Domaine a Monticello ou autre part?

J'en ai fait, depuis peu—arranger un Modêle.

D'après le Mechanisme (c'est a dire *mis* en Mouvement) des Moulins d'ici, il est probable, qu'un Mechanisme *mouvant* de la même proportion, que le Mien et celui du prince de Bauden pouroit mettre 4 pairs de Meules ordinaires en Mouvement &c.

Mais—qu'il n'en mette en Mouvement &c que deux pairs, ou méme pas plus qu'une—il fera—eû egard a ce que coute ce Mechanisme vis a vis de l'eau a leur entretien respectif &c et en ce que le premier n'est point exposè aux inconveniens de l'eau—il fera, dis je, toujours plus que l'eau, ainsi qu'il a effectivement prouvè sur le Domaine du prince de Bauden près de Carlsruhe, ou il y avoit aussi un Moulin a l'eau.

La Construction d'un Moulin a Maïs, qui devroit fournir toutes les donneès d'un Exemple—ne pourroit—outre l'emplacement, et un log-house pour le Comencement, se monter, qu'a 1300 Gourdes en Supossant, que çe mechanisme mouvant couteroit ici le triple, et les 2 paires de Meules avec leurs appareils 1000 Gourdes.

Permettez moi de Vous presenter mes respects intimement sinceres et profonds. REIBELT

EDITORS' TRANSLATION

MISTER PRESIDENT! Baltimore [12] Mch. 1805

In Europe, in a porcelain, creamware, and faience factory on the upper Rhine that was destroyed in the last revolutionary war, I had a glaze mill with six beams and eight pairs of grindstones, two and one-half feet in diameter. Its powering mechanism was extremely simple, requiring an area of only 30 square feet and very little maintenance (five dollars a year). It could be used for every kind of mill, without exception. It was not of water, or wind, or steam, or horses, or overall of any of the known means, yet it perfectly replaced the functions of water without any of the disadvantages.

In 1788, I gave the secret to my friend, the late brother of the elector of Baden. From this plan he built a mill very near Karlsruhe with the same powering mechanism and dimensions: three pairs of ordinary grindstones, one to grind barley for his brewery, another to make flour for his household and factories, and the last one to press oil.

The mill, owned by his son, was still functioning when I left the Rhine.

The powering mechanism cost the prince and me about 100 piastres.

Might it be useful for you to have a similar one on your estate at Monticello, or elsewhere?

Since then, I have had a model constructed.

Based on the mechanism (in other words the operation) of mills here, it is likely that a powering mechanism of the same dimensions as mine and the prince of Baden's could operate four pairs of ordinary grindstones, etc.

Even if it operated only two pairs, or even a single grindstone, it would still produce more than water, considering its cost by comparison to water, their comparative maintenance, etc., and the fact that this mill is not subject to the disadvantages of water. The prince of Baden demonstrated as much on his estate near Karlsruhe where there was also a water mill.

The construction of a corn mill could serve as an example. Besides the land and a log house to begin with, the cost should not exceed $1,300, assuming that the powering mechanism would cost here three times as much, while two pairs of grindstones and related equipment would cost an additional $1,000.

Allow me to offer you my deeply sincere and profound respect.

REIBELT

RC (DLC); torn at seal; addressed: "A Son Èxcellencè Monsieur le President des Etats unis Thom. Jefferson à Monticello"; franked; postmarked Baltimore, 12 Mch., and Washington, 18 Mch.; endorsed by TJ as received 21 Mch. and so recorded in SJL.

To Abner Ritchie

Sir, Washington Mar. 12. 05.

Having referred to the Superintendant your letter of Feb. 9. I have recieved from him the answer of which the inclosed is a copy. it appears, as I conjectured in my former letter, that the US. have no interest in the question between the representatives of Byrne & Beatty, should not intermeddle, but to leave to them to settle their right to the money in their own way. Accept my salutations & respects.

Th: Jefferson

PoC (ViW: Tucker-Coleman Collection); at foot of text: "Mr. A. Ritchie"; endorsed by TJ. Enclosure: Thomas Munroe to TJ, 24 Feb.

my former letter: TJ to Ritchie, 14 Feb.

To John P. Van Ness

Dear Sir Washington Mar. 12. 05.

The case of mr Peacock has been duly considered. had we been permitted to yield to circumstances of commiseration for his wife & family certainly there is no case in which they have been more deeply felt. but the public security will not allow these considerations to confer entire impunity. the judges who sat on his trial, & the attornies who assisted in it declare they can offer no circumstance justifying an immediate pardon. to grant it in such a case would be not a mitigation of the severity of the law where it's letter does what it's spirit did not mean, & for which purpose the power of pardon is confided to the Executive, but it would be to suspend the intended operations of the law, and to leave the nation exposed to unrestrained wrong. the discharge of mr Peacock at this time therefore cannot be admitted, nor can we now say exactly at what period precisely the rigours of justice may with propriety be made to yield to more pleasing considerations. but it may be useful for mrs Peacock to know that if the happiness of herself & family can be advanced by her retiring to her friends, the term of her husband's confinement will certainly not be lengthened one day by that circumstance. as you have been so kind as to be a mediator in this case I have trusted you would convey in the most acceptable way this information to the parties interested. accept my salutations and assurances of respect. Th: Jefferson

PoC (DLC); at foot of text: "Colo. Van Ness."

Robert Ware Peacock's confinement was briefer than expected. He escaped from the Washington jail on 22 Mch. A $100 reward for his return apparently went unclaimed, for later in the year William Thornton received a letter from Peacock written from Bath, England, in which he observed that his "*expedition was fortunate*" and "the harbinger of future prosperity" (*National Intelligencer*, 25 Mch.; Madison, *Papers, Sec. of State Ser.*, 10:439-40; Vol. 41:574-5n).

MEDIATOR IN THIS CASE: see Petition of Eliza Peacock and Petition of John P. Van Ness and Others for Robert Ware Peacock, both 3 Jan., and TJ to Van Ness, 9 Jan.

To Ann Welsh

MADAM Washington Mar. 12. 05.

Your letter of Nov. 23. came to my hands in December. I took measures for obtaining information of the nature of the case which was the subject of it and to know whether it admitted remedy. I found it was one of those for which no provision had ever been made, but it has not been till now in my power to answer you. altho' the case belongs solely to the legislature, yet it is the duty of my place to make those observations which may place their conduct on it's just ground. the old Congress had engaged to give half pay for life to all their officers who should serve through the war. those whom you represent, having fallen during the war, no right of half pay could arise in their case. after the war, the officers entitled to half pay commuted it for a fixed sum; but no one not entitled to half pay could be entitled to the commutation which was the equivalent for it. the merit of those you represent appears to have been great. but a legislature must act by general rules, and never do for one person what they would not do for every other under the same circumstances. to give the commutation in your case could not be done but under a previous general rule that they would give it to all officers who fell or died in their service during the war. this has never been done by any nation: and it would be a vast undertaking for ours. no one can say what it would add to the national debt. I suggest these observations to you as well to remove all supposition that the representatives of the nation, in making no provision for this case are acting contrary to justice & precedent, and for the tranquility of your own mind, which will be better satisfied on observing that the failure to obtain your request is not the effect of an arbitrary dispensation of the public justice. certainly it would have been more pleasing to me to have found your[1] case among those which come within the scope of legal provision. Accept my salutations & best wishes TH: JEFFERSON

RC (NHi: Gilder Lehrman Collection at the Gilder Lehrman Institute of American History); at foot of text: "Mrs. Ann Welsh." PoC (DLC).

TOOK MEASURES: see Dearborn to TJ, 3 Dec. 1804.

[1]TJ here canceled "application."

From John Davis

SIR Philadelphia, March 13, 1805.

Amidst the important multiplied engagements that necessarily employ your thoughts, I congratulate myself with the most lively satisfaction that you could spare one moment to my importunity for the patronage of your name to my Indian Tale. It is now in the press, a plate is engraving for it, & it will be published with every allurement of paper & type. That it may deserve to be in the hands of those who have imagination to be awakened, & sensibility to be moved, has been my study.

I am, Sir, with great respect, Your much obliged, & most obedient humble Servant, JOHN DAVIS.

RC (DLC); endorsed by TJ as received 21 Mch. and so recorded in SJL.

PATRONAGE OF YOUR NAME: Davis cited TJ's subscription in the front matter of *Captain Smith and Princess Pocahontas*. He wrote: "The author is proud to subjoin the suffrage of the President of the United States of America," and he printed a slightly altered version of TJ's letter of 8 Mch. Davis also used TJ's endorsement to promote his novel later in the year (*Captain Smith and Princess Pocahontas, An Indian Tale* [Philadelphia, 1805], unnumbered page of testimonies; *The First Settlers of Virginia, An Historical Novel* [New York, 1805], vii).

From Albert Gallatin

DEAR SIR Wednesday [13 Mar. 1805]

The enclosed is Robt. Williams's letter respecting the sales of land for taxes in the Mississippi territory under late West's influence.

Respectfully Your obt. Sert. ALBERT GALLATIN

RC (DLC); partially dated; addressed: "The President of the United States"; endorsed by TJ as a letter of 13 Mch. 1805 received that day and "West's conduct selling lands" and so recorded in SJL. Enclosure not found.

To Stephen W. Johnson

Washington Mar. 13. 05.

Th: Jefferson presents his compliments to mr Johnson & acknoleges the reciept of his letter in the moment of his departure on a short visit to Monticello. it cannot but be gratifying to him to find his name connected with useful things, and entertains a due sense of mr Johnson's favorable opinion, in proposing to him a dedication which cannot but be flattering to him. he asks leave to enter his name as a subscriber.

RC (CSmH).

HIS LETTER: Johnson to TJ, 5 Mch.

To William Pryce

Washington Mar. 13. 05.

Th Jefferson presents his respects to the revd. mr Pryce, acknoleges the reciept of his book, and prays him to inform him of the price, and whether to remit it to himself or to pay it to any one here. he is in the moment of a short visit to Monticello; but mr Pryce's note will find him in either place.

PoC (MHi).

ACKNOLEGES THE RECIEPT: see Pryce to TJ, 9 Mch.

To Puckshunubbee and Others

MY CHILDREN. March 13. 1805.

I learn with great satisfaction that you have leased to us three stations of one mile square each on the road from the Chickesaws to Natchez, and one on the Pearl river: and you desire me to send you a paper under my own hand to shew to your warriors that these lands are not sold, but lent. I now accordingly declare that the property in these lands remains in your nation, that they are lent to us for a rent of four hundred pounds weight of powder annually, and that your nation has a right to take them back at their pleasure: and this paper, now signed by my own hand will be evidence of these things to future generations. we will, according to your desire, settle but one white family on each station, and take care that they conduct themselves peaceably & friendly towards you; or being made known to me that they do otherwise, they shall be removed. they will be placed there merely for the accomodation of our paper carriers and travellers.

My children. You have asked whether I did not promise to send you ploughs to enable you to improve in husbandry? I did promise it, & immediately sent the ploughs: but by a mistake in forwarding them, they were delayed some time before we knew of it. you must however have recieved them before this time.

You ask if I did not promise to send to your deputation ten rifles for yourselves and other deserving warriors? I did not promise it. you said they would be acceptable: but I said nothing in reply. but altho I did not promise, yet, to shew my good will to you, I will send you the rifles.

You ask if we will allow commissions to you according to your rank, and medals and commissions to such chiefs as you may appoint to assist in the government of your country? it has not been a custom with us to give commissions to our friends among the red men: and as it is a new thing; we will take it into consideration. we wish to do what is agreeable to you if we find we can do it with prudence.

We shall be willing to give medals to a certain number of the distinguished chiefs who aid you in the government of your country, and who manifest dispositions to preserve peace & friendship between your nation and ours. we wish you therefore to recommend such to us.

My children, persevere in your friendship to the United States. we will never injure you, nor permit you to be injured by any white people, and we trust you will take care that none of our people are injured by yours. encourage among you the cultivation of the earth raising of cattle, spinning and weaving, and we will assist you in it. with plenty of food & cloathing you will raise many children, multiply, be strong and happy. may the great spirit protect & prosper you in all your just pursuits. farewell. TH: JEFFERSON

PoC (DLC); at head of text: "Thomas Jefferson President of the United States to Pukshanubby, Mingo-Humastubbe, Oakchummy, Tuskamiabby and Pushamattaha, Chiefs of the Choctaw nation." Notation in SJL: "Choctaws. a letter."

For Puckshunubbee, Homastubbee, Oak Chummy, and Tuskamiubbee, see Vol. 41:402n; Vol. 42:111n. Pushmataha (ca. 1764-1824) rose to prominence among the Choctaws through his prowess as a warrior and eloquence as a speaker. By 1805 he had joined Puckshunubbee and Homastubbee as one of the three principal Choctaw chiefs, playing a leading role in treaty negotiations with the United States in 1805, 1816, and 1820. A steadfast ally of the United States, Pushmataha opposed Tecumseh's call for a Native American confederacy and later sided with U.S. forces combating the Creeks and Seminoles. He died in Washington while visiting as part of a Choctaw delegation and was buried in the Congressional Cemetery with military honors (ANB; ASP, *Indian Affairs*, 1:749; Greg O'Brien, *Choctaws in a Revolutionary Age, 1750-1830* [Lincoln, Neb., 2002], 32, 100, 111; Gideon Lincecum, *Pushmataha: A Choctaw Leader and His People* [Tuscaloosa, Ala., 2004], 72-4).

I LEARN WITH GREAT SATISFACTION: agent Silas Dinsmoor recently forwarded several communications from the Choctaws to the War Department. A 27 Aug. 1804 letter from Dinsmoor (received 9 Oct.) enclosed "a Conference with the Chactaws & their Petition to the President." Letters written on 5 and 8 Jan. 1805 (both received 20 Feb.) enclosed, respectively, an "address of Cultivators of lands &c" and "a talk of the Chiefs relative to lease of lands &c." Neither Dinsmoor's letters nor their enclosures have been found (recorded in DNA: RG 107, RLRMS).

In December 1803, Dearborn discussed the establishment of STATIONS on Choctaw lands with a visiting delegation that included Puckshunubbee and Homastubbee (Vol. 42:108-12, 130-1n). For the DELAYED shipment of plows and other implements and tools promised to the Choctaws, see Vol. 42:130n.

To Isaac Briggs

DEAR SIR Washington Mar. 14. 05.

Your letter of Feb. 9. comes to hand in the moment of my departure on a short visit to Monticello. I have time therefore only to thank you for the information it contains, and to pray you to continue it, as it is impossible for me to govern without information. I wish to know every thing & then do what I find is right. on your information I have reliance.—your map & report arrived 3. or 4. days only before Congress rose. I communicated them. they were entirely disposed to compensate your labour, but they had past the stage of appropriations. an effort was made to insert an appropriation in the Post office bill which was still unpassed; but it was declared to be so unprecedented, & so dangerous to let appropriations be slipt into bills so much out of their due course that it was struck out, and it was too late to introduce it otherwise. it lies over therefore for next session. in the mean time mr Gallatin says you need not suffer for the money, as you are authorised to draw as surveyor, & may draw the more largely, to be allowed in your future accounts. I have written to Govr. Claiborne about the location & survey of La Fayette's lands. pray attend to it, as you would were it my case. it is nearer my heart than my own concerns. Accept my affectionate salutations. TH: JEFFERSON

P.S. the members talked of allowing 1000. or 1200. D. for expences & services of yourself & assistant, leaving the partition of it to you.

RC (NHi: Gilder Lehrman Collection at the Gilder Lehrman Institute of American History); at foot of text: "Isaac Briggs"; endorsed by Briggs. PoC (DLC); postscript, in margin, added separately to RC and PoC; endorsed by TJ.

VISIT TO MONTICELLO: TJ departed from Washington on 14 Mch. and arrived at Monticello on the 17th, expending $16.03 on the journey (MB, 2:1148-9).

I COMMUNICATED THEM: TJ to the House of Representatives, 23 Feb. See also TJ to James Holland, 22 Feb.

WRITTEN TO GOVR. CLAIBORNE: TJ to William C. C. Claiborne, 10 Mch.

To William C. C. Claiborne

Dear Sir Washington Mar. 14. 05.

Your letter of Jan. 29. was recieved yesterday, and I have just time to drop you a line as I am setting out on a short visit to Monticello. you apologise to the Secretary of state for troubling him with documents in confutation of the Accuser. we perfectly understand the game which is playing against you, we know every man concerned in it, and I only lament, sincerely lament the name of one man found among them, and from whom I had expected much better things. but you do right in sending evidence against such documents as the Accuser No. 3. has published; because it enables us to understand the truth of the transaction. one of the deputies returned from hence will probably join that faction actively. the others are dissatisfied, but they are virtuous men who will do nothing wicked.

I desired you some time ago to enter into conferences with the Marquis di Casa Calvo, or, if necessary, a correspondence with Governr. Folk for their acquiescence in our sending the post-rider who is to go from hence by Cartersville, Pr. Edwd. C. H. Athens, Tuckabatche, Fort Stoddert & the mouth of Pearl river to N. Orleans, thro' a corner of the territory mutually claimed by them & us, that is to say from Fort Stoddert to the lowest bluff on Pearle river. while the country is the subject of negociation we think it honorable that each party should innovate nothing without the consent of the other. they have not observed this as to the road from Mobile to Baton rouge. settle this matter immediately as our rider will set out within a week to explore & establish his route. he will be with you almost as soon as this letter.—I have appointed Thruston of Kentucky & Duffield of Tennissee your 2d. & 3d. judges (they speak French) James Brown District attorney, and mr Gurley Recorder. Accept my friendly salutations and assurances of great esteem & respect.

Th: Jefferson

PoC (DLC); at foot of text: "Govr. Claiborne."

you apologise to the secretary of state: Claiborne wrote to Madison on 26 Jan., enclosing a copy of the third essay by "Public Accuser," which accused the governor of ignoring the militia and of assisting in the elopement of an army officer with the teen-aged daughter of a local family. Claiborne also enclosed statements by others describing his conduct in the latter affair. "I feel as if I was trespassing upon your important duties," he told Madison. "But when you perceive the malignity of my opponents, I trust you will excuse the desire I manifest to keep the Executive advised of my answers to the charges exhibited against me" (Madison, *Papers, Sec. of State Ser.*, 8:507-9; Jared William Bradley, ed., *Interim Appointment: W. C. C. Claiborne Letter Book, 1804-1805* [Baton Rouge, 2002], 160-5; *Orleans Gazette, For the Country*, 26 Jan.).

NAME OF ONE MAN: probably John B. Prevost, whom TJ appointed a judge for Orleans Territory in 1804 upon the recommendation of James Monroe. Soon after his arrival at New Orleans, Prevost aligned with Edward Livingston, one of Claiborne's principal critics in the territory (Vol. 43:31; TJ to Prevost, 20 July 1804; Claiborne to TJ, 10 Dec. 1804; Isaac Briggs to TJ, 9 Feb. 1805).

THE DEPUTIES: Pierre Sauvé, Jean Noël Destréhan, and Pierre Derbigny, the delegation that presented the Louisiana memorial to Congress (TJ to Claiborne, 2 Dec. 1804).

SOME TIME AGO: TJ to Claiborne, 7 Jan.

To William Dunbar

DEAR SIR Washington Mar. 14. 05.

Your letters of the 2d. & 15th. of Feb. arrive just in the moment I am setting out on a short visit to Monticello. it will be necessary for us now to set on foot immediately the Arcansa & Red river expedition, Congress having given an additional appropriation of 5000. D. for these objects generally. I think you were not able to get any person in your quarter the last autumn fitted for the astronomical part of the undertaking. I have desired Genl. Dearborne to propose it to a mr Pease in the post office, who is fully equal to it, or if he will not accept, then to a mr Wily professor of an academy here. he will write to you fully on this subject, as my departure obliges me to leave to him the settling with you all details, not having time myself to read your journal before I set out. Accept my acknolegements for your services & assistance, my friendly salutations and assurances of great esteem & respect. TH: JEFFERSON

PoC (DLC); at foot of text: "Mr. Dunbar."

An act of 3 Mch. that authorized funds for obligations in treaties included an ADDITIONAL APPROPRIATION "for the purpose of exploring the Indian country, and of ascertaining proper and convenient places for establishing trading houses"; see TJ to the Senate and the House of Representatives, 13 Feb.

Seth PEASE, surveyor and mathematician, was a brother-in-law of Gideon Granger. He had gained extensive surveying experience in western New York and the Western Reserve in Ohio (RS, 1:216n). Presbyterian minister David Wiley (WILY) was the principal of the Columbian Academy in Georgetown (Vol. 36:435n). In October 1804, they and Abraham Bradley, Jr., made astronomical observations that William Lambert used to calculate latitude and longitude (William Lambert, *Calculations for Ascertaining the Latitude North of the Equator and the Longitude West of Greenwich Observatory, in England, of the Capitol, at the City of Washington, in the United States of America* [Washington, D.C., 1805], 6; Lambert to TJ, 15 Dec. 1804).

To Peter Kuhn, Jr.

SIR Washington Mar. 14. 05.

I found at Turin in the year 1787 a red wine called Nebioule, which I considered equal to any wine made in Europe. it is produced in the neighborhood of Turin, is there well known, and considered as the best wine of their country. it accordingly holds the first rank at the tables of the rich there. desirous of obtaining some of it, and having no correspondent there, I have presumed it might not be inconvenient for you to procure it for me, and that your connections in the US. might render a paiment of your draught on me to any correspondent of yours in the US. as convenient as to remit the money now under uncertainty as to the amount, & the practicability of the commission. if you can procure & send me 200. bottles I shall esteem it a favor & will answer your draught for it on demand. the wine should be in strong bottles, well corked & cemented, and addressed for me to the Collector of the customs of the port at which the vessel may enter. you know the ports most convenient to this place. Accept my salutations and assurances of respect.

TH: JEFFERSON

PoC (MoSHi: Jefferson Papers); at foot of text: "Mr. Peter Kuhn consul of the US. at Genoa"; endorsed by TJ.

NEBIOULE: TJ first encountered wines made from the Nebbiolo grape during his tour of southern France and northern Italy in the spring of 1787 (Vol. 11:435).

From Joseph Nourse

SIR. Treasury Department Register's Office March 14th. 1805

I do myself the honor to transmit herewith, two copies of the receipts & expenditures of the United States for the year 1803.

I have the honor to be with great respect Sir. Your Obedient humble servt.

JOSEPH NOURSE. Rr

RC (DLC); at foot of text: "The President of the United States"; endorsed by TJ as received from the Treasury Department "(Nourse)" on 17 Apr. and so recorded in SJL; also endorsed "Receipts & expenditures." Enclosure: *An Account of the Receipts and Expenditures of the United States, for the Year 1803. Stated in Pursuance of the Standing Order of the House of Representatives of the United States, Passed on the Thirtieth Day of December, One Thousand Seven Hundred and Ninety-One* (Washington, D.C., [1804]).

From Giovanni Fabbroni

EXCELLENCE Florence en Toscane ce 15 Mars 1805

La bonté que Vous eutes de m'envoyer en 1782 votre excellent Ouvrage, modestement intitulé Notes on Virginie, est une circonstance si flatteuse qu'on ne peut pas l'oublier. J'ose Vous rappeller aujourdhui mes sentimens, qui sont ceux de La reconnoissance la plus vive, de la veneration la plus exalteé, en prenant La Liberté de vous faire hommage d'un livre qui peut en quelque sorte vous interesser; parce qu'il offre une partie de la Statistique de ce Païs: Son titre est = *Dei Provvedimente Annorarj* = Je le remet avec cette Lettre a Mr Appleton Consul des Etats Unis à Livourne; pour Vous le faire passer. Le sujet n'y est pas traité aûssi dignement qu'il le faudroit; pas même avec la force et le stile qu'il auroit exigé: Mais j'y ai mis toute la verité historique etayeé par l'evidence des faits. J'ai affecté de produire des faits tirés de L'Espagne, parcequ'il etoit à propos de persuader une nouvelle Cour: J'ai eu la consolation de voir dissipée [la] tempête reglemantaire, qui nous menaçoit. Des nouveaux maux sont venus affliger ce pauvre Païs deja fatigué par les changemens politiques. Nous avons eu des tremblemens de terre qui ont endommagé quelques unes de nos villes, et des inondations qui ont submergé plus que 60 milles quarrées de terreins richement cultivés.

En dernier Lieu une fievre maligne bilieuse a paru à Livourne, et les Ennemis de notre petit commerce ont crié à *la fievre Jaune*! et ont jetté l'epouvante si loin autour de nous, que presque toute L'Europe nous regarde comme des pestiferés. Il y a six àns que les circonstances ont detourné les Magistrats de soigner La netteté d'une ville aussi peuplée que Livourne. Les egouts y etoient presqu'obstrués, Les fossées remplies de boue &c. Voilà ce qui a fait naître d'elle meme La Maladie, que Vos Ecrivains ont appellée Endemic Yellow *fever not contagious*, trop differente de celle qu'on a nommée *Yellow Pestilential fever*. Il a été evident que celle de Livourne n'a eù aucun caractère contagieux, ni par l'attouchement des Malades, ni par celui des Marchandises. Je sais qu'on a avéré à Philadelphie, que la fievre jaune pestilentielle ne donne point son miasme au papier à ecrire, et que celui ci ne La communique point. Il vaudroit la peine pour La sureté du Commerce, et pour la tranquillité des Nations, qu'on fit des expèriments repetés pour assurer quelles sont les marchandises, qui sont susceptibles de recevoir, et transmettre La contagion, et quelles ne le sont pas. C'est depuis 15 ans que nous observons dans nos trois Lazzarets les effets des marchandises, qui nous viennent de tous les points de l'Amerique, non seulement des endroits suspects mais de ceux même où regne la Maladie; et jamais aucune de nos Gardes destinés à s'assurer par un maniement long tems continué, si ces marchandises sont infectées, n'a donné Lieu au plus petit soupçon de maladie. Je ne suis pas instruit si on a etabli à Philadelphie Le Bureau de Santeé qu'on avoit projecté: Il seroit du plus grand interêt pour le Commerce des Etats Unis d'instituer exprès une suite d'experiences dirigées à prouver si la fievre jaune pestilentielle communique Son *Seminium pestif* aux Marchandis, et à quelles; savoir: si seulement les matières animales, telles que les Laines, Les soies, et non pas les matieres vegetales, telles que Le coton, le lin &c: et si ce *Seminium* les penetre, combien de tems peut il y rester actif. Ces faits une fois bien averés, on sauroit a quoi s'attenir; on sauroit si une quarantaine quelconque est necessaire; si peu de jours d'observation seroient suffisans, ou s'il faudroit une quarantaine rigoureuse. Le Commerce y gagneroit beaucoup; et la confiance des Nations se rassurereoit contre ses peurs excessives qui les font agir à caprice, et d'une maniere qui ne fait pas l'eloge à La raison humaine. La fievre de Livourne n'a pas été contagieuse; elle n'a pas même été epidemique; car Le premier jour que sur la crainte mal fondée de nos Voisin nous determinames d'enfermer ces malades, dans un Hôpital particulier, on n'en trouva que 14 a y enfermer, le premier jour; et Le total qui y est entre, durant plus d'un mois qu'il a été en activité, n'a outre passé le nombre de 165! Quoique celà, La Ville de Livourne fut declarée complettement nette le 21. Xbre: On passà de la nouvelle chaux aux chambre des infirmes, on purgea les hardes dans les Lazaret: Et nos voisins continuent à nous interdire toute espece de commerce mediterranéen jusqu'à ce jour, de crainte que La maladie se renouvelle au Primtems! C'est un sujet qui est digne d'occuper le Chef d'une grande Nation, qui procure à celle ci L'honneur de donner des leçons à La trop vieille, et craintive Europe. J'ai en attendant celui d'être avec La plus haute estime, et le plus profond respect

de Votre Excellence Tres humble et très obeissant Serviteur

Jean Fabbroni
Surintendant du Musée;
directeur du monnoyage,
membre de la deputation Sur les Finances

EDITORS' TRANSLATION

Excellency, Florence, Tuscany, 15 Mch. 1805

Your kindness in sending me your excellent work, modestly entitled *Notes on Virginia*, in 1782 is such a flattering occurrence that one cannot forget it. Now I dare renew my feelings of intense gratitude and exalted veneration by taking the liberty of giving you a book that might be of interest because it provides statistics about this country. The title is *Dei provvedimenti annorarj*. I am giving it to Mr. Appleton, consul of the United States in Leghorn, with this letter to transmit to you. The subject is not treated as seriously as it should be, or with the power and style it requires, but I included all the historical truth that can be supported by facts. The book gives the impression of drawing facts from Spain because that was the appropriate way to convince a new court.

I was consoled when the legislative storm that threatened us dissipated, but new misfortunes have come to afflict this poor country which is already exhausted from political upheaval. Earthquakes damaged some of our cities, and floods submerged more than 60 square miles of richly cultivated land. Then a malignant bilious fever broke out in Leghorn and the enemies of our modest trade shouted *yellow fever!* creating terror so far around us that almost all of Europe views us as plague victims. Six years ago circumstances prevented the magistrates from safeguarding the cleanliness of a populous city like Leghorn. Sewers were almost blocked, trenches filled with mud, etc. From this emerged the sickness your writers have called endemic noncontagious yellow fever, entirely different from pestilential yellow fever. Leghorn's fever was clearly not contagious through contact with patients or merchandise. I know that in Philadelphia pestilential yellow fever was determined not to be transmitted by writing paper; that does not spread it. To ensure trade and reassure nations, it would be worthwhile to undertake multiple experiments to find out which goods are susceptible to receiving and transmitting the contagion and which are not. For 15 years, in our three quarantine areas, we have observed the effects of goods coming to us from all parts of America, not only places that were suspect but those where the sickness prevailed. None of our guards responsible for determining through extended contact whether any goods were infected has given even the slightest hint of sickness. I do not know whether the health bureau has been established in Philadelphia as planned. It would be in the interest of U.S. commerce to initiate a series of experiments designed to determine whether pestilential yellow fever transmits its pestiferous seed to goods, and if so, which ones; whether only animal products like wool and silk are affected, and not vegetable products such as cotton, linen, etc. And if this seed does infiltrate them, how long does it remain active? Once these facts are determined, we would know what to expect; we would know if a quarantine is needed, if a few days' observation would suffice, or if a rigorous quarantine is required. Trade would benefit greatly and nations would be reassured from the excessive fear that makes them act capriciously in ways that do not reflect human reason. The Leghorn fever was not contagious; it was not even an epidemic. On the day we first admitted patients to a special hospital, because of the ill-founded fear of our neighbors, we found only 14 patients to admit. The hospital operated for more than a month and during all that time the total did not exceed 165! The city of Leghorn was declared completely clean on 21 Dec. Patients' rooms were sanitized with lime; clothes from the quarantines were destroyed; yet our neighbors continue to ban all Mediterranean trade, for fear that the illness might return in the spring!

This subject deserves the attention of the head of a great nation, thanks to whom your country gives lessons to a too old and fearful Europe.

Meanwhile, with the highest esteem and deepest respect of your excellency, I have the honor of being your very humble and obedient servant.

JEAN FABBRONI
Superintendent of the Museum,
Director of the Mint, Member
of the Finance Ministry

RC (DLC); torn, text in brackets supplied from Dupl; endorsed by TJ as received 22 May and so recorded in SJL. Dupl (same); at head of text: "Seconde"; endorsed by TJ as a letter of 15 May received 2 Aug. and so recorded in SJL. Enclosure: Fabbroni, *Dei provvedimenti annonarj* (Florence, 1804). Enclosed in Thomas Appleton to TJ, 22 Mch.

DE M'ENVOYER EN 1782: TJ sent Fabbroni *Notes on the State of Virginia* in 1785 (Vol. 8:161, 260-1).

TEMPÊTE REGLEMANTAIRE: possibly a reference to French demands that Etruria forgo its longstanding neutrality and crack down on British shipping at Leghorn (Paul Marmottan, ed., *Documents sur le royaume d'Étrurie [1801-1807]* [Paris, 1900], 51-3; Paul Marmottan, *Le royaume d'Étrurie [1801-1807]* [Paris, 1896], 140-2).

Fabbroni added a postscript to the Dupl: "Je prends la Liberté de joindre à ce *double* une brochure que je recois de la Presse dont ce meme moment 26 mars" (that is, "I take the liberty of adding to this duplicate a brochure that I have received from the press this moment, 26 Mch."). He was possibly enclosing his *Ricerche sulla quina*, on cinchona, an edition of which was published in Milan in 1805. The Dupl and pamphlet were conveyed in a letter of 1 May from Appleton to TJ.

From Gideon Granger

DEAR SIR Genl post Office Mar: 15th. 1805

Inclosed I transmit a Letter from Rufus Easton Esq with various other documents which relate to Louisinia. They were by him intrusted to my discretion and I presume you will not deem the perusal an Useless labor.

I Am, Sir, your most Affectionate friend GIDN GRANGER

RC (DLC); endorsed by TJ as received 21 Mch. and so recorded in SJL. Enclosure: Rufus Easton to TJ, 17 Jan., enclosing his confidential communication on Louisiana District.

Notes on Personal Finance

[4 Feb.-15 Mch. 1805]

1805			
Feb.	4.	in bank—1.19	
		Salary for Nov.	2083.33
	5.	Note to be discounted (2000)	1979.
		balance ante	4062.33

			1.19	
		Note to be taken up	1500.	1501.19
				2561.14
paimts.	✓	Lemaire	600.	
	✓	Daugherty	207.28	
		J. Barnes.	[ ] + 150	
	✓	Pairo	24	
	✓	Dufief	36.50	
	✓	Brown & co.	416.	
	✓	Perry	200.	
	✓	Short	500.	
	✓	Jefferson	150.	
	✓	Jones & Howell	249.33	
		Newspapers		
		Reibelt		
		Fernandes	152.25	
		Latrobe		
	✓	Yznardi	194.85	
Mar.	15.	Jones & Howell	144.47	

Actual statement.

Feb.	5.	in bank 2561.14		
	8.	Lemaire		600
		Daugherty		200
		Short		500
	9.	Ducombe		36.50
	10.	Tucker		600.
	11.	Pairo		24.
		Lilly		200.
	12.	Jones & Howell		249.33
	20.	Smith		50.
	23.	cash		30.
				2489.83
				2561.14
		balance in bank		71.31
Mar.	4.	Salary for Feb.		2083.33
		note to be discd. (2000)		1979.
				4133.64
		note of Jan. to take up		1500.
		balance in bank		2633.64
	5.	J. Barnes	380	

7. Lemaire	600	
Is. Coles. salary 150		
cash 100	250	
cash. Fernandes Cary, Byrne, Reibelt	321.615	
8. cash	50.	
9. Short	500	
11. cash	530	2631.615

MS (CSmH); entirely in TJ's hand, including bracketed blank.

NOTE TO BE DISCOUNTED: TJ took loans of $2,000 at the Bank of the United States on 6 Feb. and 5 Mch. The NOTE TO BE TAKEN UP may have been one of $1,500 at the same bank on 5 Dec. 1804. TJ took another $1,500 loan at the bank on 8 Jan. (MB, 2:1141, 1144-5, 1147).

Payments on 8 Feb. to Étienne LEMAIRE and Joseph Dougherty (DAUGHERTY) were applied toward Lemaire's President's House accounts from 6 Jan. to 2 Feb. and Dougherty's accounts for forage, smithing, and contingencies. The 7 Mch. payment to Lemaire was applied toward his President's House accounts from 3 Feb. to 2 Mch. (same, 1145-6).

TJ received $150 from John BARNES on 25 Jan., another $30 on 6 Feb., and $200 on 2 Mch. He paid Barnes $380 for the total on 5 Mch. (same, 1144-7).

Thomas W. PAIRO was a Washington dry goods merchant with a store in the Seven Buildings. TJ paid him $24 for wine on 11 Feb. (same, 1146; *National Intelligencer*, 9 Nov. 1804).

BROWN & CO.: for the complicated arrangements regarding TJ's payment of $416 to William Brown & Co., which eventually involved a $600 draft by Treasurer of the United States Thomas Tudor Tucker on the collector at Richmond, see TJ to George Jefferson, 19 Dec. 1804, 4 Jan., 10 Feb., and 11 Feb. 1805.

TJ paid JONES & HOWELL $144.47 on 4 May (TJ to Jones & Howell, 4 May; MB, 2:1152).

On 20 Feb., TJ gave $50 to Alexander SMITH as a donation toward erecting a Baptist church in Alexandria (same, 1146).

From William Short

March 15. [1805]

Jefferson Prest.—to return his draught for endorsement &c

FC (DLC: Short Papers); partially dated; entirely in Short's hand, consisting of an entry in his epistolary record. Recorded in SJL as received from Philadelphia on 21 Mch. 1805.

HIS DRAUGHT: see TJ to Short, 11 Mch.

From Thomas Appleton

SIR Leghorn 16th. of march 1805

By the desire of Mr. Mazzei I have shipped on board the schooner Dolphin Capt. Williams for Philadelphia, one case of Vine cuttings, and four small boxes of strawberry-plants, which I have directed to the care of Mr. Muhlenburg Collector of that port; to be forwarded to you.—I have enjoined on the captain a very particular Attention to the plants, which he has obligingly promised me to fulfill.—In the course of the present month I shall receive the montepulciano wine which will be sent by the first Vessel after for Baltimore, or Philadelphia.—I have this day receiv'd a letter from Malta in date of the 25th. of february which contains the following passage "Commodore Barron is here in a very dangerous State of health.—The Constitution, President, Constellation and Essex frigates with the usual Brigs and Schooners form the squadron."—

I have the honor to be with the highest respect Your devoted Servant.
Th: Appleton

RC (DLC); at foot of text: "Thomas Jefferson esquire President of the United States of America &c &c"; endorsed by TJ as received 27 May and so recorded in SJL. Enclosed in J. P. G. Muhlenberg to TJ, 25 May 1805. FC (Lb in DNA: RG 84, CR, Leghorn).

TJ did not have success with the STRAWBERRY plants sent by Philip Mazzei; see TJ to Mazzei, 18 July 1804, and J. P. G. Muhlenberg to TJ, 25 May 1805.

Samuel BARRON suffered from liver disease from his arrival in the Mediterranean in September 1804 until he returned to the United States in May 1805 (Madison, *Papers, Sec. of State Ser.*, 9:153; Joseph Barnes to TJ, 8 Oct. and 24 Dec. 1804).

From Elisha Avery

Sir, New York, March 16, 1805.

The time which has elapsed since I had the honor of communicating with You Sir, would lead You to expect as soon as the present, the arrival of the *papers* proposed to be transmitted to You. Fearing lest you might mistake the cause of this delay, I take the liberty Sir, of informing You that it has been occasioned by an indisposition, which has prevented my reaching as Yet, the abodes of my friends.—Soon after I had the honor of seeing You, I attempted to proceed on my Journey to the Northward, but a violent cold with which I was then afflicted becoming extreemly inveterate, I was obliged to discontinue my route, & have since suffered a very severe pleurhetic illness. I am however nearly recovered, & now on my way, & hope soon to be enabled to forward you the certificates proper for the purposes of which I had the pleasure of conversing with you &c—Meanwhile I remain Sir

Most Respectfully Your Obedt Srvt
E. Avery

RC (DNA: RG 59, LAR); endorsed by TJ as received 28 Mch. and so recorded in SJL.

PAPERS: see TJ to Avery, [17 Feb.].

From Isaac Briggs and Robert Williams

MY DEAR FRIEND, Washington M.T. 16th. of the 3rd. mo. 1805

Being informed that the office of United States' Attorney for the district of Orleans is now vacant, I presume to mention for that appointment Lewis Kerr now resident in New-Orleans. He is a man of genius and very handsome acquirements—of sound integrity and pure republican principles. So far as I am capable of judging, he possesses considerable and competent professional skill, having been employed, as is said, for the last 13 years of his life in the study and practice of the law. In relation to this point I am aided by the opinion of others more capable of judging than myself. But as to his native genius, his education and principles, I am authorized, from an intimate acquaintance of 18 months, to bear unequivocal testimony.

Accept renewed assurances of my respect and affectionate regard.

ISAAC BRIGGS

I perfectly agree, with Mr. Briggs as to the within opinion relative to Mr. Kerr. ROBERT WILLIAMS

RC (DNA: RG 59, LAR); at head of text: "Duplicate"; at foot of text: "Tho. Jefferson President U. States"; endorsed by TJ as received 23 Apr. and "Kerr Lewis to be Atty for Orleans distr." and so recorded in SJL. FC (MdHi); lacks addendum by Williams.

From William Dunbar

DR. SIR Natchez 16th March 1805

I have the pleasure of transmitting you the continuation of the Journal of Occurrences & remarks, but not yet the Conclusion, it is perhaps proper that I should make you an apology for its extreme length, as all that is really important might be comprised in a few sheets—my object has been this,—seeing that the late small expedition is prefatory to others of much greater extent & importance, and knowing that in very many particulars the future must resemble the past, I conceived it to be one of the useful purposes of the excursion just completed to collect into one point of view the various incidents small as well great which are to be expected and provided for on any future occasion; I conceived it therefore to be my duty to place before your view many little particulars which tho' not altogether uninteresting to Goverment, would most undoubtedly appear both prolix & trivial to an ordinary reader: time has not admitted of any attempt to improve or amend, so that it has of necessity been transcribed in its original garb, which it is hoped will be accepted as an apology for imperfections & probably repetitions which are some times unavoidable in a Journal, when the same objects have a 2d or a 3d time presented themselves under different points of view—

It is also proper that I should observe to you that the greatest harmony subsisted between Dor. Hunter & myself; the Doctor is a good & a worthy man, it is however observable that he is of a very warm temper, I found upon the arrival of the boat from new orleans that the Doctor & the Lieut. had not discovered the secret of pleasing each other, most probably the fault of the young Gentleman; this was a sufficient cause for not admitting the Lieut. to be of our party, if a superior reason had not prevailed, that is, not conceiving myself authorized to deprive the service of a commisioned officer.—It would appear that the Doctor's chemical re[. . .][ha]ve been generally applied to the Object of making money, I there[fore] [. . .] him in the light of an Excellent practical Metalurgist but not a [min]eralogist this is what he has himself told, in the last particular I failed in obtaining from the Doctor's knowledge the advantages I had promised myself. I persuade myself that this information will not be received by you as if intended to diminish the Doctor's merits in your view, far from it I have a high esteem for the Doctor, but I proceed on the principle that it is my duty to make known every particular to *You* that you may be furnished with data on which to found future expectations. a number of specimens were collected to be taken round by the Doctor in order that you might have the satisfaction of judging of their properties from your own view, the Doctor being arrived at New orleans writes me that Govr. Claiborne had already sent you a number of specimens from the washita collected by a Richard King; from which circumstance the Doctor conceived it to be superfluous to carry you those specimens & left them at N.O. to be sent to me; I am persuaded that mr. King has never thought of collecting any specimen from the hot springs & probably has only sought for metalic or chrysaline specimens, or any thing possessing a shewy appearance. I have therefore requested the Gentleman at N.O. with whom the Doctor left the specimens to forward them to him at Philada. in order that the first intention of presenting them to you may be fulfilled—

Dft (Lb in Ms-Ar: William Dunbar Papers); in Dunbar's hand; torn; at head of text: "Thos. Jefferson P.U.S. Washington City." Recorded in SJL as received 23 Apr.

JOURNAL: see Dunbar to TJ, 15 Feb.

RICHARD KING: see William C. C. Claiborne to TJ, 1 Nov. 1804.

From John Keemle

SIR, Philada. March 16th. 1805.

Having read Your communication to Congress, in which you Noticed the lead Mines in Louisianna, I was induced to make a trial of calcining raw into red lead. Having succeeded in the experiment, I shewed a sample of it, to Tench Cox Esqr. who informed me, that he would forward it to you, with information, that if Congress should think it proper and advantagious to the interest of the United States to give Employment to some persons, to manufacture the raw lead from the mine into red and white on the spot that I would furnish you with a draught of the proper construction of the furnaces Necessary for the purpose; or that I would go myself and superintend their construction.

Should you be authorized, to select and appoint any persons for the above work, may I beg the favour of being remembered by you. If my Revolutionary services, and afterwards the confidence of my fellow Citizens, in electing me a member of the Legislature of this State, can carry any recommendation, let me notice them to you without vanity & presumption

In common with your republican fellow Citizens, I sincerely congratulate you on your re-election to the Presidential Seat of Your Country.

With considerations of high Esteem, I remain your friend and Humble Servt.—

JOHN KEEHMLE

RC (DLC); at foot of text: "Thos. Jefferson Esqr."; endorsed by TJ as received 8 Apr. and so recorded in SJL.

John Keemle (ca. 1753-1830), also spelled Keehmle in several of his signatures, was a veteran of the American Revolution and a Philadelphia doctor who sold medicines, surgical tools, paints, and glass. Allied with William Duane's faction of the Republican Party, Keemle received support from the city's general ward committee for a seat in the state's General Assembly, where he served in the 1803-1804 term. Over the course of his life, Keemle remained active in the Philadelphia community and chaired veterans' committees. During the remainder of TJ's administration, Keemle continued to write to the president seeking a federal job (*Aurora*, 13 Aug. 1803; *Poulson's American Daily Advertiser*, 5 June 1805; Philadelphia *National Gazette and Literary Register*, 24 Sep. 1824; Philadelphia *Pennsylvania Inquirer*, 16 Feb. 1830; *Journal of the Fourteenth House of Representatives of the Commonwealth of Pennsylvania, Commenced at Lancaster, on Tuesday, the Sixth Day of December, in the Year of our Lord One Thousand Eight Hundred and Three, and of the Commonwealth the Twenty-Eighth* [Lancaster, Pa., 1804], 3; Madison, *Papers, Pres. Ser.*, 2:172-4, 187-8; Keemle to TJ, 1 Oct. 1807 and 4 Aug. 1808).

LEAD MINES IN LOUISIANNA: see Annual Message to Congress, 8 Nov. 1804.

Keemle's interest in RED LEAD likely stemmed from its use as an ingredient in paint dye, the manufacture of glass, and certain medical treatments (John Hunter, *A Treatise on the Venereal Disease* [Philadelphia, 1791], 125-6; William Spotswood, *The Golden Cabinet: Being the Laboratory, or Handmaid to the Arts; Containing Such*

Branches of Useful Knowledge, As Nearly Concerns All Kinds of People; From the Squire to the Peasant: And Will Afford Both Profit and Delight [Philadelphia, 1793], 10, 95, 166, 185).

From Thomas Lomax

DEAR SIR Pt. Tobago Mar. 16. 1805.

You will be pleased to excuse my troubleing you with this Address. It is made in behalf of my friend Mr. Humphrey B. Brooke, who is considered as one of the best Surveyors in our State. He will be thankful if there are any Appointments to be made in his Line, to any of our new Countries, to receive one. I can safely assert, that he would be found, fully adequate to any Business of the kind. If this should be the means of rendering him a Service, it will afford me great pleasure. I am with Sentiments of the highest Esteem,

Dr. Sir Yor. Mot. Obdt. Humbl. Servt. THO. LOMAX

RC (DNA: RG 59, LAR); endorsed by TJ as received 11 May and "Brooke Humphrey B. to be Surveyor" and so recorded in SJL.

From James Mease

SIR Philadelphia 16th. March 1805

Your highly esteemed favour of the 11th. inst. came to hand on friday but I am sorry to say the box containing the modells of the mould boards, which you mention were sent did not arrive by the mail stage. As I set no small value upon them, I have set on foot an inquiry respecting the box, and hope to recover it. I regret that you did not inform me whether the cast mould plate, appeared to be made right, because I have had a similar one framed and am now using it every day. I find that it is very advantageous to have the face of the plate well secured, as the rough surface tends to hold the earth longer than is necessary, and hence, as I mentioned in my letter of november last, the pulverized soil of my potatoe ground which was a little moist, mounted up, and fell over between the handles of the plough.—I intend to make another pattern with a sharp toe, and think I can improve the mode on which my present plough is framed. All the farmers to whom I shewed it, agree with those in your part of the Country, in preferring the sharp toed plate or mould board.—

I regret very sincerely to learn from Dr. Mitchell, that the grand and patriotic attempt of a national board of agriculture has failed, because I think immense advantages to the interests of the Union would have resulted from it, if it had been continued with spirit. But without any extraordinary penetration, I predicted, when the measure was first proposed, that it would fail, unless an active well informed Secretary could be obtained who without having any ambition except that of the public good, would devote the whole of his time to the duty of his appointment. Such a character I feared was not to be found at Washington. I hope another attempt will be made, and that by Congress, who should allow a salary to the Secretary, and a sum of money annually for the purposes of the institution.—The old Society of Philadelphia in consequence of my exertions has been revived, and from the present zeal exhibited will be carried on with spirit.—

I am very Sincerely your obliged and very humble Servt

James Mease

RC (DLC); at foot of text: "The President of the U States"; endorsed by TJ as received 25 Mch. and so recorded in SJL.

NATIONAL BOARD OF AGRICULTURE: the American Board of Agriculture had been established in February 1803 with Madison as president and Isaac Briggs as secretary. Samuel Latham Mitchill was one of the vice presidents (Vol. 37:339-40; Vol. 40:637-8; Vol. 42:219-20).

OLD SOCIETY OF PHILADELPHIA: formed in 1785, the Philadelphia Society for Promoting Agriculture fell into "a long sleep" before being revived in the winter of 1804. Mease was secretary in the spring of 1805 (*Memoirs of the Philadelphia Society for Promoting Agriculture*, 1 [1808], i-iii; *Poulson's American Daily Advertiser*, 10 June).

From Joseph Barnes

Livorno Mar. 17th. 1805

On the 16th Feb. per the Ship Hannah Cap. Yardsley of Philada. I did myself the honor of addressing Mr Jefferson from Florence enclosing a duplicate of my Letter of Decemr. 24th. 1804—with some trifling remarks—Accompany'd by a Letter for Mr Madison. As the Quarantine in the Roman State was 40 days, I remained in Florence, and got a friend to make application to the Government to endeavor if Possible to obtain permission to pass by performing a Short Quarantine—all his endeavors however having proved fruitless, I judged it expedient to return to Livorno, and take my passage by Sea directly for Sicily; and Should have been on Board this evening had I not reced. a Letter from Mr Gibbs of Palermo, brot. by a Vessel which made the Voyage in four days, an extract of which is as follows. I immediately communicated the contents to Mr Appleton; and having a Letter to answer Mr Cathalan of Marseilles I took care to give him the same information—"Extract of a Letter dated Palermo Mar. 6th 1805." "Cap. Pottit, of H.B. Majesty's Sloop Termagant, informed me that he Met off Sardinia about Twenty days ago two Tripoline Cruizers—Commodore Barron has in consequence dispatched all the Vessels he could Spare in pursuit of them. The Commodore is Still very ill, tho' gone to Malta and His Sicilian Majesty has refused the Gun Boats; probably by your personal attendance & application in Naples some thing may Nonetheless again be Effected.—

"I have removed the Vice Consul as you requested, & invested myself with the Power you Sent me dated jan. 16 1804 Which I Should have done before but expected the pleasure of Seeing you daily; tho' I well know the unfortunate events which have Occurred.—The Presant Secretary of State at Naples being a frenchman, you will of course provide yourself with the requisites—We have had no arrivals here since my last, nor any thing new. I quote the prices of every article at foot" &c &c—.

Three weeks Since the Emperor of the French has been daily expected in Italy, however Since the advice of the Great Armament having Sailed from England they write that his journey here is Suspended 'till the last of next month. Monr. Beauharnois is arrived in Milan: who they expect here will marry the Queen of Etruria—Those reports are however, more matter of Speculation, nevertheless that great changes will take place thro' all Italy is *not* doubted by any.

Where the English fleet is destined we cannot form any just Idea as yet: Some think for Lisbon, others Sicily, & others Germany to Unite with the Prussians & Swedes—indeed 'tis conjectured by many that *Mexico* is the grand object; a Short time however will demonstrate.—

The division of Italy by the French Cabinet will be a very important Stroke against any Coalition that may be opposed to France; for this Simple reason, after the Governments are established, all who may join the Standard of any power against France will naturally be consider'd Rebels & treated Accordingly; consequently, it will *add* near 18 Millions of Subjects indirectly to the French Empire, and necessarily diminsh the Force oppos'd to the French in the Same ratio, which virtually will be a double loss to them.—

From Letters recd. this day 'tis reported, tho' not to be relied upon, that the French troops in Milan had recd. orders to March immediately for Verona, and that the Fortresses of Turin were order'd to be put immediately in a State of defence and garrisoned fully.—

For this part of the world 'tis unquestionably a very perilous moment—A Short time will determine the Events which fare Likely to take place on the Continent of Europe—As to me, I have Some doubt whether the Emperor of Germany will go to War, provided he can possibly avoid it, *not* having any General of Celebrity to Command his Troops nor resources to Sustain a War and a *want of Energy* in the Government.—In regard to myself, I shall not trouble Mr Jefferson with any further observations, except being Still perfectly persuaded that I could be extremely useful were I appointed as Auditor of the Accounts of the different Consuls; & of Agents of the U.S Squadron in Italy, Sicily & Malta: as well as to collect Commercial information—And, as I have before Suggested, I would undertake it with pleasure for the *Simple expences*, which would not be great; and the Saving which would result to the Government would be considerable, independent of the information I Should be able to communicate. On my arrival in Naples I flatter myself notwithstanding all the difficulties that I Shall be able to obtain the Gun-Boats for Commodore Barron; Should money be necessary in a Corrupt Government like that; I Shall venture to advance it, the object being important;—and I hope Soon to have it in my power to write from Sicily that I have got our Vessels put on the Same footing as the English.

With the highest consideration & respect I have the honor to be Mr Jefferson your obedt. sert J: BARNES

NB. I have recd. a Letter Yesterday from Vienna which States that the Emperor of Germany, the Archduke Charles, & the Ci-devant Grand Duke of Tuscany will Visit Venice and their Italian possessions the begining of April—This does not Portend War between the two Emperors but a Partition of Territory—

RC (DLC); addressed (clipped): "Thomas Jefferson President of the United [. . .] Washing[. . .]"; postmarked Philadelphia, 20 May; with Barnes's notation: "per favor of Mr. Woodmass Schooner Dauphin of Philada."; endorsed by TJ as received 22 May and so recorded in SJL.

LETTER FOR MR MADISON: see Madison, *Papers, Sec. of State Ser.*, 9:45-7.

I HAVE REMOVED THE VICE CONSUL AS YOU REQUESTED: Barnes previously expressed dismay at the conduct of the individual acting as consul at Palermo, who he believed was acting on behalf of a rival. His correspondent, Abraham Gibbs, had also been designated navy agent at Palermo by Edward Preble (NDBW, 4:140-1; Vol. 40:627).

SECRETARY OF STATE AT NAPLES: Antonio Micheroux (Harold Acton, *The Bourbons of Naples [1734-1825]* [London, 1956], 488-9).

EMPEROR OF GERMANY: that is, Francis II, Holy Roman Emperor and newly proclaimed emperor of Austria. His brothers were CHARLES, archduke of Austria, and Ferdinand III, formerly Grand Duke of Tuscany (Peter H. Wilson, "Bolstering the Prestige of the Habsburgs: The End of the Holy Roman Empire in 1806," *International History Review*, 28 [2006], 723-6; A. W. Ward, G. W. Prothero, and Stanley Leathes, eds., *The Cambridge Modern History*, 13 vols. [New York, 1903-12], 13: tables 33 and 73).

From Thomas T. Davis

SIR Jeffersonville. Indiana Territory March 17th 1805

A Company of Gentlemen from different States in the Union have formed themselves into a Company for the purpose of Cuting a Cannal around the Falls of Ohio from this side of the River—. An Object highly important to the Western World. Capt. Thair one of the Company is here and others are Hourly expected: But they will not begin this work untill the Legislature of this Territory will incorporate them. The Object therefore of this Letter is to request you to appoint the Legislative Council of This Territory as soon as possible, that the wish of the Company may be effected. I have Written this Letter at the request of Capt. Thair who manages for the Company: And I am so fully impressed with the utility & importance of this Cannal that I unite with him heartily in beging the appointments of Legislative Counsellors may be made speedily. The situation of some Landed property through which this Cannal must pass makes it essential for the Company to be incorporated. The River Ohio and the Waters West of it is much higher now than they have been for Several Years Ships have passed the Rapids without difficulty. The Quantity of Wild Pigeons in this Quarter exceed Heavier Calculation. I am Respectfully your Oblgd.

THO. T DAVIS

RC (DLC); endorsed by TJ as received 8 Apr. and so recorded in SJL.

The Indiana Canal COMPANY began a campaign to attract investors in 1804. Led by Benjamin Hovey, a group of interested parties petitioned Congress early in 1805, requesting they either be granted a parcel of public lands for the effort or be allowed to purchase those lands on special terms. A Senate committee reported favorably on the proposal on 28 Jan. 1805, but recommended no action be taken until the group was legally incorporated. Hovey and his associates brought a petition to the Indiana territorial legislature on 6 Aug., and on 17 Aug., the legislature passed an act incorporating the company. In addition to naming George Rogers Clark, John Brown, Jonathan Dayton, Aaron Burr, Hovey, and seven others as a board of directors, the act set potential toll rates and allowed for the sale of 20,000 shares at $50 each. Despite the act of incorporation, the effort to build the canal stalled (Lexington *Kentucky Gazette*, 19 Dec.; JHR, 5:51; ASP, *Miscellaneous*, 1:419; Gayle Thornbrough and Dorothy Riker, eds., *Journals of the General Assembly of Indiana Territory, 1805-1815* [Indianapolis, 1950], 63-4, 78, 81, 89, 94; Francis S. Philbrick, ed., *The Laws of Indiana Territory, 1801-1809* [Springfield, Ill., 1930], 154-63; *History of the Ohio Falls Cities and their Counties*, 2 vols. [Cleveland, 1882], 1:47).

LEGISLATIVE COUNCIL: see Davis to TJ, 20 Feb.

From James Madison

DEAR SIR Washington Mar. 17. 1805

I inclose two letters from Monroe recd. since your departure. The intermediate ones referred to, of the 16 & 18. of Decr. are not yet recd. I inclose also a Letter of Decr. 24. from Armstrong; who I am pleased to find understands the language in which the honorable & honest policy of this Country ought to be expressed. you will find that I obey the wish of Govr. Claiborne in taxing you with a lengthy communication from him rendered necessary by the persevering & elaborate attacks of his political adversaries. Fowler of Kentucky shewed me yesterday two letters one from James Brown, the other from Bradford the Editor of the newspapers. Brown without indicating any personal ill will agst. the Govr[1] appears to concur fully in denonouncing his want of talents and weight of Character. He confirms the views given by others of the quiescent disposition of the Louisianians.

Bradford is bitter, wishes it to be inferred from circumstances which necessarily mean nothing unusual, that the Govr. endeavored to give him a sop, in the job of public printing, and declares that if no removal takes place, the federal party will gain the upper hand of those attached to the administration, among whom he classes himself as one of the most zealous. His letter intimates that he had in a previous one mentioned two persons whom he does not name[2] as fit successors to Claiborne; but that he would name as preferable to all others, Chancellor Livingston in whose character he finds all the desirable qualifications.

Cathalan having been attacked, very unjustly I dare say, because the Accuser is notoriously of a worthless character, and sent a voluminous justification of himself. I do not trouble you with more of it, than the inclosed letter from Barnes, which is worth your perusal as it throws light on his own character. Lee has also written a long letter for a like purpose, which I inclose on account of some intelligence contained in it.

With respectful attachment, I remain Yrs.

JAMES MADISON

RC (DLC); at foot of first page: "The President"; endorsed by TJ as received from the State Department on 21 Mch. and "Barnes' ltr to Cathalan Monroe's Nov. 8. Dec. 20. Armstrong Dec. 24. W. Lee Dec. 20. Claiborne. Jan. 19." and so recorded in SJL. Enclosures: (1) James Monroe to Madison, Paris, 27 Nov. 1804, reporting that French support of U.S. rights to Florida has been threatened by Napoleon's favorable reaction to a formal protest by Spain; Monroe encloses a copy of his response to Talleyrand of 8 Nov., which reiterates the terms of the Louisiana treaty, reminds France of its promise to support U.S. claims, and endeavors to show the common interest of all three nations in "promoting an amicable adjustment of our differences"; Monroe hopes that his candor and expressions of friendship will encourage a similar response by the French (Madison, *Papers*, *Sec. of State Ser.*, 8:329-33). (2) Monroe to Madison, Bayonne, 20 Dec., announcing "that Spain has declared war agnst England at the instance of France" and sharing rumors of the Spanish king's willingness to abdicate in favor of one of his sons with Manuel de Godoy as regent (same, 410). (3) John Armstrong to Madison, Paris, 24 Dec., stating that he has presented his credentials to the French government and remarking on Talleyrand's bad treatment of Monroe; French officials have intimated that negotiations would go more smoothly "if *certain persons* could be sufficiently *gratified*," to which Armstrong has responded with disbelief that the French would dishonor either themselves or the United States by such a practice; Napoleon has yet to respond to the communications sent by Armstrong and Monroe; Armstrong speculates that the delay is a result of Napoleon's irritation with the United States, which Armstrong attributes to Jerome Bonaparte's marriage, American trade with Santo Domingo, "the freedom *with which he is treated* in *our journals*," and above all, the negative effect of U.S. prosperity on the emperor's attempt to extinguish democratic principles in France (same, 417-19). (4) William C. C. Claiborne to Madison, New Orleans, 19 Jan., defending himself against charges of incompetence and of subservience toward Spanish officials; Claiborne accuses Daniel Clark of perpetuating the attack out of resentment for not having obtained an appointment, and Edward Livingston and John B. Prevost of having joined in the opposition to him; he encloses newspaper clippings of the accusations and documents related to a breach of authority by the Marqués de Casa Calvo (same, 487-92; *Terr. Papers*, 9:371-7). (5) Joseph Barnes to Stephen Cathalan, Jr., Marseilles, 15 Apr. 1803, explaining his reasons for traveling to France with his vice consul, E. J. Newton, which included making connections in anticipation of opening a banking and commercial enterprise in Sicily (RC in DNA: RG 59, CD, Marseilles); for accusations against Cathalan by William Baker of Boston, which included charges related to Cathalan's issuing of a passport to Newton, an English subject, see Madison, *Papers, Sec. of State Ser.*, 8:79-80. (6) William Lee to Madison, Bordeaux, 20 Dec., defending himself against accusations made by Pierre Guestier, a Bordeaux wine merchant, that Lee was involved in the seizure of the *Joseph & Phoebe* by offering protection to the ship's consignee in return for a share of his profits and by denouncing the ship as British in order to share profits from the seizure with the customs official; Lee encloses statements from Robert R. Livingston, Fulwar Skipwith, and the director of customs; he informs Madison of Monroe's probable arrival in Bayonne and of news from Spain (same, 411-13).

[1] Preceding three words interlined.
[2] Preceding five words interlined.

From Philip Mazzei

17 Marzo, 1805,
alle 4 della mattina.

STIMSSMO, E CARMO. AMICO,

Mr. Appleton non seppe prima di ieri, che lo Schooner Dolphin, Capn. William, partirà domattina per Filadelfia; ed io non potei averne avviso prima di $\frac{1}{2}$ giorno. Fù impossibile di preparare il tutto con certezza di evitare sbagli, avendo dovuto impiegar troppe persone per essere in tempo, e trovar i mezzi per farne la spedizione stamattina di buon'ora, essendo necessario che la Cassa e le 4 cassette sieno a Livorno prima delle ore 11. Avevo preparato un numero di peschini di varie qualità, ma la febbre gialla in Livorno, gli inconvenienti che ce ne ànno impedita la libera comunicazione, e finalmente una rottura dell'argine del fiume Arno, che per quasi 2 mesi à tenuta allagata la campagna fra Pisa, e Livorno per la circonferenza di circa 80 miglia quadre, non à permesso di potergli mandare in tempo, e cavandogli di terra adesso, morrebbero certamente.

La brevità del tempo non mi permette di dir'altro per ora. Mi conservi un posto nel suo cuore, e mi creda con vera stima, e col più cordiale affetto &c.

EDITORS' TRANSLATION

MOST ESTEEMED AND DEAREST FRIEND, 17 Mch. 1805, 4 A.M.

Mr. Appleton did not learn until yesterday that the schooner *Dolphin*, Captain Williams, will set sail tomorrow morning for Philadelphia and I did not receive notice of this before noon. It was impossible to get everything ready with the certainty of avoiding mistakes. Too many people were needed to be ready on time, and means had to be sought for the shipping to happen early this morning, since the chest and the four boxes had to reach Leghorn before 11 in the morning. I had set aside a certain number of peach trees of different qualities, but the yellow fever in Leghorn and the difficulties that have hindered communications with the city, as well as the breaking of an embankment along the river Arno—which for two months has kept the countryside between Leghorn and Pisa in a radius of about eighty miles under water—have made it impossible to ship them on time. If I were to uproot them now, they would certainly die.

The short time I have does not allow me to say more at this moment. Please, keep a place for me in your heart, and know that I am, with true esteem and the most cordial affection, yours etc.

Dft (Archivio Filippo Mazzei, Pisa, Italy); in Mazzei's hand. Recorded in SJL as received 27 May.

From John Tyler

DEAR SIR; Green-Way Charles City March 17 1805

Now that our Country is in so prosperous a Situation, politically speaking, and the Republican Interest so well establish'd by your unequivocal Election to the Chair of State, permit me once more to congratulate you, and once more let it be in my power to do the same, if I shou'd live, by your third promotion if you shou'd live, and then I think the Victory over aristocracy will be compleat. "It will not do that the Traytor shou'd be merely trodden under foot but the Treason must be entirely abolish'd."+ For yet does that evil Spirit rear its monstrous Head whensoever an opportunity offers, of which the Georgia Speculations afford the strongest imaginable proof. The support given to such an unparrelleld instance of fraud on the People's Rights and such a dereliction of honor, and duty as the Act of the Georgia Legislature exhibits, evinces the most profound ignorance of Facts and principles, or the basest depravity—Surely these things must have their reward. But perhaps it may not be charitable to attribute bad motives to any One but from the most incontestable proof

Since I began this Letter I receiv'd your Address to the Senate and Members of Congress on your Inauguration which without flattery in my Opinion adds a Lustre to the whole of your Life if any thing cou'd be necessary to highten your public Character, which more and more is making its way into the Hearts of the People—The soundness of the reasoning, and the temper and philanthropy with which it is express'd must and will have the happyest effect on every person not so vicious as to persist in Spite of light and truth in a perverse Opinion—I hope experience will prove the justness of that sentiment which supposes a Republic may be happy and yet extensive, at least for Centuries to come, under just and wise Laws, and a just and wise administration—Surely a stranger is not so much to be relied on as a Neighbor, as our own family are govern'd by the same Laws and principles—It is very weak therefore to refuse a present good for fear of a future mischief—"Sufficient for the day is the Evil thereof"—After we have so happily attain'd our great object, a Stable republican Government, acquired New States, sinking our public debts and yet diminishing the Taxes, it is impossible but the country must be soon United, and without a *Mausoleum* of Stone or Brass these things will live in the honest page of History to the latest time—while they wou'd moulder into dust—.

I correspond with very few at your City and while I am writing this I know what an intrusion it will be on those Moments of your Life which are so precious to our Country. Yet I cannot help offering this small tribute of my Esteem for your Person and Character and do not think it too much trouble and condescension to receive a Letter from an old acquaintance once or twice a year although he cannot add one single Laurel to your Crown of Glory, but who really Loves his Country and all good Men as ardently as ever did a Grecian or Roman Patriot—I sincerely hope your Health and Happiness will long remain unimpar'd, both for your own sake and also for your Country,

+Cicero of Cæsar and Anthony

and that you may live to conquer by your integrity all evil speaking and printing, lying and Slandering, without the aid of Sedition Laws.

I am much delighted to find how honorably our little Navy has acquitted its self, but dear enough do[1] we pay for the visionary scheme of protecting Trade at such a distance, beside the possibility of involving our selves in quarrels with other Nations.

It is a fine thing for us to talk about, that our Citizens rather than be made slaves blow'd them selves up; but had they been cultivating the Earth how much more beneficial to themselves and Families their labour wou'd have been—I wou'd permit a Man to carry his Vessel where he pleased but he shou'd do it at his own risque—The advantages arising from the Trade so much contended for will not shortly compensate for the loss of Life and Treasure already expended—But this is going from my design in a Letter only meant as a congratulatory One—I hope a peace may be forced with Tripoli and our Citizens releas'd from their Chains, and then we may have time to avail our selves of all the advantages arising (in an honest Way) from the great *Battle Royal* in the old world—I have been at no feasts on the 4th instant, but my single Daughter Martha Jefferson and my son Wat Tyler & self have not fail'd to drink to your health and long life, but we have determin'd not to make you an *Emperor*, believing it wou'd not be so honorable to your self or Country—

I am with sincere regard JNO. TYLER

RC (DLC); endorsed by TJ as received 25 Mch. and so recorded in SJL.

John Randolph had recently revived the longstanding controversy over the mid-1790s attempt by GEORGIA to sell some of its western lands. One of his principal targets was Gideon Granger, an investor in one of the interested land companies (Granger to TJ, 28 Jan.; Randolph to TJ, 4 Mch.).

SUFFICIENT FOR THE DAY IS THE EVIL THEREOF: Matthew 6:34.

NAVY HAS ACQUITTED ITS SELF: given the subsequent, misleading reference to U.S. citizens blowing themselves up, Tyler likely alluded to the destruction of the *Philadelphia* (Vol. 43:39n).

[1] MS: "to."

From William Bartram

SIR Kingsess near Philadelphia March 18th. 1805

I have taken the liberty to cover a Letter for Your Excelly. from Mr. Alexander Wilson accompanying a fine and accurate drawing of two rare Birds, which he lately procured when on a tour through the No.eastern parts of the State of Nw York to view the Catarach of Niagara Mr. Willson shewed me the birds well preserved: The Jay seemes to differ from Mr. Pennants Corvus cinorius. Arct. Zool. And the Butcher Bird Lanius Excubitor Linn. Mr. Wilson excited by motives of benevolence, from a high opinion of Your personal & Publick character, requests me to convey to you this offering as a testimony of his esteem & affection.

Some time past Your worthy friend Doctr. Barton soon after his return home from Virginia informed us, that it was your wish to have the horns of the Stone Buck, (Capra Cervicapra?) I am directed by my brother to assure you that you are perfectly wellcome to them, and should have sent them, but living so remote from Philadelphia, have not yet found a safe mode of conveyance.

We have, a horn of a species of Cervus from the coast of Hudsons Bay, brought and presented to my father by Capt. Swain, who many years since, made a voyage thither, when on a descovery of a N. Western passage across our Continent, Tho' this horn appears to have belonged to an adult, it is singularly small & light, & must have shaded the brows of a very small Animal. I beg leave to repeat that you are wellcome to both these specimens, and wish for an oportunity of safe conveyance.

I sincerely unite with my friend W. and every True American in congratulations, for Your reelection to the Presidency of U. States

On wishing You a long and happy Life, beg leave to subscribe Your Excellencys Sincere Friend WILLIAM BARTRAM

RC (DLC); endorsed by TJ as received 6 Apr. and so recorded in SJL. Enclosure: Alexander Wilson to TJ, 18 Mch.

William Bartram (1739-1823), the son of John Bartram, Sr., was a naturalist who explored the American south in the 1760s and 1770s. After returning to Philadelphia, Bartram settled at the family estate in Kingsessing Township on the Schuylkill River, where he operated a botanical garden and later, in 1791, published an account of his journeys. A printed proposal for Bartram's travel narrative is in TJ's papers, and TJ was a subscriber to the publication. The two men knew one another from the time TJ spent in Philadelphia, and they regularly corresponded about seeds and plants (ANB; William Bartram, *Travels through North & South Carolina, Georgia, East & West Florida, the Cherokee Country, the Extensive Territories of the Muscogulges, or Creek Confederacy, and the Country of the Chactaws* [Philadelphia, 1791; Sowerby, No. 4029]; DLC: TJ Papers, 56:9532-3; MB, 1:759; Vol. 26:167-8, 272-4; Vol. 29:4-5, 117, 136, 319, 389-92; Vol. 30:232-3; Vol. 31:89-90; Bartram to TJ, 29 Oct. 1808).

Benjamin Smith BARTON visited Monticello in 1802 (Vol. 38:532).

CAPT. SWAIN: in 1753 and 1754, Charles Swaine commanded two voyages from Philadelphia in search of the Northwest Passage (Leonard W. Labaree and others, eds., *The Papers of Benjamin Franklin*, 43 vols. [New Haven, 1959-], 4:380-4).

From Bishop James Madison

DEAR SIR March 18h 1805 Williamsburg

I have enclosed a Letter from Mr Brackan, who was appointed Administrator for Mr Bellini, to Mr. Mazzei, which, he informs me, gives a particular State of the affairs of our deceased Friend.—It appears, from what Mr Brackan says, that there is Property remaining to the Amount of nearly £300.

A Certificate of the Death of Mr Bellini is forwarded by this Post to Govr Page, with a Request, that he wd. cause the Seal of the State to be affixed, & then to transmit it to you—

I congratulate our common Country upon your Re-election; & am Dr Sir, with sincerest Respect & Esteem

Yr Friend & Sert. J MADISON

RC (DLC); endorsed by TJ as received 25 Mch. and so recorded in SJL, but as a letter of the 25th. Enclosure: John Bracken to Philip Mazzei, not found.

FORWARDED BY THIS POST: see John Page to TJ, 20 Mch.

From Alexander Wilson

SIR Kingsess March 18th 1805

I beg your acceptance of a small trifle in Natural History which though imperfectly executed is offered with all the sincerity of affection to the best Friend and brightest ornament of this happy Country. If It afford You a moments amusement I shall think myself amply rewarded.

On my return from a visit to the Falls of Niagara in October last I killed two Birds on the shores of the Mohawk river and conceiving them to be little known, particularly the Jay, I have taken the liberty of transmitting under favour of Mr. Bartram as faithfull a sketch of them as I was capabable of taking The Jay approaches nearly to the *Corvus Canadensis* of Linnaeus and *Le Geay brun* of Buffon differing however in the colour and article of crest so much as to seem to be a distinct species. From several other Birds found while on the same Tour I am inclined to believe that many subjects still remain to be added to our Nomenclature in the Ornithology of the middle and northern states.

Permit me now to ask your Excellency's forgiveness for this intrusion. Rejoicing with a gratefull Country in the prospects of Reaping the fruits of your Pre-eminent services for many years I implore Heaven to bless and preserve a live so honourable to Science and so invaluable to the Republican institutions of a great and rapidly increasing Empire and beg leave to Subscribe myself

With the deepest veneration Your Excellencys sincere Friend and humble Servt ALEX WILSON

RC (DLC); at foot of text: "His Excelleny The President"; endorsed by TJ as received 6 Apr. and so recorded in SJL. Enclosed in William Bartram to TJ, 18 Mch. Enclosure not identified, but see below.

Alexander Wilson (1766-1813) wrote and illustrated the nine-volume *American Ornithology: or, The Natural History of the Birds of the United States*, which was published between 1808 and 1814 and provided the first comprehensive description of American birds (Sowerby, No. 1022). TJ was a subscriber of the work. Born into a weaver's family in Paisley, Scotland, Wilson initially made a name for himself by writing poems extolling pastoral values and critiquing the working conditions in textile mills. He immigrated to the United States in 1794 and after a time settled in the Philadelphia area, where he became friends with William Bartram, who inspired him to pursue his studies of American fowl. On the day of TJ's first inauguration, Wilson delivered a public oration extolling the new president's commitment to liberty (ANB; Clark Hunter, ed., *The Life and Letters of Alexander Wilson* [Philadelphia, 1983]; *Port Folio*, new ser., 7 [1812], 34-47; Alexander Wilson, *Oration, On the Power and Value of National Liberty. Delivered to a Large Assembly of Citizens, at Milestown, Pennsylvania, on Wednesday, March 4, 1801* [Philadelphia, 1801]; TJ to Wilson, 9 Oct. 1807).

SMALL TRIFLE IN NATURAL HISTORY: in a letter of 26 Mch., Wilson described the drawing he sent to TJ. "The two nondescript birds which I killed on the Mohawk, attracted the notice of several naturalists about Philadelphia," he wrote. "On the 4th of March, I set to work upon a large sheet of fine drawing paper, and in ten days I finished two faithful drawings of them, far superior to any that I had before. In the background, I represented a view of the Falls of Niagara, with the woods wrought in as finely as I possibly could do" (Hunter, ed., *Alexander Wilson*, 235).

From Matthew Wilson

Martch the 18th. 1805
Mead:Ville Crawford County & State Pennsylvania

DEAR SIR

I hope you will pardon my Asureance in Troubleing your Excellancy with the Reeding these few lines, but as they come from the hand of a true Republican an Old Soldier & Volintier & A Sincier friend to his Cuntery, you will be pleased to Reed them and Return Me an Answer as Soon as possable—

it has pleased the Almighty God to Gift me with a great portion of Natural Engenuity So that I can Contrive & Compleet Any thing I Undertake The greatest Power & the wonderfullest branshes of ingenuity are yet to be found in My opinion There is five powers namely Water—Wind—Steem or fire—Weights & Springs. By these All mills

& machenery whatever Actuates—there Remains yet One to be found which I Cann See affar of but I am not Able to reetch to it—for the want of a bite of the Root of all Evill—but the Evill Lyes in Useing it to answer Evil purposes I call it the Power of "pressuar," By which a time peise may be made smaller than Common Watches to revolve as Long as the Works will Last without any thing but Ragulating—Likewise Timepieses may be made for Sailing on Sea that will Effectually Compleet Longsitude also Cariages May be made that the Loading or preshuar of its Load will be the means of its Valosity—Also A Boat May be Calculated that the preshuar of the Load will forse it against the Currant—Likewise be Usefull for Spinning ingines and all Sutch Matchinary the World has Vulgarly Called it the Perpetual motion but I Call it the power of pressuar (I have already found it on water & by wind I have Calculated A boat to go against the Currant the Stronger the Currant the faster its motion against it by means of the Currant & its own Action—Also A Wheel cariage that Will runn Against the Wind the Stronger the Wind blews the faster its motion Against it—On these same prinsiples will the power of pressuar work when Rightly Constructed

I will State it fair in the Rure of Three to those Who Do not Credit the finding of this power—

If Water—and Wind can be made work Against Each other—Why not Weights and Springs—

The 2d Day of February Last I was in Lanchester with Mr. Elicut Secretary of the Land office an Old Aquaintanc of mine I told him My Entention and asked him to assist me With a Little Money to Enable me to make an Experiment he refered me to Our Assembly I also conversed with Severals of them but found they were not Willing to venture Any thing Upon Unsertantyes without they could Reep immediate Benefit So I advansed no further

I Also told Mr. Elicut of a Discovery I made Last September On the Bank of Lake Erie in York State of a Large body of Iron Oar which is A Grand Object for Som Able Men to Come And Start Iron Works where there is thousands of Tunns of Oar Lying in Water mark Washed out of the Slate Rocks Ready dug for mans Use And the Best Seat for forges at the Rappids of the outlet of the Lake that is in the Union: I Could Wish that the United States Would Embark into that busness for Castings and Iron Could Be transported By Water Over All our Western Cuntery By Water Cariage—

I was 42 years Old When I maryed in 1797—has now five Smal Children in Eight years Next June my Wife is then 25 year & I 50—but Very Stout for my Age. I am A Building A Grist Mill Upon A new

Construction from the foundation She is to go without Cog—or round or wheel—Multiplication of Works Dipresuates Strenth is My Creed—that that Costs the Least & Does the Most Execution is the best Envented plann

I Look Up to Your house As A Son to A Father for A Littl assistance & I will bring you the power of pressuar Dead or Alive if alive it Will be Usefull to the World I ad no more but Remains your Affectionot Wellwisher MATTHEW WILSON

N:B I Send this Letter by post from Mead ville Direct your Letter to th care of Joseph Hackney Mead ville.

RC (DLC); endorsed by TJ as received 26 Apr. and so recorded in SJL.

Matthew Wilson (1755-1844) was born in Chester County, Pennsylvania, and served as a private and sergeant in the Continental line from 1776 until his discharge in 1778. After the war, he filed a claim for service as a frontier scout and captain in a Pennsylvania regiment. He relocated several times, but by 1820 resided in Morgan County, Ohio, where he died (DNA: RG 15; Virgil D. White, *Genealogical Abstracts of Revolutionary War Pension Files*, 4 vols. [Waynesboro, Tenn., 1990-92], 3:3893).

From Joel Barlow

DEAR SIR London. 19 March 1805—

I believe I took the liberty of mentioning to you in a letter last summer, before I left Paris, that the ill state of my wife's health was the sole cause of my not embarking for America that season, and that we were coming to England for medical advice, with the intention of passing the winter here, & embark this spring if possible. This is what we expect to accomplish. Her health now promises to enable her to support the voyage, & we hope to sail in May.

But my taking this country in my way has, I find, subjected me to a great deal of calumny in France. Some Americans, as well as Frenchmen, in Paris have endeavoured to connect me with the operations of Mr. Fulton in this country, tho these operations took place before my arrival here, & tho I never had any personal interest+ or connection even with his projects.

A knowledge of these reports having been communicated to me by Mr. Lee of Bordeaux, I have addressed to him a letter on that subject, the copy of which I take the liberty of enclosing to you. And as it is possible that the slanders which this letter is meant to oppose may reach America & even get into the public papers, I desire you would have the goodness to make such use of it as in your opinion my reputation may require, should it even be to give it the same publicity that the stories which occasioned it may have had in that country.

I am, Dear Sir, with great respect, yr. obt. Sert.

JOEL BARLOW

+I mean no other interest than a patriotic one. For I still think, as I have before mentioned to you, that if his theory can be reduced to practice, it will give to America her cheapest mode of defence, & greatly diminish, in all countries, the instruments of despotism & the provocatives to war.

RC (DLC); at foot of first page: "Mr. Jefferson"; endorsed by TJ as received 12 June and so recorded in SJL. Enclosure: Barlow to William Lee, London, 15 Mch., thanking Lee for advising him of the criticism being expressed in Paris regarding Barlow's move to England and his rumored intrigue with Fulton; Barlow reiterates the reasons for his move and his lack of involvement in any of Fulton's projects; he defends Fulton as a patriot who wants only "to check tyranny, diminish the frequency of wars, and promote the interest of America" and is willing to work toward that purpose "in whatever country he can find a footing for his machines" (Tr in same; in Barlow's hand).

LETTER LAST SUMMER: Barlow to TJ, 26 June 1804.

Fulton moved his OPERATIONS on submarine warfare from France to England in May 1804 and signed a contract with the British government in July. The Barlows were still in Paris as late as August (E. Taylor Parks, "Robert Fulton and Submarine Warfare," *Military Affairs*, 25 [1961-62], 178; Vol. 44:261).

From Mathew Carey

SIR

Philada. March 19. 1805

Your favor of the 7th. covering a Check for ten $\frac{37}{100}$ Dollars, the amt. of the Books forwarded you some time since, I duly recd.

By Capt D. Bensson I sent you on Thursday last, two copies of the New Testament, the best 12mo. Edition printed here. There is an octavo edition, considerably superior.

Your obt. hble. servt.

MATHEW CAREY

Thomas Jefferson, Esqr. president U.S. bot. of M Carey 2 Testements, Long Primer—$1.

RC (MHi); at head of text: "Thomas Jefferson, Esqr. President U.S."; endorsed by TJ as received 25 Mch. and so recorded in SJL.

From Francis Macy and Others

ESTEEMED FRIEND Nantucket the 19 of 3 mo 1805

As the Office of Collector of customs at Nantucket has been some time Vacated by the Death of Stephen Hussey, and feeling anxious that a Suitable Person for the benefit off Goverment, as well as the Quiet of a large Majority of the Inhabitants of this place might be Appointed to Suceed him, and having Information that Jered Coffin at Hudson is Recommended[1] to fill the Office we cannot but Express our our desire (if our Information is Correct) that he may not be the person to fill the office believing it would not tend to the advantage of Goverment nor meet the wishes of the Inhabitants of this place, we perceiving that Capt Daniel Coffin has been Recommended by our worthy Friends Micajah Coffin one of the House of Representatives and Isaac Coffin a Senator from this to the General Court, we Cannot but Unite with their Recommendation, believing that Daniel Coffin is the most Suitable man within our County being a man that is Ardent for the present order of things,—

with Sentiment of Esteem we are your Friends—

FRAN MACY
SETH COFFIN
PAUL GARDNER JNR.
SHUBAEL COFFIN
OBADIAH FOLGER
GILBERT COFFIN
LATHAM GARDNER
Select Men of the Town of Nantucket

RC (DNA: RG 59, LAR); at foot of text: "Thomas Jefferson Esqr. President of the United States"; endorsed by TJ as a letter of 9 Mch. from "Coffin Seth et al." received 17 Apr. and so recorded in SJL with notation "Danl. Coffin to be Collector"; also endorsed by TJ: "Coffin Danl. to be" and "Coffin Jared not to be," connected by a brace to notation "Collectr. Nantucket."

Francis Macy (1750-1817) became a Nantucket County justice of the peace in 1811. Seth Coffin (1753-1830) was a whaling captain and Paul Gardner (1755-1835) a merchant and importer. Shubael Coffin (1754-1821) represented Nantucket in the Massachusetts General Court from 1809 through 1812. Ship master Obadiah Folger (ca. 1755-1821) became county treasurer in 1812. Merchant and ship owner Gilbert Coffin (1759-1843) was a state legislator in 1813. Latham Gardner (1760-1830) served for many years as the island's town clerk and register of deeds. The seven signers were all Republicans and lifelong residents of Nantucket (*New-Bedford Mercury*, 30 Apr. 1813, 2 Nov. 1821; Lydia S. Hinchman, *Early Settlers of Nantucket* [Philadelphia, 1901], 289; *The Massachusetts Register and United States Calendar for the Year of Our Lord 1811, the Thirty-Fifth of American Independence* [Boston, 1811], 98; *The Massachusetts Register and United States Calendar for the Year of Our Lord 1812, the Thirty-Sixth of American Independence* [Boston, 1812], 98; Benjamin Sharp, "Nantucket's

Representatives in National and State Legislatures," *Proceedings of the Nantucket Historical Association: Seventeenth Annual Meeting* [Nantucket, 1911], 30-1; *Nantucket Inquirer*, 23 Jan., 25 Sep. 1830, 4 Nov. 1835; *Whalemen's Shipping List*, 9 Dec. 1873; Nantucket Historical Association finding aids for Worth Family Papers, 1743-1912, Gardner Family Papers, 1717-1911, Ships' Papers Collection, Micajah Coffin Papers-Charles Congdon Collection, 1671-1844, Account Books Collection).

TJ had already appointed DANIEL COFFIN to be collector at Nantucket (TJ to the Senate, 26 Feb.; Vol. 45: Appendix I).

[1] MS: "Reommended."

From James Oldham

SIR— Richmond 19th. March 1805.

Your favor of the 11th. I receivd yesterday and am very thankful for the information which it contains; as Mr. Galligo had frequently ast me Respecting the ornement, I thot it would be some wat satisfactory to thim to se the information Which you have pleasd to give; and I shew him your Letter of the 11th. Which gave him every satisfaction that was Nesary: he desird me to proceed as I thot moast proper, Which I think will be best to wat your return to Washington.

I think the ornements of your parlor Frize will sute mine the best, if I recolect rite the depth of your Frize is nearly equal with mine which is 8 I.—the ornements are in the Juish Stile, but I amagin that will make no difference with Mr. Galligo.

Unfortunately for me Last nite about Twelve Oclock my Plank-kiln Took fiar and was intirly consumd. the hole amount of Plank was 3050 Feet Which was all prime; 1000 of it was perchasd for the purpose of doing your dores and sashes, Which I intend to be my own Loss: if with conveniance you can give me a draft out of my own wages for a £11. 12 s. which is the cost I shall be very thankful: Shall go into the cuntery to day and perchace as much more to try it a second time.—This would of bin had I of bin Sucsesful, the Last kill that should of had to dry for Mr. Galligos. use, it happened so strangly that am not Able to account for it: Mr. Galligo Bares his misfortune with the graites patience as says I must Try it gain. I have hurn he should say that he conceived it not owing to any inattention or negglect by myself.—

Adue and may Heaven Bless You. Your moast Humble and Obt Sevt. JAMES OLDHAM

RC (DLC); at foot of text: "Thoms. Jefferson Esqr."; endorsed by TJ as received 21 Mch. and so recorded in SJL.

From Caesar A. Rodney

HONORED & DEAR SIR, Wilmington March 19th. 1805.

I received your favor of the 8th. inst: by the mail on the subject of mr Cope's new theory of the magnet & shall embrace the earliest opportunity of making the communication to him which you desire.

You are well acquainted with the material facts & circumstances relative to the ship Favourite & her cargoe, which was by the weather cast ashore near Lewistown. We have been engaged in the trial of a court, which is not yet concluded, between the owners & those who claim as the salvors of the cargoe, for a week past.

Among other grounds of defence on which we resist this claim of salvage, to a moiety of the cargoe, we shew that the salvors by their mal-conduct have forfeited the cargoe to the U.S. by a breach of the revenue laws. That altho' the U.S. may relinquish to us this forfeiture, because we were innocent, yet then we receive the property from their hands & not from those of the salvors, the plain English of whose claim, is in fact nothing more nor less than this: For having forfeited the *whole* of your cargoe to the U.S. we now claim of you the value of a moiety.

On the second day of the trial, the District judge (G. Bedford) delivered to us a letter from judge Winchester to him, containing a summary of a case, together with the arguments of council & the decision of the court, determined by himself.

This adjudication extends the whole lenth of deciding that *salvage goods* are not liable to the payment of duties & can not therefore be forfeited by any misconduct of the salvors.

I have sent on to Mr. Gallatin a copy of the above letter, considering the revenue of the U.S. as deeply affected by such a decision, & have taken the liberty to give you a sketch of the business.

What Bedford's decision will be I know not but the District Attorney & myself are determined to use every exertion to protect the interests of the U.S.

With great esteem & regard I remain Dr. Sir Yours Very Sincerely

C. A. RODNEY

RC (DLC); endorsed by TJ as received 25 Mch. and so recorded in SJL.

For the case arising from the salvage of the ship (FAVOURITE), see TJ to George Read, Jr., 10 Feb.

James WINCHESTER, the federal judge for the district of Maryland, sent a summary of a case involving the ship *Blaireau*, which he ruled on in July 1803. The *Blaireau* was a French vessel, disabled en route from Martinique to Bordeaux by a Spanish boat and subsequently salvaged by a British ship, part of the crew of which sailed the *Blaireau*, at heavy risk, to Baltimore. Although that case, which ultimately was appealed to the Supreme Court, mostly involved questions related to the amount and distribution of the salvage, Winchester did rule "that salvage goods were not dutiable." In a response to Rodney's letter of 19 Mch. (not found), GALLATIN recalled having "heard of the decision in the case of the Blaireau" and of a similar case. The distinction, as he understood it, was that the salvage did not involve goods being imported from a foreign port (since their original destination was not the United States). The salvage of the *Blaireau* could be treated "on the same principle that fish & oil taken at sea by American vessels pay no duty." The salvage of the *Favorite*, by contrast, involved a ship bound for an American port and disabled in American waters, so U.S. revenue laws should apply (William Cranch, *Reports of Cases Argued and Adjudged in the Supreme Court of the United States, 1801-1815*, 9 vols. [Washington, D.C., 1804-17], 2:240-71; 4:355-6; Gallatin to Rodney, 22 Mch., in Gallatin, *Papers*, 10:754).

BEDFORD'S DECISION: the district court at Wilmington ruled against the federal government's contention that the cargo salvaged from the *Favorite* should be treated as a forfeiture and ordered the sale of the goods so that salvage could be distributed. The decision was upheld by the circuit court. Gallatin, who had authorized Rodney's employment as a co-counsel to U.S. attorney George Read, continued to pursue the case, fearing that the "decision of the Delaware district judge leaves the revenue officers in a very awkward situation, injures the revenue itself, and encourages plunderers." In a unanimous Supreme Court opinion delivered on 9 Mch. 1808, however, John Marshall ruled that the "libels filed on the part of the United States were properly dismissed" (Gallatin, *Papers*, 10:782; 11:287; 13:365; Wilmington *Mirror of the Times, & General Advertiser*, 8 May 1805; Cranch, *Reports*, 4:347-66; Herbert A. Johnson, Charles T. Cullen, Charles F. Hobson, and others, eds., *The Papers of John Marshall*, 12 vols. [Chapel Hill, 1974-2006], 7:166-72).

From John Boyle

SIR Lancaster Kentucky March 20th 1805

Since my arrival at home I have been informed that Joshua Lewis Esqe of this State is desirous of receiving an appointment as a commissioner in the District of Louisiana under the law for ascertaining & adjusting the titles to land in that country—The difficulty of procuring men who to the other requisite quallifications add that of a knowledge of the French Language has induced me to name to you Mr Lewis as a person well quallifyed to fill with propriety the office of commissioner. Mr Lewis is a man of Academical education was regularly bred to the profession of Law & has practiced with credit in the courts of this State for several years—

He is a man of strict honour & integrity & a genuine republican in principle—I am informed & believe that he early acquired a knowledge of the French language and that he yet speaks it with considerable correctness & fluency

In short I have no doubt that Mr Lewis if he should meet with the appointment would discharge the duties of the office with fidelity & ability

I am with sentiments of the profoundest respect & esteem your obt st
JOHN BOYLE

RC (DNA: RG 59, LAR); addressed: "The President Of the U States Washington"; franked; postmarked Lexington, Kentucky, 5 Apr.; endorsed by TJ as received 24 Apr. and "Lewis Joshua to be a Comr. Westwd." and so recorded in SJL, where it is connected by a brace with John Breckinridge and Buckner Thruston to TJ, 5 Apr.

From John Page

DEAR SIR Richmond March 20th. 1805

At the request of President Madison I now transmit to you the Certificate which you had requested him to have authenticated by annexing the Seal of the State.

I am with great respect & Esteem your mot. obedt.

JOHN PAGE

RC (DLC); endorsed by TJ as received 28 Mch. and so recorded in SJL. Enclosure not found, but see TJ to Bishop James Madison, 10 Mch., and Madison's reply of the 18th.

From William Pryce

Wilmington March 20th. 1805.

W. Pryce, presents his respects to His excellency Thomas Jefferson Esqr, apologises, for the neglect, in his last, and informs that the price of the life of Christ &c is $4.00, which he will please to remit here, by any convenient opportunity that may offer.

RC (MHi); endorsed by TJ as received 28 Mch. and so recorded in SJL.

HIS LAST: Pryce to TJ, 9 Mch.

The PRICE offered to subscribers in the original proposal was $4.50. In his financial memoranda under 3 May 1805, TJ recorded payment for the book (Easton, Md., *Herald and Eastern Shore Intelligencer*, 8 Nov. 1803; MB, 2:1152; see also TJ to John Barnes, 12 Aug. 1805).

From Zadok Cramer

Pittsburgh, March 21, 1805

Zadok Cramer hopes he will justly appreciate the honor conferred on him by Thomas Jefferson in the receipt of his very polite note of the 8th 2 mo. in which he says he "subscribes with pleasure for a copy of Brown Dictionary of Bible, proposed to be printed at Pittsburgh"

N.B. Enclosed is a printed proposal for said work.

RC (DLC); endorsed by TJ as received 1 Apr. and so recorded in SJL. Enclosure: proposal dated 22 Feb. for *A Dictionary of the Holy Bible* (printed copy in same).

NOTE OF THE 8TH 2 MO.: TJ to Cramer, 8 Mch.

From Charles Philippe Magnan

MONSIEUR Philadelphie le 21 Mars 1805

Je prends la liberté de vous adresser la présente pour vous aviser avoir remis à la poste deux plis qui m'ont été recommandés par Monsieur Gouan Proffesseur de Botanique & membre de l'Institut national à Montpellier qui a eu l'honneur de jouir chez lui de quelques heures d'entretient avec Vous lors de votre dernier voyage en france; j'ai l'avantage de le connaitre très particulièrement & c'est lors de mon séjour chez lui en me rendant de Marseille à Bordeaux qu'il me remit ces objets y joignant une lettre que vous trouverez inclus & dans la quelle il veut bien réclamer votre protection en ma faveur, j'en suis on ne peut plus flaté & permettez, Monsieur, que dans ce moment je prenne la liberté d'en user en vous demandant, si rien ne s'y oppose, une protection de votre Gouvernement pour me mettre en sécurité contre les corsaires dans un voyage à St. Thomas que je vais effecteur. je ne vous laisserai pas ignorer que je parle un peu l'Anglais, en cas que ce fut nécessaire, j'ai vingt cinq ans & d'une taille ordinaire, plustôt au dessous. je vous serai infiniment reconnaissant de ce service. Il m'aurait été bien agréable que mes affaires m'eussent permis d'avoir l'honneur de me présenter à vous pour avoir l'avantage de vous connaitre & je vous prie de ne pas m'oublier si d'autres occasions se présentaient ou je dus réclamer votre protection.

Je vous prie de me croire, Monsieur, avec la plus haute Considération, votre très humble & obeissant serviteur

CHLES. PHILIPPE MAGNAN FILS

P.S. Chez Monsieur William Cramond Philadelphie

EDITORS' TRANSLATION

SIR, Philadelphia, 21 Mch. 1805

I am taking the liberty of sending you this letter to inform you that I mailed two envelopes that were entrusted to me by Mr. Gouan, professor of botany at Montpellier and member of the National Institute, who had the honor of enjoying a few hours of conversation with you in his home during your last trip to France. I have the good fortune of knowing him very well. It was during my stay at his home en route from Marseilles to Bordeaux that he gave me these objects with the enclosed letter. In it, he asks for your protection on my behalf. I am exceedingly flattered. Allow me, Sir, to take the liberty of using his recommendation to ask for your government's protection, if possible, to ensure my safety from pirates on a trip I am taking to St. Thomas. Let me add that I speak a little English, should that be necessary. I am 25 years old, of average height, or slightly below. I would be infinitely grateful for this favor. If my plans had allowed, I would have been very pleased to have had the honor of introducing myself and having the good fortune of meeting you. I beg you not to forget me if other occasions arise when I might need to request your protection.

With the highest consideration, Sir, I beg you to believe me your very humble and obedient servant. CHLES. PHILIPPE MAGNAN, JR.

P.S. Care of Mr. William Cramond, Philadelphia

RC (DLC); at head of text: "Monsieur Jefferson Président des Etats unis d'Amérique à Washington"; endorsed by TJ as received 28 Mch. and so recorded in SJL. Enclosure: Antoine Gouan to TJ, 28 Oct. 1804.

Charles Philippe Magnan of Marseilles was an amateur painter and a nephew of a prominent medical doctor in Paris (Vol. 44:614-15).

WILLIAM CRAMOND ran a counting house at the corner of Third Street and Cypress Alley in Philadelphia (James Robinson, *The Philadelphia Directory for 1805* [Philadelphia, 1804], n.p.).

From Thomas Appleton

SIR Leghorn 22nd. March 1805

About five years since I requested my brother in law Samuel Emery of Philadelphia to make enquiry for a certain Carlo Bellini, a tuscan by birth, and who left this country nearly forty years ago for Virginia.—By information he rec'd from you Sir, it appear'd, that this person was then professor of languages in St. Mary's college, and a short time after, a letter was handed me from Bellini containing one for his sisters in Florence.—from that period, they have not had any direct intelligence from him; but they have been lately inform'd by Mr. Mazzei, that their brother is since dead.—I mention these circumstances to apologize for my now inclosing you a Memoria which I have this day receiv'd from his Excellency the Governor of Leghorn, by order of the government of Florence and in behalf of the two sisters Bellini,—I should not trouble you Sir on this business if through any other channel I could obtain for them the information which is the object of the Memoria. I therefore now inclose you the original, and have ventured to assure the Governor, that in due time I shall be able to reply to it.—

I have this moment receiv'd from Mr. Fabbroni the inclosed book and letter which he desires I would *transmit* to you.—

I have the honor to be with Sincere respect your devoted Servant.—

TH: APPLETON

RC (DLC); at foot of text: "Thomas Jefferson. esq. President of the U: States of America"; endorsed by TJ as received 22 May and so recorded in SJL. FC (Lb in DNA: RG 84, CR, Leghorn); dated 21 Mch.; at foot of text: "sent by the Scho. Dolphin Capt. Williams." Enclosures: (1) "Memoria," 21 Mch., from the government of Etruria to Appleton, relating a request from Luisa and Aurora Bellini to confirm the death of their brother Carlo Bellini; they ask when his passing took place, whether he made a disposition concerning his estate, and who might be in possession of any inheritance he left; the government asks Appleton to report any answers in due course (MS in DLC: TJ Papers, 148:25805; in Italian). (2) Giovanni Fabbroni to TJ, 15 Mch., and enclosure.

ST. MARY'S COLLEGE: Carlo Bellini had been a professor at the College of William and Mary (Vol. 38:214n).

In his letterbook, Appleton included a note of 21 Mch. to TJ, covering the enclosure of Giovanni Fabbroni's BOOK AND LETTER. A received copy has not been found, and the letter is not recorded in SJL (FC in DNA: RG 84, CR, Leghorn; at foot of text: "Thos. Jefferson, esqr. President of the U: States of America Washington" and "Sent Via Scho. Dolphin").

From Joseph Dougherty

DEAR SIR Geor. Town Mar. 22. 05

only this morning I recd. your letter Dated culpeper C: H. Mar. 16th. I went imediately to Mr Main & brot. the 4000 thorns. on enquireing at the stage office I met a young man with whom I am well acquainted going from here to Richmond immediately in the Stage I purchased a box and packed. the thorns. which he will be particular in delivering from his hands. on planting those thorns Sir. you will please to observe the directions of mr. Main. that is to plant them one inch lower than the yallow part which is conspicuous otherways they will not do well. Sir your packages left Alexa. in good order in a vessel bound to Richmond on Sunday last the 17th inst.

Dear Sir whilst mr. Burwell was at the Presidents House he requested of me to find him 2 young pointer Dogs which I did. the time is now expired I was to take them away but I know not what to do with them. If Sir you Should see him please to remind him so that he may Direct me as they are reserved for him

The family is all well I am happy to hear of the Success of the cart and chair

Sir your Hble servt.

JOS DOUGHERTY

RC (MHi); endorsed by TJ as received 28 Mch. and so recorded in SJL.

YOUR LETTER: not found and not recorded in SJL.

Thomas MAIN operated a nursery near Georgetown. In a letter of 13 Mch., he asked Dougherty to pay $38 to a third party "as the full amount of my Accot. for Trees and plants sold to the President and delivered on the 8th. Inst." In his financial memoranda, TJ recorded giving this amount to Dougherty on 11 Mch. The THORNS were intended as fencing at Monticello (RC in MHi, endorsed by TJ: "Main Tho"; MB, 2:1148).

At some point, likely before he began using the polygraph exclusively, TJ wrote detailed instructions for securing a CHAIR to the mechanism of a carriage or cart (PrC in MHi; entirely in TJ's hand; undated; blurred and faint; includes drawings).

From David Gelston

SIR, New York. March 22d. 1805

Enclosed is Capt. Lee's bill of lading for 5 boxes, 2 cases and one small sample box of wine and 3 boxes of sweetmeats—

I also shipped yesterday on board the Schooner New York, Nathaniel Thomson Master one pipe of Lisbon wine to the care of Messrs. Gibson & Jefferson at Richmond—

The present, are the first opportunities I have had since the arrival of the wines that appeared to me proper to risk—

The duties with the expenses on the whole as soon as collected will be forwarded, the packages appear to be in good order, I wish them safe to hand—and have

the honor to be—with great respect Sir, your obedient servant

DAVID GELSTON

RC (MHi); at foot of text: "Thomas Jefferson President United States"; endorsed by TJ as received 28 Mch. and so recorded in SJL. Enclosure not found.

For the shipment from William LEE, see Lee to TJ, 12 Sep. 1804.

To John Benson

Monticello Mar. 23. 05.

Th: Jefferson took the liberty of desiring that a box or package of plants should be sent by the stage from Washington to Fredericksburg addressed to the care of mr Benson. he now asks the favor of mr Benson to forward them by the stage to Milton with a recommendation of them to the particular care of the driver. he expects they may arrive at Fredericksburg about the time this note does. he presents to mr Benson his salutations & good wishes

PoC (MHi); endorsed by TJ as a letter to Egbert Benson and so recorded in SJL.

John Benson (d. ca. 1815) became postmaster of Fredericksburg in 1802 after the removal of Federalist Timothy Green. At that time he was described as poor, with a large family, and "quite respectable." Benson operated the city's principal tavern and livery, the Old Stage Office. TJ lodged at the tavern during his days traveling to and from Philadelphia in the 1790s. On those occasions when he used the stage from the capital to Fredericksburg, TJ would have his enslaved servant Jupiter meet him at Benson's livery with horses for the trip on to Monticello. This sometimes required days of waiting by Jupiter and enabled Benson to collect boarding fees (Williamsburg *Virginia Gazette* [Dixon & Nicolson], 20 Nov. 1779; Baltimore *Republican; or, Anti-Democrat*, 17 May 1802; Norwich *Connecticut Centinel*, 14 Sep. 1802; George H. S. King, "General George Weedon," WMQ, 20 [1940], 248; MB, 2:912, 957, 966, 987; RS, 1:14n; Vol. 29:436).

MR BENSON: TJ wrote Benson a number of letters from 1805 to 1812, each one endorsed as a letter to Egbert Benson. His endorsement on letters from Benson varied (Benson to TJ, 26 Mch. 1805, 25 Mch., 15 Aug. 1807, 18 Nov. 1808, 3 Mch. 1809, 8 Apr. 1812).

From Peter Lenox

SIR Washington City 23d March 1805

The bearer of this letter is Mr. Richard Barry, With whome, I have Contracted to do your Painting, and whome I wish & have know dought, will endeavour to give you—Compleat satisfaction

Sir I am with the greatest Respect and best wishes

PETER LENOX

RC (MHi); at foot of text: "Mr Thomas Jefferson Eqr."; endorsed by TJ as received 28 Mch. and so recorded in SJL with notation "by Barry."

To James Madison

DEAR SIR Monticello Mar. 23. 05.

Yours of the 17th. was recieved on the 21st. I consider Armstrong's letter as giving us the result of the two intemediate letters of Monroe not recieved and that we may anticipate the effect of his mission. on it's failure as to the main object, I wish he may settle the right of navigating the Mobile, as every thing else may await further peaceable proceedings. but even then we shall have a difficult question to decide, to wit, whether we will let the present crisis in Europe pass away without a settlement

Barnes's letter strengthens the intimations we have recieved that he is but a wandering adventurer. his perpetual absence from his post offers just cause of superseding him whenever a good subject offers. Lee & Claiborne seem both pestered with intriguants. but as far as we see the conduct of both is without blame. in the case of Claiborne we must shew that however thankfully we recieve personal informations as to our officers, we will not permit them to be written down by newspaper defamation.—the use of an 8vo. Polygraph obliges me to write on paper of that size. Affectionate salutations.

TH: JEFFERSON

RC (DLC: Madison Papers); at foot of text: "Mr. Madison." PoC (DLC); endorsed by TJ; with canceled endorsement of a letter of 12 Apr. to Dabney Carr. Notation in SJL: "Armstrong. Monroe. Barnes. Lee. Claiborne." Enclosures: letters of James Monroe and John Armstrong to Madison (see Madison to TJ, 17 and 27 Mch.).

SUPERSEDING HIM: in a letter of 11 May, Madison informed Joseph Barnes that his lengthy absence from Sicily, combined with the greater convenience of splitting the island between two consulates, had encouraged the administration to appoint Abraham Gibbs consul at Palermo and John Broadbent consul at Messina. Barnes's commission was now defunct. Commissions dated 20 Mch. had already been sent to Gibbs and Broadbent, and a commission of the same day went to Frederick Degen at Naples (DNA: RG 59, MPTPC; Madison, *Papers, Sec. of State Ser.*, 9:342-3; Vol. 33:585-6).

From John Stricker

SIR Baltimore March 23d. 1805

Enclosed I have the honour to hand you Captn Manns receipt for three barrels of Perry, which were delivered to me by Captn Matthews, who received them from Mr Langdon of New-Hampshire, with directions to put them into some persons hands here that would forward them to you—

In consequence of which directions Captn Matthews placed them under my care, and I avail myself of the first packet going to Washington to forward them to your Excellency—

I have the Honour to be with great respect yr Excellencys obedt servant
JOHN STRICKER

RC (MHi); endorsed by TJ as received 17 Apr. and so recorded in SJL. Enclosure: Zachariah Mann, Baltimore, 23 Mch., acknowledging the receipt on board the schooner *Providence* of three barrels of perry, "in good order which I promise to deliver in like order at Washington to the President of the United States or to his order he paying me the Customary freight for the same" (MS in same).

John Stricker (1759-1825), a Baltimore merchant, was the city's U.S. navy agent from 1801 to 1810. As a brigadier general in the state militia in the War of 1812, Stricker led Maryland forces at the battle of North Point in 1814 (James Robinson, *Baltimore Directory, for 1804* [Baltimore, 1804], 62; *Maryland Historical Magazine*, 9 [1914], 209-18; Philadelphia *Gazette of the United States*, 14 Oct. 1801; JEP, 2:147).

From John Francis Vacher

SIR
New York March 23d 1805

I was Just about adressing Your Excellency on the forwardness of my work and anticepating the Satisfaction its variety presents when the enclosed of Mr Jonathan Dayton appear'd: a copy of which I transmitted to the Secretary of the treasury, with my application in behalf of my Son for the Agency of the Board of Commissioners, to be established at St Loüis, or in any other office under the Same law, but St Loüis to have the preference; and wait for my Son's arrival from New Jersey to ascertain his intention thereon. his presence here, and his strong desire to Serve his Country, have not only prompted him to approve of my Steps but yet to make a personnal application for the Same office to the Secretary by the Same post which conveys the present

It would have been more Satisfactory to my feelings had this favour Sprung from my political friends, either in new Jersey or in this State; and Yet it must be pleasing to me that a person Whose political Conduct I reprobated *in propria persona* but with decency, Should of his own accord, do me good without my even dreaming of it.

My Son is going on twenty four Years. I began his education by Sending him to canada where he Stay'd nearly one Year, wherefrom he brought a good french accent, that he has rather improved, and I make no doubt that a year's application in a french town, would render him so capable, as to find no difference between him and french natives. he translates it as well as any one in America, he has the Knowledge which the ancient and french languages may prompt to the Spanish, has had a Collegiate education; and Suffer'd not a little in Philadelphia by the prosecutors of the System of terror, I Suppose on my account as well as on his own. he has Studied the law for five Years. he is honest or else I would not countenance him in any thing. he possesses a beautifull Orgon, and his Masters think him fit for the Bar; and he is an attorney at law in New Jersey Since last fall.

I enclosed in my adress to the Secretary of the Treasury, recommendations from Doctr Mitchill, and from Mr Fairlie, then our Vice Mayor; and Yet although I was honor'd with a letter from You last Year and recommended by the two Gentlemen whose Character is well established, was I not Satisfyed in my mind to direct You the present unless I Should be further recommended. when luck brought in the City our very respectable Exgovernor the Vice president of the United States, whose very great favour is here annexed.

Should your Excellency in Consequence of my Incapacity to tender my Son any further pecuniary Service So as to carry him through the perillous path young and poor attorneys have to follow, and that he and my-Self Should appear to you worthy of your attention, I hope he Shall behave to do Justice to the appointment, in case the Secretary of the treasury Should have presented his Name in good time to Your Excellency. and Should any thing disapoint my expectation, I beg of you to believe that as Interest has never been a motive for me; in this world of Misery, of anxiety, of error, that I will never be deterr'd from admiring your talents, your virtue, and Your good and great and humane Soul. for if I have ever had it in my mind to have been in a Situation a little above my common mediocrity it has been with no other desire than to have been able to have had the Sight of you once in Every two or three weaks, and to have had the Chance to frequent Sober, desinterested and learned Men. but So scarce alas! they are about here, that which Side Soever a man turns him-Self, he Sees nothing but depravity. ô Albany!!

What follows was to be the begining of the letter I contemplated to adress you—before Mr Dayton's Favor.

at my return to this City I Saw every where your portrait under different impressions. Some of them had no Inscription, Some had one of Some fourteen or sixteen long lines. I thought to offer you the following with the hope that in future the artists may have them under Your portrait

De la fière Albion la tirannique chaine,
fut brisée a sa voix.

*{Il fait / Il fit} de l'age d'or reparaitre les loix
Et L'embellissement de la Nature humaine.

---

but Such is the difficulty in versification that though it appears at a glance beautifull, reflection will lead us into numberless deffects and all writers will more or less fall into them. for example here is Voltaire's Inscription

"Le *celebre ecrivain*, dont tu vois la gravure
Sur le bord du leman *fit admirer Sa voix*
L'apollon de nos Jours il fut l'ami des roix
Et le peintre de la nature"

each line Signifies the Same thing—Dont tu vois la gravure—is needless. the first Six lines of the henriade of that great writer, of that very humane Man! the priests of this Country, Stigmatise so much without having Seen a line of his precious works, are deffectuous in that kind of pleonasm. Henry 4th reign'd on france by right of Conquest—knew how to conquer, confounded—which is also here to conquer, the *league* Mayene and Spain—and was the conqueror of his Subjects. I was guilty of a most absurd pleonasm in the last letter I had the honor to adress you. but it was gone, and I know that it is impossible for me ever to attain english idiom, unless I Should make a Study of it.

Line 19th of the first canto of the Gaitiade I had the honor to present to You—it reads *Et toi Monticello.* that Italian word, was a great[1] Burthen on my Shoulders; & have finally gallifyed it. and line 20—du Monde les delices—although that inversion has nothing desagreeable, yet it is not elegant, besides, I never liked the Shortness of the Episode. as to the work, it goes on, It has eight cantoes already; and much longer than what I had first projected, So much is to be Said on our beautifull revolution!

please to believe Sir that, had I been a man with dispositions, to flatter and to heap gold; that I would have Stay'd in france, or here, I would have prostituted my Self to the altar of plutus, during the funding System. the very money I spent to send and to keep, my Son to canada with that of his Mother's Journey at *trois rivieres* to fetch him back, would have brought me several thousands of acres of land from my fellow Soldiers. no. I refused. I would not touch at the bane. the woods, the solitude; where my three daughters have finally dragg'd me from: Sobriety to exces, have had more charms for me. therefore Sir please to think, it is your virtue that I admire! and that happy medium, reason! that Sister of the gods which leads you. why did I not take general washington for the hero of the poem? his name his great now, he deserves much for his *cunctator*ship, for his exertion at trenton and princeton, but he forsook he Sacrificed! his Soldiers to vanpires. he may in many respects be compared to lewis the 14th particularly in his vanity. why did I not throw my-Self under the wings of Mr adams? no. I waged an eternal war to his principles; and to those of his vile and barbarous Satellites, at the risk of my life, it is publick in Morris County. Judge pennington from new Jersey was present, when I braved a whole hord of usurers and tories at new ark, at the eve of the Sedition law, by pertinent observations where I expected a Second time, to find my-Self, in a very uncertain existence. but Such are Men that many of our former adherents here, after having amass'd gold, scarcely know me, whilst others are Selling their Country, the honor of america, at albany, and that for 2 or 3 hundred Dollars. wonderfull! arnold was a virtuous Man, to Such a villanous baseness. finally Mr adams will have his dues, for his appeal to the godess of liberty, and mutilate her so wretchedly, as he has done to Squeeze down hundred thousand dollars more, which he miss't.—here follows the alteration in the episode in Canto first

Et toi de Monticelle en bien-faits si feconde,
Source de la Splendeur des delices du Monde
Ô terre! qui di front de tes monts Sourcilleux,
reçus du haut Olympe, et de la main des Dieux
pour ces vastes États le plus bel apanage;
et pour le Monde entier le savant et le sage.
Puissé-Je etre inspiré par Ses actes humains.
Puisse ma Muse encor, aux Sons des chants divins,
Du chantre Mantouan D'homère et de pindare;
rendre graces aux dieux d'un present aussi rare,
Dans les nobles vertus de ton nouveau Solon.
et que favorisé de la cour D'apollon
Je celèbre mon vers atteignant cette Sphere
ton pupille, ton nom Jusqu'au bout de la terre.

Nombres armonieux du Chantre Mantouan,
Qui sutes illustrer les bords du Caïetan.
Rivages fortunés de la grande Hesperie:
où ce chef des troyens qui fuyant Sa patrie,
en remplissant les vœux des dieux et des Destins
avant de voir les bords des antiques latins;
perd Sa mere de lait. pour illustrer la cendre
du Sein qui le nourrit aux rives du Scamendre.
Pieux, reconnaissant dès l'age du berceau,

Eleve a Sa nourrire un Superbe tombeau.
par le quel depuis lors, cette belle contrée
fut, et Sera du nom Gaïete honorée.
Et qui Sutes encore avec tant de grandeur
peindre la bienveillance adoucer la fureur
du Monstre qui nourrit et remus et Romulé
dans un antre proffond Sur les bords de L'albule.
Et reunir encore en leur Sublimité,
A la perseverance a tant de piété
Les actes de valeur, les Amours de cet homme!
Celebrer les heros, et les sages de Rome
Et pour plaire au tiran de L'univers Connu
Imprimer l'air du vrai par un charme ingenu
aux contes merveilleux de ces antiques ages!
Que n'eussiez vous pas dit des heros et des Sages:
La gloire et la Splendeur de cet autre univers
et du sage Surtout qui m'inspire ces Vers,
qui fit naitre un empire aussi grande que le votre
et d'un seul trait de plume il nous en donne un autre?
Magiques Precepteurs de L'antique Albion
De l'ebre et de la Gaule et du Septentrion:
Bordes du merveilleus des rives du Bosphore
Du Nil, du Zenderouth, des Peuples de L'aurore!
Charmes de L'univers! charmes de tous les tems
Que neussent pas chanté vos Sublimes accens?
Eussiez-en devant vous un aussi beau Modele
Que L'est L'astre brillant des cieux de Monticelle.
Par Minerve *Inspiré le peuple* en fit le Choix &c.

Canto the viiith roils upon George's lunacy, the Shade of Sully appears to Franklin, instructing him with the Character of the King the Queen—and court of france, their love intrigues. franklin relates to the Queen how venus Settles the woods of america, fashionable way of love making in new england. this with extracts of the two antecedent cantoes will make the subject of another adress, which I beg of your Excellency to accept and as there is a little room lef in the Sheet I will inser a few lines on the unacountable coquetery of Some american ladies extracted from canto viii *vers 593*

Le Sage cependant ayant repris haleine
constant dans Ses desseins pour complaire a la reine,
reprend son entretient, et disant "parmalheur
il est de ces beautés qui manquant de candeur,
Soit pour Se faire un nom, Sont encor par Vengeance,

Sous les dehors trompeurs d'une belle apparence.
ont l'art d'envelopper pour remplir leurs objets
L'amant de bonne foi dans leurs obscurs projets;
Qui dès que son amour par de faits Se déclare
ces filles de Medée ont l'ame assez barbare
d'arracher le bandeau de leur ressentiment
et d'exposer les faits du malheureux amant."
Belles si vous voulez que vôtre modestie
triomphe de L'erreur de la Coqueterie.
Que vos charmes divins, ne Servent que d'éclat
aux plus austeres loix de votre célibat.
Sachez que la pudeur et non de feintes larmes
Sont contre L'indiscret vos plus puissantes armes.
Fut-ce un Seigneur, un prince! un Seul de vos regards
Anéantit la Fougue ou d'hercule ou de Mars
Et qu'il n'est de milieu qui celèbre ou qui blesse
entre les sentiments de phedre et du lucrece.
Et qu'els que de vos feux puissent être les traits
faites vous une loi de les taire a Jamais.
car de L'homme toujours vous etes la victime:
lui qui sait que ce feu n'est ni vice ni crime
que lorsque Sa fureur porte à des attentats:
Quant à phedre et didon ne les imitez pas.
Mais comme la ses travaux presque inconpréhensibles,
la nature vous fit et tendres et Sensibles.
Et qu'amour dans le fort de vos Jours perilleux
venant vous inonder d'un torrent de Ses feux,
D'ès l'elan d'une course un peu trop effrenée;
vous prive des douceurs d'un heureux hyménée
Meprisant de troquer vos charmes pour de l'or
imitez de polly le courageux essor
Dont l'histoire franklin pour votre independance
raconta comme Suit a la reine de France &c

I am with Respect Sir of Your Excellency Your Excellency's Most obedient and very humble Servant JOHN F. VACHER

EDITORS' TRANSLATION

[*From Canto I*:]
And you of Monticello, so fertile in good deeds,
Source of the splendor of the world's delights,
O earth! which from the face of your furrowed mountains
Received from high Olympus, from the hands of the gods,

The best privilege for these vast states
And for the whole world, the scholar and sage.
May I be inspired by his human acts.
May my muse, borrowing once again the divine song,
Of the poet of Mantua, Homer, and of Pindar,
Thank the gods for such a rare gift.
May my verses reach that sphere as I celebrate
In the noble virtues of your new Solon,
Favored by Apollo's court.
Your pupil and your name to the ends of the earth.
  Harmonious rhythms of the Mantuan singer
Who brought prestige to the banks of the Caïetan,
Blessed shores of the great Hesperides
Where the Trojan leader, fleeing his country
To fulfill the wishes of gods and fates
Lost his wet-nurse before reaching the shores of the ancient Latins.
Pious and grateful since childhood,
He built a superb tomb to her
To immortalize the ashes from the milk
That had nourished him on the banks of the Scamander.
This beautiful country was and will forever be honored with the name of Caieta.
With such grandeur he also knew how to depict good will
And calm the fury of the monster that nourished Romulus and Remus
In a deep cave on the Tiber's shores.
  He also knew how to unite
Sublime piety with sublime perseverance,
The acts of valor and the loves of this man!
He could celebrate the heroes and wise men of Rome
And please the tyrant of the known world;
Convey with disarming charm an air of truth
To the marvelous tales of ancient times!
What would you not have said of these heroes and sages:
The glory and splendor of that other universe
And of the sage, above all, who inspires my verses,
Who gave birth to an empire as large as yours
And with a single penstroke gives us another?
  Magic preceptors of ancient Albion
From the Ebre to Gaul and the north;
The marvelous shores of the Bosporus,
The Nile, the Zayanderud, and peoples of the East?
The charms of the Universe! Eternal charms.
What would you not have sung with your sublime accent
If you had had before you as worthy model
The brilliant star of the Monticello sky?
Inspired by Minerva, the people chose, etc.

[*From Canto VIII*:]
  The Sage however, finding never-ending inspiration
In his plan to please the queen
Resumes his conversation, saying "Alas,

There are some beautiful women who lack candor.
Whether to make a name for themselves, or out of vengeance,
Under the deceptive mien of a beautiful appearance,
They envelope their well-meaning lovers
In their dark designs.
As soon as he demonstrates his love in acts
These daughters of Medea are savage enough
To rip the cover from their resentment
And expose the acts of the unfortunate lover."
You are beautiful if you wish your modesty
To triumph over the error of coquetishness.
May your divine charms serve only to illuminate
The most austere laws of your chastity.
Know that modesty rather than feigned tears
Is the strongest weapon against indiscretion.
Even if it is a lord, a prince! One of your glances
Can extinguish the rage of Hercules or Mars.
Between the sentiments of Phaedra and Lucretia there is no middle ground which celebrates or wounds.
Vow to keep them forever secret
For you are always the victim of a man.
He knows this passion is neither vice nor crime
Until its furor leads to acts.
Imitate neither Phaedra nor Dido.
Nature in her almost incomprehensible way
Made you tender and sensitive.
When love comes with the speed of an all-too-terrifying race
To flood you with a torrent of fire
In the midst of your perilous days
And deprives you of the sweetness of a happy union,
Refuse to trade your charms for gold,
And imitate the courageous flight of Polly
Whose story Franklin for your independence
Thus related to the Queen of France, etc.

RC (DNA: RG 59, LAR); at foot of text: "His Excellency Thomas Jefferson Esqr President of the United States"; endorsed by TJ as received 1 Apr. and so recorded in SJL. Enclosure: Jonathan Dayton to Vacher, 10 Mch., from Washington; Dayton has recommended Vacher's son to Gallatin for a position on one of the land commissions in Orleans Territory or Louisiana Territory; he advises St. Louis as a preferred location and believes that although less well paid than the position of clerk, the job of "Agent" would "be more in line with your son's profession, and be less troublesome" (Tr in same). Other enclosure not found.

MY APPLICATION IN BEHALF OF MY SON: in a letter of 16 Mch. to Gallatin, Vacher recommended his son, Francis Vacher, as a land commissioner at St. Louis, with Natchitoches as a second choice. He also enclosed a recommendation of 16 Mch. from James Fairlie, who informed Gallatin that the younger Vacher had "considerable talents," and a letter of 15 Mch. from Samuel Mitchill, who praised the elder Vacher's consistent republicanism and private worth. In a subsequent letter of 23 Mch. to Gallatin, the elder Vacher enclosed a letter of the same day from his son to Gallatin, requesting a commission at St. Louis or another office and pledging "by an upright conduct to do honor to your appointment" (RCs and Tr in same; Francis Vacher to Gallatin, 23 Mch., endorsed by TJ: "Vacher Francis. to be Agent or Comr. Louis").

DE LA FIÈRE ALBION: that is, his voice broke the tyrannical chain of the proud Albion. He restored the laws of the golden age.

VOLTAIRE'S INSCRIPTION: "The famed writer, whose image you see on the shore of Lake Geneva, was admired for his voice. The Apollo of our times, he was the friend of kings and the painter of nature."

LAST LETTER: Vol. 43:153-8.

DU MONDE LES DELICES: that is, the delights of the world.

CUNCTATORSHIP: that is, a strategy of delay, inspired by the Latin nickname for a Roman consul who fought Hannibal through attrition rather than pitched battle (OED; *Oxford Classical Dictionary*, s.v. Fabius Maximus Verrucosus, Quintus).

CHANTRE MANTOUAN: Virgil. Much of the canto Vacher composed involves a gloss on the *Aeneid*, including the reference to the bay at Gaeta (LES BORDS DU CAÏETAN), where Aeneas was said to have erected a tomb to his wet-nurse, Caieta (*Aeneid*, 7.1-4).

RACONTA COMME SUIT: Vacher elaborated on the story Benjamin Franklin told to Marie Antoinette in a different canto, which he enclosed in a letter of 13 May to TJ.

[1]Vacher interlined "heavy" and connected the two words with a brace.

To George Jefferson

DEAR SIR Monticello Mar. 24. 05

I now inclose you the Manifests of my tobo. made the last year at Poplar forest, being 29 hhds weighing 46,402. ℔ nett, the whole of which I expect is with you before this. from these are to be taken 3 hhds ducked which you have already sold. you mentioned that you thought you could get 7. D. for the residue on reasonable credit. if you can get that on 2. or 3. months credit, I shall be willing you should let it go.

I have this day drawn on you for forty dollars in favor of James Oldham. accept my affectionate salutations TH: JEFFERSON

PoC (MHi); at foot of text: "Mr George Jefferson"; endorsed by TJ. Enclosures not found.

YOU HAVE ALREADY SOLD: see Jefferson to TJ, 28 Feb. and 4 Mch.; MB, 2:1149.

From James Mease

SIR Philadelphia March 24. 1805

I have the pleasure to announce the arrival of the little box, containing the models of your mouldboard, for which I return my most sincere thanks—It came to hand yesterday.—I regret that I did not see the bearer of it, to express my obligations for his Care of it.—

With my sincere respect I remain your obliged humble servt

JAMES MEASE

RC (DLC); at foot of text: "The President of the United States"; endorsed by TJ as received 1 Apr. and so recorded in SJL.

LITTLE BOX: TJ to Mease, 11 Mch.

Notes on Blinds for Monticello

1805. Mar. 24.

instead of the Venetian blinds before planned for South Piazza, substitute these

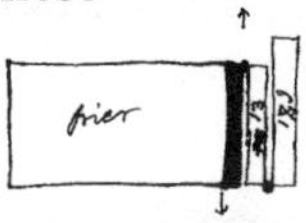

62. I.
50. I.
65. I.

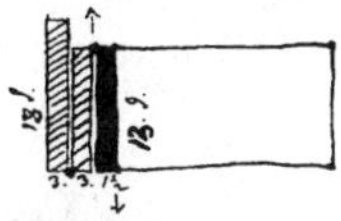

the height of each blind 4 f. to wit to top of impost, because the lining of the jamb fills up the projection of the impost, and makes all flush. the jamb is but 13. I. thick

---

2. sashes from floor of Piazza to top of impost = 8 f .825 I. both to slide up.

height of sashes. Upper one. upper rail	2.I.		breadth of sash.
			1.75 + .25 × 4 +
			1.75 + 11.75 × 5
			= $63\frac{1}{4}$ I.
	.25		each sash then
	.25		will contain 15.
		I.	panes $11\frac{1}{2}$ by 15. I.
lower do. lower rail } upper rail }	1.	3.	
	.25		
	.25	3.	
lower rail	2.		
6. panes of 15. I. each	7–4		
	8–0		

[*on verso*:]

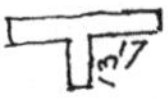

4 f - $5\frac{1}{2}$

arches & Jambs of the Porticle before the door of S.W. Bow room

the imposts & arches are of the same height as those of the brick arches 5 f - 5 I

the plinth of the piers is 5. I. high & projects $\frac{5}{8}$ I.

MS (MHi); entirely in TJ's hand; see Nichols, *Architectural Drawings*, No. 147p.

TJ sketched out a separate design for VENETIAN BLINDS for one of Monticello's piazzas, but likely opted for the design above (MS in MHi, undated, entirely in TJ's hand, see Nichols, *Architectural Drawings*, No. 147r; TJ to James Oldham, 14 June). TJ sketched a "manner of fixing Venetian blinds in the Porticos" that used hinges and hooks to enable the shades to be folded halfway up or fully out of the way (MS in same, undated, entirely in TJ's hand; Nichols, *Architectural Drawings*, No. 147s).

The SOUTH PIAZZA was intended as a greenhouse and required a good means of regulating light. A small structure that TJ termed a PORTICLE adjoined each side of the piazza nearest the cabinet, or BOW ROOM, and library. The porticles, built by John Hemings, were designed to admit air and light while preserving privacy (Jack McLaughlin, *Jefferson and Monticello: The Biography of a Builder* [New York, 1988], 321-5).

To James Oldham

Monticello Mar. 24. 05.

Th: Jefferson with his salutations to mr Oldham and his regrets for the loss of the plank mentioned in his letter of the 19th inst. incloses him an order on Gibson & Jefferson for forty dollars

PoC (DLC); endorsed by TJ. Enclosure not found; on this date, TJ recorded the payment to Oldham for $40 (MB, 2:1150).

From Amos Stoddard

SIR, St. Louis, 24th. March 1805.

I have the honor to forward you the enclosed Vocabulary of the Scioux language; furnished me by Mr. Crawford, at the request of Captn. Lewis.

Such information as I have received of Captn. Lewis, I transmitted to the Secretary of war by the last mail. Permit me to add here, that the Scioux Chiefs from the River Demoine, invited to the seat of Government by him, have just arrived. Their intention was to join those expected from the Missouri—but as the latter will not probably reach this place till about the middle of May, the former have resolved to return home. I have favored this resolution, because part of them belong to the same nation, and because I conceived the visitors would be more numerous than the policy of the Government dictated. Any arrangements made with those from the Missouri, will be considered as obligatory on those from the Demoine.

I am, Sir, with sentiments of high respect, your very hume. Servant,

AMOS STODDARD,
Captn & Agt. for Captn. Lewis

RC (DLC); at foot of text: "The President of the United States"; endorsed by TJ as received 10 May and so recorded in SJL. Enclosure not found; see Amos Stoddard to TJ, 29 Oct. 1804.

From Joseph Anderson

DEAR SIR— Soldiers Rest—Jefferson County 25th March 1805

On the Morning I left George Town—I adressd you a note—relative to George Duffield Esquire, in Which I informd you, I woud Write you again on the subject, after my arrival in Tennessee—On my way home I stop'd at Greenville—where Mr Duffield lives—for the purpose of seeing and converseing with him—and thereby learning more Certainly his knowledge of the french Language—But on seeing him—painful to relate—I found him much affected by intemperate drinking—I therefore in a few Minutes, left him as I found him—and upon making inquiry from several Gentlemen upon whom I cou'd depend—I was informd he had lately become a good deal adicted to intoxication—A thing extremely mortifying—to his friends as you may suppose—and ruinous to his future agrandizement—he was an ornament to Society—and universally esteemd—his Education has been of the first kind, this Country cou'd afford—he was not only a Correct Classic Scholar—but was well vers'd in the Sciences and polite literature—he was a well informd historian—and possessed extensive information upon—great National and political subjects—he also speaks the french Language—in the study and reading of which I am told he takes—(even now) much delight—but I fear he is lost to himself and to Society—tis greatly to be lamented, and nothing but the Obligations—which I feel I owe to you—cou'd induce me—to make this communication—but the recommendation, which I gave him, in my note to you—without knowing of the unfortunate circumstance—I have mention'd—now impells me—to give you this further information—As I ever have, and always shall hold myself responsible for the Conduct of every gentleman—I may take leave to Offer—to your patronage—This letter is written in haste—and I have not leisure to Correct or Copy it—I must therefore rely on your goodness, to pardon its defects—

accept assurances of my most sincere respect and Esteem

JOS: ANDERSON

RC (DNA: RG 59, LAR); endorsed by TJ as received 23 Apr. and "Duffield George. a sot" and so recorded in SJL.

I ADRESSD YOU A NOTE: Anderson and John Rhea to TJ, 5 Mch.

From James Bowdoin

Boston Mar. 25th. 1805.

I cannot resist, Sir, the disposition which I feel of writing to you, from the renewed instance of your politeness & condescension, in readily dispensing with my attendance at Washington, from motives, which refer to my Health: this indulgence, rather than to accept of my Resignation, demands from me my most respectful acknowledgments; and you will permit me upon the occasion to present you with my sincere thanks for the favour.—

From the desire I had to fullfill your expectations & to pay my respects to you, I put myself too forward at several times when in a State of convalescence; & thereby greatly retarded my general Recovery: and perhaps it is owing to this circumstance exclusively, that I cannot now have the pleasure to visit Washington, and that I shall be obliged to wait for my instructions here. Conceiving the outlines of my mission to be now settled, I shall avail myself of the first suitable vessell, which I can procure to take me & my family to Spain; and I calculate to be in compleat Readiness to embark by the 1st. of May & certainly not to exceed the tenth; it being understood that a suitable vessell can be had, of which I am told, there is no doubt: if I embark at that time, I think, I may safely calculate upon being at Madrid, by the 1st. of July. Mr. Madison has suggested to me, that the Events of Mr. Munroe's special mission to Madrid are not yet known, in the U.S. & that he has recd. no advices from him since Octo. last, when he was at Rotterdam; from which circumstance it may happen, that I may meet Mr. Munroe before he may have quitted Madrid, & thereby become acquainted (*minutely*) with his negociations, whether successful or not: if to this circumstance be added the extreme heat of the climate of Spain in the months of July & August wch. render travelling in those months almost impracticable, I ought to urge my departure as much as possible: I could wish for Letters of introduction from the spanish & french ministers, if they have acquaintances at Madrid; & likewise a general letter to the Consuls of the United States in the different ports of Spain to afford me any assistance in their power to facilitate my Journey to Madrid. I have had the ports of Lisbon, Coruna, St. Andero & Cadiz severally recommended to me, but from the best intelligence I can collect from Books & personal information, I think St. Andero would be the best port to proceed to, & after that either Lisbon or Coruna: but I must have some reference to the destination of the vessell, on which I may embark.—Be assured Sir to find in me a heartfelt disposition to promote the public interest, & the success of your administration, as well as to extend your personal fame & honour, from a conviction of its propriety.—Will you permit me to make you a tender of my services in procuring for you any Specimens of the arts, either in Sculpture or painting; & although I am no adept, yet from having been in Italy & having viewed the works of the best masters, if you would entrust me with your commissions, I would execute them in the best manner in my power. Accident having thrown in my way a handsome peice of modern Sculpture, a Cleopatra copied & reduced from the ancient one now at Paris, which for many years lay at the Palace of Belvidere at Rome, as I think it for the fineness of its marble & the neatness of its workmanship & finishing, among the best of the modern peices of Sculpture, you will much oblige me, if you will do me the favour to accept it & to place it in a corner of your hall at Monticello; for which purpose I shall take the liberty of shipping it to you by the first convenient opportunity: I was told it was purchased of a french Commissary in Italy, who wanted money; & that it had been taken from the apartments in the vatican, which were built by Pope Ganganelli Clement the 14th., who was liberal as a Pope, & distinguished as a man of Taste & Learning. With Sentiments of grateful attachment I have the honour very respectfully to subscribe myself

Sir, Your devoted & ob. Servt. James Bowdoin

RC (DLC); at head of text: "Thomas Jefferson Esqe. President of the United States"; endorsed by TJ as received 17 Apr. and so recorded in SJL. FC (MeB: James Bowdoin Letter Book); dated 22 Mch.

DISPENSING WITH MY ATTENDANCE: on 23 Nov. 1804, Bowdoin wrote to TJ that ill health had delayed his plans for visiting Washington prior to departing for Spain. To Madison, he more openly questioned the wisdom of his coming at all, given the weather and his health. Although Madison continued to encourage the visit, on 28 Feb. Bowdoin wrote that he was not physically able to withstand the trip. He offered to resign "if the journey to Washington shd. be indispensable to the public service." Madison responded on 14 Mch. that TJ had agreed to "dispensing with such a visit in case the obstacles to it should not be removed" (Madison, *Papers, Sec. of State Ser.*, 9:11-12, 44, 71-2, 133; Bowdoin to TJ, 23 Nov. 1804).

THE FAVOUR TO ACCEPT IT: TJ recorded the gift in his painting catalog as "a Cleopatra in marble." He later amended the identification to "Ariadne reclined on rocks of Naxos" after noticing a likeness of the sculpture illustrated in his copy of Augustine Legrand's *Galeries des antiques* (Paris, 1803; Sowerby, No. 4243). In entering the correction in his catalog, TJ wrote that the figure wore a bracelet on her left arm, which, "taken for an asp, long occasioned the belief that this figure represented Cleopatra procuring death by the bite of this reptile" (Susan R. Stein, *The Worlds of Thomas Jefferson at Monticello* [New York, 1993], 238; Catalogue of Paintings, undated MS in ViU).

From William C. C. Claiborne

Dear Sir, New Orleans March 25th. 1805

The late Indian Agency which has been confered on Doctor John Sibly has occasioned an investigation of his private character, and I discover that it has received many injurious reproaches. Mr. Bradford the Editor of the Orleans Gazette has addressed to me a Letter upon the subject, which I deem it a duty to lay before you, more especially since in some of my former Letters to you, I spoke respectfully of Doctor Sibly, and I recollect to have mentioned him as a proper person to fill a seat in the Legislative Council. I have myself no knowledge of the Doctors *private character*, nor did I ever learn until lately any serious exceptions *to it*. He passed a few Weeks in the Mississippi Territory in the year 1802, and was occasionally at my House: I was pleased with him as an agreeable companion, and a man of information; I have since received many interesting Letters from the Doctor which contained as I supposed much valuable information. The reputation of the Doctor in North Carolina can readily be acquired from some of the Gentlemen of that State. Of his general conduct here, I cannot give any Testimony; there are however other Citizens who speak of him equally as disrespectful as Mr. Bradford, and there are others again who represent him as a Man of integrity and profess a friendship for him.

I persuade myself that when you consider the motive which has induced me to address you this Letter, you will excuse the Liberty I have taken;—I have always been careful in recommending persons for Office, and whenever I should be so unfortunate as to have named in my Letters to you, an unworthy character, you may be assured, it has arisen from my being myself deceived. I still hope Doctor Sibly is not unworthy of your Patronage—The characters of the best of men have been misrepresented;—of the Doctors private reputation I have no personal knowledge, but as serious exceptions to it were stated by Mr. *B*. I esteemed it a duty to enclose you *his* Letter.

The Council are yet in Session; among the good acts which they will draft, I hope there will be one for the support of Public Schools, and upon liberal principles. Many African Slaves are introduced into the settlement of *Baton Rouge*, by the way of Pensacola and Mobile, and *from Baton Rouge*, they pass into Louisiana; these abuses are seen and regretted, but (under existing circumstances) cannot be prevented.

I pray you to accept the best wishes of Dear Sir your faithful friend!

William C. C. Claiborne

RC (PHi); in a clerk's hand, signed by Claiborne; at foot of text: "Thomas Jefferson President of the United States"; endorsed by TJ as received 21 May and so recorded in SJL. FC (LU-Ar: Claiborne Letter Book). Tr (DNA: RG 59, TP, Orleans). Enclosure not found.

INDIAN AGENCY: on 13 Dec. 1804, writing with the president's authorization, Dearborn asked John Sibley "to act occasionally" as U.S. agent to secure the friendship of the various Native American tribes in the vicinity of Natchitoches. He was authorized to hold conferences and to distribute presents and supplies, for which Sibley would receive four dollars per day. James M. Bradford's *Orleans Gazette*, citing Sibley's rumored lack of "moral character" and harshly criticizing "those who possess executive confidence" for recommending such a person to the president, attacked the appointment (*Terr. Papers*, 9:352-3; *Orleans Gazette, For the Country*, 9 Mch.).

MY FORMER LETTERS: Claiborne to TJ, 10 and 29 Jan.

From Henry Dearborn

SIR Washington March 25th. 1805

I have the honour of enclosing a letter recently received from the Marquis Lafayett,—by the closing paragraph, it would appear that he would have no objection to an appointment in lower Louisiana,—I presume that Genl. Armstrong was authorised to sound him on the subject,—I have sent Genl Scotts commission to him, with some instructions, and requested him to set out for Louisiana as soon as he can possibly make it convenient,—I have written to Mr. Dunbar & given him full powers to form arrange & direct an exploring party, I have forwarded commissions to Genl. Robertson & Dinsmore, with instructions for holding the treaties with the Chocktaws & Chickasaws,—I have by the advice of Mr. Gallatin appointed Mr. Davy of Philadelphia as principle Agent for superintending the Indian factory business generally,—I have agreed to allow him two thousand dollars a year & he has consented to undertake the business, all which I hope will meet your approbation,—Mr. Madison informs me that from late dispatches from Mr. Munroe & Genl. Armstrong, it appears that we have no remaining hope of obtaining West Florida, except by an equivalent, from the western part of Louisiana.

with sentiments of respectfull esteem I am Sir Your Obedt. Huml Servt.

H. DEARBORN

RC (DLC); at foot of text: "The President of the United States"; endorsed by TJ as received from the War Department on 28 Mch. and "Lafayette. Scott. Dunbar. Robertson & Dinsmore treat Choct. Chick. Davy Indn. com." and so recorded in SJL. Enclosure: see Enclosure No. 1 at Lafayette to TJ, 1 Dec. 1804.

SCOTTS COMMISSION: on 13 Mch., during a congressional recess, TJ appointed John B. Scott of Virginia colonel and brevet commandant of the regular army troops and militia in the district around Cape Girardeau in Louisiana. Dearborn sent Scott his commission and instructions as to his duties on 19 Mch. The Senate took up Scott's appointment in December 1805, but postponed discussion of it repeatedly. It was postponed indefinitely on 21 Apr. 1806. (Appendix I; *Terr. Papers*, 13:105-6, 107-8; JEP, 2:8, 10, 19, 20-1, 35).

WRITTEN TO MR. DUNBAR: on 25 Mch., Dearborn wrote to William Dunbar at the "direction of the President of the United States" with instructions for an expedition up the Red River. Dearborn asked Dunbar to recruit "the most suitable persons," including George Hunter. They would be assisted by a contingent of soldiers from Fort Adams. Dunbar was to see to the construction and outfitting of a boat and could draw on the War Department for a total of up to $5,000 for the expenses of the expedition. Dearborn cautioned him not to advance beyond "the first considerable ridge or high land" to avoid approaching too close to Spanish settlements around Santa Fe. Dunbar was to seek information in particular regarding the distance between the Red and Arkansas Rivers. Dearborn advised him that John Sibley, who had $3,000 in trade goods available, would likely be interested in making contact with Native American groups along the Red River and could assist Dunbar in obtaining guides. "It will be desirable to set out as early as possible," Dearborn noted (FC in DNA: RG 107, MLS).

ROBERTSON & DINSMORE: James Robertson of Tennessee and Silas Dinsmoor of New Hampshire, U.S. agents to the Chickasaw and Choctaw nations, were appointed on 13 Mch. to negotiate land cessions with those nations. Dearborn sent the commissioners instructions on 20 Mch. In exchange for a sum covering debts to the Scottish mercantile trading firm Panton, Leslie, & Co., the Choctaw were to cede lands between the Mississippi and Big Black Rivers. In exchange for a lump sum and annual payments made to an important leader, the Chickasaw were to cede lands north of the Tennessee River between the Duck River and the Mississippi. Robertson and Dinsmoor concluded arrangements with the Chickasaw on 23 July and a treaty of limits was signed on 16 Nov. with the Choctaw, but in neither case were lands along the Mississippi included (Appendix I; ASP, *Indian Affairs*, 1:697, 700, 749, 750; William S. Coker and Thomas D. Watson, *Indian Traders of the Southeastern Spanish Borderlands* [Pensacola, Fla., 1986], 255-8).

MR. DAVY: Dearborn wrote to William Davy on 19 Mch. to accept Davy's offer to undertake "the Superintendence of the Public Trading Houses with the Indian Nations" and to sketch the terms of the position. He wrote again on 26 Mch. to confirm the appointment and to give more detailed instructions (Dearborn to Davy, 19 Mch., in DNA: RG 107, MLS; Dearborn to Davy, 26 Mch., in DNA: RG 75, LSIA).

LATE DISPATCHES FROM MR. MUNROE & GENL. ARMSTRONG: see Madison to TJ, 17 Mch.

To John Wayles Eppes

DEAR SIR Monticello Mar. 25. 05.

Yours of the 22d. by Martin is recieved together with the horse. in the exchange we have made my own knolege of the horse recieved is sufficient to prevent all after-claims as to his soundness. should he become unsound [. . .] so frequently the lot of horses the loss must be mine, without affecting you.

With respect to the land at Poplar forest you are free to enter into occupation of it when you please. the only wish I have relative to it is, that as I destine it for one of your children it may be so occupied or leased as not to wear it out. a due portion of rest unpastured or in clover not too closely pastured will always keep it in heart, so that when they recieve it it shall be of value. when that shall be is a point I have never settled: but it will depend on considerations which will weigh equally on your mind as on mine. I presume you can hardly meditate to put improvements on it of so much value as to exceed the annual profit.

I rejoice to hear of the health of the dear children, and of the family at Eppington, we are all well here except Patsy, and she is recovering flesh and strength. by a careful regimen her stomach is getting better. at times however it becomes deranged, and shews itself immediately by it's effect on her spirits. so great a derangement of that organ cannot but leave us anxious as to it's course. we depend solely on prudent diet and moderate exercise to strengthen the whole system and this portion of it with the rest.

Mar. 26. I had written thus far before it occurred to me that whether the lands had been laid off, or how laid off had escaped my recollection. I knew that as mr Randolph's original portion had been at the N.W. end of the tract, I had directed the additional parcel to be laid off adjoining that, and that yours was to be at the South East end, my plantations occupying the middle part. I have searched my papers & have found in a letter of Clarke's that they had accordingly laid off 450. as. for mr Randolph adjoining his former parcel, and considering his as of double the value by the acre, of that in the S.E. end, he had marked out 903. as for you. I had recieved his letter & plat just as I was setting out for Washington, and not having time to look at them, had put them by & never seen them since. I find on examination that as he proposed to lay off the 900. as. for you, he left about 500. of mine surrounding it in a long narrow useless belt cut off from the body of my tract which would have been injurious to me, and useless to you. the inclosed plat therefore will shew you the alteration I propose by laying off yours in a compact body at the South East end. the land there is of the second quality of red land, fine for grain & lying levell. the line which I propose will give you $1137\frac{1}{2}$ acres which I am confident are of greater value than the 903. proposed by Clarke; but if they are not the line shall be made to include more, so as to be of equal value; my only object being to keep the residue in a body so as to admit future subdivision to the best advantage.

Present me affectionately to mr & mrs Eppes & be assured of my sincere & constant attachment. TH: JEFFERSON

PoC (CSmH); faint; at foot of first page: "Eppes J. W." Enclosure not found.

YOURS OF THE 22D: a letter from Eppes dated 22 Mch. is recorded in SJL but has not been found.

For the EXCHANGE of a horse for TJ, see Eppes to TJ, 16 July 1804, and TJ to Eppes, 7 Aug. 1804. TJ paid Samuel D. Purviance $120 through Eppes "for a bay horse which formerly belonged to Capt. Dyson" (receipt of 16 Dec. 1804, MS in DLC, endorsed by TJ: "Purviance. rect. for 120. D. horse"; MB, 2:1142).

For arrangements in TJ's planned bequest of LAND AT POPLAR FOREST to his daughters' families, see Vol. 35:418-20; Vol. 37:448; Vol. 43:582-4.

LETTER OF CLARKE'S: probably a letter from Bowling Clark, TJ's overseer at Poplar Forest until 1801, relating to land parcels in Bedford and Campbell Counties (see Vol. 24:280n; Vol. 28:537-8, 553-4; Vol. 29:52; RS, 5:88).

From John Strode

[25 Mch. 1805]

My Son Tom has just Sent me a Letter inclosing a few of the Seed of the soft Simblin or Quash, which He humbly intreats the President to accept, together with Ardent prayers for His health & Felicity.

I was not fortunate enough to receive the Letter &c or know anything of them untill they had been several days at Our Cot. House, and then a private Gentleman who intended for Albemarle Coty. kindly offerd to carry this for me to Charlottesville, which hurried me or my Letter had certainly been more correct & the Model some thing better finish'd. I expected the Wood was very well seasond, but now I am going to enclose it, find it has Sprung a little well knowing Good & Worthy Sir you will benignly account for and pardon every defect & every Weakness which Originates in the good intentions of the Heart my poor Wishes however Ardent, are but small among the many thousands which are continual breathd for your health & felicity

JOHN STRODE

at last the above mentioned Gentleman has declined his Journey on Acct of the appearance of Rainy Weather in consequence this goes by post.

RC (MHi); undated, but see enclosure; addressed: "Thomas Jefferson esquire President of the United States"; endorsed by TJ as a letter of 25 Mch. 1805 received 8 Apr. and so recorded in SJL.

ENCLOSURE

Description of a Moldboard Plow

Culpeper 25 March 1805

I am favourd with a present of intrinsic Value; the estimation of which is encreased by coming from a character who with Just propriety fills the first place in the gift of Man! tho' great that expression, I proudly boast transcendantly more; It is from Thomas Jefferson; a name, which will I believe duribly Stand the test of Time; when that of Presidents Emperors and Kìngs are eventually obliterated. I wd thank you Sir if I had Language to express the feelings of my elated Heart.

Were I ever so much a proficient in the Science of Apology, wd. not on this Occasion presume to exercise it; altho' indeed there is before me, with Respect to my Judgement or Opinion of a plough, a very fair opportunity; the more especially as the concentrated ingenuity and experience of the Wisest and best of Men have down to the present age been drawn to that important Subject; but rather, implicitly obey your command, by Simply Stating the little I know of the business, for which I am some indebted to observation & experience, but more to Necessity, the Legitimate Parent of invention; of my sort of Mould board herewith is a Model; as I may have Occasion to mention both of Yours & also Mine; for distinction, I will call your broad toed Mould board A, the Narrow toe'd B, & that herewith C. A & B may be among if not the very best constructions of human Wisdom; but clearly enough are fitted for different purposes. A must be fixt on the plough so that its Toe shall immediately follow the Wing of the Share; the Coulter having Cut the turf perpendicularly and the Share horizontically, that Mould board then is of all others best calculated to take it up & turn it over with least Resistance; the only objection to its construction is, that it would make the Wood work and Bar of the Share too long & too heavey for common use; but whether, in very Stiff Swardy Land, that inconvenience wd. not be fully compensated by the ease it would take up the Sod & turn it over, is with me matter of uncertainty, to be determined by fair experiments, at any rate there are two purposes in which it would most certainly excel; One of which is where the Farmer wishes to turn the sod completely over, and give it (for the intended Crop) no other ploughing; the other is for pairing up handsome green turf for the purpose of Sodding the bank of ditches, falls of Gardens &c. B. Will admit of a shorter lighter and more convenient plough, because its narrow Toe is well calculated to come forward on the top of the Wing of the Share, and therefore the Wood work may be Shorter lighter and indeed Stronger; but as its Shape begins to turn the Sod as soon as it is partially cut by the Share, and must of course be forced forward while a part of the turf is yet uncut or immediately as cut; undoubtedly on that account meets with more resistance than A; but they both have on the top a curve given them, which if any way essential, is more than I can discover; if not, that curve must have a tendency in some degree to impede the Operation. If a plough is to enter and turn over the Surface of the earth on the principle of a Wedge, the Smoother and Straighter the Sides of that Wedge, the easier it may be introduced and carried forward, in which respect it is that C differs chiefly from B, another is the curving figure of the piece taken out of the tail part of C, which I conceive to add to its facillity, as well as laying the Sod over neater and better; of this however I am not absolutely certain, as I never used one of another Shape, but well aware that theory is so frequently at variance with practice, I will make the experiment. A & B are I presume calculated to be of Cast Iron, C of Wood; the Sort, (tho' not altogether out of Choice) I always use, for which purpose I always select a tree that twists or winds naturally into the very shape I wish it. In mentioning of the Wood work of a plough as above, Shall be understood Such as is best calculated for the Barshare, & size for two Horses. am an indifferent Slow hand to draw any thing, and not a moments time to Spare, will endeavour to discribe mathematically, such as I use, as if standing on a plane Vizt. the Beam from the Tenon that goes into the hande to the

Middle	of the Mortice for the upright post	1	foot	10 In
thence	to the hole for the screw brace		"	4 "
"	to fore part of the Coulter Mortice		"	7
"	to the Clevis[1] pin hole	2	"	0
	to the end being the length of the head		"	7
		5	feet	4 In.

to diverge, from the Coulter Mortice to the Clevis pin hole (to the right) at Rate of an angle of 9 Degrees. Its Size will depend on the goodness of the timber which ought to have a Natural Cast, and to Swell handsomely against the Mortices where Strength is wanting and largely again, & handsomely, at the head where the Clevis is to be fixt. all the other parts putting off as Small as will admit for proper Strength. the Handles 4 feet 2 In: long, bevelling from the hindend of the Beam at the Rate of an Angle of 130 Deg: The Upright post 1 foot 4 In long, clear of both tenons starting forward at an Angle with the Beam that is taking the Angle behind the post at the underside of the beam, of 105 Degrees. The Barshare, its Bar, from the tail Screw to the fore part of the Mortice, 1 foot 2 Inches; thence to the point 1 foot 3 In; the Length of the Wing along the edge 1 foot 6 In:, and diverging from the point of the Bar at the Rate of 35 Degrees which will cause the broadest part at the hind end to be about 10$\frac{1}{2}$ Inches, when New; *great care Should be taken* that the Share be so framed on the Upright post and left handle that when the plough is in its proper posture on a plane that the distance of the head of the Beam (exactly against the Clevis pin hole) from that plane will Measure 14$\frac{1}{2}$ Inches, if for Midling Horses, if Very Large Horses, a Small Matter more not exceeding One Inch may be discretionally Allow'd; and the Lower end of the two Handles Should be so far firmly Seperated by proper pins as to cause the Lower end of the tale of the Mould board to be 9 Inches from the opposite side of the Bar, for that part should always be a little Narrower than the broadest end of the Wing of the Share or it will work very hard, and will throw the Sod too far, for the Sod in falling over not Only gains its own width but also gains its thickness. I am sorry I cannot well describe the head piece of this plough and its Regulating Clevis, the Head Should Swell to the end 4$\frac{1}{2}$ Inches Wide, 7 In from the end is the hole of the Clevis pin (as above), passing perpendicularly thro' the Beam, within one Inch of the End is 3 other perpendicular holes tho' smaller than the Clevis pin hole and at equal distance from each other, on a Scribe made by putting One foot of the Compasses in the Center of the Clevis pin hole, the other foot extending as above within one inch of the end of the head then Scribe a Circle in which at equal distance lay off the three smaller holes, to be bored as above, perpendicularly, then let the Clevis be made with holes at ends of its two Shanks to Receive the Large pin thro', then a Cross plate being welded on it by the Smith and turnd in a circular manner So that 3 holes may be punched in it exactly corresponding with the 3 holes in the head of the Beam but the end of the *Clevis* moves perpendicularly Round the end of the head which ought to be circular with 3 or 4 Notches in it, in one of these Notches the first Large Link unites the plough to the Swingle tree to which the horses is fixt, so that the ploughman may cause his plough to go deeper or Shallower by moving that link higher or Lower in those Notches—but the peculiar advantage of the thing is having it in his power to increase or decrease His furrow by Means of a Small pin in any one of the holes at the point or end of the head. for if there be at that place 3 holes in the Clevis and 3 corresponding as above in the Beam that Enables him to make 9 alterations at pleasure; and for tending of Indian is a very great advantage; because, altho' the Horse Should walk on making the first furrow 12 Inches from the Corn the plough may be Set by that Clevis to throw the Mould upon it, for the Second furrow it may in a Moment be alterd &c.

Another[2] improvement is the Regulating back band, which consists in the usual way of a broad Strap of Leather about 4 Inches Wide & Something longer than those in Common use, but without any Loop at the end extends down the Horses Side within the Chain that is between the Chain and his Side, On this Strap near each end are Sewd three Narrower Straps, Suppose a little more than Inch wide each with Buckles to them and corresponding Straps with holes in them a little higher up the back band to buckle to; two of these Narrower Straps go Round the Chain the third one goes through a link of the Chain, they all three buckle up higher or lower at descretion of the ploughman, and has many advantages attending it.

Of folly & its offspring Vanity, this poor tedious performance is guilty enough, of which however the humble performer is not so Solicitious if this thing does not appear to border too much on the confines of Arrogance. It merits not an Answer or one Moment of Your invaluable time, but when I have the felicity of Seeing you again at my poor Cot, I may have honor of an Oppty. of explaining, what I cannot so well do On paper. with all perfect and due Regard Good & Worthy Sir I am Yr. most Obdt JNO STRODE

RC (DLC); dateline inserted at head of text; at foot of text: "Thomas Jefferson Esqe. Prest. U:S:."

COT: cottage (OED).

[1] MS: "Clvis."

[2] Strode here canceled "Small."

From Peachy R. Gilmer

DR SIR. [before 26 Mch. 1805]

Mr. Carr informed me that you wished to know whether a man by the name of Dominick Gilmer had ever lived with my father, I can assert very confidently, that no such man has been a member of our family within fifteen years. that I never before heard the name, and that there is not a person of that name in any branch of the family

I shall be very happy to furnish you with 30 gallons of cyder if you like the flavor of it; particularly if you will accept it on the same terms, that my frds have taken what I have hitherto disposed of, as a mark of my respect and esteem.

Accept my most freindly wishes P. R. GILMER

RC (DNA: RG 59, LAR); undated; endorsed by TJ as received 26 Mch. 1805 and "Gilmer Rodomenic. not known to the family" and so recorded in SJL.

CARR: likely either Peter or Dabney Carr.

DOMINICK GILMER: see Rodominick H. Gilmer to TJ, 23 Dec. 1804, in which Gilmer reminded TJ of his "personal acquaintance with you while I lived at Doctor Gilmer,s near your country seat."

From John Barnes

SIR. George Town 26 March 1805.

The inclosed, recd Yesterday is presented. you for your Government.—The Painter—Mr Dougherty—informed me was in Town a few days ago.—said he abt. to set out for Monticello—in a day—or two—I desired Mr D. to tell him—I wished to see him—not having called. presume he is on his way to M.

The within Articles I hope will reach Rd: & M. in time for a seasonable use of them—

with due Respect to the good family I am Sir your most & very obedt: servt. JOHN BARNES

RC (ViU: Edgehill-Randolph Papers); at foot of text: "The President U States at Monticello"; endorsed by TJ as received 4 Apr. and so recorded in SJL. Enclosure not found, but see below.

INCLOSED: a letter from John Taggart, probably to Barnes, enclosing an invoice for paints and oils. See TJ to Barnes, 5 Apr., and TJ to Taggart, 2 May.

PAINTER: Richard Barry arrived at Monticello on 28 Mch. The ARTICLES being shipped through Richmond to Monticello included supplies needed by Barry and estimated by TJ in Notes on Painting at Monticello, at 2 Dec. 1804 (MB, 2:1150; TJ to Barnes, 5 Apr.).

From John Benson

DR SIR, Fredericksburg 26 March 1805

Your esteem,d favour of the 23rd current was duly received, and its contents punctually attended to. I hope the box will be safely delivered to you.

Permit me Sir to congratulate you, on your reelection, Accept my best wishes for your heath & happiness, with Sentiments of esteem, I am very respectfully your Obt Servt J Benson

RC (MHi); endorsed by TJ as received from "Benson J" on 28 Mch. and so recorded in SJL.

To William C. C. Claiborne

Dear Sir Monticello Mar. 26. 05

On the 14th. inst. being the moment of my departure on a short visit to this place, I wrote to you on the subject of locating the lands of General Lafayette, and particularly to have immediately surveyed the vacant lands adjacent to the canal of Carondelet on both sides, & either touching, or near to the city. if I recollect rightly they were upwards of 600. as. I omitted, what I meant to have observed, that I did not mean to include the commons to which you supposed the city entitled. and altho' I did mean to include the lands on both sides, to & under, the Canal, yet it was merely to comprehend the whole in *one* parcel, so as to let it count but as *one* thousand acres, and not as *two* parcels to count as *two* thousand. there shall be no opposition to the public having a road or street of sufficient width on each bank. it would be very contrary to the General's character & to my wish to oppose the public convenience. Accept my friendly salutations; and my reiterated request to take care of my friend who has deserved so well of this country Th: Jefferson

PoC (ICN); at foot of text: "Governor Claiborne"; endorsed by TJ.

THE 14TH. INST.: that is, TJ to Claiborne, 10 Mch.

From William C. C. Claiborne

Dear Sir, New Orleans March 26th. 1805

Mr. Robinson a passenger on Board the Brig Enterprize Bound for Baltimore has promised to convey to you a Barrell of excellent Brown Sugar, Manufactured by Mr. Fortier a respectable Planter of this Territory.

Mr. Fortier has requested me to forward to you this Sugar, and to pray your acceptance of it as a Sample of the Production of this fertile District—

I am my Dear Sir with great Respect Your faithful friend

Wm. C. C. Claiborne

RC (MHi); at foot of text: "Thomas Jefferson President of the United States"; endorsed by TJ as received 24 Apr. and so recorded in SJL. FC (LU-Ar: Claiborne Letter Book).

To Richard Fitzhugh

DEAR SIR Monticello Mar. 26. 05.

Immediately on my arrival at home I sent to three different persons to whom I had given the large oat the last year. every one of them had already sown the whole of what they had. after the next harvest however I shall be able to secure you some & will attend to it. I have taken the earliest moment in my power to copy Triplett's survey for you which I now send; and I sincerely wish you success in the road proposed. Accept my friendly salutations & respects to mrs Fitzhugh

TH: JEFFERSON

PoC (MHi); at foot of text: "R. Fitzhugh esq."; endorsed by TJ. Enclosure: copy, not found, of survey of road by John Triplett (see below).

Richard Fitzhugh (1766-1821) lived at the Oak Hill estate on a portion of the Ravensworth tract, a 22,000-acre grant in Fairfax County given to his great-grandfather, William Fitzhugh, in 1694. TJ sometimes stayed at Oak Hill during his trips between Monticello and Washington. Fitzhugh was a farmer and, according to the 1820 federal census, owned 50 slaves (Stella Pickett Hardy, *Colonial Families of the Southern States of America* [New York, 1911], 227; *Daily National Intelligencer*, 31 May 1821; MB, 2:1071n, 1123n).

TRIPLETT'S SURVEY of the road between Stevensburg and Georgetown circulated among interested parties beginning in the early 1790s as plans for the federal city took shape. TJ received a copy from Ferdinando Fairfax in September 1792 and used it and related materials to advocate for a straight and level route that would improve connections between the area around Washington and central Virginia (Vol. 24:269, 368; Vol. 29:431-32, 529, 530; "The road from the ferry landing opposite Georgetown to Stevensburg from actual survey by Capt John Triplett" and "Distances from the ferry landing opposite Georgetown," in DLC: TJ Papers, 233:41695, 41696, in TJ's hand).

MRS FITZHUGH: Susannah Meade Fitzhugh (*Alexandria Gazette*, 2 July 1856; Hardy, *Colonial Families*, 227).

From Albert Gallatin

DEAR SIR 26 March 1805

The bad arrangement of districts on the Lakes had heretofore prevented the organisation of the district of Erie which includes Cayoga. A representation was made on that subject to Congress and a law was obtained which, amongst other things, authorizes you to designate the port of entry & delivery for the district of Erie. Cayoga is the most proper place for that purpose, and I mentioned to you that as soon as

I could hear of a proper character for the office I would submit the appointmt. to you. This of course has anticipated the request of the assembly of Ohio, as it will give them not only a port of delivery but one of entry at Cayoga. It may be expected that the district will be organised in the course of the spring.

I have nothing new to mention. The Treasury is poor; and if all the bills come at once from France, it will be difficult even with the assistance of the Bank to meet them. A loan of about one million & half will be necessary: but I think we will be able to repay it in the course of the year. Mr Livingston's arrangements on that & some other subjects have not been the best possible; and much do I fear that his interference & schemes respecting Florida have done much to prevent Mr Monroe's success in Spain.

With sincere attachment & respect Your obedt. Sert.

ALBERT GALLATIN

RC (DLC); at foot of text: "The President of the United States"; endorsed by TJ as received from the Treasury Department on 1 Apr. and "Cayuga. state of treasy. Livingston. Flowers" and so recorded in SJL. Enclosure: Thomas Moore to Gallatin, 25 Mch., recommending Thomas Flowers for appointment as lieutenant of the revenue cutter at Philadelphia (DNA: RG 59, LAR; endorsed by TJ: "Flowers Thos. to be Lt. of a revenue cutter").

REQUEST OF THE ASSEMBLY OF OHIO: see Edward Tiffin to TJ, 27 Feb.

From Frédéric L. Hammer

MONSIEUR LE PRÉSIDENT, Strasbourg, le 26. Mars, 1805.

Permettez que je profite d'une occasion qui se présente par Mr. Winkelblech, Membre respectable de notre Société d'Agriculture, Sciences et Arts du Département du Bas Rhin, pour Vous addresser les voeux, que cette Société m'a autorisé d'emettre en son nom comme les siens. Ils tendent à s'entourer de toutes les lumières et de tous les moyens, qu'elle peut se procurer, et que l'on veut bien lui confier, pour les repandre sur cette partie de l'industrie et des connaissances humaines, qui en est la plus intéressante, et les communiquer à nos concitoyens agricoles. Je suis infiniment flatté de l'honneur d'être son organe auprès de Vous, en Vous la recommandant et Vous priant de vouloir bien l'honorer de votre bienveillance en la personne de Mr. Winkelblech, son membre, qui s'est offert, et que j'ai invité au nom de la Société, de nous enrichir de tout ce qui peut intéresser l'agriculture et les sciences, dans les pays si interessants qu'il va visiter. Il s'est chargé d'une liste de graines de plantes et surtout d'arbres, inconnus chez nous, que j'ai addressée au jardinier grenetier Kin, qui parcourt lui même les vastes contrées de Vos Etats, pour y ramasser ces graines et ces plantes.

La protection que Vous accordez aux sciences en général, et principalement à la première productrice et nouricière d'un état, le zèle et la connaissance profonde avec lesquels Vous l'embrassez Vous-même, m'est un garant sûr, que Vous ne la bornez pas au pays et à la nation industrieuse, qui a le bonheur d'être gouvernée par un tel chef. Notre Département, un des plus intéressants de la france par sa situation, son sol et l'industrie de ses habitants, est aussi propre à recevoir de nouvelles lumières, qu'il l'est peut-être d'un autre côté d'en pouvoir repandre.

En accueillant favorablement nos voeux, Vous nous donnerez l'espoir, Monsieur le Président, que Vous agréerez aussi nos offres de réciprocité et notre desir de pouvoir Vous être agréable en quelque chose. Je désirerois en mon particulier obtenir l'occasion de Vous prouver les sentiments de respect, avec lesquels j'ai l'honneur d'être

Monsieur le Président Votre très-humble et très-obéissant Serviteur,

F. L. Hammer,
Professeur d'histoire naturelle, &c.

EDITORS' TRANSLATION

Mister President, Strasbourg, 26 Mch. 1805

Allow me to take advantage of an opportunity offered by Mr. Winkelblech, a respected member of the Société des Sciences, Agriculture et Arts of the department of Bas-Rhin to send these wishes on behalf of the society. By bringing together as many enlightened minds as it can find and as many resources as one is willing to give, the society seeks to share them with this branch of industry and human knowledge—the most interesting one—and with our compatriots in agriculture. I am infinitely flattered by the honor of serving as the society's liaison to you. I recommend it to you and ask your good will in honoring it in the person of its member, Mr. Winkelblech. He offered, and I invited him in the name of the society to enlighten us about everything related to agriculture and science from the fascinating countries he is going to visit. He has with him a list of plants and, especially, trees that are unknown in our region. I sent it to the gardener and seed merchant Kin, who travels through the vast regions of your states, asking him to gather these seeds and plants.

The protection you give to science in general and notably to the major motor and nurturer of a state, the zeal and deep knowledge with which you yourself embrace it, is a sure sign to me that you do not limit science to the industrious nation that is fortunate to be governed by such a leader. Our region, one of the most interesting in France because of its location, terrain and industrious inhabitants, is as ready to receive new knowledge as to disseminate it.

By graciously accepting our good wishes, Mister President, you will allow us to hope that you will also look favorably on our offers of reciprocity and our desire to be helpful to you in some way. I would like to have a personal opportunity to demonstrate the respect with which I have the honor of being, Mister President, your very humble and obedient servant.

F. L. HAMMER
Professor of Natural History, etc.

RC (DLC); endorsed by TJ as received 3 June 1819 and "Professeur d'Hist. nat. et membre de la societé d'Agriculture sciences et arts du Departemen du Bas Rhin" and so recorded in SJL. Enclosed in Christopher Winckelblech to TJ, 25 May 1819.

Christophe Winckelblech (WINKELBLECH) belatedly discovered this letter among his effects after "A serie of misfortune" that transpired in the years after his emigration from Basel in 1805 (RS, 14:325-6; Vol. 44:270-2).

From Benjamin H. Latrobe

DEAR SIR, Wilmington March 26th. 1805.—

I have kept the enclosed letters by me above a Week, doubtful how to act respecting the subject of them. If in sending them to You I act imprudently,—my heart assures me, that the high opinion I have of your candor alone has led me into this imprudence, and that the sincerest & most respectful sentiments accompanies them.—By them it will appear that the sum I mentioned to You in the conversation I had with You on the subject, of 4$ ℔ day, was the compensation expected by Mr Lenthall,—although I did not then say, that he had made those terms himself.—In the warmth of his temper he feels himself offended at the appearance of undervaluing his services,—which are certainly of infinite importance to the public, and which could not be rendered by any other person with whom I am acquainted. The Labor of this Year will certainly be greater than that of any of the two preceding. Perhaps, on considering that Mr Blagden, to whom formerly 3$ 67 Cents ℔ day were paid, had only the superintendance of the Stonecutters, while of Mr Lenthall it may be asked, *quae pars operis, nostri non plena laboris*,—you will think that the remaining 2/6 might be added to his Salary.—The difficulty, should this be your opinion, will be in changing[1] the former decision; upon which I presume Mr Munroe has by this time already acted.—It must be observed that Mr Blagden had also a house found him by the public, as is now the case with Lenthall who has removed his family into the Office, which I have rented of Mr Carroll till the 1st. of Octr. for 100$. Should you under all circumstances agree to the raising his wages;—4$ 67 Cents for the present Year would bring up the deficient $33\frac{1}{3}$ Cents of the last two Years.—He will have the superintendance of the Treasury fire proof independently of the works at the President's house & in the North wing,—for all which, in Philadelphia his wages would not be under 5$ ℔ day.—

As to the sentiments he expresses in his letter concerning my situation, they are evidently unauthorized by any thing I have ever said to him on the subject; and I am confident that your opinion of me does me this justice at least, to render it unnecessary for me solemnly to disclaim them.—My engagement at Washington is an engagement of grateful attachment to your person,—not of interested views, to the public. Were it the latter, I should long have declined it on account of the calumnies to which it subjects me, & the ill will from my employers here which I incur by it.—I also consider, that though I certainly can carry on the business by my agent, *absent*, as well as present,—yet the American public, not understanding the nature of mental & scientific labor, are unwilling to pay for any thing but personal attendance, & would be shocked were I to make the European charge of 5 ℔ Cent on the money expended.—Perfect candor is the safest as well as most respectful mode of treating even the highest Officers of the State. I have therefore suffered Mr Lenthall's letter to go forward with all its faults of waspish and angry expression, independently of which it does no dishonor either to his head or his heart.

I have taken care that the letters of which I have made duplicates to Mr Appleton & to Mazzei shall be forwarded by separate opportunities. Since my arrival I have been very ill & almost entirely confined to the house. My leisure has been employed in forwarding the necessary drawings & instructions to Mr Lenthall with whom I shall not correspond on the subject of the enclosed letter till I hear again from You.—I find many[2] difficulties in the arrangment of the connecting portico of the public offices with the Presidents house which however I do not despair of conquering.

With the sincerest respect I am Your obedt hble Servt

B Henry Latrobe

RC (DLC); at head of text: "The Pr. UStates"; endorsed by TJ as received 1 Apr. and so recorded in SJL. Enclosures not found.

HIS SERVICES: in appointing John Lenthall clerk of the works at the Capitol with TJ's approbation in 1803, Latrobe assumed full responsibility for Lenthall's conduct and delegated to him authority to judge the fitness of George Blagden and other employees in fulfilling their contracts (Latrobe, *Correspondence*, 1:284-5).

QUAE PARS OPERIS, NOSTRI NON PLENA LABORIS: an adaptation of Virgil, *Aeneid*, 1.460, "Quae regio in terris nostri non plena laboris," with Latrobe here meaning "what part of the work is not filled with our labor."

LETTERS: TJ to Thomas Appleton and to Philip Mazzei, both 10 Mch., enclosed in TJ to Latrobe of that date.

[1] Word interlined in place of "correcting."

[2] MS: "may."

To Wilson Cary Nicholas

Dear Sir Monticello Mar. 26. 05.

Your favor of the 10th. was recieved only the last night. I now return you the letter to Colo. Newton, which I will pray you to deliver & use your influence to induce an acceptance. it is in truth only asking him to become responsible for his son, which he would of course do were the office given to his son directly: & it will relieve me from a painful dilemma. should he however refuse, be so good as to inform me of it, and you may at the same time address your letter of resignation to mr Gallatin, only confining the knolege of the fact as much as you can between Colo. Newton & yourself, that the appointment may be made before any sollicitations can be forwarded.

The divisions among the republicans which you speak of are distressing. but they are not unexpected to me. from the moment I foresaw the entire prostration of federalism, I knew that at that epoch more distressing divisions would take it's place. the opinions of men are as various as their faces, and they will always find some rallying principle or point at which those nearest to it will unite, reducing themselves to two stations, under a common name for each. these stations or camps will be formed of very heterogeneous materials, combining from very different motives & with very different views. I did believe my station in March 1801. as painful as could be undertaken, having to meet in front all the terrible passions of federalism in the first moments of it's defeat & mortification, and to grapple with it until compleatly subdued. but I consider that as less painful than to be placed between conflicting friends. there my way was clear & my mind made up. I never for a moment had to balance between two opinions. in the new divisions which are to arise the case will be very different. even those who seem to coalesce will be like the image of clay & brass. however under difficulties of this kind I have ever found one, & one only rule, *to do what is right*, & generally we shall disentangle ourselves without almost percieving how it happens. Accept my affectionate salutations. Th: Jefferson

RC (CSmH); at foot of first page: "Mr. Nicholas." PoC (DLC); endorsed by TJ. Enclosure: TJ to Thomas Newton, 6 Dec. 1804, updated to 25 Mch. and with postscript added (see 6 Dec.).

like the image of clay & brass: in the second chapter of the book of Daniel in the Bible, Daniel interpreted a dream of King Nebuchadnezzar in which a great statue, made of gold and silver with thighs of brass, was struck down because its feet were made of iron mixed with clay, which do "not cleave one to another" to provide the strength to withstand a blow. Daniel interpreted the statue as representing a kingdom.

From William P. Robinson

SIR March 26th. 1805

I am writing to a person who should from his unparaleled Virtue have the Esteem of all Mankind. Secundum Initium. I am now Eighteen Years of age full far advanced to be in Business of some kind I had in Contemplation some time ago of entering myself in Fredericksburg with some of the Merchants but finding no Vacancy has forced me to call on you for Assistance. I hope the Reflorescency of your Mind will not suffer you to leave a Youth (without a Father or a Friend) in Despair I hope you will not think it unworthy your Attention to answer this Letter as I should be happy of being well employed. I am &c your

with the greatest Respect WM. P. ROBINSON

RC (MHi); endorsed by TJ as received 1 Apr. and so recorded in SJL.

SECUNDUM INITIUM: from the beginning.

From Elisha Avery

MONSIEUR, Pomfret, March 27, 1805.

Je transmets sous ce plie deux certificats touchant l'objet dont J'ai deja eu l'honneur de m'entretenir avec vous: ces papiers me se sont presentés en passant par les demeures des personnes qui les ont ecrites. Je conte de procurer d'autres recommendations dans cet Etat, lesquelles J'aurois voulu pouvoir expedier avec celles-ci, mais l'eloignment où sont ceux qui devront me les donner m'empeche de les recevoir sans quelque delais. Craignant Monsieur, que vous ne puissiez soupçonner de negligence de ma part, J'ai cru devoir vous transmettre tels rensiegnmens, que j'ai pu obtenir Jusqu'à present: Si ma santé me l'eut permis, Je vous aurois donné avant ce Jour, des preuves plus satisfactoires.—

Les Messieurs qui m'ont fourni ces certificats, ne sont peut-être pas trés connus hors de Cet Etat, quoique ici leur temoinage reçoive le plus grand credit. Monsr Granger pourroit vous rendre compte de leur charactere.—Je dois partir aujourd-hui pour Boston, Je prendrai avec moi une lettre de raccommendation Au General Hull d'un de ses Amis particuliers, esperant par-cela ainsi que par mes connaissances à Boston, de me Justifier aupres de lui un plein titre à sa confiance—A mon arrivée dans cette Ville-la Je me ferai le plaisir de consulte avec le Docteur Eustis et ne doute pas Que Je ne puisse l'engager à s'interester à mon égard.—Les connaissances que j'ai à Boston sont principalement des commercans, et peu connus dans le public; Ils n'en sont pas moins accrédité chez eux, et leur temoinage y Jouit de la meilleure foi—

Mais comme il foudrait *à eux* pour etablir leur merite à vos yeux, des preuves en leur faveur, Je pense Monsr que je pourrai me mieux servir de leur bonne volonté devant le Genl Hull *lui-même* que les connoit, qu'en vous donnant la peine de vous en enformer.—S'il pouroit vous plaire Monsieur lorsque Vous aurez reçu cette lettre, de vous intereser en ma faveur, en autant que de me proposer au Genl Hull; J'ai toute confiance que je pourrai oter facilement à son esprit, toute hesitation à m'accorder la place à laquelle vous aurez en la bonté de me nommer.—

Ce n'est pas sans peine Monsieur que je vois dans cet Etat et un trop grand nombre d'hommes tellement aveuglés à leur propres intérêts, qu'ils ne puissent voir que ce que leur vient des ennemis de leur bonheur et de leur prosperité—Je me felicite cependant de croire que les principes que Je cheris y ont fait et font de progres.—

J'ai neanmoins à regretter Monsr que le veritable intérêt de l'Etat et de la Nation ou ne parrait pas y posseder assez de soutien du coté des talents. Les Amis du General Government sont honêtes et zelés, mais Je crains que leurs efforts ne soient pas trés bein appuiés par l'habilité, et par les grands ressorts de l'esprit. J'ai pourtant la consolation d'apprendre, qui l'opposition contre les Chefs *de l'Union* devient de Jour en Jour beaucoup plus foible, et que malgre l'obstination du parti dominant, l'intérêt de la patrie se fait apperçevoir et sentir dans les acts et dans les vues de l'Administration

Les habitans de Connecticut ont été et sont trés tenaces de son regime interieur, et tout changement leurs paroit inutile sinon onereux:

Les Federalists proffitent de cette circonstance pour se maintener; Ils representent les intentions des Republicains, comme hostiles à toutes leurs regles etablir, et le Clergé n'aide pas peu à créer cette idée.

Il est certain cependant, et J'en cheris la pensée, que l'erreur se devoile, que la verité s'Empare du mensonge et de l'intrigue; et que la volonté de cet Etat se montrera bientot d'accord avec la Volonté Generale.—Vous me pardonerez Monsr. ces observations, et si elles sont mal-placées, c'est un defaut du jugement et non de coeur.—Comme vous m'avez fait accroire Monsr de la Connaissance de la langue françoise étoit essentiel à mon projet, Je prends la liberté de m'en servir ici, Afin que vous pussiez mieux Juger de mes Qualifications sur ce point.

J'ai l'honneur de Vous Saluer, & Suis Monsieur Votre trés respectueux et Obdt. Serviteur E. Avery

N.B. Je resterai à Boston Jusqu'a ce que Je sache la disposition du Presidet a mon egard.—

EDITORS' TRANSLATION

Sir, Pomfret, 27 Mch. 1805

I am enclosing two certificates regarding the topic I have already had the honor of discussing with you. These papers were given to me when I visited the homes of those who wrote them. I plan to obtain other recommendations in this state. I would have liked to include them here but the people live too far away for me to obtain them without delay. Fearing, Sir, that you might suspect negligence on my part, I thought I should transmit the information I have received to date. If my health had permitted, I would have provided more satisfactory letters before now.

The gentlemen who furnished these attestations may not be very well known outside this state, but their word inspires the greatest trust here. Mr. Granger could give you an account of their character. Today I must leave for Boston. I will take a letter of recommendation to General Hull from one of his close friends, hoping to earn his trust through that as well as through my acquaintances in Boston. When I arrive, I shall have the pleasure of consulting Dr. Eustis. I do not doubt that I can inspire him to take an interest in my situation. My acquaintances in Boston are principally merchants who are not well known to the public, but they are no less respected in their circles and their word is trusted.

Since it is necessary to justify their merit in your eyes, I believe, Sir, that I could share their favorable recommendations with General Hull, who knows them, to spare you the trouble of inquiring yourself. When you receive this letter, if you are willing to take an interest in me and recommend me to General Hull, I am fully confident I can readily overcome any hesitation he might have about appointing me to whatever position you are kind enough to designate for me.

It is painful, Sir, to see too many men in this state who are so blinded by their own interests that they see only what comes from the enemies of their happiness and prosperity. I take heart, nevertheless, in believing that the principles I cherish have made headway and continue to do so.

I however regret, Sir, that talented people do not seem to defend the true interests of the state and the nation. Friends of the federal government are honest and enthusiastic but I fear their efforts are not backed up by skill or by the vital force of reason. Yet I am consoled to learn that opposition to the leaders of the Union is growing weaker every day. Despite the obstinacy of the dominant party, the government's acts and opinions are seen to reflect the nation's interest. The inhabitants of Connecticut continue to hold on to their local regime and to believe that all change is useless if not burdensome. The Federalists take advantage of this to stay in power. They portray the Republicans as hostile to their established rules, and the clergy plays no small rule in fostering this idea.

Yet it is certain, and I cherish this knowledge, that error is unveiled, that truth conquers lies and intrigue, and that Connecticut's wishes will soon be in accord with the general will. Forgive me for these observations, Sir. If they are inappropriate, it is a weakness of judgment, not of heart.

Since you led me to believe that knowledge of French was essential for my project, I am taking the liberty of using it here so you may better judge my qualifications in this domain.

I have the honor of saluting you, Sir, and am your very respectful and obedient servant. E. Avery

N.B. I will remain in Boston until I know the president's decision concerning my situation.

RC (DNA: RG 59, LAR); endorsed by TJ as received 17 Apr. and so recorded in SJL. Enclosures: (1) Statement by Lemuel Grosvenor, dated Pomfret, Connecticut, 26 Mch., attesting to Avery's being "an active upright and intelligent Young Gentleman," qualities Grosvenor witnessed in their correspondence while Avery was in Europe over the prior six years (RC in same). (2) Statement by Daniel Putnam, dated Brooklyn, Connecticut, 26 Mch., attesting to Avery's character, deportment, and integrity, "so far as I have had knowledge thereof" (RC in same; at foot of text: "The President of U. States").

From Jacob Crowninshield

Dear Sir Salem 27th March 1805

Having received from you far greater attentions than I was any way intitled to, and having a sincere disposition to give my best services in Support of your Administration I had determined previous to leaving Washington to accept the appointment with which I had been honored, almost at every sacrifice, and I then flattered myself I should be able to surmount all the obstacles which seemed opposed to my speedy return. It is now about ten days since I joined my family in Salem and I am truly sorry to inform you that I find Mrs. Crowninshield in so low a state of health that it would be quite unsafe for her to undertake a journey even for the distance of a few miles from home. During the whole winter while I was absent she has been in very ill health, she has been confined to the house for some time past and is now seldom able to leave the room, and it is painful for me to add from the nature of her complaints I could have little hope that she would soon recover her health even if the journey to the South could be attempted, and to Seperate myself from her in her present situation will be impossible, indeed I am bound by every consideration not to leave her during her sickness.

Surrounded with a family of young children, with ardent attachments to a retired life and with a sincere conviction that her happiness is deeply involved in the determination Mrs. C. would have consented at any time with great reluctance to the removal from Masstts. still I believe it would have been in my power to overcome every objection, if her health had been even tolerably good but it is unfortunately so much the reverse of this that I am compelled to remain with her, and of course to give up all thoughts of visiting Washington during the present Summer.

I have not come to a precipitate determination but I have calmly and deliberately considered the subject, and finding I can not enjoy the company of my wife and children in Washington I am reduced to the necessity of informing you that I can not accept the office lately assigned to me, I beg you at the same time to be assured that I make this communication with deep regret, and I hope when I have the pleasure of seeing you again I shall be able to convince you that I have acted as I ought to, and as most men would have done who were placed in a similar situation.

I will now only tender my sincere acknowledgments and request permission to express my best wishes for your health and happiness, and with assurances of the highest esteem and respect

I subscribe myself your devoted and obliged servt.

JACOB CROWNINSHIELD

RC (DLC); addressed: "Thomas Jefferson President of the US Washington"; endorsed by TJ as received 17 Apr. and so recorded in SJL; also endorsed by TJ: "declines office of Secy. of Navy." Dft (Mrs. Charles L. Hoskins, Seneca Falls, New York, 1950).

CAN NOT ACCEPT THE OFFICE: Robert Smith agreed to remain as secretary of the navy. Because TJ never went through the process of having Smith reinstated through the Senate, older government records sometimes list Crowninshield and not Smith as secretary of the navy during TJ's second administration (Noble E. Cunningham, *The Process of Government under Jefferson* [Princeton, 1978], 70; Benjamin Perley Poore, *The Political Register and Congressional Directory: A Statistical Record of the Federal Officials, Legislative, Executive, and Judicial, of the United States of America, 1776-1878* [Boston, 1878], 216; TJ to the Senate, 2 Mch.).

From Jacob Crowninshield

Salem Masstts. 27th March 1805

Jacob Crowninshield presents his respects to Mr. Jefferson & has the honor of informing him that he has received his note of the 11th inst and will with great pleasure procure the quintal of dumb-fish and send it by the first vessel as directed or to the nearest port in Virginia. J.C regrets that he has been obliged to come to the resolution expressed in his letter of this days date, but he rests himself on Mr. Jefferson's candour, & trusts he will be excused as soon as Mr. Jefferson considers the unfortunate & delicate situation in which he is placed. With the most sincere regard Jacob Crowninshield begs leave to tender to Mr. Jefferson the homage of his high respects and consideration.

PS. JC has taken the liberty to give an opinion to Mr. Smith that the common coasting vessels, of which we have so many in all capital sea ports, would answer very well in the room of the gun boats to go to Tripoli (if the latter could not be spared) & with some improvement and alterations which could be readily made they would be preferable

New York can furnish any number immediately, the North river sloops of from 60 to 80 tons drawing but little water might be selected in preference. These vessels I should suppose could be dispatched in a week or ten days after they were purchased, & I feel confident they will accomplish every thing expected from them in the meditated attack on Tripoli & its Marine force. They might sail in a fleet together or depart by single vessels as they were fitted or prepared for the expedition.

RC (DLC); addressed: "Th. Jefferson President of the U States"; endorsed by TJ as received 17 Apr. and so recorded in SJL. Dft (Mrs. Charles L. Hoskins, Seneca Falls, New York, 1950); postscript only; written at foot of Crowninshield to TJ, 27 Mch. (first letter).

From James Madison

Dear Sir Wasington Mar. 27. 1805

I recd. on monday evening your favor of Mar. 23. with the return of Armstrong's & Monroe's letters first sent you. I cannot entirely despair that Spain notwithstanding the support given by France to her claim to W.F. may yield to our proposed arrangement, partly from its intrinsic value to her, partly from an apprehension of the interference of G.B. and that this latter considn may, as soon as France despairs of her pecuniary object, transfer her weight into our scale. If she should persist in disavowing her right to sell W.F. to the U.S. and above all can prove it to have been the mutual understanding with Spain that W.F. was no part of Louisiana, it will place our claim on very different ground, such probably as could not be approved by the World, and such certainly as could not with that approbation be maintained by force.

If our right be good agst. Spain at all, it must be supported by those rigid maxims of technical law, which have little weight in national questions generally, and none at all when opposed to the principles of universal equity. The world would decide that France having sold us the territory of a third party, which she had no right to sell, that party having even remonstrated agst. the whole transaction, the right of the U.S. was limited to a demand on France to procure & convey the territory, or to remit pro tanto the price, or to dissolve the bargain altogether. I am pleased to find that Talleyrand's letter is silent as to the W. Boundary. This circumstance is the more important as Monroe's letter to which Talleyrand's is an answer, expressly names the Rio Bravo as the W. limit of our claim.

The importance of some arrangement with Spain opening the Mobille to our trade, is sufficiently urged as in every event to be seriously pressed, in the instructions already in the hands of Monroe.

Inclosed are the letters from Cathalan which were sent me for perusal—a paper not before recd from Monroe—a letter from C. Pinkney—and two from Jarvis with their inclosures, except the letters from the forger of draughts in Preble's name, which have been put into the hands of the Secy. of the Navy; & a letter from Dr. Lattimore

Yrs. with respectful attachment JAMES MADISON

RC (DLC); at foot of first page: "The President of the U States"; endorsed by TJ as received from the State Department on 30 Mch. and "Monroe. Pinckney. Jarvis. Lattimore" and so recorded in SJL. Enclosures: (1) Probably Stephen Cathalan, Jr., to Madison, 22 Sep. 1804, enclosing other documents, including Cathalan's defense of his conduct (see Madison, *Papers, Sec. of State Ser.*, 8:79-81; Cathalan to TJ, 22 Sep. 1804). (2) Probably Charles Pinckney to Madison, 8 Dec. 1804, reporting that the question of war between Spain and Great Britain is "yet decided"; should Spain choose war, the country's commerce "will be ruined"; Pinckney anxiously awaits permission to return to the United States, which in a year's time will fly the "only neutral flag in the world"; in a postscript, he refers to the possible British intention to expel the Dutch and French from the West Indies, which has led the Spanish to contemplate opening their ports in the Caribbean and South America (Madison, *Papers, Sec. of State Ser.*, 8:360-2). (3) Probably William Jarvis to Madison, 5 Jan., from Lisbon; he assumes that the administration has learned of the Spanish declaration of war against Great Britain but will enclose a copy of the declaration and expects that the enclosed letter from Pinckney contains the news; he reports on some ships at Lisbon, including the *Constitution*, which needs new sails and a bowsprit; the captain also hopes to add to his crew, a difficult task because of the war; Jarvis encloses some extracts of a message he received about allegations injurious to his reputation, and his response; he forwards a letter from James Simpson; in a postscript, he adds that Joseph Rademaker, Portugal's consul general and chargé d'affaires to the United States, will sail soon to New York; Jarvis believes Portugal will remain neutral (same, 8:455-7; NDBW, 5:255-7). (4) Jarvis to Madison, 19 Jan., from Lisbon; he reports on the progress of repairs to the *Constitution* and of efforts to add to the frigate's crew and encloses correspondence with the foreign minister on obtaining an anchor; he also encloses correspondence involving himself, Captain John Rodgers, and British consul James Gambier on British seamen serving on American vessels; Jarvis adds some information on a Moroccan vessel in port and another in Sétubal, speculates that Prussia may reject Moroccan terms of tribute, and advises "some measure of precaution" if "two or three Vessels can be spared"; he relates a conversation on the individual who may have perpetrated the fraud on Mackenzie & Glennie of London and encloses potential samples of the person's handwriting; he also encloses a copy of a British announcement of a blockade at Cadiz and a duplicate of the Spanish declaration of war; the "alarm about this Country being involved in the War seems to be daily subsiding" (same, 5:291-3; Madison, *Papers, Sec. of State Ser.*, 8:493-5). (5) William Lattimore to Madison, 19 Mch., from Norfolk, concerning the grants of land Congress made available for use of Jefferson College in Mississippi Territory; Lattimore warns of competing claims for the lands in question and requests that no patent be issued until the matter is resolved by Congress (same, 9:149-51).

W.F.: West Florida.

PRO TANTO: as far as it goes (Bryan A. Garner, *Black's Law Dictionary*, 8th ed. [St. Paul, Minn., 2004], 1259).

TALLEYRAND'S LETTER: see Pinckney to TJ, 28 Jan., and Madison to TJ, 17 Mch. The PAPER from Monroe may have been a memoir consisting of capsule descriptions of the treaties transferring portions of Louisiana and Florida and a statement of how the treaties supported U.S. arguments that the eastern boundary of Louisiana was the Perdido River. Monroe enclosed the paper in his letter of 8 Nov. 1804 to Talleyrand (Tr in DNA: RG 59, DD, Spain; Madison, *Papers, Sec. of State Ser.*, 8:333n).

FORGER OF DRAUGHTS: see Madison to TJ, 16 Aug. 1804.

From Robert Smith

SIR, Washington Mar 27. 1805

Commodore Preble[1] has in the most importunate and impressive manner entreated me to recommend to you the promotion of Masters Commandant Charles Stewart and Isaac Hull to the rank of Captains in the Navy. mr. Stewart I personally know. His manners are those of a well bred Gentle man. He has had the advantage of a Classic liberal Education and is considered by all an elegant Officer—Mr. Hull I do not personally know; but his Character in the Navy is remarkably high. He is admired by all who know him. He is a favorite Nephew of our good friend Genl Hull who interests himself much in his advancement. These two Gentlemen have commanded the two Brigs in our Medn. Squadron and have upon all occasions so distinguished themselves for their bravery and judgment that in the Opinion of their Commodore they have just claims upon their Country for promotion. By this kind of manifestation of our good will to the Officers of the Navy we not only strongly attach them to us but we inspire them with a zeal that will lead them on to the most glorious deeds. Indeed I fear unless we do something of this sort we will lose these two very valuable Officers. They are both too far advanced in life to remain in their present grade. And let me suggest to you what I have learned since I have been in the Navy Department, that it requires many years experience and great attention to make such Officers as these Gentlemen are. If you should consider it proper to gratify Commodore Preble (and let me add) myself in this instance, you will have the goodness to sign the Commissions herewith sent and return them to me to be forwarded by a store Ship which will sail about a week hence. Be persuaded, Sir, I would not thus press this subject, were I not well satisfied that those two promotions would be attended with great advantages and that they are in every respect strictly proper. Respectfully Your Obed. Sevt.

RT. SMITH

RC (DLC); endorsed by TJ as received from the Navy Department on 30 Mch. and "Sterett and Hull to be Captains" and so recorded in SJL.

PROMOTION OF MASTERS COMMANDANT: Charles Stewart and Isaac Hull were promoted to captain in April 1806 (NDBW, *Register*, 26, 53).

[1] Word interlined in place of "Barron."

From Antoine Vosse

SIR

Philadelphia 28th Mar 1805

In your next philosophical publication please to inform the Citizens how many *beans* make five and take three away! The solution of this very important question may be of equal benefit to the United States as the discovery of a bloody Arena or the formation of a dry Dock.

With Compliments to Sally I remain, Dear Sir Your Obedient and humble Servant

ANTOINE VOSSE

RC (DLC); at foot of text: "Mr Thomas Jefferson"; endorsed by TJ as received 4 Apr. and "scurrilities" and so recorded in SJL; also endorsed by TJ: "(Pseudonymus)."

In the months after TJ's 17 Oct. 1803 annual message to Congress, Federalist newspapers lampooned his call for Americans to remain neutral in the face of the "BLOODY ARENA" produced by war in Europe. In addition to using the phrase to critique TJ's reputed pro-French tendencies, these writers increasingly tied it to their opposition to the expense of the purchase of Louisiana (*Charleston Courier*, 31 Oct. 1803; Utica, N.Y., *Patriot*, 7 Nov. 1803; Boston *Columbian Centinel*, 19 Nov. 1803; *Connecticut Post and New Haven Visitor*, 15 Dec. 1803; *Trenton Federalist*, 30 Apr. 1804; Vol. 41:538).

To Charles François d'Anmours

DEAR SIR

Monticello Mar. 29. 05.

I recieved by mr Derbigny with very great pleasure your letter of Sep. 30. it was not delivered till Dec. 11. & mr Derbigny informed me you would be gone from N. Orleans before an answer could reach it.

had I known of your being there, I should not have failed to drop you a line to recall our antient acquaintance. the present will go to the care of Govr. Claiborne, and is merely to express to you the continuance of my esteem, & the regret that distance & your retired situation cuts off all intercourse but that of mutual recollection. it will always give me pleasure to hear from you, & to recieve any information which your position & knolege of affairs will enable you to give. I am satisfied you will be disposed in this way to serve those among whom you are, and to enable me to do whatever would be useful or agreeable to them and to convince them we consider & wish to treat them as our brethren. Accept my affectionate salutations & assurances of constant esteem & respect. TH: JEFFERSON

PoC (DLC); at foot of text: "The Chevalr. D'Annemours."

To William Darlington

Monticello Mar. 29. 05.

Th: Jefferson presents his salutations to Mr. Darlington & his thanks for the pamphlet he has been so kind as to send him on the mutual influence of habits & disease which he shall peruse in the first moments of leisure with the pleasure so interesting a subject promises.

RC (Lucius Wilmerding, Jr., Princeton, 1946); addressed: "Doctr. William Darlington Westchester. Pensva"; franked; postmarked Milton, 30 Mch. PoC (DLC); endorsed by TJ.

THANKS FOR THE PAMPHLET: Darlington to TJ, 11 Mch.

To Henry Dearborn

DEAR SIR Monticello Mar. 29.05.

Your favor of the 25th. came to hand yesterday, and I now return the letter of La Fayette with a similar one under cover to me, which he desired me, if I thought it proper, to hand on to you as the channel through which he wished to have it conveyed to Congress. considering it as proper & believing it will have a favorable effect I comply with his request in now inclosing it.

You remember it was proposed that Pease should have the offer of the direction of the Arcansa expedition. does he undertake it? if he does not, it might be well to enquire into Parson Wiley's fitnesses, & if you find them sufficient, authorise him to proceed.

I wish mr Gallatin & yourself may not have been misinformed as to Davy. I knew a little & heard a great deal of him in the days of Liston. he was at the door of every party, but most, & most devotedly at that of Liston. since that I have only understood generally that he is an insincere man, of principles not to be trusted, and peculiarly obnoxious to one section of the republicans of Philadelphia. indeed I was strongly cautioned against his appointmt. to this office as one which he would turn to the purposes of England and benefit of his own private commerce. however we will try him. this will give us time to consider whether this office may not be put on a better footing. I had supposed this officer should be considered as the Director of all the Indian commerce, that he should be a person of perfect commercial knolege & experience, but withdrawn from private commerce, that he should be considered as a high officer of secondary grade in your office, where with the aid of a single clerk he might keep the accounts of all the factories be able to tell at any moment the state of their affairs, & from thence, under your advice, as from head quarters, direct all purchases & supplies and keep up the necessary correspondence. if it be thought he should be at the place of purchase & make all the purchases personally, this would give to the place of his residence the monopoly of that commerce. I acknolege I never had been able to think of a person with the necessary qualifications: but since I began to write these sentences, John Mason comes into my head, of mercantile education & experience, withdrawn from commerce, residing at the seat of government and possessing so much the public confidence as to take all responsibility from us. nor do I suppose his occupations at the bank leave him less time to spare for it, than Davy's occupations with his private commerce. however we shall have time enough to consider whether this arrangement would be the best? whether he would be a fitter person? & whether he would accept it? should this be hereafter thought expedient, Davy could hardly consider such a change, made on general considerations, as meaning a dissatisfaction with him. I observe the federal papers are giving out the word to their party how to avail themselves of the schisms arising among our friends. they will join the minority, let their principles be what they may, because the minority alone will give a price by compromise of principle & office. unable to prevent these schisms, we should carefully avoid siding with either, and give our confidence to both equally. Accept my affectionate salutations & assurances of great respect.

TH: JEFFERSON

RC (MH); at foot of first page: "Genl. Dearborne." PoC (DLC). Notation in SJL: "Departmt. War. Fayette. Pease. Wily. Davy." Enclosures: Lafayette to TJ,

1 Dec. 1804, and Enclosure No. 1 listed there.

For Seth PEASE and David WILEY, see TJ to William Dunbar, 14 Mch.

From Jones & Howell

RESPECTED FRIEND Phila. 29th March 1805

We have Shipp'd to the address of Gibson & Jefferson agreeable to Your orders Some time Since given

80 Bundles 2-0-0-0 Nail rods

at $126—	$252.00
porterage—	1.33
	$253.33

these rods Should have been Shippd: by the first of this month, or at least by the first Vessels after the Navigation open'd but was Omitted through A mistake of the person. who had it in charge. You will we hope excuse us. this Vessel will Sail on Sunday.

we are very Respectfully Your Friends JONES & HOWELL

RC (MHi); at head of text: "Thomas Jefferson Esqr."; endorsed by TJ as received 4 Apr. and so recorded in SJL with notation: "80. bund. rod shipd. Mar. 29. 253.33."

YOUR ORDERS: TJ to Jones & Howell, 9 Dec. 1804, 12 Feb. 1805.

From William Keteltas

DR SIR. New York 29h March 1805

Perceivng that two Commissioners Are to be Appointed for upper Louisiana, and Advised to make the follng Appeal to Your Magnanimity and Patriotizm Under *Injuries unmerited* and *Unparrelled*—Injuries Which it becomes Me to forgive Considering the frailties of humanature—I should Consider it a favour Conferd. by the President, to have one of those places If they Are disposed of, Should Any other Present Equally Respectable &, honorable, I hope to Merit the Presidents Consideration

Havg a family, It is Important for Me to Know should I Obtain an Appointment, the fact before the 1st of May, to Make Arrangments Accordingly The President May be Assured of My personal Esteem and Respect, Uniform Attatchment too, And firm support of his Administration Which has been frank, and sincere Under All Circumstances

Yours &c WM KETELTAS

RC (DNA: RG 59, LAR); at foot of text: "Thomas Jefferson Esqr President United States"; endorsed by TJ as received 6 Apr. and so recorded in SJL; also endorsed by TJ: "to be a Western Commr."

To James Madison

DEAR SIR Monticello Mar. 29. 05.

Your packet came to hand yesterday with the letters of Monroe, Armstrong, Coburn, Zeigler & Baldwin. altho' I presume the appointment of Baldwin would be proper, yet as Zeigler continues to act it may lie awhile. I inclose you a letter from a mr Thomas of Indiana inclosing a proclamation of Govr. Harrison and the names of 10. persons out of whom 5 are to be named as Counsellors. who he is I know not, nor does he say. whether he is in any office, & whether his communication is official or private, whether this is the formal communication on which I am to act, is the question. perhaps this may be found out at Washington. if it is official & requires immediate action, be so good as to consult with the other gentlemen & name the 5. who are to be commissioned. Armstrong's stile of correspondence is satisfactory, but he is already forgetful of the temper of his country, & proves how readily we catch the hue of those around us. I have recieved a short letter from Fayette saying only that he had committed a long one to Livingston explaining his purposes & situation, & covering the power of Attorney which I now inclose. I had thought the 600. as. on the Canal of Carondelet too valuable to await this instrument & had desired Claiborne to have it located and surveyed immediately and to draw on me for the expence. what has passed shall be communicated to you on my return. Dupont writes me that he will be over in the spring & probably La fayette with him.

Accept affectionate salutations. TH: JEFFERSON

RC (DLC: Madison Papers); at foot of text: "J. Madison." PoC (DLC). Notation in SJL: "Monroe. Zeigler. Baldwin. Coburn. Thomas. Armstrong. Fayette." Enclosures: (1) Jesse B. Thomas to TJ, 1 Mch., recorded in SJL as received from Lawrenceburg, Indiana Territory, on 28 Mch. but not found. (2) Copy of power of attorney authorizing Madison to locate lands and execute documents on Lafayette's behalf (not found, but see Madison, *Papers, Sec. of State Ser.*, 8:148n).

YOUR PACKET: TJ did not record receiving a letter from the State Department on 28 Mch. In the package, he may have received James Monroe's letter of 16 Dec. 1804 to Madison, in which Monroe detailed his efforts to gain the good offices of France and his difficult interactions with Robert R. Livingston (same, 386-402). A letter of 30 Dec. from John ARMSTRONG was recorded in SJL as received from Paris on 28 Mch. but has not been found. It is possible TJ was recording Armstrong's letter of 30 Dec. to Madison, in which Armstrong confirmed the French government's denial that West Florida should be treated as part of Louisiana, pointed out that the French "left wholly unnoticed" other points of negotiation between the United States and Spain, and suggested that American goals might best be accomplished "by means, purely our own" (same, 428-31). The other cited enclosures in the packet involved potential appointments: John Coburn to Madison, 28 Feb. (RC in DNA: RG 59, LAR; endorsed by TJ: "Coburn John. Kentucky to mr Madison to be in Judiciary or land office in Western govmt speaks French"); David Zeigler to Madison, 4 Mch. (RC in same, 1:497-8; endorsed by TJ: "Zeigler David resigns as marshal Ohio Baldwin Michl. recomdd."); and Michael Baldwin to Madison, 8 Mch. (RC in same; endorsed by TJ: "Baldwin Michl. to mr Madison to be Marshal Ohio"). See also Madison, *Papers, Sec. of State Ser.*, 9:76-7, 103-4, 121-2.

William Henry Harrison's PROCLAMATION of 5 Dec. announced that Indiana had passed into the second grade of territorial governance and called for an election on 3 Jan. to choose nine members for the house of representatives. Those elected were to convene on 1 Feb. to choose candidates for the legislative council. The assembly, which counted Jesse B. Thomas among its members, selected the following council candidates, from whom TJ was to choose five: Benjamin Chambers of Dearborn County, Marston Green Clark and Samuel Gwathmey of Clark County, John Hay and Jean François Perrey of St. Clair County, John Rice Jones and Jacob Kuykendall of Knox County, James Henry and James May of Wayne County, and Pierre Menard of Randolph County (Logan Esarey, ed., *Messages and Letters of William Henry Harrison*, 2 vols. [Indianapolis, 1922; repr., New York, 1975], 1:112-13, 126-8; William Wesley Woollen, Daniel Wait Howe, and Jacob Piatt Dunn, eds., *Executive Journal of Indiana Territory, 1800-1816* [Indianapolis, 1900], 72-3; Thomas T. Davis to TJ, 20 Feb.).

SHORT LETTER FROM FAYETTE: Lafayette to TJ, 1 Dec.

DUPONT WRITES ME: Pierre Samuel Du Pont de Nemours to TJ, 1 Jan.

To Charles Philippe Magnan

SIR Monticello Mar. 29. 05.

I recollect with great pleasure the short time I passed so agreeably with Doctr. Gouan at Montpelier, and am gratified by his recollection of me, and thankful for the seeds he has been so kind as to send me, & to you for the care you have been pleased to take in forwarding them. I should have been still more so had it been in my power to have furnished you with the letters of protection you desire, as a guard, doubtless, against hostile rovers on the sea. but the strictness of our rules forbids them to be given but to citizens of the United states, and I must be the last to set an example of acting against our own rules. indeed a protection to any other would not be respected by the officer of a foreign power. Accept my salutations & best wishes for a pleasant and safe voyage TH: JEFFERSON

PoC (DLC); at foot of text: "M. Ch. P. Magnan fils"; endorsed by TJ.

SHORT TIME I PASSED: during his travels through southern France, TJ spent 11 May 1787 with Antoine Gouan in Montpellier (Vol. 11:444).

THANKFUL FOR THE SEEDS: see Magnan to TJ, 21 Mch.

To John Tyler

DEAR SIR Monticello Mar. 29. 05

Your favor of the 17th. found me on a short visit to this place, & I observe in it with great pleasure a continuance of your approbation of the course we are pursuing, and particularly the satisfaction you express with the last inaugural address. the first was from the nature of the case all profession & promise. performance therefore seemed to be the proper office of the second. but the occasion restricted me to mention only the most prominent heads, & the strongest justifications of these in the fewest words possible. the crusade preached against philosophy by the modern disciples of steady habits induced me to dwell more in shewing their effect with the Indians than the subject otherwise justified.

The war with Tripoli stands on two grounds of fact. 1st. it is made known to us by our Agents with the three other Barbary states, that they only wait to see the event of this to shape their conduct accordingly. if the war is ended by additional tribute they mean to offer us the same alternative. 2dly. if peace was made, we should still, & shall ever, be obliged to keep a frigate in the Mediterranean to[1] overawe rupture, or we must abandon that market. our intention in sending Morris with a respectable force was to try whether peace could be forced by a coercive enterprize on their town. his inexecution of orders baffled that effort. having broke him, we try the same experiment under a better commander. if in the course of the summer they cannot produce peace, we shall recall all our force except one frigate & 2. small vessels who will keep up a perpetual blockade. such a blockade will cost us no more than a state of peace, & will save us from increased tributes, and the disgrace attached to them. there is reason to believe the example we have set begins already to work on the dispositions of the powers of Europe to emancipate themselves from that degrading yoke. should we produce such a revolution there we shall be amply rewarded for what we have done. Accept my friendly salutations & assurances of great respect & esteem.

TH: JEFFERSON

PoC (DLC); at foot of first page: "Judge Tyler."

[1] TJ here canceled "prevent."

Petition for Charles, with Jefferson's Order

TO THE PRESIDENT OF THE UNITED STATES

We the Undersignd subscribers take the liberty of representing to the President of the United States, that Negroe Charles, a slave, the property of one Henry Nicholson of the Town of Alexandria, was at a Court held for the County of Alexandria, in November term last, Convicted of having Burglariously broken and enterd the dwelling house of one Thomas White in the Town of Alexandria aforesaid, with an intent to steal the goods and chattells of the said White—And he hath been accordingly condemnd to Suffer death for the said crime, and his execution directed to take place on the tenth day of May next, as will appear by a Certificate from the Clerk of the Court herewith exhibited—The Undersignd Subscribers further represent, that the circumstances given in evidence upon the trial were barely sufficient to authorise the Jury to find a Verdict against the said Negroe Charles, and taking the said circumstances into consideration, together with the severity of the Law inflicting the punishment of death for offences of that kind, they look upon the said Negroe Charles as a fit and proper object of pardon and recommend him as such to your Excellency—

THO, SWANN Atty. at Law.
EDM: J. LEE atty. at Law.
GEO. YOUNGS. Atty. at Law
R. J. TAYLOR Atty at Law
HENRY HIORT Atty at Law.
G. DENEALE CLERK of the Court

The Undersigned Judges of the Circuit Court of the District of Columbia respectfully recommend to the President of the United States to Grant a Pardon to negro Charles in the within Petition mentioned on the ground therein stated—

30 March 1805.

W KILTY
W. CRANCH
N FITZHUGH

concurred in by

WR: JONES JR.
U.S. Atty. for D. of Cola.
L SUMMERS D Marshal

[*Order by TJ*:]
Let a pardon issue

TH: JEFFERSON
Apr. 23. 05.

note, it's safe & speedy[1] transmission to the marshal should be particularly attended to

RC (DNA: RG 59, GPR); petition in Thomas Swann's hand, signed by all; judges' recommendation in a clerk's hand, signed by William Kilty, William Cranch, and Nicholas Fitzhugh; concurrence in hand of Walter Jones, Jr., signed by him and Lewis Summers. Recorded in SJL as received 22 Apr. from Alexandria with notation "Charles, negro. petn. for pardon." Enclosure not found.

In a petition for freedom filed in June 1805, Charles reported having been "imported" in spring 1801 from Maryland to Alexandria, where he was imprisoned and sold to a man who transported him to South Carolina. Charles escaped back to Maryland but was again "imported" to Alexandria and jailed. Henry Nicholson, a local soap manufacturer who would later be a member of the town council, purchased him for the cost of the jailer's fees and paid an additional $300 to the South Carolina buyer. Nicholson then manumitted Charles, and on 26 Aug. 1801, the two entered an agreement whereby Charles, described in their contract as a "free Man" previously "the property of Henry Nicholson," became Nicholson's indentured servant for 10 years. Possibly by a mistake in his indictment for burglary or by an intentional deception on the part of Nicholson, Charles was tried as a slave. Had he been tried as a free person, he would have been subject to Virginia's penal reform statute of 1796, which eliminated capital punishment for all crimes committed by free persons other than first-degree murder. Slaves remained subject to older statutes that made burglary a capital offense, a punishment that was not pursued in all such cases. Subsequent to the pardon, Nicholson sold Charles to two North Carolina men for $222, prompting Charles's freedom suit, which he pursued from the Alexandria jail. In late May 1805, Charles marshaled evidence in service of two claims. First, his petition argued that his importation to Alexandria had violated the Virginia state ban on slave importation, under which any slaves found to have been illegally imported were emancipated. Second, he presented evidence of his manumission by and indenture to Nicholson. On 19 June, Charles was released to Nicholson's custody upon payment of the jailer's fees. A summons issued by William Kilty on 29 June characterized the case between Charles and Nicholson as "depending and undetermined" (MSS in Vi: Local Government Records Collection, Arlington County Court Records, Judgments [Freedom Suits], 1795-1858, box 1; *Alexandria Gazette*, 8 July 1811; William Waller Hening, ed., *The Statutes at Large; Being a Collection of All the Laws of Virginia*, 13 vols. [Richmond, 1809-23], 4:326; 9:471-2; Samuel Shepherd, ed., *The Statutes at Large of Virginia, from October Session 1792, to December Session 1806*, 3 vols. [Richmond, 1835-36], 2:5-6; Miller, *Alexandria Artisans*, 2:7; Philip J. Schwarz, *Twice Condemned: Slaves and the Criminal Law of Virginia, 1705-1865* [Baton Rouge, 1988], 19, 122-3, 216).

FIT AND PROPER OBJECT OF PARDON: on 20 Apr. Summers, the deputy marshal, wrote from Alexandria to an unidentified recipient (perhaps Jacob Wagner). Referring to the petition for clemency, "which I trust will have the desired effect," Summers stated that Daniel C. Brent, who was away, "has requested me to desire of you to send the Pardon (shold one be granted) to me at this place." The recipient would "add to the obligation by informing me of the probable success of the applycation, shold it have come to your knowledge, and apprizing me of any additional documents that may be deemed necessary" (RC in DNA: RG 59, GPR). TJ pardoned Charles on 23 Apr., staying all legal actions against him stemming from the burglary charges (FC in Lb in same).

[1] TJ interlined the preceding word and ampersand.

From Charles Willson Peale

Dear Sir Museum March 30th. 1805.

I have not been unmindful of the conversation we had on Stone ware for the purpose of cookery, and in Baltimore I went to the manufactory of such ware and obtained a list of their prices with the intent of sending it to you, under the Idea that you might wish to order some covered stew pans for the use of your Kitchen in lieu of those made of Copper, which may at times be neglected to be tined and thus used, be detrimental to health. Since my arrival here I have seen in a Store some Vessels in the form of stew pans with covers, I eagerly enquired the price of them, but questioning the Woman who owned the Shop about the use made of them, she replyed to keep butter in. that it would not stand the fire, indeed it would be dangerous to use them for Cooking, as heat made them break with a report loud as the firing a Pistol. I then enquired[1] what was the quality of the New York Stone ware, and it is but little better than that of Baltimore. Both these manufactories have their ware of a different colour from that made in England; the latter being of a redish brown, and the American of a cenerious colour. The English Stone ware will stand the fire well, and if such ware will answer the purpose of Cooking generally, it certainly ought to be prefered to Pans made of Copper, however well they may be tined.

Respecting the dressing of Racoon Skins, I have begun an essay of dressing two Skins; they will be made good strong leather, such Skins are often very greasey which must be cause of some trouble in the dressing of them. The Furriers tell me that they frequently have the Racoon skins dressed, but not with allum, the only method I have practiced in dressing of Skins with the hair on them.

Since I sent you the Small Polygraph, I have had one made for my use, my Son Rembrandt has made an important improvement, it enables me to write this Letter with this Small Machine: by placing the Paper diagonally, and after writing one half the Letter, than changing the place of each sheet to write the lower half, But it is absolutely necessary to have the Pens made distant from each other half the length of the paper.

I therefore herewith send you a new Pen bar, which you will, I hope find no difficulty of puting in the place of the other. The enclosed sheet will shew you the direction we have given to the lines for placing the paper. Some pieces of paper appears to be necessary to be placed under such parts of the letters as are not doubled, other wise the Pens must be frequently adjusted.

April 1st. Since writing the above, we have contrived a Bar to hold the paper more firmly in its place, therefore I send a Catch and that bar with the Penbar in a Small box directed for you. The ketch to be let into the bottom edge of the Gallows so as to embrace the bar along the dotted lines, on the enclosed paper—The lines on this paper is drawn from the Machine I now write with. After the top of your letter is written, to begin the other half of it, put the NE. corner of it underneath the Gallows by an opening between the Gallows and the board you write on. I forget that I need not be so particular to you. a few minutes tryal will give the best situation, and perhaps you may vary the direction of the lines from mine. I shall only say further that a small heavy bar appears to be necessary to keep the uppermost paper down more particularly at the NE. Corner when you are writing the lower half of your Letter. The bar now sent may be used to advantage when writing the octavo size. Thus, put a Screw to receive the notch of sd. bar near the hinge and close or rather nearly so, to the bottom of the Gallows, and to hold the other end of the bar have a *Pin* projecting from the Gallows of such a hieght from the board you write on as to press down on the paper, by pushing the bar under the sd. Pin. This Pin & the Screw must have holes made opposite them so that no injury may be done in shuting up the machine. I find no difficulty in writing this letter, but a little pull at bottom when the machinery is at the utmost stretch.

The Pen-Bar which this now sent, is to take the place off. may be sent with you old Polygraph, which, I presume you mean to send me that I may put the improved Machinery to it.

I am anxious to hear how you like your small Machine, I thought it wrote correctly, but I had only a few minutes for tryal of it, having sat up untill 2 O'Clock to have it ready for the Post going at 7.

I have not yet come to any determination of going to France, but when I do will communicate it to you in time to give you the opportunity of writing such letters as you may please to send by me. and recieve your commands generally.

Accept my salutations and believe me Your friend

C W Peale

RC (DLC); at foot of text: "His Excellency Thos. Jefferson Esqr."; endorsed by TJ as received 8 Apr. and so recorded in SJL. PoC (Lb in PPAmP: Peale-Sellers Papers). Enclosure not found.

SINCE MY ARRIVAL HERE: Peale returned to Philadelphia in mid-February after a visit of about seven weeks to Baltimore and Washington. While in the capital, he and his son Rembrandt waited on the president on several occasions. In January, Peale twice dined at the President's House (Peale, *Papers*, v. 2, pt. 2:785, 793, 798, 806; Vol. 45: Appendix II; Peale to TJ, 18 Dec. 1804).

Peale contemplated GOING TO FRANCE in the spring of 1805 to settle some exchanges with the natural history museum in Paris and to dispose of the mastodon skeleton, but the trip never materialized (Peale, *Papers*, v. 2, pt. 2:808, 832, 835).

[1] MS: "equired."

From Edwards Pierce

SIR, Charleston 30th March 1805,

It gives me much pleasure to find that the People of the United States have chosen a second time, a Gentleman to preside over them, who is studious, & anxious, to lessen our Duties & Taxes as much as possible; which induces me to think, you will not be displeased with the Liberty I now take, of sending you *a new System of Taxation*, by which the present, or any *larger* Amount of the Expences of Government can be annually discharged, which are now paid by the present System of Taxation,—My meaning is, That this shall be the only mode of Taxation, with two Exceptions only, vizt Postage on Letters, and Tonnage on Vessels; and instead of laying Duties on the Tonnage of Vessels as at present, that all Duties of Tonnage on American Vessels shall cease; & to lay a Tonnage Duty on foreign Vessels only, & that Duty not to be as high as it now is.—Whatever is the Amount that is laid ℔ Ton on foreign Vessels, take from that Amount, the Amount which is laid on American Vessels, & lay the Difference only on foreign Vessels; which will give to American Vessels the same Advantage, which the present System of Duties on Tonnage of Vessels gives them.—This will induce other Nations to put the Tonnage Duties on American Vessels on the same footing, & tend to introduce a more pacific & friendly System, amongst the Nations of the civilized parts of the World.—

Incredible as it must appear to you Sir, until I explain this new System of Taxation, yet it is a Fact; *That no Article which will be sold, ought to be sold higher on Account of the Duty which I propose should be laid*, than 10 ℔ Cent; and the Advantages to this Country in other respects would be astonishing.—

As no Duty would be paid on any Article imported, nor any Excise, the Importers of Merchandize could import a larger Quantity of Merchandize with the same Capital,—the wholesale Dealers could purchase a larger Quantity of Merchandize from the Importers with their Capitals; and the Retailers a larger Quantity with their Capitals.—

The Money which is now locked up in the Treasury Department for a time, & kept out of Circulation, would by this System be thrown into the hands of the Public; & no Specie in the United States would be kept locked up, except that which each individual kept locked up in his Chest, or which he deposited in Bankers hands for safe keeping.—This System would also tend to keep the Specie in this Country, but I am afraid we could not carry this System into Execution in the United States, without the Assistance of our Bank Notes, but if so, it is not on that Account worse than our present System of Taxation, as our present Duties & Taxes are paid with them.

There is another Advantage which would also arise from this new System of Taxation, that Remittances could be made *for a short time*, with the Government paper which would be issued in order to carry this System into Execution, to every part of the United States, by remitting with such Government paper, a Draft payable in Specie or Bank Notes for the Amount of the Duty thereon.—

When I resided in my native Country, (Great Britain,) Specie was paid at the Bank of England for their Bank Notes when demanded, which I hear is not now the Case; Then the Bank of England Notes would often circulate through one hundred persons hands & upwards, before any person would carry the same to the Bank to demand Money for them; which was the Case in this City with our Bank Notes also, till lately, but our Banks finding such large Calls on them for Specie for their Notes, for the purpose of sending the same to the East Indies, and Europe, now give but a *small* proportion of Cash in payment of Drafts on them, and the remainder in Bank Notes;—*but if this System is adopted*, & supposing that there is in the United States *a sufficient Quantity of Specie* with which the Duties of this new System might be paid, the 12th holder of the Government paper, which would be issued to carry this new System into Execution, would be paid with Specie for the same; but if not, said Government paper would be sunk by being paid to the 12th holder with Bank Notes.—Part of the national Debt might also be sunk each year by this System, as will plainly appear Sir, when I have fully described it to you.—The Quantity of Government Paper which would be issued each year for this purpose, would answer the end of Bank Notes for the *very short time* it would remain in Circulation, so that Trade might be carried on with more facility for ready money.—Each paper that was issued, would be sunk & discharged with Specie or Bank Notes, as soon as it had passed through the hands of the public Creditor, & the hands of ten other Persons, as the 12th holder of each Government paper would be paid the Money for the same; which 12th holder should be compelled by Law to deliver the same to some Treasury Officer, (of which one at least should be appointed in every City & Town in the

United States,) who should forward such paper to the Treasury Office that issued it; where when it was examined & found to be genuine, it should be cancelled; & if found to be forged, it should be traced to the Forger, who should be punished agreeably to Law.—For the more easy Detection of Forgeries, each Holder (beginning with the Public Creditor,) should be obliged to write his Name on the back of said Government paper before he passed it away; of Course the first Signature on the back of the paper (if forged) should be considered as the Forger; & the 12th Signature would be the Name of the person who had been paid the Amount of the same.—

Whether it was War or Peace, the Duty on the Government paper would *always be the same*, that is 10 ℔ Cent on the Amount of the paper issued.—

The public Creditor (to whom the paper was issued in payment of what was due to him,) should pay no Duty thereon when he paid the same away; but if he afterwards took it in payment of Merchandize sold, or on any other Account, he should when he afterwards paid it away, pay the same Duty of 10 ℔ Cent thereon that any other person paid.—

I propose that the Government paper issued, should be called *Government Certificates*; which should certify that such an Amount was due to such a person (expressing his Name) by the Government of the United States.—And in order to make the Certificates more negociable, each Certificate should be issued for the Sum of 10 Dollars,* so that the Duty which each of the 10 persons, who paid the Duty, would have to pay on the same (after it had passed out of the hands of the public Creditor,) would be 1 Dollar; which would make up the 10 Dollars, the Amount of the Certificate.—The Person who had paid the last tenth part of the Duty, would pay away the Certificate to some other person with the 10 Dollars.—This last person should deliver the Certificate to the Treasury Officer, of the City or Town in which he lived; who should forward it to the Treasury Department for it to be examined & cancelled.

On the Margin of each Certificate should be stamped the Figures 1, 2, 3, 4, 5, 6, 7, 8, 9, 10.—After the public Creditor had endorsed any Certificate & paid it away without paying any Duty with it, the next person that paid it away, should cut off the figure 1, & give one

*When Government paid the public Creditors with these Certificates, if the Sum to be paid to any Creditor was short of the Sum of 10 Dollars, such public Creditor should give the Change of a ten Dollar Certificate in Money to Government, which Change could be applied to the paying some Expenses of Government, which on a Number of payments in that Situation would amount to a very considerable Sum of Money.—

Dollar with it when he paid it away,—the second that paid it away should cut off the figure 2, & give 2 Dollars with it,—the third person cut off the 3, & give 3 Dollars,—the fourth person the 4, & give 4 Dollars,—the fifth person the 5, & give 5 Dollars,—the sixth person the 6, & give 6 Dollars,—the seventh person the 7, & give 7 Dollars,—the eighth person the 8, & give 8 Dollars, the ninth person the 9, & give 9 Dollars—the tenth person the 10, & give 10 Dollars; so that each person who paid the Duty would sink 10 ℔ Cent on the Amount of the Certificate; which 10 ℔ Cent each would lay on the Amount of the Goods they sold for such Certificate.—

This System of Taxation would greatly lessen the Number of Revenue Officers.—

Though no Duties or Excise on Merchandize imported would exist after this System took place, there should still be Custom Houses, in order that every Importer should declare there on Oath, the Value of the Goods he imported; & every Exporter the Value of what he exported, by which Government would be able to ascertain the Balance of Trade of this Country.

I hope Sir, I have explained my System so as that you may fully comprehend my meaning, should you wish for any further Explanation, you have only to let me know the same.—

with the greatest Respect & Veneration, I remain sir, Your most obedt Servant EDWARDS PIERCE.

PS.—

The Custom Houses could receive the Duties on Tonnage of Vessels as at present.

RC (ViW: Tucker-Coleman Collection); endorsed by TJ as received 17 Apr. and so recorded in SJL. Enclosed in Gallatin to TJ, 23 Apr.

To Gideon Granger

Monticello Mar. 31. 05.

Th: Jefferson asks the favor of the Postmaster genl. to let no papers be sent from his office to him at this place after the post which shall leave Washington on Friday next, the 5th. of April. he presents him his salutations.

PoC (DLC).

To Robert Smith

Dear Sir Monticello Mar. 31. 05.

Your favor of the 27th. was recieved yesterday proposing to advance Lieutenants Sterett and Hull to be captains, nobody feels more strongly than I do the desire of encouraging by just rewards the enterprize of our officers, and especially should I be gratified by the promotion of Lt. Sterett who first taught our countrymen that they were more than equal to the pirates of the Mediteranean. but I have not here the means of knowing what is the number of Captains the laws permit us to have, nor whether we already have them. I remember that by one act we were to reduce the number to nine; but whether the small vessels added to our navy allows additional captains I know not; nor do I recollect with sufficient certainty the number we have. I have however signed the commissions, because you have I presume satisfied yourself that the measure is both proper & lawful, or you can satisfy yourself, having all the means at hand. if it be clearly allowed by the law, you will deliver the commissions. if it be doubtful it will be better to take time to consider & consult about it; as to have to revoke the measure would do much more harm than the taking time to keep in the right.

I shall leave this on my return within a fortnight & would wish nothing to be sent me after the departure of next Friday's post (Apr. 5.) Accept my affectionate salutations and assurances of great esteem & respect Th: Jefferson

PoC (DLC); at foot of first page: "The secretary of the navy." Notation in SJL: "Sterett & Hull."

TJ mistook Andrew sterett for Charles Stewart (Smith to TJ, 19 Apr.).

equal to the pirates: on 1 Aug. 1801, Sterett, in command of the schooner *Enterprize*, captured a Tripolitan corsair after a three-hour battle. TJ had personally congratulated Sterett on his accomplishment (Vol. 36:3).

reduce the number: the Naval Peace Establishment Act of 3 Mch. 1801 reduced the number of captains in the U.S. Navy to nine (U.S. Statutes at Large, 2:111).

additional captains: neither of the laws approving additional schooners, brigs, and gunboats for the navy, dated 28 Feb. 1803 and 26 Mch. 1804, expanded the officer corps (same, 206, 292).

the number we have: as of 1 Jan. 1805, the navy had 10 captains due to the promotion of Stephen Decatur, Jr., the previous year for his meritorious service in the destruction of the captured frigate *Philadelphia* (Christopher McKee, *A Gentlemanly and Honorable Profession: The Creation of the U.S. Naval Officer Corps, 1794-1815* [Annapolis, 1991], 473; Vol. 43:476; Vol. 44:703-4).

Statement of Salary from Benjamin H. Latrobe

[March 1805]

Salary of the Surveyor of the public Buildings

Dr.			Cr.	
Decr. 29 to March 1st.	60 days.		By one Years pay 1804.	1.700
April 17th.	9		Balance, loss on this Engagement	86.62
July 1.	13			1.786.62
Oct. 20.	11			
Decr. 13.	15			
	108 days			
To. 108 deduct salary from Ches: & Del. Canal Co @ $3.500 ⅌ Annum		1041.12		
To Jo. Lenthall		400.00		
To travelling expenses		68.00		
To extra expenses at Washington		215.00		
To $\frac{1}{8}$ of DeMun's salary (Clerk) @ 500		62.50		
		1.786.62		

MS (DLC); undated; in Latrobe's hand; endorsed by TJ as received March 1805.

Notes on Appointments

[March 1805]

✓ James Wilkinson of Maryland Governor of the territory of Louisiana from the 3d. day of July next for 3. years then next ensuing unless sooner &c.

✓ Joseph Browne of New York Secretary for the Territory of Louisiana from the 3d. day of July &c.

✓ Return Jonathan Meigs of Louisiana,
✓ John B. C. Lucas of Pensylvania
✓ Rufus Easton of New York
} to be judges of the court of the territory of Louisiana from & after the 3d. day of July next.

✓ James Brown late of Kentucky, now of Orleans to be Attorney of the US. for the district of Orleans.[1]

✓ George Duffield of Tennissee to be a judge of the Superior Court, of the territory of Orleans.
he resides at Greeneville in Greene county Tennissee[2]

✓ John Thompson of Kentucky to be Register of the land office in the territory of Orleans on the red river or it's waters

✓ John W. Gurley of Orleans
or
✓ James Tremble of Tennissee
or
} to be Register of the land office in the Territory of Orleans on both sides of the Missisipi exclusive of the red river & it's waters

Benjamin Sebastian of Kentucky
or John Kennedy of Tennissee[3]
} Recorder for the territory of Louisiana.

Hezekiah Huntington of Connecticut to be Attorney for the US. in the district of Connecticut.

John B. Scott of Virginia to be a Colonel Commandant in the territory of Louisiana.

Consuls. ✓ Henry Hill junr. of New York for the island of Cuba.
✓ Edward Carrington of Rhodeisland at Canton.
qu. ✓ James M. Henry of Virginia to be Agent at Jamaica. v. Savage

6. Commissioners for Louisiana, Red river & Misipi
J. Dawson of Virga
Benj. Sebastian of Kentucky
John Kennedy of Tennissee
Noah Lester
or Pomeroy } of Connecticut
Richard Parrot. Columbia. to be a justice of peace

MS (DLC: TJ Papers, 155:27139); undated, but see below; entirely in TJ's hand.

Almost all of the names on this list had been recommended as candidates for appointment before or during March 1805. TJ forwarded the names with check marks next to them in a letter of 11 Mch. to Madison, which adopted some of the same phrasing as the notes above, as in the description of James Wilkinson's appointment and in the discussion of the residence of GEORGE DUFFIELD. At some point, Gideon Granger brought to TJ's attention the possibility of nominating HEZEKIAH HUNTINGTON to succeed Pierpont Edwards as U.S. attorney for Connecticut. A letter of 25 Jan. from Robert Fairchild, Elijah Boardman, Epaphras W. Bull, and James Stevens assured Granger that Huntington's appointment would meet with "universal approbation" from the state's Republicans. On the verso of the letter, TJ wrote: "Huntington Hezekiah to be District Atty Connecticut v. Edwards. G: Granger says Huntington & Spalding stand on the most eminent ground of any republican lawyers in the state. Huntington. poor, a uniform & persecuted republicn. Spalding, rich. & not coming foward till after victory" (DNA: RG 59, LAR). TJ likely added the name of JOHN B. SCOTT late in the month after William Branch Giles recommended Scott in a letter of 12 Mch. that is recorded in SJL as received 21 Mch. with the notation "John B. Scott to be Commdt." but has not been found. That letter probably enclosed a recommendation of 10 Dec. 1804 from Abraham B. Venable to Giles (DNA: RG 59, AOC; endorsed by TJ: "Scott Genl. John B. to be Commandt. Louisiana v. Kennon").

Under the provisions of an act passed on 2 Mch., Orleans Territory was to have two land offices and Louisiana District one, with each land office assigned two COMMISSIONERS. TJ appears to have been compiling a preliminary list of candidates for these commissions from individuals who had requested or been recommended for other positions. John Dawson, for example, had expressed interest in the governorship of Michigan Territory, and Noah Lester and Ralph POMEROY had also applied for positions there. By the end of April, when TJ forwarded his selections for the land commissions to the State Department, candidates were at least partially based on deliberations that occurred in April (U.S. Statutes at Large, 2:327-8; Lester to TJ, 9 Feb.; Pomeroy to TJ, 17 Feb.; Dawson to TJ, 12 Mch.; Gallatin to TJ, 18 Apr.; TJ to the State Department, 30 Apr.).

[1] Entry interlined.

[2] Sentence interlined.

[3] Sebastian's and Kennedy's entries here have been marked through with a large "X."

From John Davis

SIR, April 1, 1805

I take the liberty to send you my second pamphlet. I shall be enabled the middle of this Month to send you Captain Smith & the princess Pocahontas. My Notice of it is so popular in Virginia that, even from Williamsburgh, there have been sent me the names of 50 Subscribers.

I believe I shall be favoured by the "Philosophical Society" of this City with the transcript of a Manuscript intituled "The Genealogy of Pocahontas": This together with Captain Smith's Letters to Queen Anne (confirming my Story) will form a good appendix, and be

Confirmations strong as proofs of holy Writ.

I am, Sir, With profound respect, Your extremely obliged, & most obedient Servant,

JOHN DAVIS.

RC (DLC); endorsed by TJ as received 17 Apr. and so recorded in SJL, where TJ recorded it as received from Philadelphia. Enclosure: the "second book" of *The Philadelphia Pursuits of Literature: A Satirical Poem* by Juvenal Junius, published in Philadelphia in 1805 (see *Aurora*, 27 Mch., and Davis to TJ, 1 Mch.).

POPULAR IN VIRGINIA: Davis listed the names of more than 30 subscribers from Williamsburg in the back matter of *Captain Smith and Princess Pocahontas*. An appendix also included a letter of support from Williamsburg professor Louis H. Girardin (*Captain Smith and Princess Pocahontas, An Indian Tale* [Philadelphia, 1805], 147-8, 159-73).

In an appendix, Davis recounted his unsuccessful attempt to view a manuscript from the American Philosophical Society on the GENEALOGY OF POCAHONTAS that purportedly established that TJ's son-in-law Thomas Mann Randolph was descended from Pocahontas (same, 134-5; see also undated manuscript by Thomas Mann Randolph, "Notes on the Genealogy of Pocahontas," in DLC: TJ Papers, Series 6, Randolph Family Manuscripts).

Davis also included a June 1616 letter of petition that John Smith claimed to have written to QUEEN ANNE on behalf of Pocahontas (*Captain Smith and Princess Pocahontas*, 125-30).

From Gideon Granger

DEAR SIR General Post Office April 1st. 1805

I have now the honor to enclose a continuam of Mr Eastons communication, and the pleasure to inform you that the New Orleans mail, via Fort Stoddart, will, at furthest, be in opperation by the 15th of May next.

I pray you to accept my congratulations on the brilliant success of our friends in New Hampshire and on our certain prospects in Massachusetts—

With great esteem and respect Yours affectionately

GIDN GRANGER

RC (DLC); at foot of text: "The President"; endorsed by TJ as received 4 Apr. and so recorded in SJL.

For Rufus Easton's previous COMMUNICATION, see Easton to TJ, 17 Jan.

ENCLOSURE

Continuation of Rufus Easton's Communication on Louisiana

Communication—continued

Should a sentiment that prevailed among some members of Congress last winter and which originated from the Landed interest be carried into effect it would prove injurious to the United States—ruinous to the Western Country and infringe the rights of the people—it is the disposition to retard the progress of settlement on the west side of the Mississippi to which I allude—It will require no argument to prove this—it depends on fact—For should the western bank of the Mississippi remain unsettled the first disturbance or rupture with the Indian Tribes would either totally cut off the navigation of the river or render it too perilous to carry on that communication and intercourse so absolutely necessary between the upper and lower country to transport to market its vast produce—No benefit would be derived from the Lead mines rich sources of wealth to the country and the manufacture of Salt iron and various other articles needful to a large portion of the settlements on the east side of the Mississippi not having a sufficient supply of those articles would be prevented and that equality of rights and privileges the brightest ornaments of a Republican government destroyed—

It might be just as well as good policy in the national Legislature to mark a certain line of Longitude including all the settlements west—and say to the emigrant or to the citizen—*this far mayest thou go but no farther.*

A strong frontier settlement would thereby be formed sufficient in a short time to protect itself against the ravages of the Indians, should any dare to molest—the navigation of the Mississipi secured and the general prosperity of the United States felt from an enhanced value of the public lands in the interior—

Notwithstanding there may be solid objections to giving a representative form of Government to the Orleans territory—yet from the manners habits and dispositions of the People of this District I would propose that here as the best form—Independent of the large majority of Americans already amongst us who are attached to this mode of Government the greatest equality prevails among the French inhabitants—a civil quiet people—easily governed—and although they are ignorant of the principles of every species of Government their attachment might be gained to the most republican form—

Saint Genevieve is the only village over which a Priest can have any influence—and from the liberality of the Parsons sentiments who is settled there no difficulty could be apprehended from him—

One branch of the Legislature to be composed of a member from each district with the addition of one more for every five hundred Electors to be chosen by the Citizens from their body, would be most desirable—the remainder of the Government might be for the present in all respects the same or similar to the first grade of Territorial Government within the United States—Except that the Governor should have power only by his negative to suspend the operation of a Law till the opinion of Congress thro the Representation of a Territorial Delagate should be had thereon—

The office of Commodant of Districts can be of no manner of use here—surely it cannot be the intention of our Government to drive the settler from his possession without a trial or without a hearing—and it is confidently believed that resistance to the Sheriff or any other civil officer will prove less frequent in this Country than in any portion of the Union—

The salaries of these officers distributed among the militia as a reward for actual time spent in military improvement would prove far more beneficial—or probably an equivalent satisfaction for the services of those who have it in charge to prosecute on behalf of the United States with the means of procuring the attendance of witnesses would more happily and promptly tend to the due administration of justice and the prevention of those *offences* which it has been intended these Commodants should remove.

In the Indiana Territory the attorney General has little more than nothing for his services—a witness gets nothing for his attendance and no means are provided for reimbursing the expences of the person who undertakes the subpoenaing of witnesses on a criminal prosecution—

A man in an honorable line of life, has been almost four years under our arrest upon a charge of perjury—no witness has as yet appeared against him, and the judge refused to discharge the defendant because the witnesses did not attend—The intentions of the Judge may be pure and upright, but the constitution and the Law becomes a dead letter—While the guilty escape the innocent are punished—I do not mention this as a solitary instance numerous cases of the kind might be stated—

The Government notwithstanding the security of the law in that case provided will be troubled by unauthorised settlers upon the public Lands. It was the general practice before the first day of October last for every emigrant coming to the country to settle down upon the public Lands and the same practice has obtained more or less since that time—The law on this subject was well known in this country early in May last—It had been promulgated thro the channel of various newspapers which circulated here—and we find the *convention rational* debating upon the Sanguinary act as they stile at the commencement of September last yet the memorial states they are to be punished for breach of laws they never knew and to suffer imprisonment for disobediance to such as they have not the means of knowing—That the Laws have not been published in the French Language may be considered a serious as well as a just complaint—

These *squatters* upon the public Lands it will be impossible for the Commodants to remove from their habitations unless it be at their own peril—There is no means to determine from the records whether the settler had legal right or not to settle—he may have a lawful permission from a Spanish Commodant in his pocket there is no method to compel him to shew his authority except in a court of Law—and how will the expences of the lawsuits be defrayed? A Government like this has no funds—it has not the means of raising any—The District must look to Congress and to them alone for money to discharge the public Burthens—It may be easily foreseen that the same difficulties which hitherto have existed in the Indiana will exist here in the administration of Public justice—

A very considerable revenue may in time be drawn from the Lead mines in this Country. At this time they are worthy the attention of the Government—The Gentleman who has written the disertation lately published on those mines would very gladly accept the agency on behalf of the United States without a Salary or any other reward than the exclusive privilege of purchasing in the mineral which would belong to the United States should congress think proper to pass a law to Lease or work the mines at a certain tax payable in mineral—

Suppose only 980,000 lbs of mineral to be annually taken from the mines (a less quantity than has been for several years past dug at those mines) at 25 Cents tax on each hundred weight would produce yearly 2,450 Dollars which at 2 Dlls. per Cwt the estimated value of mineral will purchase 122,500 lbs—

The profit in smelting this quantity of mineral will be a sufficient compensation to the Superintendant and the sum of 2,450 Dollars would annually be recived into the public Treasury without any expence to the United States.

This calculation is made on the supposition that the Public agent should engage in the smelting business—I venture to say that the Executive branch of the Government could not select a more capable and trusty character than Moses Austin Esquire who is now extensively engaged in that business and who would readily accept the proposition from the Government—

R. EASTON

MS (DLC: TJ Papers, 148:25853-9).

The PRIEST to whom Easton referred was probably James Maxwell, who was vicar general for upper Louisiana and resided in the Ste. Genevieve settlements before and after the cession to the United States (Carl J. Ekberg, *Colonial Ste. Genevieve: An Adventure on the Mississippi Frontier*, 2d ed. [Tucson, Ariz., 1996], 407-10).

THE JUDGE in question was either Thomas T. Davis, Henry Vander Burgh, or John Griffin, who traveled from Indiana Territory to hold courts in Louisiana District (Logan Esarey, ed., *Messages and*

Letters of William Henry Harrison, 2 vols. [Indianapolis, 1922; repr., New York, 1975], 1:88-9, 170-1; *Terr. Papers*, 7:188-9).

LAW ON THIS SUBJECT: section 14 of the act "erecting Louisiana into two territories," which barred settlement on any lands belonging to the United States (U.S. Statutes at Large, 2:287-9). For the meetings held in September 1804 and the resulting MEMORIAL, see William Henry Harrison to TJ, 6 Nov. 1804, and Easton to TJ, 17 Jan.

DISERTATION LATELY PUBLISHED: *A Summary Description of the Lead Mines in Upper Louisiana*, by MOSES AUSTIN, published in Washington in 1804.

To James Madison

DEAR SIR Monticello Apr. 1. 05.

Yours of the 27th. is recieved. I put Lattimore's letter into my bundle of Agenda to be acted on in due time. Monroe's, Pinckney's & Jarvis's are now returned. I suspect that Pinckney gives us the true design of Gr. Br. to be to oust the French & Dutch from our quarter & leave the Spaniards & Portuguese. it is possible she would rather see these two last in possession of the Southern continent than any other nation. it is really of good augury that Taleyrand should have been silent about the Western boundary of Louisiana, & I have no doubt Monroe will make the most of it. should it end in our getting the navigation of the Mobile only we must make our protestation to Spain that we reserve our right which neither time nor silence is to lessen & shall assert it when circumstances call for it. in the mean time propose the keeping it in statu quo, unsettled. I shall be glad that nothing be forwarded to me here after the mail which leaves Washington on Friday the 5th. Accept my affectionate salutations & assurances of constant esteem & respect. TH: JEFFERSON

RC (DLC: Madison Papers); at foot of text: "Mr. Madison." PoC (DLC). Notation in SJL: "Lattimore. Monroe. Pinckney. Jarvis. Louisa." Enclosures: see Madison to TJ, 17 and 27 Mch.

From James Madison

DEAR SIR Washington Apl. 1. 1805

I find by a letter just recd. from Mr. Tomkins that he declines the appointment lately given him; so that it will be necessary for you to think of another Successor to Judge Hobart. Writing at present without having the letter by me I can not inclose it

A decree of Genl. Ferrand commanding at St. Domingo dated the 5th. of Feby. has just been forwarded from N. York, which transcends every former instance of barbarous misconduct towards neutrals. It subjects to *death* all persons on board vessels allied as well as neutral, bound *to* or *from* ports occupied by the blacks, *or* found within two leagues of any such port; and the trial in those cases is to be by *military commission*. The decree is to operate after the 21. of April. Turreau is on an excursion to Baltimore. On his return which will probably be in a day or two: I shall make this atrocious proceeding the subject of a conference with him, and shall urge his interposition immediately with Ferrand. It will of course be a subject of proper representation to the French Govt; but a remedy thro that circuit must not be waited for. Will it be proper for this Dept. to address directly to Ferrand a warning agst. the execution of the decree on Citizens of the U. States? The conversation with Turreau may perhaps decide this question.

With respectful attachment Yrs. truly JAMES MADISON

RC (DLC); at foot of text: "The President"; endorsed by TJ as received from the State Department on 4 Apr. and "Tomkins declines. Ferrand's decree" and so recorded in SJL.

LETTER: Daniel Tompkins wrote to Madison on 27 Mch. to turn down TJ's nomination as U.S. district judge for New York (RC in DNA: RG 59, RD; addressed in Madison's hand: "The President of the United States Monticello"; endorsed by TJ: "Tomkins Danl. D. declines commn. of judge").

The DECREE issued by General Louis Ferrand, commander of the French forces at Santo Domingo, was part of a wider French effort to constrain Haiti's commercial connections and ultimately to overturn the new nation's independence. It was directed in particular at merchants based in Curaçao, St. Thomas, and the United States. Madison received a translated copy from merchant John F. Brown in New York, to whom it had been sent by the acting consul in St. Thomas, Owen Ewers. Summary accounts of the decree were current in American newspapers by early April, and a translation circulated by the middle of the month (Julia Gaffield, *Haitian Connections in the Atlantic World: Recognition after Revolution* [Chapel Hill, 2015], 30-50, 126, 131; Madison, *Papers, Sec. of State Ser.*, 9:189, 133-4; Baltimore *American, and Commercial Daily Advertiser*, 1 Apr., 12 Apr.).

CONFERENCE: Madison wrote to French minister Louis Marie Turreau on 4 Apr. to protest Ferrand's actions (Madison, *Papers, Sec. of State Ser.*, 9:210-11).

From Archibald McDonald

[on or before 1 Apr. 1805]

To his Excellency Thomas Jefferson President of the United States
The Humble Petition of Archibald McDonald Humbly Sheweth

That your Petitioner has served the United States Ten years from St Clears defeat to the year 1802. then discharged and now Infirm and having a sickly wife and unable to support himself and family without the Assistance of a Son which is now under age and enlisted in the states service, which was of great support before enlistment to myself and family, your Petitioner humbly implores the assistance of his Excellency in order to gain his Sons discharge he being under Age and would be of great Assistance he helping to support a distressed family, if your Petitioner should be so happy as to get his discharge your Petitioner shall be in duty bound to Ever pray

ARCHIBALD MCDONALD

The under named Subscribers will certify the *service* of the above Petitioner, and the books at the War Office can testify the same—

E SMITH
JOHN SMITH
ROBT. WOOD

RC (MHi); undated; attestation in McDonald's hand, signed by Smith, Smith, and Wood; endorsed by TJ as received 1 Apr. and so recorded in SJL with notation "petn to discharge son as infant."

Archibald McDonald lived in Winchester, Virginia. He likely served as a private in Lieutenant Colonel William Darke's regiment, which was levied for Arthur St. Clair's expedition into the Northwest Territory in 1791 (DNA: RG 94, Compiled Service Records of Volunteer Soldiers Who Served from 1784 to 1811; Washington, *Papers, Pres. Ser.*, 8:55-7).

From Neill McPhaill

MAY IT PLEASE YOUR EXCELLENCY.—
MOST HOUNOURED SIR Fort Mifflin April 1st. 1805

To accept the Pettition most Humbly Adressed By me the Pettitioner Thereof and Hopes Most Worthy Sir that Your Excellency will Grant the Requist of Sir Your Faithfull Servent Being forwarded and Bore Date the first of January Last Stating My Situation and the Place of my Nativity—Supposing Sir that my letter of Pettition Hath not Reached Your Excellency—. I Hope to Merit the Reguard of your Person in this As my Desire is Not for Pomp or Riches More then the Support of my Family as Natures Law Binds me to be their Support: and Sir the Grade I Posess is that of Corporel in the Company of my worthey Captn. Jas. Read Stationed at Fort Mifflin, and all my Desire is Onley to Gain the Rank of Cadett in Either this Regt or any of the Infantry

I ame Solitious to Gain the Santion of Your Excellency as my Desire is to Serve under a Republican authority During my Life—america hath Been an asylum to me and the Republican Sentiments I Enjoy hath made me Free as in all Spheres of Life I ame at Liberty—I also

Remark that I ame fully aquanted with the Deciplin of Infantry—in forming and Desplaying as Having Served in Great Britain Several Years
Sir
the aid I Requair I will with the Strickist Attention Observe with Fedility if Conferd Upon Your Servant And I Request the fiavour of an answer to Sir this Pettion and hope to Be forgiven for my Boldness in Writing and in the Familliar mode of my application—I Have Remarked in my Last that I have a Small Family to Support which is the Cause of my Pettition
Perhaps the spirit of Philanthrophy may overcome adversity as it is the Paternal Frend of men I Solicit
Most Worthey Sir I. Requist Your Answer and Aid—

I For Ever must Remain with Fedelity and Desires to Serve with Respect As your Humble and Obedient Servt.

NEILL MC.PHAILL

RC (DLC); endorsed by TJ as received 19 Apr. and so recorded in SJL.

Neill McPhaill left the military within two years of his letter to TJ and after having served five years under Captain James Read. In 1807, he wrote to Dearborn from Columbiana County, Ohio, to apply for re-enlistment as a commissioned officer in the artillery or infantry, but his request was denied (12 Oct. 1807, in DNA: RG 94, Letters Received by the Office of the Adjutant General, 1805-1811).

McPhaill's letter of the FIRST OF JANUARY has not been found but is recorded in SJL (see Vol. 45:735).

From John Milledge

SIR, Executive Department, Georgia. Louisville, 1st. April, 1805.

I have the honor to transmit you agreeably to the wish of the legislature of this state, a schedule of the claims of the citizens of Georgia, against the creek nation of Indians. The respective claims are established on the oath of one or more disinterested persons, and deposited in this office. You will also find transmitted a copy of the Journal of the commissioners appointed by me to claim and receive from the Indians negroes and other property as mentioned in schedule, the journal fully states the result of their mission; and information particularly important, in as much as it points out the place at which the Uchee creek or river empties into the Chatahoochie, which is some distance below that mentioned in the deed of cession and agreement, between the United States, and Georgia.

I have the honor to be with the greatest respect & consideration, yr. mo. obt. servt. JOHN MILLEDGE

FC (Lb in G-Ar: Governors' Letter Book); at foot of text: "Thomas Jefferson, President of the United States, City of Washington." Recorded in SJL as received 23 Apr. Enclosures not found.

CLAIMS: in conformity with an 11 Dec. 1803 resolution by the Georgia legislature, Milledge had appointed commissioners to meet with the Creeks and demand the return of property taken at various times from the citizens of Georgia, or restitution. In his message to legislators on 5 Nov. 1804, the governor reported that the mission was unsuccessful and presented copies of his instructions and an extract from the commissioners' journal to prove that their exertions "were not wanting" in the matter (*Columbian Museum & Savannah Advertiser*, 24 Nov. 1804). For Milledge's earlier communication on the subject of claims against the Creeks, see Milledge to TJ, 5 Aug. 1803.

For the terms of the 1802 CESSION AND AGREEMENT regarding Georgia's western land claims and the location of its western boundary, see TJ to the Senate and the House of Representatives, 26 Apr. 1802.

From João F. Oliveira Fernandes

MONSIEUR Norfolk 1er. d'Avril 1805

La branche dé Commerce, que j'ai établi, pour fixer dans cette Ville un de mes plus proches parents, m'ayant procuré l'honneur de recevoir vos Ordres, comme commerçant, pour une petite Commission, dont le Montant, je viens de recevoir; permettes, Monsieur, que je profite L'occasion pour m'addresser à vous comme philosophe naturaliste, et vous envoyer un produit du Regne Animal; le quel n'etant pás si rare pour óccupér une place dans votre Cabinet d'Histoire Naturelle, Vous será peût-être util dans vos prómenades rustiques, pendant votre séjour à Monticéllo.

Excusér, Monsieur, je vous en prie, la libérté que je prends: (Mes intentions n'etant pàs d'autres, que Cèlles qui doit avoir un etranger desiroux de temoigner son respect et sà reconnoissance envers le digne Chef d'un Peuple, parmi le quel il á trouvé un asyle dans Ses malheurs;) j'espere que Vous vous daignerés rendre justice à la pureté des Sentimens de la plus haute consideration et estime avec les quels j'ai l'honneur d'être

Monsieur Votre tres humble et tres Obéissant Servtr.

JEAN F. DE OLIVEIRA FERNANDES

EDITORS' TRANSLATION

SIR, Norfolk, 1 Apr. 1805

The business that I have established for settling one of my close relatives in this city has afforded me the honor of receiving your orders for a small commission. Allow me, Sir, to take advantage of this occasion to address you as a wise natural philosopher and to send you a product of the animal kingdom. Although it is not rare enough to occupy a place in your natural history collection, it might be useful in your country walks at Monticello.

I beg you, Sir, to forgive my forwardness. My intentions are simply those of a foreigner who wishes to show his respect and gratitude toward the worthy leader of a people among whom he found refuge from his misfortunes. I hope you will look kindly upon the sincere sentiments of respect and esteem with which I have the honor of being, Sir, your very humble and obedient servant.
JEAN F. DE OLIVEIRA FERNANDES

RC (DLC); at head of text: "Monsieur Thomas Jefferson"; endorsed by TJ as received 18 Apr. and so recorded in SJL.

UN PRODUIT DU REGNE ANIMAL: a walking stick fashioned from an animal bone with a gold handle. The object and Oliveira Fernandes's letter became separated, so that when the walking stick arrived in the summer of 1805 its origin was at first a mystery. TJ bequeathed it to Madison, who passed it on to Thomas Jefferson Randolph (Stein, *Worlds*, 428-9; Anne Cary Randolph to TJ, 11 July 1805; TJ to Oliveira Fernandes, 28 Feb. 1806; Oliveira Fernandes to TJ, 15 Mch. 1806).

Petition of Simon Stedecorn, with Jefferson's Order

TO THE PRESIDENT OF THE UNITED STATES—

The Petition of Simon Steadicorn humbly represents—That your Petitioner some time in the year 1804 was indicted in the County of Alexandria in two instances for assaults charged to have been committed by him upon One Christian G. Pasche, and at the November term last the said Indictments were tried, and your Petitioner was find in one case Twenty five dollars and the Costs and in the other the sum of one Cent and the Costs. all which will more fully appear by a short copy of the Judgments herewith exhibited—Your Petitioner saith that when the Judgmts. aforesaid were renderd against him he was committed to Goal in the said County of Alexandria and was by the Judgment of the Court to remain there untill he paid the said fines and Costs—Your Petitioner saith that he is intirely insolvent, and wholly unable to pay the said Judgments or any part thereof, and hath ever since his commitment aforesaid been wholly unable to pay the same—Your Petitioner saith that he is old and feeble, and from the confinement which he has sufferd together with the severity of the Winter he hath been brought to the point of death, and altho he is now somewhat better he is still in a very sickly state of health—Your Petitioner hath no hopes of being able to procure from any friend or acquaintance or any one else the means of discharging the said Judgments and consequently hath no hopes of a release from his present confinement but by the interposition of your Excelency, who possesses exclusively the power of extending to your Petitioner the priveledge of a release from Goal by a remission of his fines—and your Petitioner Humbly hopes that the said benifit may be extended to him &c. SIMON STEDECORN

County of Alexandria Sct:

Simon Steadicorn appeared before me a Justice of the peace for the County aforesaid and made oath that the several matters and things in the foregoing Petition containd are true—Given under my hand this 1st. day of April 1805. A FAW

As Goaler of the County of Alexandria I hereby Certify that the within mentined Simon Steadicorn has been confind as within stated— JAS. CAMPBELL

I believe the facts stated in the within Petition to be true— L SUMMERS D M

Believing the facts stated in the within petition to be true we respectfully recommend to the President of United States to grant the prayer thereof W. CRANCH.
N FITZHUGH

[*Order by TJ*:]

Apr. 9. 1805:

Let a pardon issue TH: JEFFERSON

RC (DNA: RG 59, GPR); petition in a clerk's hand, signed by Stedecorn; attestation in the same hand, signed by Abraham Faw; following Faw's attestation, the following text was canceled: "We the undersignd subscribers do hereby Certify we beleive the several matters set forth in the within Petition are true as therein stated"; certifications by James Campbell and Lewis Summers in their hands and signed by them; recommendation of judges in William Cranch's hand, signed by Cranch and Nicholas Fitzhugh. Recorded in SJL as received 8 Apr. Enclosures not found.

TJ pardoned Stedecorn on 17 Apr., remitting his fines and fees (FC in Lb in DNA: RG 59, GPR).

From George Jefferson

DEAR SIR Richmond 2d. April 1805.

Your favor of the 24th ultimo inclosing the manifests of your Tobacco I have received.

I have been endeavouring to make sale of the Tobacco, but as yet have not been able to do it at your limits; the most I am offered being 40/. on a credit of 120 days.—Impressions somewhat unfavorable with respect to the quality of your crop having been made on the minds of some persons who saw the duck'd Hhds, I thought it advisable to accede to the proposal of a Gentleman to open two hhds—on seeing which he declined taking it at your price; the Tobacco not being at all well assorted.—had some of the most indifferent even been burnt, I am confident that the remainder would have sold for as much as the whole will now command—but for that, there would be no necessity, as it might be stem'd (if the Overseer would take the trouble) by which mean there would be no loss sustained on that part, but a great gain in the remainder. On this subject however I believe I once before took the liberty of writing to you.

As you do not stand in immediate want of money, I think it will be best, notwithstanding what I have said, still to hold the Tobacco at the price you ask, as I think it rather probable than otherwise, that some advance in our Market may be expected.

I am Dear Sir Yr. Very humble servt. GEO. JEFFERSON

RC (MHi); at foot of text: "Thomas Jefferson esqr."; endorsed by TJ as received 4 Apr. and so recorded in SJL.

To Charles Smith

SIR Monticello April 2. 05

Mr. John Perry informs me he is indebted to you about one hundred & thirty pounds by bond now due, and that you would be willing to give him time on obtaining security. I am willing to be his security and to make the paiment for him in the first week of January next; if that shall be sufficient inducement to you to give him that time. this present letter shall bind me accordingly if you chuse to accept it as security. witness my hand this 2d. day of April 1805.

TH: JEFFERSON

PoC (MHi); at foot of text: "Mr. Charles Smith"; endorsed by TJ. Notation in SJL: "130. £ for J. Perry. Jan. 06."

JOHN PERRY INFORMS ME: Perry's letter of 27 Feb. 1805 has not been found (Vol. 45:737). In his financial memoranda TJ recorded the security for Perry under 3 Apr., but then canceled the entry with a notation "Not concluded" (MB, 2:1150).

From William Clark

Sir Fort Mandan April the 3rd. 1805.

It being the wish of Captain Lewis,[1] I take the liberty to send you, for your own perusal the notes which I have taken in the form of a journal in their original state. You will readily perceive in reading over those notes, that many parts are incorrect, owing to the variety of information received at different times, I most sincerely wish that leasure had permited me to offer them in a more correct form.

Receive I pray you my unfained acknowledgements for your friendly recollection of me in your letters to my friend and companion Captn. Lewis. and be assured of the sincere regard with which I have the honor to be.

Your most obedient and Humble Servent Wm Clark

RC (DLC); at foot of text: "The President of the US"; endorsed by TJ as received 13 July and so recorded in SJL. Dft (MoSHi: William Clark Papers, Clark Family Collection); in Clark's hand, with alterations in Meriwether Lewis's hand; dated 1 Apr. Enclosed in Lewis to TJ, 7 Apr. Enclosure not found, but see below.

The journal that Clark enclosed to TJ has not been positively identified. On 2 Apr. Clark noted his intention to send his journal to TJ, advising that it would cover the period "from the 13th of May 1804 untill the 3rd of April 1805" (Moulton, *Journals of the Lewis & Clark Expedition*, 2:14-17; 3:328).

[1] In Dft, Lewis interlined the preceding seven words in place of "As Capt Lewis has not Leasure to <*Send*> write a correct coppy journal of our proceedings &c."

To Thomas Claxton

Dear Sir Monticello Apr. 3. 05.

The inclosed applications from & on behalf of a mr Meer, relating to matters under your superintendance, I inclose them to you to do therein what you find best for the public interest, and add my salutations and assurances of esteem. Th: Jefferson

PoC (DLC); at foot of text: "Mr. Claxton"; with "Washington" in dateline overwritten to read "Monticello"; endorsed by TJ. Enclosures not found, but see below.

The applications were probably enclosed in John Meer to TJ, 23 Mch., not found (Appendix iv).

To Henry Dearborn

Dear Sir Monticello Apr. 3. 05.

I inclose you letters from P. Choteau & a mr Hay giving information of Capt Lewis. the information given by the former of the combination forming among the Machicoux (the Indians about Michigan I presume) is worthy attention. I wonder neither Governr. Harrison nor Wells have noted it. if true it may be proper for us to send a talk to each of the tribes, explaining our real intentions as to their lands, and our determination to consider the combination proposed as a proof of unfriendly intentions which we shall meet in a due manner. I have recieved two other quires of mr Dunbar's journals, but have not yet read them. I will bring them on with me. I have desired that nothing may be forwarded to me here after the 5th. as I shall be with you in a fortnight. Accept affectionate salutations & assurances of constant friendship & esteem Th: Jefferson

RC (PHi: Daniel Parker Papers); at foot of text: "Genl. Dearborne." PoC (DLC). Notation in SJL: "capt. Lewis. Machicoux. Dunbar." Enclosures: (1) Pierre Chouteau to TJ, 12 Feb. (2) John Hay to TJ, 12 Feb.

To Albert Gallatin

Dear Sir Monticello Apr. 3. 05.

Your favor of 26. March is recieved and I learn with real concern the danger that a temporary loan may be necessary, because we know how it will be perverted to throw dust in the eyes of the people. however if no other expedient can be used we must meet it—I have no expectation that Monroe will be able to get any acknolegement of boundary which we can admit. the next best measure will be to obtain a free use of the rivers of either party rising within the limits of the other, and that neither party shall either settle or fortify within the disputed country, until the limits can be fixed. this will give us time to await & avail ourselves of events.—I presume the appointment of Flowers may wait my return in the mean time the other may be heard from. I have desired the Postmaster Genl. to forward nothing to me here after the 5th. inst. as I expect to be with you in a fortnight. Accept affectionate salutations & assurances of constant friendship & respect. Th: Jefferson

RC (NHi: Gallatin Papers); at foot of text: "Mr. Gallatin." PoC (DLC). Notation in SJL: "loan. Monroe. Flowers."

To Benjamin H. Latrobe

DEAR SIR Monticello Apr. 3. 05.

I return you mr Lenthal's letter, on which the most painful observation is that it furnishes proof in addition to suggestions which have been recieved that he is not always in a state of temperance. should he take this turn, he would be a real loss. I have by this post desired mr Munroe to settle his account @ 4. D. a day, back from the beginning because that seems to have been his own desire. I am writing with a Polygraph made for billet paper. it is 11. by 15. I. but I have made a model for mr Peale showing that for the same sized paper it may be reduced to 8. by 12 I. I set out in ten days on my return to Washington. Accept friendly salutations & assurances of esteem & respect. TH: JEFFERSON

PoC (DLC); at foot of text: "Mr. Latrobe"; endorsed by TJ. Enclosure not found, but see Latrobe to TJ, 26 Mch.

MADE A MODEL: see TJ to Charles Willson Peale, 5 Apr.

To Thomas Munroe

SIR Monticello Apr. 3. 05.

The representations I have recieved satisfy me that mr Lenthall ought to be allowed 4. Dollars a day from the beginning. be so good therefore as to settle with him accordingly, or if a settlement has been made, to correct it in conformity herewith. Accept my salutations & assurances of esteem TH: JEFFERSON

P.S. I have desired that nothing may be forwarded to me here from the Post-office after the 5th.

RC (ViU). PoC (DLC); endorsed by TJ.

REPRESENTATIONS I HAVE RECIEVED: see Benjamin H. Latrobe to TJ, 26 Mch.

To Edward Tiffin

SIR Apr. 3. 1805

Your letter of Feb. 27. was recieved on the 26th. of March with a resolution of the General assembly of Ohio on the subject of a port of delivery at the mouth of Cayahoga. Congress had at their last session authorised the President to designate a port of entry & delivery for the district of Erie. considering Cayahoga as the most proper place for the purpose, I have concluded on that as the designation. in the course of the spring we expect to be able to organise the district. I am happy in being thus able to inform you that the General Assembly of Ohio will see their wishes carried into effect.

Accept my respectful salutations & assurances of great esteem and consideration. TH: JEFFERSON

RC (OClWHi); at foot of text: "Governor Tiffin." PoC (DLC).

TJ received Tiffin's LETTER on 21 Mch., not 26 Mch.

From Andrew Burns

SR. MAY IT PLEASE YOUR EXCELLANCY

Washington, Georgia April the 4th 1805

In consequence of a passage I saw some time past in the National Inteligencer: Wherein it appears that Congress had Directed your Excellancy to send some suitable Person to Louisiana to survey the Lead Mines of that Contry: also to ascertain the Lattitude and Longitude of them. Together with the Quantity and Quallity of the Oars—I wrote to General Meriweather Member of Congress from the State of Georgia upon the Subject. But fearing he May have left the Federal Cyty Ere my address Could arive.—I have thought proper thus to lay my views before your Excellancy

Which are these. Should your Excellancy see proper to appoint me I would go in Person, and do any thing, or Every thing Your Excellancy might require of me, touching the premises, aforesaid

The whole of the Georgia, Congressional, Representation, are personnally aqueant with me. And I trust I Should have their Suffrage as an Honest man—But as Some of them, as well as your Excellancy may not be aqueant with my Capability as an Artist. Suffer me to Inform your Excellancy in the first place, that I have been bred to the Silver Smith and Jewler Buisnes—In addition to Which I have Made oars and Fossils the Subjects of my Investigation. Aided in Pursuits of this kind By Professor Gellerts Metallurgick Chemestry I have been Successful in many Instances. But the mines or Banks of the Oars being out of my reach I was never any thing the Better—My aqueantances generally think me somewhat scientifick. But Still they may not know that I am Capable of Ascertaining the Lattitude & Longitude of a place. or that I understand Astronomy—As a proof of my Sapience, in that line Suffer me to predict to your Excellancy that there will be an Eclips of the Sun on the fifteenth day of June 1806 Eleven Oclock in the moring at this place. It will be total in the

Northern States. The Axis of the Earth at that time 5.° 30′ East of the Axis of the Ecliptick the Moons Lattitude No. descending the Sun in 25.° 45′ of Gemini

I have had the Honour in my time of filling many places of Publick Trust Which my Contry Men Can Attest

Suffer me further to add that *Should I be apointed* An old Gentln. Bred in the Mines of Wales and Cornwell of course us'd to the Smelting and refining of Oars. Will accompany me His Name is Charles Devaraux He was Brought from Waels by Collo. Chissel and wrought in his Lead Mines on New River—He, that is Devaroux Says That During Our Revolutionary War he Sold your Excellancy twenty thousand weight of Lead which you purchased for the Troops This Devaroux directed them works on New River during the War.

Inclosd I have thought proper to transmit Your Excellancy a Map of Louisiana, The Materials Collected and aranged by myself. The Authorities are Peleret De. Anvil Mitchel Billen & De. la. Ro[. . .] Together with Every Latter Information I could Collect on the Subj[ect]

Not Supposing in this I communicate any-thing New to your Excellancy—It is done Barely with a View to Show that I have Made the Geography of that Country in Some Measure my Studdy

Now the buisnes is have I done right: or have I done wrong: I dont know—One thing I know—That my Intentions are Pure And that amongst the many thousands that Compose the Agregate of the American Census there is not a Bosom more Ardenly Glows with the Amor Patri. or that is more firmly attached to the present happy Administration. than that of Your Excellancies

Most Devouted and Verry Humble Servant ANDW. BURNS

The later part the Honourable General James Jackson Can Attest I Should be happy to have a Reply

RC (DNA: RG 59, LAR); torn; at head of text: "Thomas Jefferson Esqr. President of the United States"; endorsed by TJ as received 30 Apr. and "to survey or explore" and so recorded in SJL. Enclosure not found.

Andrew Burns was among the early settlers of the area of Georgia that became Wilkes County. He later paid taxes on about 1,400 acres in that county and another 1,200 acres in Richmond County, as well as on four enslaved persons. Aligned with the revolutionary cause, he was elected a member of the First Provincial Congress of Georgia in 1775 and subsequently filled a number of leadership positions: justice of the peace, representative of the county to the state executive council, and state commissioner in at least two negotiations held with the Creeks (*Columbian Museum & Savannah Advertiser*, 22 Dec. 1797; Merrill Jensen, John P. Kaminski, Gaspare J. Saladino, and others, eds., *Documentary History of the Ratification of the Constitution*, 28 vols. to date [Madison, Wis., 1976-], 3:217; Grace Gillam Davidson, comp., *Early Records of Georgia: Wilkes County*, 2 vols. [Macon, Ga., 1932], 1:124; 2:60, 71-2; George White, comp., *Historical Collections of Georgia: Containing the Most Interesting Facts, Traditions, Biographical Sketches, Anecdotes, Etc. Relating to Its History and Antiquities, from Its First Settlement to the Present Time* [New York, 1854], 65, 123, 682; Vol. 34:593-4).

PROOF OF MY SAPIENCE: Burns's prediction was off by one day. A solar eclipse, total in the northern states, occurred on 16 June 1806 (*New-England Palladium*, 17 June 1806).

The AUTHORITIES Burns consulted for his map were likely Jean Palairet, Jean d'Anville, John Mitchell, Jacques Nicolas Bellin, and Louis Delarochette, all of whom produced maps of North America during the eighteenth century.

From David Gelston

SIR, New York April 4th. 1805

By the Ship Independence, from Leghorn, I have received a letter from Mr. Appleton, enclosing bill of lading for two boxes tuscan wine, said to contain one hundred bottles—

When opportunity offers I shall ship them to Alexandria or Georgetown, unless, you direct otherwise—

I have the honor to be, with great respect, Sir, your obedient servant DAVID GELSTON

RC (MHi); at foot of text: "Thomas Jefferson President United States"; endorsed by TJ as received 17 Apr. and so recorded in SJL with notation "100. b. vino del Carmine. Leghorn."

From Wilson Cary Nicholas

DEAR SIR Norfolk Apl. 4. 1805

I last night had the pleasure to receive your favour of the 26th. of march, your letter was delivered to Col. Newton this morning. he accepts the appointment. I this day write to Mr. Gallatin to request that I may be permitted to resign, and that my resignation may take place the 26th. of this month, by that time the business of the office will be as nearly up, as it is possible it ever shou'd be. In taking leave of this subject forever, I feel that I owe you an apology for the trouble that I have given you. Upon your goodness I rely for my[1] pardon. Be assured my Dear Sir, that no time or circumstances, can ever erase from my heart, the recollection of the weight of my obligations to you. The situation of the Pennsylvania & New York, and strong indications of the same spirit existing here, and elsewhere, gives me the most poignant concern. Can it be possible that our country is destined to go through the miseries that the revolution brought upon France? and that we are in the same way to be deprived of our liberty? I pray to God this may not happen, before it does, I am sure thousands, and thousands, of our best Citizens must be deprived of their lives. I fear it will be scarcely possible for you to avoid being embroiled with one of these parties, if an appointment shou'd be to be made in Pennsa. your preference of a man of either party, will be considered as making your election between them.

I am Dear Sir, with the greatest respect & esteem Your devoted

W. C. NICHOLAS

RC (DLC); endorsed by TJ as received 11 Apr. and so recorded in SJL.

[1] Nicholas here canceled "forgiveness."

From Samuel Smith

SIR/ Baltimore 4. April 1805

Mr. James Lowrey Donaldson, a young Gentleman of the Bar, of very handsome talents, has a disposition to reside in the Western Country. he has been 4 Years a practising Lawyer—and Studied four years prior thereto.—his Character is unblemished his Connexions respectable—his Politicks has been proved by some handsome pieces in the public Papers. they are Republican. his Age about 25—Permit me to recommend him as a Gentleman every way worthy of being appointed as One of the Commissioners for Ascertaining the Titles in Louisiana,—and to assure you that I shall feel myself particularly Obliged, and the public as benefited by the service that I Consider him Capable of rendering—My Brother Can give you any farther information that may be required respecting Mr. Donaldson

I am Sir/ your Mo. Obedt. Servt. S. SMITH

RC (DNA: RG 59, LAR); endorsed by TJ as received 17 Apr. and "Donaldson James Lowry to be Comr. Louisa." and so recorded in SJL.

On 5 Apr., James Lowry DONALDSON wrote to Smith's BROTHER, Secretary of the Navy Robert Smith, asking him to recommend Donaldson for a Louisiana commissioner's appointment. In addition to nearly eight years of legal study and practice, Donaldson had "some acquaintance" with the French language and "a slight smattering" of Spanish. Donaldson's father, William Lowry, wished to move with his family to Louisiana, and Donaldson's appointment would allow him to support the "numerous family" that would accompany him (RC in DNA: RG 59, LAR; endorsed by TJ: "to be Comr. Louisa.").

To John Barnes

Dear Sir Monticello Apr. 5. 05

Your favor of Mar. 26. was recieved yesterday and I now return you mr Taggert's letter, retaining his bill. the painter has been here about a week, and we are able to get some paints in the neighboring stores, for the present. I imagine those of Philadelphia are about now arriving in Richmond & may be here in a week or ten days. I expect to be with you about the 17th. health & weather permitting. accept my affectionate salutations & assurances of constant esteem

Th: Jefferson

PoC (Mrs. Edwin Page Kirk, Charlottesville, Virginia, 1956, on deposit at ViU); at foot of text: "Mr. Barnes." Enclosure not found, but see Barnes to TJ, 26 Mch.

From John Breckinridge and Buckner Thruston

Kentucky April 5. 1805.

Mr. Joshua Lewis of Jessamine County in this State having an intention of visiting Louisa., & being willing to serve as a Commr under the act of the last session of Congress for adjusting the titles to lands there; I can certify, that Mr. Lewis is a Gentn. of good Character, respectable Connections, good understanding & education, a practising Lawyer; & possesses the Confidence of his County, having often represented it in the legislature of this State.—I am informed, that he understands the French language, but can only speak from Information knowing nothing of that language myself

John Breckinridge

Kentucky April 5th. 1805.

The above Representation of Mr Lewis I believe to be just; In Addition I know that he has a tolerable knowledge of the French Language being able to translate with considerable Ease, and I think with a little practice would speak it fluently.

B. Thruston

RC (DNA: RG 59, LAR); written on the same sheet; endorsed by TJ as received 24 Apr. and "Lewis Joshua to be Comr. Westwd." and so recorded in SJL, as two letters connected by a brace with John Boyle to TJ, 20 Mch.

Buckner Thruston (1763-1845), originally of Gloucester County, Virginia, graduated from the College of William and Mary and then moved to Lexington, Kentucky, where he opened a law practice. After Kentucky became a state in 1792, Thruston served as the first clerk of the state senate and as a district and circuit court judge. In 1804, he was elected to the U.S. Senate, resigning the seat in 1809 to become judge of the circuit court of the

District of Columbia, a position he held until his death (*Biog. Dir. Cong.*; Lexington *Kentucky Gazette and General Advertiser*, 27 Nov. 1804; Vol. 32:570).

John Brown sent TJ a recommendation for Joshua Lewis that he had received from a member of the Dufour family in Kentucky. Written on 16 Apr. at First Vineyard, the letter stressed both Lewis's knowledge of THE FRENCH LANGUAGE and his skill at pronunciation (RC in DNA: RG 59, LAR; endorsed by TJ: "Lewis Joshua. to be Register Louisa.").

From Christian VII, King of Denmark

Denmark, 5 Apr. 1805. The king formally recalls Peder Blicher Olsen as resident minister and consul general to the United States.

Tr (DNA: RG 59, NL, Denmark); 2 p.; in a clerk's hand, in Latin; at head of text: "Copia"; at foot of text: "Ad Presidem Statuum confœderatorum Americo Septentionalis" ("to the president of the United States of America"); endorsed by Jacob Wagner; enclosed in Peder Pedersen to Madison, 15 Aug. (RC in same). Recorded in SJL as received 22 Aug.

The recall was at the request of Blicher Olsen, who had departed from the United States in 1803 on a leave of absence for reasons related to his health (Madison, *Papers, Sec. of State Ser.*, 10:214; Vol. 40:493-4).

From James Madison

DEAR SIR Washington Apl 5. 1805

Yours of the 1st. instant has been recd. with the letters of Jarvis Monroe & Pinkney. I had a conversation yesterday with Turreau on the subject of Ferrand's decree. He was perfectly rational and accommodating, expressed a wish to receive without delay a note from me on the subject, and promised to interpose as requested. He regretted that Logan's motion to prohibit the trade with St. Domingo, had not succeeded; observing that the Blacks had lately been enabled by American supplies to advance agst. Ferrand, & that the violence of his proclamation had been probably inspired by that circumstance. The Baltimore paper of yesterday, serves to confirm this circumstance, & with the addition, that the French are likely to be driven out of the Island. Inclosed is a copy of Ferrand's Edict, and of the letter I sent to Turreau. His answer has not yet been recd.

Yrs. with respectful attachment JAMES MADISON

RC (DLC); at foot of first page: "The President"; endorsed by TJ as received from the State Department on 8 Apr. and "Ferrand's decree. Tureau. Yrujo" and so recorded in SJL. Enclosures: (1) Proclamation of Louis Ferrand, 5 Feb. (see Madison to TJ, 1 Apr.). (2) Madison to Louis Marie Turreau, 4 Apr., arguing that Ferrand's proposed actions clearly violate accepted diplomatic norms and requesting that Turreau act to restrain him (Madison, *Papers, Sec. of State Ser.*, 9:210-11).

LOGAN'S MOTION: on 27 Feb. Senator George Logan of Pennsylvania sought to submit a bill "to suspend trade and intercourse with the island of St. Domingo." Because the act to regulate the clearance of armed merchant vessels was under consideration, Logan's motion did not carry (JS, 3:461; U.S. Statutes at Large, 2:342).

BALTIMORE PAPER OF YESTERDAY: likely the *Federal Gazette*. Relying on reports from arriving merchant vessel captains in early April, U.S. newspapers reported that Haitian forces were advancing against the remaining French forces in Santo Domingo. By mid-month, however, accounts suggesting that a French evacuation was imminent had been debunked (Baltimore *American and Commercial Daily Advertiser*, 4 Apr.; *New-York Evening Post*, 6 Apr., 13 Apr.; New York *Daily Advertiser*, 8 Apr.; *Poulson's American Daily Advertiser*, 12 Apr.).

To Charles Willson Peale

DEAR SIR Monticello Apr. 5. 05.

Your 8vo. Polygraph arrived at Washington just in time for me to bring it on here, where I have used it and still use it constantly. altho' the machinery will require your rectification to make it quite a good one, yet it is sufficient to shew that the reduction of size is not only practicable, but useful in proportion to it's reduction, for those who travel. I have therefore bestowed some attention on it, and being here amidst my workmen, I have had a model made, by which it appears that for the sized paper on which I now write (5. by 8. I)[1] the *horizontal* rhomboids will work perfectly, & shut up within the internal dimensions of 11. by 7. I. & if half inch stuff be sufficient the external dimensions will be 12. by 8. the one I now write with is near 15. by 11. I. I cannot say how the vertical machinery may answer, but I see no difficulty in shortening the sides of the rhomboids there. I shall carry both this Polygraph & my model to Washington, & forward them thence to you by the stage: praying you instead of the one returned, to make me one as near to my own model as you can.

The former desk Polygraph which you made for my use at this place, I shall send hence by water to Philadelphia, according to your request, to have the machinery reformed to the new manner. as one is wanting for the office of the President's Secretary, I think to appropriate this to that purpose, and will direct mr Claxton, who has the purchasing of furniture for the President's house, to pay for it. of course the paiment I made for it some time ago may be considered as the price of the new portable one I now desire for my own private use. Accept my friendly salutations TH: JEFFERSON

RC (TxU). PoC (DLC); at foot of first page: "C. W. Peale"; endorsed by TJ.

YOUR 8VO. POLYGRAPH ARRIVED: Peale had sent the polygraph by mail stage on 8 Mch. (Peale to TJ, 6 and 8 Mch).

PAIMENT I MADE: see Peale to TJ, [on or before 28 Jan. 1805].

[1]TJ here canceled "it may."

From Joseph Browne

SIR New York April 6th. 1805

I have received by the Hands of Colol. Burr a Commission by which You have honored me with the appointment of Secretary of the Territory of Louisiana; after mature consideration I accept it; and pray you will permit me to tender you my most respectfull homage therefor—

Altho' my pursuits for some Years past have been more of a Philosophical, than statistical or political nature, I trust my conduct in this Office will merit and obtain your future patronage—

If on my voyage to or during my residence at this *Land of Promise* any Observations should occur which may be deemed usefull to humanity, or conducive to a knowlege of our Country, I shall beg Permission to communicate them to you.

May you in health long continue to possess the confidence and affection of your fellow Citizens— JOSEPH BROWNE

RC (DNA: RG 59, AOC); at foot of text: "Thomas Jefferson The President of the United States"; endorsed by TJ as received 17 Apr. and so recorded in SJL; also endorsed by TJ: "accepts as Secy. of Louisa."

Joseph Browne (1758-1810), a British-born physician, served as a member of the Pennsylvania line during the Revolutionary War. In 1782 he married Catherine de Visme at The Hermitage near Paramus, New Jersey. At the same ceremony Aaron Burr married de Visme's half-sister, Theodosia Prevost. The two men were linked politically thereafter. In 1798 Browne proposed a system by which drinking water for New York City would be drawn from the Bronx River, a plan that he and Burr advocated together, which led to the establishment of the Manhattan Company. In 1804, Browne campaigned for Burr's election as governor of New York. Once established in St. Louis as territorial secretary, Browne served as acting governor of the Louisiana Territory during James Wilkinson's absence, during which time he made efforts to distance himself from the rumors of his brother-in-law's potentially questionable activities. He was replaced by Frederick Bates in April 1807 (Mary-Jo Kline, ed., *Political Correspondence and Public Papers of Aaron Burr*, 2 vols. [Princeton, 1983], 1:lxvi, 400; 2:835; *Terr. Papers*, 14:3, 98-101, 117).

To Thomas Carr, Jr.

DEAR SIR Monticello Apr. 6. 05.

I recieved on the 19th. Ult. your letter and statement of my account with Colo. Bell. The articles of it which are not in my statement are the following

1800. June	22.	paid per note to Reuben Perry	£ 3
	28.	paid per order to George Wash	£ 3
July	3.	$7\frac{1}{2}$ galls. whiskey	1–12–9
	8.	$17\frac{1}{2}$ galls. do.	3–10–9

the two last I have no doubt are right. I kept no account myself of store articles. but of articles of cash & orders I kept exact account and am confident the two first articles are wrong. if the do. means paid to Perry & Wash I have their settlements with me in which they neither credit, nor do I charge any such sums. if the do. means only a paiment to myself the silence of my memm. book is satisfactory evidence to me that I recieved no such sums. I imagine you have charged these sums merely on finding some note of mine among Colo. Bell's papers asking such sums. but I am persuaded no such entry was made in his books as paid. if there is, I shall certainly admit it. but you know Colo. Bell sold nails for me, and I drew on him for small sums as I wanted them. very often he had not money to pay them, but still did not return my note, which between him & me was never attended to. I have little answers to such notes now, assuring me he had not a dollar to furnish me. therefore the bare finding such a note of mine among his papers is no evidence at all that he sent me the money. whenever he sent the money my entries shew it, and so I have no doubt the entries in his books do. if there be such, made at the time, & not afterwards merely on finding such notes, I shall suppose I have made two omissions of money recieved in 6. days, which is more than I have done in 40. years. I will ask the favor of you to look into these two charges & let me know on what they are founded. Accept my friendly salutations.

TH: JEFFERSON

RC (ViU: Carr-Cary Papers); at foot of text: "Mr. Thos. Carr."

Thomas Carr, Jr., was TJ's agent for the sale of nails at Charlottesville. He also handled some of TJ's financial transactions, including cash payments and settling his taxes and court fees in Albemarle County (MB, 2:939n, 1028, 1030, 1107, 1108; Vol. 30:574n, 601n; Vol. 31:384n; Vol. 32:341-2; Vol. 41:405).

The LETTER from Carr to TJ has not been found.

MY ACCOUNT WITH COLO. BELL: Thomas Bell died in October 1800. He had been part of TJ's nail distribution network, transmitted and stored goods for him, and handled some financial transactions.

According to TJ's financial memoranda, on 19 June 1800 TJ gave REUBEN PERRY an order on Bell for $10 and on 28 June gave GEORGE WASH an order in full on Bell for 38 shillings and 8 pence (MB, 2:1022; Vol. 29:371n; Vol. 32:254).

To George Jefferson

DEAR SIR Monticello Apr. 6. 05.

Your favor of the 2d. is recieved & I thank you for the admonition as to my tobo. I shall hand it on to my overseer with a proper charge. I should be for holding out for 7. D. unless you should foresee a permanent fall of price. I expect there are or will very soon be with you the following articles

10. packages from Washington. sailed Mar 17.
5. Nos. [No. 1. being 12. bands] from Phila. sailed Mar. 20
a pipe of wine from N. York, sailed Mar. 21.
80. bundles nailrod from Phila. sailed Mar. 31.

the first & second parcels I should be anxious to recieve before I leave this, which will be on the 14th. the wine should come by the most trusty hand; the nailrod by those we usually employ. my painter, now at work here is so much in want of the articles on the next page, that I must pray you to procure them in Richmond & forward them by the Milton stage which will be leaving Richmond immediately after you recieve this. Accept affectionate salutations. TH: JEFFERSON

7 ℔ red lead.
7. ℔ stone ochre
2. ℔ Umber
2. ℔ Terradisiana
6 ℔ litharge
2 ℔ rose-pink
4. oz. Prussian blue
6. oz. white vitriol
6. books of gold leaf.
25. ℔ whiting.
5. oz. Vermilion.
6. small sash brushes.

PoC (MHi); brackets in original; at foot of text: "Mr. Jefferson"; endorsed by TJ.

MY PAINTER: Richard Barry (see Peter Lenox to TJ, 23 Mch.).

From John Pittman

SIR, Alexandria April 6th: 1805

A real respect for your Excellency, and a regard for my own duty, seem equally, to require that I should take the liberty of suggesting to your recollection, the subject of an address which I had the honor to present to you from the Citizens of Alexandria relative to Colonel Francis Peyton. The reply you were pleased to make at the time the address was handed, was that you would take it under consideration and make known the result to some one of the Committee—No communication on the subject having been yet received, as far as I am informed, I presume the affair has escaped your recollection.

The time at which I shall consider myself bound to make a final report of this business, is on the last Saturday of the present month, when a battalion muster is to take place in pursuance of a notice given in May 1804; and it is therefore that I feel particularly solicitous of presenting the subject at this time, again to your thoughts; and I shall think myself personally obbliged, if your leisure and inclination should permit you to make the proposed communication, prior to the said period.

I have the honor to be Sir, Your sincere Obbt.

JOHN PITTMAN

RC (DLC); at foot of text: "Thomas Jefferson Esqr: President of the United States"; endorsed by TJ as received 17 Apr. and so recorded in SJL.

John Pittman (d. 1829) worked as a clockmaker and watchmaker in Falmouth, Virginia, before moving to Alexandria, where he was a goldsmith and silversmith. Active in the town's militia, he was chosen to house the militia's arms in 1802 (Fredericksburg *Virginia Herald*, 28 Nov. 1793, 26 Sep. 1829; *Alexandria Advertiser and Commercial Intelligencer*, 1 Sep. 1801; Miller, *Alexandria Artisans*, 2:37).

For the effort by members of the Alexandria militia to remove FRANCIS PEYTON as commander, see Dearborn to TJ, 7 Dec. 1804.

To William Bartram

DEAR SIR Monticello Apr. 7. 05.

Your favor of the 18th. of March was recieved here yesterday. it covered mr Wilson's, with his elegant drawing, which being dated from the same place with your's, I take the liberty of putting the answer under your cover. I thank you for the specimens of horns you so kindly offer me, & which I will accept with thankfulness. altho' I have never had time to think of a cabinet, yet I have collected some articles of a durable kind and requiring no other care than safe-keeping. may not the small horn you mention be either the Capra depressa or the Reversa of Linnaeus, which Buffon (24. 190) denies to America? if it be, it is an additional proof of the superior accuracy of Linnaeus. I dare say you know that Westward of the Misipi there is an animal of the Capra kind; & tho by some it is called a deer, & by some a goat that would not authorise us to call it the Cervicapra of the East, to which the other pair of horns you have belong. the Osage Indians shewed me a specimen of it's leather, superior to any thing of the kind I ever saw. their manner of dressing the leather too deserves enquiry, as it recieves no injury from being wet. I count on special information as to this animal from Capt Lewis, and that he will enrich us with other articles of Zoology, in which he is more skilled than in botany. the prickly lizard which I recieved from the Osages, & forwarded to mr Peale you have doubtless seen, and found to be a great singularity. Accept my friendly salutations, & assurances of great esteem & respect

TH: JEFFERSON

P.S. lest you should be at a loss about the conveyance of the horns, if you will be so good as to deliver them to my friend mr Vaughan I will ask the favor of him to address them to Messrs. Gibson & Jefferson at Richmond to be forwarded to Monticello. I will also desire him to be so good as to have them put into a box for greater safety.

RC (MBU: Edward C. Stone Collection); at foot of first page: "Mr. W. Barton." PoC (DLC). Recorded in SJL as a letter to William Barton. Enclosure: TJ to Alexander Wilson, 7 Apr.

MR WILSON'S: Wilson to TJ, 18 Mch.

AN ANIMAL OF THE CAPRA KIND: Lewis and Clark first spotted the mountain goat, or *Oreamnos americanus*, on 24 Aug. 1805 (Moulton, *Journals of the Lewis & Clark Expedition*, 5:160, 164n).

THE PRICKLY LIZARD: see Vol. 43:453n.

From Meriwether Lewis

DEAR SIR. Fort Mandan, April 7th. 1805.

Herewith inclosed you will receive an invoice of certain articles, which I have forwarded to you from this place. among other articles, you will observe by reference to the invoice, 67. specimens of earths, salts and minerals; and 60 specimens of plants: these are accompanyed by their rispective labels expressing the days on which obtained, places where found, and also their virtues and properties when known. by means of these labels, reference may be made to the Chart of the Missouri forwarded to the Secretary at War, on which, the encampment of each day has been carefully marked; thus the places at which these specimens have been obtained may be easily pointed out, or again found, should any of them prove valuable to the community on further investegation. these have been forwarded with a view of their being presented to the Philosophical society of Philadelphia, in order that they may under their direction be examined or analyzed. after examining these specimens yourself, I would thank you to have a copy of their labels made out, and retained untill my return. the other articles are intended particularly for yourself, to be retained, or disposed off as you may think proper.—

You will also receive herewith inclosed a part of Capt. Clark's private journal, the other part you will find inclosed in a seperate tin box. this journal is in it's original state, and of course incorrect, but it will serve to give you the daily detales of our progress, and transactions. Capt. Clark dose not wish this journal exposed in it's present state, but has no objection, that one or more copies of it be made by some confidential person under your direction, correcting it's gramatical errors &c. indeed it is the wish of both of us, that two of those copies should be made, if convenient, and retained untill our return; in this state there is no objection to your submitting them to the perusal of the heads of the departments, or such others as you may think proper. a copy of this journal will assist me in compiling my own for publication after my return. I shall dispatch a canoe with three, perhaps four persons, from the extreem navigable point of the Missouri, or the portage betwen this river, and the Columbia river, as either may first happen; by the return of this canoe, I shal send you my journal, and some one or two of the best of those kept by my men. I have sent a journal kept by one of the Sergeants to Capt Stoddard, my agent at St. Louis, in order as much as possible to multiply the chances of saving something. we have encouraged our men to keep journals, and seven of them do so, to whom in this respect we give every assistance in our power.—

I have transmitted to the Secretary at War, every information relative to the geography of the country which we possess, together with a view of the Indian nations, containing information relative to them, on those points with which, I concieved it important that the government should be informed. If it could be done with propriety and convenience, I should feel myself much obliged by your having a copy taken of my dispatches to the Secretary at War, on those subjects, retaining them for me untill my return. By reference to the Muster-rolls forwarded to the War Department, you will see the state of the party; in addition to which, we have two Interpreters, one negroe man, servant to Capt. Clark, one Indian woman, wife to one of the interpreters, and a Mandan man, whom we take with a view to restore peace between the Snake Indians, and those in this neighbourhood amounting in total with ourselves to 33 persons. by means of the Interpreters and Indians, we shall be enabled to converse with all the Indians that we shall probably meet with on the Missouri.—

I have forwarded to the Secretary at War, my public Accounts rendered up to the present day. they have been much longer delayed than I had any idea that they would have been, when we departed from the Illinois, but this delay, under the circumstances which I was compelled to act, has been unavoidable. The provision perogue and her crew, could not have been dismissed in time to have returned to St. Louis last fall without evedently in my opinion, hazarding the fate of the enterprise in which I am engaged, and I therefore did not hesitate to prefer the sensure that I may have incurred by the detention of these papers, to that of risking in any degree the success of the expedition. to me, the detention of those papers have formed a serious source of disquiet and anxiety; and the recollection of your particular charge to me on this subject, has made it still more poignant. I am fully aware of the inconvenience which must have arrisen to the War Department, from the want of these vouchers previous to the last session of Congress, but how to divert it was out of my power to devise.—

From this place we shall send the barge and crew early tomorrow morning with orders to proceed as expeditiously as possible to St. Louis, by her we send our dispatches, which I trust will get safe to hand. Her crew consists of ten ablebodied men well armed and provided with a sufficient stock of provision to last them to St. Louis. I have but little doubt but they will be fired on by the Siouxs; but they have pledged themselves to us that they will not yeald while there is a man of them living.

Our baggage is all embarked on board six small canoes and two perogues; we shall set out at the same moment that we dispatch the barge. one or perhaps both of these perogues we shall leave at the falls of the Missouri, from whence we intend continuing our voyage in the canoes and a perogue of skins, the frame of which was prepared at Harper's ferry. this perogue is now in a situation which will enable us to prepare it in the course of a few hours. as our vessels are now small and the current of the river much more moderate, we calculate on traveling at the rate of 20 or 25 miles pr. day as far as the falls of the Missouri. beyond this point, or the first range of rocky Mountains situated about 100 miles further, any calculation with rispect to our daily progress, can be little more than bare conjecture. the circumstance of the Snake Indians possessing large quantities of horses, is much in our favour, as by means of horses, the transportation of our baggage will be rendered easy and expeditious over land, from the Missouri, to the Columbia river. should this river not prove navigable where we first meet with it, our present intention is, to continue our march by land down the river untill it becomes so, or to the Pacific Ocean. The map, which has been forwarded to the Secretary at War, will give you the idea we entertain of the connection of these rivers, which has been formed from the corresponding testemony of a number of Indians who have visited that country, and who have been seperately and carefully examined on that subject, and we therefore think it entitled to some degree of confidence. Since our arrival at this place we have subsisted principally on meat, with which our guns have supplyed us amply, and have thus been enabled to reserve the parched meal, portable soup, and a considerable proportion of pork and flour, which we had intended for the more difficult parts of our voyage. if Indian information can be credited, the vast quantity of game with which the country abounds through which we are to pass leaves us but little to apprehend from the want of food.—

We do not calculate on completeing our voyage within the present year, but expect to reach the Pacific Ocean, and return, as far as the head of the Missouri, or perhaps to this place before winter. You may therefore expect me to meet you at Montachello in September 1806.—

On our return we shal probably pass down the yellow stone river, which from Indian information, waters one of the fairest portions of this continent.

I can foresee no material or probable obstruction to our progress, and entertain therefore the most sanguine hopes of complete success. As to myself individually I never enjoyed a more perfect state of good health, than I have since we commenced our voyage. my inestimable friend and companion Capt. Clark has also enjoyed good health generally. At this moment every individual of the party are in good health, and excellent sperits; zealously attached to the enterprise, and anxious to proceed; not a whisper of discontent or murmur is to be heard among them; but all in unison, act with the most perfect harmony. with such men I have every thing to hope, and but little to fear.

Be so good as to present my most affectionate regard to all my friends, and be assured of the sincere and unalterable attatchment of

Your most Obt. Servt. MERIWETHER LEWIS Capt.
1st. U'S. Regt. Infty.

RC (DLC); at foot of text: "Thomas Jefferson President of the UStates"; endorsed by TJ as received 13 July and so recorded in SJL. Enclosure: William Clark to TJ, 3 Apr. Other enclosure printed below.

The CHART OF THE MISSOURI was made up of 29 half-sheets, now lost, upon which Clark had recorded the course of the river, supplemented by daily measurements of latitude and longitude (TJ to Dearborn, 14 July 1805; TJ to Volney, 11 Feb. 1806; Moulton, *Journals of the Lewis & Clark Expedition*, 1:7).

The PARTY that left Fort Mandan on 7 Apr. consisted of about two dozen sergeants and soldiers; interpreters George Drouillard and Toussaint Charbonneau; Charbonneau's wife, the Shoshone woman Sacagawea; their child, Jean Baptiste Charbonneau; an unidentified Mandan man; and Clark's slave York (same, 4:9, 11).

SNAKE INDIANS: that is, the Shoshones (Sturtevant, *Handbook*, 13, pt. 2:902, 967).

PUBLIC ACCOUNTS: on 16 July, the War Department received a communication from Lewis at Fort Mandan dated 6 Apr. transmitting "his Accts. for 1805 and Rects." (recorded in DNA: RG 107, RLRMS).

Clark composed a MAP of the western portion of North America between the 34th and 54th parallels by combining accounts and sketches provided by various traders and Native Americans with information and observations gathered by members of the expedition. The map is no longer extant (TJ to the Senate and the House of Representatives, 19 Feb. 1806; Moulton, *Journals of the Lewis & Clark Expedition*, 1:8-9).

ENCLOSURE

Articles Sent from Fort Mandan

Invoice of articles forwarded from Fort Mandan to the President of the United States through Captn. Stoddard at St. Louis and Mr. H. B. Trist the Collector of the Port of New Orleans.

No.	Package	Contents	
1.	Box	Skins of the Male and female Antelope, with their Skeletons. *came. P.*	
"	do	2 Horns and ears, of the Black tail, or Mule Deer. *came*	
"	"	A Martin Skin *came* containing the Skin of a weasel *came. P.* and three Small squirels of the Rocky Mountains & the tail of a Mule deer fully grown. *came.*	
"	"	Skeleton of the Small, or burrowing wolf of the Praries, the Skin haveing been lost by accedent. *some skeletons came, not distinguishable. sent to P.*	
"	"	2 Skeletons of the White Hare. *as above. P.*	
"	"	A Mandan bow with a quiver of arrows, *came* the quiver containing Some Seed of the Mandan tobacco. *came*	
"	"	A carrot of Ricara tobacco. *came*	
2.	Box	4 Buffalow robes, *came* and an ear[1] of Mandan corn.	
3.	Box.	Skins of the Male and female Antelope, with their Skeletons *undistinguishable. P* and the Skin of a brown, or yellow Bear.	
4.	Box	Specimens of earths, Salts, and Minerals, numbered from 1. to 67.	*came A. Ph. Society*
"	"	Specimens of plants numbered from 1. to 60.	*came.*

"	"	1 earthen pot, Such as the Mandans manufacture, and use for culinary purposes. *came*
"	"	1. tin box containing insects, mice &c.
"	"	a Specimen of the fur of the Antilope.
"	"	a Specimen of a plant, and a parsel of its roots, highly prized by the natives as an efficatious remidy in the cure of the bite of the rattle snake, or Mad dog.
in a	Large Trunk	Skins of Male and female Braro, or burrowing Dog of the Praries, with the Skeleton of the female. *came. P.*
in a	large Trunk	1 Skin of a red fox containing a Magpie. *came.*
		2 Cased Skins of the white hare. *came. P.*
		1 Minetarre Buffalow robe, *came* containing some articles of Indian dress. *came.*
		1 Mandan Buffalow robe, *came* containing a dressed Skin of the Lousirvea *came* and two cased Skins of the burrowing Squirels of the praries. *came P.*
		13 red fox skins. *came*
		4 horns of the mountain ram, or big horn.[2] *came.*
		1 Buffalow robe painted by a Mandan man representing a battle which was faught 8 years sence, by the Sioux & Ricaras, against the Mandans, Minetarras & Ahwahharways. *came.*
6	Cage	Containing four liveing Magpies. *1. came P.*
7	do.	Containing a liveing burrowing Squirel of the praries. *came. P.*
9	do.	Containing one liveing hen of the Prarie.
10	—	1 large par of Elk's horns connected by the frontal bone.

MS (DLC: TJ Papers, 148:25876); undated; in William Clark's hand; notations by TJ in italics.

Clark recorded a nearly identical list of the ARTICLES sent to TJ in his field notes under the date 3 Apr. (Moulton, *Journals of the Lewis & Clark Expedition*, 3:329-31). Many of the specimens sent by Lewis and Clark arrived, in varying condition, at the President's House in August 1805 while TJ was at Monticello (Étienne Lemaire to TJ, 12 and 20 Aug.; Dearborn to TJ, 15 Aug.; TJ to Lemaire, 17 Aug.). Following his return to Washington in October, TJ inventoried what had arrived and began to disburse the items to appropriate specialists while awaiting the arrival of the remaining articles. He sent the skins, skeletons, and surviving live animals to Charles Willson Peale (noted in the list printed above as "P"). The mineral and plant specimens went to the American Philosophical Society, with a request that the seeds be sent to horticulturalist William Hamilton. TJ retained a number of the articles for himself, intending them for an "Indian Hall" he was planning for Monticello (Jackson, *Lewis and Clark*, 1:239-40; Paul Russell Cutright, *Lewis and Clark: Pioneering Naturalists* [Urbana, Ill., 1969], 349-92; TJ to Peale, 6, 9, and 21 Oct.; TJ to Hamilton, 6 Nov.; John Vaughan to TJ, 21 Jan. 1806).

MARTIN: that is, a marten, a member of the weasel family (Moulton, *Journals of the Lewis & Clark Expedition*, 3:330, 331n).

BURROWING WOLF OF THE PRARIES: coyote (same, 3:87-8, 330; 4:112-13).

WHITE HARE: white-tailed jackrabbit (same, 3:70, 73n, 330).

For an inventory of Lewis and Clark's specimens of MINERALS and PLANTS received by the American Philosophical Society, see same, 3:462-78.

MICE: Benjamin Smith Barton reported finding "two specimens of an extremely minute quadruped" in the box of plants sent by Lewis, which he identified as a shrew (Barton to TJ, 27 Dec. 1805).

SPECIMEN OF A PLANT: narrow leaf purple coneflower (see Description of a Plant by Meriwether Lewis, 5 Mch.).

BRARO, OR BURROWING DOG OF THE PRARIES: badger, or *blaireau* in French (Moulton, *Journals of the Lewis & Clark Expedition*, 2:429, 431n; 3:330; TJ to Peale, 6 Oct.).

MINETARRE: another name for the Hidatsas (Moulton, *Journals of the Lewis & Clark Expedition*, 3:193-4n, 205-6n, 404-5).

LOUSIRVEA: the lynx, or *loup cervier* in French (same, 256-7, 330; TJ to Peale, 9 Oct.).

BURROWING SQUIRELS OF THE PRARIES: prairie dogs (Moulton, *Journals of the Lewis & Clark Expedition*, 3:54n, 330-1; Cutright, *Lewis and Clark*, 79-80; TJ to Peale, 6 Oct.).

The Awaxawi (AHWAHHARWAYS) were a division of the Hidatsas (Moulton, *Journals of the Lewis & Clark Expedition*, 3:193-4, 202, 403-4).

HEN OF THE PRARIE: sharp-tailed grouse (Cutright, *Lewis and Clark*, 375).

[1] Preceding word underlined by Clark.

[2] Preceding two words underlined by Clark.

From Benjamin Waterhouse

SIR Cambridge April 7th. 1805.

Ever since I received your short but Ciceronean Epistle, it has seldom been long out of my mind. It made an impression I cannot get rid of; and therefore, in the true spirit of that religious sect among whom I was educated, I cannot hold my peace. It may be deemed impertinent, but you must excuse the impulse. On this head I say, as did the celebrated Edmund Burke to my kinsman Dr. Fothergill "I have reason every day to be thankful that I was educated by Quakers."

When I read your wish, expressed in a manner peculiar to yourself, for a successful opposition of this organ of Virginia influence, and *every other injurious to our physical, moral, and political well being*, I longed for as much of the spirit of Tacitus, as your epistle exhibits of that of Tully, that I might give the history of men and parties at this time in this quarter. Then perhaps you and others in the South would see that the men among us most distinguished for talents, character and years abhor that odious vapour of calumny, which has appeared among us, and even tainted the walls of some of our Temples. The genius of a Tacitus would be able to trace out the cause, & display, in true colours, the effects of that disposition which does the least honour to the human heart. An historian thus inspired would predict that if Virtue could not, at once, exorcise this malignant spirit, Time infallibly would.

Laying under the black imputation of being a moderate man, or a lukewarm federalist, I have long since been excluded from the solemn feasts and *clamorations* of the outrageous party men. Yet when opportunity allows I never fail denouncing this odious, this wicked calumniating spirit, this worse than "*Virginia influence*," by declaring that what is morally wrong cannot be politically right.

I am continually receiving additional evidence of the pernicious effects of tobacco. In a letter on this subject from our venerable countryman Mr. Adams, he says "Having been a great offender in the use of this weed, in some parts of my life, I may not be an unprejudiced judge I have found Tobacco to be a very dangerous vegetable, extremely apt to steal upon a man & urge him to very pernicious excesses. In addition to its physical effects, it consumes an enormous proportion of precious time, & prevents application both to business & to study, in a very criminal degree. It has also very hurtful effects on the memory. I would give any thing for the time that has been stolen from me by this thief. I have often been injured by a thoughtless excess, & now after a frequent use of it, for *three score* years, (having learnt it at 8 years of age, when skaiting on ponds of ice) I am unable to take into my mouth a morsel bigger than a swan-shot, without sensible & immediate injury."

Had it been determined that my friend Mr. Bowdoin should have visited Washington, and he continued to have urged me to accompany him, I should have rejoiced at the opportunity of paying my respects to you in person. But it is ordered otherwise and I can do it only with my pen. BENJN. WATERHOUSE

RC (DLC); endorsed by TJ as received 17 Apr. and so recorded in SJL.

CICERONEAN EPISTLE: see TJ to Waterhouse, 9 Mch.

KINSMAN: Waterhouse was the son of Hannah Proud, John Fothergill's cousin (Betsy C. Corner and Christopher C. Booth, eds., *Chain of Friendship: Selected Letters of Dr. John Fothergill of London, 1735-1780* [Cambridge, Mass., 1971], 9, 472n).

TULLY: a common anglicization of Marcus Tullius Cicero.

John Adams inveighed against the consumption of tobacco in A LETTER to Waterhouse in February 1805, though using slightly different phrases than those noted here (Adams to Waterhouse, 13 Feb. 1805, MHi: Adams-Waterhouse Letters, 1784-1837).

To Alexander Wilson

SIR Monticello Apr. 7. 05.

I recieved here yesterday your favor of Mar. 18. with the elegant drawings of the new birds you found on your tour to Niagara, for which I pray you to accept my thanks. the Jay is quite unknown to me. from my observations, while in Europe, on the birds & quadrupeds of that quarter, I am of opinion there is not in our continent a single bird or quadruped which is not sufficiently unlike all the members of it's family there to be considered as specifically different. on this general observation I conclude with confidence that your Jay is not a European bird.

The first bird on the same sheet I judge to be a Muscicapa from it's bill, as well as from the following circumstance. two or three days before my arrival here a neighbor killed a bird, unknown to him, & never before seen here as far as he could learn. it was brought to me soon after I arrived; but in the dusk of the evening, & so putrid that it could not be approached but with disgust. but I retain a sufficiently exact idea of it's form & colours to be satisfied it is the same with yours. the only difference I find in yours is that the white on the back is not so pure, and that the one I saw had a little of a crest. your figure, compared with the white bellied Gobemouche 8. Buff. 342. Pl. enlum. 566. shews a near relation. Buffon's is dark on the back.

As you are curious in birds there is one well worthy your attention, to be found or rather heard[1] in every part of America, & yet scarcely ever to be seen. it is in all the forests, from spring to fall, and never but on the tops of the tallest trees from which it perpetually serenades us with some of the sweetest notes, & as clear as those of the nightingale. I have followed it miles without ever but once getting a good view of it. it is of the size & make of the Mockingbird, lightly thrush-coloured on the back, & a greyish-white on the breast & belly. mr Randolph, my son in law, was in possession of one which had been shot by a neighbor. he pronounces this also a muscicapa, and I think it much resembling the Moucherolle de la Martinique 8. Buffon 374. Pl. enlum. 568. as it abounds in all the neighborhood of Philadelphia, you may perhaps by patience & perseverance (of which much will be requisite) get a sight, if not a possession of it I have for 20. years interested the young sportsmen of my neighborhood to shoot me one; but as yet without success. Accept my salutations & assurances of respect.

TH: JEFFERSON

RC (PPAmP: Sol Feinstone Collection of the David Library of the American Revolution); at foot of first page: "Mr. Wilson." PoC (DLC). Enclosed in TJ to William Bartram, 7 Apr.

PL. ENLUM.: *Planches enluminées*, the plates accompanying the Comte de Buffon's *Histoire naturelle*.

[1] Previous three words interlined.

From Stephen Cathalan, Jr.

My most Respected Dear Sir! Marseilles the 8th. april 1805

Since my Respects of the 8th. December Last, I had the misfortune of Supporting Two Irreparable Losses in my Family;

Mrs. Cathalan my Beloved wife, on the 28th. January Last, & my old Respectable Father, on the 17th. Last february, Left this world! Soriously Regretted by me, my old mother, & my Daughter!

a Great Comfort for my Remaining Family, was the Concern that their & our acquaintances, & the American Citizens then at Marseilles, took in our affliction; 23 american vessels whereof 5 to my address, where then in this Port & about fifty american Masters or Citizens, in Marseilles, they all empressed themselves to pay their Memory, Respect, on Board their vessels, & in assisting to their Respective funerals, I acknowledged to them my Gratitude; it is my duty to mention You this Circumstance, & at Same time to Inclose you a Copy of the epithaph I caused to be engraved on their Tombs!

never Such a number of american vessels had frequented this Port, nor was I So much Busied, than at that Fatal Epoque, to dispatch them, at their own Satisfaction, till a few Days past;

this is the Cause which has prevented me to address you Sooner on this melancolic Subject;

The remainder of my Family Joins me in their Best wishes & prayers to the allmighty, for the Preservation of your Precious Days, During many Succeeding Years, in Good health, with their most Respectfull Compliments;

I have the honor to be with great Respect Sir Your most obedient humble & Devoted Servant Stephen Cathalan Junr.

RC (DLC); at foot of first page: "his Excellency the most honorable Thomas Jefferson President of the united States"; endorsed by TJ as received 5 Aug. and so recorded in SJL. Dupl, not found, enclosed in Cathalan to TJ, 9 May. Enclosures: epitaphs of Charlotte Angleys Cathalan and Stephen Cathalan, Sr. (MSS in same: TJ Papers, 147:25679-80; undated; in French; in Cathalan's hand).

From Archibald McDonald

Your Excellency Winchester April, 8th. 1805

By your direction I have ascribed these lines to inform you or to put in remembrance of my Petition I presented to you at mount assylia near Charllottesville in Albemarle County concerning my Son John McDonald who is enlisted in the first Battalion of Royal Artillery in

Captain McClennings Company now lying in Baltimore or else where your Excellency will please to accept of my most Sincere thanks for the kindness I receiv'd of your Excellency when I presented my Petition and shall still bear in mind your great kindness if I should be so happy as to get my Sons discharge, your most Humble Petitioner will for Ever remember your great Benevolence and Wishing your Excellency all the enjoyments of this World and happiness of the next when time shall be no more ARCHIBALD MCDONALD

RC (MHi); addressed: "His Most Excellency Thomas Jefferson Chief Magistrate and President of the United States of America"; franked; endorsed by TJ as received 19 Apr. but recorded in SJL as received 18 Apr.

MY PETITION: McDonald to TJ, 1 Apr. A letter to TJ from one Mary McDonald, dated 11 May at Winchester, is recorded in SJL but has not been found (Appendix IV).

A JOHN MCDONALD (b. ca. 1787) of Winchester, Virginia, served as a private in the First Infantry Regiment from 1810 to 1815, during which time he was disciplined repeatedly for drunkenness and other derelictions of duty (DNA: RG 94, Registers of Enlistments in the United States Army, 1798-1914).

From Scipion Jérôme Bexon

MONSIEUR LE PRÉSIDENT. Paris ce 9 avril 1805.

Les Etats-unis ont déja offert à l'Europe et à toutes les Nations civilisées, l'Exemple de la Sagesse dans leur législation, comme dans leur Gouvernement, et ils Semblent avoir approché plus que toute autre nation du but vers lequel doivent tendre toutes les Loix, celui du bonheur des hommes et de l'utilité des peines dont la société a été obligée de menacer les méchans.

C'est aussi vers ce but que les Essais de mon travail ont tendu, et que les approbations qu'ils ont reçues de plusieurs Souverains m'ont encouragé à continuer.

Je désire bien vivement, Monsieur le Président, que quelques unes de mes pensées se trouvent en rapport avec Celles dont l'application contribue à la prospérité et au bonheur des Etats qui Se felicitent de vous avoir pour Chef, et que l'apperçu de l'ouvrage dont j'ai l'honneur de vous faire hommage, puisse être digne de Votre attention.

J'ai l'honneur d'être avec un profond Respect, Monsieur le Président, Votre très humble & très obéissant Serviteur. BEXON

EDITORS' TRANSLATION

Mister President, Paris, 9 Apr. 1805

The United States has already given Europe and all civilized nations an example of wisdom in legislation and governance and seems to have come closer than any other nation to the goal toward which all of its laws strive: human well-being and useful punishment with which society needed to dissuade evil-doers.

This is also the goal of my essays. The approval of several sovereigns has encouraged me to continue writing.

I fervently hope, Mister President, that some of my ideas might resonate with the ones that enhance the prosperity and happiness of the country that is blessed to have you as leader and that the work I have the honor of giving you might be worthy of your attention.

With deep respect, Mister President, I have the honor of being your very humble and obedient servant. Bexon

RC (DLC); at head of text: "A Monsieur Jefferson Président des Etats-unis"; endorsed by TJ as received 3 July and so recorded in SJL.

Scipion Jérôme Bexon (1750-1825), a French jurist, was the editor of legal journals and author of several works, including *Parallèle du code pénal d'Angleterre avec les lois pénales françaises* and *Développement de la théorie des lois criminelles* (*Dictionnaire*, 6:373; Sowerby, No. 2697).

From George Jefferson

Dear Sir Richmond 9th. Apl. 1805

I send by the Stage all the articles for which you wrote except the Terradisiana, of which there is none in Town. The carriage I have paid.

I forwarded a few days ago every thing of yours that was here; they will be with you I expect before you receive this.

Your Tobacco I shall hold up for 7 dolls, as I do not think there is any prospect of its falling.

You will receive inclosed, your account made up to the first of this month—shewing a balance in our favor of $:56.\frac{52}{100}$.

I am Dear Sir Yr. Very humble servt. Geo. Jefferson

Mr. Burwell is in Town—he desires me to inform you that he shall set off tomorrow to Washington

RC (MHi); at foot of text: "Thos. Jefferson esqr."; endorsed by TJ as received 11 Apr. and so recorded in SJL.

for which you wrote: TJ to Jefferson, 6 Apr.

From William Lattimore

SIR, Norfolk, April 9th, 1805.

Since my arrival in this place, I received from Messrs. Wm & John Peirce, of the Tombigbee settlement, a talk from three chiefs of the Creek nation, relative to the Island of Nannii Hubbá, which I have thought it proper to inclose to you.

With sentiments of very great respect I am, Sir, Your Obt. Servant

WM. LATTIMORE

RC (PHi: Daniel Parker Papers); at foot of text: "The President of the United States"; endorsed by TJ as received 17 Apr. and so recorded in SJL with notation "W." Enclosure not found.

William Lattimore (1774-1843) was the delegate to Congress from Mississippi Territory from 1803 to 1807 and again from 1813 to 1817. Born near Norfolk, Virginia, and trained as a physician, he had been recommended to TJ by William C. C. Claiborne as "a well informed, modest man" with "purely republican" political principles (*Biog. Dir. Cong.*; DAB; Vol. 41:227).

Brothers William and John PEIRCE were early inhabitants of the Tensaw settlement. They resided near Nanna Hubba Island, located at the confluence of the Alabama and Tombigbee Rivers (David Mathews, *Why Public Schools? Whose Public Schools? What Early Communities Have to Tell Us* [Montgomery, Ala., 2002], 49-53; *Terr. Papers*, 5:254, 284, 294).

From G. H. Le Prétre

VOTRE EXCELLENCE.— Philadelphie 9e. Avril 1805—

Pendant le cours de ma vie, jai Souvent eu occasion de m'adresser a des personnes elevées—aux quels les mortels ont confiés leur Sort.

Mais je puis dire dans la Sincérité du coeur & de la vérité, que jamais je ne me Suis approché d'un homme avec plus d'estime, & de respect qu'en vous écrivant.

Vous étes Philosophe & en meme tems le chef de l'amérique. Jai lu & relu votre ouvrage.—Jai frémi d'indignation, quand un misérable plagiaire, ou gazetier, Se Servant de Sa liberté d'imprimer, comme le meurtrier Se Sert du couteau—a osè vous diffamer. Vous Président d'une nation naissante, doux, bénin, Philosophe—titre que Marc Auréle envioit—vous navès rien.—Puissent les hommes étre assès Sages pour ne jamais confier leur interret qu'aux Savans—cette qualification doit étre Suffisante pour bien mériter deux. Dumoins elle l'est a la Chine—elle l'etoit dans la Grèce & a Rome lorsque l'homme Se glorifioit d'étre.

Je vous envoye le prospectus d'un ouvrage que je me propose de faire publier. Vous me favoriserès en y mettant votre nom—il Sera d'effectueax comme toutes les productions humaines.

L'amerique est devenue ma patrie par adoption, je la chéris comme le centre & le refuge de la liberté. Elle na pas encor toutes les habitudes qui doivent consolider une Republique—Je mefforce a prouver aux hommes qu'ils ne peuvent être heureux Sans être vrais, justes & bienveuillans. Je n'ai dautre moyen a le faire, que par l'imprimerie.

J'écris dans la langue française parceque d'après Diderot, & de l'aveu des plus grands philosophes de l'Europe—elle Seule est la l'angue que l'on puisse appeller la langue du Sage.—

Je Suis avec considération De votre Excellence Le très humble & obeissant Serviteur— G. H. Le Prétre. M.D.

EDITORS' TRANSLATION

Your Excellency, Philadelphia, 9 Apr. 1805—

In the course of my life I have often had occasion to address eminent people to whom mortals entrusted their fate.

But I can say in all truth and sincerity that I have never approached a man with more respect and esteem than I do in writing to you.

You are a philosopher, and at the same time the leader of America. I have read and reread your works. I have raged with indignation when a pathetic plagiarist or gazetteer dared defame you, wielding his freedom of the pen as a murderer wields his knife. As the serene, compassionate president of a nation that is coming into being, as a wise man—a title Marcus Aurelius envied—you do not own anything. May men be wise enough to entrust their well-being only to the learned. This one qualification must be sufficient to justify their trust. At least it is in China, and it was in Greece and Rome in the age when men were proud to live there.

I am sending you the prospectus of a work I plan to publish. You would honor me by adding your name. It will be imperfect like all human productions.

America has become my adoptive country; I cherish it as the heart and refuge of liberty. It does not yet have all the customs needed to unify a republic. I seek to prove that people cannot be happy unless they are truthful, fair, and benevolent, and publishing is my only means of doing so.

I am writing in French because, according to Diderot and the greatest European philosophers, it is the only language one can call the language of wisdom.

With respect, your excellency, I am your very humble and obedient servant.

G. H. Le Prétre, M.D.

RC (Vi); below dateline: "Poste restante" (general delivery); endorsed by TJ as received 17 Apr. and so recorded in SJL. Enclosure not found.

From J. P. G. Muhlenberg

Sir Philadelphia April 9th. 1805

The enclosed Note, handed me by Consul Obrien I have the Honor to transmit to the President, & at the same time to inform Him, that the Box alluded to in the Note is deposited in the Custom House Store until the President shall be pleasd to direct how it is to be dispos'd of.

with sincere, & perfect Respect I have the honor to be Sir Your Obedt Servt
P Muhlenberg

RC (MHi); at foot of text: "The President of The U States"; endorsed by TJ as received 17 Apr. and so recorded in SJL with notation "Fitzpatrick figures." Enclosure: William Kirkpatrick to Richard O'Brien, Malaga, 4 Feb., asking him to take charge of a box, carried on board the *Martha*, containing "Six clay Figures made in this Place, Two representing a man & woman dancing the Bolero, to the music of the Guitar which is played by a third Person, A Smugler & his Mistress, All five in the proper spanish Dress, which the People they represent wear on festival days, to make up half a Dozen Another Common figure has been added"; Kirkpatrick wishes O'Brien to present these "objects of Curiosity" to the president and hopes they will merit his approbation (RC in MoSHi: Jefferson Papers; addressed: "Richard OBrien Esqe"; endorsed by TJ).

From James Oldham

Sir Richmond 9th. Aprail 1805.

This day week I recevd your faver of the 24th. Ultimo with an order inclosed for 40 Dollars, which am Sir exceeding thankful for; I have thot whilst you were at monticello it would be as well to apply for the Dementions of the Dores, which at your Lasure you will Please to faver me with, in Fore days the Plank will be sufficiently dryd and I intend to begin them immediatly.

I must beg the faver of you Sir, on your return to Washington, if perchance you should se Loyer Gantt to aske him to be so good as to indever to make a close of the Business which is depending betwen the estate of Jacson and my Self.

With Respect I Have the Honr. to be Sir, Your Obt. Huml. Sevt.
Jms. Oldham

RC (MHi); addressed: "His Excelency Thoms. Jefferson Esqr. Prt. U. Sts. Monticello"; franked and postmarked; endorsed by TJ as received 11 Apr. and so recorded in SJL.

estate of jacson: presumably the late carpenter Jonathan Jackson. In 1804, Jackson's estate was sold at public auction by Thomas Beall, who, along with John Mackall Gantt, was a trustee of the District of Columbia (*Washington Federalist*, 22 Feb. 1804; Vol. 34:647n; Vol. 36:418).

To Charles Willson Peale

Dear Sir Monticello. Apr. 9. 05.

My letter of the 5th. had been written but not sent off when I recieved yours of Mar. 30. with the new penbar. this finds me so near my departure for Washington that all is now hurry. I have not time therefore to change the penbars for trying the Diagonal writing; & I should not be without fear of deranging the machine, & losing the use of it while I yet stay & while I have much to write. I have no doubt however from what I see as well as from your information that the medium sized polygraph (such as I now write with) may be made to write on either 4to. or 8vo. paper. but while one is at their stationary post, the large size is most convenient, & for travelling the Minimum is all important. I adhere therefore to the model I shall forward you for my travelling Polygraph. I find no inconvenience in using the 8vo. paper in ordinary, & if one has to write to a punctilious correspondent, who might consider his dignity implicated in the size of the paper on which he is addressed, one may write an 8vo. page on a 4to. sheet as I do now, which leaves a good margin for dignity. the desk-polygraph shall be sent by water. the one I now write on, with my model I will carry on to Washington & forward thence by the stage. the new pen-bar shall be returned with the one or the other as I find it pack best. Accept my friendly salutations.

Th: Jefferson

RC (TxU); at foot of text: "Mr. Peale." PoC (DLC).

From Nicholas King

Sir Washington 10th. April 1805

Men of Science have of late years attended to Meteorological occurrences under the expectation, that from a series of observations, may be deduced some theory beneficial to Society: every hint therefore, leading to this object will I am sure be so well received by you, as to supercede the necessity of an apology for its communication.

Supposing the enclosed specimen of a Meteorological Chart exhibits the different Phenomena, in a manner more concise and intelligible than the tabular form in which registers are generally kept; I transmit it to you, as a better judge than I can be of its merit; and because, if it afford the means of a more distinct classification and arrangement of the facts necessary for framing a useful system, it will sooner be perfected by the improvements which your information on the subject may suggest, than by what my slight knowledge affords.

So difficult appears the arrangement of the information furnished by meteorological journals from the variety of causes operating and to be attended to at the same time—the almost impossibility of connecting them all in the same train of reasoning however accustomed to abstruse speculation the mind may have been & however tenacious the memory is of facts,—that little progress seems to have been made in reducing this branch of science to a regular System. It is so important to the agriculturalist to ascertain the changes about to take place in the weather from observations to be made on the atmosphere, that the subject has always received a considerable portion of their attention; and men of science have lately brought to their aid all those inventions which can be the means of furnishing correct data.

Many Gentlemen who have kept records of their observations, seem only to have in view the comparison of Climates, and their influence on the human constitution; attending to the prevalence of particular winds, the temperature and gravity of the atmosphere, the quantity of rain, &ca. at different seasons, in order to obtain general results. In doing this however they have collected a mass of information capable I believe of being digested into a system of still greater utility to mankind. It is only by viewing the operation of all the Natural causes in connection that we can acquire such a knowledge of their effect as will be useful; it being from this combination of causes, and not from their individual action that the phenomena we observe are produced. The state of the atmosphere as it is affected by the quantity of the electric fluid and moisture is seldom noted, perhaps from the difficulty in constructing instruments which shall be capable of measuring it, and which will bear an accurate comparison with other instruments of the same nature.

Considering how much more readily the ideas we receive through the medium of sight and touch are recalled by a linear representation of the objects which caused them, than by words; and, that Charts have with advantage been constructed to facilitate the acquisition of Historic and chronological knowledge, it suggested the peculiar fitness of this mode of deliniation for registering Meteorological facts and observations. Almost all the information we collect on this Subject may be pourtray'd as it is received: much is acquired by measurement, and can therefore again be deliniated by a graduated scale; and, form a chart or picture capable of transmitting ideas in a manner bearing much similitude to that in which they were received, and without the intervention of words sometimes doubtful in signification. By a chart therefore containing scales or measures corresponding with the observations, and where the continuation of a line shall represent the progress of time and the measure of the thing under consideration; and where adjunctive circumstances are denoted by colour, or appropriate characters, we have in one view all the facts in our possession, and which the mind can have to reason upon; and from which its general deductions are to be drawn.

On these principles I have drawn the Chart, from observations made by Mr. Dunbar near the Mississippi, in the year 1799. Philosophers believe in the Lunar theory of the tides; and Husbandmen have in almost all ages believed in the influence of the Moon on the weather, and on vegetation; I have therefore added the phases of the moon during the period embraced by the chart, that her attraction, if any, may be noted, or how far it is counteracted by other and more powerful causes.

On examining this chart an exact coincidence will be found between the depression of the Mercury in the Barometer and the approximation of rain. So true an indication of these changes will the barometer be found, as to deserve the attention of all those whose business is affected by them. The Chart suggests another observation of some apparent importance: that variations in temperature as indicated by the thermometer, occur from the same causes which affect the barometer, but in a contrary manner: the elevation of the mercury in the latter being accompanied by a proportionate decrease of temperature and falling of the Mercury in the former instrument,—and this, independent in a great measure of the quarter from which the wind blows during the unsettled weather of Feby. March & April we observe the greatest variation in the gravity and temperature of the atmosphere, its weight decreasing as the warm season approaches. When the Weather becomes settled, in June and July and the barometer nearly stationary, something like an atmospheric tide is observed: It may not however arise from the same cause with the tides of the ocean; for, in a fluid so rare and so elastic as the atmosphere, the effects of expansion and condensation by the solar heat, may be more powerful and observeable than what takes place from the attraction of Gravity.

I am Sir, with the greatest Esteem & respect, yours truly

NICHS. KING

RC (DLC); at foot of text: "Th: Jefferson. Pres: U.S."; endorsed by TJ as received 20 Apr. and so recorded in SJL. Enclosure not found.

OBSERVATIONS MADE BY MR. DUNBAR: TJ transmitted William Dunbar's meteorological observations, kept from 1 Feb. 1799 to 31 Jan. 1800 and sent to TJ on 29 Nov. 1800, to the American Philosophical Society (Vol. 32:262).

Notes on Henry Aborn and Thomas Aborn

[after 10 Apr. 1805]

Aborn Henry. to be Consul. Martinique

Aborn Thomas was one of the Midnight appmts as Coml. Agent to Cayenne. he is of R.I. no comn. ever went. Henry Aborn must have assumed the deputn witht authority.

MS (DNA: RG 59, LAR); in TJ's hand, undated; written as an endorsement to Tr of Robert Allyn and others to Henry Aborn, Saint-Pierre, Martinique, 8 Feb. 1805 (see below).

In their letter of 8 Feb., Robert Allyn and 16 shipmasters and American merchants urged Henry Aborn, who had previously functioned as deputy vice commercial agent at Cayenne in French Guiana, to seek the position as commercial agent at Saint-Pierre on MARTINIQUE. From Providence, Rhode Island, on 10 Apr., Benjamin West sent Gideon Granger the copy of their letter on which TJ made the notes printed above. Identifying Aborn as his pupil, West requested Granger to inquire with the State Department if TJ had already appointed someone to the post in Martinique (RC in same).

John Adams named THOMAS Aborn as commercial agent at Cayenne on 24 Feb. 1801. TJ reappointed him in June 1801 and January 1802, but when Aborn arrived in Cayenne in February 1802, Governor Victor Hugues refused to recognize him as an official agent of the United States and Aborn, who was in poor health, returned to the United States (Madison, *Papers, Sec. of State Ser.*, 2:56; 3:347; Vol. 33:172; Vol. 34:146-7, 266; Vol. 36:332).

From Barthélemy Lafon

MONSIEUR Nouvelle Orléans le 11. Avril 1805.

Votre surprise sera sans doute grande en recevant une petition dun étranger inconnu. La démarche que je fais, différenté des moyens ordinaires que l'on emploie pour solliciter une place, ma parû néanmoins celle que je devois employer préférablement a toute autre, devenant directe. La protection que vous accordez aux Arts, les faveurs que vous prodiguez aux Artistes, l'encouragement que vous donnez aux talents, sont les motifs principaux qui m'y ont déterminé. Habitant depuis quinze ans la Louisiane, où je n'apportai pour toute fortune que dix ans d'étude, je me suis constamment adonné au génie, et a l'étude du Pays. La premiere partie a été mon occupation dominante, huit ans consécutifs m'ont vu m'occuper de la Géographie locale, et quelques uns de mes travaux sont déjà parvenus jusques dans la chambre des représentants; mon Seul bien-être, ma Seule fortune étant fondés sur ce genre de travail, c'est le motif qui me porte a solliciter au près de vous, la place darpenteur général de la Louisiane. Mes qualités morales et physiques ne vous sont point connues; mais s'il est nécessaire d'informations, je prandrai la liberté de vous citer toutes les personnes honorables de la Nouvelle-Orléans, Messieurs le Gouverneur, les Membres du Conseil Législatif, par ordre desquels je viens de dresser la Carte du Territoire d'orléans, sur une échelle de huit pouces par dégré; Messieurs les officiers Municipaux, pour qui je dresse en ce moment une carte d'un [. . .] au lieue de la Corporation de la [Ville?]; Messieurs le Maire, et Juges du Territoire qui m'honorent de leur société: je vous citerai plusieurs étrangers, et entre autres, Monsieur Dumbard des Natchez, dont la correspondance m'éclaire tous les jours; si enfin, il fallait apporter d'autres titres qui pussent vous déterminer a m'accorder cet Emploi, je connais les langues Espagnolle et Anglaise, la premiere devenant indispensablement nécessaire à un Arpenteur général, la vérification des titres, touts faits en Espagnol depuis quarante ans, en exigent la connaissance.

Ce Sont les Seuls titres que j'ai l'honneur de vous présenter; remettant à votre loyauté, et au désir que vous avez de faire prosperer les connaissances, prouvés par toutes vos actions, la réussite de ma demande

Recevez les vœux les plus sincères de celui qui a l'honneur d'être avec la plus haute estime et considération

Monsieur Votre très humble et très Obéïssant Serviteur

LAFON

EDITORS' TRANSLATION

SIR, New Orleans, 11 Apr. 1805

You will undoubtedly be very surprised to receive this petition from an unknown foreigner. My approach is unlike the ordinary means of applying for a position, but it seemed the best one because the most direct. The protection you provide for the arts, the benefits you bestow upon artists, and the encouragement you give to talent are the principal reasons that convinced me to do this. I arrived in Louisiana 15 years ago with no resources except 10 years of education. Since then I have devoted myself entirely to working as an engineer and to studying this country. Engineering has been my primary occupation. I devoted eight consecutive years to local geography and some of my work even reached the House of Representatives. Such work has provided my one livelihood, my only income. This is what prompts me to apply for the position of chief surveyor of Louisiana. You are not familiar with my character and qualifications, but should you need information, I take the liberty of citing all the honorable people of New Orleans; the governor and members of the legislative council for whom I just drew up a map of the

Orleans territory on a scale of eight inches per degree; the municipal officers for whom I am currently drawing a map of [. . .] at the site of the municipal government; the mayor of the city and judges of the territory who honor me with their company. I shall name several foreigners, and among others Mr. Dunbar of Natchez, whose correspondence enlightens me daily. If other qualifications could persuade you to award me this position, I know Spanish and English, the former becoming indispensable for a chief surveyor to verify deeds since they have been written in Spanish for the past 40 years.

These are the only attributes I have the honor of presenting you. I entrust the success of my request to your integrity and to the desire you have shown in all your actions to help knowledge flourish.

Accept, Sir, the most sincere wishes of someone who has the honor of being, with the highest esteem and respect, your very humble and obedient servant.

LAFON

RC (DNA: RG 59, LAR); torn; at head of text: "A Monsieur Thomas Jefferson Président des Etats Unis de L'amérique"; endorsed by TJ as received 17 June and "employment" and so recorded in SJL.

Barthélemy Lafon (1769-1820) was born near Paris and emigrated to New Orleans about 1790. Apparently well-educated as an architect and surveyor, Lafon received numerous commissions for public works projects during the last years of Spanish governance. Staying busy after the United States assumed control, he executed the plan for an expansion below the city and developed an idea for another new neighborhood backing up against the river—the area eventually known as the lower Garden District. He also planned the town of Donaldsonville, across the river from Baton Rouge. In 1806, Isaac Briggs named him deputy surveyor for Orleans County, a position he held for three years. During the War of 1812, he inspected and suggested improvements for New Orleans's defenses. In addition to his architectural, engineering, and surveying pursuits, he compiled directories of the city for 1807 and 1809. Lafon acknowledged two children he had with a free woman of color. His auctioned estate included a plantation of some 24,000 arpents bordering Lake Pontchartrain and 21 enslaved persons (Glenn R. Conrad, ed., *A Dictionary of Louisiana Biography*, 2 vols. [New Orleans, 1988], 1:476; Mary Louise Christovich, Roulhac Toledano, and Betsy Swanson, eds., *New Orleans Architecture*, 7 vols. [Gretna, La., 1971-89], 1:8-12, 31; Gilbert C. Din and John E. Harkins, *The New Orleans Cabildo: Colonial Louisiana's First City Government, 1769-1803* [Baton Rouge, 1996], 190, 247-8, 253; Harold D. Moser and others, eds., *The Papers of Andrew Jackson*, 10 vols. [Knoxville, 1980-], 3:152n, 471; *Orleans Gazette; and Commercial Advertiser*, 26 Mch. 1806; New Orleans *Courrier de la Louisiane*, 1 Jan. 1821; Lafon, *Calendrier de commerce de la Nouvelle-Orleans, pour l'année 1807* [New Orleans, 1806]; Lafon, *Annuaire Louisianais pour l'année 1809* [New Orleans, 1808]).

CARTE DU TERRITOIRE D'ORLÉANS: Lafon's draft became the basis for *Carte générale du territoire d'Orléans comprenant aussi la Floride occidentale et une portion du territoire du Mississippi*, which he published in New Orleans in 1806.

The CORPORATION, or Conseil, de Ville was the new, elected city government created by the territory's legislative council to replace the municipal body appointed by French prefect Pierre Clément Laussat (Eberhard L. Faber, *Building the Land of Dreams: New Orleans and the Transformation of Early America* [Princeton, 2016], 209-11).

To James Madison

DEAR SIR Monticello Apr. 11. 05.

Yours of the 5th. came to hand on the 8th. & I now return the papers it covered. Ferrand's decree is serious & I have more hope of it's being corrected by Tureau than by Buonaparte. I shall be with you by the middle of the next week, & therefore defer to verbal explanation every thing public. I shall leave my daughter in a state not immediately threatening nor yet clear of serious anxiety. a weakened stomach is the basis of her complaint, & great debility the consequence. she goes about however, is chearful, & keeping her sufferings to herself, her friends know their extent incidentally only. we have had two very fine rains within the last fortnight. the trees are all leaved here, but in the neighborhood generally only the poplar. our first Asparagus was Mar. 27. the 1st. Whippoor will Apr. 2. the 1st. tick & the Dogwood blossoms on the 4th. my affectionate salutations to mrs Madison & yourself & assurances of cordial esteem & respect

TH: JEFFERSON

RC (DLC: Madison Papers); place written in dateline as "Monticllo"; at foot of text: "Mr. Madison." PoC (DLC). Notation in SJL: "Ferrand." Enclosures: see Madison to TJ, 5 Apr.

I SHALL BE WITH YOU: TJ departed from Monticello on 14 Apr. and arrived in Washington on 17 Apr. His expenses for the journey totaled $14.48 (MB, 2:1150).

From Joseph B. McKean

SIR, Philadelphia April 11th: 1805.

Mr; Clement Penrose has, I understand, been recommended to your Excellency as a fit person to be appointed Register, under the Act of Congress "For ascertaining and adjusting the titles & claims to Lands within the territory of Orleans and the district of Louisiana." Although, I have not had the pleasure of a very intimate acquaintance with Mr; Penrose, yet, from his character & talents, his knowledge of the French and German languages, I presume he is competent to discharge the duties of the office. I have therefore taken the Liberty to recommend him to your Excellency for the appointment.

I have the honour to be with great respect Your Mt. Ob St.

J. B. M;KEAN

RC (DNA: RG 59, LAR); at foot of text: "His Excellency Thomas Jefferson Esqr."; endorsed by TJ as received 17 Apr. and "Penrose Clemt. to be Comr." and so recorded in SJL.

Lawyer Joseph B. McKean (1764-1826) was the son of Pennsylvania governor Thomas McKean and the brother of Sarah McKean Irujo, wife of the Spanish minister. He served as state attorney general from 1800 to 1808 and as a judge in the district court of Philadelphia beginning in 1817. At the time of his death, McKean was president of that court and was described as "learned, undefatigable patient and candid" (Cornelius McKean, *McKean Genealogies, from the Early Settlement of McKeans or McKeens in America to the Present Time, 1902; With Portraits Representing the Different Branches of the Family* [Des Moines, 1902], 118-19, 122; John Hill Martin, *Martin's Bench and Bar of Philadelphia: Together with Other Lists of Persons Appointed to Administer the Laws in the City and County of Philadelphia and the Province and Commonwealth of Pennsylvania* [Philadelphia, 1883], 26-7, 78-9; *Poulson's American Daily Advertiser*, 5 Sep. 1826).

A FIT PERSON: Tench Coxe recommended Clement Penrose in an undated letter to Madison. Coxe described Penrose as the nephew of "Mrs. Genl. Wilkinson," about 34 years old, with a background in law and an acquaintance with the German and French languages (RC in DNA: RG 59, LAR; endorsed by TJ: "Penrose Clement B. Comr. Louisa. Tenche Coxe to mr Madison"). See also Madison, *Papers*, *Sec. of State Ser.*, 9:233-4.

To Dabney Carr

DEAR SIR Monticello Apr. 12. 05.

I was lately summoned as a witness in a case wherein mr Craven Peyton was a party, to appear on some day of the ensuing district court at Charlottesville; but my public duties requiring my immediate return to Washington, for which place I set out the day after tomorrow, it will not be in my power to attend. believing I could know nothing of any matter of controversy between the parties, I enquired & was told it was supposed that some money paid by me to mr Peyton was supposed to be for the use of Colo. Charles L. Lewis. this supposition is entirely without foundation. the money was paid to mr Peyton on an unsettled account existing between him & me, and having no relation to the affairs or interests of Colo. Lewis, but purely to those between him mr Peyton[1] & myself, nor is any person but mr Peyton answerable to me for them. I know that this letter can be no evidence in the controversy; and am willing to put it's contents into the form & under the solemnities of a deposition if it be desired. I have stated what I know merely that the parties may judge whether it can avail either. Accept my affectionate salutations.

TH: JEFFERSON

PoC (CSmH); at foot of text: "Mr. Dabney Carr."

Charles Lilburne LEWIS was both TJ's first cousin and his brother-in-law, having married TJ's sister Lucy. Lewis was also the father-in-law of Craven Peyton and the brother of Elizabeth Lewis Henderson, the widow of Bennett Henderson (Boynton Merrill, Jr., *Jefferson's Nephews: A Frontier Tragedy* [Princeton, 1976], 50, 59, 344, 347; Vol. 28:474n).

[1] Preceding two words interlined.

From Joachim F. Eckard

Sir — Philadelphia 12th. April 1805.

A scientific Gentleman at Copenhagen gave me in charge, when I was there last Winter, to convey to your Excellency the inclosed with a small Package containing some ancient coins, which he has begged your Excellencys permission to offer as a token of his great respect.

I have felt as highly gratify'd to have been honourd. with this commission, as I feel happy in this opportunity of most respectfully joining with my countrymen in paying you the tribute of my homage and veneration

I most humbly beg permission to sign Your Excellencies Most obedient and most humble Servant

J. F. Eckard
Danish V. Consul at Philadelphia

RC (DLC); at head of text: "His Excellency Thomas Jefferson Esquire President of the United States &.c. &.c. &.c. &.c."; endorsed by TJ as received 18 Apr. and so recorded in SJL. Enclosure: Nicolai Henrich Weinwich to TJ, 30 Oct. 1804.

Joachim Frederick Eckard (d. 1827) was a Danish merchant from the island of St. Thomas who settled in Philadelphia and married into a local family. Eckard sold goods sourced from the Baltic, offered his services as a translator, and served as the Danish vice consul (*Relfs Philadelphia Gazette*, 21 Mch., 5 May 1803; *Poulson's American Daily Advertiser*, 27 Aug. 1805; Philadelphia *National Gazette and Literary Register*, 5 Jan. 1821, 15 Oct. 1827).

From Thomas Worthington

Dear Sir — Chilicothe April 12th 1805

Soon after I returned I was informed the marshal of this state Major David Zeigler had resigned his office. I am requested by two Gentlemen of this place (Mr Michael Baldwin & Mr Joseph Kerr) to name them to you as candidates for this vacancy. With Mr Baldwin you are acquainted Of Mr Kerr I have only to observe that he is a man of property reputable character and qualified to discharge the duties of the office He is at present a Senator in the State Legislature from the county in which I live Give me leave to refer you to Mr Gallatin who is acquainted with[1] this gentleman for further information

I beg Sir you will accept my most sincere wishes that your present term of office may end with accumulated honour to yourself & satisfaction to your country. and that you may live long in the enjoyment of health happiness & the confidence of a grateful country I have nothing important to communicate we are all peace here & as happy as new setlers can be

I am with the most sincere esteem & respect your obt st

T Worthington

RC (DNA: RG 59, LAR); endorsed by TJ as received 26 Apr. and "Baldwin Michael. Kerr Joseph to be Marshal" and so recorded in SJL.

An additional recommendation in favor of MICHAEL BALDWIN came from U.S. district judge Charles Willing Byrd. Writing to Madison on 15 Mch., Byrd lauded Baldwin's merits as a government officer and attorney, and his "demeanour as a man" (RC in DNA: RG 59, LAR; endorsed by TJ: "Baldwin, Michl. Marshal v. Zeigler").

[1] MS: "with with."

From William Eustis

Sir, Boston April 13th. 1805.

Mr Thomas Lewis Junr. goes to Washington to explain to the department of State and to ask assistance in recovering a claim for captured property which appears to me to be attended wth. circumstances equally novel and extraordinary. He will be anxious to have the honor of paying his respects to you, and I have assured him of the pleasure with which you will receive one of our most respectable and constant friends.

At the same time I offer you the respect and esteem of your obedient Servt.

William Eustis.

RC (DLC); at foot of text: "Thomas Jefferson President of the United States"; endorsed by TJ as received 9 May and so recorded in SJL.

NOVEL AND EXTRAORDINARY: in 1800, a ship owned by Thomas Lewis & Son was captured by French privateers and condemned at Guadeloupe. Although the firm successfully appealed to the Council of Prizes in Paris for restitution, the government in Guadeloupe refused to honor the award of $17,862 "untill the publication of Peace between France and England be Officaly declared" (Madison, *Papers*, *Sec. of State Ser.*, 9:336-7; 10:560-1).

From Tucker Moore Woodson

Sir Charlottsville April 15th. 1805.

Inclosed you find a letter written by Joseph Woodson now resident at Manchester. My acquaintance with this young Man will not justify my saying any thing for or against him—Yet I feel it a duty owed to all to promote so far as I can the hapiness of my fellow man. This duty otherwise than letting Known the wish he expresses for serving his Country & himself could not be discharged

I am Sir Most Respectfully yr Ob Servant T M Woodson

RC (DNA: RG 59, LAR); endorsed by TJ as received 30 Apr. and "Woodson Joseph to be employed in Navy" and so recorded in SJL. Enclosure: Joseph Woodson, Jr., to Tucker Moore Woodson, 27 Mch., Manchester, Virginia, mentioning their "consanguinity" and asking that his request for a naval appointment be put to the president; "I trust to your friendship for your influence with Mr Jefferson" (RC in same; endorsed by TJ).

Tucker Moore Woodson, a distant relative of TJ, was a considerable landowner in Albemarle County. He and his wife, Martha Eppes Woodson, moved to Kentucky in 1804 and ultimately resided in Jessamine County (Edgar Woods, *Albemarle County in Virginia* [Charlottesville, 1901], 357, 391; WMQ, 1st ser., 10 [1901-2], 47-8, 188; G. Glenn Clift, comp., *Kentucky Obituaries, 1787-1854* [Baltimore, 1977], 113).

From Robert Stewart

Honored Sir, Philadelphia, April 16th, 1805.

The favorable account my brothers William and John, gave me of that country, occasined me to wish for an oppertunity to settel in it—I therefore solicit you to indavour to get me a situation, as overseer of a plantation in your neighbourhood. It not being in my power to stock a farm.

I can bring recommendation from Messrs Patterson and Cochran, whom I served my apprenticeship with; & all the others who, I have worked for.

From the many favors my family hath received from you; I expect you will not forget me.

If you can get me such a situation you will be so kind as to let my father know and he will let me know when to come.

If you could have imploy for me I should prefer it to any other.

Your's &c: Robert Stewart.

RC (MHi); endorsed by TJ as received 19 Apr. and so recorded in SJL.

Robert Stewart was presumably the son of the Monticello blacksmith, William Stewart.

MESSRS PATTERSON AND COCHRAN: Stewart may have apprenticed for the Philadelphia printing firm Patterson & Cochran, which was in operation in 1799 and 1800. One of the proprietors, Hugh B. Cochran, continued the business with a different partner (*Robinson's Philadelphia Register and City Directory, for 1799* [Philadelphia, 1799], n.p.; Cornelius William Stafford, *The Philadelphia Directory, for 1801* [Philadelphia, 1801], 80; Philadelphia *Universal Gazette*, 9 Jan. 1800).

MANY FAVORS: TJ recommended William G. Stewart for a midshipman's warrant in the navy and may have employed John Stewart as a painter at Monticello (MB, 2:1126; Vol. 38:62-3).

From William Shippen

DEAR SIR, [before 17 Apr. 1805]

I have known Major Penrose a long time—believe him to be a good republican—a man of considerable talents, a man of integrity & polite manners & think him qualified for the place he solicits.

I am Dr. Sir with sentiment of Respect Your obed Servt

W. SHIPPEN

RC (DNA: RG 59, LAR); undated; endorsed by TJ as received 17 Apr. 1805 and "Penrose Clement to be Comr." and so recorded in SJL.

From "A Democrat"

[on or before 17 Apr. 1805]

Mem arem for Aeminor monon ex in espe for mon et Contra asume jour in datu foromonoso fallalia discordio Rama tivon desto Ces morid et mon et munda—Rebuble arc nor for these: Jontuficul Romana—Rex Robertus 3d in de anno domine 1403—

Ex in animanu for this dater forum informa alluse Justus

Let the hero of Carters hill decipher this if he can, If he does then and not till then is he fit to fit out Gun Boats and know the effects they can produce

Dry docks good things—never get wet Saving plan[k] are for the good of the people—Sly dog do n't mind them—resign at the end of this 4 years with Grace

A DEMOCRAT

RC (DLC: TJ Papers, 149:25991); undated; at foot of text: "T Jefferson Esqr"; addressed; endorsed by TJ as an anonymous letter received 17 Apr. 1805 and so recorded in SJL; also endorsed by TJ: "a fool."

HERO OF CARTERS HILL: a slighting reference to TJ's avoidance of capture by the British cavalry in 1781; see TJ to Gallatin, 21 June, and Vol. 4:267-8n.

From John Keemle

SIR, Philada. April 17th. 1805.

Being in company with Mr. T. Cox a few days ago, he informed [me that] he had not forwarded the sample of calcined re[d le]ad to You, according to promise. I was somewhat disp[leased] on hearing it. I immediately told him to Let me have it, and I would forward it to you myself, for it was not attended with any expence to as all letters and packages to you were free of postage.

Mr. Cox not sending it according to promise, is a mystery—which I cannot develope. He has no Cause to suspect me of applying for his office, for I never was an office hunter, though often advised to it, by my friends, as more deserving of one than many who have held lucrative offices, and who never fought and suffered in our revolution as I did. But as I am now getting old; and a large family to maintain, I think I may with more freedom solicit an appointment, than in my Younger Years; or those, who at no time rendered any service to establish our independence, or grown up since that memorable peri[od.]

From Governor Mc.Kean, I cannot expect any favour, for he was highly displeased, at my speaking and writing against the Judges, when I was in the Legislature last Year. He censured me severly about it. I replyed—"I acted agreeable to the dictates of conscience in that buisness."

Enclosed Sir, I send you the sample. Should the lead mines be worked for the benefit of the states; or any other vacancy occur I request to be remembered.

With considerations of high esteem, I am Yours. &c. &c.

John Keehmle

RC (DNA: RG 59, LAR); torn; at foot of text: "Thos Jefferson Esqr."; endorsed by TJ as received 20 Apr. and "for office" and so recorded in SJL.

according to promise: see Keemle to TJ, 16 Mch.

highly displeased: an anecdote published in several Federalist newspapers claimed that during the debate in Pennsylvania over the impeachment of the state supreme court judges, Thomas McKean insulted Keemle's intelligence (*New-York Commercial Advertiser*, 19 May 1804; see Anonymous to TJ, 28 Jan. 1805).

From Samuel Smith

Sir/ [on or before 17 Apr. 1805]

I did myself the honor to recommend for your Attention Mr. James Lowrey Donaldson a Gentleman of the Bar of this City for the Office of Commissioner to Ascertain the Titles to Land in Louisiana—I have taken some pains to ascertain the Character of Mr. Donaldson, and find it unblemished—his talents are highly estimated by Gentlemen well acquainted with him, & his Capacity to fill the Office with Ability, not doubted,—his Father Colo Lowrey Commands one of our Regiments of Militia, and means to remove to that Country with his

Son—the Politicks of both, republican—the son has written some useful pieces—I feel much interested in his favor, and shall Consider his appointment a very particular favor Conferred on—

Your friend and Obliged servt S. Smith

Mr. Donaldson's name was Changed from Lowrey—for the reversion of an Estate—

RC (DNA: RG 59, LAR); undated; endorsed by TJ as received 17 Apr. 1805 and "Donaldson to be Comr." and so recorded in SJL.

DID MYSELF THE HONOR: Smith to TJ, 4 Apr.

From Albert Gallatin

Sir, Treasury Department 18th April 1805

I have the honor to transmit Adam Gantz' petition praying for a pardon, the effect of which will be the remission of a penalty incurred by reason of an infraction of the revenue laws, and his releasment from confinement. His former petition had on your suggestion been returned to him in order that the district judge's certificate, which accompanies this, might be obtained.

I have the honor to be with the highest respect Sir Your obedt. Servt. Albert Gallatin

RC (DLC); at foot of text: "The President of the United States"; endorsed by TJ as received from the Treasury Department on 19 Apr. and "Gantz pardon" and so recorded in SJL.

FORMER PETITION: see Gallatin to TJ, 2 Feb., and TJ's reply on 4 Feb.

ENCLOSURE

Petition of Adam Gantz, with Jefferson's Order

To the Honerable Albert Gallatin Secrety. of the Treasury of the United States

Adam Gantz of the City of Baltimore respectfully shewes to your Honor that being encouraged by the Honorable Judge Winchester from intimations of relief given to him by his Excellency the President, your Petitioner is encouraged to beg your attention to this his petition and to the enclosures submited with it, The distress and actual suffering of a wife and several helpless Children who are dependant upon your Petitioners personal Exertions for the necessaries of Life are the real Excuses offered by your Petitioner for the pressing solicitude with which he entreats the interference of your Honor, your Petitioners case was lately submited to his Excellency the President with a hope that he could, and if so your Petitioner did not doubt, but that he would grant your Petitioner relief—He was pleased to intimate as your Petitioner is informed that application ought to be made to the Treasury Department but that, altho', your petitioner should be entirely unable to pay yet it might not be proper to interfere to relieve him, from all punishment, and your Petitioner having been for some time locked up in Jail where he must at mercy remain, unless by the Clemency of your Honor directed to be Liberated it is therefore most respectfully and earnestly prayed that your Honor will be pleased so to order

ADM GANTZ
12 Apl. 1805

I hereby certify that Adam Gantz of the City of Baltimore hath been for thirty days past and now is confined in the prison of Baltimore County upon a writ of capias ad satisfaciendum at the suit of the United States—.

THO: RUTTER
Marshal of Maryld District
10 April 1805

To the Honoble: James Winchester
Maryland district. April 11. 1805.

I do hereby certify, that in my opinion Adam Gantz has been sufficiently punished by the term of imprisonment he has suffered for the offence of which he was convicted, provided he indemnify the United States from Costs of conviction and imprisonment.

J WINCHESTER
Judge Maryd. dist

[*Order by TJ*:]
Apr. 20. 05.
Let a pardon issue

TH: JEFFERSON

MS (DNA: RG 59, GPR); petition in a clerk's hand, signed by Gantz; Thomas Rutter's and James Winchester's certifications in their hands, on a separate sheet, with order added by TJ at foot. Certifications enclosed in Winchester to Gallatin, Baltimore, 11 Apr. (RC in same).

INTIMATIONS OF RELIEF: Winchester's 11 Apr. letter to Gallatin, now mutilated, stated that "In conversation with the President of the [United States], on the subject of a petition of Adam [. . .] my statement of facts, he stated to [. . .] the prayer of the petition could not be [. . .] but that under all circumstances the [. . .] should [be] reduced as far as was [consistent] with justice to the public, and the [. . .] of Gantz—and desired me to certify [. . .] opinion of the extent of punishment which the offence of Gantz required."

In a letter to Jacob Wagner, 22 Apr., Edward Jones wrote that "Mr. Gallatin to whom the petition in question was referred by the President, is inclined to think that Gantz had been concerned in landing of goods without a permit from the Custom House, but as his recollections on that point [. . .] too imperfect to be relied on," he advised inquiring of William MacCreery for more information (RC in same; torn).

TJ pardoned Gantz on 1 May and remitted his $400 fine "so far as the United States are interested in the same" (FC in Lb in same).

From Albert Gallatin

Dear Sir 18th April 1805

I enclose the following papers

1. Rufus Easton's communications returned
2. Recommendations in favor of Vacher of New York for some of the land offices in Louisiana.—For the office of commissrs. in upper Louisiana there are two other applicants—Lucas who, being poor, is afraid the expences there will be more than his salary as judge and, I conjecture, will not be able to accept that office unless he also obtains the other—Clement Penrose of Philada. a nephew of Mrs. Wilkison who intends moving there. I know nothing of him except that he is honest & speaks very good French: he is independent in his circumstances & having a growing family is induced to go in order to make provision for his children. As the office of Register commences only on 1st Septer. I detained Trimble's[1] commission till your return, in order that, you might take a general view of the whole subject at once:—also recommendation in favor of Fromentin—
3. Recommendations in favor of Muse, & application by Brett Randolph, who had been formerly warmly recommended by John Randolph. His not being appointed post-master at Fredericksburg gave him, I think, some disgust.
4. A letter from M. Lyon & a note from Gen. Dearborn respecting the vacancy of collector at Massac. Either the man recommended by M. Lyon or the commanding officer must be appointed. The place is a sinecure of 250 dollars; the only duty that of granting two or three registers a year to vessels built below Louisville
5. A recommendation in favor of J. Saunders as 2d mate of the revenue cutter of Philadelphia. You received at Monticello a recommendation for 1st mate on which you wrote that you would act on your return
6. recommendation in favr. of M. Baldwin as marshal of Ohio
7. Papers relative to the establishment of Sacket's harbour as an additional port of entry on Lake Ontario as authorized by a former law. From an investigation of the subject & late conversation with Mr Tillier who resided several years on Black river, I have no doubt of its being the proper place; and, on the whole, it is probable that A. Sackett himself will do for collector.
8. Letters from Mr Nicholas respecting E. Randolph, one of which you have already seen. I wish to consult you before the propositions are adopted or rejected

With great respect & attachment Your obedt. Servt.

ALBERT GALLATIN

RC (DLC); at foot of text: "The President of the United States"; endorsed by TJ as received from the Treasury Department on 18 Apr. and "Louisa. officers. Brett Randolph. Officer of customs Massac. Saunders. Baldwin Sackett. W. C. Nicholas" and so recorded in SJL. Enclosures: (1) Communications of Rufus Easton on upper Louisiana (see Easton to TJ, 17 Jan.; Gideon Granger to TJ, 1 Apr.). (2) See John Francis Vacher to TJ, 23 Mch. (3) Probably William Polk to Gallatin, 6 Mch., from Somerset County, Maryland, recommending his son-in-law, Eligius Fromentin, as "well qualified to fill almost Any Office that may be Vacant in" Louisiana (RC in DNA: RG 59, LAR; endorsed by TJ: "Fromentin Eligius for office in Louisa. Judge Polk to mr Gallatin"). (4) Matthew Lyon to Gallatin, 2 Apr., from Bedford, Pennsylvania, concerning the need for a customs official at Fort Massac; Lyon understands that Captain Daniel Bissell has orders to remove from his post and that the situation requires an official to give registers to vessels descending from there; he recommends Gideon D. Cobb, a "Steady Man," and will act as his security (Gallatin, *Papers*, 10:778-9). (5) Probably Jared Mansfield to Gallatin, 23 Mch., from Marietta, Ohio, adding his "testimony to that of Others" in favor of Michael Baldwin's appointment as marshal of the Ohio district; Mansfield asks that Gallatin pass on his recommendation to the president (RC in DNA: RG 59, LAR). Other enclosures not found, but see below.

Among the enclosed documents recommending Francis VACHER for one of the new western land offices may have been a letter from John Brown to Gallatin. Brown mentioned Vacher as a good candidate, as well as Clement Penrose (RC in same, 1:1162-3; endorsed by TJ: "Brown John to mr Gallatin"). John B. C. LUCAS discussed his financial needs with Gallatin some time before leaving Washington, and in a letter of 4 May to Madison repeated his request to be named a land commissioner in the Louisiana Territory, in addition to his appointment as territorial judge. If not granted the position, he would have to decline his judicial commission (RC in same; endorsed by TJ: "Lucas John B. C. to be Commr. Louisa").

The COMMANDING OFFICER at Fort Massac, Daniel Bissell, had been appointed collector in January 1803 (Norman W. Caldwell, "Fort Massac: The American Frontier Post, 1778-1805," *Journal of the Illinois State Historical Society*, 43 [1950], 279-80; Vol. 39:315).

RECEIVED AT MONTICELLO: Gallatin to TJ, 26 Mch.

FORMER LAW: "An Act to make Beaufort and Passamaquoddy, ports of entry and delivery; to make Easton and Tiverton, ports of delivery; and to authorize the establishment of a new collection district on Lake Ontario," approved on 3 Mch. 1803 (U.S. Statutes at Large, 2:228-9).

Wilson Cary NICHOLAS had been interceding on behalf of Edmund Randolph in the latter's defense against U.S. claims for a shortfall in his accounts as secretary of state. After Gabriel Duvall, the arbitrator, ruled against Randolph in November 1804, Nicholas assumed control of Randolph's property and agreed to reimburse the government in four installments. He may have discussed the plan in letters of 3 Mch. and 3 Apr. to Gallatin (not found). In a response of 11 Apr., Gallatin expressed broad approval of the plan but worried that "there is some difficulty respecting the dispensation of the negroes" and wondered if Nicholas's "assumption shall be taken in lieu of the lien on the real estate." Gallatin viewed the plan as beneficial to the United States, but, as Nicholas's friend, he regretted it. At some point, TJ obtained a document, dated 1 Jan. 1804, listing some of Randolph's ideas for the arrangement with Nicholas. Randolph was to cede land and slaves to Nicholas while retaining control over pork and tobacco raised on the land (MS in MHi, in Edmund Randolph's hand; Gallatin, *Papers*, 10:806; John J. Reardon, *Edmund Randolph: A Biography* [New York, 1975], 356-7; Duvall to TJ, 20 Nov. 1804).

[1] MS: "Thrimble's."

From Albert Gallatin

SIR Treasury Department 18th April 1805

I have the honor to enclose a letter received from Mr Granger in behalf of the owners of the "Connecticut reserve," and a copy of instructions previously given on that subject to the Surveyor General.

The principle assumed in the instructions is that if the land adjacent to the reserve shall be purchased by the United States, the boundary line or lines dividing the reserve from the lands of the United States shall be surveyed altogether at the expence of Government; but that the indian boundary lines dividing the reserve from lands not purchased by the United States shall be surveyed at the expence of the owners of that reserve; Government in the last case, defraying only the expence of a proper agent who is to attend for the purpose of ensuring correctness in running the line.

That principle appears consistent both with equity & with the existing laws which authorise the surveying of lands purchased from the Indians for the United States and of no other lands. As the company who own the lands seem to entertain a different idea & to suppose that the boundary lines ought, at all events, to be surveyed at the expence of the United States, I beg leave to submit the subject to your decision.

I have the honor to be with the highest respect Sir Your obedt. Sert.

ALBERT GALLATIN

RC (DLC); at foot of text: "The President of the United States"; endorsed by TJ as received from the Treasury Department on 19 Apr. and "Connecticut reserve" and so recorded in SJL. Enclosure: Gallatin to Jared Mansfield, 4 Apr.; reminding Mansfield of prior instructions to send an assistant surveyor to attend the running of boundary lines of the Connecticut reserve, Gallatin informs the surveyor general of U.S. plans to purchase the tract lying between the reserve and the northern boundary of the "military tract"; if that land is obtained, the United States can assume the expense of surveying the southern boundary of the reserve, but if not, the company owning the reserve must defray the expense of running the line; no matter what, surveying the western boundary of the reserve is the company's responsibility (Gallatin, *Papers*, 10:790). Other enclosure not found.

For negotiations between the United States, several Native American tribes, and directors of the CONNECTICUT RESERVE, see Henry Champion and Others to TJ, 28 Feb.

From John Rhea

SR, Sullivan Courthouse April 18th. 1805

Three weeks after having the pleasure of seeing You—I was at the place and had the conversation promised—from what passed there is every reason to believe that business will be right—of which I would have wrote sooner but waited to hear of the arrival of the papers, but as Yet they have not been heard of by me—

In conversation with Mr Anderson respecting the intended treaty with the cherokee Indians—a question presented itself—If General Smith being heretofore elected a Senator of the United States—should act as a commissioner of that treaty—can it be objected as a reason to preclude him from taking his senatorial seat in the ninth congress? I only mention this—and for taking the liberty so to do I hope You will excuse me.

I am with Sincere Esteem & respect Yr Obt Servt

JOHN RHEA

RC (DLC); at foot of text: "The President of the United States"; endorsed by TJ as received 30 Apr. and so recorded in SJL.

THAT BUSINESS: possibly Rhea and Joseph Anderson's recent recommendation of George Duffield for a judicial appointment in Orleans Territory (see Anderson and Rhea to TJ, 5 Mch.; Anderson to TJ, 25 Mch.; and Rhea to TJ, 24 May).

In April 1804, TJ had appointed Daniel SMITH and Return Jonathan Meigs commissioners to treat with the Cherokees for land cessions in Tennessee, Kentucky, and Georgia (ASP, *Indian Affairs*, 1:699; Vol. 43:231-2, 680). The previous year, the Tennessee legislature elected Smith to represent the state in the U.S. Senate commencing 3 Mch. 1805. He would take his seat in the Ninth Congress on 2 Dec. (*Journal of the Senate at the First Session of the Fifth General Assembly of the State of Tennessee* [Knoxville, 1803], 21-2, 24-5; JS, 4:3-4).

From Robert Smith

SIR, Nav Dept. 18 April 1805.—

I have to request your signature to the commissions herewith sent for Lieuts. Haraden and Magrath. one of these officers is required for the J. Adams, the other for one of the gunboats now fitting for service.—

I am very respectfully, Sir, yr. ob St.— RT SMITH

RC (DLC); in a clerk's hand, signed by Smith; at foot of text: "The President of the United States"; endorsed by TJ as received from the Navy Department on 18 Apr. and "Commns." and so recorded in SJL. FC (DNA: RG 45, LSP).

From Henry Dearborn

SIR War Department. April, 19th. 1805

I have the honor of proposing, for your approbation, the appointment of Jonathan Williams, as a Lieut. Colonel in the Corps of Engineers.

Accept, Sir, the assurances of my high respect, and consideration

H. DEARBORN

PrC (PHi: Daniel Parker Papers); in a clerk's hand, signed by Dearborn; at foot of text: "The President of the United States." FC (Lb in DNA: RG 107, LSP).

From Henry Dearborn

SIR [19 Apr. 1805]

I have informed Col Williams that it a new nomination must take place, and that I have doubts as to the propriety of his being appointed to a higher grade than a Lt. Col, but would not oppose his having a higher grade if you should think it advisable. I have such information from the Officers of the Corps as to induce a belief that the reappointment of Col Williams will give satisfaction & pleasure to the Corps.

Yours, H. DEARBORN

RC (DLC); undated; at foot of text: "the President of the United States"; endorsed by TJ as received from the War Department on 19 Apr. 1805 and "Colo. Williams" and so recorded in SJL.

From Gottfried Heise

MAY IT PLEASE YOUR EXCELLENCY &C. &C.

Dommitzsoh near Torgau in the Electorate of Saxony 19 April 1805

As the US have obtained, by the acquisition of Louisiana, so much uncultivated and fertile[1] land, and as I hope they will allot a part thereof for the cultivation of the German Evangelical congregations; they may be desirous of obtaining a number of German cultivators. Among these am I and my family. Will your Excelly. permit me to explain my proposal, which shall be realised without delay as soon as your Excy. shall be pleased to grant my wishes in this respect. I therefore humbly pray you to hear my proposal and my wishes.

My proposal. I shall come as Evangelical Lutheran preacher with a german congregation which I shall collect in Germany, and which shall consist of a company of substantial husbandmen and Artizans: we shall purchase for ourselves in Louisiana a District containing many acres of land,[2] build farm houses upon it for ourselves and bind ourselves to fulfill all the laws of the U.S. The name of the place shall be *Treufelden* [Fields of Faith] which may constantly remind the Inhabitants of the place, of their faithfulness to the Religion of Jesus and to the U. States

My wishes. That your Excy. should send me, in order to the happy accomplishment of this work, a patent wherein the following shall be secured: —

1st. That the Evangl. Lutheran German[3] colony at Treufelden in Louisiana may at their discretion locate and Survey the quantity they may chuse of uncultivated fertile land and also of forest lying therein; That they shall have an acre of land, be there wood thereon or herbage, or any thing else, with the appurtenances, for dollars shillings: That they shall pay for the same in two portions, half immediately and the other half in yearly instalments; That they may subdivide, as they think proper, among themselves the lands contained in their patent; That they shall be in all respects subject to the ordinary law of the land; but that they shall have the privilege of ordaining and using bye-laws not contrary to the laws of the land: That they shall not be taxed until after the term of ten years from the date of their patent; that they shall have every freedom and Support in trade, liberty of hunting on the lands belonging to the company, right of fishing in all Streams, rivers &c. &c. lying in and near the Same, free religion and worship, Security and protection of property and the privilege of voting in the affairs of the U.S. after the expiration of years.

2. That your Excy. should lend me with the above writing of assurance, a pass as well in the german as in the English and French languages of nearly the following import: —

That Mr. G. L. Heise, elected preacher by the North American, Evangelical, Lutheran, German Congregation in Louisiana, who is at present in Germany, wishes before his departure from Germany to make a journey through Saxony, Franconia, Swabia and Westphalia, as well with a view to examine the various earths, stones and waters of the various mineral springs, and to collect specimens of each for a comparison with those of North America and to be able to give instruction by exhibiting them;—as also with a view once more to visit his friends and learned correspondents; and take leave of them, and that he intends to take his daughter Amalia with him on this journey; That finally he intends, with his wife and children, to prosecute his voyage to North America, on which he will also take some friends, by way of Hamburg &c. &c.

3. There are many thousand poor families of farmers & mechanics in Germany. If they could better their condition in America, they would come: but I wish to obtain from you the explanations and instruction for that purpose, that I may *privately* explain it to the people, for it cannot be openly done, the Princes not permitting emigration.
4th. Your excy. will make the purchase money per acre as low as possible, in order that the substantial husbandmen whom I shall collect may see a palpable gain before them.
5. As I am not a rich man, I wish to obtain, after I shall have well accomplished the business, a recompense in land as property for my children of whom I have nine.

I have forwarded this letter through Mr. Fr. W. Müller at Bremen & his correspondents in America. I beg for the determination through this or another safe and expeditious medium and remain with the deepest respect, your Excellency's most obed. servt.

MR. G. L. HEISE,
Naturalist & Theologian

Tr (DLC); a translation in Jacob Wagner's hand (see Wagner to TJ, 27 July [first letter]); brackets in original. RC (same); in German; at head of text: "Excellenz, Hochstgeehrtester Herr Präsident, Hochgeneigter gnädiger Gönner"; endorsed by TJ as received 20 July and so recorded in SJL. Enclosed in Wagner to TJ, 3 Aug.

MY PROPOSAL: TJ thanked Wagner for the translation, deeming the letter "not worth the trouble" (TJ to Wagner, 9 Aug.). Heise wrote again on 26 Apr., duplicating the text of the letter of 19 Apr. with an introductory paragraph. TJ referred that document also to Wagner, who replied in a note: "This letter is a duplicate of one J.W. had the honor to translate, in the summer, containing a proposal from a Mr. Heise to carry a colony from Germany to Louisiana. He now adds, that he has discovered a method of preserving potatoes, the secret of which he offers for sale" (RC in DLC; in German; endorsed by TJ as received 19 Oct. and so recorded in SJL).

[1] Canceled: "fruitful."

[2] Wagner here canceled "cultivate it and."

[3] Wagner here canceled "congregation."

To George Jefferson

DEAR SIR — Washington Apr. 19. 05.

In your letter of Feb. 12. you asked me whether you should engage my bacon as usual from Colo. Macon. I considered the question as answered by a letter which I had written two days before & you had not recieved at the date of yours. this requested you to procure me 100. *hams* of Colo. Macon, & to have them forwarded as soon as they should be fully cured: it being material that they should be recieved as soon after that as possible in order to take precautions against the fly. the object of the present is merely to ask the favor of you to drop me a line of information on the subject. Accept my affectionate salutations.

TH: JEFFERSON

PoC (MHi); at foot of text: "Mr. Jefferson"; endorsed by TJ.

To J. P. G. Muhlenberg

Washington Apr. 19. 05.

Th: Jefferson presents his respectful salutations to Genl. Muhlenberg, whose letter of the 9th. he found on his arrival here. he will thank him to forward the package he recieved from mr Kirkpatrick (by Capt. Obrien) by any vessel which may be coming round from Philadelphia to this place or neighborhood, as it's contents will not bear a transportation by land.

PoC (MHi); endorsed by TJ.

From Martha Jefferson Randolph

MY DEAREST FATHER Monticello April 19 1805

Mr Randolph's election is almost certain the polls stand, Alb. TM.R 503 W.L. 140. Amh. TM.R. 390. WL. 474. which leaves Mr Randolph a majority of 279, so that independant of his influence in Fluvanna which is great, he is safe. we are all well, but I am moored here till thursday as he[1] stopped a day with us on his way to Fluvanna where he now is, of course I am obliged to stay till his return. the weather is very favorable to your new plantations but many of the thorns I am told are certainly dead. adieu My Dear Father it is so late I am in danger of Losing the post yours most tenderly MR.

RC (ViU: Edgehill-Randolph Papers); endorsed by TJ as received 23 Apr. and so recorded in SJL.

W.L.: Walter Leake, also of Albemarle County, later governor of Mississippi (Dunbar Rowland, *Encyclopedia of Mississippi History*, 2 vols. [Madison, Wis., 1907], 2:63).

AMH.: Amherst County.

For TJ's new planting of THORNS, see Joseph Dougherty to TJ, 22 Mch.

[1] Randolph here partially canceled "[bare]ly."

From Robert Smith

SIR, Ap. 19. 1805.

In the course of a few days the sailing instructions and other communications will be forwarded to the Commanding Officer of the John Adams. Having but your qualified approbation of the accompanying commissions I deem it proper to return them to you for that reconsideration which you may be pleased to give them. I would only remark that I have not Considered the *peace*-establishment-Act the Rule of our Conduct with respect to the number of Officers or men in the prosecution of the War against Tripoli. Under the provisions of that Act only two thirds of the full complement of Seamen could be attached to our frigates and only 9 Captains—36 Lieutenants & 150 Midshipmen could be in service. Whereas we have always given as was essentially necessary, the full complement of men to each frigate and we have now in actual service fifty Seven Lieutenants. Congress having manifested a disposition to prosecute the War against Tripoli with vigour and the Executive having put in Commission the requisite number of vessels to effectuate that intention, the necessary Complement of Lieutenants was of course attached to each vessel amounting as before stated to fifty Seven. There is not any Law that restrains the President from appointing such Captains or Lieutenants as he in his judgment may deem proper.

It may not be improper to repeat to you that mr Stewart and mr. Hull are the two Gentlemen that command the two Brigs now in the Mediterranean

Respectfully RT SMITH

RC (DLC); addressed: "The President"; endorsed by TJ as received from the Navy Department on 19 Apr. and "Stewart & Hull" and so recorded in SJL. Enclosures not found.

SAILING INSTRUCTIONS: on 24 Apr., Smith ordered the frigate *John Adams*, then in New York, to sail with Gunboats Nos. 6 and 7 for the Mediterranean (Smith to James Lawrence and Peter S. Ogilvie, 17 Apr., FC in Lb in DNA: RG 45, LSG; NDBW, 5:537-8).

REPEAT TO YOU: see Smith to TJ, 27 Mch.

TWO BRIGS: Charles Stewart commanded the *Siren*, Isaac Hull the *Argus* (NDBW, *Register*, 26, 53).

To the State Department

The following Commissions to be issued
Michael Baldwin of Ohio to be Marshal of Ohio
Thomas Newton senr. of Virginia to be Collector for the port of Norfolk &c.

Th: Jefferson
Apr. 19. 05.

PoC (DLC). Notation in SJL: "Nomns. Baldwin. Newton."

Michael BALDWIN wrote to Madison on 29 May, acknowledging the receipt of his commission and thanking the president "for the honor conferred upon me" (RC in DNA: RG 59, AOC; torn; endorsed by TJ: "Baldwin Michael. accepts [. . .]").

From Matthew Walton

Sir, Ky. Springfield April 19th. 1805—

You may remember that a few days before I left the City of Washington I handed to you a recommendation from the Kentucky delegation, recommending Mr Felix Grundy & Mr. John Thompson as fit persons to fill the appointment of commissioners to adjust the Claims to lands in Louisiana under an act of the last Congress, I having my doubts whether they woud serv have conversed with Mr. Grundy on the subject, & find he is willing to serve if appointed in the uper District, unless his not understanding French accurately is a surmountable difficulty I cannot help reminding you that I am convinsed you cannot make an appointment that will Give more Satisfaction, he is a Lawyer of as high standing as any in this state, & a man of profound education & one I think I can answer will do the duty accurately if appointed

I am Sir your most Obt. Servant

Matthew Walton

RC (DNA: RG 59, LAR); endorsed by TJ as received 21 May and "Grundy Felix to be Comr." and so recorded in SJL.

RECOMMENDATION: Kentucky Members of the House of Representatives to TJ, 28 Feb.

To Carlos IV, King of Spain

Great and Good Friend,

I have made choice of James Bowdoin one of our distinguished citizens and lately our Charge d'Affaires at the Court of your Majesty, to reside near your Majesty in quality of Minister Plenipotentiary of the United States of America. He is well apprized of the friendship which we bear to your Majesty and of our desire to cultivate the harmony and good correspondence, so happily subsisting between us. From a knowledge of his fidelity, probity and good conduct, I have entire confidence that he will render himself acceptable to your Majesty, and give effect to our desire of preserving and advancing on all occasions the interest and happiness of the two Nations. I beseech your Majesty therefore to give full credence to whatever he shall say on the part of the United States, and most of all when he shall assure your Majesty of their friendship and wishes for your Majesty's prosperity: and I pray God to have your Majesty in his safe and holy keeping

Written at the City of Washington, the Twentieth day of April in the year of our Lord one thousand Eight hundred and five.

TH: JEFFERSON

FC (Lb in DNA: RG 59, Credences); in a clerk's hand; at foot of text: "To Our Great & Good Friend His Catholic Majesty"; below signature: "By the President of the United States of America" and "James Madison Secretary of State." Not recorded in SJL.

Madison enclosed the RC in a letter of instructions to James Bowdoin dated 20 Apr. (Madison, *Papers*, *Sec. of State Ser.*, 9:259-61).

From Pierre Chouteau

MONSIEUR.— St. Louis le 20 Avril 1805.—

Je vous ai annoncé par ma derniere lettre L'arrivée de plusieurs chefs Sioux que je n'avois pas encore vus; peu aprés le depart du courier Mr crawford m'a annoncé leur arrivée et me les a amenés; Je les ai renvoyé dans leurs nations avec quelques petits presents dont ils ont été satisfaits et ai remis a l'automne prochain a leur faire connoitre les intentions du gouvernement relativement à leur voyage a Washington city dont ils ont été flattés par les ordres du capne Lewis, mais ils preferent eux mêmes entreprendre ce voyage dans L'automne plutot que dans le tems des chaleurs: Mr crawford m'a remis en même tems un compte de depenses occasionnées par la descente de ces sauvages à St. Louis, Je ne l'ai point accepté et L'ai envoyé à Mr Le general Dearborn dont j'attendrai les ordres a ce sujet je lui ai en même tems observé que Mr crawford en obtenant de moi l'année derniere un permis pour traiter chez les Sioux ne m'a point alors parlé de son projet de faire descendre des chefs de cette nation ni des ordres qu'il pouvoit avoir reçu à ce sujet du capne Lewis. Je lui aurois alors donné communication des ordres et instructions que j'ai reçu du Gouvernement

et qui m'enjoignent de ne permettre le depart d'aucuns chefs de nations sauvages sans une permission Speciale. Je Joins ici une lettre que j'ai recu dernierement du chef osage Les Cheveux blancs, il paroit que la division s'accroit toujours entre les differents partis de cette nation et je sens combien ma presence y est necessaire pour y retablir l'harmonie et faciliter le passage de L'expedition que le gouvernement se propose de faire par la riviere des arkansas, mais j'ai été forcé de reculer mon voyage par L'arrivée d'un parti consequent de Sakias qui sont venus demander Le prisonier de leur nation detenu a St Louis, Les Veritables intentions de cette nation ne sont pas bien connues et il est a craindre que partant mecontens ils ne se portent a quelques excès, Je sais aussi qu'un autre parti de cette même nation et plus consequent encore est sur la riviere des grands osages dans le dessein de m'arretter dans mon voyage où peutêtre seulement pour frapper sur les osages, Je prens a ce sujet toutes les informations possible et suivant ce que J'apprendrai, comme je considere mon voyage chez les osages comme absolument indispensable pour remplir les intentions du gouvernement je compte demander au commandant des troupes en garrison a St. Louis une escorte de dix soldats pour assurer au pavillon americain le respect qui lui est du et que par une habitude contractée Sous notre ancien gouvernement le Sauvage paye plus volontiers a L'uniforme des troupes de Ligne. Si Le commandant me refuse je prendrai alors toutes les precautions en mon pouvoir pour empecher les Sakias d'executer leurs mauvaises intentions dont je ne Suis pas certain mais que j'ai tout Lieu de presumer.
La nouvelle officielle de votre ré-élection a la place de president des Etats Unis a comblé les voeux de tous nos citoyens et particulierement Le mien, le bonheur de la haute Louisiane et de ses habitans nous paroit assuré dès ce moment

J'ai l'honneur d'etre avec le plus profond respect Monsieur. Votre très Humble et très obeissant serviteur Pre. Chouteau

EDITORS' TRANSLATION

Sir, St. Louis, 20 Apr. 1805

In my last letter I announced the upcoming visit of several Sioux chiefs whom I had not yet met. Soon after the letter was sent, Mr. Crawford announced their arrival and brought them to me. I sent them back to their nations with some small gifts which satisfied them and I deferred until autumn a decision about the government's intentions concerning the trip to Washington City with which Captain Lewis's orders had flattered them. They themselves prefer to travel in the fall rather than during hot weather. Mr. Crawford also gave me a list of the costs these natives incurred on their trip down to St. Louis. I did not accept it but sent it to General Dearborn and will await his instructions on the matter. I also explained that when Mr. Crawford obtained a permit from me last year to trade with the Sioux, he did not discuss his plan to bring the nation's chiefs here or any orders he might have received from Captain Lewis. If he had, I would have informed him of the government's orders and instructions not to allow chiefs of any native nation to depart without special permission.

I am enclosing a recent letter from the Osage chief White Hair. Apparently the rift between the different factions of this nation continues to grow. I realize how much my presence is needed to restore harmony and to facilitate the expedition the government proposes to undertake on the Arkansas River, but I had to delay my trip because a large delegation of Sacs has come to claim one of their nation who is imprisoned in St. Louis. This nation's true intentions are unclear. If they leave unsatisfied they may be inclined to do something rash. I also know that another, even larger faction of the same nation is still on the Osage River and plans to stop me on my journey, or perhaps only to attack the Osages. I am obtaining all the information I can. Based on what I learn, and since I consider my trip to the Osages absolutely indispensable to fulfilling the government's wishes, I plan to ask the commander of the St. Louis garrison for an escort of 10 soldiers to ensure that the American flag receives the respect it deserves. The natives give respect more willingly to troops in uniform, a habit they acquired under our previous government. If the commander refuses, I will take whatever precautions I can to prevent the Sacs from carrying out the evil intentions that I have reason to suspect, even though I cannot be sure of them.

The official news of your re-election as president of the United States fulfilled the wishes of all our citizens, and especially mine. From this moment forward, the happiness of Louisiana and its inhabitants seems assured.

With the deepest respect, Sir, I have the honor of being your very humble and obedient servant.

PRE. CHOUTEAU

RC (DLC); at head of text: "Mr T. Jefferson Presidt of the United States"; endorsed by TJ as received 1 June and so recorded in SJL. Enclosure: White Hair to Chouteau, 20 Mch., from "Grande Rivierre"; White Hair informs Chouteau of the bad tribe ("mauvaise nation") from the other side of the Mississippi who have attacked the Osages twice, the first time killing five men and the second time 10 people; he asks Chouteau to inform the president ("mon grand Pere") that he has ordered his people to keep the peace but at the risk of his warriors' morale; he discusses Great Track, who has attempted to make him a laughingstock by declaring himself the great chief of the Osages; White Hair hopes Chouteau will speak with the Arkansas band and with his village; time is short, and he should hurry (RC in same; in French; in a clerk's hand).

Chouteau discussed an expected delegation of SIOUX leaders in his letter of 2 Mch.

COMMANDANT DES TROUPES: James Bruff.

To Albert Gallatin

Th: J. to mr Gallatin Apr. 20. 05.

I wish that when Muse was appointed to Tappahanoc we had known that Brett Randolph would accept of it. he is a very worthy & needy man, & one for whom it would be a good act to do something.

Colo. Lyon's applications have been so many & so unsuccessful that, all other qualifications being equal, I should like to prefer the person he recommends: if you know nothing against him. in that case if you will furnish me his *title* I will direct a commission

Saunders's recommendation is returned, approved.

Baldwin's commission is directed to be made out.

The establishment of Sacket's harbour & appointment of Sacket himself is approved.

Colo. Newton's commission is directed to be made out.

On the Western appointments generally we will converse on some occasion.

RC (NHi: Gallatin Papers); endorsed by Gallatin. PoC (DLC). Notation in SJL: "Br. Rand. Sanders. Sacket." Enclosure: see Gallatin to TJ, 18 Apr. (second letter).

person he recommends: Gideon D. Cobb.

To Albert Gallatin

Th: Jefferson to mr Gallatin Apr. 20. 05.

I think the instructions are perfectly just which provide that if a purchase be made of the Indians adjacent to the Connecticut reserve by the US. the public should be at the expence of surveying all the lines circumscribing their purchase. but if they make no purchase, then those for whom the survey is should pay the expence. it has been sometimes made a question whether Seller or Buyer should be at the expence of measuring & marking the lands: but never whether a third person should who has no right in the lands. I approve therefore of the instructions, and return the papers.

PoC (DLC). Notation in SJL: "Connecticut purchase." Enclosures: see Gallatin to TJ, 18 Apr. (third letter).

To John Mackall Gantt

Washington Apr. 20. 05.

Th: Jefferson presents his respects to Judge Gantt, and on behalf of James Oldham a former client of mr. Gantt and now in the employ of Th:J. takes the liberty of asking whether he can give any information on the subject of Oldham's claim against Jackson's estate, or to whom Th:J. can address himself to obtain information which will be thankfully recieved

PoC (DLC); endorsed by TJ.

John Mackall Gantt (1762-1811) was a trustee and bankruptcy commissioner for the District of Columbia before receiving an appointment to the Maryland judiciary in 1803 (Edward C. Papenfuse, Alan F. Day, David W. Jordan, and Gregory A. Stiverson, eds., *A Biographical Dictionary of the Maryland Legislature, 1635-1789*, 2 vols. [Baltimore, 1979-85], 1:344; Vol. 34:647; Vol. 39:497-8).

A FORMER CLIENT: see James Oldham to TJ, 9 Apr.

To David Gelston

Washington Apr. 20. 05.

Th: Jefferson presents his compliments to mr Gelston, acknoleges the reciept of his letter of the 4th. (since his return to this place) and will thank him to forward the two boxes of wine to this place or neighborhood by the first vessel. he will also, at his convenience, be so kind as to inform Th:J. of the reimbursements he has to make him.

PoC (MHi); endorsed by TJ.

From Lafayette

MY DEAR FRIEND Auteuïl 30h Germinal 20h April 1805

Here I am With my Son and daughter in law Who is Going to increase our family. Her father is to Stand God father to the child and if He is a Boy We intend taking the liberty to Give Him Your Name—You Have No Greater Admirers in the World than My two friends Tracy and Cabanis Who live Quietly in this Village, Going Now and then to an Insignificant Senate and Employing their time in philosophical pursuits. Tracy Has Given a New Edition of His ideology Which He is Happy to See through me presented to You—Besides this offering of the Author I inclose a short Extract from a long dissertation by dupuis—This abridgement Has been Made by tracy—

But He drew only a few Copies and from Motives of deference to His Mother did not put His Name to it—I thought this little Work Might for Some Moments Entertain You. I am With the Most Affectionate Respect Your Grateful friend LAFAYETTE

Dupl (DLC); at head of text: "duplicate"; endorsed by TJ as received 6 July and so recorded in SJL. Enclosures: (1) Antoine Louis Claude Destutt de Tracy, *Éléments d'idéologie, Première partie . . . Seconde édition* (Paris, 1804), with inscription on half title page, "presenté a Mr. Jefferson par l'auteur" (Sowerby, No. 1239). (2) [Destutt de Tracy], *Analyse raisonnée de l'origine de tous les cultes, ou religion universelle* (Paris, 1804), an abridged version of *Origine de tous les cultes* by Charles François Dupuis and first published in 1796 (Sowerby, No. 1296).

INCREASE OUR FAMILY: George Washington Lafayette and his wife, Françoise Émilie Lafayette, the daughter of Destutt de Tracy, were expecting their second child. A daughter, Charlotte Mathilde du Motier de Lafayette, was born on 7 May (Arnaud Chaffanjon, *La Fayette et sa descendance* [Paris, 1976], 171).

French physician and medical writer Pierre Jean Georges CABANIS lived in Auteuil and served in the *Sénat* (Vol. 38:525n).

To G. H. Le Prétre

Washington Apr. 20. 05.

Th: Jefferson presents his salutations to Mr. Le Pretre and subscribes with pleasure to his book. he now returns the subscription paper.

PoC (Vi); endorsed by TJ. Enclosure not found.

From Thomas Paine

DEAR SIR New Rochelle (N.Y) April 20 1805

I wrote you on 1st. Janry from N. Rochelle, mentioning my intention of spending part of the Winter at Washington; but the severity of the Winter and the bad condition of the roads and rivers prevented me, and I stopped at N. York. I wrote you from that place a second letter of more than nine pages on a variety of subjects accompanied with a Hamburgh Gazette and a letter from a revolutionary Sarjent at Kentucky. On the 18th. Febry., which I judge was about a fort'night after my second letter was sent, I recd a letter from you of the *fifteenth Janry* acknowleging the receipt of my first letter of Janry 1st. but of the second letter, enclosing the Hamburg Gazette and also proposals from a Hamburgh Merchant to bring German redemptioners to New

Orleans I have heard nothing. I did not put the letter into the post-office myself but I sent it by a friend who assures me he delivered it

The enclosed half sheet marked No. 1 is part of a letter which I began the latter part of last Summer but as I then intended to make further experiments I suspended finishing it, for I do not permit the *whole* of my mind, nor ever did, to be engrossed, or absorbed by one object only. When I was in france and in England since the year 1787, I carried on my political productions, religious publications, and mechanical operations all at the same time; without permitting any one to disturb, or interfere, with the other.

The piece No. 2 is part of a third letter which I began after the receipt of yours of Janry. 15. This confusion and interference of dates arise from the uncertainty I am in with respect to the fate of my second letter.

I intend continuing my letters addressed *to the Citizens of the United States*. The last (No. 7,) published the summer before last was chiefly on the Affairs of New Orleans. I distinguish those letters from others of a less public Character, such as the remarks on Governeur Morris's funeral Oration on Hamilton, That on the Louisiana Memorial, & the piece to Hulbert,

The reflections which Hulbert threw out with respect to your letter to me by Mr Dawson arose from some half equivocal qualifying paragraphs which appeared I believe in the National intelligencer before my arrival. Dr. Eustis said to me at Washington more than two years ago. "*Those paragraphs, and which are supposed to be under Mr Jefferson's direction, have Embarrassed to Mr Jefferson's friends in Massachusetts. They appeared like a half denial of the letter or as if there was something in it not proper to be owned, or that needed an apology.*"—I was myself offended at one which I saw while in Paris and which determined me not to come by a National Ship. It was copied from the National Intelligencer into a Baltimore federal paper and introduced into that paper with the words in Capitals "Out at last." It owned the receipt of a letter from me in which I expressed a wish to return by a National Ship, and the paragraph concluded thus,—"*permission was given*"; as if the giving it, was an Act of Charity, or of great condescension; at least it had the appearance of apologising. Hulbert introduced the subject of the letter by way of convicting you of something you had appeared to disown, or given cause to your friends to disown. I have given Hulbert the dressing he deserved, and you the credit the letter merits; but had no equivocation been made about the letter Hulbert could not have made the use of it he did.

Yours in friendship THOMAS PAINE

RC (DLC); at foot of text: "Thomas Jefferson President of the United States"; endorsed by TJ as received 26 Apr. and so recorded in SJL.

I WROTE YOU: Paine to TJ, 25 Jan.

I INTEND CONTINUING MY LETTERS: on 7 June, Paine's eighth letter addressed to the citizens of the United States was published in the *Aurora General Advertiser*. In it, he attacked the principles of the Federalist Party. Paine's previous essay, NO. 7, was published in the 14 May 1803 edition of the same paper.

For Paine's REMARKS on Morris's FUNERAL ORATION and the Louisiana MEMORIAL, see notes at Paine to TJ, 25 Jan.

On 31 Jan., Massachusetts Representative John W. HULBERT delivered a blistering attack against TJ and Paine during a legislative debate on whether to cancel the *New-England Palladium*'s printing contract after it published an alleged libel against the president. Paine's response to Hulbert appeared in the 12 Mch. issue of the *Aurora* (Boston *Repertory*, 8 Feb.).

YOUR LETTER TO ME: Vol. 33:358-9.

NATIONAL SHIP: on 29 July 1801, the *National Intelligencer* published a story regarding the origins of Paine's desire to return to the United States by way of an American frigate (Vol. 32:191).

ENCLOSURES

I

Unfinished Letter No. 1

DEAR SIR [summer 1804]

I will first give you an account of my own operations and then pass on to such other matters as may occur.

I am settled down on my farm at New Rochelle 20 Miles from N York. It is a pleasant and healthy situation commanding a prospect always green and agreeable as New Rochelle produces a great deal of grass and hay. The farm contains three hundred acres, about one hundred of which is meadow land, one hundred grazing and tillage land, and the remainer wood land. It is an oblong about a Mile and half in length. I have sold off sixty one Acres and an half for four thousand and twenty dollars. With this Money I shall improve the other part, and build an addition 34 feet by 32 to the present dwelling house which is small. The additional part will be one room high from the ground (about 11 or 12 feet) divided into apartments with a workshop for my mechanical operations. The upper part of this will be flat as the deck of a ship is, with a little slope to carry off the rain. It will be enclosed with a palisade all round, and covered with arched rafters shingled as the roof of a house is, down to within about 7 feet of the deck or floor. This part will then serve for an observatory and to live on in summer weather; and with screens, or light shrubs in light cases on casters to move easily I can set off what rooms I like in any part, alter them as I chuse, and be as retired in the open air as I please.—The roof of my kitchen is decayed and must be taken down, and I intend putting a semicircular roof over it; by which means that which is now the Garret, in which you can scarcely stand right up but in the middle, will then be spacious and commodious; and I have an Idea, that appears to me well founded, that a Garret with an arched roof will not be hot in summer like one covered with a roof on strait rafters, because the sun's rays striking on an arched roof will be thrown off, on a similar principle that in a concave they are concentrated; but a strait raftered roof presents almost a right-angled surface to the sun's rays and the heat of them passes through. I have observed that the round metal globe or ball on the top of andirons does not retain heat. The present form of roofs is unpleasing to the eye and nothing can make them otherwise; but an arched roof will be an ornament without and commodious within, and support itself better than a strait raftered roof. This is my opinion but experience must decide.

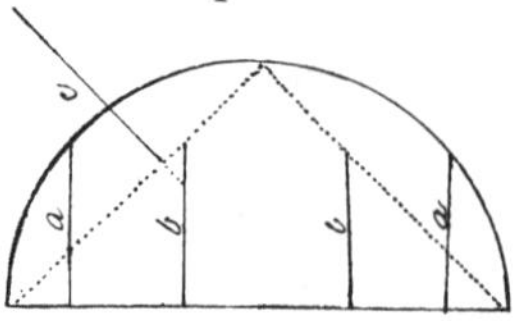

This figure shews the different capacities, between an arched roof, and a strait raftered roof.—If the perpendicular line a represents a man's height, he cannot stand up-right under a strait-raftered roof but between the lines b and b. In the arched roof all the way from a to a. The diagonal line c represents a ray of the sun striking at right angles on a strait-raftered roof. The heat of it must either be reflected back on the ray or pass through the roof. The arched roof will, I think, have a disposition to scatter them. I have made a Model in paste-board of an Arched roof on a base of 32 inches (half an inch to a foot) which equals my expectations. It shews the method of forming arched rafters, which may be done two ways. One by using narrow boards edgeways cut into short pieces in the direction of the radius and of two or three thicknesses to breah joints. This is on the principle of the dome over the Corn Market at Paris adapted to a square building, and I wonder they should not have thought of applying it; but they began with a dome and then they left off as if it was applicable to no other figure. The second figure in the Margin represents a narrow board cut in the direction of the radius. The piece cut off serves as a pattern for cutting all the pieces which when put together form a polygon the corner of which may be sawed or chisseled off.

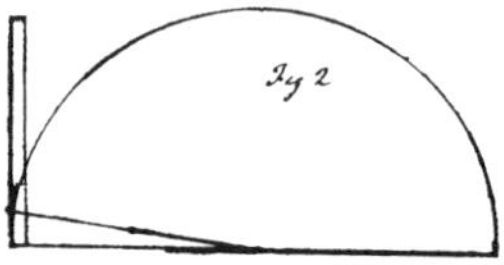

The other method of making arched rafters is to bend a board flatways to the curve that is wanted, then bend another board over it and nail them together they will then keep that curve, because the upper board being a portion of a larger Circle than the under one, the two confine each other to the curve. The thickness may be encreased at pleasure.This method is expeditious. I shall roof my kitchen in this Method—and the new part by the former method.

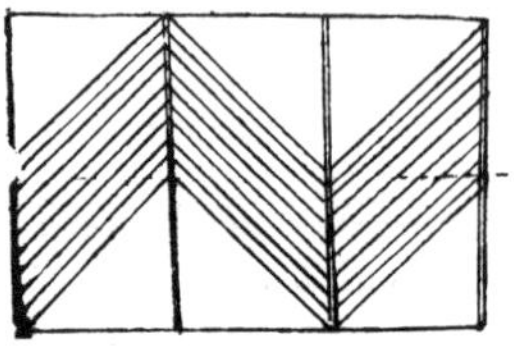

This is one of the Methods of making Oak floors in france. It is firm and of a handsome appearance.

RC (same); in Paine's hand, undated (see covering letter); at head of text: "No. 1."

CORN MARKET: the Halle aux Bleds (Vol. 38:619-21).

II

Unfinished Letter No. 2

DEAR SIR [February 1805]

Yours of the 15 Janry. in answer to mine of the 1st of that Month did not reach me at N. York till the 10th of Febry. occasioned by its having lain in the Post office at Philadelphia, where, according to my letter of the 1st Ult I intended to be. Since which I have written you a second letter from N. York, a lengthy one of more than 9 folio pages enclosing a Printed Proclamation of the Senate of Hamburg respecting the class of persons we call German Redemptioners. I also mentioned a proposal of a Hamburg Merchant at New York to bring them to Louisana at 12 Guineas per head. Capt. Charles Rogers with whom I have been acquainted about 7 Years tells me they can be brought for ten Guineas. He will not sail from N.Y. till April, and will in the course of his Voyage be at Hamburg. I mention these things to you because I think it is interesting to you to be informed of them. The settlement of Louisana is a great object.

I see all the niceties and difficulties you mention respecting Domingo, yet I see no other way out than by some kind of compromise, such as that of Domingo agreeing to give france a Monopoly of her Commerce for a term of Years. The Americans, as I have before said, would, I suppose, be the Carriers on both sides. and the trade having got into that Channel would most probably go on so by choice after the term was expired. I know that the expedition against Domingo was so very unpopular in france that even Victory was held to be a loss, and I think it not improbable that Bonaparte would be glad if something could turn up to bring him out of the scrape without loss of Reputation. This is what Lord North hoped to do by his conciliatory propositions.

I know that the United States, as a Government, cannot with propriety move in it originally, but I wish the matter to get into conversation in an indirect manner. This would be one way of "*keeping the lead line a head and sounding as we go.*" The more distantly it began the better. For my own part I had rather be the vindicator of such a measure than the proposer. When I address a piece to the public I feell myself on my own ground, but when Government is to be the actor I had rather suggest a thought, if a good one occurred, than publish it. It is the best way to succeed.

In my last I spoke of Captain Landais, and if I recollect right (for I have no copy of that letter) I spoke of Dr. *Miller*, instead of saying Dr. *Mitchel*, knowing him. If nothing be done for him in Congress you would do a good thing to give him some appointment in Louisana. He is fit for that Station, and is a remarkable strong, hearty, active Man of his age which is full 70 Years. He speaks english well; was too much of a patriot for Bonaparte, and one of the fraternity of Theophilantropists in Paris. I wish, if it suits you, you would talk with Dr Mitchel on this matter.

RC (same); in Paine's hand, undated (see covering letter); at head of text: "No. 2."

SECOND LETTER: Paine to TJ, 25 Jan.

In 1778, LORD NORTH authorized the Carlisle peace commission to negotiate a reconciliation with the Americans (Alan Valentine, *Lord North*, 2 vols. [Norman, Okla., 1967], 1:499-534).

FRATERNITY OF THEOPHILANTROPISTS: Theophilanthropy was a form of deism that received sponsorship from the French Directory (R. R. Palmer, *The Age of the Democratic Revolution: A Political History of Europe and America, 1760-1800*, rev. ed. [Princeton, 2014], 637).

To Charles Willson Peale

DEAR SIR Washington Apr. 20. 05.

According to my letter of the 5th. from Monticello, I sent the desk-Polygraph by water viâ Richmond, addressed to you; & brought with me your 8vo. one, & my model which are now sent to the stage office to be forwarded. in making one for me according to my model, I leave to yourself entirely the thickness of the stuff, so that whatever that is more than half an inch, will be added to the dimensions: and so indeed is every thing else about it left to you, because my model is but theory and you have to decide on the practicability. as it is intended to be carried backwards & forwards on my journies to & from Monticello, every half inch of unnecessary size is sensible in stowing it away. on remounting the Desk Polygraph I would not wish the Vertical Rhomboids to be lowered, & consequently shortened in order to pass under the cover: because that shortening contracts the sphere of it's action, & I would rather use it without a cover, or make the whole front of the cover open back, if necessary. it might seem as well that I should take at once the one you remounted here for mr Beckley. but the drawers &c of that are not as convenient; and the open wire cover, which I have, was made to fit that forwarded to you, and does not fit this one. I have suspended seeking an opportunity of sending Volney's Polygraph in expectation of your going. should that be uncertain or at a distance be so good as to inform me & I will seek some other opportunity. Accept my friendly salutations.

TH: JEFFERSON

RC (TxU); at foot of text: "C. W. Peale esq." PoC (DLC); endorsed by TJ.

John BECKLEY, who had adopted the polygraph for his own use, also helped publicize it by inviting members of Congress to his office to observe the Peale and Hawkins patent polygraph and "have an opportunity of judging how far the instrument merits their approbation" (*National Intelligencer*, 21 Jan.; Peale to TJ, 30 Oct. 1804).

From Oliver Evans

Sir Phila April 21st. 1805

Mr. George Clymer who I have found to be fertile in origional ideas has communicated to me his idea of a new mode of attacking an enemy by sea which appears to promise fair to insure a complete victory over the Tripolitans because they would be totally unprepared for such an attack and would have to surrender or be killed as they would be able to make no defence he is willing to communicate his discovery in case a complete victory is not gained this season over them it is kept a profound secret, untill it be known whether it would be adopted

Sir your most Obdt Huml Servt Oliver Evans

RC (DLC); at foot of text: "Thos Jefferson Presadent of the United States"; endorsed by TJ as received 24 Apr. but recorded in SJL as received 25 Apr.

clymer: see George E. Clymer to TJ, 15 May.

To Hughes & Allen

Gentlemen Washington Apr. 21. 05

Mr. Cathalan of Marseilles, by letter of Dec. 20. informed me that he had shipped some wines & other articles for me on your ship the New Orleans, which had sailed the day before, bound for Norfolk. having never yet heard of the arrival of the vessel, I take the liberty of asking information from you respecting her, & my articles on board her, if you can give any. Accept my respectful salutations.

Th: Jefferson

RC (MHi); at head of text: "Messrs. James H. Hughes & William Allen of Philadelphia"; at foot of text in hand of J. P. G. Muhlenberg: "Mr. B. Wilsons information" and "The Ship New Orleans met with a heavy gale of Wind soon after she sailed & put into Port Mahon to refit having received much damage, was expected to sail from thence for Norfolk when repaird." PoC (MHi); endorsed by TJ. Recorded in SJL with notation "returned. no such house." Enclosed in TJ to Muhlenberg, 21 Apr.

James H. Hughes and William Allen were Norfolk merchants (Stephen Cathalan, Jr., to TJ, 9 Aug. 1805; *Alexandria Daily Advertiser*, 13 June 1805).

letter of dec. 20: Stephen Cathalan, Jr., to TJ, 8 Dec. 1804 (second letter), with postscript of 20 Dec.

To George Jefferson

DEAR SIR Washington Apr. 21. 05.

One of the sky-lights of my house requiring a pane of glass $4\frac{1}{2}$ feet diameter I procured two such at the Boston glass works which were sent on. They were broken however in some part of their route—being very badly packed I got the favor of a friend there to make another effort, & to see to the package. they are now on their way to Richmond as you will percieve by mr Cutts's letter now inclosed. will it be in your power to take any precautions for their being safely landed & carried by hand to your warehouse. when there, be so good as to retain them until some person calls with an order from mr Higginbotham, to whom I now write to engage the most trust-worthy person in that business to take charge of them, offering treble portage if safely delivered. it will be requisite that they shall be carried from your warehouse to the batteau by hand, the expence of which I shall not regard: because if once they can be got safely to Monticello, the supply will suffice for ages. Accept my affectionate salutations.

TH: JEFFERSON

PoC (MHi); at foot of text: "Mr. George Jefferson"; endorsed by TJ. Enclosure: probably Richard Cutts to TJ, 13 Apr., recorded in SJL as received from Boston on 20 Apr. but not found.

TO WHOM I NOW WRITE: TJ to David Higginbotham, 21 Apr., recorded in SJL, but not found.

To Nicholas King

SIR Washington Apr. 21. 05.

I recieved yesterday your favor of the 10th. with the meteorological chart inclosed. it is one of the several ingenious representations which the linear mode has enabled us to make, & is much more satisfactory to the eye than numbers. there is another species of meteorological table which I have seen suggested somewhere & have often wished I had time & materials to form. for the Maritime states of N. America for instance, from Florida to Canada inclusive, draw first a vertical column for the months & their days; and a line across the paper for every day of the year. make a 2d. column for the flowering, leafing, fruiting, falling of different kinds of trees & other vegetables, the appearance & disappearance of birds, reptiles, insects, frost, ice, & whatever indicates the progress of season. then add a column for each of the states on the sea coast from South to North and extend a line from each phenomenon noted in the 2d. column, horizontally or rather obliquely through each state column on the day on which that phenomenon appeared there. this would give the most perfect idea possible of the advance of the season from South to North & it's recess in Autumn. but to procure the materials should require a careful observer at every degree at least from 25.° to 50.° of latitude. it would then be curious to make a similar one on any given parallel of latitude, say $37\frac{1}{2}$° (as a middle term) from East to West, in order to ascertain the effect of the elevation & depression of the country on the progress of the seasons. the effect we know to be very great. the Maryland & Virginia line on the Eastern shore for instance is within a few minutes of the latitude of Monticello. but I imagine their season is 10. days or a fortnight ahead of mine. Accept my friendly salutations.

Th: Jefferson

PoC (DLC); at foot of text: "Mr. Nicholas King."

To J. P. G. Muhlenberg

Washington Apr. 21. 05.

Th: Jefferson presents his respects to Genl Muhlenberg, and not knowing, but from the letter of mr Cathalan, that there are such merchants at Philadelphia as Hughes & Allen, he takes the liberty of putting a letter to them under cover to Genl. Muhlenberg of whom he asks the favor to have the letter delivered if there be such persons & if not to inform him of it.

PoC (MHi); endorsed by TJ. Enclosure: TJ to Hughes & Allen, 21 Apr.

From Philippe Reibelt

Monsieur le President! Baltimore le 21 Avr. 1805.

Venant d'apprendre par les Gazettes, que Vous etez de retour a la Capitale, je m'empresse, de Vous en presenter mes felicitations sinceres—j'ose en même tems Vous observer, que le petit paquet (contenant Plutarque de la Jeunesse, et 1 Vol. des Oeuvres de Plutarque nouv. edit. de Cussac) dont Vous m'avez marquè le 7 Mars, qu'il me sera renvoyè de Suite—ne m'est pas encore parvenu; et je Vous prie d'accepter mes respects les plus profonds et les plus cordiales

Reibelt.

P.S.

Si dans votre famille on desirait d'avoir un parfait Gouverneur des enfans—je pourrois Vous en adresser un—recomandable Sous tous les rapports, qui apres avoir fait des grands Voyages en Europe, et pris le Grade de Docteur en Droits, etait avocat a Liége—Il possede les langues francaise, allemande, Italienne, Espagnole, Anglaise, Latine, et grecque—et est capable de donner des instructions dans toutes les branches de Literature. Un homme rare pour ses Talens, ses Connaissances, et sa Moralite—Il a quittè notre pays par principe.—

EDITORS' TRANSLATION

MISTER PRESIDENT! Baltimore, 21 Apr. 1805

Learning from the newspapers that you are back in the capital, I hasten to present my sincere congratulations. At the same time I dare point out that I have not yet received the small package (containing Plutarch for young readers and one volume of Plutarch's Works, in the new Cussac edition) that you indicated on 7 Mch. would be returned to me immediately.

Please accept my deepest and most cordial respect. REIBELT.

P.S. If someone in your family is looking for the perfect tutor, I can send you someone who is excellent in every way. After traveling extensively in Europe, he earned a law degree and practiced law in Liège. He knows French, German, Italian, Spanish, Latin, and Greek and can teach all branches of letters. His talent, knowledge, and morality make him a rare man. He left our country as a matter of principle.

RC (DLC); endorsed by TJ as received 23 Apr. and so recorded in SJL.

From Robert Brown of Washington

SIR, Apl. 22th 1805.

I hope your honrable Body Will Concider My Misfortune in the publick work Since your honner Discharged Me from the Barrecks I never got aney work since in the City Worth a naming though Mr Voss is Work Was thought Beter Work than the Barrecks I am informed that Conl, Wartton has Menthend that the walls of the Barricks that is, uncoverd this four years is Beter work than was Don Last Year By Voss though the purser was Much More in favour of Voss I should Be Willing to Do the work at the Navey yard By the Day Without trying to Mack aney Speat on the Publick it is Well None By Docter thorntin And Sevral others that I was imployed as fore man at the house your honour Livs in at Present to the Chimneys Was finished and above all others Worked in the plac though I Say it I could Never Be shenshred for aney Mis Conduct what Ever I have Laid out my all in this City and hav Made Som purchesis for a fue Lots the Money is Due this Summar Sir I should not trobeld you honour But no Use in Spacking to aney one But you for Mr Smith i have Menthend it to him But you honor is the onley person to put me in To the work or not at toll if your honnar Be so kind as to give me a fue Lins to hosoever that I may aply to By Geting the Work i Shall be In gutey Bound to Ever prey if I went aney thing Astray at the Barrecks it was not intentily Don Mr Voss Complaned to Mr Smith when the Gust put Down four of the arkade arches of the Barreks or your honner Never Should Been trubeld in the Busness if the Walls of the Navey Yard was Examned as i hav Don the publick Wood find them indifrently Don By aney Brickwork in the City I have Been a sitison this twelve years its well None that if that Report of the Baricks had not tacken plase that i should Be aponnted one of the foremen at the Captal I never Was a man that Enterdferd With aney pollitícks What Ever But was the industres Man i hope I have Don Nothing a miss But What Your honour Will forgive all so there is fore hundred Dollars Rimanes to Be paid me if you honner will Do With me as the publick Don with Mr McNanze in the Carpenter work of the Baricks in short if So Concered i will taek two Dollars pr Day and Keep the time as i Don at the house your honour Livs in I now Wate for a Entervue With your honner I am you Most Obet Set,

Robt, Brown

RC (DLC); addressed: "The Right Onrebele the presedent of United States"; endorsed by TJ as received 22 Apr. and so recorded in SJL.

Robert Brown (d. 1815) was a Washington bricklayer who made his home on F Street. In 1801, he and partner Lawrence Pearson were contracted to do the brickwork on the new navy yard barracks. The quality of their work was questioned and a number of repairs were demanded on TJ's instructions. By 1806, Brown had found work laying brick at the President's House (*Daily National Intelligencer*, 30 July 1814, 28 Dec. 1815; "Monies Expended on the President's House," 1806, 1807, 1808 [FCs in DNA: RG 53, RES]; Vol. 35:417, 512; Vol. 36:668).

MR VOSS IS WORK: local builder Nicholas Voss handled the brickwork for a navy yard warehouse contracted in 1803 (Robert Smith to Thomas Tingey, 25 Apr. 1803, in DNA: RG 45, MLS; Madison, *Papers*, *Sec. of State Ser.*, 2:46n).

CONL, WARTTON: Franklin Wharton, commandant of the Marine Corps (Vol. 43:114).

On 31 Oct. 1801, Robert Smith authorized a $500 payment to Charles McNantz for CARPENTER WORK done on the new barracks (DNA: RG 45, MLS).

From Stephen Cathalan, Jr.

My most Respected
Dear Sir! Marseilles the 22d. april 1805—

I beg Leave to allow me to address you my warmest & most Sincere Congratulations on your Réelection to the Eminent Charge of President of the United States of America; it was indeed a Reward dûe to your Long, Continued past Services, in the Sundry Stations, Which So honorably you had filled during so many years, with no other Ambition, than the Prosperity and Wellfare of the United States, & your fellow Citizens;

They had already felt the advantages bèstowed on them and to the United States (to which Louisiana has been Joined) in the four years past of your First Presidency, in which you have proved to all the world, that a Man placed at the head of a Government, may acquire a more Solid & lasting Glory, by an Economic & Fatherly Administration in the Interior, & in Settling the differences with other Nations, by Treaties Grounded on Justice and mutual Interest, than by Wars and Conquests.

Could the Electors make a better Choice, than to Continue to Put at their head, the Same, who wants four and Probably Eight Years more, to Perfectionate and Compleat the Great Objects, he has already Laid the foundations? & who Could better execute & Carry to a Perfection Such vast Plans, than the Author himself?

The (*but Few*) Dissenters of the General oppinion, Soon will be convinced that their own Interest is to Join by a *Sincere* Reûnion, the Great Majority of the People to Support Strengthen & Bless you as the best Safe keeper of the Constitutional Government.

it is then the Whole Body of the Nation of America, which is to be Congratulated, for having Continued you as President!

may my Services Continue to be agreable to you, Sir,! I will encrease my best endeavours, in fullfilling the Duties of the office you have Confided me, with, as much as it will lay in my Power;

begging the Allmighty to Preserve many years your Precious Days!

I have the honor to be always at your Commands & with Great Respect Sir Your most obedient humble & Devoted Servant

Stephen Cathalan Junr.

RC (DLC); on printed letterhead in the form of the seal of the United States for the commercial agency and naval agency at Marseilles; at foot of first page: "His Excellency The most Honorable Thomas Jefferson President of the United States"; endorsed by TJ as received 5 Aug. and so recorded in SJL. Dupl, not found, enclosed in Cathalan to TJ, 9 May.

From George Jefferson

Dear Sir Richmond 22d. Apl. 1805

I am by to nights post favor'd with yours of the 19th, and have in reply to inform you, that previous to the receipt of your letter authorizing it, (I believe the day before) I engaged your usual supply of bacon from Mr. Macon; as he called on me to know if it would be wanted, applications having been made to him by others.

I represented to him the necessity of your getting it early, and stated the reason—he informed me it was not then sufficiently cured—but I have lately received it, and have been looking out for a Vessel for Washington, but have not as yet been able to meet with one. if I do not shortly, it shall be sent to Norfolk to be forwarded from thence

I am Dear Sir Yr. Very humble servt. Geo. Jefferson

RC (MHi); at foot of text: "Thos. Jefferson esqr."; endorsed by TJ as received 24 Apr.; recorded in SJL as received 25 Apr.

From Lafayette

My dear friend Auteuil 2d floreal April 22d 1805

Your Letter, June the 27th, With a post Script of the 11th. July, is the Last from You I Have Received—there I found New Motives for Grateful feelings and Serious thoughts—it Became the Matter of Conferences With Mm. Livingston, Monroe, and Armstrong, Where Each of Us Endeavoured to Guess and follow What Would Have Been, on the Spot, Your Sense of public duties and personal Situations—they Have Since, and I Have also writen to You—But My Chief Dependance was on a Letter of Anterior Date, Where the principal Objects Had been Anticipated, and Which they Have Been pleased to Convey—General Armstrong Has no Doubt, He Even thinks there are Intelligences of its Arrival—Yet, to Avoid Repetitions, I Beg Leave to Inclose a Copy of it—I Warmly Wish an Answer Might Come Before Mr. Livingston's departure.

I Have However Been on the point not to Wait for it—Not that on this Side of the Atlantic Matters Are Changed—The political Situation is Generally and Individually the Same—The Scrupules I Expressed, the Ideas I Hinted at, Are, Notwithstanding Appearances, Rather Strengthened—and While the Late Mortality in the State of Orleans, the Loss of Governor Claiborne's Lady and Children do not Lessen the Hesitation of My family With Respect to me, Mine With Respect to them, and that of their Respective families and friends

With Respect to All, it Happens that the Late changes in the Organization of Louisiana may in a Measure Change Your Views upon the probable Services of One Man—Under the Circumstances I ought to Wait for Your Answer to My Observations—But General Armstrong Having Suggested the idea, Upon Motives of private interest, for me to Embark with Mr Livingston, I Could Not Resist the temptation, Nor on Account of my pecuniary Affairs, for which You, M. Madison, and M. Gallatin Are Better Qualified and More Eager than Myself, But in the Happy prospect to Revisit America, and for the Sake of An Interview with You, Both of Which Would Afford me Inexpressible delight.

All objections were Set a Side, But One Relative to this Government Which I Undertook to Clear out, the other founded Upon the probability of Being taken at Sea, And I Made it the object of a writen Consultation, and When I found it Was prefered, of a Confidential Conference With General Armstrong and Mr Livingston Now Returned to Paris.

We did fully Discuss What Had past formerly, When my American Rights as a Citizen and a General Were, Unavailing to Shorten My five Years Emprisonement Untill Being Claimed and Released By a french treaty I Have Afterwards Reassumed My Civil, and, on Half pay, My Military Station in france—it Was observed that My principal Ennemies then Had Been the Actual prime Minister of Great Britain, and the King Whose peculiar Hatred to me Was, in the Expressed Opinion of Mr pitt Himself, totally Unmanageable—We Examined Whether in the Almost Certainty of Being Visited at Sea, there Was An Admiral or Captain of a Ship Who Would forbear, With Respect to Me, At Least a provisory Application of a too Well known Article of the treaty With England—General Armstrong Had only *Hopes* that on Going I should Escape discovery—Mr Livingston thought there Was Very Little Chance for that Hope, and if it failed, did Not Believe that Either the flag or Himself Could defend me Against the dreaded Construction of the Article and its Consequences—Both Were of Opinion that a Return to france Became, from the Awakened Attention of the British Cruisers, Still more dangerous—So that My intended Visit Would produce to me a Relapse in Captivity, and to the United States a political incident of a disagreable Nature.

I do not Here Mention an Objection Applicable to Me, With respect to this Government and An other Not Wholly UnApplicable to Louisiana Both of Which Mr. Livingston Will fully Explain.

Let me only Conclude in Saying that, Every thing Considered, We Were Unanimous in the Opinion that I should give Up my Plan of an Interview With You—As Nothing But public Service of A positive Call from You Could Warrant the Almost Unavoidable Risk—and as Mr Livingston Will in a few days Afford the Safest And fullest Opportunity of a free Communication, I Am Going to Say a few Words on Colonel touzard's particular Case:

You know, My dear friend, He Has from the Beggining fought With Us in the Cause of American Liberty—I Was Highly pleased With His Zeal on a tedious duty Among the Indians—He Had His Right Arm, when My Aid de Camp, Shot of in one of the Most Gallant Actions of the War, and After He Had been promoted and Emploïed by His Native Country I Heard With Pleasure He Was Returned into the American Service, Had Married An American Lady, and Became alltogether An American Citizen. on My Return to Europe, it Was a Great Satisfaction for me to See Again My old fellow Soldier—I Heard from Him He Had Served in the West Indias; But Intended to fix Himself, with his Family, in the United States.

Some time After He wrote to Me that, Having Been proposed by *talleyrand* for the Consulship of New Orleans, and Notwithstanding the Merits of His Brother With Bonaparte, de forgues, patronised by *fouché* Had been prefered to Him—I knew deforgues only by Hear Say and Had a Question on His Account put to *fouché* Who Sent me Word I Should Be, in Every Respect, Satisfied With de forgue's Conduct in America—in the Mean While touzard Informed Me that He Was Standing for the Chancellorship, that His friend the Minister of finance Had told Him His own Good Will and that of talleyrand Would be Counter Acted By the Minister of the police, But that He Was Sure a Letter from Me Would Insure His protection. I of Course wrote it, and Mr Fouché Was pleased to Ask the place in His Own Name. So that Colonel touzard was Appointed.

I Had Not Hitherto Connected the Name of that Officer with Any idea of Recent parties in America—that He was a Soldier of the Revolution, a Citizen, father of a family in the United States, that He Belonged to them Still More than to His Native Country and Intended to Become a Settler in the State of Orleans Were the only Considerations that Struck me—The More So as the few Words He Had Had the Opportunity to tell Me Respecting Your person, My obligations to You, and Your Unquestionable Resolution were full of Respect to You, and perfectly Concordant With My Own Sentiments.

I Have been Since told there Were Some Circumstances Which Would Render His Appointment Not So Agreable as I Had thought—I frankly Called Him to Account for it—He Answered He Had Been Attached to Men, My Intimate friends, Whose Memory I Cherished, But that He Was Stranger to parties, that altho His Displacement from the Army Had Been the Occasion of a publication for Which He Had, in the time, Be Very Sorry, He Was Sensible You Had No ill Disposition towards Him, and that His Behaviour in Every Instance, public and private, Would Convince You that America Never Had a More Sincere patriot than He is, Nor You a More Respectful Admirer—There Was an other Article Upon Which I Had an Explanation With Him—it is the Colonial doctrine About Slavery—I found He Had been a planter, and An Officer in Le Clerc's Army, Nor did He Appear to Me free from prejudices on that Head—But He Gave me His Honor that What Ever were His Ideas Respecting the West Indias He firmly believed Louïsiana Might Be Worked By free Hands, and that on this point as Well as on Every other He Would to the Utmost of His Abilities Contribute to forward Your philantropic Views.

He Also Has Assured me that in Whatever Case You think proper to Honor Him With Any part of Your Confidence Respecting My private Concerns, He Will think Himself Doubly Bound to preserve and promote the principle that No Speculation Can Be By Me Admitted But those Which tend to better the fate and Insure the freedom of the Men Employed Upon it.

I am Going to write to Mr Madison Respecting My Louïsiana Affairs—I Hope the powers of Attorney are Long Ago Arrived—as our friend will Communicate My Letters I Refrain from Repetitions But Beg Leave Once More to Offer My Affectionate Grateful thanks not only for the Immense Service I owe to the Donation in General, But for Your kind Minute Care to Render Each part of it As profitable as possible.

Mr Madison Will Recieve a Note Respecting a piece of Ground Highly Valuable Which I Have, By Chance, discovered to Exist at New Orleans, and Which May Have Hitherto Escaped the Notice of Government.

I Hope My Official Letter of Thanks Has Long Ago Been Received—Yet I Will Inclose a Copy of it Which I Submit, as Well as the duplicate Sent, to Your friendly Enlightened Judgement.

Colonel touzard is Charged With a parcel of Books Wherein I Have Inclosed a Letter Requesting, or Rather Anticipating the permission, if My Expected Grand-Child is a Boy, to Give Him Your Name.

Your Reelection Was Unquestionable—Yet I Have Heartily Enjoyed its Almost Unanimity—We Had Your Admirable Speech printed Here—I Was the More pleased With it as it Was perfectly Suited Not to the Situation, But to the Wants of this part of the World, and of Course to the feelings of those Who Can Not Give Up the Hope of its final Enfranchisement.

Adieu, My dear, Respected friend, Accept with Your Usual Affection, the Warm Attachment, profound Gratitude, and tender Regard of Your friend LAFAYETTE

RC (DLC); at head of text in an unidentified hand: "Copd." Recorded in SJL as received 3 July. Enclosures not identified, but see below.

A LETTER OF ANTERIOR DATE: TJ to Lafayette, 30 Mch. 1804 (Vol. 43:140-1).

THE IDEAS I HINTED AT: see Lafayette to TJ, 8 Oct. 1804.

ARTICLE OF THE TREATY WITH ENGLAND: Lafayette likely referred to the 17th article of the 1795 Jay Treaty, which concerned the detaining of vessels on the high seas for carrying enemy property (Miller, *Treaties*, 2:258).

OBJECTION APPLICABLE TO ME: Lafayette possibly referred to the situation he would be in should there be a conflict between the United States and a Franco-Spanish alliance over the Floridas (Madison, *Papers, Sec. of State Ser.*, 9:501-3).

COLONEL: Anne Louis de Tousard (Vol. 36:296n).

Tousard's BROTHER, Antoine Étienne Tousard, had served as an engineer in Napoleon's expedition to Egypt and later became a baron of the French Empire (Georges Six, *Dictionnaire biographique des généraux & amiraux français de la Révolution et de l'Empire, 1792-1814*, 2 vols. [Paris, 1934], 2:506-7).

DE FORGUES: François Louis Michel Chemin Deforgues was appointed to the French consulship in New Orleans (Tulard, *Dictionnaire Napoléon*, 582).

SOME CIRCUMSTANCES: following the downsizing of the army in 1802, Federalists alleged that Louis Tousard was fired because of his politics. However, Meriwether Lewis's classification of officers for the 24 July 1801 War Department list of officers indicated that Tousard was "professionally the soldier without any political creed" (*Philadelphia Gazette & Daily Advertiser*, 5 Apr. 1802; Vol. 36:296n).

ATTACHED TO MEN: Tousard had long been friendly with Alexander Hamilton (Syrett, *Hamilton*, 26:54).

WRITE TO MR MADISON: see Madison, *Papers, Sec. of State Ser.*, 9:276-80.

Lafayette granted Madison THE POWERS OF ATTORNEY over his American lands (same, 8:144-48).

NOTE RESPECTING A PIECE OF GROUND: probably "Note sur un Terrain de la nouvelle Orleans appartenant aux Etats unis," which Lafayette appears to have enclosed in his letter of this day to Madison. Based on information that Lafayette received from a New Orleans merchant then in Paris, the note described a plot of approximately 50 acres near the city, owned by the government and consisting of cleared land and cypress forest. The land was estimated to have a value of 300,000 francs (MS in DLC: TJ Papers, 137:23726, endorsed by TJ: "Fayette Duplicate"; see Madison, *Papers, Sec. of State Ser.*, 9:276-7).

A LETTER: see Lafayette to TJ, 20 Apr.

To Benjamin H. Latrobe

Dear Sir Washington Apr. 22. 05.

Having returned a few days since, I called on mr Ludlow to have the offices for this house now begun, he told me he awaited your instructions, papers &c and would write to you immediately. having three months now before our Autumnal recess I should be glad this work could be pushed on such a scale as to compleat one end at least while I am here. having given you the only sketches I had of the design, I must ask the return of them in order to recollect my own views respecting the work, and to recieve an answer as soon as convenient. Accept my friendly salutations. Th: Jefferson

PoC (DLC); at foot of text: "Mr. Latrobe"; endorsed by TJ.

From Thomas Munroe

Monday 22d Apl.

T Munroe respectfully enquires of the President whether the sheet iron charged in the enclosed bills, or either of them, was ordered by him for his private use—. The bills have been presented to me for payment, but there has been no such parcel of iron ordered for public use I am informed

RC (DLC); addressed: "President US"; endorsed by TJ as received 22 Apr. and so recorded in SJL. Enclosures not found.

To Henry Dearborn

Th: J. to Genl Dearborne Apr. 23. 05.

Will you be so good as to peruse the inclosed and have some conversation with me on it to-day?

RC (PHi: Daniel Parker Papers); endorsed by Dearborn. Not recorded in SJL. Enclosure not identified.

From Henry Dearborn

SIR, April 23d. 1805

Genl. Mason has not yet received an Answer from Col Peyton, but he expects one immediately, and as soon as he receives it, he will wait on you.

Yours H. DEARBORN

RC (DLC); addressed: "The President of the United States"; endorsed by TJ as received from the War Department on 24 Apr. and "petn agt Peyton" and so recorded in SJL.

John MASON was brigadier general of the District of Columbia militia (Vol. 37:699).

From Pierre Samuel Du Pont de Nemours

Paris 3 Floréal An 13.
[i.e. 23 Apr. 1805]

MONSIEUR LE PRÉSIDENT,

Il m'est extrêmement pénible de ne pouvoir encore porter moi même à Votre Excellence l'hommage du plaisir que me fait pour l'Amérique et pour le Monde, votre Ré-Election, dont au reste je ne doutais nullement: Car, chez une Nation sage, On ne perd pas le fruit de ses oeuvres.

Je saisis du moins la premiere occasion de vous le faire passer.

Ma Lettre vous sera remise par Mr de Forgues, qui a êté en France un ami chaud, on disait en ce tems là trop chaud, de la Liberté et de la République. Mais peuvent-elles être trop aimées?

On l'envoie Consul à la Louisiane. Dans l'esprit du Gouvernement qui l'a nommé, c'est un honorable exil.

Il l'embrasse comme l'entrée dans un Port de salut.

Et je crois que Votre Excellence aura sujet d'être satisfaite de la conduite qu'il tiendra dans cette place.

Nous avons commenté ensemble votre admirable discours au Congrès, sur lequel je vous écrirai plus au long par Mr. Le Chancelier Livingston.

Je me proposais d'accompagner cet Ambassadeur.

Mes amis de France ont *stoppé* mon Voyage en mettant devant moi un devoir positif.

J'ai les papiers de Mr. Turgot; et c'est une obligation essentielle de ma vie de les mettre en ordre, d'en faire imprimer ceux dont il aurait pû désirer la publication, de les lier ensemble par de petites Préfaces, d'ajouter des Notes historiques et autres à ceux dont elles pourront augmenter l'utilité.

C'était un des premiers travaux que je comptais faire aux Etats Unis.

On m'a demandé, avec une trés grande justice, de quel droit j'exposerais cette collection précieuse des œuvres de mon illustre Ami à retraverser pour la troisieme fois l'Océan, à périr avec moi, ou sans moi, â être perdue pour le Genre humain.

J'ai pâli et rougi de ce qu'on avait êté obligé de me le dire. Cette conjuration, non pas magique mais céleste, a fixé mes pieds à la terre.

Je compte qu'un an bien employé suffit au Travail qu'elle me prescrit.

Aussitôt que j'aurai satisfait à ce devoir, si je ne le paye pas de ma tête, ce qui dans les données de l'Europe est possible, je cours auprès de vous et je m'y attache jusqu'à ce que sous votre protection nous ayions rempli l'autre devoir que vous m'avez impôsé, et sur lequel vous avez applaudi à mon premier essay; jusqu'à ce que nous ayions dans votre Patrie, qui pour lors deviendra la mienne, effectué l'organisation complette de l'éducation nationale, que je vois sans surprise que vous n'oubliez pas.

Dieu bénira votre Présidence!

Vous connaissez mon profond respect et mon inviolable attachement.

Du Pont (de Nemours)

Madame Du Pont se recommande à votre souvenir dont elle est digne.

Je vous remercie de la marque de bienveillance et de justice que vous avez donnée à mon second Fils: celui d'*Eleutherian-mill.*

EDITORS' TRANSLATION

Mister President, Paris, 3 Floréal Year 13 [i.e. 23 Apr. 1805]

It is extremely painful for me not to be able to tell your excellency in person how pleased I am about your reelection, for America and the world. Of course there was never any doubt since a wise nation does not forfeit the fruit of its efforts.

I take this opportunity, however, to convey my thoughts.

Mr. Deforgues will bring you my letter. In France he was an ardent friend of liberty and the Republic. At the time people called him too ardent, but is it possible to love these things too much?

He has been named consul in Louisiana. In the spirit of the government that named him, it is an honorable exile. He embraces it as he would the entrance to a safe harbor, and I think your excellency will be pleased with his conduct there.

He and I have discussed your admirable speech to Congress, about which I shall write at greater length via Chancellor Livingston. I had contemplated accompanying the ambassador, but my friends in France precluded my trip by confronting me with an obligation.

I have Mr. Turgot's papers; and it is an essential duty of my life to organize them and publish the ones he wished to see in print, connecting them with short prefaces and adding notes on historical and other elements to help readers.

This was one of the first projects I intended to do in the United States, but I was asked, quite justifiably, what right I had to expose this precious collection of works by my illustrious friend to a third ocean crossing, where it could perish, with or without me, and be lost to the human race.

I was dismayed and embarrassed they even had to ask. That conjuration, which is not magical but celestial, anchored my feet to the ground.

I estimate that a year of solid work will suffice to complete the task. If I do not perish in the process, which is possible in the current situation of Europe, I shall hasten to you as soon as I have finished my task and remain there until, under your guidance, you and I have fulfilled the other duty you imposed upon me and for which you praised my first effort: establishing national education in your country, which by then will have become mine. I am not surprised to see that you have not forgotten it.

God bless your presidency!

You know my deep respect and unwavering loyalty.

Du Pont (de Nemours)

Madame Du Pont respectfully asks to be remembered to you.

Thank you for your kindness and fairness on behalf of my second son, the one in Eleutherian Mills.

RC (DLC); at head of text: "a Son Excellence Thomas Jefferson Président des Etats Unis"; endorsed by TJ as received 11 Oct. and so recorded in SJL.

VOTRE ADMIRABLE DISCOURS AU CONGRÈS: Second Inaugural Address, 4 Mch.

LES PAPIERS DE MR. TURGOT: see Vol. 43:394n.

From Albert Gallatin

Dear Sir April 23d 1805

Will you have the goodness to inform me whether Judge Bruin of the Mississippi territory is dead. Such report prevails & prevents our paying his salary for the first quarter of this year, for which he drew before it had become due. The holder of the bill has been waiting some days till we could ascertain the fact. If it be so, it is also necessary to know when he died—

With great respect Your obedt. Sert. Albert Gallatin

RC (DLC); addressed: "The President of the United States"; endorsed by TJ as received from the Treasury Department on 23 Apr. and "Bruin" and so recorded in SJL.

Judge Peter Bryan BRUIN was not dead, but frequent court absences due to his intemperance would culminate in his resignation from the bench in 1809 (Robert Williams to TJ, 10 Aug.; *Terr. Papers*, 5:489-90, 510, 597, 615, 650).

From Albert Gallatin

Dear Sir 23d April 1805

I enclose the sketch of an Act for organizing the new district of Sacket harbour in conformity with the act of 3 March 1803 (6th Vol. page 273). If you approve of the form, and division, a fair copy shall be prepared for your signature.

Pierce's plan of a depreciating paper is returned. Herman Husband the Pennsylvania madman proposed a similar one to the legislature of that State in the year 1779: only his paper, instead of depreciating at a regular rate each time it passed in the hands of another man, was to depreciate, instead of bearing interest, regularly every day so as to be worth nothing at the end of three years. Pierce's paper is to be worth nothing when it shall have passed through the hands of ten persons. It is evident that such paper, without the assistance of severe tender laws, will be worth nothing from the day it is issued. But supposing such laws to exist & to be enforced; what do such plans amount to? If the depreciation be very gradual, say one per cent or one per thousand, instead of ten per cent, on each payment, it is perfectly similar to a stamp duty on receipts, notes &a. If the depreciation be at the rate of ten per cent, as suggested by Pierce, it is the Spanish Alcavalla.

With great respect Your obedt. Sert. Albert Gallatin

RC (DLC); endorsed by TJ as received from the Treasury Department on 23 Apr. and "Sacket harbor. Pierce" and so recorded in SJL. Enclosures: (1) Draft order for establishment of Sackets Harbor, New York, as a port of entry, not found (see Gallatin to TJ, 18 Apr., second letter). (2) Edwards Pierce to TJ, 30 Mch.

spanish alcavalla: that is, alcabala, a system of sales taxes operating throughout the Spanish empire. Although it varied locally, the tax could be as high as the 10 percent Castilian rate, which is what Gallatin seems to have had in mind (J. Michael Francis, ed., *Iberia and the Americas: Culture, Politics, and History: A Multidisciplinary Encyclopedia*, 3 vols. [Santa Barbara, Calif., 2006], 1:57-8).

From Albert Gallatin

Sir Treasury Department 23d April 1805

I have the honor to enclose two accounts of certain contingent expences incurred by Governor Claiborne, which he has transmitted to this office. The only appropriation for contingencies in the territory of Orleans was made by the act of 3d March last and is in the following words "For incidental and contingent expences of the legislative council and of the secretary of the said territory, two thousand dollars"

The contingent expences of various kinds which were incurred by Governor Claiborne prior to the first day of October 1804 were chargeable to the fund of twenty thousand dollars created by the second section of the Act providing for the expences of the civil Government of Louisiana, passed March 19, 1804. The accounts for that period are not yet settled; nor can they be settled until the principles of settlement shall have been decided upon by the President, under whose direction the expenditure of that sum was placed. But the fund being amply sufficient to cover all the expences thus incurred, there will be no difficulty arising from want of authority or appropriation, in settling the accounts for that period.

It is only for expences incurred subsequent to the first day of October 1804, when the form of Government established by the Act of March 26, 1804, took place that any difficulties occur. The sum for contingencies is only two thousand dollars, and is applicable only to such as relate to the legislative council and to the Secretary's office. It is not believed, however, that there be any expectation on the part of that council, that any portion of their contingent expences shall be defrayed by the United States: and the whole sum of two thousand dollars may, with the approbation of the President, be applied to the executive department. Still, it seems confined by the words of the law to the Secretary's office: and there are several items in the enclosed accounts which have never been allowed to the Governors of other territories, and cannot by any forced construction come within the meaning of the appropriation. Indeed the necessary expences properly pertaining to the Secretary's office would remain unprovided for, if the sum intended for that object should be applied to others.

It is true that there are some expences arising from the peculiar situation of the Governor of Orleans, such as the allowance to an interpreter, and the repairs of the Government house, which ought perhaps in justice to be provided for. Others, such as that of a private Secretary, appear altogether inadmissible. But in respect even to those which, though not yet provided for, appear reasonable, Governor Claiborne should be apprized that there is no fund to defray them, and he should also be informed of the precise manner in which it is intended that the appropriation should be applied. As he sends regularly his accounts, he may justly complain should they remain longer in our hands without any communication being made to him of the objectionable parts. Permit me, therefore, to call your attention to the subject and to request such instructions as may enable me to write to the Governor.

I have the honor to be with the highest respect—Sir Your obedt. Servt.

ALBERT GALLATIN

RC (DLC); at foot of text: "The President of the United States"; endorsed by TJ as received from the Treasury Department on 23 Apr. and "Govr. Claiborne's accts." and so recorded in SJL. Enclosures not found.

For a summary of William C. C. Claiborne's CONTINGENT EXPENCES, see TJ to Gallatin, 24 Apr.

ACT OF 3D MARCH LAST: that is, "An Act making appropriations for the support of Government" for 1805, enacted on 1 Mch. (U.S. Statutes at Large, 2:319).

From Dominique Joseph Garat

à Paris le 3 floreal an 13 [i.e. 23 Apr. 1805]

Le sénateur garat à Monsieur jéfférson Président des états unis de l'amérique

je n'ai aucun titre personnel, Monsieur le Président, pour vous recommander un de mes compatriotes et un de mes amis; mais je n'ai pu oublier que je vous ai vu assez souvent, dans ma jeunesse, chez m. dalembert et chez madame hélvétius; et j'ai pensé que les noms de ces personnes qui avoient de l'amitié pour moi pouvoient me donner au pres de vous des droits que je n'ai point par moi même.

si m. déforgues vous étoit connu, Monsieur le président il n'auroit aucun besoin de vous etre recommandé; il auroit déja votre éstime et votre amitié: vous vérriés dans son cœur tous ces sentimens qui remplisent le votre, tous ces principes avec les quels vous gouvernés l'Amérique et aux quels elle doit son bonheur.

m. déforgues a rempli les postes les plus importans de la république françoise dans les tems ou pour la servir il falloit etre prés à mourir pour élle: il ne l'auroit jamais quittée s'il n'avoit jamais vu dans son sein que des dangers pour sa vie; aujourdhui il pase avec joie dans ce nouveau monde qui ést nouveau, sur tout, depuis que vous présidés à ses déstinées.

La place q'uil va remplir ést tres subordonée sur tout si on la compare à ses talens; elle l'occupera pourtant des intérets de la France et de ceux de l'Amérique; et soiez sur, Monsieur le président, q'uil cherchera toujours les intérets de son païs dans le point ou ils s'accorderont avec les intérets du votre. il ést du petit nombre de ces ames distinguées pour les quelles l'amour meme de la patrie n'ést que l'amour de l'humanité.

m. déforgues vous dira, Monsieur le président combien il y a de françois pour les quels votre nom ést une consolation et une éspérance; il vous dira combien il ést béni parmi nous celui qui fait des principes de la démocratie les fondemens de la sagesse et des prospérités d'un grand peuple. l'autorité d'un pareil éxemple manquoit aux plus sublimes théoriés; vous la leur donnés; et c'ést, je crois, le plus grand bien qu'on fut faire à l'espéce humaine.

Vous civilisés par degres vos sauvages malgré leurs *antiphilosophes*: nos antiphilosophes et nos sauvages le sont apparament plus que les vôtres; il n'y a aucun moien de leur pérsuader que les méilleures loix sont celles qui etablissent et conservent entre les hommes *l'équité* et *l'égalité* qui ne sont guere qu'une seule et meme chose; ils ne veulent voir la véritable civilisation que là ou ils voient un maitre et des sujets. Ah! Monsieur, quelle place vous occuperé dans l'histoire et ce qui vaut mieux encore dans les cœurs!—adieu Monsieur receves mes salutations et lexpréssion de mes vœux sinceres pour la prolongation d'une vie que vous rendes si utile à vos semblables. GARAT

EDITORS' TRANSLATION

Paris, 3 Floréal Year 13 [i.e. 23 Apr. 1805]

Senator Garat to Mister Jefferson, President of the United States

I have no authority, Mister President, to recommend one of my compatriots, one of my friends, but I could not forget having seen you rather often, in my youth, at the homes of Mr. d'Alembert and Madame Helvétius. I thought the names of these people, who considered me a friend, might give me some authority in your eyes which I do not have in my own right.

If you knew Mr. Deforgues, Mister President, he would not need any introduction; he would already have your esteem and friendship. You would see in his heart the same sentiments that fill your own, all the principles with which you govern America and to which it owes its happiness.

Mr. Deforgues held the most important positions in the French Republic at a time when to serve the Republic meant to be ready to die for it. He would never have left France if he had not seen that his life was in danger. He has come joyfully to this new world which has been new, above all, since you began presiding over its destiny.

The position he will occupy is quite subordinate, especially compared to his talents. But it will involve him in the interests of France and America. You can be sure, Mister President, that he will always seek the interests of his country in the places where they intersect with the interests of yours. He is among that small number of distinguished souls for whom love of country is but love of humanity.

As Mr. Deforgues will tell you, Mister President, your name offers hope and consolation to so many Frenchmen. He will tell you how much we bless the name of the person who bases the wisdom and prosperity of a great people upon democratic principles. Until now, the most sublime theories lacked the authority of such an example. You provide it, and I believe this is the greatest good one can give the human race.

You civilize your natives step by step, despite their anti-philosophers. Our anti-philosophers and natives are apparently worse than yours. There is no way to convince them that the best laws are the ones that establish and preserve equity and equality, which are one and the same thing. They do not want to see true civilization except where there are masters and subjects. Ah, Sir, what a place you will occupy in history and, even more significantly, in human hearts! Farewell, Sir. Accept my greetings and my sincere wish that the life you make so useful to your fellow human beings will be a long one.

GARAT

RC (DLC); endorsed by TJ as received 11 Oct. and so recorded in SJL.

From the Labourd region of France, Dominique Joseph Garat (1749-1833) trained in the law and, while living in Paris in the 1770s and 1780s, became a contributor to the *Encyclopédie méthodique* and the *Mercure de France*. He authored several historical essays that soon earned him a position as a professor of history at the Lycée de Monsieur in 1785. Chosen to represent Labourd at the 1789 meeting of the Estates General, Garat subsequently served in several positions in the French government, took part in the Thermidorian reaction against Maximilien Robespierre, and supported Napoleon Bonaparte's coup against the Directory. In the early 1800s, Garat served as a senator and, in 1808, became a count of the empire. Later in life he authored a history of the Basques, which was published posthumously (Tulard, *Dictionnaire Napoléon*, 773-4; Charles Coulston Gillispie, *Science and Polity in France: The End of the Old Regime* [Princeton, 1980], 191; Michel Duhart, *Dominique-Joseph Garat [1749-1833]* [Biarritz, 2009], 390; Vol. 15:169-70).

LES POSTES LES PLUS IMPORTANS: during the French Revolution, François Louis Michel Chemin Deforgues held a number of positions before heading the Ministry of Foreign Affairs from June 1793 to April 1794 (Tulard, *Dictionnaire Napoléon*, 582).

From George Jefferson

DEAR SIR Richmond 23d. Apl. 1805

The inclosed I forward for your acceptance.

Yr. Very humble servt.

GEO. JEFFERSON

RC (MHi); at foot of text: "Thos. Jefferson esqr."; endorsed by TJ as received 26 Apr. and so recorded in SJL with notation "C. Peyton 201. D." Enclosure: order of Craven Peyton, not found (see TJ to Jefferson, 28 Apr.).

In his financial memoranda under 28 Apr., TJ recorded: "Assumed to pay Geo. Jefferson the first week in Aug. 201. D. for Craven Peyton. Note this is for 2. shares in the warehouse at Milton" (MB, 2:1151).

From J. P. G. Muhlenberg

Philadelphia April 23d. 1805

Agreeably to the contents of the Note, I had the honor to receive from The President, I made enquiries relative to the Owners of the Ship, New Orleans from Marseilles—& can not find that such a firm as Hughes & Allen exists in this City, but I believe the information, stating that the Ship had been damag'd and oblig'd to sail into Mahon is correct.

with Perfect Respect I have the honor to be The Presidents Obedt servt

P MUHLENBERG

RC (MHi); at foot of text: "The President of The U States"; endorsed by TJ as received 25 Apr. and so recorded in SJL.

THE NOTE: see TJ to Muhlenberg, 21 Apr.

At some point, James Simpson, U.S. consul at Tangier, provided INFORMATION that after sailing from Marseilles the *New Orleans* was damaged in heavy winds and put into Mahón for repairs. A "Captn. Davis" corroborated the account and reported that the ship was believed to be en route to Norfolk (MS in MHi; undated; in a clerk's hand, with corroborative note by Muhlenberg and his heading: "Note from Mr. J Simpson").

From Charles Willson Peale

DEAR SIR

Museum April 23d. 1805.

Your Model for a very small Polygraph is now before me, to give a proper answer on it, I must first make some machinery to try if it is possible to write to the bottom of 8vo. Paper, and then find room within the Gallows when put down with said machinery. At present it really appears to be impossible for want of height in the perpendicular as well as lengths of the horizontals, however it is deserving trial, which shall be done without delay.

I write this letter with a size that pleases me, for although it is only one Inch longer than the Polygraph you have returned with your Model, yet I can write with ease the whole of this page without mooving the Paper.

This I am enabled to do by making the Pen-bar longer than is usial

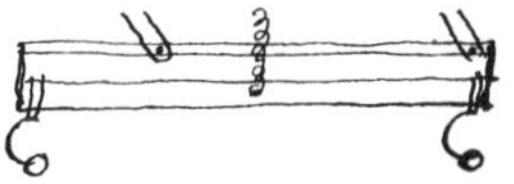

with such parallels, thus, giving 2 Inches greater length to the left hand Pen, which additional length does not prevent the Machinery being put as before. The distance between these Pens is $7\frac{1}{2}$ In. Post paper one Sheet laid on the other a good margin distance, exactly extends to the extreme edges of the board I write on, and this my guide for placing the Paper. It is my Son Rembrandts 2d. invention, and much more agreable than that of placing the Paper diagonally to only write one half the page and then mooving it write the other half.

I am still unable to determine whether I can go to France this Spring greatly as I wish it, and important as it appears to me in affording such an extensive opportunity of advancing the interests of the Museum.

It may happen that my Son Rembrandts service on some occasion abroad may be acceptable, in which case, I would be glad he could accompany me, a short residence in France, or Itally would greatly improve him & certainly would enhance his reputation. Knowing your wish to encourage young men of Genius, I take the liberty of bringing my Son into your notice and remembrance.

Mr. Pinchon will I fear go too soon, if his being a Frenchman is not an exception, it would certainly be a good opportunity. If I can manage some of my family concerns, I mean to make this voiage as soon as possible, in which case I shall give you the earliest notice.

As the Polygraph you return, by way of Richmond, is more convenient in the Drawers, it certainly will be best that I should fit the machinery to it for your use, more especially as I hope to execute it better than that which was intended for Mr. Beckley. I shall write more fully after I have made tryal on the Model—yours affectionately

C W Peale

RC (DLC); at foot of text: "His Excellency Thos. Jefferson Esqr."; endorsed by TJ as received 24 Apr. but recorded in SJL as received 25 Apr. PoC (Lb in PPAmP: Peale-Sellers Papers).

REMBRANDTS 2D. INVENTION: Rembrandt Peale had also developed pens with a greater ink capacity (Charles Willson Peale to TJ, 19 Aug. 1804).

From Robert Smith

Sir. Nav Dep 23 April 1805

I request your signature to the enclosed commissions.

I am with great respect Sir, yr mo ob st Rt Smith

RC (DLC); at foot of text: "President of the United States"; endorsed by TJ as received from the Navy Department on 24 Apr. and "Lts. commns" and so recorded in SJL. FC (Lb in DNA: RG 45, LSP).

From Louis Marie Turreau de Garambouville

le Mardy 23. [i.e. 23 Apr. 1805]

Le General Turreau presente l'hommage de Son Respect a Son Excellence Monsieur Le Président de Jefferson. A luy envoye Ses Journaux et Ses Remerciemens.

EDITORS' TRANSLATION

Tuesday, the 23d

General Turreau sends his respects to his excellency President Jefferson, along with his newspapers and his thanks.

RC (DLC); partially dated; endorsed by TJ as received 23 Apr. 1805. Enclosures not found.

Louis Marie Turreau de Garambouville (1756-1816) was a French soldier and diplomat. After serving in the French army during the American War for Independence, he returned to France and was a captain in the infantry at the start of the French Revolution. He rose through the ranks quickly. By the end of November 1793 he was named commander-in-chief of the Army of the West. In that position he presided over efforts to suppress the rebellion in the Vendée and became known for his harsh tactics in the region. Denounced and jailed in the aftermath of the fall of Robespierre, he defended himself in print and was released. He resumed his military career in 1797, and led troops in Switzerland and Italy. After peace was declared, he was named a Grand Officer of the Legion of Honor. Napoleon appointed him minister plenipotentiary to the United States in 1803. He arrived at the capital in November 1804. His wife, Marie Angélique Lequesne Ronsin Turreau, followed several months later. Her arrival only added to his poor reputation with Washington locals as the brutal suppressor of the Vendée rebellion. "They live in quarrel," wrote one congressman. "He is a savage." Turreau beat her, often so severely that her cries could be heard from the street. The situation escalated until, with Turreau's permission but without his promised financial support, city officials moved Marie Angélique Turreau to safer quarters in Georgetown. She lived there in poverty from late 1806 until March 1809, when William Thornton raised the funds to see her back to France. "'Tis disgraceful that such a man should be the representative of a nation," William Plumer wrote, but he, like the rest of official Washington, continued to accord Turreau the courtesies of his rank. As for TJ, Plumer wrote that the president "very prudently" took no notice of Turreau's private affairs. The French minister's working relationship with TJ's and Madison's administrations remained professional and without political incident. In 1811, when Napoleon decided he needed a younger, more energetic representative in Washington, Turreau was recalled. He returned to France and once again served in the army until Napoleon's final defeat (*Biographie universelle, ancienne et moderne*, new ed., 45 vols. [Paris, 1843-65], 42:300-3; Charles M. Wiltse and others, eds., *The Papers of Daniel Webster: Correspondence*, 7 vols. [Hanover, N.H., 1974-86], 1:77; Everett Somerville Brown, ed., *William Plumer's Memorandum of Proceedings in the United States Senate, 1803-1807* [New York, 1923], 521, 555-6; Anna Maria Brodeau Thornton diary, 18-19 Mch. 1809, in DLC: Anna Maria Brodeau Thornton Papers; Peter P. Hill, *Napoleon's Troublesome Americans: Franco-American Relations 1804-1815* [Dulles, Va., 2005], 84; Vol. 42:416n).

From Joseph Wheaton

EXCELLENT SIR 23. Apl. 1805

the bearer Mr. Kimball, from Hanover New Hampshire, is very desirous to See the President, to have an oppertunity of a few moments—to State Some business of considerable importance to himself, (and as he Say's beneficial to the country) his native defidence is Such as Seems to require Some Sort of introduction—he has no acquaintance in this place—if the President can afford him a few minutes it will be very gratefully recd. by him.

your faithful & Obedient Servant JOSEPH WHEATON

RC (DLC); endorsed by TJ as received 23 Apr. and so recorded in SJL.

MR. KIMBALL: possibly Increase Kimball, a tinware manufacturer from Hanover, New Hampshire, who received a patent for a nail cutting machine on 1 May (*List of Patents*, 53; *Dartmouth Gazette*, 8 Feb. 1805; Boston *American Traveller*, 27 Sep. 1856).

From George Andrews

SIR New York April 24th 1805

by Mrs. Andrews I was informed you wished to see me I am extremely sorry it is my Lot to be from home the want of sufficient imployment, in Washington City has rendered it necessary for me to remain here some time to transact Business the Various Building I am employed for will not I fear be finesed until the midle of may the execution of work for which renders my personal attendance necessary but if you will be pleased to Honour me with your Commands I shall endeavour to execute them as promply as possible Sir the communication. you were pleased to Honour me with respecting Mr Oldham orders I recd and return you my sincere and respectfull acknowledgements for your Goodness so strongly manifested towards me I trust I shall ever retain lively sentiments of gratitude understanding that an apropriation has been made by Congress for the purchase of furniture for your accomodation I have taken the Liberty of mentioning that any Window cornices that may be wanting for your House I can get Manufactored in as handsome a Stile as any I presume can be obtained and on as Good terms my professional pursuits having led me into some knowledge of most of the Fine Arts if any particular pieces of Furniture Looking glasses &c. are wanting if no other arrangement has been made I trust I could at least I would endeavour to give as much satisfaction as any other Person any communication you will be pleased to Honour me with Mrs Andrews will forward me. with Sincere and respectfull acknowledgements

I am your obedit servt GEORGE ANDREWS

RC (MHi); at foot of text: "Thos Jefferson Esqr"; endorsed by TJ as received 29 Apr. and so recorded in SJL.

Irish immigrant George Andrews (ca. 1765-1816) first set up shop as a "composition manufacturer" in New York during the mid-1790s. In 1799 he became a naturalized citizen and that same year he expanded his business to Baltimore. After James Hoban commissioned his work for the President's House in 1800, Andrews relocated to Washington. Soon after, TJ turned to Andrews for architectural ornamentation needed at Monticello, and he would continue to do so through 1807, sometimes sending detailed preparation notes to the artisan. Andrews also earned commissions for the Octagon House and for Riversdale in Prince George's County. He supplied ornamentation for the President's House into the Madison administration. Active in local affairs, Andrews was an officer in the district militia, a city commissioner, and chair of the Washington Building Committee, and he served as a city tax collector (Mrs. Edward J. Chapin, "Naturalizations in Federal Courts, New York District, 1790-1828," *New York Genealogical and Biographical Record*, 97 (1966), 7; New York *Columbian*, 23 Aug. 1816; Baltimore *Telegraphe and Daily Advertiser*, 17 May 1799; Baltimore *American*, 13 Apr. 1801; Orlando Ridout V, *Building the Octagon* [Washington, D.C., 1989], 77, 92-3, 123; Boston *Independent Chronicle*, 7 July 1806; *Alexandria Daily Gazette, Commercial & Political*, 15 May 1811; *National Intelligencer*, 12 May 1809, 21 May 1811; *Daily National Intelligencer*, 30 June 1814, 14 Sep. 1815; MB, 2:1167, 1198; Vol. 35:30-1; Vol. 40:80-1; Vol. 43:536).

YOU WISHED TO SEE ME: see TJ to James Oldham, 11 Mch.

Congress appropriated $14,000 for the PURCHASE OF FURNITURE (Thomas Claxton to TJ, 1 Mch.).

Statement of Account with James Cheetham

1803		To the proprietors of the American Citizen	Ds
August	5	To a Copy of the "letter to a Freind."	$ 0.37½
Decr.	9	To a Copy of Aristides	.50
1804			
Jany.	1	To 8 Mo. Citizen @ $8 per Ann	534
	"	To 8 Mo. Evening Post @ $8 per Ann	5.34
	23	To a Copy of the reply to Aristides	.50
Feby	13	To my remarks on the Merchants bank	25
May	24	To a file of the Watch Tower Bound & lettered.	7—
Decr.	3	To a Copy of letters on our affairs with Spain	.50
1805			
Apl	1	To 1 Year & 3 Mo Citizen @ $10 pr. an	12.50
	"	To 1 Year & 3 Mo Evening Post @ $10 pr. ann.	12.50
			$ 44.80½
		1804. Apr. paid by mr Richards	*19.*
			25.80½

New York April 24. 1805.

RC (DLC); in a clerk's hand, with text and figures in italics in TJ's hand; at head of text: "His Excellency Thomas Jefferson"; endorsed by TJ: "19. D. not credited were to be pd in Apr. 1802 by mr Richards for J. Barnes. *25.80*$\frac{1}{2}$ remitted by mr Barnes May. 10. to Ludlow."

LETTER TO A FREIND: Cheetham, *A Letter to a Friend on the Conduct of the Adherents to Mr. Burr* (New York, 1803; Sowerby, No. 3445).

William Van Ness, using the pseudonym ARISTIDES, wrote *An Examination of the Various Charges Exhibited Against Aaron Burr, Esq.* in 1803 (Vol. 42:150-1n).

REPLY TO ARISTIDES: Cheetham, *A Reply to Aristides* (New York, 1804; Sowerby, No. 3447).

REMARKS ON THE MERCHANTS BANK: Cheetham, *Remarks on the "Merchants' Bank," Respectfully Submitted to the Legislature of the State of New-York* (New York, 1804; Sowerby, No. 3328).

Cheetham published LETTERS ON OUR AFFAIRS WITH SPAIN as a pamphlet in New York in 1804 (Sowerby, No. 3311).

To Albert Gallatin

DEAR SIR Washington Apr. 24. 05.

I have no information of the death of judge Bruin, altho I have letters & newspapers from Natchez to Mar. 24. in some of which it would certainly have been mentioned if true. I return you the instrument for Sacket harbour approved. with respect to Claiborne's accounts I think his situation so totally different from that of all other governors as to justify peculiar indulgences. the office of the Secretary of the territory is so completely the office of the Governor, that it requires no great latitude of construction to identify them, because there is not a single official act of his which may not properly emanate through the Secretary. even the dispatching an express is the business of the Secretary; & this particular charge is so important that it ought to be justified if any latitude of construction will admit it. his account stands thus.

Expresses &c	700.	these 3. articles, which seem to belong to the office amount to 2100. D. which is 100. D. over the appropriation.
Stationary &c	700.	
Translator of Fr. & Span.	700.	
Private Secretary	800.	not allowed by the law.
Indian Interpreter	350.	this ought not to stand in his account as Governor but as Indian agent. it belongs to his account with the War department, where the pay of Interpreters is allowed if deemed reasonable, but I am volunteering in opinions which belong to the ordinary jurisdiction of the treasury: therefore I wish them to be recieved only as suggestions & as if they came from any other person.

affectionate salutations. TH: JEFFERSON

P.S. the papers from Tombigbee are on a subject new to me.

P.P.S. I omitted to observe on the article of repairs of the government house, that the US. have houses, lands & other property there, some leased on rent, some in their own possession & which they must keep in repair. the rents seem a proper fund for doing this so far as they will go. the only question is whether the repairs made by Claiborne were necessary for the preservation of the house, or it's occupation. he cannot be chargeable with necessary repairs.

RC (NHi: Gallatin Papers); at foot of text: "Mr. Gallatin"; endorsed by Gallatin. PoC (DLC). Notation in SJL: "Bruin. Claiborne."

CLAIBORNE'S ACCOUNTS: See Gallatin to TJ, 23 Apr. (third letter).

From Albert Gallatin

[24 Apr. 1805]

Congress did not act on the memorial herein alluded to: the boards of commissrs. have not been consolidated and Mr Nicholas having arrived at New Orleans in March is probably by this time at the Tombigbee.

Whether the construction given by the Commissrs. (Kirby, Chambers & Nicholas) to the law was correct or not I cannot say, because the memorial stated only general grounds of complaint of which, without a knowledge of the facts, it was impossible to judge. The most active supporters of the memorial which is now supported by Gilmore, Grew and Harwell, were, however Cato West & his friends at Natchez. I believe they were afraid that if the same principles which had governed Kirby in Mobile were adopted by the Commissrs. at Natchez, it would curtail their extensive claims; and the memorial of the Legislature to Congress was perhaps less intended for the purpose of obtaining a revision of Kirby's decisions, than for that of influencing, by the fear of a similar denunciation, the expected decisions of Rodney & Williams. This induced me to write to those two Gentlemen that without pretending to decide on the correctness of every determination of the Mobile commissrs., yet there was every reason to believe, (both on account of their integrity & intelligence) that they had given to the law in general its true construction. On one point indeed which was specified I have no doubt they had. It is true at the same time that the whole amount of land, claims to which they have recognized, does not exceed 37,000 acres exclusively of pre-emption rights; but an additional number will be recognized this spring under the act of last year. That those people will be very troublesome must be expected from their habits & situation— A.G.

RC (DLC); undated; endorsed by Gallatin: "Memorandum on the Tombigbee petitions" and "*Note* No answer necessary to either; the act of last Session being a sufficient answer to both"; endorsed by TJ as received from the Treasury Department on 24 Apr. 1805 and "Tombigbee petns." and so recorded in SJL.

MEMORIAL HEREIN ALLUDED TO: that is, the memorial of the Mississippi Territory legislature to Congress, 14 Dec. 1804 (*Terr. Papers*, 5:361-7; Rodominick H. Gilmer to TJ, 23 Dec. 1804, 4 Mch. 1805). In addition to Rodominick Gilmer's letter of 4 Mch., TJ received two additional communications from Tombigbee on 23 Apr.: one that he recorded as from "Grew & Harwell" on 3 Mch., probably meaning Ranson Harwell and someone whose last name may have been McGrew, and Joseph Thompson and others to TJ, 19 Feb. Neither has been found (see Vol. 45: Appendix IV).

For criticism of the CONSTRUCTION given by the commissioners east of Pearl River to the 1803 law regulating land grants and the disposal of public lands south of Tennessee, see Gilmer to TJ, 23 Dec. 1804. Congress revised the act in March 1804 and again in March 1805 (U.S. Statutes at Large, 2:303-6, 323-4). On 11 Mch., Gallatin sent the most recent revision to Thomas RODNEY and Robert WILLIAMS, the commissioners west of Pearl River at Natchez, and emphasized that their authority did not extend to claims east of Pearl River. Gallatin mentioned this in light of the recent complaints received from the inhabitants of Washington County, which might induce them to make new applications to the board at Natchez and thereby "create great confusion" if acted upon by Rodney and Williams. Gallatin had "every reason to believe" that the commissioners east of Pearl River had performed their business "with correctness and in perfect conformity with the true meaning of the law" (*Terr. Papers*, 5:388-9).

From Albert Gallatin

DEAR SIR Ap. 24 1805

I had written to have the Hatteras shoals examined. I would like to know who Mr Tatham is & to see his section of the Mississippi light house. On that subject I am still embarrassed notwithstanding Latrobe's report which I send together with Lafon's drafts & explanations. Shall the octogon or square form be preferred? Shall the building be left open or weatherboarded? Shall we use Mississippi cypress or more northern timber? How can a contract be made, or even proposals be issued, unless Mr Latrobe himself will draw it, in order to ensure the necessary size &ca of the several timbers? We have no model by which to go.

With great respect Your obedt. Servt. ALBERT GALLATIN

RC (DLC); at foot of text: "The President of the United States"; endorsed by TJ as received from the Treasury Department on 24 Apr. and "Tatham on shoals of Hatteras" and so recorded in SJL. Enclosure: Barthélemy Lafon, "Plans, mémoires et devis du phare du Mississipi," consisting of seven architectural sketches illustrating a lighthouse's foundation piles, platform, framework, elevation, sectional view, and a completed tower; Lafon's "observations" on the project and his design for it; and itemized cost estimates totaling $13,867.41 (MS in DNA: RG 26, Lighthouse Plans; 12 p.; in French). Other enclosure not found, but see below.

William TATHAM, an acquaintance of TJ, had recently returned to the United States after spending about nine years in Europe. He was staying in Georgetown and may have shared with the administration some thoughts on navigation of the North Carolina coast. Gallatin was soliciting plans for a lighthouse to be constructed near the mouth of the Mississippi River, and at some point Tatham conveyed his ideas on lighthouse lanterns (G. Melvin Herndon, *William Tatham and the Culture of Tobacco* [Coral Gables, Fla., 1969], 376-89; Latrobe, *Correspondence*, 2:69-71; Tatham to TJ, 17 May).

William Brown, the collector at New Orleans, enclosed LAFON's plan in a letter of 14 Jan. to Gallatin, who shared it with Benjamin H. Latrobe. Latrobe's report on the plan apparently criticized Lafon's design, which called for a four-sided, open-air structure made from cypress wood. Latrobe favored an octagonal stone structure, the basis for his initial proposal after Gallatin hired him as architect for the project (Gallatin, *Papers*, 10:482; Michael W. Fazio, "Benjamin Latrobe's Designs for a Lighthouse at the Mouth of the Mississippi River," *Journal of the Society of Architectural Historians*, 48 [1989], 232-4; Latrobe, *Correspondence*, 2:30-1, 69-71).

To George Hay

DEAR SIR Washington Apr. 24. 05.

The inclosed papers respecting Thomas Logwood will sufficiently explain themselves. the law having clearly manifested it's intention that his punishment should not be death, I consider myself as executing that intention in relieving him from a confinement which would induce death. and I would wish him to be informed that it is not our intention to have him remanded to jail so long as he behaves well & unsuspiciously, & confines himself within the limits prescribed of his own land. I suppose the power to make this change in the place of his confinement to be a portion of that power which the law gives of changing a prison in cases of necessity: but should it on investigation be adjudged as amounting to a pardon, it is still a duty to take the measure. not knowing how far Logwood's correct use of this indulgence may be relied on, and aware that the state in which he resides may apprehend peculiar danger from this relaxation, I pray you, before a word be said on the subject, to submit it to the Governor & council. if they are of opinion that Logwood's condition does not need this indulgence, or that the public safety does not admit it, return me the papers, and let things remain as they are. if they think otherwise, be so good as to return me the papers with information of their approbation, except the warrant for his enlargement to be delivered to the Marshal. Accept my friendly salutations & assurances of great respect & esteem TH: JEFFERSON

PoC (DLC); at foot of text: "George Hay esq." Enclosure: TJ to the U.S. marshal for Virginia, Joseph Scott, 24 Apr., offering a conditional pardon to Thomas Logwood; TJ understands that Logwood, imprisoned "under strict confinement," is "languishing with disease," which threatens his life "unless freer use of air and exercise be allowed him"; TJ authorizes Scott to allow Logwood "to transfer himself to his ordinary residence," where he is to remain "in custody of the law" (FC in DNA: RG 59, GPR; in a clerk's hand, including signatures of TJ and Madison; at head of text: "Note—the following remission was never actually issued"; not recorded in SJL). Other enclosures not identified, but see below.

Among the enclosed PAPERS may have been certifications by the clerk of the U.S. district court of Virginia concerning verdicts on four of the five indictments against Logwood for counterfeiting notes of the Bank of the United States. A motion for an arrest of judgment on the first verdict was denied and Logwood was ordered imprisoned for nine years and ten months at hard labor beginning on 24 May 1804, while a motion for an arrest of judgment on the second verdict was upheld. No motions were presented on the third and fifth verdicts, for each of which Logwood was sentenced to an additional month at hard labor (FCs in DNA: RG 59, GPR; Vol. 43:218-20).

RETURN ME THE PAPERS: a letter of 8 May from Hay was recorded in SJL as received from Richmond on 12 May, but has not been found.

To Thomas Munroe

Aprl 24. 05.

Th: Jefferson presents his compliments to mr Munroe. he recieved some time ago a parcel of sheet iron from mr Latrobe but, without knowing exactly how much, he had supposed it double the quantity stated in the papers furnished by mr Munroe. at least he thinks he ordered double the quantity. nevertheless presuming this to be what was furnished him, & which was ordered on his private account, he will answer it to mr Lenthall. he returns the account in the name of the Superintendant, and retains that stated against himself. he presumes it was stated in both forms, to meet the case either the one way or the other as it should be.

RC (DNA: RG 42, LRDLS). Not recorded in SJL. Enclosure not found.

Samuel Mifflin, Benjamin H. Latrobe's partner, billed TJ for two boxes of SHEET IRON near the end of 1804. On 5 May, TJ paid John LENTHALL $178.25 for the order (MB, 2:1152; statement of account with Mifflin and Latrobe, 24 May 1803-12 Dec. 1805, in MHi). In a letter of 18 May to Lenthall, Mifflin acknowledged the payment and explained that the "two accounts sent you were for the same parcel of Iron" (RC in MHi; endorsed by TJ: "Latrobe & Mifflin's rect. for 174.25 sheet iron May 18. 05").

To Joseph H. Nicholson

Wednesday. Apr. 24. 05.

Th: Jefferson asks the favor of mr Nicholson to dine with him to-morrow, en petite comité.

RC (Rosalie S. Magruder, Cambridge, Massachusetts, 1961). Not recorded in SJL.

From John Page

DEAR SIR Richmond Apl. 24th. 1805

I submit the inclosed Plan of a Society to your consideration—At your leisure your Ideas repecting it will be acceptable to your sincere Friend & obedt. Servant JOHN PAGE

P.S.

As I have taken a Copy for Mr. Tucker, you need not return the Original. He is busily employed in collecting Pamphlets &c &c already.

J.P.

RC (DLC); endorsed by TJ as received 27 Apr. and so recorded in SJL. Enclosure: St. George Tucker to Page, 14 Apr. from Richmond, stating: "Agreeably to your request I have sketchd out the plan we were talking of lately. If you think it worthy of transmitting to Mr. Jefferson, or any other friend, you will be pleased to do it. Should it meet with approbation in whole, or in part, it would be my wish to recieve any additional hint which he may think proper to give. Having no copy, I could wish, if approved, it might be returned to me; if otherwise, it will be of no importance" (RC in same; addressed: "For Mr. Page"). Other enclosure printed below.

ENCLOSURE

Proposal for a National Library

Plan of an American historical, political, & philosophical Society, for collecting, preserving, multiplying and encouraging Memorials relative to the political, civil, & national history of the United States, & of America in general.

The objects of the society may be

1. To collect all the authentic histories, voyages, journals, memoires, maps, and other memorials which have been published in Europe and America relative to the discovery, settlement, establishment, progress & improvement of the several States, Colonies, provinces, & Islands in America; including such as relate to the aboriginal inhabitants, their customs, manners, and character; and such also as relate to the geographical, topographical, & natural history of the American continent and Islands, with their respective productions

& commerce.—And to preserve the same in well bound books, methodically arranged, according to their respective subjects & dates, in a public Library, to be established at the Seat of the Government of the U.S.

2. To collect, preserve, & arrange in like manner, all the Charters, Constitutions, Laws, Journals, and other memorials relative to the Government, civil institutions, civil history, & military operations, of the several Colonies now forming the United States, antecedent to their separation from the crown of great Britain, and from that period to the conclusion of the peace with that Government in 1783. together which such essays and controversial writings as were published either in Europe or America at any time from the commencement of the Disputes between the two Countries, and all memoires, Manuscripts, & other memorials respecting the same that can now be procured or obtained, either in America or Europe.

3. To collect, preserve, & arrange in like manner, all the Journals, Acts, proceedings, & propositions of the Congress of the united States, & of the several States, respecting the former Confederation, or the present Constitution of the United States, and all the Laws, and Acts of the Governt. of the United States, and of the respective States, since the adoption of the federal Constitution; and all Reports, Journals, Speeches, controversial essays, & occasional, or periodical publications, relative thereto, (including newspapers) which have heretofore appeared, or may hereafter appear, so far as the same can be collected.

4. To obtain a Charter of incorporation—to erect a Library, and appoint a Librarian to arrange, and keep the Books, and to preserve them from decay, by having them bound which may need it; &ca. &ca.

5. To chuse a standing committee annually, (of whom three, at least, Should reside at the Seat of Government) whose charge it might be to select, and publish, annually or oftener, one or more volumes of a Museum, printed in octavo, and bound, in which extracts, abridgments, or entire copies of such of the Collections of the society might be published, for the use of the members, and all other persons willing to purchase them, as they may judge more important, interesting, or curious. Each member of the Society to recieve one Copy gratis.

6. The Library to be open every day, sundays excepted, for six hours, and all persons admitted therein gratis.—and such as may chuse to take copies or extracts from any of the Books in the Library to be permitted to do so, gratis; but no book to be taken out of the Library.

7. To publish a complete catalogue of all the Collections of the Society, methodically arranged, annually. Copies of which to be furnished the members of the Society, gratis.

8. That standing committees be appointed in the principal town's of every state for the purpose of purchasing the objects of the Institution within the state, in which they reside.

9. That the Society from time to time reprise such scarce & valuable books, as they may think proper, and publish the same for the benefit of the fund—that the members be furnished with copies of such books at an under-rate.

10. That every person at the time of becoming a member shall pay   Dollars, and   dollars ℔ annum afterwards.† and a Treasurer appointed at the Seat of Government to collect & Account for the same to the Society.

11. That Donations from Congress, from the State Legislatures, or from Individuals, either of money, Books, or other objects of the Society be accepted—and suitable returns made of the publications by the Society.

† It is submitted, with what sums it might be proper to fill up these blanks?

MS (DLC: TJ Papers, 148:25891); undated; in St. George Tucker's hand.

From Henry Rose

Dr Sir Alexandria 24th April 1805

As the season is approaching when the musters of the year must commence, I find it necessary and with reluctance to resign the Commission with which you have honoured me, as Major of the 2d Legion of Militia of this District A consideration the reverse of that which led me to accept it operates with me at present, to which may be added a sterile hope that my aid would contribute, under existing circumstances, to the organisation of the Militia of this place—The persecution with which I have been followed since my acceptance of the Commission has caused me to loose all confidence in the line of my profession, with a few exceptions, and knowing the temper of the people with whom I am unfortunaetly connected & upon whose good opinion I am entirely dependant at the same time feeling a full assurance that their spirit of intollerance will not be changed while I adhere to a system to which there is little probability of reconciling them, prudence would direct that I should not continue longer in the station—I have thought there was an obligation upon me thus candidly to assign the reasons that actuate me in this instance

With assurances of respect & esteem I am most obedient & hume. Servt.

Henry Rose

RC (PHi); endorsed by TJ as received 26 Apr. and so recorded in SJL.

resign the commission: TJ appointed Alexandria physician Henry Rose a major in the District of Columbia militia in July 1802. A Republican, Rose had recently been elected president of the Alexandria common council (*Alexandria Expositor, for the Country*, 4 Mch.; *Alexandria Expositor*, 24 Apr.; Vol. 33:395n; Vol. 38:680; Vol. 42:576n).

From William Short

April. 24. [1805]

Jeffn. P.—recd. his note from Monti.—inclose a copy of accot.—hope he will understand it—know not at this moment between France—Niagara—& Virginia mountains—Mr. Barnes & library—beg him to value the works of Raynal & Palladio.

FC (DLC: Short Papers); partially dated; entirely in Short's hand, consisting of an entry in his epistolary record. Recorded in SJL as received from Philadelphia on 26 Apr. 1805. Enclosure not found, but see TJ to Short, 4 May.

NOTE FROM MONTI: likely TJ to Short, 23 Mch., which is recorded in SJL but has not been found.

From Robert Smith

[24 Apr. 1805]

Promotions in the Navy of the United States shall take place by Seniority or by appointment in the following proportions Vizt:

Captains, Masters Commandant, and Lieutenants shall be appointed one Half by Seniority and one half by the Choice of the President who in the exercise of such Choice will be altogether influenced by considerations of the respective professional merits of the several Officers thus to be promoted.

Admirals (when the appointment of such Officers shall by Congress be deemed necessary) shall each and every of them be appointed by the Choice of the President without respect to seniority.

RC (DLC); undated; endorsed by TJ as received from the Navy Department on 24 Apr. 1805 and "reguln for promotions"; recorded in SJL as received 25 Apr.

From Madame de Corny

paris le 25 avril. [1805]

Je vous prie, monsieur, de recevoir mes Compliments Sur la réelection qui vous nomme president des Etats unis, c'est bien la nation qui vous choisit puisque toutes les voix etoient pour vous, jaurois facilement prevu ce resultat, et davance je pouvois vous Adresser mes felicittations, je donne un Soupir a montechello

Vous ete si loin des petits interêts que je ne crains point de vous parler de Mde churche sa santé deperits, elle a eprouvé des pertes si Sensible et si repettée que tout mon desir est de la voir Seloigner pour quelques tems, sa tristesse est si grande que je ne crains plus pour elle mon extrême solitude, jay fini avec le monde, elle a, a Sen plaindre. notre reunion peut luy etre utille parler a un homme detat des interets de mon Coeur c'est un hommage que je rend a sa bonté joignez y, je vous en prie, celuy de tous les sentiments destime et damitie que je vous ai Voué, et qui ne cesseront jamais.

DE CORNY

EDITORS' TRANSLATION

Paris, 25 Apr. [1805]

I beg you, Sir, to accept my compliments on your reelection as president of the United States. You are indeed the nation's choice since all voices were for you. I could easily have predicted this result and congratulated you in advance. I breathe a sigh for Monticello.

You are so far beyond pettiness that I do not fear telling you about Madame Church. Her health is failing; she has undergone such deep and repeated losses that my only wish is for her to get away for a while. Given her great sadness, I no longer fear that my extreme solitude would be a problem for her. I have finished with the world, but she has cause to lament. It would do her good to be here with me.

In sharing my sentiments with a statesman, I pay tribute to your goodness. Add to that, I beg you, all the feelings of respect and friendship that I have and will never cease to have for you. DE CORNY

RC (DLC); partially dated; endorsed by TJ as received 3 July 1805 and so recorded in SJL.

DAVANCE JE POUVOIS VOUS ADRESSER MES FELICITTATIONS: Corny to TJ, 2 Feb. 1804.

ELLE A EPROUVÉ DES PERTES: Angelica Schuyler Church, who suffered from frequent bouts of illness, mourned the deaths of her eleven-year-old son Alexander in August 1802, her mother, Catherine Van Rensselaer Schuyler, in March 1803, and her brother-in-law and close friend Alexander Hamilton in July 1804 (*New-York Evening Post*, 27 Aug. 1802; Syrett, *Hamilton*, 26:93-4; Philip John Schuyler to Angelica Church, 4 Aug. 1804, MS in ViU: Papers of Angelica Schuyler Church; Vol. 36:549).

To Albert Gallatin

TH: J. TO MR GALLATIN. Apr. 25. 05.

In answer to your queries I would say

1. the square for the lighthouse on the Missisipi is preferable to the Octagon. in brick or stone the Octagon is strongest, but not so in wood. it is all but impossible to make an Octagon of wood, that will stand at all.

2. the building should be weather boarded, because, as mr Latrobe observes, the lift of the wind is as dangerous as it's direct impulse, and because it will protect the frame from rotting.

3. I should certainly prefer Atlantic pine & workmen to Missisipi cypress & their workmen. the difference of price is a sufficient justification. Is not Lafon qualified to give such a specification of the building as will suffice for a contract?

But fears, much greater than the above, assail me from mr Latrobe's observation that the worm will in a few months destroy the piles. we know that this actually took place with the bridge at Newport. therefore if there be a possibility of building with stone or brick, I should be for preferring it. does the worm enter wood below the mud of the bottom? if it does not, would it not be possible to cut off the piles at the surface of the mud, & raise the work on that with stone to the top of the water? this suggested for enquiry.

PoC (DLC). Notation in SJL: "light H. Misipi."

YOUR QUERIES: Gallatin to TJ, 24 Apr. (second letter).

LATROBE'S OBSERVATION: in his report to Gallatin, Benjamin H. Latrobe apparently warned about the likelihood that shipworms, which burrow through wood immersed in salt water, would destroy the foundation of a structure subject to inundations (Latrobe, *Correspondence*, 2:31n).

From Craven Peyton

DEAR SIR — Stump Island Apl 25th. 1805

James L. Henderson arrived hear a few days past I obtained his deposition & forwarded it to M. Hay. he braught with him Deeds from the Three Youg Girls for their warehouse shears with himself & Mothar as their security to ratify aftar becomeing of age also. Bullocks deed compleat for all the interest including the ware house. which leaves onley three Now to execute deeds, Henderson made but a short stay. I paid him Four hundred dollars in young Negroes for the four shares in the warehouse I got them at such a reducd. price that I am in hopes the purchase will be satisfactorry to you, one of the other shears bought of Anderson the tittle being rathar in the doubtfull. he is bound to refund the purchase money if it is not made secure, I will forward all the deeds to you as soon as they are recorded, Anderson applied to John Henderson for his interest in the 15 Acres he instantly said it was for me & he woud. not sell at Any price, on Andersons saying that he baught it for himself the othar observed he woud. considar & give him An Answer. at the last district term the Court & Jury pronounced. his administrataship to of been so fraudulently conducted as to lay himself liable for all the debts yet unpaid due from his Fathar, which must push him Out of all proparty of all discriptions, I am extremely sorry to be compelled to draft on You but have taken the longest time I coud. & have given the drafts in favour of Geo. Jefferson supposing it woud. be more agreeable to you although the Money is to be pd off to Men in Richmd. which I have requested him to do. the amt. is £260. Sixty in 90 days & the 200. in Sixty days if you will be so Obligeing as to name it to M. Jefferson & he can pass his word to those in Richmd,

with great respt Yr Mst. Obt C PEYTON

RC (ViU); endorsed by TJ as received 30 Apr. and so recorded in SJL.

THE THREE YOUG GIRLS: Bennett Henderson's daughters Frances, Lucy, and Nancy Crawford of Shelby County, Kentucky, deeded their interests in the Henderson warehouse, totaling $300, to Peyton on 25 Feb. (MS in ViU, in a clerk's hand, endorsed by TJ: "Frances L. Lucy L. Nancy. for Warehouse & lot to Craven Peyton. 1805. Feb. 25. 300. D James L. & Elizab. Hend. to Peyton. warranty"; RS, 1:460-1, 463; 5:422-4).

BULLOCKS DEED: Henderson's daughter Elizabeth Bullock and her husband, John H. Bullock, conveyed her warehouse share in a deed of indenture to Peyton on 26 Feb. for a total of $500, which included $100 for the Henderson warehouse (MS in ViU; in a clerk's hand; endorsed by TJ: "John H. Bullock and Eliza deed to Craven Peyton 1805 Feb. 26 500. D. for all the lands, warehouses, storehouse, mill & lots").

From Charles Pougens

Paris, Quai Voltaire, No. 10.
ce 5 floreal an 13. 25 avril 1805 (V. style.)

MONSIEUR

J'ai eu l'honneur de vous fournir l'Encyclopedie Methodique on par ordre des matières Jusques et y compris la 67e. livraison. Depuis Ce tems il a paru les livraisons 68 et 69 Je vous prie de me donner vos ordres. Non seulement je les exécuterai avec zèle par suite de mon devoir, Mais aussi à raison de ma sincere admiration pour votre personne.

Ci joint deux Catalogues, Choisissez disposez tant pour vous que pour vos amis. Sur l'un des deux est le nom de Mr françois Cocheris fils mon successeur vu que je me suis retiré des affaires pour reprendre les travaux de mon Dictionnaire Etymologique et raisonné de la langue française dont je m'occupe depuis 25 ans. Mais je me suis reservé la vente de mes magazins actuellement existans et le service de quelques personnes distinguées.

Veuillez Monsieur, prendre en Considération le fait suivant.—J'ai déposé Chez Mr J. Kaumann chargé des affaires de la Maison James Dupuy à New York deux Caisses livres FLP Nos. 1. et 2. Ces Messieurs ont le Catalogue et peuvent le mettre sous vos yeux Ce sont tous bons ouvrages Courans, nouveaux et bien choisis. Le prix de ces deux Caisses qui sont très fortes s'éleve à la somme de Cinq mille trente neuf livres six sols Tournois ou environ Deux cent dix livres Sterling monnaye d'Angleterre. Ce prix est très doux même pour Paris. Chaque volume ne reviendrait guère l'un dans l'autre qu'à deux Shillings. Il y aura ensuite le port à payer et je Crois aussi quelques droits. J'ai pensé que je pourrais beneficier en les envoyant hors d'Europe. Je m'en rapporterai sur cela à votre décision. Mon but intérieur étant de retourner entièrement aux lettres, J'aimerais à terminer toutes mes affaires et je les laisserai au susdit prix net qui est le prix Coutant si vous Croyez que la Chose soit bien ainsi. Mon opinion est que ces livres en très grande partie vous Conviennent. Mon desir bien vif est de m'en déffaire par la raison que je viens de vous soumettre

J'ai l'honneur, Monsieur de vous saluer avec Respect.

POUGENS

Vu l'eloignement Je voudrais ne me défaire de ces deux caisses que toute à la fois et ne point les diviser.

EDITORS' TRANSLATION

Paris, Quai Voltaire, No. 10
SIR, 5 Floréal Year 13, 25 Apr. 1805 (old style)

I had the honor of providing you with the *Encyclopédie Méthodique* up to and including the 67th installment. Since then parts 68 and 69 have been published. Please give me your instructions. I will follow them assiduously, not only out of duty but also out of admiration for you.

Attached are two catalogs. Make selections for you and your friends. One bears the name of Mr. François Cocheris, Jr., my successor, since I have retired from business to continue the *Dictionnaire etymologique et raisonné de la langue française* that I have been working on for 25 years. I continue to be responsible for selling my current stock and serving certain distinguished individuals.

Please note, Sir, that I left two cases of books, FLP 1 and 2, with Mr. J. Kaumann, representative for the New York firm of James Dupuy. These gentlemen have the catalog and can show it to you. They are all good, recent books, new and well chosen. The price of the two hefty cases is 5,039[tt] and 6 sols, which is approximately £210 sterling in English money. It is a very reasonable price for Paris. Each volume costs barely two shillings all told with transportation costs and, I believe, some duties. I thought I could benefit by sending them outside Europe. I will act according to your wishes. Since my fundamental goal is to return entirely to writing, I would like to conclude all my business and am willing to sell the books at cost if that is acceptable to you. I believe you will find them appropriate on the whole to your needs. My fervent wish is to part with them for the reason I just explained.

I have the honor, Sir, of sending you my deepest respect.

POUGENS

Given the distance, I would like to sell the two cases together, not separately.

RC (DLC); in a clerk's hand, signed by Pougens; on printed letterhead, including dateline with blanks for date filled by clerk; at head of text, printed: "Charles Pougens, Membre de l'Institut National de France, Correspondant de l'Académie Impériale des Sciences de S. Pétersbourg, de la Société Royale de Gottingue, etc., etc., à" continuing in clerk's hand: "Monsieur Jefferson"; endorsed by TJ as a letter of 13 Mch. received 12 Aug. and so recorded in SJL. Enclosures: see below.

DEUX CATALOGUES: Pougens may have been enclosing the latest version of his catalog, published as *Extrait du catalogue des livres de fonds et d'assortiment de Ch. Pougens* in either 1804 or 1805; a two-sided sheet, *Notice de livres*, which appeared annually; or the four-page *Catalogue des livres qui se trouvent chez Charles Pougens*, printed in 1805. Pougens's successor released a two-sided sheet in 1805, *Livres de fonds et d'assortiment de François Cocheris fils, successeur de Charles Pougens.*

For the DICTIONNAIRE ETYMOLOGIQUE, see Vol. 40:513n.

To William Strickland

DEAR SIR Washington Apr. 25. 05.

When you were in America you appeared to set some value on the form of a mould-board which I had proposed & used, a model of which I afterwards sent to the board of Agriculture at London. having found that in moist earth the broad spread of the toe was apt to accumulate earth on it, I tried the making it with a sharp toe but exactly on the same principle. in this form it has met great approbation here, and the rather as it admits a shorter plough-share. a good opportunity occuring of sending a model to you by a person going to London, I accordingly confide to him a box containing a model for yourself, and another which I pray you to lodge in the office of the board of agriculture, among their models. they will both be left in the hands of mr Monro, our Minister at London, to be delivered to your order. I send this trifle the rather as it gives me an opportunity I am always glad to avail myself of of assuring you of my constant & high esteem, and tendering my friendly salutations.

TH: JEFFERSON

PoC (DLC); at foot of text: "William Strickland esq."; endorsed by TJ. Enclosed in TJ to William Tunnicliff, 25 Apr.

For TJ's SHARP TOE moldboard, see TJ to Samuel Harrison Smith, 21 Feb.

To William Tunnicliff

SIR Washington Apr. 25. 05

I avail myself with thankfulness of the opportunity your kindness offers of procuring certain articles from London, which I have long wanted, and only waited a special opportunity to acquire. you will find a list of them on the next leaf. I have been less scrupulous in enlarging it because you mentioned it as your wish to bring your property from England in some other form rather than money. I suppose these articles may cost about twenty guineas.

Having a friend in York, mr Strickland, eldest son of Sir George Strickland of that place, to whom I wish to send the model of the mouldboard of a plough with which he was much pleased when he was at my house in Virginia, I have put one for himself into a small box, & another into a second for the board of agriculture in London, of which we are both members, & which he will recieve & present. I ask the favor of you to take charge of these with the letter addressed to him, & to leave them with mr Monroe our Min. Plen. at London; unless you should propose to lengthen your journey to Stafford as far as York, in which case you would do me a favor by presenting them youself. Accept my thanks for the kind proffer of your services on this occasion, my wishes for a safe & pleasant voyage & return, and my salutations.

TH: JEFFERSON

PoC (CSmH); at foot of text: "Mr. Tunnicliff." Enclosure: TJ to William Strickland, 25 Apr. Other enclosure printed below.

William Tunnicliff was proprietor of the Eastern Branch Hotel from 1796 to 1799 and the Washington City Hotel from 1799 to 1804. A native of England, he came to Washington in the 1790s as a surveyor and draftsman, working for Robert Morris's land syndicate. He may have been the creator of topographical surveys and maps of several English counties published between 1787 and 1791. Tunnicliff sold his hotel interest to Pontius D. Stelle in 1804 and apparently entered the mercantile trade. Writing to TJ in 1810, he recalled the "little articles" he procured in London for the president and reminded him of his desire to secure a clerkship in an executive department for himself and his son (RCHS, 7 [1904], 79, 84-5, 90; 69-70 [1969-70], 39; RS, 2:142-3; MB, 2:1033, 1055n, 1170, 1184; Vol. 32:392n; William Jones to TJ, 3 Aug. 1805).

ENCLOSURE

List of Items to Be Acquired in London

Baxter's history of England. the 8vo. edn would be preferred, if there be one	0–15–0
Combrun on brewing [this is a 4to. vol. published some 40. or 50. years ago, & much desired.]	0–15–0

Adams's geometrical & graphical essays by Jones. 2. v. 8vo.		0–14–0
Adams's introdn to practical astronomy or the use of the Quadrants & Equatorials		0–2–6
Arrowsmith's 4. sheet map of Europe do Asia do Africa	on linen with rollers &, varnished. about	
Olmedilla's map of S. America by Faden.	do.	4–14–6
Jones's New 18 I. British globes with the new discoveries to 1800. in common plain frames of stained wood		7–7–0
with a compass fitted to both the frames of do.		6.
& a pr of red leather covers		1–4–0
A new portable drawing board & seat (the board foldg up for the pocket & the legs formg. a walking stick)		0–18–0
for the 2. last articles see W. & S. Jones's catalogue No. 30. Lower Holborn. London.		
an additional telescope for an Equitorial. see drawg.		2–2–0
double turning plates for an Equatl. to stand on see drawg.		0–10–6
		19–8–6

MS (CSmH); entirely in TJ's hand, including brackets. Enclosed drawings not found.

COMBRUN ON BREWING: English brewer Michael Combrune published *The Theory and Practice of Brewing* in 1762. The work promoted the application of scientific methods, including the use of thermometers, to the brewing trade. A revised edition was printed in London in 1804 (DNB; Sowerby, No. 1206).

ADAMS'S INTRODN TO PRACTICAL ASTRONOMY: "An Introduction to Practical Astronomy" was the title of the fourth essay in George Adams, Jr.'s *Astronomical and Geographical Essays*. W. and S. Jones of London offered the essay for sale as a separate title, sewed, with two plates, for two shillings and six pence. The scientific instrument firm had acquired copies of and copyright to several of Adams's works following his death in 1795, with partner William Jones subsequently revising and publishing new editions of Adams's writings. To increase business, the firm included catalogs of their wares in the back of these volumes (Sowerby, Nos. 3718, 3797; DNB, s.v. "Jones, William (bap. 1762, d. 1831)"; s.v. "Adams family"; "A Catalogue of Optical, Mathematical, and Philosophical Instruments, Made and Sold by W. and S. Jones, [No. 30,] Lower Holborn, London," printed in Adams, *Astronomical and Geographical Essays*, 5th ed., corrected and enlarged by William Jones [London, 1803]).

OLMEDILLA'S MAP: *Mapa Geográfico de América Meridional* by Spanish cartographer and engraver Juan de la Cruz Cano y Olmedilla was initially printed in Madrid in 1775. The map was soon after suppressed by Spanish officials, however, allegedly over concerns that it did not support Spain's territorial claims in America. TJ managed to acquire a copy in 1786, spending "from ten to twenty guineas" for it. He subsequently forwarded his copy to English engraver William Faden to be duplicated for Congress and government offices. Faden's edition of the map did not appear until 1799. TJ never recovered his copy of the original (Thomas R. Smith, "Cruz Cano's Map of South America, Madrid, 1775: Its Creation, Adversities and Rehabilitation," *Imago Mundi*, 20 [1966], 49-78; Vol. 10:211-17; Sowerby, No. 3857).

To Thomas Munroe

Apr. 26. 05.

Th: Jefferson presents his compliments to mr Munroe he has this moment seen a wooden house building in F. street near mr Hobens' which seems indubitably beyond the limits allowed. he prays him to have it examined, & if found unlawful, to have injunctions instantly served on all liable to them.

RC (DLC: District of Columbia Papers); written on verso of an address cover with "President of the United States" in an unidentified hand. Not recorded in SJL.

BEYOND THE LIMITS ALLOWED: see TJ's Proclamation Extending Building Regulations in the City of Washington, 28 Dec. 1803.

From Robert Smith

SIR, [26 Apr. 1805]

The Enclosed is a Copy of the letter addressed to Mr John Randolph respecting the two Brigs—

Respecty. RT. SMITH

RC (DLC); undated; addressed: "The President"; endorsed by TJ as received from the Navy Department on 26 Apr. 1805 and "the 2. brigs" and so recorded in SJL. Enclosure not found, but see below.

TWO BRIGS: an act of 26 Mch. 1804 "further to protect the commerce and seamen of the United States against the Barbary powers" had authorized the purchase or construction of "two vessels of war, to carry not more than sixteen guns each." The administration sought an appropriation of funds for the use of those vessels against privateers along the coast. At the beginning of the next session of Congress, John Randolph's Committee of Ways and Means reported a bill that appropriated an extra $250,000 for the navy's expenses in 1805. The bill became law on 11 Dec. (U.S. Statutes at Large, 2:291-2, 348; JHR, 5:187; Vol. 43:63-4; Notes on a Cabinet Meeting, 8 July 1805).

To James Bowdoin

DEAR SIR Washington Apr. 27. 05.

Your favor of Mar. 25. has been duly recieved. I regret that the state of your health renders a visit to this place unadvisable. besides the gratification we should have felt from personal considerations the perusal of the correspondences, for some time back, with the governments of Europe most interesting to us, by putting you in possession of the actual state of things between us, would have enabled you to act under all emergencies with that satisfaction to yourself which is derived from a full knolege of the ground. but I presume you will find this supplied, as to the government to which you go, by the papers of the office at Madrid. our relations with that nation are vitally interesting. that they should be of a peaceable & friendly character has been our most earnest desire. had Spain met us with the same dispositions, our idea was that her existence in this hemisphere & ours, should have rested on the same bottom; should have swam or sunk together. we want nothing of hers: & we want no other nation to possess what is hers. but she has met our advances with jealousy, secret malice, and ill faith. our patience under this unworthy return of disposition is now on it's last trial: & the issue of what is now depending between us will decide whether our relations with her are to be sincerely friendly, or permanently hostile. I still wish & would cherish the former; but have ceased to expect it.

I thank you for the sentiments of esteem you are so good as to express towards me, and the mark of it you wish me to place at Monticello. it shall be deposited with the memorials of those worthies whose remembrance I feel a pride & comfort in consecrating there. with my best wishes for the restoration of your health & for a pleasant voyage I tender you my friendly salutations & assurances of great esteem & respect. TH: JEFFERSON

RC (MHi); addressed: "James Bowdoin esq. Boston"; franked and postmarked. PoC (DLC).

To Mathew Carey

Washington Apr. 27. 05.

Th: Jefferson presents his compliments to mr Carey, and incloses him the price of the two testaments which he found here on his return to this place.

RC (MH); endorsed. Not recorded in SJL.

TWO TESTAMENTS: TJ enclosed one dollar to Carey for two copies of an edition of the New Testament that had recently been printed in Philadelphia (MB, 2:1151; Carey to TJ, 19 Mch.).

From Albert Gallatin

DEAR SIR April 27th 1805

The following is the designation of the office at Sacket's harbour—With great respect Your obedient Servt.

ALBERT GALLATIN

Augustus Sacket of New York, Collector of customs for the port of Sacket harbour

Do— Inspector of the revenue for the sd. port

Commissions awarded as soon as convenient

RC (DLC); addressed: "The President of the United States"; endorsed by TJ as received from the Treasury Department on 27 Apr. and "Sacket Augustus Collector & Inspector Sacket harbor" and so recorded in SJL.

From Albert Gallatin

DEAR SIR April 27th 1805

I enclose a letter received from Govr. Harrison on the subject of the salt springs; and a copy of a letter previously written to him, but which he had not yet received at the date of his own. Must we wait for further information & for his answer, or take any other steps?

With great respect Your obedient Sert. ALBERT GALLATIN

A copy of the contract is enclosed. There is also bond with security for its performance

RC (DLC); at foot of text: "The President of the United States"; endorsed by TJ as received from the Treasury Department on 29 Apr. and "Salines" and so recorded in SJL. Enclosures not found.

SALT SPRINGS: for recent discussions regarding the lease of the Wabash saline, see Gallatin to TJ, 24 Dec. 1804 and 16 Feb. 1805, and TJ to Gallatin, 26 Dec. and 17 Feb.

From Thomas Munroe

Saturday Evening 27 April 1805

T Munroe presents his best respects to the President. He encloses Messrs Lenthall & Blagdins report concerning the wooden House building on F street; and, as the District Attorney is not in the City respectfully asks whether it would be advisable to bring the present case before one of the Judges of the Court to ascertain whether an injunction will be granted, and also whether the Court on return of the Summons, or on a hearing of the case will countenance the evasions of the proclamation which are practiced by putting frames together, and making hipp'd roofs to two story buildings so as to bring the eve within twelve feet of the cill; or whether the Attorney had better be consulted on the Subject

RC (DLC); endorsed by TJ as received 27 Apr. and so recorded in SJL. Enclosure not found.

CONCERNING THE WOODEN HOUSE: see TJ to Munroe, 26 Apr.

To Thomas Munroe

TH:J. TO MR MONROE. [27 Apr. 1805]

I do not know whether it is the practice here to issue a subpoena of injunction without a bill filed. if it is, it would be best to take out one immediately against the master Carpenter & the owner or employer. if it is not the custom, then the case should be stated by letter immediately by post to the Atty of the District, & a bill derived from him without delay. the evasion of putting 2. frames together is too palpable to need consultation.

Mr. Gallatin wishes you to call on him, to explain to him exactly the situation of the High-way fund, & the manner in which you have given in your accounts.

RC (DLC: District of Columbia Papers); undated, but likely a reply to the preceding document. Not recorded in SJL.

To Robert Patterson

DEAR SIR Washington Apr. 27. 05.

I have learnt *indirectly* that mr Boudinot will shortly resign the office of Director of the mint. in that event I should feel very happy in confiding the public interests in that place to you. will you give me leave to send you the commission in the event of mr B's resignation? I pray you to consider this as confidential, as what you write me shall be. Accept my friendly salutations. TH: JEFFERSON

P.S. I should be sorry to withdraw you from the college; nor do I conceive that this office need do it. it's duties will easily admit your devoting the ordinary college hours to that institution. indeed it is so possible that the mint may some time or other be discontinued that I could not advise a permanent living to be given up for it.

RC (NjGbS); addressed: "Mr. Robert Patterson College Philadelphia"; franked and postmarked. PoC (DLC).

RESIGN: Elias Boudinot's tenure as director of the Mint, beginning in 1795, entered a stormy stage after 1801, when some members of Congress criticized the Mint for its expense and sought to close it. Though Boudinot quieted detractors by cutting costs, a new degree of tumult emerged when he and Mint treasurer Benjamin Rush became embroiled in a private disagreement over the will of Boudinot's son-in-law. Over the course of the dispute Rush accused Boudinot of graft. Though he was ultimately vindicated, by spring 1805 Boudinot had served for over a decade and was anxious to retire (George Adams Boyd, *Elias Boudinot: Patriot and Statesman, 1740-1821* [Princeton, 1952], 240-51).

WITHDRAW YOU FROM THE COLLEGE: Patterson was professor of mathematics at the University of Pennsylvania (DAB).

Petition of John Peacock, with Jefferson's Order

The Petition of John Peacock most respectfully Represents.

That at the circuit Court for the county of Washington in the district of Columbia, at December Term 1804, Your Petitioner was convicted of Larceny, & by the said Court was sentenced, to suffer corporal punishment, & to pay one hundred dollars fine, with costs of Court & Prison fees—

That your Petitioner, in pursuance of said Sentence, received his punishment the same day it was ordered; & has given up a horse, (the only property he possessed) in part payment for his fine & the fees of Court—and that for the balance thereof he has since been confined in the Prison of said County, where he had been before confined, for nearly four months.

That your Petitioner is utterly unable to pay the balance of his fine &c—that he has a family in this city, distressed by his separation from them, And

Therefore prays your Excellency will be pleased to remit the said balance of fine & fees,—restore him to his family,—the pursuits of honest industry, for his own & his family's support & promises that his future life shall evince his attachment to the laws & government of his Country—

And as in duty bound your Petitioner will ever Pray &c—

JOHN PEACOCK

Washington City
27th. April 1805

We the Jurors who were charged with John Peacock's Case, believe what he has stated in his Petition to the President of the United States, to be literally true; & we cheerfully join in the Prayer of it, with a hope it may be granted—

ROBT. TILLEY
CLOTWORTHY STEPHENSON
CHARLES JONES
WILLIAM WORTHINGTON JUR.
JOHN BRIDGES.
JONATHAN MONROE
THOS. SANDERS
ISAAC DAWES
MATHW. DELANY
QUINTIN BAIN
JOHN KROUSE
ROBERT BROWNE
HENRY INGLE

We the Subscribers inhabitants of this City & its vicinity, from what we know from information, believe that John Peacock has resided for near thirty years in the State of Maryland, & that he is by no means an abandoned Character; but on the contrary, the general tenor of his life has been, (with only an exception or two) sober, moral & industrious—and therefore hope the Prayer of his Petition will be granted—

The Horse mentioned by Peacock was never in the possession of the Marshal or any of his Deputies; but was put into the custody, of one Sutton by the magistrate who committed him.

DANIEL C. BRENT
M. D.C.

A Colt taken from John Peacock at the time of his commitment was taken charge of by Robert Sutton, what he did with him I do not know

CORNS. CONINGHAM
May 16. 1805

The Undersigned Judges of the Circuit Court of the District of Columbia, being satisfied that the within petitioner is unable to pay his fine and fees, and that he has suffer'd the corporal part of the Judgment, in addition to a long confinement in prison, respectfully recommend to the President of the United States a compliance with the prayer of the petition.

W KILTY
W. CRANCH.
August 9th. 1805.

I have reason to beleive that the Petitioner is a proper object of mercy—

WR: JONES JR. U.S.
Atty Dist: Cola.

[*Order by TJ*:]

Let a pardon issue

TH: JEFFERSON
Aug. 16. 05.

RC (DNA: RG 59, GPR); in a clerk's hand, signed by Peacock; at head of text: "To the President of the U. States"; attestation of jurors in an unidentified hand, signed by all; attestation of city inhabitants in an unidentified hand, unsigned; Daniel Carroll Brent's testimony written at foot of Peacock's petition; Cornelius Coningham's testimony written at foot of jurors' attestation; recommendation of the judges in William Cranch's hand, signed by Cranch and William Kilty.

TJ's pardon, dated 12 Aug., remitted Peacock's fine and costs and discharged him from any further proceedings (FC in Lb in same).

To Charles Willson Peale

DEAR SIR Washington Apr. 27. 05.

Your favor of the 23d. is recieved. I think the improvement by your son, of lengthening the pen-bar to the left is an excellent one. by lessening the breadth of the rhomboids or parallels, it lessens the projection of their corners when folded up, and of course permits a shortening of the polygraph from East to West. I think it will enable you to reduce that dimension to 16. I. in the clear (being the double breadth of letter paper) and 10. I. from North to South in the clear. and such a reduction is really important even for those not meant to be carried about. the one I am writing with, tho' a most excellent one, is inconvenient from it's occupying so great a space on a table, to wit 22. by 32. I. when by the new improvement 17½ by 24½ would do, which is but ⅔ of the area. I think you will find on trial that 2. vertical rhomboids of 5. I. each, will command the whole page in my model, and

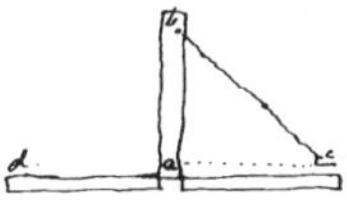

shut up within the space. because the gallows a.b. being 8. I. in the clear, and the paper board a.c. the same, the line b.c. is but $8\frac{3}{4}$ I., and requires 2. rhomboids of 5. I. only, which will certainly shut up on the North board a.d. because 3. five inch rhomboids do that in the model. I think therefore that 5. I. rhomboids will command the whole of the South board, & shut up on the North one. but still this is theory; while you will be controuled by the law of practice. I have, since my return, thoroughly tried the desk polygraph you left here. it does not at all command the page. I do not wonder at Mr. Beckley's returning it, & think it would not be for your interest to sell it till you have had it in your own hands. I will therefore have a box made for it, & will forward it to you by water with the box of minerals. the Polygraph for mr Volney must be reserved for some vessel bound to Havre, that it may get to Paris by water. Accept affectionate salutations.

TH: JEFFERSON

RC (TxU); at foot of text: "Mr. Peale." PoC (DLC); endorsed by TJ.

To John Pittman

SIR Washington Apr. 27. 05.

On the reciept of your former letter, I referred it to the Secretary at war, who soon afterwards reported on it. the constant pressure of business during a session of Congress prevented my answering it during that term, and indeed occasioned it to be mislaid so that I cannot now lay my hand on the report. it's substance however was that the law having provided suitable tribunals for the trial of all members of the military or militia, all complaints which would go to their removal, should be carried before those tribunals. altho' the President has a power to remove without trial, it is one which the public interest requires should be reserved only for very extraordinary cases, & particularly those where a court from improper motives should refuse to do it's duty. it is for the public good that military officers should feel secure that their honour can not be touched but on a regular trial before a tribunal of their brother officers. Accept my respectful salutations.

TH: JEFFERSON

PoC (DLC); at foot of text: "Mr. John Pittman"; endorsed by TJ.

YOUR FORMER LETTER: not found, but see Dearborn to TJ, 7 Dec. 1804.

From Thomas Mann Randolph

Dear Sir, Edgehill April 27. 05.

Martha may now be said with certainty to have recovered perfectly. She has had no cough or complaint of any kind, nor ever a sentiment of debility or languor, for many days and has regained no inconsiderable degree of flesh. Her appetite and digestion are both right and her spirits as good as ever they were. Her strength has returned so well and she has got so much accustomed to the open air again that my apprehensions of fresh colds and farther debility and emaciation, their sure consequences, are entirely removed. I have had no uneasiness about her, except the fear of such accidents, since her first recovery, for none of the appearances have been to my mind seriously alarming. The children are all in the most perfect health.

The elections in this district terminated on Monday last in Fluvanna. The polls have been, *Alb.* TR. 503. W.L. 140. *Amh.* TR. 390 W.L. 474 *Fluv.* TR. 282. W.L. 56 leaving a majority of 505.

with sincerely affectionate attachment yr. &c.

Th: M. Randolph

RC (ViU); endorsed by TJ as received 30 Apr. and so recorded in SJL.

recovered perfectly: from a stomach ailment that had persisted for months (TJ to Martha Jefferson Randolph, 28 Jan.; TJ to Madison, 11 Apr.).

the polls: see also *National Intelligencer*, 6 May, and Martha Jefferson Randolph to TJ, 19 Apr.

To Oliver Evans

Sir Washington Apr. 28. 05.

Your favor of the 21st. is recieved in which you mention that mr Clymer has concieved a means which would ensure victory over our enemies the Tripolitans, but not to be communicated until it be known whether it would be adopted. ever glad to recieve every information & hint which may be employed to the public good, it would yet be against my duty to do it on the previous condition of engaging that it shall be adopted, without knowing what it is. indeed, unacquainted myself with Nautical matters, I could only refer it to the judgment of the Officer who would be entrusted with the execution of it. with this freedom reserved, I should with pleasure recieve any communication which yourself or mr Clymer suppose might be used to public advantage. and in any event I recieve from you with thankfulness this proof of attention & affection to the public service. Accept my friendly salutations & assurances of great respect & esteem

TH: JEFFERSON

PoC (DLC); at foot of text: "Mr. Oliver Evans"; endorsed by TJ.

To William Henry Harrison

DEAR SIR Washington Apr. 28. 05.

I recieved some time ago from mr Jesse B. Thomas, Speaker of the H. of Representatives of Indiana, a certificate of the election of ten persons out of whom I am to name five for the legislative council. the names being new to me, and utterly uninformed of every character, it would be to substitute chance for choice were I to designate the five. I therefore send you an instrument designating the five who are to compose the council, but leaving a blank for their names to be filled up by you. in doing this I can only recommend an adherence to the principles which would have governed myself in making the selection. 1. to reject dishonest men. 2. those called federalists. even the honest men among them, are so imbued with party prejudice, so habituated to condemn every measure of the public functionaries that they are incapable of weighing candidly[1] the pro and the con, of any proposition coming from them, & only seek in it the grounds of opposition. their effect in the public councils is merely to embarras & thwart them. 3. land-jobbers are undesirable. it is difficult for them, even with honest intentions, to act without bias in questions having any relation to their personal interests. the principle of distribution merits respect, where there is not too great a disparity between two candidates. I observe the legislature have paid a just attention to it. those in the county of Wayne being now out of the territory, we have of course but 8. out of which the 5. are to be named.

Your favor of Mar. 29. is just recieved. commissions issued early in March to the judges of Louisiana. the map of the Arcansa mentioned in your letter has not come with it, but will I suppose find it's way here. accept my thanks for it. we hear rumours of combinations among the Indians on both sides the Missisipi for objects not explained to us. I credit them the less as you say nothing of them. these coalitions merit great attention and should be prevented if possible. justice, favor, & interest must all be kept in activity to counterwork them. liberalities and patronage to chiefs of influence may be necessary & cannot but have effect. if each tribe can be satisfied that they have a sure & separate reliance on the justice & liberality of the government of the union, they will probably see their safety and prosperity better secured by that than by a dependance on rival tribes: and in this they shall not be disappointed. the general approbation given to our[2] measures respecting the Indians, shews that they are in unison with the sentiments of the[3] great body of our nation, & that there is no danger of a departure from them. the Little Turtle is indisposed. ambition will account in some degree for his efforts to produce a great confederacy; but perhaps we also may have been defective in our kindnesses to him. a liberality towards him which would not be felt by us, might prevent great embarrasment & expence. the Delawares & Piankeshaws will of course keep aloof from these plots, & attached to us, because we are maintaining their independance.

Accept my friendly salutations & assurances of great esteem & respect TH: JEFFERSON

P.S. be so good as to inform me of the names you insert in the instrument of designation, that they may be recorded here.
May 1. 05. the map is this moment come to hand.

PoC (DLC); at foot of first page: "Governor Harrison." Enclosure not found.

For the letter from JESSE B. THOMAS and the list of legislative council candidates, see TJ to Madison, 29 Mch.

Following the division of Indiana Territory by Congress in January 1805, the COUNTY OF WAYNE became part of Michigan Territory (Thomas Worthington to TJ, 10 Jan.).

Harrison's FAVOR of 29 Mch. has not been found. Harrison sought a territorial judgeship for David Coupland, his brother-in-law (Appendix IV; Harrison to TJ, 5 July 1806).

RUMOURS OF COMBINATIONS: see Pierre Chouteau to TJ, 12 Feb. and 2 Mch., and TJ to Dearborn, 3 Apr.

LITTLE TURTLE: see TJ to Dearborn, 16 Dec. 1804, and Notes on Indian Affairs, Tripoli, and Great Britain, at 8 Jan. 1805.

[1] Word interlined.
[2] Word interlined in place of "the."
[3] Preceding three words interlined.

To George Jefferson

DEAR SIR Washington. Apr. 28. 05.

Your favor of the 23d. is recieved & I now return you mr Peyton's order accepted payable the first week of August. this I presume will make only the week's odds with you, while it makes a month's odds with me, as I settle & pay the first week of every month for the whole month. considerable paiments for the beginning of July render an anticipation then not convenient. Affectionate salutations.

TH: JEFFERSON

PoC (MHi); at foot of text: "Mr. George Jefferson"; endorsed by TJ.

From Benjamin H. Latrobe

Dear Sir Wilmington, April 28h. 1805.

On my return home,—for a few hours today,—to my family, I had the honor to receive both your letters of the 8th. & the 22d. April.—I feared that in the letter to which your first is an answer, I had exceeded the bounds of propriety, in my wish to go to the extent of my duty.—I beg to acknowledge with gratitude the manner in which you have received, & answered my letter.—I hope sincerely that the surmise against Mr Lenthall is unfounded. He is exceedingly disliked in the city, on account his unbending disposition, & may be misrepresented. The hint however will make me very watchful over him, & will be useful.—

I have been for the last three weeks entirely without assistance even of a Clerk at our Canal, otherwise the designs of the connecting building would have been forwarded before now. I have bestowed much labor upon them already, and find my self exceedingly puzzled how to determine the exact mode of accomodating the two ends of the wing between the Presidents house & the Treasury to each other so as to answer the object of each in the best manner.—I can now promise all the drawings & directions by 8th. of May but not sooner, if they are to be complete,—for on the 30th. April & the 3 or 4 following days our directors meet to wind up the accounts of the first Year, & I have still to prepare for them & afterwards to attend them, & am most unfortunately deprived of the assistance of the principal Clerk of the Works.—

It appears that many hindrances to the rapid progress of the works have occurred, especially in the want of bricks. I write constantly to Lenthall on these subjects and shall be in Washington myself about the middle of May.—

With the most respectful sentiments I am Your much obliged hbl Servt B Henry Latrobe.

RC (DLC); at head of text: "The President of the U.S."; endorsed by TJ as received 30 Apr. and so recorded in SJL.

your letters of the 8th.: TJ's letter to Latrobe of 3 Apr., which Latrobe mistakenly referenced, answered Latrobe to TJ, 26 Mch.

From Alexander Ogle

Ogle's Mill Bourbon County,
Kentuckey Apr. 28th. 1805.

HONOURED SIR,

With the most Sincere & highest Respect as Your Fellow citizen & a Stranger—I hereby address You as my Fellow Citizen, a Gentleman whom I have never had the pleasure to be personally acquainted with, but by Character, and as a Needy Man (I hope) on the most Excellent grounds I may with Propriety also Style You—my Friend, and therefore have used the freedom to trouble You with this Scrawl, in hopes that Your Excellency will have it in his Power and be Pleased to favour his petitioner some way—as in his Opinion may appear most p[ro]per,—on hearing my Situation, a Sketch of my Life, my Sentiments [& W]ishes; I have resided in this place about Nine Years & five Months [un]der conderable embarrassments, through various disappointments, [. . .]ses & Afflictions by death Sickness &c. have been anxious—for eight years [. . .], to some other part of the new Country, but was prevented for want of Specie to purchase Lands and so detained here yet, tho' I still feel anxious to go hence and experience some other Climate, I am a Man of a weak Constitution have a Wife and five Children & a few Negroes, a small tract of Land and a Mill, I was born in New Castle County, S. Deleware the 25th. Decr. 1759. Moved with my Father and family to Monokesy Creek—seven Miles above Frederick Town in the Spring—65, where I lived (his only Son) Thirty Years and a half—at the Mills known by our name, and came to this State with my Family in the Fall—95, to the Place where I now live,—which was purchased particularly for me—by a Connection of mine, when Lands were selling higher here than ever before or since, I consequently Obliged to take, And with the refunding pay to him for the same, Rebuilding all the Mill-works a large Dam and other necessary plain dwelling houses &c. together with the untowardness of a part of my Connections—on Monokesy, (probaly to benefit themselves), in making use of a peculiarty in my Father's Will res[pec]ting my Portion of his Estate and preventing me (several Years) from selling [the] same so soon and to as good a purpose as I otherways might have [. . .] which unavoidably Involved me to a considerable disadvantage in [. . .] State, I had for a considerable lenghth of time before I left Maryland contemplated coming to some part of the back Country, to get more Land for myself and family—than I was likely to own there, And tho' (I think) I can say in truth I have always been Sober, Industrious and Carefully engaged at my business, Yet I have not obtain'd as much as I sold there; About three years ago I adventured to send three Boat-loads of Flour to New Orleans, (I blieve) of excellent quality as any that ever went out of this State, and what with it's being a little damaged by the difficult Navagation of our small Rivers, the Glut of the Market then and the Caprice of the Spaniards who were then in possession of that place,—and lost thereby about two thousand dollars, And by the loss of three houses by fire and other damage by water together about three thousand dollars more, and having lost several of my Children[1] here too, my eldest Daughter in her third Year being drowned, my second and Darling Son at about seventeen Years of age—last Fall with the Nervous Fever, at which time myself and four other of my Sons & two black persons suffered [mu]ch with the same Disease, Having experienced that the Soil here (tho' ric[h and] the Climate too—is neither well adapted to produce wheat of a [. . .] quality, and (I believe) will not in half or a whole Century to come [. . .]ich Illy answers my occupation, being in the habit of Millering, the [pre]cariousness of sending our produce so great a distance to market, and in this rich soil the scarcity and meaness of the timber in many places, the innumerable disputes about the Titles of Land in this State, and what appears to be worst—as a general Vexation is the Imperious carriage and the unjust & Wicked disposition of some of my Neighbouring fellow citizens, particularly—Professor of Religion (somewhat like St. Paul false brethren), all join'd together makes me Desire much to seek my Fortune in the Louisania Country, I began house keeping in the year 1783, and tho' I never was so much attach'd to any place to be unwilling to exchange it for another, Yet, I have only moved once in the above space of about twenty-one Years, I have seen Dr. John Sibley's report of said Country which to me appears reasonable and encouraging, have also seen Mr. John Fowler's circular Letter in which I noticed the account of an allowance of some [. . .] to persons ("actual Settlers on the 20th of December 1805. Which as [I am] not able at present to purchase Land—with Cash—would well suit [me] I have a small Cargo in a boat now lying in Licking, waiting a rise of [wa]ter, and intend (if I live), to go along and before I return, to explore some part of said Country—in hopes to find an Alsyllum for the reception of myself and Family,—Have for several years past contemplated going to see the Louisania Country even while held by the Spanish Government, and since with abundantly more pleasure, and had thoughts frequently about a year ago of writing to You on the Subject of my going there with my Family, and to purchase some Land soon as my Circumstance would admit, and under the Sanction of Your Excellency to have Enjoyed the benefit of some Office, But that time has elapsed,

And now, Sir, I crave the Favour of some one the smallest, If, (from the experiment of inquiry and Just recommendation of any of my Friends & Acquaintence) You should think proper to bestow on me, at least, Sir, in case my Life is spared to go and see said Country, and there can be any Land obtain'd by me, and it's agreeable to You—Please to recommend me to some of your Friends there, and write me a Letter, probably it might find me at the Natchus or on Red River, I know none [who] live in that Country except Mr. James Brown (Atty.) of this State [. . .] Mr. Sibley by Character only, I wish, (Fearing the diseases prevalent in the [warmer?] Climate), particularly to see the Red River and three or four hundred Miles up it, where if I can get Land well suited for small grain, [. . .] and Navigating water, will be willing to Build a Mill and occupy it there; If You, sir, may think me worth Your Notice—and covenience serves, pray inquire by some Friend or otherways at some of the Gentlemen in Frederick Town of the Traits of my Character, Names, Schley, Mantz, Steiner, Butler, Buckey, Hauer, Ritchie, Brunner, Miller, Revd. Wm. Perkinson, and M. Bartgis, in George Town—Beatty and Hedges, and of Majr. G. M. Bedinger & Govr. James Garrard of this State, and Your Petitioner will always acknowledge Your Friendship with Thankfullness—at least; I am a Religionist of the Regular Babtist order, and a full & firm Republican in principles of State policy, or, Government, Feel comfortably serene & firmly established in the ground of my Hope for Future happiness, and pratise Religion without Biggotry or Sophistry, & that too with Toleration for my Friends of every other Denomination, I have [tri]ed—(since I can remember), to Conduct myself in a plain, civil, and [. . .] Honest way—so far in my Life, have been a Soldier midling early [in] the American Revolution, and a True Whig ever since the Fall 1776, [m]uch disgusted on hearing the Tories and British prisoners—say, that "tho' we (Americans), made so much ado in Opposing the British Government about their Stampt-acts &c.—the time was not far distant when we would be Obliged tamely to submit to the like Acts &c. under our own Government," which to my great Mortification was the Case for a while, which pieces of Admistration with some parts of the Treaty stipulated with the British and known by the name of Jay's—has made me more ashamed than any thing the American Government has ever yet done since the declaration of Independance, I don't know that I can—with propriety—censure Genral Washingtons proceedings in the administration of Government, Am confident that I have not the smallest ground of such Complaint against my Friend the present President of the United States of America; But have much regretted the large apparent shew of a Struggle, in the Reign of Mr. John Adams—and not only by him but a great many others in the general Community, for an Establishment, (as I apprehended), to blend the Religious and [Civi]l codes of Laws—partially together, which I presume, can never po[ssibly] be done in the nature of things, consistant with Reason and Just[ice] But am happy under the present Aministration, on account of the [Just] and Complete toleration of Religious principle as well all other Civil [ri]ghts,—allowed by the Laws of our General Constitution, as also every other thing that is right and necessary to be pratised by Yourself as the Administrator; As to Mr. Thomas Paine, I can't join with my Friends of the Presbyterian and Baptist denominations to ridicule his Religious tenets,—But conclude that in a coming day neither him or I will have reason to complain that our teeth is on Edge by the other having ate sour grapes, And that I am undoubtedly under particular Obligation to thank the Almighty, that ever Tom. Paine was in America, and that he has done so much good—first & last—for the happiness of the People therein, as also for all the good done our Country by other Men, acting as Counsellers or Rulers—Justly as all good Men ought and will do, either in Matters of State Policy and the Execution of Just, Civil Laws, or, in Religion: If you should think proper, Sir, You [ha]ve full permission to publish this Epistle from the words in the [twen]tieth line in the third page "I am" to the word religion last mentioned [on] this page inclusive, And I hope—on Your considering the great lenghth of time in which we have not particularly wrote to each other and my being a Dependant creature of GOD and my fellow Men, that You will Excuse my Freedom in thus writing to You, and in my Necessitous situation afford me some relief, I can (I think), with the greatest solemnity vouch for the truth of what I have wrote, tho' I fear the diction is Ill, I am, Honoured Sir, with the Sincerest Respect as above Your Most Obt. Servant

ALEXANDER OGLE

RC (DLC); torn; at foot of text: "His Excellency Thomas Jefferson Esq. President of the U.S. of America"; endorsed by TJ as received 17 May and so recorded in SJL.

Alexander Ogle (b. 1759) served in the Delaware militia during the American Revolution. After leaving Frederick, Maryland, he operated a flour mill and a saw mill in the vicinity of Paris, Kentucky, both of which he sought to sell beginning in 1815 (DNA: RG 93, Compiled Service Records of Soldiers Who Served in the American Army During the Revolutionary War; Paris *Western Citizen*, 4 Feb., 29 Apr., 10 June 1815).

DR. JOHN SIBLEY'S REPORT: possibly that which Sibley sent to the Medical Society of North Carolina, in which he described the Louisiana Territory's flora and fauna. Sibley also wrote a descriptive letter to printer Joseph Gales that was widely publicized (Salem, Mass., *Salem Register*, 2 Jan. 1804; North Carolina *Wilmington Gazette*, 17 Jan. 1804; Vol. 42:213).

MR. JOHN FOWLER'S CIRCULAR LETTER: Kentucky congressman John Fowler wrote a public letter to his constituents on 5 Mch. Among other topics, he discussed developments in Louisiana, including the creation of commissions that were to combat speculation by confirming the claims of those who were "actual settlers" as of 20 Dec. 1803. The commissioners were to issue titles in 640-acre parcels (Noble E. Cunningham, Jr., ed., *Circular Letters of Congressmen to Their Constituents, 1789-1829*, 3 vols. [Chapel Hill, 1978], 1:405-9).

[1] Ogle wrote "Chil-" at the end of a line but then failed to complete the word on the next line.

To Robert Williams

DEAR SIR Washington Apr. 28. 05.

A few days since, came to hand, from mr Philander Smith, Speaker of the H. of R. of the Missisipi territory, a certificate of ten names, out of which I have to select five for the legislative council. the names & characters being equally unknown to me, it would be to substitute chance for choice were I to undertake the designation. I therefore inclose you a blank instrument of designation which I will pray you to fill up with the names you think best, & to inform me of the names you insert that they may be recorded here. the distractions in your legislative bodies are not well understood here. but I presume you will think it for the public good to have an eye in your selection, to the healing of them, but more especially to the securing a sound preponderance of those who are friendly to the order of things so generally approved by the nation. men hostile to that, & whose principal views are to embarras & thwart the public measures, cannot be too carefully kept out of the way of doing it. I do not mean by this to proscribe honest, well meaning men, heretofore federalists, and now sincerely disposed to concur with the national sentiment & measures. of such I am persuaded you have some who merit just confidence. Accept my friendly salutations & assurances of great esteem & respect

TH: JEFFERSON

PoC (DLC); at foot of text: "Governor Williams." Enclosure: blank commission of appointment for the legislative council of Mississippi Territory, dated Washington, 29 Apr. 1805; the appointees were to serve until no later than the end of the next session of the Senate (MS in same; in a clerk's hand; signed by TJ and countersigned by Madison; with seal of the United States).

The letter from PHILANDER SMITH to TJ, 8 Mch., has not been found (see Vol. 45: Appendix IV). On 6 Mch., the Mississippi House of Representatives chose TEN NAMES as nominees for the territory's legislative council: Daniel Burnet and William Downs of Claiborne County, Thomas Hinds and James Stewart of Jefferson County, Alexander Montgomery and Joseph Sessions of Adams County, Henry Hunter and Joshua Baker of Wilkinson County, and Lemuel Henry and William Buford of Washington County (Natchez *Mississippi Messenger*, 15 Mch.; Madison, *Papers, Sec. of State Ser.*, 9:120-1).

Williams returned the INSTRUMENT OF DESIGNATION without naming any appointees; see Williams to TJ, 25 Nov. 1805.

From William Bartram

[before 29 Apr. 1805]

Sketch of the

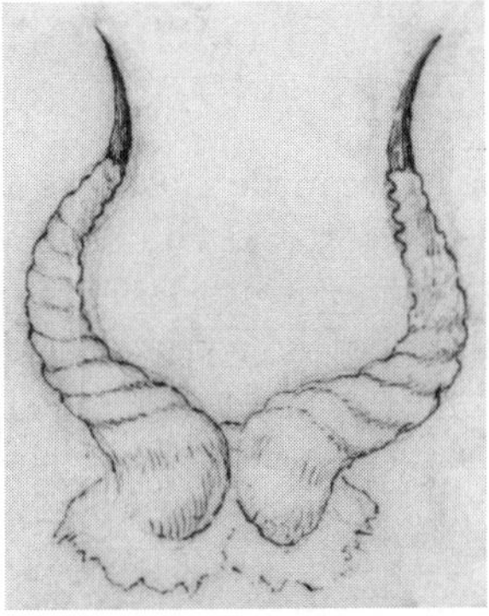

N 1. Horns of The Antilope as they stood upon a part of the Frontal bone of the Cranium when we recieved them, but have since parted from each other, & may be reunited. They were mutilated when we recieved them, in the manner they now appear. One horn is yet intire & perfect in figure.

No. 2. The other is a single horn of a species of *Cervi* from Ter de Labrador, or *Hudsons Bay*. they are small & remarkeble in being so flat & thin. This horn is also mutilated, the Rats having eat off the points of the Antler.

We have added a few other articles to fill the Box.

No. 3. appears to be a species of Chama—petrifyed, it was found in lower Jersey. many feet under the surface of the Earth in a heteroginous stratum, of Sea-Shells of various Genera and species* combined & cemented, into vast ponderous masses, with other recrements of the Ocean, together with Alumenous vitriolie, & ferraginous concretes

Phytolithus ligni, a piece of Petrifyed Wood said to be Holly, found on the Banks of Cape Fear River where I have seen large Trees in this state of transmutation

Zoophyta corallina.

*of the great variety of sea-shells & other lestacious rermi composing these masses, few appear'd to be of the same sorts now found on our Sea coasts, and dont exist, unless in so great depth of water as to elude our reserches

WM. BARTRAM

RC (DLC: TJ Papers, 155:27163-4); undated; addressed: "His Excelly. Thomas Jefferson President United States"; endorsed by TJ: "Natural History."

HORNS OF THE ANTILOPE: Bartram offered TJ these specimens in his letter of 18 Mch. This letter likely accompanied the box that John Vaughan mentioned in his 29 Apr. letter to TJ.

CHAMA: a genus of bivalve mollusks (OED).

From John Cone

SIR [before 29 Apr. 1805]

I am in the Mercantile Business at the mouth of White river in the County of Windsor and State of Vermont—we find our Selves in this part of the Courntrey Dayley Imposed on by the alteration of Our Currancey of money which is alltogather Bank bills—I wish your Excellecy would Recommend to the Pressidents and Derecters of the Severl Banks in the United States to Alter the [sis]e of thare bills and make thare bills of one Sum All of one sise—

Bills Sise

	Inches							
$100.	8 by	7½	$10–	5½	4½	$4–	3	2½
50–	7½	7	9–	4½	4	3–	3	2¼
40–	7	6½	8–	4	3½	2–	3	2
30–	6½	6	7–	3½	3	1–	3	2¾
25–	6	5½	6–	3½	3			
20–	5½	5	5–	3½	2¾			

I think if thare is Some such way taken it will Pervent the alteration of bills and the Common People not so Liable to be Imposed on as thay will know them by the Sise, unless thay are Counterfet

I Remain a True Friend To my Cuntrey and Your Humble Servent

JOHN CONE

RC (DLC); undated; torn; at head of text: "To the Honnerble Thomis Jefferson Esqr.—Commender in Chief in and over the United States of Ammarica"; endorsed by TJ as received 29 Apr. 1805 and so recorded in SJL.

John Cone (1770-1831) conducted his mercantile business at Hartford, Vermont. After a series of financial setbacks, including a stint in jail for debt in 1808, he left Vermont and opened a new store at Clarendon, New York, where he resided until his death (William Whitney Cone, *Some Account of the Cone Family in America* [Topeka, Kans., 1903], 328-9; Windsor *Spooner's Vermont Journal*, 29 Nov. 1803, 20 June 1808; Randolph, Vt., *Weekly Wanderer*, 8 July 1805).

From Jean Baptiste Biot

SIR, [on or before 29 Apr. 1805]

Though I have not the honour of being known to you, I take the liberty of making a request, which, the generous interest you take in every thing that is useful, inclines me to hope you will readily grant.

I have lately published, in conjunction with Mr Humboldt, a memoir on terrestial magnetism. We have, I beleive, discovered the law which governs the dip of the compass in different latitudes. The knowledge of which law must prove extremely useful to Philosophy, particularly in determining the longitude of places, where fogs prevent the possibility of observing the stars. Since the printing of our memoir, I have learnt, that Tobias Mayer, the celebrated astronomer of Gottingen, has entertained a similar idea; tho' he had never published it, and his son has had the goodness to send me an extract from the notes he left on this subject. But since the time of Mayer, observations have been greatly improved, and the voyages to the South sea have afforded a fund of materials which he did not possess. I have myself, since the publication of our memoir, profited by these discoveries so as to modify and perfect our theory. And without vanity I may say, that our results coincide more and more with actual observations so as to render it extremely probable that we are in possession of all the laws of terrestial Magnetism. I include the variation itself. But we are desirous of being well acquainted with the different dips of the compass. In North America, we think, the dip must be greater than in other places in parallel latitudes. And as a new expedition to your country is proposed, I venture, Sir, to request that you would invite the Phil: Soc: to add their remarks from observations on the variation of the compass, the needles dip and the degrees of magnetic force.

For this purpose it will be necessary to construct an excellent *variation* compass; and observations are to be made by changing the poles as pointed out by Mr Colomb. in the 4th vol. of the Memoirs of the Institut. in the Philosophical & Mathematical Sciences. This method was adopted by Captn Cook in his voyages, agreably to the instructions he received from Mr Cavendish; and is very expeditious and exact.

It will likewise be necessary to observe the very minute oscillations of the needle, so as to establish the degree of the magnetic powers. This observation must be repeated in the plane of the Magnetic Meridian, and in the perpendicular plane; for from these data the needles dip may be again calculated and verified as indicated in our memoir.

Lastly, these observations ought to be multiplied as much as possible, not only in North America, but in different parts of the United States, and in Philada itself. But it is of the utmost importance, that they be conducted with the greatest accuracy, so that we may depend upon the results as upon those of Captn Cook and Mr Humboldt. And too much care can not be employed in the construction of the compasses, and in the choice of the persons intrusted with these experiments.

Such, Sir, is the request I have to make. To this letter are added two copies of the memoir. You will please to accept of one, and to present the other to the Phil: Soc: of Philada. If ever I desired that it should contain useful truths, it is now, that I have the honour to present it to the sincere friend of Justice, Science and Humanity.

Accept Sir, the homage of my profound respect. BIOT

RC (PPAmP); undated; at head of text: "Biot member of the National Institute of France to Mr Jefferson President of the United States." Recorded in SJL as received 3 July. Enclosure: Alexander von Humboldt and Jean Baptiste Biot, "Sur les variations du magnétisme terrestre a différentes latitudes," *Journal de physique, de chimie, d'histoire naturelle et des arts*, 59 [Paris, 1804], 429-50. Enclosed in Pierre Samuel du Pont de Nemours to TJ, 29 Apr.; enclosed in TJ to Caspar Wistar, 6 July.

Jean Baptiste Biot (1774-1862) was a prominent mathematician, physicist, and textbook author who held a number of teaching and research positions in France. He was elected a nonresident member of the National Institute of Arts and Sciences in 1800 and a full member in the mathematics section three years later. He investigated a variety of subjects, including magnetism and the velocity of sound. His most significant scientific research was in the study of light polarization, for which the Royal Society of London awarded him the Rumford Medal in 1840. In 1803, John Wheatcroft, Sr., had informed TJ about Biot's report on a meteorite that had landed in Normandy (DSB, 2:133-40; Vol. 41:430-2).

TOBIAS MAYER: Mayer's 1760 essay on magnetism, *Theoria Magnetis*, provided the first "proof and experimental verification of the validity of the inverse-square law of magnetic attraction and repulsion" (Eric G. Forbes, ed., *The Unpublished Writings of Tobias Mayer*, 3 vols. [Göttingen, 1972], 3:7).

Mayer's SON, Johann Tobias Mayer, was a professor of physics at the University of Altdorf (Forbes, *Tobias Mayer [1723-62]: Pioneer of Enlightened Science in Germany* [Göttingen, 1980], 205).

MR COLOMB: although Charles Augustin de Coulomb's most notable work on magnetism was published in the 1780s, in 1802 he proposed a new method for determining the balance point of a compass (DSB, 3:439-47; Charles Augustin de Coulomb, "Nouvelle méthode de déterminer l'inclinaison d'une aiguille aimantée," *Mémoires de l'Institut national des sciences et arts. Sciences mathématiques et physiques*, 4 [1802], 565-84).

ADOPTED BY CAPTN COOK: Henry Cavendish issued instructions to James Cook to record the variation of the compass during the explorer's third voyage to the Pacific Ocean (Christa Jungnickel and Russell McCormmach, *Cavendish* [Philadelphia, 1996], 167n; James Cook and James King, *A Voyage to the Pacific Ocean*, 3 vols. [London, 1784], 3:493-530).

PHIL: SOC: OF PHILADA: at the July 1805 meeting of the American Philosophical Society, the members discussed Biot's proposal and referred it to Robert Patterson and Thomas T. Hewson (APS, *Proceedings*, 22, pt. 3 [1884-85], 377).

From Pierre Samuel Du Pont de Nemours

Paris 10 Floréal 13.
[i.e. 29 Apr. 1805]

Monsieur le Président,

J'ai eu l'honneur d'écrire ces jours derniers à Votre Excellence deux lettres par Mr de Forgues: l'une d'introduction pour lui même, l'autre pour vous exprimer mon sincere regret de ce que je suis obligé de séjourner encore un an en Europe et vous en exposer le motif.—C'est un très grand sacrifice que je fais; mais aussi le fais-je à un très grand devoir que j'ai à remplir envers la mémoire de Mr Turgot;

J'avais compté pouvoir remporter en amérique ses papiers qui ont déja fait le voyage et le retour. Mais on m'a fait sentir l'imprudence de les exposer une troisieme fois sur l'océan. Et l'âge, et un peu de mauvaise santé, me commandent de ne pas reculer le travail que j'ai à faire à ce sujet.

Dès qu'il sera terminé, la mauvaise santé même, si elle ne s'améliore point, ne sera pas une raison qui puisse m'empêcher d'aller finir mes jours dans une terre de Liberté, gouvernée par un véritable Philosophe. Elle sera un motif de plus pour m'y conduire.

D'ailleurs j'espere qu'il me restera encore assez de forces pour concourir à organiser sous vos ordres l'éducation publique: seule institution qui puisse rendre durables les sociétés politiques en donnant aux bonnes maximes de morale et de gouvernement, et à l'essai des devoirs civils, cette sanction de l'habitude qui enracine par tout le monde des préjugés religieux et totalement dénués de raison, qui serait par conséquent bien plus puissante pour inculquer des règles de conduite dont la raison peut chaque jours démontrer l'utilité.

Je joins ici une lettre et deux exemplaires d'un Mémoire de notre Collegue Biot de l'Institut national, qui vous prie, Monsieur le Président, et la société philosophique de vouloir bien vous occuper d'une suite d'observations sur l'inclinaison, la déclinaison et l'intensité des forces magnetiques dans votre continent.

J'ai ôsé lui promettre que son invitation serait bien accueillie.

Je vous remercie de nouveau des bontés que vous avez témoignées à mon fils pour notre manufacture de *Gun-Powder*.

J'ai traduit votre discours que nos gazettes ont volontairement mutilé. Nous le ferons imprimer à deux colonnes, l'anglais d'un côté, le français de l'autre.

Votre belle experience sur la liberté de la presse, et votre tableau des anti-philosophes sauvages, qui ressemblent tant aux anti-philosophes européens; ne peuvent être trop répandus. Le dernier sera cité demain dans un discours de l'abbé Morellet à une seance publique de l'Institut.

Madame Du Pont et moi présentons à Votre Excellence nos plus profonds respects et notre plus inviolable attachement.

Du Pont (de Nemours)

EDITORS' TRANSLATION

Paris, 10 Floréal Year 13
[i.e. 29 Apr. 1805]

Mister President,

I recently had the honor of writing your excellency two letters by Mr. Deforgues: one introducing him and the other expressing my sincere regret at having to prolong my stay in Europe for another year and explaining why. It is a great sacrifice for me, but I do so because of the very great duty I must fulfill toward the memory of Mr. Turgot.

I had counted on being able to bring his papers to America, but since they have already traveled back and forth across the ocean, I was made to understand the imprudence of exposing them to a third ocean voyage. Age and some health problems impel me not to postpone my necessary work on this project.

As soon as it is finished, not even ill health, if it does not improve, will prevent me from going to live out my remaining years in the land of liberty, governed by a true philosopher. Indeed, ill health would be an additional reason to take me there.

Moreover, I hope to have sufficient strength to organize public education, under your guidance. That is the only institution through which civil societies can perpetuate themselves, by instilling the principles of ethics and governance and the practice of civic responsibility and by rooting out the ingrained habits of irrational, religious prejudices. Education is all the more powerful because it inculcates rules of conduct whose usefulness is demonstrably visible every day.

I am enclosing a letter and two copies of a report by our colleague Biot from the National Institute. He asks, Mister President, if you and the philosophical society would be willing to undertake a series of observations on the inclination, declination, and intensity of magnetic fields on your continent.

I took the liberty of assuring him that his request would be well received.

Thank you again for the kindness you have shown my son for our gunpowder factory.

I translated your speech which our newspapers deliberately mutilated. We will print it in two columns, English on one side, French on the other.

Your admirable experiment with freedom of the press and your description of the wild anti-philosophers, who very much resemble European anti-philosophers, cannot be widely enough disseminated. That description will be cited in a speech tomorrow by Abbé Morellet at a public session of the Institute.

Madame Du Pont and I offer your excellency our deepest respects and most enduring loyalty.

Du Pont (de Nemours)

RC (DLC); at head of text: "A son Excellence Thomas Jefferson President des Etats unis"; endorsed by TJ. Recorded in SJL as received 3 July. Enclosure: Jean Baptiste Biot to TJ, [on or before 29 Apr.], and enclosure.

DEUX LETTRES: Du Pont to TJ, 23 Apr., and a letter of introduction for François Louis Michel Chemin Deforgues, not found.

From John Hunter

HONORED SIR/ Fairfax County Virginia 29th. April 1805

If your Excellency will please to recolect on the 9th. of November 1803. I waited on you for your Councel respecting a balance of a years rent due me from the Estate of John Fitzgerald, late Navel Officer Alexandria So. Potomac. When I shew'd you my claim, you advised me to apply to the Member of our District, which I did, & enjoyn'd Mr. John Randolph with him in my application, and have lost my claim. Now Honored Sir as I have heard lately, that it is your intention to withdraw that Office from the person who now is in possession of it, Mr. Charles Simms; should you wish to displace him; can I, tho' a stranger to your Excellency, with any degree of confidence solicite your interest for that appointment, To the faithful fulfilment and due performance of which, I will render your Excellency very sufficient security. I have a lott, the same which Colo. Fitzgerrald occupyed on Fairfax Street while Navil Officer, quite centrical for the business.—

Of this request, I hope you will consider, and when convenient you will please drop me a line which the present bearer will bring at your pleasure. I could wish myself better acquainted with you, but if this request should merit your answer which I hope for; will wait on you soon after, should you require a recommendation, I hope to furnish you with one to your sattisfaction; this Sollicitation is in behalf of my Son who is a sober Man and can afford a good recommedation, well acquainted in business, about 27 years old, the bearer is very well acquainted with us both.—I am with the greatest esteem your Excellencys obt. and very hble servant JOHN HUNTER

RC (DNA: RG 59, LAR); endorsed by TJ as received 29 Apr. and "to be Collector Alexa" and so recorded in SJL.

John Hunter (1746-1815) was born in Ayr, Scotland. He immigrated to Fairfax County and resided at Ayr Hill in a town of the same name (now Vienna, Virginia). Hunter later traveled back to Scotland, where in 1811 he chaired a George Washington birthday dinner in Edinburgh for "a select party of American Gentlemen and their friends." It was at that celebration that the Earl of Buchan read his 10 July 1803 letter from TJ, which made public the former president's disillusionment in the outcome of the French Revolution (Bernard Burke, *Genealogical and*

Heraldic History of the Landed Gentry of Great Britain & Ireland, 2 vols. [London, 1879], 1:837; Charles A. Mills, *Hidden History of Northern Virginia* [Charleston, S.C., 2010], 93; *Relfs Philadelphia Gazette*, 16 Apr. 1811; *Columbian Phenix: or, Providence Patriot*, 29 June 1811; *National Intelligencer*, 10 Aug. 1811; RS, 4:153).

MEMBER OF OUR DISTRICT: Joseph Lewis presented Hunter's petition to the House of Representatives on 9 Nov. 1803. John Fitzgerald, who was the customs collector at Alexandria from 1793 to 1799, died insolvent and his property was subsequently seized by the U.S. government. Hunter claimed £40 owed him by Fitzgerald. The House denied the claim (*Alexandria Daily Advertiser*, 11 Nov. 1803; JHR, 4:440, 443; Vol. 35:683n).

MY SON: Perhaps George Washington Hunter, born in 1776, and one of four sons (Burke, *Genealogical and Heraldic History of the Landed Gentry*, 1:837; *Alexandria Gazette*, 29 Mch. 1856).

From Wilson Cary Nicholas

DEAR SIR Norfolk Apl. 29. 1805

Permit me to request that the appointment of my successor may be made as soon as possible, beleiving that it wou'd be perfectly convenient to you, to make the appointment before that time, I had fixed my departure from this place for the 26th. and made several appointments that require me to be in Albermarle as early as possible. and I do not think it wou'd be proper, either in respect to the public or myself, that I shou'd leave this, until I have made a transfer of all the public property in my hands to my successor. Col. Newton having informed me that he had determined to accept the office, I saw no motive for concealing that you had made him the offer of the place, on the contrary I supposed it better that it shou'd be known, as my preparations to wind up the business, had discovered my intention of resigning; if it had not been at the same time understood that you had offered that place to Col. Newton, you wou'd have had a great number of applications for the office. to prevent that, I prevailed upon the Col. to let me mention that the offer had been made to him; this he consented to at length, but with reluctance. and I beleive he now feels a little awkward at not having received the appointment. If it was wrong that your offer of the place to Col. Newton shou'd be known, it was my fault and not his, and I beg you to be assured that my only motive was a wish to save you trouble. in your letters you only required it to be concealed in the event of his not accepting. If you do not approve of the course we have pursued, I yet flatter myself you will pardon an unintentional error.

I am with the greatest respect & esteem Dear Sir, Your devoted hum. Servt. W. C. NICHOLAS

RC (DLC); endorsed by TJ as received 4 May and so recorded in SJL.

ACCEPT THE OFFICE: Thomas Newton wrote to TJ on 6 Apr. in a letter not found (see Appendix IV). TJ asked Gallatin to issue a commission on 20 Apr. (TJ to Gallatin, 20 Apr. [first letter]).

From Benjamin Rush

DEAR SIR, Philadelphia April 29th. 1805.

Mr Boudinot having lately built a house at Burlington in the state of New Jersey, and purposing to remove there with his family in the Course of two months, it is presumed he intends to resign the Directorship of the mint of the United States. Should this be the Case, I have been induced by the wishes of all the Other Officers of the mint, as well as by Other Considerations, to solicit the favor of being his Successor. Large Sacrifices made during our Revolution, more recent losses incurred by the Clamors, and Calumnies which have followed my new, and (Once) unpopular Opinions in medicine, a numerous family, and the near approach of that period of life, in which the labors of my profession must be performed with difficulty, will render the Appointment peculiarly acceptable to Dear Sir Your Sincere Old friend BENJN: RUSH

PS: I beg the Contents of this letter for the present, may be private.

RC (DNA: RG 59, LAR); endorsed by TJ as received 2 May and "to be Director of mint" and so recorded in SJL, but as received 1 May.

OPINIONS IN MEDICINE: by the mid-1790s, drawing on the ideas of William Cullen and John Brown at Edinburgh, Rush had developed a unitary theory of disease that connected bodily symptoms to the excessive actions of blood vessels. He adopted an aggressive course of treatment for yellow fever that centered around purgatives, bloodletting, and cold water, and he championed the notion that the fever originated from rotting matter left in Philadelphia's streets (ANB).

From Robert Smith

SIR, Nav Dept. 29th April 1805.

I request your signature to the 2 Commissions for Surgeon's Mates (for the J. Adams) herewith enclosed.—

I am resptflly sir yr mo ob st. RT SMITH

RC (DLC); in a clerk's hand, signed by Smith; at foot of text: "The President of the U.S."; endorsed by TJ as received from the Navy Department on 29 Apr. and "Surgeons" and so recorded in SJL. FC (Lb in DNA: RG 45, LSP).

The COMMISSIONS were for Isaac Kipp and Augustus C. W. Love. Love's commission was returned as a dead letter. He officially resigned on 23 Jan. 1806. Kipp served on the *John Adams* until his dismissal in August (DNA: RG 45, LSO; NDBW, *Register*, 30, 32).

From Madame de Tessé

a Aulnay ce 29 avril 1804 [i.e. 1805]

je vis dans L'incertitude que mes Remerciemens Reiterés vous soient parvenus, Monsieur, je crois bien que vous ne doutés pas de ma Reconnoissance mais vous pouvés être incertain du Resultat de vos bons soins et j'en suis affligée. sachés donc au moins par mr. Livingston que jai sauvé La pluspart de vos plans, que jai une petite forest de chênes et de noyers, plus de Tulipiers que ne Lesperois, et que vos Rosiers ou eglantiers se developpent en ce moment avec abondance.

Le cornus florida que je sais être L'arbuste favori de mr. jefferson sera placé dans L'endroit de mon jardin ou je me Livre aux plus doux souvenirs. car je suis honnoreé de ses bontés et de mon attachement quand je me Retrace le temps le plus heureux de ma vie que ne fut pas celui de ma jeunesse.

vous croiés bien, Monsieur, que jai appris avec joie La justice qui vous avoit eté Rendue. c'est une foiblesse dont on ne peut se defendre. on aime a voir porter aux grandes places les personnes qui en sont dignes et on s'etourdit sur le malheur qui les accompagne.

en devenans sexagenaire depuis mon Retour dans ma patrie, j'ai fondé mon Repos sur L'habitude de me considerer comme voyageuse plustót que comme habitante de cette terre dont la pluspart de mes amis ont disparu, et dont la societe est etrangere aux idées qui ont Rempli ma vie. je sens quelle finiroit asses doucement si je Laissois mr. de La fayette dans une situation paisible et honnorable. c'est vous dire que je L'aimerois pres de vous; mais trop de Risques, trop d'affreux Risques se presentent en traversent les mers.

que diriés vous de moi si je le considerois avec sa famille comme L'empire Romain et si je vous Remettois ses interets de toute espece par le

ne quid detrimenti capiat Res Publica?

je crois ne pouvoir trop abreger une lettre d'un bien mince interêt dans la foule de celles qui vous parviendront par mr. Livingston. mais il me Reste a vous presenter L'hommage de mr. de Tesse. daignés L'agréer avec L'assurance de L'attachement sincere Reconnoissant et profond que vous a conservé, Monsieur, votre tres humble et tres obeïssante servante. NOAILLES DE TESSÉ

EDITORS' TRANSLATION

Aulnay, 29 Apr. 1805

I live in uncertainty, Sir, not knowing whether my repeated thanks have reached you. I am sure you have no doubt about my gratitude, but am dismayed that you might not be aware of the results of your generosity. Know at least, through Mr. Livingston, that I saved most of your plants. I have a small forest of oak and walnut trees, more tulip trees than I had hoped for, and your rose or wild rose bushes are now growing vigorously.

The flowering dogwood, which I know to be Mr. Jefferson's favorite bush, will be planted in the place in my garden where I dwell on my sweetest memories, for I am honored by his kindness and loyalty. When I recall the happiest time of my life, it is not my youth.

Believe me, Sir, I was overjoyed to learn that justice had been rendered to you. We cannot protect ourselves from the weakness of wanting to see worthy people elevated to the highest ranks and being stunned when these people encounter misfortune.

Having become a sexagenarian since returning to my country, I have found peace by considering myself a traveler rather than a resident in this land from which most of my friends have departed and whose society is alien to the ideas that have shaped me. I sense that my life would end serenely if I could leave Mr. Lafayette in a peaceful, honorable situation. That is to say I would like him to be near you, but crossing the sea entails too many risks, too many horrible risks.

What would you say about me if I considered him and his family like the Roman empire and entrusted all his interests to you according to the principle of

Ne quid detrimenti capiat res publica?

I believe a letter of such slight import cannot be too short, given all those you will receive from Mr. Livingston, so I conclude by extending Mr. de Tessé's good wishes. Please accept them, Sir, with the assurance of the deep, sincere, grateful devotion of your very humble and obedient servant.

NOAILLES DE TESSÉ

RC (MoSHi: Jefferson Papers); misdated; endorsed by TJ as received 3 July 1805 and so recorded in SJL. Enclosed in Lafayette to TJ, 1 May.

VOS PLANS: for the plants TJ sent to Madame de Tessé in November 1803, see Vol. 41:644-5.

NE QUID DETRIMENTI CAPIAT RES PUBLICA: may the state suffer no harm (Julius Caesar, *Civil Wars*, 1.5).

From John Vaughan

D SIR Philad: 29 April 1805

I have received a small box from Mr Bartram which I shall the pleasure of forwarding by the first Vessel for Richmond to Mess Gibson & Jefferson

By Mr Hunter I have Sent on a few Certificates of admission to the Amn Phil. Socy. to be signed & returned as Soon as convenient

I have had the Satisfaction of hearing from Mr Dunbar who is preparing a paper for the society as soon as he has completed his Official papers—We are very anxious to collect all the Materials we can to complete the 2d pt. of the 6th Vol which we wish to commence printing Very shortly.—I have this day forwarded two Official letters from the society.—I flatter myself that we shall be able hereafter to publish a half Volume regularly—You have very much in Your power, & by communicating yourself, or giving the Direction to the Communication of others as you have hitherto done you will essentially serve us.

Having only just learnd that M Hunter was going—You will I hope excuse this hasty manner of adressing you

I remain with respect Your ob. Serv. JN. VAUGHAN

RC (DLC); at head of text: "Thomas Jefferson President US."; endorsed by TJ as received 3 May and so recorded in SJL.

A SMALL BOX: see William Bartram to TJ, [before 29 Apr. 1805].

6TH VOL: APS, *Transactions*, 6 (1809).

TWO OFFICIAL LETTERS: Thomas C. James to TJ, 1 Mch., and a communication from the American Philosophical Society dated 15 Feb. but not found (see Vol. 45: Appendix IV).

To Joachim F. Eckard

SIR Washington Apr. 30. 05.

Mr. Patterson safely delivered me your letter of the 12th. inst. with that of mr Weinwich; and the box of Roman coins he was so kind as to send me. the desire which this valuable present manifests of aiding the advances of science in this region, cannot I think be better fulfilled than by depositing it with the American Philosophical society which I shall accordingly do. will you permit me through you to convey to him the inclosed letter mentioning this disposition of them, and returning him the thanks so justly due to him; and at the same time, with proper acknolegements to yourself for the care & trouble of your agency herein, to salute you with assurances of great respect & consideration. TH: JEFFERSON

PoC (DLC); at foot of text: "Mr. Eckhard"; endorsed by TJ. Enclosure: TJ to Nicolai H. Weinwich, 30 Apr.

THAT OF MR WEINWICH: see Weinwich to TJ, 30 Oct. 1804.

I SHALL ACCORDINGLY DO: see TJ to Caspar Wistar, 30 Apr.

From Thomas Munroe

Tuesday 30th April [1805]

T. Munroe's best respects to the President

Being informed that Mr. Jones was not in Alexandria, and fearing that it might be several days before a bill could be recd from him, and that the House building on F street would be finished in the mean time TM has drawn the enclosed himself & would file it for an injunction early tomorrow if he was sure it was a proper bill—If the President under these circumstances will be pleased to pardon the trouble of looking over it at his leisure & should approve of it TM will immediately call on Judge Kilty with it—.

RC (DLC); partially dated; endorsed by TJ as a letter of 30 Apr. 1805 received that day and so recorded in SJL. Enclosure not found.

From Robert Patterson

Sir, Philada. April 30 1805

Your unexpected & very flattering favour of the 27th. demands my most grateful acknowledgements.

My long services in this institution, & the respect I have always experienced both from the trustees & students, so strongly & justly attach me to the seminary, that the offer of a more lucrative employment could not of itself induce me to have it. But, happily, in the present instance, this, as you are pleased to suggest, would not be required. And I must confess, that I am not insensible to the honest republican pride of being thought worthy of notice, and serving in any office under the present Administration—I shall therefore, Sir, make no hesitation in accepting the appointment you have been pleased to mention, should a vacancy occur, by a voluntary resignation. Whether, in that event, I shall be found qualified to perform the duties of the office is more than I can promise—This, however, I *can* promise—that the utmost exertions in my power to justify the confidence you may repose in me shall not be wanting.—

With sentiments of the highest esteem, I have the honour to be, Sir, Your most Obedient Servant Rt. Patterson

RC (DNA: RG 59, LAR); endorsed by TJ as received 2 May and so recorded in SJL.

To Philippe Reibelt

SIR Washington Apr. 30. 05.

On my return here I found the Plutarque de la jeunesse 4. vols. and the 5th. vol. of the Plutarque d'Amyot, of which I keep the former & return the latter. when I came to examine more at leisure the Annales des Beaux arts, I found it did not give a compleat idea of the gallery of Paris, & that I had been too hasty in returning the Manuel du Museum. if therefore this last remains still on hand I shall be glad to recieve it by the stage.

Altho' naturally fond of mechanics, my present occupations forbid me to indulge in them. still the account given in your letter of the mill erected near Carlesruhe moved neither by water, wind, horses, steam or any other of the known means, excites curiosity sufficient to ask a communication, if it be not a secret, & can be given in writing without too much trouble to yourself. but if a secret, I am far from asking the communication. I thank you for the information respecting a Governor for children. but my family is not in a situation to need one. Accept my salutations. TH: JEFFERSON

PoC (DLC); at foot of text: "Mr. Reibelt"; endorsed by TJ.

YOUR LETTER: Reibelt to TJ, 12 Mch.

To John Rhea

DEAR SIR Washington Apr. 30. 05.

Agreeably to the recommendation of Mr. Anderson & yourself I sent to mr George Duffield a commission as a judge of the territory of Orleans. I have since learnt with great pain & from an authority not to be doubted that mr Duffield has contracted a habit of drinking to a degree which renders him unfit for a judge. by the constitution the present commission continues only to the end of the next session of Congress. the tenure for life is given only to that which issues on my nomination of him to the Senate, and their approbation. but if the fact abovementioned be true, as I believe it to be without doubt, my duty will not permit me to nominate him to the Senate. it would be an act of friendship to let him know this, as the repairing to his station might derange his present affairs, & the being recalled from it affect his reputation. under these circumstances I have thought it my duty to put it in your power to endeavor that he might be saved from these disagreeable circumstances by[1] resignation. should he conclude not to accept the sooner it is made known to me the better, that the office may be filled.

I have appointed mr Tremble one of the Commissioners for the territory of Louisiana. Accept my friendly salutations & assurances of great esteem. TH: JEFFERSON

PoC (DLC); at foot of text: "The honble Mr. Rea."

RECOMMENDATION: Joseph Anderson and Rhea to TJ, 5 Mch.

I HAVE SINCE LEARNT: Anderson to TJ, 25 Mch.

[1] TJ here canceled "an immediate."

To the State Department

Commissions to be made out

Christopher Ellery of Rhodeisland to be Commissioner of loans for the state of Rhodeisland.

Augustus Sacket of New York, to be Collector & Inspector of revenue for the port of Sacket harbour.

Gideon D. Cobbs of Indiana to be Collector at Massac.

Benjamin Sebastian of Kentucky
John Coburn of Kentucky } Comrs. for land titles in the Eastern district of Orleans

---

John B. C. Lucas of Pensylvania
Clement B. Penrose of Pensylva } Comrs. for land titles in Louisiana

James Lowry Donaldson of Maryland. Recorder for Louisiana.

James Tremble of Tennissee
Francis Vacher of New Jersey } Comrs. for land titles in the Western distr. of Orleans

TH: JEFFERSON
Apr. 30. 05.

PoC (DLC). Notation in SJL: "Nomns. Ellery. Sacket. Cobbs. Sebastian. Coburn. Lucas. Penrose. Donaldson. Tremble. Vacher."

In a letter of 29 June 1804, TJ had offered Christopher Ellery the position of COMMISSIONER OF LOANS, contingent upon the office's return to Providence from Newport (Vol. 43:670). Ellery declined the offer and instead pursued the Newport collectorship (Ellery to TJ, 13 Nov., Jonathan Russell and others to TJ, 30 Nov., and Ellery to TJ, 13 Jan., all not found [see Vol. 45: Appendix IV]; Ellery to TJ, 22 Feb.).

BENJAMIN SEBASTIAN and JOHN COBURN were both judges in Kentucky (Vol. 36:620-3; Vol. 39:148n).

To Nicolai Henrich Weinwich

SIR Washington Apr. 30. 1805.

The box containing 150. pieces of Roman coins in bronze which you were so kind as to address to me, has been safely delivered. the desire expressed in the letter accompanying it, that it should be made use of in such way as may be most advantageous for the literati of the US. cannot be better fulfilled than by depositing it with the American Philosophical society, which I shall accordingly do. the philanthropic disposition manifested, by this valuable present, to aid our young but rising nation in it's advances towards science, is worthy of a legitimate member of the republic of letters, which, banishing geographical limits, comprehends all countries in one fraternity. in my own name, as well as for the American Philosophical society, permit me to return you the thanks to which you are so justly entitled, and to salute you with assurances of great consideration & respect.

TH: JEFFERSON

PoC (DLC); at foot of text: "M. Weinwich." Enclosed in TJ to Joachim F. Eckard, 30 Apr.

THE LETTER: see Weinwich to TJ, 30 Oct. 1804.

To Caspar Wistar

DEAR SIR Washington Apr. 30. 05.

I have recieved from a scientific gentleman in Copenhagen a box containing 150. pieces of Roman coin in bronze of different sizes from the reign of Augustus to that of Theodosius, comprehending a space of 400. years. though addressed to me personally, I am sure I shall better fulfill the enlarged views of that gentleman by placing them where they may be of more extensive use. I ask permission therefore to deposit them with the American Philosophical society, believing them to be well worthy it's acceptance. the giver is mr Nicolai Henrich Weinwich Secretary & member of the Royal society of heraldry & genealogy in Denmark Fellow of the Royal society of sciences in Drontheim, & corresponding member of the Northern society of arts & sciences in London; to whom I have written returning him just thanks, & informing him of the disposition I have made of them. Accept my salutations & assurances of great respect & esteem.

TH: JEFFERSON

P.S. to prevent injury by rubbing I shall send them by water.

RC (PPAmP); addressed: "Doctr. Wistar Philadelphia"; franked and postmarked; endorsed for the American Philosophical Society. PoC (DLC).

I HAVE RECIEVED: see Nicolai Henrich Weinwich to TJ, 30 Oct. 1804.

Notes on Newspaper Subscriptions

[April 1805]

	.1805.		
Boston.	Chronicle	3.	
	Democrat	4.	
	Aegis	3	
	Salem register	3	
Hartford.	Babcock	2.50	
N. York	Hudson bee	1.	
	Alby. Register	3.	
	✓ Cheetham	19 + 25.80½	} remitted by mr B.
	✓ Morng Chronicle	8.	
		46.50	
Phila.	Poulson	8	
	Mc.Korkle		
Balt.	✓ Eveng. Post Cook.		
	✓ American		
Alexa	Dinsmore	6	
Fred. T.	Colvin	5.	

MS (MHi); partially dated; addition to Cheetham entry after receipt of James Cheetham to TJ, 24 Apr.; entirely in TJ's hand.

REMITTED BY MR B.: TJ added this notation on or after 7 May, when he gave funds to John Barnes for payments including $33.805 to Cheetham for "newspapers & pamphlets" (MB, 2:1153; Cheetham to TJ, 24 Apr.; Barnes to TJ, 3 June [first letter]; Vol. 43:147-8).

William M'Corkle (MC.KORKLE) was the editor of the Philadelphia *Freeman's Journal* beginning on 12 June 1804 (Brigham, *American Newspapers*, 2:908).

John COOK & Co. established the *Baltimore Evening Post* on 25 Mch. 1805 (same, 1:230-1). On 14 May, the firm invoiced the president seven dollars for the paper for a one-year subscription ending 25 Mch. 1806 (MS in MHi; endorsed by Barnes for payment).

The Baltimore AMERICAN was published by William Pechin and Leonard Frailey beginning 1 Jan. 1803 (Brigham, *American Newspapers*, 1:224). The firm submitted an invoice to TJ for five dollars on 16 May 1805 for a 12-month subscription through 16 Aug. 1805 (MS in MHi; endorsed by Barnes for payment).

From Thomas Appleton

Sir Livorno 1st. May 1805.

I had the honor of addressing you on the 3d. of September 1804 by Mr: Vigano who went passenger in the Schooner John Adams for Philadelphia, conveying at the same time a small bundle of the yellow cotton seed of Malta.—also on the 4. of January last by the way of Newbury Port accompanying it with various garden-seeds from the same island.—likewise on the 1st. of february, and forwarded by the Brig Independence to the care of David Gelston esq. Collector of New York two cases containing together one hundred bottles of Vino del Carmine.—on the 25th. of the same month I again wrote you by the Ship Hannah for Philadelphia in which I informed you the result of my application for the bust of Genl. Washington.—In my respects of the 16th. of March I mention'd having shipp'd by the desire of Mr. Mazzei in the Schooner Dolphin to the care of A. Muhlenburg esq. Collector for Phila. one Case of Vine Cuttings and four small boxes of Strawberry plants.—by the same vessel and in date of the 21st. of the same month I took the liberty Sir to inclose you a Memoria from the Tuscan government address'd to me in behalf of the heirs of Carlo Bellini late professor of languages in the College of St. Mary's in Virginia:—in this package was likewise inclos'd a letter and a book which I was desired by Mr. fabbroni of florence to forward to you.—

By the Brig Eliza Capt St clair bound for New York, I have address'd to the care of David Gelston esq. ten Cases containing 473. bottles of Montepulciano wine. I have reason to think it will prove superior to that I sent last year, as the wines of 1804 in Tuscany were generally of a better quality than the year preceding.—There is a vast quantity of wine sold under the name of montepulciano, but that which I now forward was produced on grounds formerly belonging to the order of Jesuits and sold for the benefit of govt. in 1773. at the time that institution was abolish'd.—I am compell'd to defer sending the account of its Cost and charges, as I have not yet reciev'd it from florence.—

I now inclose you a letter and pamphlet which Mr: fabbroni has requested I would forward to you.—the other small pamphlet has been sent me by the government, as you will perceive it treats on the fever which lately prevail'd in Leghorn.—Yesterday His Holiness the Pope, arriv'd at florence in his way to Rome. and on the 15th. the King of Italy will make his entrance in our Capital.—not a Republic or a Kingdom in Italy but has already sent the most respectable of their citizens or their subjects to compliment him.—every curate of a Village is enjoin'd to appear at the door of his church, with all the officers which may appertain to it in their most splendid robes to salute him as he passes. in short, there are no honors that the church or State can confer, but are prepar'd for him.—I have the honor to be with very Sincere respect

your devoted Servant, TH: APPLETON

RC (DLC); at foot of text: "Thomas Jefferson, esqr Prest. of the U: States &c"; endorsed by TJ as received 2 Aug. and so recorded in SJL; also endorsed by TJ: "Montepulciano. on grounds formerly the Jesuits. Maccaroni. Parmesan." FC (Lb in DNA: RG 84, CR, Leghorn); at foot of text: "N.B. inclos'd the bill of the wine." Enclosures: Giovanni Fabbroni to TJ, 15 Mch., and enclosure.

3D. OF SEPTEMBER 1804: Appleton's letter dated 3 Sep. 1804 was presumably lost at sea with Giuseppe Timpanari Viganò. Appleton enclosed a copy, dated 2 Sep., in his letter to TJ of 6 July 1805 (see Appleton to TJ, 2 Sep. 1804).

For the MEMORIA regarding the heirs of Carlo Bellini, see Appleton to TJ, 22 Mch. 1805.

COLLEGE OF ST. MARY'S: that is, the College of William and Mary (Vol. 38:214n).

Napoleon Bonaparte became KING OF ITALY with the transformation of the Italian Republic into the Kingdom of Italy in 1804. His coronation took place at Milan on 26 May (Philip Dwyer, *Citizen Emperor: Napoleon in Power* [London, 2013], 185-8).

ENCLOSURE

Invoice for Wine

Postscriptum
at the moment of the departure of the vessel I have receiv'd the Note of the wine.—

		Pavolis.
The Cost of the wine together with the transportation 120 miles by land		642–
the transportation from florence by the Arno, with porterage, bottling, Cases, Straw, Corks, ropes, transporting on board &ca. &ca.	.–	241–
for 473. black bottles		243–
	Pavolis.–	1126–
	Dollars	
N:B. 9. pavolis and a half make a Spanish dollar. the amt. in dollars.—	118.½–	
which is precisely one quarter of a dollar each, including the bottle.		

RC (MHi); undated. FC (Lb in MB: Thomas Appleton Account Book); dated 6 Apr. 1805; with additional details, including the information that the wine was Montepulciano obtained from Chevalier Bucelli of Florence; notation at foot of text: "Cr. By a bill of excha. drawn by James Madison and endors'd to me by the President for 250. Doll on Liverpool, which I having sent for payment produced 260 Doll: 95 Cents."

PAVOLIS: paolis were silver coins produced in Tuscany from the sixteenth to the nineteenth centuries (OED).

From James Leander Cathcart

Wednesday evening [1 May 1805]—

James L. Cathcart presents his respects to Mr. Jefferson and requests him to accept a few Flower seeds & fruit kernels from Italy—

RC (DLC); partially dated; endorsed by TJ as received 2 May 1805 and so recorded in SJL.

James Leander Cathcart (1767-1843) emigrated from his native Ireland as a young child. He served briefly as a midshipman on a Continental frigate but was taken prisoner by the British. During the 1780s, he worked on merchant vessels, but after his schooner was captured by Algerians in 1785, he was sold into service in Algiers. Making the best of his situation, he worked as a clerk in a series of increasingly important positions, eventually becoming the Christian secretary to the dey of Algiers. In that capacity he aided negotiations that led to the release of American captives there, including himself. Cathcart returned to the United States in 1796 and lived in Philadelphia, where he met TJ, who later characterized him as "a man of very sound judgment & fearless." Named consul to Tripoli by John Adams, Cathcart served in that position until the outbreak of war between Tripoli and the United States. TJ named him consul at Algiers in 1802, but the dey rejected the appointment, and the following year he was appointed consul at Tunis. Again, his appointment met disapproval, and TJ was forced to rescind it. From 1807 to 1815, Cathcart served as U.S. consul to Madeira, followed by a two-year stint as consul at Cadiz. In later years, he worked at the Treasury Department in Washington (DAB; *Daily National Intelligencer*, 9 Oct. 1843; JEP, 2:46; 3:20-1; Vol. 36:557; Vol. 42:351-3).

PRESENTS HIS RESPECTS: Cathcart returned to the United States at the end of February and had been in Washington for about a month. He dined at the President's House on 29 Apr. (*National Intelligencer*, 3 Apr.; Madison, *Papers, Sec. of State Ser.*, 9:87-8; Appendix II).

From Jean Henry De Croisœüil

MONSIEUR LE PRÉSIDENT. Norfolk 1er May 1805.

Permettez à un français passager en cette ville et vivant dans l'obscurité, de s'élever un instant jusqu'à votre Excellence et de lui offrir un juste tribut d'hommages. c'est moins comme au chef d'un état puissant que j'ai l'honneur de les adresser, que comme à l'ami au protecteur des arts et des lettres. ils n'ont cessé d'être cultivés dans ces tems de calamités dont le seul souvenir afflige encore, et en ont allégé le poids. lorsque la religion fondait en larmes et qu'un crêpe funebre voilait le temple de la justice, l'homme pieux priait en secret et le sage étudiait dans le silence. le terme de nos malheurs fut le moment ou l'on put professer hautement les principes antérieurs à tous les tems. bientôt au siecle de la démence succéda le regne de l'ordre, et la société redevint une nouvelle copie de la création.

La persévérance dans le bien constitue seule l'homme vertueux, les ouvrages d'Esprit sont les exercices du talent, une bonne action ne sera donc pas plus la vertu qu'on bon mot ne sera de l'Esprit. mais la Vertu, Mr. le Président, vous le savez, a besoin des talens pour composer le vrai mérite. lorsqu'il se trouve dans la représentant d'une grande nation, c'est alors qu'il en devient la pierre fondamentale, alors il est à lui seul une puissance; ses actions, qui ne diffèrent que par leur plus ou moins d'importance, reçoivent toutes son empreinte. son esprit est une source de lumieres pour ses contemporains, et sa vie un modele pour les générations futures.

Deux grands états se disputent aujourd'hui l'empire et semblent avoir pris pour devise, plutôt périr que de ne pas commander. l'un emprunte des deux mondes ce qui lui manque pour rivaliser avec l'autre, puissant par lui même. celui cy par son immobilité ma majestueuse a lutté jusqu'à présent avec sureté contre toute l'activité de l'autre toujours inquiet, toujours dans les craintes, mais toujours debout et dans la plus respectable attitude. tous deux nous offrent un spectacle allarmant, se font une guerre sans combats, négocient sans paix, commercent sans s'enrichir. loin du sage toute idée de destruction. les grandes associations d'hommes sont les plus beaux chef d'œuvres de la raison humaine, et méritent notre respectueuse admiration.

Cette situation critique est la conséquence des événemens passés qui ont saisi d'étonnement toutes les nations, et ne peuvent être expliqués qu'en remontant à l'arbitre souverain des peuples et des rois. j'ai tenté de les décrire. je me suis armé d'un poinçon de fer, j'ai parcouru les fastes horribles de notre histoire, et en ai tracé les événemens en caracteres de sang. l'effrayante complicité des crimes et de la puissance de la france a pétrifié les ames et glaçé les cœurs. le ciel a suspendu le cours de ses vengeances et a opéré un prodige instantané. près de l'abyme ou j'ai vu ma patrie, un jeune heros chargé de toute sa gloire, l'a fermé, pour ainsi dire, d'un seul coup de son bras, et a consolé la france couverte de deuil. la sagesse prémier don du créateur, le courage, la force l'ont fait le plus grand homme de l'Europe. par lui la tranquilité a été rétablie dans son paÿs, par lui la paix a été donnée aux deux mondes, et son bonheur n'a plus été redoutable qu'à ses ennemis.

C'était avec une plume d'or qu'il fallait peindre ces dernieres merveilles, je le sais; mais que je serais flatté si cette production de mes faibles talents méritait un moment votre attention! peut être avez vous vu, Mr. le président dans la gazette de Norfolk l'annonce de la cinquieme partie des annales de la révolution française. peut être que l'avertissement a déja été honnoré de votre regard. je le devrais à Mr. Girardin dont vous connaissez la belle plume qui a relevé mon ouvrage par sa traduction brillante. je ne me suis point proposé dans cette cinquième partie de louer, encore moins de juger le premier Consul de france Napoleon Buonaparte. je rapporte les faits assez éloquens par eux mêmes. pour le louer d'une maniere digne de lui pour le bien juger, il faudrait être ou grand Ministre ou grand roy.

l'éclatant diadême, le plus beau de l'Europe qui ceint aujourd'hui son front, le juste prix de ses hauts services, de ses talens signalés, le soumet à un joug superbe qu'il porte avec honneur, et précipite dans l'abyme de sa gloire sa nombreuse famille. Votre personne offre un aspect plus doux et plus flatteur. Votre place éminente vous impose des devoirs plus satisfaisans: l'estime et la considération de l'univers couronnent vos nobles fonctions.

Je suis avec un respect profond Monsieur le Président De Votre Excellence Le très humble et très obéissant Serviteur

J. H. De Croisœüil

EDITORS' TRANSLATION

Mister President, Norfolk, 1 May 1805

Allow a Frenchman, living in obscurity and passing through this city, to come forward for a moment and offer your excellency the praise you deserve. The homage I have the honor of addressing is directed less to the head of a powerful state than to the friend and patron of arts and letters. During the calamitous times whose memory still afflicts us, the arts and letters continued to be practiced and they lightened our burden. When religion dissolved into tears and a mourning crape veiled the temple of justice, the pious prayed in secret, the wise studied in silence. Our sufferings ended when we could openly proclaim eternal principles. The reign of order will soon replace the century of folly, and society will once again become a fresh image of creation.

The virtuous man is defined by his perseverance in goodness. Works of wit are manifestations of talent. One good action does not constitute virtue any more than one witticism constitutes intelligence. But as you know, Mr. President, virtue needs talent to create genuine merit. When it occurs in the representative of a great nation, it becomes the fundamental bedrock and he himself becomes a force. All his actions, of greater or lesser importance, are imprinted with his virtue. His mind is a source of enlightenment for his contemporaries and his life is a model for future generations.

Today two great states compete to be empires and seem to have adopted as their motto, better to perish than not to command. One borrows what it lacks from both worlds to compete with the other, which is strong on its own. Until now, the latter, in its majestic immobility, has confidently resisted all actions by the other one, which is ever anxious, ever fearful, but always standing in the most respectable stance. The two provide an alarming spectacle: they wage war without combat, negotiate without peace, and trade without profit. The wise man has no desire to destroy. The great communities of humankind are the most beautiful masterpieces of human reason and deserve our respectful admiration.

This dire situation is the consequence of past events that awed all nations and can only be explained by returning to the sovereign judge of peoples and kings. I have attempted to describe them. I armed myself with an iron stamp; I have studied the terrible displays of our past and traced the events in blood. The terrifying complicity between power and crime in France has petrified souls and frozen hearts. Heaven has suspended the course of vengeance and worked a sudden miracle. Near the abyss where I saw my country, a young hero filled with honor closed it, so to speak, with a single wave of his arm and consoled a grieving France. Wisdom, the first gift of the creator, along with courage and strength, made him the greatest man in Europe. Through him, peace was restored to his country. Through him, peace was restored to both worlds. Only his enemies feared his success.

It would take a golden pen to depict these recent marvels, I know. But how flattered I would be if this product of my feeble talent deserved a moment of your attention! Perhaps you saw, Mr. President, the announcement in the Norfolk Gazette of the fifth volume of the annals of the French Revolution. Perhaps you honored the announcement with a glance. I am indebted to Mr. Girardin, whose fine pen you are familiar with and who enhanced my work with his brilliant translation. In this fifth volume, I did not seek to praise, and even less to judge the first consul of France, Napoleon Bonaparte. I relate facts that are sufficiently eloquent on their own to praise him in a manner he deserves. To judge him accurately would take either a great minister or a great king.

The sparkling diadem, the most beautiful of Europe, which now crowns his head, while a worthy tribute to his distinguished service and acknowledged talent, burdens him with an imposing yoke. He wears it with honor, but it precipitates his large family into the abyss of his glory. You provide a more gentle and pleasing mien. Your eminent position imposes more satisfying duties upon you. The respect and esteem of the universe crown your noble functions.

With deep respect, Mister President, I am your excellency's very humble and obedient servant. J. H. De Croisœüil

RC (DLC); endorsed by TJ as received 8 May and so recorded in SJL.

Jean Henry De Croisœüil (d. 1806) was married to the daughter of a close friend of Josephine de Beauharnais (later the empress of the French), all of whom were from the French Antilles. De Croisœüil wrote a five-volume history of the French Revolution, at least part of which was composed during a stay in Grenada in 1802, but only the fifth volume and an excerpt from the third volume were published while the remainder has not been found. The published excerpt indicated abiding respect for Louis XVI, and the fifth volume reflected De Croisœüil's pride in the military and political accomplishments of Napoleon Bonaparte (Biographical information in Archives Nationales, Paris; Caroline d'Arjuzon, *Madame Louis Bonaparte* [Paris, 1901], 224-5; Jean Henry De Croisœüil, *Revolutionary Annals, or History of the French Revolution, from the Convocation of the States-General to the Treaty of Amiens, in 1802. Part V. Buonaparte, during the First Three Years of His Consulate*, trans. L. H. Giradin [Norfolk, Va., 1805]).

Form for Warrants

Sir, Washington [on or before 1 May 1805]

Be pleased to advance to Dollars out of the fund appropriated by the Act of Congress of last session entitled "An Act to provide for the accommodation of the President of the United States";[1] of which fund he is appointed Agent and is to render his accounts to the Treasury.

Dft (DLC); undated; in a clerk's hand, with revision by TJ (see note 1 below); at foot of text: "To the Secretary of the Treasury"; endorsed by TJ: "Claxton Thos. warrts. issued to him 1805. May 1. 4000. D."

For the ACT OF CONGRESS approved 3 Mch. 1805, see U.S. Statutes at Large, 2:346, and Thomas Claxton to TJ, 1 Mch.

[1] Remainder of sentence interlined by TJ in place of "for which sum he is to be charged and held accountable."

To George Jefferson

Dear Sir Washington May. 1. 1805.

I suppose we may by this time conclude that my tobacco will not fetch 7. Dollars: and foreseeing no circumstance likely to raise the price soon, I propose that you should sell it for 40/ for any credit not exceeding 90. days. indeed the shorter the term of paiment you may be able to obtain, the more convenient to me, as I have calls which would render it a sensible accomodation. Accept affectionate salutations.

Th: Jefferson

PoC (MHi); at foot of text: "Mr. George Jefferson"; endorsed by TJ.

From Lafayette

My dear friend Auteuïl 11th floreal May the 1st 1805

Mr Livingston is Going—I Heartily Lament Not to Accompany Him—it is Necessary for me to Hope You Will Approve My Motives, Not only those I Have Stated in former Letters; the Copies of which I Beg Leave to Inclose, But those also Which in Confidential Conversations He Will More Particularly Explain—my Heart is Known to You, My dear friend, and if You think You Have to Blame me for Mistaken Notions, I am Sure You Will partake in and feel for the principles Upon Which I Have Acted—it is Needless to Add I am impatiently Waïting for Your Answer—Mr Livingston Will Soon Meet You, and Altho He Cannot Be in Some Respects So Sanguine as I am, He Seems Equally Sensible of a public inconvenience Attending My immediate Concern in the politics of Louïsiana for Which I Refer Myself to Him.

I Have Sent to You the Copy of A public Letter of thanks, Which, if You Approve of it, Might I Believe Be printed as the Best Way to Express My Gratitude to Congress and the people at Large—I Have Calculated it on purpose, and it May Very Well Appear on Both Sides of the Water.

My Invalid Wife Has Been these past days Very ill—the Humour Which preys Upon Her Was Brought inside, a Circumstance Which, if not Immediately Attended to, might Become Very dangerous—She is Better to day, and Requests Her Most Affectionate Compliments to You—George and His Sisters Beg to Be Respectfully Remembered. Your God Son is daily Expected—Here is a Letter from Mde de Tessé to You, and One to our friend Short to Whom I Send My Best Compliments. I Live Here With Tracy, Cabanis, and Arthur O'Connor, three Excellent Men Who Love and Venerate You—When My dear daughter in law Will Be Well I Must pay another Visit to Mont d'or, and from there to My Aunt—I shall Anxiously Waït for Letters from You—Tracy Has Sent to Me His Second Volume Requesting Your Acceptance of it—as Soon as the third Comes out it Shall Be forwarded—We Had Your Speech printed in the Argus—but in the other papers they impudently Curtailed and Altered it—Two translations Are Making, one Here, the other By our friend dupont—and if the Gazettes dare not Give it One, it shall be Printed and distributed By Us. My Letters to Madison are full of pecuniary Concerns—You Have Saved me from a Situation, in point of finance, truly desperate—I still Want your friendly Exertions to Complete the Cure By a timely and proper disposal of the Munificent Ressources You Have provided for me, So as to Clear my fortune, insure A moderate Revenue, and prepare the Wealth of My Children—Advantages the More precious to Me, as they fill My Heart With all the Enjoyments of Gratitude. Adieu, My dear friend, I am Happy in the Sentiments of Admiration, Love, and Respect Which for Ever Bind me to You

Your friend LAFAYETTE

RC (PHi); at head of text: "To Thomas Jefferson"; endorsed by TJ as received 3 July and so recorded in SJL. Enclosures: (1) Probably Lafayette to TJ, 8 Oct. 1804 and 22 Apr. 1805. (2) Madame de Tessé to TJ, 29 Apr. (3) Antoine Louis Claude Destutt de Tracy, *Éléments d'idéologie. Seconde partie. Grammaire* (Paris, 1803). Other enclosures not found.

GOD SON: see Lafayette to TJ, 20 Apr.

This was the second copy of the SECOND VOLUME of *Éléments d'idéologie* sent to TJ. Destutt de Tracy previously sent

TJ a copy on 21 Feb. 1804, received on 30 Apr. 1805. See also Sowerby, No. 1239.

YOUR SPEECH: Second Inaugural Address, printed at 4 Mch.

To Thomas Munroe

May 1. 05.

Th:J. presents his compliments to mr Munroe; he is so much engaged as to be unable to read the inclosed with attention, but has no doubt it is sufficient to obtain the injunction on; & should it need any thing material afterwards, it can be amended.

RC (DLC: District of Columbia Papers). Enclosure not found, but see Munroe to TJ, 30 Apr.

From John Pittman

SIR, Alexandria May 1st: 1805

The communication which your Excellency was pleased to address to me under date of the 27th. I had the honor to receive two days afterwards. While it cannot fail to be a cause of regret to those who petitioned for the removal of Colonel Peyton from his command, that their undertaking has proved ineffectual; I indulge a hope, that, with me, they will yield a prompt acquiescence to your decision.

I pray you to accept assurances of the consideration & Respect with which, I am your Excellency's very Obedient JOHN PITTMAN

RC (DLC); at foot of text: "Thomas Jefferson Esqr. President of the U. States"; endorsed by TJ as received 2 May and so recorded in SJL.

Francis PEYTON resigned as commandant of the second legion of the D.C. militia, leading to the appointment of John McKinney, whom Pittman and others had recommended when seeking Peyton's removal (Dearborn to TJ, 7 Dec. 1804 and 19 June 1805).

From Philippe Reibelt

MONSIEUR LE PRESIDENT! Baltimore le 1er. Mai 1805.

Permettez—de Vous rappeller l'Affaire, pour laquelle j'etois adressè a Vous par le Gen. Kosciuszko il y a $2\frac{1}{2}$ Ans,—de Vous dire, que le Colonel Armstrong n'a pas repondu du tout a votre invitation au Sujet de la *Patente originale*, qui est dans ses Mains—et de Vous prier, de vouloir bien lui ecrire iterativement, a çe, qu'il remette enfin cette Patente en Vos Mains, desquelles je serois alors sur de la recevoir.

Je suis tres fachè, d'etre forcè de vous causer çette peine, mais il ne me reste autre Moyen pour avoir çet Original, que de me representer a Vous, d'autant plus que Vous avez bien voulu Vous charger Des le commencement de l'exécution des pouvoirs, que le General a pris la libertè de Vous deferer dans çette Affaire, et en consequence ecrie la premiere Lettre au Colonel pour l'extradition de cette Patente originale a Moi.

Daignez agreèr mes respects les plus profonds et les plus sinceres.

REIBELT.

P.S.

Si Vous voulez me renvoyer le paquet de Plutarque de la Jeunesse, avec le Vol. des Oeuvres de Plutarque—Je Vous prierai de le faire remettre a Mr. le Consul francais Arcambal, qui ayant beaucoup de respect pour Vous et d'amitiè pour Moi, s'en chargera volontiers; Il est aussi le porteur obligeant de çelle ci.

P.S.

Je viens de recevoir votre Lettre du 30—par la quelle je Vois, que le Plutarque de la jeunesse Vous convient.

J'ai vendu—il y a quelques jours les derniers Exempl. du Manuel du Museum &c mais j'en attend, et je vous en enverrois par consequent l'exemplaire, que Vous desirez, aussitot, que j'en aurois recu.

Le Moulin en Question—au reste une idee extremement simple—n'est pas du tout un secret entre Vous et Moi—je ne suis pas elevè dans les principes et les sentimens d'un Negociant, ils me sont tout etranger mais je ne puis pas Vous en donner une Notion assez exacte par ecrit—je viendrois, aussitot, que j'en aurois le loisir Vous presenter personellement mes respects a Votre Residence, et j'apporterois alors le Modèle &c. Je serois venu avec Mr. Arcambal, si mes affaires me l'avoient permises.

EDITORS' TRANSLATION

MISTER PRESIDENT! Baltimore, 1 May 1805

Regarding the matter I wrote to you about through General Kosciuszko two and a half years ago, allow me to inform you that Colonel Armstrong did not respond to your invitation concerning the original patent which is in his hands. Allow me, too, to request that you write to him again, asking him to entrust the patent to your hands where I can be sure to retrieve it.

I regret having to cause you this trouble, but I have no other way of obtaining the original except by asking you. All the more so because you were willing to take on the patenting process from the beginning, and since the general took the liberty of deferring to you, it is you who sent the first letter to the colonel asking for the original patent to be returned to me.

Please accept my most profound and sincere regards. REIBELT.

P.S.

If you wish to return the package containing *Plutarque de la jeunesse* with the volume of Plutarch's works, please give it to the French consul, Mr. Arcambal, who will gladly take care of it, given his great respect for you and his friendship for me. He is also the gracious carrier of this letter.

P.S.

I just received your letter of the 30th in which I see that the *Plutarque de la jeunesse* meets your needs.

A few days ago I sold the last copies of the *Manuel du muséum*, etc., but I expect more and will send the one you ordered as soon as I receive it.

The mill in question, which is actually a very simple idea, is not at all a secret between us. I was not raised with the principles and sentiments of a businessman, which are totally alien to me, but I cannot convey a precise enough idea of the mill in writing. As soon as I have time, I will come to present my respects in person and bring the model, etc. I would have accompanied Mr. Arcambal if my business obligations had permitted.

RC (DLC); at foot of first page: "Vertatur" (Latin, "to be turned over"); endorsed by TJ as received 9 May and so recorded in SJL.

Reibelt was the agent for Louise Françoise Felix, the purchaser of property of Tadeusz KOSCIUSZKO on the Scioto River in Ohio (Vol. 39:93-6, 185-6, 202-3).

From John Joseph Rey

SIR George Town May 1st. 1805.

To presume that any man is inerrable, is admitting him equal to god. A well disposed man, may inadvertently err, but no sooner, he acknowledges it, than makes amendment, & ceases. The wicked, or hypocrite, never owns faults; but upon conviction of any; he fires resentment; devices bloody vengeance, & adds to his errors. The former, judging his own cause, with Justice, makes himself independant of the Law; while the latter provokes the execution of it.

Too much affluence with ones, & too much penury with others, inspires Jealousy, strife, & all sorts of licentiousness; & a Connivance thereat; rings the alarm bell, to arms. The cup of salvation is, bitter, salutary, & as precious to one, as to another; though, not equally esteemed. The safety of all, depends upon doing right; the unsafety of all, upon doing wrong; & the danger of all, in being divided.

If Serpentine malignity, allured the frail cupidity of our sinistrous genitors, to indulge their hearts, with the satiety of every illegal desire; & to erect for each, an idolatrous temple of worship; whose venemous follies, we are the heirs of: is it not our duty, as well as interest, to demolish, or convert the same into Lazarettos? yes, with all speed. May you never repent, nor be ashamed, to have lifted up, the first tool, to unroof the gins of so, accursed structures, & setting all hands at work; no doubt but your noble example will be attended with great success, throughout the land; by well disposed citizens, who are animated with similar republican principles; & willing to sacrifice self interest, to public welfare. Notwithstanding the heavy showers of rain; the sky is bright. It is vain, to question the prudence of your past administration; when your continuance, is the answer. Persevere, in repressing evil, without dismay; for, this task, was left for you; which requires more firmness, than labor. Your virtuous conduct, will conquer more nations, than all the treasures, fleets, & armies, on earth. Your name, shall be endeared, & engraven, in the hearts of a grateful posterity; & your services, shall be rewarded, with a crown of bless, in the glorious mansions of everlasting Joy: a felicity, flowing from the sincere heart of him, who has the honor, to be most respectfully,

Sir Your best well wisher J. J. Rey

P.S. the favor of admittance to the national library at the capitol, is, my humble request.

RC (DLC); at foot of text: "Mr. Jefferson"; endorsed by TJ as received 1 May and so recorded in SJL.

CUP OF SALVATION: Psalms 116:13.

To Benjamin Smith Barton

Dear Sir Washington May 2. 05.

Mr. Dunbar, during his excursion up the Washita, the last fall and winter, collected some dried specimens of plants which he has sent me in order to have them ascertained. I know I cannot dispose of them better than by transmitting them to you, with a request of the result of your investigation. he went as far as the hot springs on that river, 500. miles up it. he found their temperature 150°. of Farenheit. his journal & Dr. Hunter's furnish us with the geography of the river, accurately taken, and with a good deal of matter relative to it's natural history. I shall put them into the hands of some one to reduce into a small compas the results divested of details too long for the common reader. I shall be happy to recieve in time to incorporate into this, your information as to the plants now sent. Accept my friendly salutations & assurances of great esteem & respect.

Th: Jefferson

RC (PHi); at foot of text: "Doctr. Barton"; endorsed by Barton as received 4 May. PoC (DLC).

SPECIMENS OF PLANTS: see William Dunbar to TJ, 9 Mch.

From Joachim F. Eckard

SIR Philadelphia 2d. May 1805.

This day I had the honour of your Excellencies condescending letter with an inclosure for Mr. Weinwich, Member of the Royal Society of Sciences at Copenhagen, who therein will be highly gratified to see that your Excellency has vouchafed to accept of the Roman Coins for The American Philosophical Society, the conveyance of which letter I am very proud to have entrusted to me.

I most humbly pray for the acceptance of my best wishes for Your Excellencys health and wellfare—

most obedient and most humbly JOACHM. FREDK. ECKARD

RC (DLC); at head of text: "To His Excellency Thomas Jefferson Esquire &c. &c. &c. &c."; endorsed by TJ as received 4 May and so recorded in SJL.

CONDESCENDING LETTER: TJ to Eckard, 30 Apr.

To James Oldham

SIR Washington May 2. 05.

Mr. Gantt now lives at Bladensburg, being appointed a judge of Maryland. I wrote to enquire of him some days ago as to the situation of your affair with Jackson's estate. I presume he may be absent on some circuit, & that I shall have an answer when he returns. the ornaments for your Corinthian frize are now in hand. they are made in the same moulds with those in my Hall, far handsomer than those of the Parlour. I now inclose you the measures of my doors. be very exact, if you please, in numbering every door, as numbered in this paper, so that the number may be planed off but not rub off. mr Andrews will be very glad hereafter to execute any thing in the ornamental way which you may desire. Accept my salutations & best wishes.

TH: JEFFERSON

RC (Mary Parmenter, Orange Park, Florida, 1947); addressed: "Mr. James Oldham at mr Galligo's Richmond"; franked and postmarked. PoC (DLC); endorsed by TJ. Enclosure not found.

WROTE TO ENQUIRE: TJ to John Mackall Gantt, 20 Apr.

To Philippe Reibelt

SIR Washington May 2. 05.

I have 10. vols of the Quarto edition of the Oiseaux de Buffon, with planches enluminées: but they go only to plate 646. being 5. vols of text, & 5. vols of plates. could you undertake to import the residue of the work for me, ready bound: for otherwise binding here costs as much as the book. the books which made the subject of your last letter had been taken by the offices. I gave your letter to mr Smith Secretary of the Navy, who will see to paiment for himself & the others. he will be in Baltimore in two or three days, & should it escape his attention, you can apply to him. Accept my salutations.

TH: JEFFERSON

PoC (DLC); at foot of text: "Mr. Reibelt"; endorsed by TJ.

SUBJECT OF YOUR LAST LETTER: probably Reibelt to TJ, 29 Apr., recorded in SJL as received 30 Apr. but not found. Reibelt may have inquired about payment for five books that TJ had previously set aside for use by the executive departments (TJ to Reibelt, 23 Jan.).

To John Taggart

SIR Washington May 2. 05.

You were so kind some time ago as to purchase some oil & paints for me at the request of mr Barnes. presuming thence that it is not out of your line to do these things on commission, I take the liberty of requesting you to purchase for me 500. lbs of unground white lead, & to ship the same by the first opportunity to Richmond addressed to Messrs. Gibson & Jefferson of that place. the amount shall be remitted you by myself on reciept of the bill. Accept my salutations.

TH: JEFFERSON

PoC (MHi); at foot of text: "Mr. John Taggert"; endorsed by TJ.

John Taggart (d. 1815) had been a merchant in Philadelphia since at least 1783. His advertisements focused on the sale of wines and spirits along with "a general assortment of Wet Goods." In 1805, he began providing TJ with paint supplies for Monticello. At Taggart's request in 1812, TJ recommended his son, Francis B. Taggart, for a navy midshipman's berth (Philadelphia *Pennsylvania Packet and General Advertiser*, 18 Oct. 1783; *Relfs Philadelphia Gazette*, 26 Sep. 1804, 4 Feb., 13 Sep. 1815; ASP, *Naval Affairs*, 1:350; MB, 2:1155n; RS, 5:502).

THE REQUEST OF MR BARNES: see John Barnes to TJ, 26 Mch., and TJ to Barnes, 5 Apr.

To John Vaughan

Dear Sir Washington May 2. 05.

In your letter of Nov. 16. you express a desire to obtain for the Philosophical society an early edition of my Notes on Virginia. I found, when lately at Monticello, a single copy remaining of the original edition printed at Paris, the only one almost perfectly correct, & which never was sold, a few copies only having been printed & given to my friends. I have put this into a box addressed to mr Peale, and gone round by sea, by Capt Hand, for the use of the society.

Accept my thanks for yourself & brother for the copy of Woodward's very interesting relation. I inclose you the only interesting communication made to Congress on the subject of Louisiana now in my possession. there is an Appendix containing the laws of that province, which I do not at present find among my papers. but it would be uninteresting to the Society. I shall recollect them in future when we publish the reports of messrs. Dunbar & Hunter lately recieved, & any future ones. Accept my friendly salutations & assurances of great esteem & respect Th: Jefferson

RC (PPAmP); at foot of text: "J. Vaughan esq." PoC (DLC); endorsed by TJ. Enclosure: probably *An Account of Louisiana, Being an Abstract of Documents, in the Offices of the Department of State, and of the Treasury*, published versions of which appeared in 1803 (see Vol. 41:721n).

original edition: likely one of the 200 copies of *Notes on the State of Virginia* that TJ had printed by Philippe Denis Pierres in 1785 (Dorothy Medlin, "Thomas Jefferson, André Morellet, and the French Version of *Notes on the State of Virginia*," wmq, 3d ser., 35 [1978], 86; Douglas L. Wilson, "The Evolution of Jefferson's 'Notes on the State of Virginia,'" vmhb, 112 [2004], 103-4, 108).

woodward's very interesting relation: for David Woodard's narrative, see Vaughan to TJ, 16 Nov. 1804.

To James Leander Cathcart

May 3. 05.

Th: Jefferson presents his compliments to Mr. Cathcart and his thanks for the seeds he has been so kind as to send him, which he will endeavor to have so disposed of as to ensure the preservation of the species.

Tr (MHi: Paul L. Ford Papers); in an unidentified hand, with added typewritten note: "From a copy courteously furnished by Dr. J. S. H. Fogg, of Boston"; at foot of text: "Mr. Cathcart." Not recorded in SJL.

From Benjamin H. Latrobe

Dear Sir, Wilmington, May 3d. 1805

I herewith transmit to you my correct, & carefully collated copies of your original Sketches of the arrangement of the connecting buildings between the Presidents house and the public Offices. The originals having been drawn in very soft black lead pencils, have been so rubbed by carriage, as to be almost obliterated in some parts, and I have therefore by carefully examining every part of them made these copies, for the extreme correctness of which I think I can vouch. I feared that the originals would become entirely unintelligible had I again committed them to the post:—but I shall carefully preserve them, and bring them with me to Washington.

The designs for the whole buildings are now in the hands of my Clerk to be copied and will be sent on by Monday's post. I have the honor to be with true respect

Your faithful hble Servt B Henry Latrobe

RC (DLC); endorsed by TJ; recorded in SJL as received on 5 May. Enclosures not found.

From Audley Laurens Osborne

Sir Salisbury May 3d 1805

Be not astonished that a Young man totally Unknown to You both in name & Character, should presume to address the first Majistrate of the United States.

The peculiar circumstances under which I am placed induce a step so unprecedented. I have been regularly educated, in the best manner the University of this State could afford, of which I can produce the proper Certificates. Agreeable to the Wishes of My Father I studied law, and took the licence of a practitioner; although from an unaccountable aversion, determined never to practice the profession. I at this time hold the office of Clerk of the Pleas and Quarter Sessions for Rowan County. I am not satisfyed with an unactive life, and various reasons of a different nature, occur daily, which have determined me to leave the Society in which I am placed. I flatter myself I am capable of performing the duties annexed to several offices Subordinate to the different departments of government. I would willingly accept any imployment, which You in Your Goodness might think proper to confer on me; and which would from its immoluments support a Young man not extravagant in his ideas. By the wise measures of

Your Government an immense country is opened to the west for the reception of the enterprising. The extent of my ambition is to become serviceable to Your Administration by excercising some office in Louisiana. I have applyed to You personally, because I have no doubt but I will be attended to: I would have made known my desires in the common mode, through the influence of some of my acquaintances in Congress, but that my letters, altho politely answered have not been attended to. You will infinitely oblige one, who can justly appreciate any favour conferred on him, by obtaining for me some honourable imployment under government. You will confer an obligation by directing an answer to my letter as soon as convenient.

With the utmost respect I am Sir Your Humble. Sevt.

AUDLEY LAURENS OSBORNE

RC (DNA: RG 59, LAR); at head of text and at foot of text: "Thomas Jefferson Esqr President"; endorsed by TJ as received 10 May and "for office" and so recorded in SJL.

Audley Laurens Osborne (his first name was also rendered Adlai) was probably the son of Adlai Osborne, a prominent North Carolina attorney, political figure, and entrepreneur. The younger Osborne graduated from the University of North Carolina in 1802. In addition to his letter to TJ, Osborne wrote to Madison twice in 1805 in his unsuccessful quest for federal employment. By 1810, he was in Orleans Territory, where he came to the attention of William C. C. Claiborne, who sent Osborne into West Florida to "ascertain the sentiments" of its citizens toward American annexation of the territory. In 1811, Claiborne appointed him a judge of St. Helena Parish and the following year recommended him to Gallatin for a land office appointment, deeming Osborne to be a "very good lawyer" and possessing "great integrity of Character" (William S. Powell, ed., *Dictionary of North Carolina Biography*, 6 vols. [Chapel Hill, 1979-96], 4:399-400; John H. Wheeler, *Historical Sketches of North Carolina, from 1584 to 1851*, 2 vols. [Philadelphia, 1851], 1:119-20; Madison, *Papers, Sec. of State Ser.*, 9:317-18; 10:130-1; Dunbar Rowland, ed., *The Official Letter Books of W. C. C. Claiborne, 1801-1816*, 6 vols. [Jackson, Miss., 1917], 5:44-6, 51-3, 98; 6:131).

From Philippe Reibelt

MONSIEUR LE PRESIDENT! Balt. le 3 Mai 1805.

J'ai l'honneur, de repondre a votre Lettre de hier, que j'ecrirais incessament a la Maison a Paris pour l'Ouvrage de Buffon, tel, que Vous le desirez; je Vous prie seulement, de vouloir bien indiquer a çet effet par le premier Courier le Genre de reliure, dans lequel est mis le Commencement, que Vous avez, afin, que çela devienne egal.

Presumant, qu'il Vous fera plaisir, de parcourir les deux petits Livres cijoints—particulierement, celui relié—si toutefois Vous ne l'avez pas encore lû, j'ose Vous les presenter ad statum legendi.

Je Vous prie, d'accepter mes hommages. REIBELT

EDITORS' TRANSLATION

MISTER PRESIDENT! Baltimore, 3 May 1805

I have the honor of replying to yesterday's letter. I shall write to the Paris office immediately to order Buffon's work, as you request. I ask only that you let me know by the first messenger what kind of binding you have for the first part so the rest will match.

Assuming that you would enjoy looking over the two enclosed books, especially the bound volume, if by chance you have not already read it, I take the liberty of proposing them to you *ad statum legendi.*

Please accept my regards. REIBELT

RC (DLC); above signature: "Le Depot de Levrault, Schoell et Comp"; endorsed by TJ as received 4 May and so recorded in SJL. Enclosures (see List of Books Purchased from Philippe Reibelt, at 26 June): (1) Armand Gaston Camus, *Histoire et procédés du polytypage et du stéréotypage* (Paris, 1802); see Sowerby, No. 1136. (2) Jérémie Jacques Oberlin, *Essai d'annales de la vie de Jean Gutenberg* (Strasbourg, 1801).

AD STATUM LEGENDI: that is, for reading.

Petition of Philip M. Topham

TO THOMAS JEFFERSON PRESIDENT OF THE UNITED STATES OF AMERICA

The Petition of Philip M; Topham of Newport in the State of Rhode Island, Mariner, most respectfully represents—

That your Petitioner labours under a cruel misfortune, from which he can be no otherwise releived than by the constitutional interposition of the mercy of the executive of the United States.—

That it is now more than five years since, when in early youth, ignorant of the consequences, & seduced by the interested persuasions of others, he was induced to take charge of, & to navigate a vessel, engaged in a commerce to the coast of Africa, rendered unlawful by the Laws of the United-States.— That for this offence he was prosecuted at the instance of the abolition Society of the City of New-York, at which place he was arrested, & for eight months confined in close Jail, being unable to procure bail for the immense amount demanded.—

That when finally released from prison by the kindness of his Friends, he has been obliged for five years thro' ten terms of the courts, to wait upon this case & to contend against the combined power, wealth & influence of a numerous Society.—

That he inherited from his father Colonel John Topham, an officer who fought in the battles that secured the Liberty & independence of the United States, nothing but his patriotism & his name.—

That condemned by the necessity of attending the trials & by his obligation to his bail to remain on shore, he has been for five years without employment, in the only line, in which he was capable of earning money and is now, exhausted by the expences, he was obliged to encounter, entirely destitute.—That at length he has had a trial & at the last April term of the circuit court of the United States, for the district of New-York been cast in a Judgment that dooms him to pay Sixteen Thousand Dollars, which is in effect to condemn him to imprisonment for life.—Your Petitioner would likewise represent that the abolition Society of the City of New-York, contented with the vindication of public justice & the support of the Laws, manifested by the judgment aforesaid, and satisfied that this is the only similar transaction, in which your petioner has been engaged & that he sincerely regrets having been so engaged, that he must be doomed to unceasing & unmitigated misery, and an aged mother & a beloved wife & infant family solely dependant on your petitioner's labour, deprived of all means of sustenance & support if the judgment should be enforced against him, are generously inclined to release their half of the Penalties.—Now your Petitioner urgently prays the President of the United States that he would in his wisdom and discretion, extend to him the equity & mercy, which he is impowered by the Constitution & Laws of the United-States to exercise—And by pardoning your petioner & releasing the claim of the United-States against him, save him and his helpless family from ruin & restore him to society, & the power of obliterating by future usefulness the unfortunate indiscretion of his youth.—And he as in duty bound will ever pray.—

PHILIP M TOPHAM

Newport May 3rd. 1805

We whose names are undersigned Citizens of the State of Rhode Island and holding the stations affixed to our names, beg leave respectfully to recommend the prayer of the within Petitioner, to the tender consideration of the President of the United States, being assured by satisfactory information, that the facts therein stated are correct & that the Petitioner is an object worthy of the President's compassionate favor.— PAUL MUMFORD Lieut Governor

RC (RHi); in a clerk's hand, signed by Topham; supporting statement in a clerk's hand, signed by Mumford and 168 others, including three persons identified as state senators, eight as state representatives, and six as other state or local officers; endorsed by TJ as received 2 July and so recorded in SJL. Enclosed in Gabriel Duvall to TJ, 2 July.

In 1800, Philip Morse Topham (ca. 1777-1816), a native of Newport, Rhode Island, commanded a brig in an illegal slave-trading expedition. The New-York

Manumission Society presented a complaint to the United States Circuit Court for the District of New York, and on 4 Apr. 1805, a jury found Topham responsible for conducting a slaving voyage. The court levied a substantial fine to be split equally between the United States and the manumission society. Unable to pay the fine and thus condemned to debtors' prison, Topham, with the support of a number of prominent Rhode Islanders, frequently petitioned for his release. TJ, refusing to grant leniency until Topham had served "a due term of imprisonment," issued a pardon in 1808. Topham served as a sailing master in the navy during the War of 1812 (Craig A. Landy, "Society of United Irishmen Revolutionary and New-York Manumission Society Lawyer: Thomas Addis Emmet and the Irish Contributions to the Antislavery Movement in New York," *New York History*, 95 [2014], 202-9; Craig A. Landy, "Slaver Captain and Son of Newport: Philip Morse Topham and Jeffersonian Justice," *Rhode Island History*, 74 [2016], 72-92; *Register of the Navy and Marine Corps* [Washington, D.C., 1815], 41; Gabriel Duvall to TJ, 2 July 1805; TJ to Joseph Stanton, Jr., 15 Jan. 1806; Topham to TJ, 12 Jan., 17 Feb., 18 Aug. 1807; memorandum on pardon for Topham, 28 Feb. 1808, in DNA: RG 59, GPR).

During the Revolutionary War, JOHN TOPHAM served in the invasion of Canada and became the commander of a Rhode Island regiment (*Second Record Book of the Society of Sons of the Revolution in the State of Rhode Island* [Newport, 1902], 57-60).

List of Books to Be Imported by Philippe Reibelt

[before 4 May 1805]

books to be imported for me by M. Reibelt.
Parkins's plans of gardens. 04. Dec. 24.
Palladio. 05. Jan. 9.
Valin. Jan. 18.
Abregé de Linné par Gilibert.
Le petit magasin economique
Connaissce. des tems. 05. 06.
Bible Fr. 3. v. 8vo.
Droit naturel par Raynevel
Milton's paradise lost
Lucrece de la Grange
Seneque de la Grange
Gibbon's Decline of the Rom. emp.
Buffon Oiseaux. vol. 11. & pl. 647 & subsequent

MS (DLC: TJ Papers, 155:27108); entirely in TJ's hand; undated, but see below.

This list consisted of works TJ requested from Reibelt that the bookseller did not have in stock. In his letter of 3 May, Reibelt reported that he would be ordering from Europe the last work on the list, later volumes of *Histoire naturelle des oiseaux* by the Comte de BUFFON. See also Reibelt to TJ, 28 Dec. 1804, 10, 21, and 25 Jan., 2, 17, and 19 Feb. 1805.

To Thomas Appleton

SIR Washington May 4. 1805

Your favors of Dec. 24. and Feb. 1. are recieved, and the Vino del carmine, some time since arrived at New York, is daily expected here. I have recieved from mr Joseph Barnes 2. boxes containing 77. bottles of different wines of Tuscany & 3. bottles of oil, all intended as samples, and all arrived in perfect order, as well that in flasks as that in strong bottles: but the strong bottle is to be preferred. his Montepulciano was most superlatively good. as I make it a point to recieve no presents while in office, I must ask you to make this apology to mr Barnes, & to pay him the price of the wine. should he be unwilling or unable to tell you the amount, the cost, at the prices you have furnished, would be about 40. D. but for safety say 50. D. should this reach you before you have sent off the whole balance of my former bill in wine, that much may be deducted from it: but otherwise I will repay the sum to mr Emery on first notice of it's amount. indeed I wish this may reach you before you send off the wines for another reason: that is that you may detain them till October. if you send them off in the spring they will be exposed through the whole summer to the heats of the vessel, & of the different warehouses in our ports, & will probably be spoiled. it is essential as a general rule that delicate wines leave Europe for America towards the end of autumn.—we have never heard of mr Vigano. nor has the packet of seeds by the brig Aidar been recieved. the seed of the Winter melon will be particularly acceptable. I take the liberty of inclosing a letter for mr Mazzei. Accept my salutations & best wishes. TH: JEFFERSON

PoC (DLC); at foot of text: "Mr. Appleton"; endorsed by TJ; forwarded to David Gelston on this day (see TJ to Gelston, 5 May). Enclosure: TJ to Philip Mazzei, 4 May.

For the Italian wines recently ARRIVED AT NEW YORK, see Gelston to TJ, 28 Feb. and 4 Apr.

From William C. C. Claiborne

DEAR SIR, New Orleans May 4th. 1805

I have received your favours of the 10th. and 14th. of March, and am indeed happy to find that the ungenerous calumnies to which I have been subjected, have *not made on your mind* impressions unfavorable towards me.—I am aware that *abuse*, *much abuse* is the constant attendant on Office, under our Government; I have endeavoured to meet *it* with composure—But when I perceived a political conduct represented as vicious, which I knew to have been guided by the purest motives of honest Patriotism; and acts which in truth were benevolent and praiseworthy, represented as dishonorable, and all this done by a faction who had recourse even to subornation and perjury in order to sully my reputation, I must confess that my feelings received a wound which could alone be healed by conscious rectitude, and a belief that the confidence of the Executive in me, was not diminished. The subject of the Road through Florida has already received my attention, and I persuade myself there will be no difficulty on that point.

You may be assured, that I will not be inattentive to the Interest of General La Fayette—It is probable, that one thousand Acres may be obtained on the Canal of Carondelet; but whatever vacant Land there may be in that Quarter shall be surveyed:—Mr. Briggs is expected here in a week or two, but should his arrival be delayed I shall write him on the subject, and be governed by his instructions.—With respect to the advantages &c of the other Lands which I recommend'd, I will, very soon write you fully.

Accept D Sir the best wishes of your faithful friend

William C. C. Claiborne

RC (DNA: RG 59, TP, Orleans); at head of text: "(Duplicate)"; at foot of text: "Thos. Jefferson President of the United States"; endorsed by TJ as received 25 June and so recorded in SJL; endorsed by Jacob Wagner. FC (Lb in DNA: RG 59, TP, Orleans).

To Jones & Howell

Messrs. Jones & Howell. Washington May 4. 05.

My absence from this place during the last month & part of the preceding occasioned the remittance of 144. D 47 to be overlooked which ought to have been made to you. I now inclose you a draught of the bank of the US. here on that of Philada for that sum. Be so good as to forward for me to Gibson & Jefferson in Richmond the articles below stated, by the first vessel. Accept my friendly salutations.

Th: Jefferson

1. bundle of the best & largest German steel.
5. ℔ of sheet brass of the thickness of a playing card.
1. mill spindle $1\frac{3}{4}$ I. thick on the edge & 5. f. 7. I. long.
a bottle of the best lacker for lackering brass.

P.S. if you could get the favor of mr Stewart (who formerly chose some particular articles for me) to do the same by the above, it is probable it would better content his father who is to have the working them up.

PoC (MHi); endorsed by TJ. Notation in SJL: "144.47."

The REMITTANCE may have been for nailrod that TJ ordered in December, but which could not be shipped from Philadelphia until the Delaware River thawed after mid-February (TJ to Jones & Howell, 12 Feb.; Jones & Howell to TJ, 16 Feb.; Notes on Personal Finance, at 15 Mch.).

MR STEWART: Alexander Stewart, son of Monticello smith William Stewart; see TJ to Jones & Howell, 28 Nov. 1804.

To Philip Mazzei

DEAR SIR Washington May 4. 05.

In my letter of Mar. 10. I informed you that I wrote that day for the certificate of Bellini's death. I now inclose it. I also mentioned that on the journey I was then taking to Monticello I should get information from your attorney mr Carr & probably be able to recieve & make you the remittance for Colle. I inclose you his letter by which you will see we shall be delayed till the fall. I got my fruits all planted at Monticello, except the single plant of the Peach Apricot which was stolen by the way. however if the stones succeed I may expect a plenty from them. the advance of the season will soon determine this point. I now write to mr Appleton to delay sending my wines till October, because if they are sent off in the Spring they will encounter all the summer heats in the hold of the ship, and the warehouses of our Seaports, and wines as delicate as the Montepulciano will not stand that. in winter they will come in perfect safety; & what has come in good condition has been generally preferred to Burgundy or Bordeaux, because it combines equal flavor with less strength. I remember you brought here some white Verdea, & Muscadell, white also, which I then admired. very likely I might not think as much of them now as then, when every thing except Madeira was a novelty. but my curiosity would be gratified with a single bottle of each, were it only to ascertain the dislocation of my palate in that period. Accept affectionate salutations & assurances of constant esteem & respect. TH: JEFFERSON

RC (ViU); at foot of text: "P. Mazzei"; endorsed by Mazzei. Enclosures: (1) Death certificate of Carlo Bellini, not found (see John Page to TJ, 20 Mch.). (2) John Bracken to Mazzei, not found (see Mazzei to TJ, 12 Sep. 1805). (3) Dabney Carr to TJ, 20 Apr., not found (see Appendix IV and Mazzei to TJ, 12 Sep.). Enclosed in TJ to Thomas Appleton, 4 May.

REMITTANCE FOR COLLE: TJ sued Kemp Catlett on Mazzei's behalf to obtain payment for the purchase of Mazzei's estate near Monticello. On 11 Aug., TJ received payment of $125.94 from Catlett by Carr for the balance due to Mazzei (MB, 2:1161; Vol. 29:83n).

MUSCADELL: muscatel.

Notes on Personal Finance

May 4. in bank. Salary		2083.33	2083.33
Disct.		1979	1979.
		3979	4062.33
bank. note of Mar.		2000	2000.
			2062.33
2. Lemaire[1]	600		
2. Daugherty	65.465		
Latrobe	178.25		
3 Short	500.		
Jones & Howell	144.47		
Rapine & Conrad	11.		
Day. cyder	100.685		
cash	340.		
Burwell taxes	32.		
Polkinson	17.77		
La Bille	16.		
	2005.64		

MS (CSmH); entirely in TJ's hand; on verso of Notes on Personal Finance, at 15 Mch.

For TJ's discounted bank NOTE, see Notes on Personal Finance, at 15 Mch.

Payment to Étienne LEMAIRE, 2 May, was applied toward his President's House accounts for a balance due of $457.30. Payment the same day to Joseph Dougherty (DAUGHERTY) was for forage, utensils, smithing, and contingencies (MB, 2:1151-2).

LATROBE: see TJ to Thomas Munroe, 24 Apr.

On 3 May TJ drew checks on the Bank of the United States to RAPINE, Conrad & Co. for books and to Thomas Claxton for payment to S. D. DAY for cider (MB, 2:1152).

The carriage TAXES settled through William A. Burwell, as well as the amounts owed to Polkinhorn & Hall and to Lewis Labille (LA BILLE) for upholstery at the President's House, were paid on 7 May (MB, 2:1057, 1153; Carriage License, 7 May).

[1] Entry interlined.

Notes on Personal Finance

	estimate May 4. 05			
	draughts			
✓	bk US. Short	500.		
✓	Jones & Howell	144.47		644.47
	Checks			
✓	Lemaire	600		
✓	Daugherty	65.465		
✓	Latrobe	178.25		
✓	Rap. & Conr.	11.		
✓	Claxton for cyder	100.685		
✓	Treasury	40.		
		995.40		995.40
	cash.			
✓	Hope	263.33		
	Price	4.		
✓	Frithey	10.		
	pocket	22.67		300
				1939.87
	postponed			
	Carpenter	100		
	Polkinson & Hall	17.77		
	Lilly—	175.		
•	Hazard	231.09		
•	Cheetham	25.805	Irwin 8	
•	March	88.50		
	taxes	24.		662.165
	J. Barnes			1023.505
	La Bille 16.			3625.54

MS (CSmH); entirely in TJ's hand; written on address sheet with "The President of the United States" in an unidentified hand; notes by TJ on his bank accounts, [February 1806], on verso.

RAP. & CONR.: Rapine, Conrad & Co.

Having obtained 100 bushels of coal from the TREASURY Department "for the use of the President's household" on 3 Apr., Dougherty paid $40 to the department a month later (MS in MHi; in John Woodside's hand and signed by him for payment received 3 May; endorsed by TJ: "Treasury. coal. pd May 4. 05").

PRICE: that is, William Pryce, paid on 3 May for the book he sent TJ in March (MB, 2:1152; Pryce to TJ, 9 Mch.).

On 2 May, barber Edward Frethy (FRITHEY) sent TJ a receipt for two months "Dressing" at $5 per month (MS in MHi; in Frethy's hand, signed by William Connor acknowledging payment; endorsed by TJ).

POSTPONED: among those who waited until TJ drew funds on 7 May and asked

John Barnes to pay them were editor Peter Irving (IRWIN) for subscription dues and Mrs. John March, the bookbinder (Statement of Account with Mrs. John March, printed at 7 Mch.; MB, 2:1153).

From Thomas Sandford

SIR Campbell C House Kentucky May 4. 1805

I am informed that there is a probability that Mr. Buckner Thruston will not accept a Judgeship offered him in the Orlean district. I therefore have presumed to recommend Mr. John Coburn one of the Judges of the General Court of this state (lately Associated with Mr. Thruston), as a proper person to fill that Office. He is a Gentleman of amiable manners, handsome legal acquirements, a staunch republican, able to translate the French into the English language with considerable facility, and is in every other manner qualified to make an excellent Judge.

I have the honor to be very respectfully your Ob: Servt

THOMAS SANDFORD

RC (DNA: RG 59, LAR); endorsed by TJ as received 25 May and "Coburn John to be judge of Orleans" and so recorded in SJL.

In a letter of 17 May to an unknown recipient, BUCKNER THRUSTON asked that TJ be informed that he was declining the judgeship because of his "infirm State of Health" (RC in DNA: RG 59, LAR; endorsed by TJ: "Thruston Buckner declines as judge of Orleans"). In response to a letter of 10 June from Madison, Thruston on 1 July confirmed the rumors that he was declining the judgeship because of "Ill Health & the Insalubrity of the Climate of Orleans" (RC in same, endorsed by TJ: "Thruston Buckner declines judge's office lre to mr Madison"; Madison, *Papers, Sec. of State Ser.*, 9:447).

In a letter of 5 Apr., JOHN COBURN asked Madison to bring to TJ's attention several recommendations he was enclosing (RC in DNA: RG 59, LAR; endorsed by TJ: "Coburn John to be a judge. lre to mr Madison"). Among these recommendations was a letter of 20 Mch. from Isaac Shelby to Madison. Shelby touted Coburn as a "gentleman possessing talents & qualifications," having been a judge in Kentucky almost since its statehood (RC in same; endorsed by TJ: "Coburn John to be a judge Western. Shelby to mr Madison"). In a letter of 3 May to Madison, John Graham stated that Coburn could read French "with great facility," and although not conversant in the language at present, had been fluent previously and could be again with a "few months practice." Graham also recommended Robert Grayson as a land commissioner in Orleans Territory (RC in same, endorsed by TJ: "Coburn John as judge of Orleans. Grayson Robt. to be Comr. Louisa. Graham to mr Madison"; Madison, *Papers, Sec. of State Ser.*, 9:312-13).

To William Short

Dear Sir Washington May 4. 05.

Yours of Apr. 24. came to hand some days since, and I now return you the calculation of interest & paiments therein inclosed. the principles of this are understood & approved, and altho my occupations have not permitted me to investigate the calculations in detail, yet I have no doubt of their correctness. I have therefore inclosed you an acknolegement of the balance due Feb. 12. with a statement of the March paiment of 500. D. and that of the like sum now inclosed in a draught of the US. bank here on that at Philada, reducing the balance on the 8th. inst. to 7910. D 84 c I have made this statement chiefly to correct an error of 2. D 93 c in your letter of Apr. 24. to your own prejudice. hereafter every paiment will be easily settled in the same way, and these shall be made with as rare intermissions as my calls will permit.

I am in hopes you will settle the uncertainty of your summer movements by a decision in favor of the mountains; and that we shall come in for our share of you at Monticello during the months of Aug. & Sep. which I shall pass there, & the more agreeably if you will be one of the family. have you heard anything more of the Cahusac wine? my last letters from Consul Lee at Bordeaux were of Dec. 18. when I presume it had not been recieved there. with respect to your books, I am certain mr B. could always have the money of mr Madison on demand. those sold to mr Eppes I will pay mr B. for whenever their amount is known. I have advised him to enquire of mr Eppes the *edition* of the Palladio, because on that depends it's value. I have priced catalogues which will ascertain the worth according to the edition. Accept my affectionate salutations & assurances of constant friendship. Th: Jefferson

RC (DLC: Short Papers); at foot of text: "W. Short"; endorsed by Short. Notation in SJL: "500." Enclosures not found.

CAHUSAC: see Short to TJ, 14 Feb.

MR B.: John Barnes (Short to TJ, 24 Apr.).

From John Vaughan

Dear Sir, Philad: 4. May 1805.

I have just recieved your obliging letter of 2nd. The Society will be gratified by possessing one of the early Copies of your notes, which was not to be procured here,—& will hope in process of time to see added to a future edition the great mass of materials that you have been so indefatigably collecting—

I am much obliged by the Louisiana Document & shall be well pleased with recieving the future ones—The Society aims at collecting all that may be published worthy notice—We hope M Dunbar may have reserved some of his *Philosophic materials* for us—as our vol will go very shortly to the press we are anxious to make the work interesting & popular—

At the meeting of last Evening your letter announcing the Donation of Coins was recieved, & one of the Vice Presidents was directed to address a letter of thanks for this very valuable mark of Your attention to the Interests of the Society—Our Cabinet is beginning to assume a very Respectable appearance, we have above 800 Specimens of Minerals which Dr Seybert is now arranging & Classing—they are chiefly from abroad—To make it more interesting to Foreigners, we shall aim at augmenting it by the Treasures of our Own Country—You may occasionally have it in your power to assist us very materially.—

An Astronomical paper from Mr Ferrer was read last Evening viz Calculation of the Occultation of Jupiter by the Moon observd at the I Leon obsy Cadiz & at N Orleans 5 Jany 1799—Also observd. in the eclipses of Jupiters Satelites—to fix Longe. N. Orleans Vera Cruz, Havanah—Also—Occultation of the first Satelite of Jupiter by the Moon observd 15 Jany 1799. at I Leon and N. Orleans—applied to find Longe: N. Orleans. 3° less (or East) than by the other Calculation.—

I have shipped a box recd from Bartram on board the Schooner Ann Capt. Beck—I have enclosed one Bill of Lading to you & one to Mess Gibson & Jefferson Richmond, with direction to send it to Monticello.

I remain with respect Dear Sir Your ob. Servt & friend

JN VAUGHAN

RC (DLC); at head of text: "Thomas Jefferson President of US"; endorsed by TJ as received 6 May and so recorded in SJL. Enclosure not found.

YOUR LETTER ANNOUNCING THE DONATION OF COINS: TJ to Caspar Wistar, 30 Apr.

LETTER OF THANKS: Wistar to TJ, 20 May.

The American Philosophical Society charged one of its secretaries, Adam Seybert, with arranging MINERALS and compiling a catalog of them (APS, *Proceedings*, 22, pt. 3 [1884-85], 370-1).

ASTRONOMICAL PAPER FROM MR FERRER: the observations of José Joaquín Ferrer y Cafranga were read on 3 May at the society's meeting, referred to Robert Patterson, Francis Nichols, and Andrew Ellicott, and reported for publication on 21 June (same, 374, 375; APS, *Transactions*, 6 [1809], 221-32).

BOX RECD FROM BARTRAM: see TJ to William Bartram, 7 Apr.

To Stephen Cathalan, Jr.

DEAR SIR Washington May 5. 05.

Your letter of Dec. 8. has been duly recieved, with the bill it covered in favor of Capt Hazard for 231 D. 09 c altho he has not presented to me that of which he is the holder, yet I shall immediately place it's amount in the bank of New York subject to his order; that place being the most convenient for his residence in Connecticut. We have been very unfortunate in this last shipment by the New Orleans. she was so much damaged in the gulph of Lyons, that she was obliged to put into Mahon, where after going thro long repairs, she resumed her voyage and approaching our coast was taken by a British armed ship & carried into Halifax; under what pretexts I know not: but the cargo will be too tempting to be cleared. I will therefore pray you without delay to send me another hundred bottles of the Hermitage vierge de Jourdan, with some boxes of the fine dry figs of Marseilles & Brignolles. it may still be here in time for the meeting of Congress. for the amount of these you will be so good as to draw on me in like manner at 30. days sight. present my best respects to all the good members of your family, whom I always recollect with pleasure, and accept yourself my friendly salutations and assurances of respect & consideration.

TH: JEFFERSON

RC (Archives municipales, Marseilles, France); at foot of text: "Mr. Cathalan." PoC (MHi); endorsed by TJ. Enclosed in TJ to David Gelston, 5 May.

IMMEDIATELY: on 7 May TJ asked John Barnes to pay $231.09 to Daniel Ludlow "for Wm. Hazard holder of Cathalan's bill" (MB, 2:1153).

For TJ's inquiries regarding the SHIPMENT BY THE NEW ORLEANS, see TJ to Hughes & Allen, 21 Apr., and J. P. G. Muhlenberg to TJ, 23 Apr.

TJ had requested that Cathalan send him 100 bottles of the HERMITAGE VIERGE DE JOURDAN in July (TJ to Cathalan, 11 July 1804).

From James Leander Cathcart

May 5th. 1805

James L. Cathcart presents his respects to Mr. Jefferson & begs leave to inform him that John Woodhouse is the name of the shiper of wine at Marsalla, & Thomas Dyson that of our Agent at Syracuse, with the Agent at Palermo Mr. C is unacquainted—As Mr. Jefferson I presume only wants a small quantity for his own use of the very best quality he respectfully recommends him to write to Mr. William Higgins our Navy Agent at Malta who purchases large quantitys annually of the above mentioned wine for the use of the Officers of the

British Navy & army & is perfectly acquainted with the business & consequently most likely to succeed to Mr. Jeffersons satisfaction—

RC (DLC); endorsed by TJ as received 5 May and so recorded in SJL.

THOMAS DYSON: that is, George Dyson.

To George Dyson

SIR Washington May 5. 1805.

Having occasion to desire a pipe of the wine of Marsalla from mr John Woodhouse merchant of that place, mr Smith the Secretary of the Navy has authorised me to desire mr Woodhouse to draw on you for paiment, and your draught on the Navy department shall be placed to the credit of your account with the United States. mr Woodhouse will accordingly draw on you which I hope will be honored, and shall be reimbursed in the way proposed. Accept my salutations & respects TH: JEFFERSON

PoC (DLC); at foot of text: "Mr. Thomas Dyson Navy agent of the US. at Syracuse"; endorsed by TJ. Recorded in SJL as a letter to Thomas Dyson with notation "shd be George."

George Dyson, an English merchant, was appointed U.S. navy agent at Syracuse by Edward Preble in January 1804. William Eaton described Dyson as "a plain, frank, up and down, hospitable Yorkshireman." In 1807, with the withdrawal of American naval forces from the Mediterranean, Dyson resigned his agency and sailed for the United States to present his accounts (NDBW, 3:339, 351; 5:55; 6:430, 546-8, 552, 570).

From Oliver Evans

SIR Phila May 5th 1805

By yours of 28th ult I find I have not wrote so explicitly as to be clearly understood Mr Clymer did not mean to impose any conditions on which his communications should be made he only means to keep his project a profound Secret untill it may be put in operation if adopted because a knowledge of the mode or means of attack would give an enemy an opportunity of preparing for defense ever Since the receit of your Answer Mr Clymer has been out of the City and I do not know where to direct a letter to him as soon as he returns which I expect will be in a few days you may expect to hear from him—

Your most Obdt Huml Servt OLIVER EVANS

RC (DLC); at foot of text: "Thos Jefferson"; endorsed by TJ as received 8 May and so recorded in SJL.

To David Gelston

DEAR SIR Washington May 5. 1805.

I troubled you yesterday with a letter for mr Appleton to be sent by the John Adams, but if she be gone, to be returned to me. I take the liberty now of asking the same favor as to those inclosed addressed to Messrs. Cathalan, Higgins & Woodhouse and salute you with friendly respects.

TH: JEFFERSON

PoC (MHi); at foot of text: "David Gelston esq."; endorsed by TJ. Enclosures: (1) TJ to Stephen Cathalan, Jr., 5 May. (2) TJ to William Higgins, 5 May. (3) TJ to John Woodhouse, 5 May.

TROUBLED YOU YESTERDAY: probably a note (not found and not recorded in SJL) covering TJ's letter of that day to Thomas Appleton.

To William Higgins

SIR Washington May 5. 1805.

A wine of Marsalla in Sicily beginning to obtain credit here from it's resemblance to that of Madeira, I am desirous of trying it, and have been advised to address myself to you as most able to furnish me of the best. I therefore ask the favor of you to send me two pipes of your best, addressing them to the Collector of the customs of any port of the US. to which the vessel on which they are shipped happens to be coming. mr Smith, Secretary of the Navy authorises me to say that your draught for the amount on the Navy department shall be passed to your credit in account, which I presume will be the most commodious negociation for you as well as myself. Accept my salutations & respects.

TH: JEFFERSON

PoC (DLC); at foot of text: "Mr. William Higgins, Navy Agent of the US. at Malta"; endorsed by TJ; enclosed in TJ to David Gelston, 5 May. PoC of Tripl (same) with postscript: "June 28. 05. Original by the John Adams; Duplicate by the Huntress, which being intercepted by one of the belligerent Privateers, this Triplicate is forwarded"; endorsed by TJ.

William Higgins was a British merchant based in Malta. A polyglot with numerous connections across the region, Higgins was recommended by Edward Preble early in 1804 to serve as a naval agent for the American squadron in the Mediterranean. He was instrumental in providing aid to the officers and crew of the U.S. frigate *Philadelphia* after their capture in 1803, and, through his correspondence, conveyed widely read accounts of the American conflict with Tripoli. He continued to act as naval agent until 1807 (NDBW, 3:237, 339, 348, 351; 4:101, 123, 230, 255; 5:267; 6:95, 547; Philadelphia *Gazette of the United States*, 17 Aug. 1803; New York *American Citizen*, 24 Nov. 1804; *Newburyport Herald*, 4 Aug. 1807; Madison, *Papers, Sec. of State Ser.*, 6:605; 8:90, 102, 133).

HAVE BEEN ADVISED: see James Leander Cathcart to TJ, 5 May.

From Benjamin H. Latrobe

Dear Sir, Wilmington Del. May 5th. 1805.

I herewith transmit to You two sheets containing the drawings of the buildings proposed to connect the president's house with the public Offices on each side The heighth of Story indispensibly necessary in the fireproof of the Treasury (of which I by this post also transmit a plan to the Secy. Treasury) as well as the general appearance, & the connection of the Colonnade with the Offices at different heighths, have induced, or rather forced me to make the Column of the exact highth of the Basement story. This throws up the blocking course to the window selles of the Presidents house, & gets over all difficulties.

The only alteration of importance in the uses of the building that I respectfully submit to You, is: the shifting the stables from the South front of the range, into a Court,—forming a Center to the Wings. My reasons for proposing this removal are:

1., Because the Colonnade will probably become the constant means of communication between the Offices & the Presidents house, both in Rainy weather, and in the heat of Summer. The Stables and Coachhouses will be then a very unpleasant interruption to the walk; and indeed, as it is often necessary to tie up the horses in the open air for purposes of farriery, the South front of the Colonnade will be soiled,—and become the resort of all the disagreeable people who loiter about a Stable.

2. In the situation, which the Stables would occupy in the front of the range,—there could not possibly be a convenient Hayloft above them,—a circumstance which appears of great importance.—In the Center building this difficulty is removed.—

3. The Coachhouses present the same difficulty, as to the occasional interruption of the Walk,—and another which is still more against their proposed situation in the South front,—viz: the necessity of cleaning the carriage, and putting to, the horses in front of the Columns: and if the carriage is to be brought to the North door of the Pr. House, I do not see how it can be very handsomely driven round, without going round one or other of the public Offices.—

4. A very careful Coachman can easily draw out a Carriage through an opening of not more the 8. f 6 i;—but in the course of a very short time, haste & carelessness will undoubtedly occasion great injury both to the Carriages and to the Columns.—The intercolumniation in the Center building may be made somewhat wider than the others,

and indeed the design as presented to you is not exactly what I wish in this respect.—

Should you approve this alteration on the West side the necessity of a similar court will perhaps present itself on the East. When the ground around the president's house is dressed, a great variety of convenience will be wasted which cannot be had in the front range of buildings, and which would destroy its great utility as a passage of covered communication between the public buildings.—

I have made some alteration in the form of that part of the design which terminates the Colonnade. The pier which now meets the Walls of the 3 Building prevents the collision of the members of the Columns with the incongruous parts of the Walls, and is specially of use to disguise the difference at each end. I hope this will meet your approbation

That no time may be lost I have written to Mr Lenthall to cause immediately the necessary quantity of rough building stone to be procured & laid down on the spot, for the foundations. The South frontwall which is under the portico had, I think, best be built of Brick & plaistered. The North Wall of the coarse but durable Acquia Stone of which we quarried a large quantity last Spring in the public quarry, & which may thus be brought into use.—

I have now to solicit, that as soon as you have taken the design into consideration & determined upon it, you will please to return them with your remarks & directions in order to the being immediately put into execution.

I am with the truest respect Your faithful hble Servt.

B Henry Latrobe

RC (DLC); endorsed by TJ as received 7 May and so recorded in SJL. Enclosures not found.

PLAN TO THE SECY. TREASURY: "Design of a Fireproof Repository of Papers for the Treasury of the United States," consisting of a ground plan and sections of the structure by Latrobe, dated 27 Apr. 1805 (DLC: Prints and Photographs Division); see Latrobe, *Correspondence*, 2:63, 66.

To John Lenthall

Sunday evening [5 May 1805]

Th: Jefferson presents his compliments to mr Lenthall and sends him a letter this moment recieved inclosed from mr Latrobe. being handed him among his own he broke it open without looking at the superscription; but seeing mr Lenthall's name at the head of it, he closed it instantly & assures him on his honor he did not read one other word in it.

RC (DLC); partially dated; addressed: "Mr. Lenthall." Enclosure: Benjamin H. Latrobe to John Lenthall, 3 May (RC in DLC: District of Columbia Papers).

AMONG HIS OWN: Latrobe to TJ, 3 May, with enclosures.

ON HIS HONOR: Latrobe's six-page letter to Lenthall ended with a comment on TJ: "I am sorry that I am cramped in this design by his prejudices in favor of the architecture of the old french books, out of which he fishes every thing,—but it is a small sacrifice to my personal attachment to him to humor him, and the less so, because the style of the Colonnade he proposes is exactly consistent with Hoban's Pile,—a litter of pigs worthy of the great Sow it surrounds, & of the Irish *boar*, the father of her." After Lenthall advised Latrobe of what had occurred, Latrobe wrote to him on 11 May: "The President, might have very safely read the whole of my last letter to you, even to the litter of pigs. He is certainly one of the best hearted Men that ever came out of the hands of Nature and has one of the best heads also. But he thinks works & acts differently from others, & who ever does that must submit to abuse, let the new road he travels be ever so much shorter, clearer, & pleasanter. As a Man, I never knew his superior in candor, kindness, and universal information;—as a political character he has not his equal any where in patriotism, right intentions, & uniform perseverance in the System he has conceived to be the most beneficial for his country.—Nothing in fact exists, in his whole character, on which to fasten ridicule and censure but his *manner*, and a few oddities of appearance and of conduct which are perfectly innocent & probably very right" (RC in DLC: District of Columbia Papers).

To Charles Willson Peale

DEAR SIR Washington May 5. 05.

By capt Hand who sailed 4. days ago, I sent the desk polygraph you left here, and the box of minerals. freight paid here. in the former box is a book for mr Vaughan. with the minerals was a list of those furnished by mr King. but there were some sent me by Capt. Lewis which you will find described in the inclosed list from him. the more I reflect on the improvement of your son by projecting the pen bar of the Polygraph to the left, the more I percieve it's value in reducing the breadth of the rhomboids so that they will shut up in a box of exactly double the size of the paper you mean to write on: and I hope to hear soon that you find from experience that this important reduction of size may be made; for after all, experience must decide. a favorable opportunity occurred yesterday of convincing mr Smith, Secy. of the Navy of the utility of your Polygraph. he determined immediately to write to you for one for his private use while at Baltimore. Accept my friendly salutations & best wishes.

TH: JEFFERSON

RC (TxU); at foot of text: "C. W. Peale esq." PoC (DLC); endorsed by TJ. Enclosure: probably a Tr, not found, of the list of minerals in William Clark and Meriwether Lewis to TJ, 18 May 1804 (see below).

BOOK: *Notes on the State of Virginia*; see TJ to John Vaughan, 2 May.

Peale recorded the receipt of the MINERALS for his museum on 10 May. TJ had received from William C. C. Claiborne the specimens collected by Richard KING on the Ouachita River. William Clark and Meriwether LEWIS forwarded ore samples and a rock crystal collected by Peter Chouteau and others, including members of the Osage tribe (Peale Museum Accessions Book, in Peale Family Papers, PHi; Clark and Lewis to TJ, 18 May 1804; Claiborne to TJ, 1 Nov. 1804).

IMPROVEMENT OF YOUR SON: see Peale to TJ, 23 Apr.

To Philippe Reibelt

SIR Washington May 5. 05.

I recieved last night yours of the 3d. the volumes of the Oiseaux de Buffon which I possess are bound in that kind of binding which has been most common in France for many years, spotted, the leaves red on the edge, and double lettered on red. the two pieces you sent me on printing & the polytypage are so curious, & on so interesting an art, that I propose to keep them with your leave. I knew Hoffman well, went often to see his works, & was intimate with the Abbé Rochon having myself tried several of his processes; so that the facts in that portion of the history are well known to me. I presume you recieved my letter of Apr. 29. Accept my salutations.

TH: JEFFERSON

PoC (DLC); at foot of text: "Mr. Reibelt"; endorsed by TJ.

While in Paris, TJ subscribed to a journal that François HOFFMAN produced on the virtues of his polytype printing technique, which allowed the user to write or draw directly onto a metal plate, thus creating a more accurate representation of his or her handwriting. Hoffman also experimented with stereotype plates, and his efforts were reported by his close collaborator the Abbé Rochon (MB, 1:610; Vol. 10:318-24).

MY LETTER OF APR. 29: that is, TJ to Reibelt, 30 Apr.

To John Vaughan

DEAR SIR Washington May 5. 05.

Your favor of Apr. 29. came to hand the day after mine of May 2. was written. some parts of it therefore were anticipated. I inclose for examination a most excellent account of the Washita river written by the Chevalier D'Annemours, formerly Consul of France in Virginia & Maryland, & who has resided on the Washita now many years. he is a man of science, good sense, & truth, and may be relied on in whatever facts he states. I do not know however that it is within the plan of our society to publish topographical accounts of this nature. they will do in this as they please. if it is not of the proper character for their volume, be so good as to have the MS. returned to me, as I preserve it for public use. not being from a public officer it has not been & will not be communicated to Congress, nor otherwise to the public.

By yesterday's post I returned the Certificates signed. I will thank you for your care of the box from mr Bartram, and to have it forwarded to Gibson & Jefferson at Richmond. I salute you with friendship & respect. TH: JEFFERSON

RC (PPAmP); at foot of text: "John Vaughan esq."; endorsed by Vaughan for the APS. PoC (DLC); endorsed by TJ. Enclosure: Charles François d'Anmours, "Mémoire sur le district du Ouachita dans la province de la Louisianne" (see Pierre Derbigny to TJ, 7 Feb.).

To John Woodhouse

SIR Washington May 5. 1805.

Being informed by mr Cathcart[1] that you are settled at Marsalla for the purpose of carrying on a trade in the wines of that place which so much resemble those of Madeira, I take the liberty of asking you to send me a pipe of the first quality. be so good as to address it to the Collector of the customs of any port of the United states to which the vessel on which it is shipped may happen to be bound, who will pay charges & forward it to me. by an arrangement with mr Smith the Secretary of the Navy mr Dyson our navy agent at Syracuse will on reciept of the inclosed letter pay you the amount of your bill.[2] Accept my salutations & respects TH: JEFFERSON

PoC (DLC); at foot of text: "Mr. John Woodhouse merchant at Marsalla"; endorsed by TJ; enclosed in TJ to David Gelston, 5 May. PoC of Dupl (same); at head of text: "Duplicate. the first having gone by the John Adams"; with postscript: "P.S. it is very much the practice to brandy wines for the American market. this is by no means my taste, & I would not have a drop of brandy put into the wine unless experience has proved it will not keep without it"; endorsed by TJ with notation "Duplicte. by Huntress." PoC of Tripl (same); with variation (see note 2 below); with postscript: "June 28. 1805. Original by the John Adams. Duplicate by the Huntress, which being intercepted by one of the belligerent privateers, this Triplicate is forwarded"; endorsed by TJ with notation "Triplicate of June 28. 05." PoC of Quad (MoSHi: Jefferson Papers); with variation (see note 2 below); with same postscript as Tripl and additional postscript: "May 4. 1806. Hearing nothing in consequence of the preceding, I send this 4.plicate by the frigate Chesapeak which carries home the Tunisian Ambassador. I am the more anxious for an answer because if the wine answers expectation, I should become an annual correspondent. observing that you are in relations with Genl. Ebenezer Stevens of N. York, it would be as agreeable to me, if more so to you to pay to him your draught on me at 30. days sight. but this entirely at your option"; endorsed by TJ as a letter of 5 May 1806 and so recorded in SJL.

John Woodhouse (d. 1826) of Liverpool first traveled to Sicily in 1770 with the intent of exporting Italian soda ash to England. He changed his objective after noting that one of the regional wines resembled Madeira, an increasingly expensive but popular import to the British Isles. Woodhouse began exporting the wine in significant quantities from Marsala to England by 1773. To ensure it could resist the effects of the voyage, he fortified each pipe with 10 gallons of spirit. The resulting "Marsala" wine proved to be highly successful. In 1800, Woodhouse earned a contract with the British government to supply his wine to the Mediterranean fleet, which spread its reputation. The business thrived and Woodhouse quickly amassed a fortune (William Stigand, *Report on the Wine Produce of Sicily* [London, 1889], 10, 20-1; Leo A. Loubère, *The Red and the White* [Albany, 1978], 71-2).

[1] Preceding three words omitted in Dupl, Tripl, and Quad.

[2] Here in Tripl and in Quad, TJ added: "it is much the practice to brandy wine for the American market. this is by no means my taste, & I would not have a drop of brandy put into that sent to me."

To Samuel R. Demaree

SIR Washington May 6. 1805.

Your letter of Dec. 28. was handed to the Philosophical society, who referred the subject to a Committee, and recieved a report from them. they have inclosed me that report with a request that in communicating it to you I would at the same time convey their thanks for the attempt to promote a laudable object. a great and sudden change in the Alphabet of any language is probably not to be effected. much has been done in the English orthography from the Anglo-Saxon days to the present; tho' we must acknolege something has also been lost, as they possessed two characters which we have abandoned altho they represented sounds peculiar to our language, and now represented by characters of far different powers. still a favorable tho' slow progression in our orthography may be observed. thus, we are leaving out the *u* in favor, honor &c the *ugh* in tho,[1] thro[2] &c. the *w* and *d* in acknolege, altho' the Dictionary makers have not yet ventured to admit it. still we are not to expect that perfection will ever be obtained in this or any other way; but probably the only way in which it can ever be approached will be to encourage gradual changes in practice. Accept my salutations & respects. TH: JEFFERSON

PoC (DLC); at foot of text: "Mr. Samuel R. Demaree." Enclosure: committee report by Peter S. Du Ponceau, Anthony Fothergill, and Benjamin Smith Barton to the American Philosophical Society, 1 Feb. 1805, on Demaree's proposed alterations to the English alphabet; stating "that usage is the only lawful Sovereign of language, & that it cannot be controuled by any authority, how ever powerful or Arbitrary," the committee is of the opinion "that the evil, if it be one, is not to be remedied by the efforts of this or any other similar Society" (MS in PPAmP).

INCLOSED ME THAT REPORT WITH A REQUEST: a letter from the American Philosophical Society to TJ, 15 Feb., with notation "Demaree's communicn. alphabet" has not been found (Vol. 45: Appendix IV); see John Vaughan to TJ, 29 Apr.

[1] TJ first wrote "though" before canceling "ugh."

[2] TJ first wrote "through" before canceling "ugh."

From Albert Gallatin

DEAR SIR May 6, 1805

I enclose Mr Crowninshield's & Collector Lincoln's letters respecting a keeper of lighthouse. If you approve of George Day's appointment, please to signify it. I also enclose De Witt Clinton's letter & one from Sanford stating that Swartwout has made a partial payment—also letters from Mr Few & Lieut. Govr. Broome recommending Tallmage as a judge. From Sanford no answer has yet been received on that subject but may be daily expected. To B. Livingston I still feel averse.

With great respect & attachment Your obedt. Servt.

ALBERT GALLATIN

RC (DLC); at foot of text: "The President of the United States"; endorsed by TJ as received from the Treasury Department on 6 May and "Day. Swartwout. Talmadge. B. Livingston" and so recorded in SJL. Enclosures: (1) Jacob Crowninshield to Gallatin, Salem, 29 Apr., enclosing a copy of James Day's resignation as keeper of the lighthouse at Annisquam, Massachusetts, which also recommended his son, George Day, to be his successor; Crowninshield would not have troubled Gallatin with this "small affair," but another candidate, "a Mr. White," has been put forward, and Crowninshield suggests there are "*strong reasons*" why he should not be appointed; an earlier recommendation of George Day by Gloucester residents had been lodged with Benjamin Lincoln, who apparently did not act on the matter "from an idea that the old Gentleman had not resigned"; Crowninshield has sent the original of James Day's resignation to Lincoln in the hope that it will provide satisfactory proof of Day's intent and secure the son's appointment (RC in NHi: Gallatin Papers). (2) Statement of resignation by James Day, Gloucester, 22 Apr.; due to age and infirmity, Day is no longer able to perform his duties as keeper of the Annisquam lighthouse; he recommends his son, George Day, as a "fit & suitable" successor; in a note at the foot of the page, Crowninshield adds that the son resides on the spot, while the father is a mile away, seldom visits the light, and is "dangerously ill with a dropsy"; Crowninshield adds that James Day's earlier recommendation has been in Lincoln's office for months, and that George Day "has been the real keeper of the light for many years, & it has been faithfully kept" (MS, facsimile in Profiles in History, Beverly Hills, California, 2014; order added by TJ: "The appointment of George Day is approved. Th: Jefferson May 6. 05."). (3) Probably Lincoln to Gallatin, Boston, 30 Apr., enclosing James Day's resignation, which was handed to him by Crowninshield; the two candidates for successor are Henry White, a captain in the American Revolution, and George Day, "who has been employed under his Father as the keeper generally" (FC in DNA: RG 56, Correspondence of the Secretary of the Treasury with Collectors of Customs, Boston). (4) Probably John Broome to Gallatin, New York, 1 May; writing at the behest of "some of our Republican friends," Broome recommends state senator Matthias B. Tallmadge, a son-in-law of George Clinton, to be U.S. district judge for New York; Broome describes Tallmadge as "correct in his Politicks" and possessing "handsome talents, & a truly independent Spirit" (RC in NHi: Gallatin Papers). Other enclosures not found.

In April 1800, Congress authorized a LIGHTHOUSE at Wigwam Point in Gloucester, Massachusetts, at the entrance of Annisquam Harbor (U.S. Statutes at Large, 2:57-8). Gallatin wrote to Lincoln on 7 May, acknowledging the receipt of his letter of "the 3d ulto" and informing him that the president had appointed George Day to succeed his father as keeper (Gallatin, *Papers*, 11:26).

Gallatin wrote to DeWitt Clinton on 26 Apr. regarding John SWARTWOUT, the U.S. marshal for New York. "Information lately received" had rendered Swartwout's removal "probable," and Gallatin asked Clinton for his opinion regarding a replacement. Since the president might, "depending on Mr Swartwout's conduct, continue him some time longer in office," Gallatin instructed Clinton not to disclose the contents of his letter (same, 48:36-7).

To Robert Kinnan

SIR Washington May 6. 1805.

I return you the papers recieved from Colo. Bentley which do not ascertain the quantity of lands claimed by mr Harrison. and unwilling to insist on a condition which tho' secured by express compact with mr Ronald, may be thought hard with his family, I acquiesce in the relinquishment of the balance still due from them as an equivalent for the rightful claims of mr Harrison.

Resuming & correcting therefore the statement of Sep. 4. which I formerly sent you, at it's 6th. page, it will stand thus.

	£ s d
Principal of costs paid	148– 4–2
1800 Feb. 6. Int. on do to this date	21–17–7
	170– 1–9
balance overpd on No. 7.	59– 2–6
	110–19–3
May. 7. Int. to this date	1– 7–9
	112– 7–0
Cr. paid by Taylor	3–12–0
Balance due	108–15–0
Int. on do. till paid	

Desirous therefore of winding up this long & weighty business I will pay you the balance here stated and interest within 60. days after you shall inform me that you will thereon give me a quietus. I need not repeat here the considerations which give me a just expectation of this; as they were sufficiently explained in the communication of Sep. 4. Accept my salutations & assurances of respect & esteem.

TH: JEFFERSON

PoC (MHi); at foot of text: "Mr. Robert Kinnan"; endorsed by TJ. Enclosure not found.

Robert Kinnan had succeeded to Richard Hanson's position as agent for Farell & Jones, the English firm to which TJ was indebted as part of his share of the Wayles estate. From January 1804 to March 1807, Kinnan, who was based in Petersburg, sent TJ nine letters, none of which has been found. TJ's surviving responses suggest that Kinnan was dissatisfied with TJ's efforts to close out the debt, but ultimately he did return to the president the final bond (RS, 2:141-2; Vol. 42:625; TJ to James Lyle, 16 Nov. 1804; TJ to Kinnan, 19 Nov. 1806; George Jefferson to TJ, 24 Mch. 1807).

William BENTLEY was the administrator of the estate of William Ronald, to whom TJ had sold his land in Cumberland County in 1790. Under the terms of the sale, TJ was issued two bonds worth £538 sterling each, the first to be paid by the beginning of 1796 and the second by the beginning of 1797. As collateral for the first bond, Ronald mortgaged a 600-acre plot of land across the James River in Goochland County, and for the second bond Ronald mortgaged the land that TJ was conveying to him. Although TJ arranged to have Richard Hanson collect payment on the bonds and apply them toward his debt to Farell & Jones, Ronald's death in 1793 and the failure of Bentley to pay off the bonds embroiled TJ and Hanson in difficulties. Given the reference to Carter Henry HARRISON, who claimed a portion of the Cumberland property, Kinnan and TJ were evidently discussing payments on the second bond. TJ had believed that completing payment on the bond would close out his debt in September 1804, but apparently Ronald's heirs or Bentley himself used the Harrison claim as rationale for not making a payment to Kinnan, thereby leaving TJ responsible for the remainder of the debt (MB, 1:767-8; 2:1051; Vol. 17:569-71; Vol. 20:326; Vol. 24:576; TJ to James Lyle, 16 Nov. 1804).

The first bond became subject to a chancery decree against Bentley in 1797, and it is possible that the second bond was similarly part of a decree, although none has been found. In a set of notes recording payments made to Hanson from the Ronald estate, TJ added some of his own calculations and referred to a "2d decree" equal in value to the first. In that set of calculations, TJ indicated that a sum of £80–19–3 remained "still due" as of 5 Apr. 1799. Most of the document, which is based on a statement of 1801, relates to payments on the first bond and is identical to a copy that TJ enclosed in a letter of 26 Jan. 1810 to James Pleasants at Bentley's request (Tr in MHi, in a clerk's hand, certified by Thomas Rector on 11 May 1801 as a statement "taken from Mr. Hansons," with TJ's calculations of payments on the first bond on verso and other calculations on separate sheet; RS, 2:184-6; Vol. 29:476-8).

FORMERLY SENT YOU: probably TJ to Kinnan, 17 Sep. 1804, recorded in SJL but not found.

CR. PAID BY TAYLOR: possibly a reference to Thomas Augustus Taylor, who purchased TJ's Elk Hill property, the sale of which also became part of TJ's payment plan (Vol. 24:21-2).

From Lafayette

My dear friend Auteuil 16h Floral May the 6th 1805

Mr Rapatel aid de Camp to General Moreau is Going to America where He Wishes His Services May Be Accepted. He is an officer Distinguished By His Interest His Character and Several Actions of Eclat. His Numerous Brothers are, as Well as Himself faithfully Attached to the Patriotic Cause. The Honor He Had to Serve in Gl Moreau's family ought to Have Recommended Him at Any time and With Every Body in france—The Reverse Has been the Case, and While He Has Refused Advantageous offers in foreign Armies which He feared Might one day or other Be at War With His Native Country, He Eagerly Wishes to Be Employed in the Service of the United States. I Generally Discourage Such Notions, Knowing How few places You Have to Give and How Many Americans Are Entitled to them. But the Situation of Mr Rapatel, His Military and private Character are So particularly Interesting that I Have With pleasure thought You Might, in the Organisation of Louïsiana, Avail Yourself of His talents as a Soldier and His Qualities as a Citizen. I am With The Most Affectionate Respect Your old Constant friend

Lafayette

RC (DLC); endorsed by TJ. Recorded in SJL as received 10 Feb. 1806 with notation "by M. Rapatel." Enclosed in Jean Baptiste Rapatel to TJ, 6 Feb. 1806.

To Martha Jefferson Randolph

My dearest Martha Washington May 6. 1805.

Your letter of Apr. 19. & mr Randolph's of Apr. 27. have given me the agreeable information of mr Randolph's success, & the more agreeable & important information that you are getting well. for the restoration of your stomach my chief dependance is on your own resolution to observe rigorously whatever regimen you find from experience to agree with you: and it will take a long course of this rigorous regimen to place you beyond the danger of relapse. to guard against cold will be more difficult. I negotiate with your friends here who enquire whether you will come the next winter, & find them readily acquiesce in the necessity of agreeing that you shall never be out of an evening. I am in hopes therefore you will come & bring the whole family. arrangements made upstairs since you were here, and additional furniture now providing will accomodate them all, and the necessity of lessening the fatigues of the table, which have borne too heavily on me, will oblige me to dine company less frequently, & to live more in a family way. a good deal of sickness is shewing itself here exactly among those individuals who were sick the last year. the same is said to be the case in the part of the country afflicted the last year. this will probably induce us to break up here a little earlier than usual: I suppose about the middle of July. as this is within little more than 2 months, I am now preparing to send off our groceries for Monticello, that they may get up the river before it falls. present me affectionately to mr Randolph & in kisses to all the dear children. to yourself tenderness without bounds TH: JEFFERSON

RC (NNPM); at foot of text: "Mrs. Randolph." PoC (MHi); endorsed by TJ.

From Philippe Reibelt

MONSIEUR LE PRESIDENT! Baltimore le 6 Mai 1805.

Votre Lettre de hier m'a ete remise aujourdhui.

1) J'ecrirais incessament pour ce, qui Vous manque des Oiseux de Buffon in 4to. &. reliè tel, que Vous le designez, a la Maison a Paris.

2) Vos desirs sont des Ordres pour Moi—les 2 Ouvrages en question sont donc pleinement a Votre disposition, quoique je les avois destines pour ma propre bibliotheque.

3) Vous me demandez, si je recus Votre Lettre du 29 Avril! je dois Vous repondre negativement—parceque je n'ai—depuis Votre retour a la Ville federale—recu de votre main respectable, qu'une Lettre du 30 Avril, et une autre du 2 Mai.

4) Mr. le Secretaire de la Marine m'a envoyè l'argent pour les Livres, que Vous aviez pris pour les differens Departement de l'etat—

5) Mais je n'ai pas encore recu le Volume des Oeuvres de Plutarque en Question.

Je Vous prie d'agreer mes hommages les plus profonds et Sinceres.

REIBELT

P.S.

J'ose Vous repeter ma demande pour la Patente originale de la terre du Gen. Koscïuszko, qui se trouve encore dans les Mains du Colonel Armstrong.

Ayant pû disposer un des Messieurs d'içi, qui avoit achetè le Manuel du Mus. fr. de me retroçeder son Exemplaire—et venant de le recevoir—Il partira avec cette Lettre çi à Votre Adresse.

E D I T O R S' T R A N S L A T I O N

MISTER PRESIDENT! Baltimore, 6 May 1805

Your letter of yesterday was delivered today.

1) I shall immediately ask the Paris office for the volumes of Buffon's *Oiseaux* that you do not have, in quarto and with the binding you specified.

2) Your wish is my command. The two works in question are thus fully at your disposal, although I had intended them for my own library.

3) You ask whether I received your letter of 29 Apr. I must reply no. Since your return to the federal city, I have received but one letter in your illustrious hand, dated 30 Apr., and a second dated 2 May.

4) The secretary of the navy paid me for the books you ordered for the various government bureaus.

5) I have not yet received the volume of Plutarch's works in question.

Please accept my deepest and most sincere regards. REIBELT

P.S.

I dare renew my request for General Kosciuszko's original land grant, which is still in Colonel Armstrong's hands.

I was able to convince one of the gentlemen here who had bought the *Manuel du muséum français* to cede his copy. Having just received it, I am sending it along with this letter to your address.

RC (MHi); above signature: "Le Depot de Levr. Sch. et Comp. a Paris"; note by TJ at foot of first page: "May. 9. 1805. inclosed him the original patent and plat" (see TJ to Reibelt, 10 May); endorsed by TJ as received 8 May and so recorded in SJL.

From James Bowdoin

SIR, Boston May 7th 1805.

I have the honour to acknowledge the receipt of your Letter of the 27th. Ultimo: & I regret extremely that such has been the State of my health, as not to allow of my proceeding to Washington, to receive the pleasure of being more intimately known to you Sir, & to the Gentlemen assisting you in the heavy burdens of government; as well as to derive those advantages so justly suggested in your Letter. But Sir, I have been obliged to yield to the necesity of the Case; and that that necesity has existed to the full extent represented in my Letters, my Physician & friends can particularly testify, & is generally well known in this city & neighbourhood.

Being upon the point of embarking for Spain; which I expect will be either this day or tomorrow, it becomes me to assure you Sir; that I shall not fail to represent to his Catholic Majesty the honourable motives, which govern your political conduct: and the particular disposition you have to preserve Peace & a good understanding with his Majesty: that you calculate upon a like friendly disposition on the part of his majestys Government:—that all causes of disagreement may be speedily done away & the most perfect confidence restored.—You may rest assured also, that I shall pay a strict & critical attention attention to the instructions, which I have, or may receive from the Department of State, & that I shall endeavour faithfully & zealously to fullfill the duties of my mission.— Permit me to notice to you Sir, that the peice of Sculpture, which you have done me the honour to accept, will be shipped to you by the first good opportunity for Washington or Alexandria. Thos. L. Winthrop Esq. my agent & near Relation will have the honour of shipping it to you. Mr. Winthrop is well known to Genl. Dearborn, & will shipp it, on receiving a few lines from Genl. Dearborn, to any particular port or person, if you shd. see fit otherwise to order it.—I have the honour to subscribe myself most respectfully, & with the highest consideration and esteem.

Sir, Your faithful & most obedt Servant JAMES BOWDOIN

RC (DLC); at head of text: "To the President of the United States"; endorsed by TJ as received 12 May and so recorded in SJL.

Bowdoin and his family sailed FOR SPAIN on 11 May (*National Intelligencer*, 20 May).

SCULPTURE: see Bowdoin to TJ, 25 Mch.

From Thomas Branagan

SIR Philada. May 7: 1805

It is with great diffidence as it respects myself, and with distinguished deference to you, that I take the liberty to send you a copy of my "preliminary Essay on Slavery"; being well convinced that the subject matter of it, will attract your attention, and perhaps; prove a stimulus to your encouraging the "Tragical Poem" which the inclosed Essay is merely intended as an introduction to.

However be that as it may, it is with enthusiastic veneration; disinterested admiration; and sincere respect for your exalted character, that I present you the Essay and will forward the Poem when Published, Whether you patronize us by your respectable signature or not—Of all the publications which may be productive of public utility, there is none more deserving of general attention; none more intrinsically momentous to the citizens of america! than the subject matter of my *Tragical Poem*.

To every nation, savage, or civilized, it must be deemed important, but to the *Body Politic* whose Very existance exclusively depends upon the purity of their political principles, it must be doubly important.

In short the lassitude of the citizens of both modern, as well as antient republics in not guarding with indefatigable assiduity, the palladiums of their respective governments, was the Radical Cause of their premature Anhilation.

Though a poor man in a pecuniary point of view, I do not by any means solicit the least assistance in that respect. If you will be so kind as to give your signature, in order to facilitate the publication; it will be considered as a special favour & will be received with unfeigned gratitude. I simply particularize my sentiments in this letter without using that formality & fulsome adulation necessary in addressing an imperial despot. May heaven bless & prosper you and as you have been may you ever continue to be a pattern to a World of despots and the means of not only keeping the glowing taper of republicanism from being extinguished but fanning it to a flame which will illuminate the benighted minds of the enslaved the wreched the degraded Sons of europe Asia and Africa. While I feel an implacable disgust & sovereign contempt for the villians who rob their fellow Creatures of all that is sacred to them I feel an ardent affection for such Characters as Who by actions as well as words prove friends to the liberties of the people and the greatest favour I can wish you is that you May have an equal share in the affections of every individual in america & the World as you have in mine & that the Supreme being may crown you with never fading laurels in paradise where I hope to have the enifible pleasure of congratulating you after we drop the burden of Mortality thus prays with Sentiments of respect & veneration

Your most Ob: hu: Sev: THOS BRANAGAN

PS if you will be so kind as to favour me with your signature you will please to forward it here—as soon as convenent direct for me No 163 South Water St. Philada.

If you should feel disinclined to give your signature your order for a few copies will be thankfull recived & punctually attended to.

RC (DLC); addressed: "The Hon Thomas Jefferson President of the United States of America"; endorsed by TJ as received 10 May and so recorded in SJL with notation "163. S. Water street." Enclosure: Thomas Branagan, *A Preliminary Essay, on the Oppression of the Exiled Sons of Africa* (Philadelphia, 1804; Sowerby, No. 1394).

Thomas Branagan (1774-1843) was born in Dublin, Ireland. From an early age he worked as a sailor on trading voyages between Britain and northern Europe. In 1790 he was part of the crew of a vessel bringing enslaved people from the Gulf of Guinea to Grenada. Branagan remained in the Caribbean for the next several years as a mariner. He worked for four years as an overseer on several plantations in Antigua before returning to Dublin to settle his deceased father's estate. Coming into conflict with his family, at least in part because of his conversion to Methodism, Branagan again left Ireland for Pennsylvania around 1798. He worked as an accountant, a schoolteacher, and a watchman. From 1804 to 1839 he wrote numerous religious and antislavery works of prose and poetry. In formulating his opposition to slavery, Branagan drew on British and American writers as well as on his own experiences and religious notions. While he argued for the fundamental humanity of Black people, he also increasingly voiced discomfort over the presence of free Black populations and advocated for their removal. Though TJ offered him only oblique encouragement, Branagan continued to send him notice and copies of his works (Thomas Branagan, *The Penitential Tyrant* [Philadelphia, 1805; Sowerby, No. 4516], [vii]-xxxvi; James Robinson, *Philadelphia Directory for 1810* [Philadelphia, 1810], 42; Robert Desilver, *Desilver's Philadelphia Directory and Stranger's Guide, for 1829* [Philadelphia, 1829], 20; Nicholas Guyatt, *Bind Us Apart: How Enlightened Americans Invented Racial Segregation* [New York, 2016], 81-4, 164; Sowerby, Nos. 1394, 1395, 4515, 4516; RS, 8:450; 12:7, 474; TJ to George Logan, 11 May; Branagan to TJ, 17 Nov. 1805, 27 Apr. 1806, 11 Feb. 1809).

Carriage License

I. RECEIPT FOR CARRIAGE LICENSE PAYMENTS, 7 MAY 1805

II. LICENSE FOR USE OF CARRIAGES, 7 MAY 1805

EDITORIAL NOTE

On 25 May 1803, the Washington city council approved an act, to begin "1 July next," that required annual licenses for the private use of carriages. Cost of the license was determined by carriage type, ranging from $15 yearly for a coach, "whether driven with a box or by postillion," to an annual fee of $2 for four-wheeled carriages "resting upon wooden spars." The statute did not pertain to those carriages employed primarily for husbandry or for carrying goods. Commercial carriages, such as those used by hackney drivers and peddlers, were licensed separately. On 7 May 1805 Jefferson paid license fees on four carriages (*Acts of the Corporation of the City of Washington, Passed by the First Council* [Washington, D.C., 1803], 45-8).

I. Receipt for Carriage License Payments

May the 7th. 1805. Recd. of Thomas Jefferson Esqr. President of the United States twelve dollars for Licence to use a Charriot in Washington City from the 1st. of July 1804 to the 1st. of July 1805

WASHINGTON BOYD
Treasurer of W. City

May the 7th. 1805 Recd. of Thomas Jefferson Esqr. President of the United States eighteen dollars for licence to use two Phaetons in Washington City from the 1st. of July 1804 to the 1st. of July. 1805.

WASHINGTON BOYD
Treasur. of W. City

May the 7th. 1805. Recd. of Thomas Jefferson Esqr. President of the United States two dollars for licence to use one Gig in Washington City from the 1st. day of July. 1804. to the 1st. of July. 1805.

WASHINGTON BOYD
Treasur. of W. City

MS (CSmH).

Washington Boyd (d. 1821) was the treasurer of the city of Washington from 1802 through 1807. In 1808, TJ appointed Boyd the marshal of the District of Columbia, a position he held until 1818. Boyd also served as an officer in the local militia and as a founding trustee of the Washington public school system (W. B. Bryan, *Various Forms of Local Government in the District of Columbia* [Washington, D.C., 1898], 18-19; F. Regis Noel and Margaret Brent Downing, *The Court-House of the District of Columbia* [Washington, D.C., 1919], 57; Baltimore *Federal Gazette*, 20 July 1802; Samuel Yorke At Lee, *History of the Public Schools of Washington City, D.C. from August, 1805, to August, 1875, Written at Request and Published by Order of the Board of Trustees of Public Schools, for the National Centennial Year, 1876* [Washington, D.C., 1876], 3; *Daily National Intelligencer*, 7 Mch. 1821).

In his financial records of this date, TJ noted giving William A. Burwell an order on the Bank of the United States for $32 for "taxes on 4. carriages" (MB, 2:1153).

II. License for Use of Carriages

City of Washington, to wit.

LICENSE is hereby granted to *Thomas Jefferson Esqr. to use one Chariot, two Phaetons and one Gig* in the City of Washington, to remain in force for one year from the *first day of July 1804.*[1] he having paid the tax therefor.

In Testimony whereof I have hereunto set my hand and affixed the seal of the City of Washington, this *seventh* day of *May* A D. one thousand eight hundred and *five*

THOMAS HERTY
Register of the City of Washington.

MS (MoSHi: Jefferson Papers); printed form, with blanks filled by Herty reproduced in italics; endorsed by TJ: "Taxes Washington. 1805. May 9. pd by W. A. Burwell & repd by check on bk. US." and with his tally of the fees by type of carriage.

[1] Date interlined in place of printed "date hereof."

From James Oldham

SIR 7th. May 05. Richmond.

Your Letter of the Second May came to hand yesterday and in very good Time, as I have Just finishd drying plank for your works: perticular attention will be paid to the numbering of the Dores as you have desird.

The good understanding you have Pleasd to Introduce between Cpt. Andrews and my Self Sir, am exceding thankful for, and will use every exertion to Introduce his composition, that my Situation will admit of.

Adue and may Heaven Bless You Your Obt Humbl. Sevt.

JAMS. OLDHAM

P.S. have taken the Liberty to inclose a Letter to Cpt. Andrews respeting Some more composition

RC (MHi); at foot of text: "Thoms. Jefferson Esqr."; endorsed by TJ as received 11 May and so recorded in SJL. Enclosure not found.

From Samuel Coleman

SIR Richmond May 8h. 1805.

If any hope had been entertained that, on an application to the Council of State, their approbation of a transmission to you, of the certificates respecting Logwood's health, by our much respected and amiable Governor, could have been obtained, that channel, as most respectful to you, would have been preferred; but as such an approbation was dispaired of, I deemed it not more a duty than a right, which I, in common with any other citizen, enjoyed, to transmit them to you myself. It will excite some surprize perhaps that the approbation of such a measure, by the Council, could be doubted. The following case not only gave rise to such a *doubt* but reduced it nearly to a *certainty* that their approbation of such a proceedure would not be had.

The first person confined in the Penitentiary was an unfortunate man by the name of Merryman, for murder, perhaps of the first degree, but the jury decided it to be of the second. For near five years his application to labour was incessant, his conduct uncommonly exemplary, and he was a creditor with the institution to a considerable amount, the produce of his labour, beyond the expences of his maintenance, which the law subjected him to reimburse. In the course of the last year he was taken with a complaint in his head and eyes, believed to be the consequence of his constant application to the business of nail-cutting, and of his close confinement. His complaint increased attended with insanity at intervals, and threatened a speedy dissolution. The physician, the keeper, and all the Inspectors of the Penitentiary, except one, who declined it for want of a knowledge of his case, joined in a representation of his situation and in a recommendation of him to the Council, *without effect*, as a proper object of mercy. In a short time afterwards he died in confinement This case Sir is not recited with a view to excite an unfavorable sentiment of the Council. They have acted from the best motives, a firm persuasion, that the penal laws of our Country are sufficiently lenient, and that the interference of the Executive, except in very extraordinary cases, is unnecessary, and may be productive of much mischief. It is stated merely to shew the reason why the certificates, respecting Logwood were not forwarded to you by the Executive.

I have the honor to be with perfect respect, your most obed Servant

Samuel Coleman.

RC (DLC); at foot of text: "The President of the United States"; endorsed by TJ as received 11 May and so recorded in SJL. Enclosures: see TJ to George Hay, 24 Apr.

Samuel Coleman (d. 1811) served as a Virginia militia officer during the American Revolution and later settled in Richmond, where he became assistant clerk of the Council of State. In addition to those duties, Coleman became deputy adjutant general of the state militia and was active in the state chapter of the Society of the Cincinnati (biographical information in Vi; Richmond *Virginia Argus*, 27 July 1803, 20 Jan. 1807, 12 Mch. 1811; WMQ, 2d ser., 12 [1932], 224).

From Oliver Evans

Sir Phila. May 8th. 1805.

I have obtained liberty of Mr. Clymer to communicate his project—he conceives that an enemy may be effectually prevented from firing a gun either cannon or small arms and be thrown into the utmost confusion by such a shower of either cold or hot water as could be thrown on them by a strong fire engine or a strong steam boiler such as I use with the power of 100 or 150 or 200 bls to the inch at the distance of 40 or 60 Yards—Hot water however cannot be thrown to so great a distance as cold, because the heat leaves it as quick as lightning after it is exposed to the open atmosphere reducing it to the temperature of 212 degrees. the heat in leaving it would disperse the column and thereby prevent it from being thrown so far—Any further communication as to the execution of the project Mr. Clymer is willing to give if required—

Your most obdt Humb Servt Oliver Evans

RC (DLC); at foot of text: "Thos. Jefferson President of the U. States"; endorsed by TJ as received 12 May and so recorded in SJL.

A STRONG FIRE ENGINE: one newspaper noted that George E. Clymer's water pump was powerful enough to lift a 24-pound cannon ball from the bottom of a well (Philadelphia *Spirit of the Press*, 12 Oct.).

From David Gelston

SIR, New York May 8th. 1805

I have this day received your letters of the 4th and 5th instant, and have handed the enclosures to Capt. Shaw—

I have the honor to be, with great respect, Sir, your obedient servant

DAVID GELSTON

RC (MHi); at foot of text: "Thomas Jefferson President United States"; endorsed by TJ as received 11 May and so recorded in SJL.

John SHAW was captain of the frigate *John Adams* (NDBW, *Register*, 49).

From Samuel Miller

SIR, New-York, May 8th, 1805.

I do myself the honor to transmit herewith a copy of two "Discourses on Suicide," lately published, at the request of some of those to whom I minister. Be pleased to accept of it as an inconsiderable offering of respect.

I have the honor to be, Sir, most respectfully, your obedient Servant,

SAML: MILLER.

RC (DLC); at foot of text: "The President of the United States"; endorsed by TJ as received 12 May and so recorded in SJL. Enclosure: Samuel Miller, *The Guilt, Folly, and Sources of Suicide: Two Discourses, Preached in the City of New-York, February, 1805* (New York, 1805; Sowerby, No. 1677).

From Stephen Cathalan, Jr.

MY MOST RESPECTED
DEAR SIR— Marseilles the 9th. May 1805

I beg your Refference to the Inclosed Copies of my Letters of the 8th. & 22d. ulto.—& to the here annexed Circular of the 1st. Inst. in which I advise the aman. Merchts. that on the 1st. June next, I will alter my Firm, as merchant, as at foot of the Same;—but as to my Consulur firm, I will continue it as before Stephen Cathalan Junr.

as it Coincides with my Commission, & it would not be prudent to change it's form, on my Certificates, in this Time of war, being long since well known as it is;

Mr. Julius Oliver a Citizen of Philadelpha., whom I have before Mentioned to you, and appointed my chancelor, having Purchased a vessel here, will be ready in Six Weeks or Two Months to Sail in her for Baltimore & Philadelphia, with a Cargo for his acct.

he will be Specialy charged by me to present Personaly to you, Sir, his and our Best Respects & Congratulations; I hope you will be so kind as to grant him an audience;—in the 15 Months, he has spent with me, he has soon been *aufait* of the detailed transactions of this Consulate, & fills His Duties to the Satisfaction of the American Citizens and of my own; he is also able to give Informations on the trade that is now Carried between the united States & Marseilles, &c &c.—he will visit the most Important Cities of the united States, & be back again here in about one year in Marseilles; my Intention is if he continues to behave well, & after he will have acquired more experience, by this Journey, to give him an Interest in my Commerce;

he, as well as I, would esteem it as a Great favor if you would Confirm and Ratify the appointment of Chancelor for this united States's Coml. agency I granted to him on the 29th. May 1804, by a Commission from you; & to Recommend him to the Persons of Distinction and in offices in the Sundry Places of the united States;

your kind attentions towards him will be Considered by me, the Same as if Conferred to my Self, as he interest me so much, that I want to advance him as much as in my Power; regretting only the honor he will have of enjoying of your Presence, & admiring your Eminent virtues & caracter, which is impossible for me to do from such a Great Distance, personally, but in Stead of Lessening, increases on the Contrary my Sincere Sentiments of Gratitude and Great Respects for you.

having the honor to be for ever Sir Your most obedient & Devoted Servant STEPHEN CATHALAN JUNR.

my Mother & Daughter's Join me in their Respectfull compliments & best wishes; I will send you by Mr. oliver a fresh Supply of Provision; I have heard that my Invoice by the Ship new orleans, has met with very bad weather & been Detained Long time at majorca.

RC (DLC); at foot of first page: "his Excellency the most honble. Thos. Jefferson President." Recorded in SJL as received 22 Aug. Enclosures: (1) Dupl, not found, of Cathalan to TJ, 8 Apr. (2) Dupl, not found, of Cathalan to TJ, 22 Apr. Other enclosure printed below.

AUFAIT: by the way.

ENCLOSURE

Printed Circular

Marseilles, the 1st. May 1805.

I had the misfortune of loosing my Father 88 years of age! he was a zealous friend to the American cause, for in the year 1775, being Agent of the Secret Committee of Congress, he determined the court of France to aid the Americans in their glorious contest against Great Britain; it is owing to his services, that I had the honor of being appointed American Consul in Marseilles in 1790, and am happy to continue of enjoying the confidence of the United States Government in that capacity; being the only son of Stephen Cathalan, he transmitted me in the year 1795, his commerce, which I have continued with success, and to the satisfaction of the Friends who confided me their interests under the firm of Stephen Cathalan Junior.

My intention being of altering my above firm, on this 1st. June next, thus, Stephen Cathalan, I beg you to take notice of it at foot.

Being already known in the United States in my official and private capacity I take the liberty of offering you a tender of my best services, in this place.

Should my House as Merchant not be well known to you I can advance that for solidity, there are none more so, or better known, it being one of the oldest in this City; the landed property I have in this place, an extensive credit (which I very seldom make use of) my Consular bond and property in the American Funds, Shares in the United States' Bank, are securities to the Merchants who may trust me the management of their concerns this way.

The war between Spain and Great Britain having put a stop to that trade this way, the Americans will carry on the greatest part of it; it is they who principally supply us with East and West Indiæ, and United States produces, as long as war Continues.

I Cannot advise you to send cargoes of a single article which may be very advantageous now, but may change before letters arrive in America, but assorted Cargoes will in general answer very well here.

The Articles I would recommend, as long as war will continue, are dry, white Codfish of small size, but must be arrived here from November to the 15th. February, to meet with advantageous Sales.—Fish Oyl of a dark Colour and Clear; Coffee, Sugars, Cocao, Indigo, Hydes, Logwood, Pepper, Yellow Nankeens and Muslins fit for Callicoes or Chintz.

Tobacco from Virginia or other States of dark, Strong well Scented long leaf, West indies, Georgia and Louisiana Cottons of a long Staple. Staves of proper length and thickness for *Brandy Pipes* and *Red wine Casks*. Wheat and Flour, when your crops affords a Supplement over your usual exportations to West indies, Spain, etc.

The consumption of Marseilles is very great, Supplying the South of France, Piedmont, etc.

We enjoy here of an Entrepot, where the imports may be sold free of duty and for reexportaion, and we hope soon to recover our free port.

This Country must be known by you for its General Exports well adapted for United States, East and West Indies and cheaper than from any other parts, Such as Brandies, Red wines, Clarified as at Bordeaux, best Verdigrease. Marseilles Soap so much reputed; Superfine olive Oil, Olives, Capres,

Anchovies, Almonds, Raisins, Saffron, Drugs, Corks, Candles, Fruits in Brandy and Glazed; Cordials and Perfumeries of all Sorts; Kid and Silk Gloves, Stockings and all Kind of Silks, Ribbonds and Millineries, etc., etc.

Should you or your Friends send Vessels or Goods here, and confide me the consignment, I hope you will be satisfied with my attention for the benefit of your interest, and you may rely on my prompt dispatch.

I have the honor to be with respect, Your most obt. and hble. Servant,

STEPHEN CATHALAN JUNR.

And on the 1st. June next. STEPHEN CATHALAN

RC (DLC); printed form, signed twice by Cathalan; endorsed by TJ as received 22 Aug.

From Albert Gallatin

DEAR SIR 9th May 1805

I enclose Mr Sandford's answer respecting a district judge. Van Wyke is certainly very young, not above 25; he is Gen. Van Cortland's nephew and has the negative recommendation of being neither a Livingston nor a Clinton. The persons proposed are therefore—

Brokholst Livingston

George Clinton junr.

Tallmage—(Govr. Clinton's son in law & would both in New York & in the State be preferred to George)

Van Wyke

I must repeat that I will not consider the revenue as very safe under B. Livingston. His decision, as a State judge, in the case of the Sandy hook beacons was very inimical, & at the time ascribed by some to E. Livingston's removal.

If you continue of opinion that Swartwout shall be removed unless he pays, and you will be pleased to direct a commission in the name of Peter A. Schenk, the person recommended by DeWitt Clinton, to be sent to me, I will transmit it to Mr Sanford, with instructions to give it, unless Mr Swartwout shall make payment within a limited time—

I have received Latrobe's plan of fire proof building, but cannot understand it fully without referring to the general sketch which he has sent you. I will do myself the pleasure to wait on you to morrow for that purpose; but I had expected that he would come & stay here a few days. Of Tatham's fitness for any actual employment I cannot judge. He has certainly genius, but the appearance of something bordering on mental derangement. I may be mistaken & would like to know.

With great respect Your obedt. Servt. ALBERT GALLATIN

RC (DLC); at foot of text: "The President of the United States"; endorsed by TJ as received from the Treasury Department on 9 May and "Vanwyck. Swartwout. Schenk. offices. Tatham" and so recorded in SJL. Enclosure: Nathan Sanford to Gallatin, 4 May, acknowledging Gallatin's letter of 30 Apr. and recommending Pierre C. Van Wyck for the office of U.S. district judge, even though he is "young in life and young in the profession"; Van Wyck will accept if appointed (DNA: RG 59, LAR; endorsed by TJ: "Van Wyck Pierre C. to be judge N.Y.").

A recommendation of George CLINTON, Jr., from Samuel Osgood, dated 7 Feb., has not been found (see Vol. 45: Appendix IV).

For the CASE OF THE SANDY HOOK BEACONS, see Gallatin to TJ, 3 Feb. 1804. Edward Livingston's REMOVAL as U.S. attorney for New York took place during summer 1803 (Vol. 38:123n; Vol. 41:63).

Gallatin wrote to DeWitt Clinton on 13 May, acknowledging his letter of 1 May and informing him that a commission for Peter A. Schenck (SCHENK) would be made out and sent to U.S. attorney Nathan Sanford, "to be used only in case Mr Swartwout shall not pay the public monies in his hands; that being the contingency on which the President has decided that his continuance in office should depend" (Gallatin, *Papers*, 11:52).

LATROBE'S PLAN: see Benjamin H. Latrobe to TJ, 5 May.

TATHAM'S FITNESS: see Gallatin to TJ, 24 Apr. (second letter).

From George Jefferson

DEAR SIR Richmond 9th. May 1805

In compliance with your direction I have for some days past been endeavouring to make sale of your Tobacco, but as yet have not been able to effect one. Mr. Rutherfoord who made the offer of 40/. at 120 days has made up his quantity, or else he says he would have taken it. I yet hope to obtain this price on a shorter credit.

Not having met with a Vessel for Washington, I have sent your hams (9 dozen in 3 Rum Hhds) to Norfolk, to be forwarded from thence by the first opportunity.—I inclose you Mr. Macon's letter, which gives an account of his mode of preserving them.—

I shall leave Town in a day or two, and shall be absent for several weeks, during which time Mr. Gibson will as usual, with pleasure attend to any of your commands with which we may be favor'd.

I am Dear Sir Yr. Very humble servt. GEO. JEFFERSON

RC (MHi); at foot of text: "Thos. Jefferson esqr."; endorsed by TJ as received 12 May and so recorded in SJL. Enclosure: William Macon to George Jefferson, 9 Apr., discussing shipment of nine dozen "bacon hams" that have been "rubed over with hiccory ashes" and packed in hogsheads and 10 more hams packed separately; Macon thinks the bacon "very fine"; he has never prevented "an insect called a Skipper" that is "never troublesome to Indifferent bacon" but breeds "only in the best"; to manage the problem, Macon hangs the hams in a dry house and after June inspects them every other week; he destroys portions with "any appearance of the Skipper" and cures those hams first; "by this manner I never lose any" (RC in same).

From Jones & Howell

RESPECTED FRIEND Phila. 9th May 1805

Your favor of 4th Inst is at hand Covering Check in the Bank for 144 $\frac{47}{100}$ which is to Your Credit.

Mr Stewart has promised to look out the articles You wrote for, and we Shall forward them. we Shall also forward You 4 Open Stoves, by order of, B H Latrobe, Sometime Since, but could not then be obtained Shall now Send them, as we have no doubt Mr Latrobe acted agreeable to Your orders

with esteem we are Your Friends JONES & HOWELL

RC (MHi); at head of text: "Thomas Jefferson Esqr."; endorsed by TJ as received 11 May and so recorded in SJL.

For Benjamin H. Latrobe's recommendations regarding the purchase of STOVES for Monticello, see Latrobe to TJ, 5 Jan.

From Richard Parrott

SIR Pretty prospect 9th May 1805

I confered with Colo. Hanson who is of oppinion that Thos. G Addison Esquire is the most proper person, on the other side of the Branch to fill the Majistracy. and in the direction to Bladensburg; there is a Doctr Fenwick who Married a daughter to the late Notly Young.

I am glad I have occasion to address you; and shall avail myself of it, to express my hapiness on having my most Sanguine expectations so far exceeded upon the change of Administration. and I do most heartily rejoice that the Wise, successful, and Virtuous acts, of the Administration, have so highly rewarded those who laboured and Suffred to effect that change.

with my fervant prears for your preservation, and that God may ever bless our Country with a Chief Majistrate whose Talents, Vigilence, moderation, and Patriotism, may, without the evils of Taxes Armies

Wars &c. better secure its prosperity and Glory; than with them I remain

Your Obd St. RICHD PARROTT

RC (DNA: RG 59, LAR); at head of text: "Thos. Jefferson Esquire President U States"; endorsed by TJ as received 9 May and so recorded in SJL; also endorsed by TJ: "Fenwick Dr. to be a justice."

From Joseph Stanton, Jr.

PRESIDENT UN. S Charlestown May 9th 1805

sir at the Special Request of a Number of the most Respectable & Unequivocal Republicans of the State R Island, as Well as from a sense of duty I owe my Country I am Impelled to Inform your Excellency of the Almost unpardonable Conduct of my once as I fondly supposed Worthy Chambermate Christopher Ellery Esqr. Who has not Ceased since his Return from the last session of Congress to Wound the Republican Interest by openly & Insidiously Joining the Federal Faction in Newport and Portsmouth Two Towns who were Nearly Equally divided in Politics, this Species of Perfidy has aded 7 federal members to Our H R—Thank Heaven the Indignation of the Citizens in every part of the State is Roused on the Question, he & his Federal Friends, Even Prevailed of my Townsman Thomas Hoxsie Esqr one of Our Senate an Unguarded weak Nerved Republican to Oppose Lt. Govr. Mumford, Said Hoxsie has Lost his Election Both as Senator & Lt Govr By a majority of 769 Mr. C E last Winter threatened our delegation in Congress, in the presence of the Postmaster General of what he Intended to do With the Assistance of his Brother in law Mr. Robins & his Federal friends. I Replied good Lord deliver me from Such Republicanism; And his Very good Friend Mr. Granger admonished him & intreated him to desist from his purpose, & told him he Behaved like a fool Repeatedly in the Course of the Evening—Sundry of our Citisens that have Been Mislead on this Occation are Returning to the Republican Standard, But the Feds exult, they Like the Trason But dispise the Traitor—you had the goodness[1] to Inform Mr. Knight Potter & my Self at the Close of the Session Previous to the last, that the martial & Loan Officer would Be Shifted when Suitable Characters were Recommended, we thanked you, & Beged you to wait untill we returned & Consulted Our friends, But Sickness & death prevented, It's now the Wish of the delegation in

Behalf of Our Best Republicans that no Shift take place till the next Session of Congress—

I am With great Respect Very truly your Hume Servt.

Jos. Stanton

we have in the present Legislature HR 24 majority, in the Senate we are unanimous

I Beg Leave to Call your Attention to the Memorial of Mr. Topham Who has Been Convicted of the Heaven daring & God provoking Traffick of dealing in Human flesh. Altho I have Been Hostile to this wicked & Impolitic trade, for 50 years, yet as mercy is Better than Sacrifice, I hope he may enjoy It at the Hands of the Executive, I had the pleasure of Serving in the Revolutionary War with his Father Colo. J Topham, Who I respected as a good Officer J S

RC (DLC); endorsed by TJ as received 19 May and so recorded in SJL.

martial & loan officer would be shifted: for the previous year's discussion regarding the location and arrangement of federal offices in Rhode Island, see Vol. 43:547, 667-8, 670, 672-4, and Vol. 44:429.

memorial of mr. topham: Petition of Philip M. Topham, 3 May.

[1] MS: "gooness."

To Richard Fitzhugh

Dear Sir Washington May 10. 05.

I recieved the day before yesterday some cow-peas from mr Randolph, by the stage, which I had desired him to send for you. the bearer now brings them, and they are in good time for planting if chequered 4. f. apart they will cover the ground: but they do not begin to run till harvest, & then get their whole growth very rapidly. I found it would be difficult by any description to enable you to make the Italian cutting knife, and having a very superior smith at home, he has made all the iron-part of one, which is now coming round by water, being too heavy for the stage. as soon as it arrives I will give you notice. perhaps a man might carry it before him on horseback; but I rather doubt it. I barely called on my return to ask how you did, my hurry not permitting me to make the least stay. be so good as to present my respects to mrs Fitzhugh, & to accept yourself my friendly salutations.

Th: Jefferson

PoC (MHi); at foot of text: "Mr. Richd Fitzhugh"; endorsed by TJ.

superior smith: William Stewart.

To Philippe Reibelt

SIR Washington May 10. 1805.

Your letters of the 3d. & 6th. had already come to hand when that of the 1st. was recieved only the last night. on recurring to my papers respecting General Kosciuzko I found among them the original patent you desire, & the plot. I therefore send them to you. they had remained here, because entirely unnecessary to the title having once been recorded. the record of title preserved in the public offices is our principal dependance here, the original in the hands of the individual being liable to destruction from many accidents.—my request of a hint as to the moving power of your machine was made only under the possibility that it could be communicated without trouble. but having arisen simply from curiosity, I cannot consent to it's employing one moment of your time.—in quoting the date of one of my letters it was by mistake that I stated it as of the 29th. instead of the 30th. ult. Accept my salutations. TH: JEFFERSON

P.S. I hope you have recd the volume of Plutarch. it is several days since it was lodged in the stage-office.

PoC (DLC); at foot of text: "Mr. Reibelt"; endorsed by TJ. Enclosures not found.

MY REQUEST: TJ to Reibelt, 30 Apr.

From John Trimnul and Oddy B. Sheldin

May the 10th 1805

This is to In form the president of the United States that the In Vin Shen of a wheel that runs perpetidle with out wind or warter or Steem that never runs down can be Repre Sinted In a Short time at the Seet of con Gress the Great Ist In vention that ever has bin found out for the use of clocks and Mills of all cinds from Six Inches to eightty feet diammeter the Greatist addition to the none world and if the Con Gress thinks proper to notice these lines In as much as to Send an answer to the same further if they think well ov our foreding such wheel mur Sheers we will In de ver to Com forward In Short time with the Same we are now In the State of west new Jersey In the County of Gloucester In the town Ship of wool wedge at the malligo mills on the head of prins Morrises River these from your friends

JOHN TRIMNUL
ODDY B SHELDIN

RC (MHi); in Trimnul's hand, signed by Sheldin; endorsed by TJ as received from Woolwich, New Jersey, on 17 May and "Perpetual motion."

John Trimnul, whose name might have been more typically listed as "Trimnel," was almost certainly the same individual identified as a prominent early resident and millwright in Woolfordtown (later Plainville) in what became Franklin Township, Gloucester County, New Jersey (Thomas Cushing and Charles E. Sheppard, *History of the Counties of Gloucester, Salem, and Cumberland New Jersey, with Biographical Sketches of Their Prominent Citizens* [Philadelphia, 1883], 214).

Oddy (or Odey) B. Sheldin (Sheldon) appears in records from Salem County, New Jersey, and the Sheldon family (*Genealogical Magazine of New Jersey*, 4 [1928-29], 166; Henry Olcott Sheldon, *The Sheldon Magazine, or, A Genealogical List of the Sheldons in America, with Biographical and Historical Notes* [Loudonville, Ohio, 1855], 14).

PRINS MORRISES RIVER: that is, the Maurice River.

From Isaac Briggs

MY DEAR FRIEND, Washington M.T. 11th. of the 5. Mo. 1805

Some time ago I received thy acceptable letter of March 14. '05. I have written to Governor Claiborne on the subject of La Fayette's lands—be assured I will sedulously attent to it.

I intended to have written to thee fully by the present mail, on several subjects, but am compelled by a press of business to defer most of them to the next, or to treat them more superficially than I wish to do.—

1. The little I was able to gather of Col. Hawkins's sentiments respecting a removal of the Indians to the westward of the Mississippi.

2. The shameful derangement of the Post office establishment as it affects this Territory. To this moment we are ignorant of the laws of last Session of Congress, except two, sent to us by the Secretary of the Treasury.

3. The political situation of the Territory. This last appearing to me likely to suffer by delay, is the principal object of the present communication.

The Republican cause has been already much weakened by the administration of the Secretary, Cato West. An ebullition of turbulent spirits has lately commenced in the news-papers. By next mail, I will send thee all the pieces, to that time, with explanatory notes.

Robert Williams has not yet received his commission as Governor, nor any *official* notice of his appointment, so as to enable him to arrange his affairs to accept &c.

From certain measures of the General Government affecting some of the near connections of the Secretary—his having high pretensions to the appointment of Governor, being so long intrusted with the administration, and being at last disappointed—render them much disposed to throw embarrassments in the way of any successor, in order to verify, if possible, what they have already said in the public prints—"That any man *sent* here must be less capable than the Secretary."—

Knowing that their intolerant little junto has lost the administration, relieves them in a great measure from their responsibility—and knowing to *whom* it is given, affords them a double opportunity to lay the ground work of faction and opposition and to barricade the avenues to a just administration, while the person against whom they fortify, may look on without the power of counteraction. In the mean time, the great mass of the people who received the news of this appointment with more than common demonstrations of joy, are in danger of being soured, in conceiving themselves still neglected by the General Government.

Accept assurances of my esteem and affectionate regard.

ISAAC BRIGGS.

RC (DLC); in Thomas Robertson's hand, signed by Briggs; at foot of text: "Thomas Jefferson, President U. States"; endorsed by TJ (torn). FC (MdHi). Recorded in SJL as received 25 June.

To James Cheetham

SIR — Washington May 11. 05

My account transmitted by you is recieved. early in the spring of the last year, I gave mr Barnes (who is kind enough to transact most of my money business for me) a list of sums to be paid for newspapers recieved in the year. among these was 19. D. for yourself. not knowing the other articles of the account I could not add what was due for them. he tells me he wrote to a mr Alexr. Richards to call & pay you that sum and shews me a letter from mr Richards undertaking it. possibly he may have forgotten it as it is not credited in your account. mr Barnes now remits to his correspondent mr Ludlow in N.Y. 25. D 80½ c the balance which, with the 19. D. paid or which will be immediately paid by mr Richards makes up the account. I have been thus particular merely to excuse myself for an apparent delinquency in letting the account run 2. years. Accept my salutations

TH: JEFFERSON

PoC (DLC); at foot of text: "Mr. Cheetham"; endorsed by TJ.

MY ACCOUNT: see Cheetham to TJ, 24 Apr.

I GAVE MR BARNES: in his financial memoranda under 31 Mch. 1804, TJ listed 14 newspapers he "Desired Mr. Barnes to pay for," including $10 for the New York *American Citizen* and $9 for the *New-York*

Evening Post to be remitted to Cheetham (MB, 2:1122-3).

For TJ's newspaper payment arrangements with Charles LUDLOW, see Vol. 37:308 and Vol. 40:554.

From John Davis

SIR, Philadelphia, May 11, 1805.

I entreat you will do me the honour to accept the enclosed volume. I have taken the liberty to prefix to it your sanction of my undertaking, and am with the liveliest gratitude,

Sir, your most obedient, most humble Servant, JOHN DAVIS.

RC (DLC); addressed: "Thomas Jefferson, President of the United States"; endorsed by TJ as received 20 May. Enclosure: probably *Captain Smith and Princess Pocahontas, An Indian Tale*, published in Philadelphia in May 1805 (*Relfs Philadelphia Gazette*, 25 May).

YOUR SANCTION: see Davis to TJ, 13 Mch.

To Benjamin H. Latrobe

DEAR SIR Washington May 11. 05.

I could not sooner return your drawings, because I could not till yesterday have a conference with mr Gallatin. some parts of your propositions being approved, some doubtful, some not satisfactory, I can only write short observations as texts for consideration, and to be discussed vivâ voce when you come here. the piers instead of half columns at the junction of the new with the old buildings are approved. that the coach house cannot permanently remain where I have planned it, is certain, because of the inconvenient distance a carriage would have to go from the South to the North front when the whole line of offices shall be closed. the upper floor of the Middle pavillions, level with the surface of the ground on the North side, and opening on it, must ultimately be destined for coach-houses. but I want a coach house immediately & hope we may the next year add 60 f. to this year's work which may be conveniently used as a coach house, while the rest of the line is unclosed, & may be converted to any other use, when further calls for accomodations shall render it necessary to build as far as the center[1] pavillions. the obstructions to the colonnade from the stables, may be prevented by giving them a North door, as horses will easily ascend or descend the terras on the North side. but the most difficult of all is the adjustment of the new connecting building to the different levels of the three existing buildings nothing can be admitted short of the terras of the offices from the Pres's House to the pavilions each way being absolutely in the level of the *floor* of the house. how it shall drop off from the last[2] Pavilion to the Treasury, and gain from the West one to the War office is the difficulty of the art which will be worthy of you to conquer. the depression of the Treasury floor favors eminently the giving the necessary height to the Treasury offices now to be built. by the bye, I observe in the drawings for the Treasury offices in mr Gallatin's hands, that the barrel of the vault runs lengthwise of the building, to wit, from East to West. I thought that you had concluded it would be better for them to run across the building from N. to S. so as to press against each other, & rest on piers or partition walls. these would take little from the internal room as they would serve to place presses against, and this arrangement would give large South windows; not indeed material for the Treasury offices now to be executed, but indispensible for those hereafter in which the officers & clerks will write. they will want doors too opening into the colonnade. my opinion is that in time they will want a double row of offices, as in my sketch given you, the passage between which will range with the colonnade. these suggestions are for your consideration: but your presence here for a few days is indispensable to consult & determine ultimately on the plans. in the mean time the digging is going on, and mr Lenthall will commence to collect the materials. in a conversation with him we found that the excellent rough building stone here is cheaper than brick in the proportion of 3. to 5. it is certainly as durable, and either of them being to be rough cast, it ought to be preferred, because it enables us to do more with our appropriated sum in the proportion of 5. to 3. which is a great matter. in hopes of seeing you here without delay, be it for ever so short a time, I shall add only my salutations & assurances of esteem & respect.

TH: JEFFERSON

PoC (DLC); at foot of first page: "Mr. Latrobe"; endorsed by TJ.

DRAWINGS FOR THE TREASURY OFFICES: see Latrobe to TJ, 5 May.

[1] Word interlined.

[2] Word interlined.

To George Logan

Dear Sir Washington May 11. 05.

I recieved last night a letter from mr Thomas Brannagan. 163. S. Waterstreet Philadelphia, asking my subscription to the work announced in the inclosed paper. the cause in which he embarks is so holy, the sentiments he expresses in his letter so friendly that it is highly painful to me to hesitate on a compliance which appears so small. but that is not it's true character, and it would be injurious, even to his views, for me to commit myself on paper by answering his letter. I have most carefully avoided every public act or manifestation on that subject. should an occasion ever occur in which I can interpose with decisive effect, I shall certainly know & do my duty with promptitude and zeal. but in the mean time it would only be disarming myself of influence to be taking small means. the subscription to a book on this subject is one of those little irritating measures which, without advancing it's end at all, would, by lessening the confidence & good will of a description of friends composing a large body, only lessen my powers of doing them good in the other great relations in which I stand to the publick. yet I cannot be easy in not answering mr Brannagan's letter unless he can be made sensible that it is better I should not answer it; & I do not know how to effect this, unless you would have the goodness, the first time you go to Philadelphia, to see him and to enter into an explanation with him. I see with infinite pain the bloody schism which has taken place among our friends in Pensylvania & New York, & will probably take place in other states. the main body of both sections mean well, but their good intentions will produce great public evil. the minority, whichever section shall be the minority, will end in coalition with the federalists, and some compromise of principle; because these will not sell their aid for nothing. republicanism will thus lose, & royalism gain some portion of that ground which we thought we had rescued to good government. I do not express my sense of our misfortunes from any idea that they are remediable. I know that the passions of men will take their course, that they are not to be controuled but by despotism, & that this melancholy truth is the pretext for despotism. the duty of an upright administration is to pursue it's course steadily, to know nothing of these family dissensions, and to cherish the good principles of both parties. the war ad internecionem which we have waged against federalism has filled our latter times with strife and unhappiness. we have met it, with pain indeed, but with firmness, because we believed it the last convulsive effort of that Hydra which, in earlier times, we had conquered in the field. but if any degeneracy of principle should ever render it necessary to give ascendancy to one of the rising sections over the other, I thank my god it will fall to some other to perform that operation. the only cordial I wish to carry into my retirement is the undivided good will of all those with whom I have acted. present me affectionately to mrs Logan, and accept my salutations & assurances of constant friendship and respect. TH: JEFFERSON

RC (PHi). PoC (DLC); at foot of first page: "Dr. Logan"; endorsed by TJ. Enclosure: probably a prospectus for *Avenia: or, A Tragical Poem, on the Oppression of the Human Species, and Infringement on the Rights of Man* (Philadelphia, 1805).

LETTER: Thomas Branagan to TJ, 7 May.

From Pierre Samuel Du Pont de Nemours

MONSIEUR LE PRÉSIDENT, Paris 12 May 1805.

Votre gravité naturelle ne vous aura pas permis d'avoir autant de plaisir pour la Médaille que notre Société d'Agriculture vous a décernée, que ma sensibilité a eu de l'hommage rendu au Philosophe Homme d'Etat de votre Pays par les Cultivateurs du mien.

Je suis sujet aux joies d'enfant; mais en cette occasion j'en ai eu une d'Adolescent, parce qu'elle tenait à un sentiment civique qui embrassait mes deux Patries, comme aussi à mon amour pour les deux sciences du Gouvernement et de la culture.

Toutes deux me portent à vous soumettre une idée que je crois utile pour finir avec équité les procès multipliés qui existent dans quelques uns des Etats unis et notamment dans le Kentucky sur la propriété des terres.

J'en ai là *cinquante six mille* acres; l'on dit que je suis le plus heureux des hommes parcequ'il y en a *seize mille* qu'on ne me conteste pas.

Le même terrein *unsettled* est réclamé par cinq ou six propriétaires: ce qui vient de ce que les concessions ont été faites, sans arpentage général, d'après les cartes particulieres que ceux qui les demandaient ont présentées au *Land-Office*; que les lignes de démarcation, désignées par des Arbres dont les pareils sont innombrables dans le Pays, n'ont rien de bien assuré; que toutes les concessions se croisent et se *surcouvrent*; et qu'il parait qu'on en a fait pour un beaucoup plus grand nombre d'acres que les limites naturelles prises à partir des Rivieres n'en contiennent réellement.

Cependant toute concession émanée de l'Etat de Virginie ou de celui de Kentucky est un titre respectable, auquel on doit toute la garantie que le territoire peut comporter.

Comment finir ces contestations fâcheuses, couteuses, et qui retardent l'établissement de la culture? Ou comment y parvenir sans faire injustice à personne?

D'abord en sachant jusqu'où s'étend la possibilité d'être juste.

On peut ordonner aux fraix des differens prétendans, possesseurs de titres authentiques, l'arpentage général de tous les Terreins dont les limites extérieures sont bien dessinées par les Rivieres et par un petit nombre de lignes droites tirées d'un embranchement, ou autre point incontestable d'une riviere, à un autre point également incontestable de la riviere voisine.

La dépense de cet arpentage devra être répartie entre tous les porteurs de titres sur des terres comprises dans ce local proportionnellement au nombre d'acres que chacun d'eux réclame.

L'arpentage général donnera la quantité d'acres contenue dans le terrein mesuré; et si les titres présentent une totalité de concessions excedant les terres qui existent effectivement dans ce canton, comme on n'a pas pu vendre ce qui n'avait point d'existence, et comme le droit est égal entre tous les concessionnaires ou acquereurs de l'Etat, on reconnaitra que chacun d'eux n'a de droit dans le canton arpenté qu'en raison de la proportion de sa concession avec la masse totale des autres concessions faites dans le même lieu.

Par exemple; si dans un terrein compris entre quatre Rivieres, ou exactement limité d'une autre maniere quelconque, il a été concédé trois cent mille acres, et si l'arpentage général fait voir qu'il n'y en a que deux cent mille, le droit de chaque concessionnaire sera réduit aux deux tiers de l'étendue mentionnée dans son titre primitif.

ces premieres bases posées, il faudra partir d'un angle ou d'un autre point parfaitement déterminé tel que le confluent de deux rivieres.—On examinera quel est le concessionnaire dont le titre, s'accordant avec ce point, serait en même tems le plus ancien de ceux qui pourraient s'y accorder comme lui; et on lui expediera un *titre nouvel* de la quantité d'acres à laquelle la reduction générale et proportionnelle lui donnera droit: titre accompagné de sa carte bien limitée.

Procédant ensuite de l'un à l'autre, on réglera les parts de ses plus proches voisins qui subiront les mêmes reductions proportionnelles; et ainsi du reste jusqu'au partage exact de tout le canton.

Alors il y aura place pour tout le monde, puisque la totalité des arpentages particuliers pourra être contenue dans l'Arpentage général.

Toutes les limites particulieres seront claires et indubitables. Tous les Procès seront finis. Et chacun des concessionnaires se trouvera le plus près qu'il soit possible du lieu où il aura désiré sa concession.

L'exécution de cette mesure sera sans difficulté pour les terreins encore *unsettled.*

Quant aux Fermes bâties et aux terres nécessaires à leur exploitation, qui peuvent se trouver dans les cantons dont pour terminer tous les procès il faudra faire ainsi une distribution, un nouveau partage, on observa de ne jamais *évincer* le possesseur actuel et de bonne foi.—La réduction proportionnelle ne pourra jamais avoir lieu sur des terreins en culture. Elle ne portera que sur les parties non travaillées. Et dans le cas où les rapprochemens, que la réduction générale des concessions aura occasionnés, placeraient la Ferme qu'un homme aura mis en valeur au delà du lieu que le nouvel arpentage général assignerait à sa concession, il sera seulement tenu de donner au Propriétaire du lot dans lequel la ferme sera établie un nombre égal d'acres à prendre au choix de ce Propriétaire dans les meilleurs de ceux encore incultes que la distribution générale accordera au Fermier dont la culture aura été respectée.

Cette indemnité de terrein pour terrein sera d'autant plus raisonnable que la Ferme construite et cultivée augmente la valeur des terres environnantes: de sorte que le concessionnaire, sur le lot duquel de telles fermes seront établies, en recevant ailleurs un nombre d'acres égal sera loin de perdre sur sa concession principale.

Je ne pousserai pas plus loin les détails de cette opération. Il est bien suffisant d'en avoir indiqué l'esprit à un homme tel que vous.

Votre Excellence verra du reste combien il importe à l'Amérique en général, et en particulier aux Etats où les concessions se croisent, de rendre les propriétés claires et sures; et de tarir la source des Procès qui, repoussant les acquereurs, sont pour l'établissement de l'agriculture un obstacle infiniment fâcheux par lequel le cours naturel de la prospérité nationale est retardé.

Agréez mes remerciemens pour toutes vos bontés et l'hommage de mon profond respect Du Pont (de Nemours)

EDITORS' TRANSLATION

Mister President, Paris, 12 May 1805

Given your characteristic modesty, you will not have taken as much pleasure in the medal our Agricultural Society awarded you as I did in the honor bestowed upon the wise leader of your country by the farmers of mine.

I am subject to childlike joys, but on this occasion I felt an adolescent pleasure because it came from the civic feeling that links my two countries, akin to my love for the two sciences of government and agriculture.

These two loves impel me to propose an idea I think would be useful for achieving an equitable resolution to the multiple lawsuits about property ownership in some states, especially Kentucky.

I have *56,000* acres there and am told I am the most fortunate of men because *16,000* of them are uncontested.

A single piece of unsettled land is disputed by five or six owners. That is because the concessions were made without a general survey, based on individual maps that applicants presented to the Land Office. The lines of demarcation are unclear because they are designated by trees, which are innumerable in the country. The concessions intersect and overlap, and there seem to be concessions for many more acres than fit within the natural boundaries of the rivers.

Yet, all concessions emitted by the state of Virginia or Kentucky have legitimate titles, which deserve all the authority the land can provide.

How can we end these regrettable, costly disputes that delay development? And how can we do so without being unfair to anyone?

By determining, first of all, what we mean by fairness.

We could authorize a general survey, at the expense of the different claimants who hold rightful titles, of all the land whose boundaries are well defined by rivers and by a small number of straight lines drawn from a fork or other uncontested points on a river, or other equally incontestable points of a neighboring river.

The cost of the survey would be shared among all the holders of titles to land encompassed in this area, proportionate to the number of acres each one claims.

The general survey would establish the number of acres contained within the measured land. If the titles to the concessions exceeded the land that actually exists within the area, since one cannot sell what does not exist, and since all the renters or buyers are equal before the law, we would recognize that each of them is not entitled to more than the proportion of his plot within all the other concessions of the same area.

For example: if 300,000 acres have been allocated in an area that lies between four rivers or is definitively delimited in some other way and the general survey indicates that there are only 200,000 acres, each grantee would be reduced to two thirds of the land specified in his original title.

Once this base was in place, we would have to begin from an angle or other precise point such as the confluence of two rivers. We would examine which grantee, whose title corresponded to this point, would be first among those whose titles might also overlap. We would send him a *new title* for the number of acres to which the general proportional reduction entitled him—a title accompanied by a clearly delimited map.

Proceeding from one to another, we would determine the proportions of his nearest neighbors, who would undergo the same proportional reductions, and so forth until the region had been precisely divided.

In this way, there would be room for everyone, since all the individual surveys could be contained within the overall survey.

All the individual boundaries would be clear and unequivocal. All the trials would be over. And each grantee would be as close as possible to the land he wanted.

Executing this measure would not present any difficulty for lands that are still *unsettled.*

As for the existing farms and the land required to exploit them, which might be in regions where it is necessary to undertake new divisions and distributions in order to resolve the trials, we would be careful never to evict a current good-faith owner. The proportional reduction would never take place on farmed land; it would apply only to unfarmed land. Wherever reductions caused by the general contraction put land one man farmed beyond the boundaries the new survey had assigned him, he would simply have to give the new owner of the plot an equivalent number of untilled acres that the new owner could choose from among the best of the untilled land, thereby preserving the farmer's cultivated land.

Trading land for land is all the more reasonable since an established, cultivated farm increases the value of the surrounding land. For this reason the original owner, on whose land such farms are built, by receiving an equal number of acres, would be far from losing on his original concession.

I will not expand further on the details of this operation. It is entirely enough to outline its gist to a man like you.

Your excellency will see, moreover, how important it is for America in general, and for the states where land grants overlap in particular, to render the property clear and secure, to remove the source of trials which, by discouraging buyers, are an infinitely undesirable obstacle to agriculture and thereby slow the natural course of national prosperity.

Accept my thanks for all your kindness and the expression of my deep respect.

Du Pont (de Nemours)

RC (DLC); at head of text: "A Son Excellence Thomas Jefferson Président des Etats unis"; endorsed by TJ as received 13 Nov. and so recorded in SJL.

LA MÉDAILLE: TJ was awarded a gold medal for his improvements to moldboard plows at the 28 Apr. 1805 meeting of the Société d'Agriculture du Département de la Seine (*Mémoires d'agriculture, d'économie rurale et domestique*, 7 [1805], xxiv, li-liii).

From Philippe Reibelt

Monsieur le President! Baltimore le 12 Mai 1805.

C'est en votre qualitè de grand Amateur et parfait Connaisseur des Arts, que je prends la libertè, de Vous adresser avec çette Lettre un petit paquet, renfermant quelques pièces, qui en partie au moins Vous feront du plaisir.

On vient a l'instant me remettre votre Lettre du 10—a la quelle j'ai lhonneur de Vous repondre incessament.

1) Je Vous prie, d'accepter mes remercimens de l'envoi de la Patente originale.

2) C'est avec un plaisir bien Sincere, que je saisirois le premier Moment, qui sera a ma disposition, pour Vous presenter personellement mes hommages, et de Vous communiquer alors le modele a la main la puissance motriçe—infiniment simple—du Moulin en question—

Soÿez en General—jusqu'a çe, que j'aurois acquis l'avantage, d'etre Connus de Vous de plus près, soÿez, je Vous prie, persuadè, que jamais il est imigrè Aux etats unis du Continent Europèen—personne plus attachèe aux principes, que Vous avez Sauvé pour l'Univers—que Moi—personne, qui aye fait des Sacrifices relativement plus importans pour çette Cause, que Moi—donc personne, qui soit penetré d'un respect plus pur pour Vous—que Moi—

3) J'ai recu le Vol. des Oeuvr. de Plutarque—et

4) j'espere, que Vous aurez recû egalement le Manuel du Mus. francais—

Permettez Moi, de Vous presenter çijoint un Catalogue d'un petit etablissement rival a Philadelphie, avec quelques remarques.

Ce sont deux frères de Lyon—cidevant Conscripts forcès pour l'armèe d'Egypte—partisans de tout ancien ordre des Choses—parfaitement profans au fait de Litterature, qui vendent a 2 et 300 pC. en Sus du prix de Paris, et se flattent de prendre le pas sur l'etablissement des Mss. Levrault, Schoell et Comp—qui n'y mettent, que 60 pC.—lesquels pour y reussir se servent de la Voie des Calomnies, dont la moins excusable est çelle, que cette Maison, ayant des Depots aux Capitales de la Russie, de la Suisse, de l'Allemagne, de la Valachie et Moldavie, et a Strasbourg—etoit sur le point de faire faillite &c.

Ils sont arrivès avec 6 Caisses de Livres, qui—comme les Catalogues respectifs le prouvent, ne renferment pas le Quart de çe que Mr. fleischer à importè, ni en Nombre, ni en Valeur litteraire.

Ce n'est pas pour ma personne, que j'ose Vous faire çes representations, c'est uniquement pour mes Amis, Composant la Maison a Paris—tous des Litterateurs tres distingués, et tres estimés—Car—Moi—je ne desire pas mieux, que de quitter aussitot, que possible, les occupations de Commerce, pour les quels je n'ai pas le moindre Gout, de remettre la direction a un beaufrere de Mr. Schoell, que j'ai demandè, et de rentrer dans la Classe bien plus Morale des Cultivateurs—autant, que çela depend de Moi, a la Louisiane—possedant mieux la langue francaise, que l'Anglaise.

Daignez Agreer gracieusement les protestations de respect, que j'ai lhonneur de Vous offrir.

REIBELT

EDITORS' TRANSLATION

MISTER PRESIDENT! Baltimore, 12 May 1805

To you, in your capacity as the perfect connoisseur and great lover of the arts, I take the liberty of enclosing a small package with this letter, containing several items that will bring you at least some measure of pleasure.

I have the honor of replying to your letter of the 10th, which was just delivered.

1) Please accept my thanks for sending the original patent.

2) It is with very sincere happiness that I shall seize the first available moment to present my greetings in person and bring you the model of the infinitely simple motor for the mill.

Until I have the good fortune of being known more personally to you, please understand that no immigrant to the United States from the European continent has ever been more attached than I am to the principles you have safeguarded for the universe; no one has sacrificed more for this cause than I have; and no one, therefore, respects you more wholeheartedly than I do.

3) I received the volume of Plutarch's works, and

4) I hope you also received the *Manuel du muséum français*.

Allow me to enclose the catalog of a small competitor in Philadelphia with a few observations. These are two brothers from Lyons whose previous experience was as conscripts drafted into the army to serve in Egypt. Biased in favor of the old order in all things, they are not at all knowledgeable about literature. They sell for 200 to 300 percent above Paris prices and presume to rival Levrault, Schoell, and Co. which marks up by only 60 percent. To succeed they resort to lies, the least pardonable of which is that this business, which has branches in the capitals of Russia, Switzerland, Germany, Wallachia, and Moldovia, as well as in Strasbourg, is on the verge of bankruptcy, etc.

They arrived with six cases of books which, as the respective catalogs prove, do not contain a quarter of what Mr. Fleischer has imported, either in quantity or literary merit.

I do not provide this description for my own benefit, but solely for that of my friends in the Paris office who are all very distinguished, respected literary figures. I desire nothing more than to retire as soon as possible from business, for which I have not the slightest inclination, to entrust the management to a brother-in-law of Mr. Schoell, as I have requested, and return to the much more ethical class of farmers. If I had my way I would settle in Louisiana, as I speak French better than English.

Please look favorably on the assurance of respect that I have the honor of offering you. REIBELT

RC (DLC); endorsed by TJ as received 14 May and so recorded in SJL. Enclosures: (1) Probably Louis Pierre Dubray, ed., *Catalogue des estampes des trois écoles, portraits, catafalques, pompes funèbres, plans, cartes géographiques, etc. qui se trouvent à Paris, au Musée central des arts* (Paris, 1801). (2) Probably the catalog published annually by the Musée Napoléon, that is, the Louvre, as *Notice des statues, bustes et bas-reliefs, de la galerie des antiques*. Other enclosures not found, but see TJ to Reibelt and to P. & C. Roche, both 17 May.

PETIT ETABLISSEMENT RIVAL A PHILADELPHIE: almost certainly the booksellers P. & C. Roche, who were advertising their business by late April (*Relfs Philadelphia Gazette*, 27 Apr.).

DEPOTS AUX CAPITALES: product of a merger between Levrault frères of Strasbourg and Paris and Schoell et Compagnie of Basel, the firm for which Reibelt worked sold books in a number of different cities. Within the soon-disbanded Holy Roman Empire, which was often called Germany, the firm operated in Leipzig, Frankfurt, and Vienna (information in Bibliothèque Nationale, Paris; William Fleischer, *Annuaire de la librairie* [Paris, 1802], preceding title page).

To Oliver Evans

Washington May. 13. 1805.

Th: Jefferson presents his compliments to mr Evans & his thanks for his letter of the 8th. which has been recieved. the questions presented by the proposition of mr Clymer are Whether the Missile powers of the Fire engine may not be used on board ship to prevent boarding, & With what matter most effectual it may be charged? these will be a subject of consideration for better judges than Th:J. is himself: he prays mr Evans to make his just acknolegements to mr Clymer & to accept himself his salutations.

PoC (DLC); endorsed by TJ.

From John Mason

DEAR SIR George Town 13 May 1805

Enclosed I take the Liberty to hand you for your consideration my Friend Hodgson's Invoice of the two Glasses which I mentioned to you some time agoe; you will be pleased remark, that in estimating these plates, by the square inch, the Frames are included, which are said to be remarkably elegant large, and richly ornamented—

I do my self the Pleasure also to send you herein a Sketch of the country and roads from this Place to Occoquan; which I have made out roughly from recollection, but which you will find accurate enough, I flatter myself, to serve as a guide in your proposed excursion—From Ward's Tavern, opposite to Colchester, to Piscataway, there is no Tavern, I have noted Mr. Graham's in Dougues Neck—and my Brother's (William Mason) on the Plat, both are near your Rout and will be extremely happy to see you

With great Respect I have the honor to be Sir Your very obt Sert

J. MASON

RC (MHi); at foot of text: "The President"; endorsed by TJ as received 14 May and so recorded in SJL. Enclosures not found, but see below.

HODGSON'S INVOICE: an 1802 inventory of Alexandria merchant William Hodgson included what he advertised as two large and superb looking glasses imported from London, with "suitable ornaments" (Miller, *Alexandria Artisans*, 1:208-9; *Washington Federalist*, 6 Aug. 1802).

EXCURSION: TJ was interested in finding the shortest route south through northern Virginia, both for "the mail & the traveller." As part of his investigation, he modified his trip home on 15 July so as to pass through Occoquan (MB, 2:1160; TJ to Nathaniel Ellicott, 7 July).

Mason and his brother WILLIAM MASON grew up at Gunston Hall near Occoquan, as did George Graham, a distant relative. Dogues Neck was the site of the family seat before Gunston Hall was built in the 1750s (Kate Mason Rowland, *The Life of George Mason, 1725-1792: Including His Speeches, Public Papers, and Correspondence*, 2 vols. [New York, 1892], 1:57; Pamela C. Copeland and Richard K. MacMaster, *The Five George Masons: Patriots and Planters of Virginia and Maryland* [Fairfax, Va., 2016], 101, 253).

To Samuel Miller

Washington May 13. 05.

Th: Jefferson returns his thanks to the revd mr Miller for the pamphlet he has been so kind as to send him, which he has perused, as he does whatever comes from his pen, with great pleasure. he salutes mr Miller with esteem and respect.

RC (NjP: Samuel Miller Papers); addressed: "The revd. Samuel Miller New York"; franked and postmarked. PoC (DLC); endorsed by TJ.

HIS THANKS: see Miller to TJ, 8 May.

From Thomas Munroe, with Jefferson's Reply

Monday morning 13 May 1805

T Munroe presents his best respects to the President—He did not until Saturday meet with a suitable person to top the trees—A beginning was made on that day (Holt the Gardner having previously given it as his Opinion that it might, at almost any time of the year, be done with safety) Some persons, however, yesterday mentioned that the sap was too much up, and that many of the trees would be killed if topp'd or trimm'd at this advanced period of the season—TM cannot think so, but not being so well informed on the subject as many others, and being unwilling to run any risk, respectfully asks the Opinion of the

President whose experience & knowledge of these things he presumes enable him to say with certainty whether there ought to be a doubt entertained about it

[*Reply by TJ*:]
I think they may safely proceed Th:J.

RC (DLC: District of Columbia Papers); addressed: "President."

Theophilus HOLT operated a nursery on the Eastern Branch (*National Intelligencer*, 23 Feb. 1807).

From John Francis Vacher

Sir New York May 13th 1805

Men born with the desire to see their fellow Creatures happy, when themselves served; their abode, the whole nature resound with the accents of their gratitude, which follows them to the grave.

I have been twenty nine Years in this Country. Your Excellency had no knowledge of me, had done me neither good nor evil; Yet perhaps no Man in the United States was more interested to your Glory than myself. this my Grateful and I dare venture to Say virtuous Familly can assert: they are equally sensible those Children, whose education has been led to follow the path of truth, as myself, to your very great favor. my Son who by chance is here has received this Day his Commission as a Commissioner in the western district of the Territory of Orleans. May he by Your example in his infant Carrier do honor to your Administration. and may Your Excellency be pleased to accept of my thanks for the Same.

I am with Respect Sir of Your Excellency's[1] Most obedient and very humble Servant John F. Vacher

P.S. who could I Submit the Sentiments of our glorious revolution to a worthier Man than to You in the two Emisphere. the emperor of France is undoubtedly the most extraordinary Character that the world ever produced as to relataid the magnanimity deriving from it. but let me be on the Side of virtue as Simply dressed as represented. however this age will witness two great wonders. the care of my Familly deprive me for the present to tender you with more than this Short Extract for the present if they can amuse You in Your short moments of respite. Gordon is my Guide. he wrote the truth. a Man Sinet to think what the english have been guilty of Since near two ages against humanity that is Since cromwell to the indirect alternative murderings of the Island of St. Domingo

Medallion Portrait by Gilbert Stuart

Ariadne

10°
15°
20°
25°
Sicily
Ætna
Spartivento
C. Passaro
Morea
Sparta
Zante
Athens
Naxia
C. Matapan olim Tenarus
Candia
Pentellaria
C. Bon
Tunis
Linosa
Malta
Lampedoza
Kerkeni
Gerbi
Lotophagi
Tozer
Tebess
Tripoli
Lebida
Mesurata
Kasr Ahmed
Sidra or Syrtis
Ras Sem
Derna
Telemata
Bengasi
Desert of Barca
Zoara
Quicksands
Augela
Gadamis
Benioleed
Ghirzé
Misselata
Gariano
Sabart
Wad-al-Jeare'
Sockna
Wadan
Sort
Soudah Desert
Sort Desert
Zala
Zeghen
Sebbah
Agaree
Telliaguess
Gerdobah
Sirua
Plain
Zillan Mt.
T R I P O L I

Tripoli

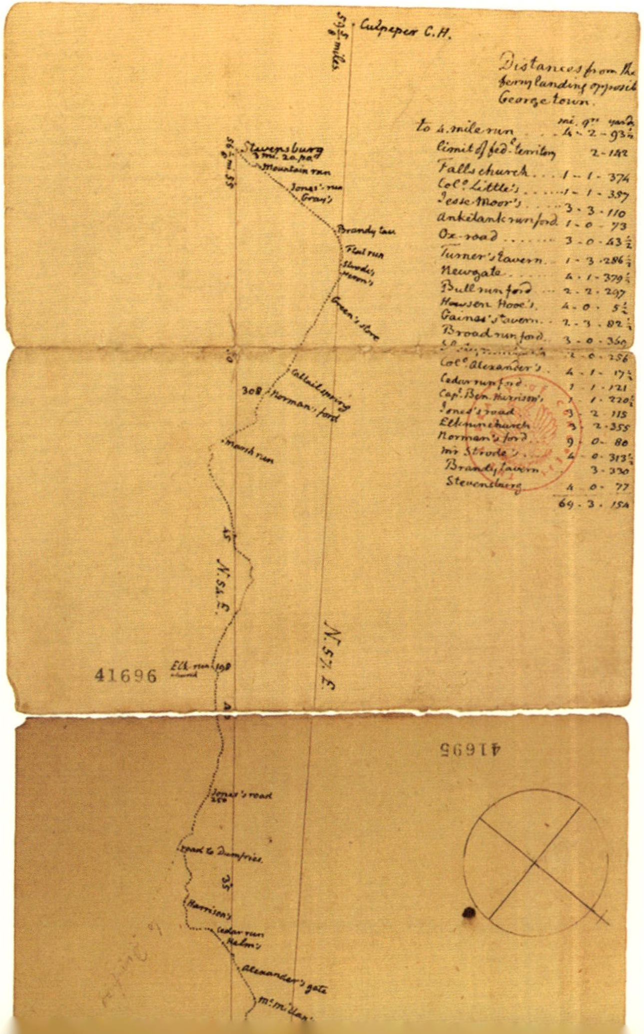

Culpeper C.H.
59 5/8 miles
Distances from the ferry landing opposite George town.
mi. qrs yards
to 4 mile run . . . 4 - 2 - 93 3/4
Limit of fedl. territory 2 - 142
Falls church . . . 1 - 1 - 374
Col. Little's . . . 1 - 1 - 397
Jesse Moor's . . . 3 - 3 - 110
Ankelank run ford 1 - 0 - 73
Ox-road . . . 3 - 0 - 43 1/2
Turner's tavern . 1 - 3 - 286 1/2
Newgate . . . 4 - 1 - 379 1/2
Bull run ford . . . 2 - 2 - 297
Hawsen Hooe's 4 - 0 - 5 1/2
Gaines's tavern . 2 - 3 - 82 1/2
Broad run ford . 3 - 0 - 369
Col. Alexander's 4 - 1 - 17 1/2
Cedar run ford 1 - 1 - 121
Capt. Ben Harrison's 1 - 220 1/2
Jones's road 3 - 2 - 115
Elk run church 3 - 2 - 355
Norman's ford 9 - 0 - 80
Mr. Strode's 4 - 0 - 313 1/2
Brandy tavern 3 - 330
Stevensburg 4 - 0 - 77
69 - 3 - 154
Stevensburg
3 mi. 20 po.
Mountain run
Jones's run
Gray's
Brandy tav.
Flat run
Strode's
Brandy tav.
Green's store
Norman's ford
308
Marsh run
45
N. 54. E.
N. 57. E.
Elk run
108
41696
41695
Jones's road
road to Dumfries
35
Harrison's
Cedar run
Alexander's gate

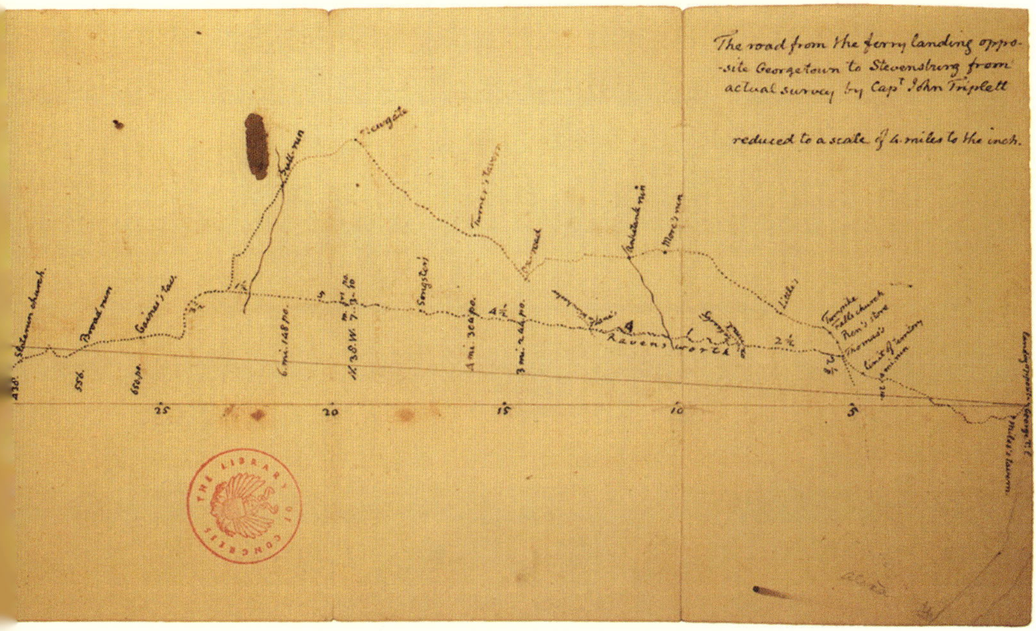

Route through Northern Virginia

Preble Medal

Thomas Jefferson by Gilbert Stuart

John Wayles Eppes

C'est Franklin qui Continue L'histoire de la Guerre a loüis XVI chant 6e vers 745

Tout près de pennyton, Seize Jeunes Bergeres;
pour eviter les pas, de ces vils insulaires;
Se cachent dans le fond de leurs sombres forêts.
Mais qu'elle en est la fin? de voltigeurs anglais
comme Si dans leurs cours manquaient encor de crimes!
vous entourent ces bois, Saisissent leurs victimes,
qui, par ces ravisseurs ont leur pudicité
immolée a l'autel de la brutalité

Helas! puissent les traits de L'histoire Suivante
de tout homme emouvoir l'ame Sympathisante;
ainsi qu'en nos etats en execration
les actes criminels du pouvoir d'albion.

Que vôtre majesté, que Sa cour toute auguste.
Que ces illustres chefs, d'un peuple grand et juste
et que tous ces pouvoirs lui portant[2] fesant amitié
puissent a ce recit être emus de pitié

Non loin d'ou le raway grossi de Ses fontaines
qui par mille contours fertilisent les plaines
et d'ou l'on voit du Sond le liquide element
baigner la cesarés et la Statenisland
Lieux ou jadis L'hymen par des Saints Sacrifices
offrait aux habitans Ses plus pures delices
que cerès et pomone comblaient de leurs egards
mais apresent livrés a la fureur de Mars.

un officier anglais force dans un étable
de l'un de nos bourgeois la demoiselle aimable
qui fesaient retentir de ses douloureux Sons
les hameaux d'alentour les plaines et les monts

oh ce pere incité par de justes alarmes
court vers Les Sons! et voir, Sa fille, ô dieux! en larmes!!
Saignante!!! et dans les bras d'un Monstre criminel
impunement Souillé du viol actuel . . . .
Et hors de blame, dit "que ton ombre Barbare
aille voir les marais de L antre du tenare!
et lui plonge a l'instant le poignard dans le Sein.

Deux autres officiers Se presentent Soudain,
qui font partir le feu de deux pieces tonnantes;
qui loge du metal les deux balles Sifflantes,
dans le Sein de se pere, et dont le triste Sort,

le reduit a languir dans le lit de la mort.
Au recit de tels faits qu'enfante la licence.
le roy, la cour touchés d'une indigne Souffrance,
dans qui même le cœur d'un tyran Sy confond.
Se Sentent tous Saisis d'un Silence proffond.
Quand dans Son char d'azur, dans la celeste plaine;
La brillante venus se presente a la reine.
qui mêlant et Son geste et Ses charmes puissants,
aux Sons articulés des plus tendres accens.
dit "ô beau rejetton de la race immortelle
du pieux chef qui Sert aux princes de modele,
Descendante d'enée et fille des cesars!
que je favorisai de mes plus chers regards.
vous dont Seulement l'air d'un Souris de tendresse,
repand chez les humains, l'amour et l'alegresse.
Ô vous ma chere fille, et dans qui par mes vœux,
furent tant prodigués mes charmes et mes feux!
Sachez que mes desirs quand Se peuple la terre,
par le celeste aiman de l'amoureux mistere;
Sont, que dans ces debats, tout Se passe Sans bruit.
Soit, Sous le voile epais des ombres de la nuit.
Soit dans des bois touffus, ou Sous un bois champêtre,
où tout près Zephir, Joue a lombrage du hetre.
et toujours Sous le Sceau du plein consentement,
de la Nymphe amoureuse et de l'heureux amant!
Mais que des forcenés aillent dans leur delire
par d'actes outrageants polluer mon empire
Sans même respecter les loix de la pudeur . . . !!
est, ce que dans mes ris J'eus toujours eu horreur;
et que dans ce forfait fletrissant la nature
mon antoinette puisse en ressentir l'injure;
elle qui des mortels dirigeant le destin
venge L'honeur blessé du Sexe americain.
Comme en calmie Se gonfle et mollement S'agite,
Le Sein majestueux, de la belle amphitrite;
a la veille de voir les furieux autans,
lever les flots au ciel, les verser en torrents.
de Même on voit celui de la belle antoinette,
d'un cœur compatissant devenir l'interprète;
qui S'emeut et S'eleve, et du qu'el les Sanglots,
font Sur le plus beau Sein verser des pleurs en flots.
Quand dans les Sentiments de cette tendre peine

Les dames de la cour se joignant a le reine.
Le bon loüis rempli d'une noble candeur.
dit alors a Franklin, "Monsieur L'ambassadeur.
vous voyez qu'el effet ne vont de mon empire,
les crimes d'albion Sur le peuple produire;
a juger du penchant du Sexe de ma cour.
pour ce Soir c'est assez. mais des que ce Sejour,
reverra rejaillir les rayons de Cynthie.
venez nous achever ce que votre patrie,
a de plus eprouvé des anglais inhumains.
et les faits eclatants des fiers americains"
fin du chant VIe

JOHN F. VACHER

EDITORS' TRANSLATION

Franklin continues the history of the war to Louis XVI
Canto 6, line 745
Close to Pennington, sixteen young shepherdesses
Hid in the depths of their dark forests
To avoid the path of these evil island dwellers.
But to what avail? As if the English infantrymen
Had not committed enough crimes in their hearts,
They surrounded their victims and seized them in these woods.
The captors immolated their modesty on the altar of brutality.
Alas! As we decry the criminal acts of Albion's power,
May the details of this story move
The compassionate souls of all men.
May your majesty and his august court,
Eminent leaders of a great and just people,
And all the powers that consider him a friend,
Be moved to pity by this account.
Not far from the surging Rahway River,
Which fertilizes plains along a thousand streams,
From which one can see the Sound
Lap against New Jersey and Staten Island,
Inhabitants once celebrated the pure delights
Of marriage through holy sacrifice.
Ceres and Pomona graced these places with their oversight
But now they are subject to the fury of Mars.
An English officer forced into a stable
The lovely daughter of one of our residents.
All the neighboring villages, plains, and hills
Echoed with her sad sounds.
The alarmed father ran toward the noise
And seeing his daughter, tearful, bleeding,
Wrongfully sullied by rape,

And in the arms of the monstrous criminal, he justly declared:
"May your barbarous shade hie to the swampy gates of Taenarus!"
And immediately plunged a dagger into the soldier's chest.
Two other officers suddenly appeared
And fired shots from two thundering guns,
Lodging the metal from two whistling bullets
Into the chest of this father whose sad fate
Reduced him to languishing on his deathbed.
Learning about the wanton acts, the king and his court,
Touched by suffering so unjust
That even a tyrant's heart can feel it,
Were stirred into deep silence.
Shining Venus in her azure chariot on the celestial plain
Presented herself to the queen
And said, with her persuasive charm and tender voice:
"O beautiful offspring of the immortal race
Of the pious leader and model to princes,
Descendant of Aeneas, daughter of Caesars,
On whom I bestowed my kindest attention,
You whose meek tender mien
Spreads love and happiness to humans,
O you, my dear daughter, upon whom I chose to bestow my charm and fire,
Know that, when the earth is inhabited by the celestial power of loving mystery,
My wish is that all disputes be silenced,
Whether under the thick veil of nightly shadows,
Or in dense forests or country woods,
Close to where Zephyr plays in a hedge's shade,
And always under the sign of full consent
Between the loving nymph and the fortunate lover!
I am horrified when crazed fanatics
Sully my empire with outrageous acts,
Breaking all the rules of decency.
May my Marie Antoinette,
Who commands the destiny of mortals,
Feel the injustice of an infamy that blackens nature
And avenge the honor of that American woman."
Just as the beautiful Amphitrite's majestic breast
Gently rises and flutters in times of calm,
On the eve of violent autumns
Which unleash heavenly storms and pour forth torrents,
So the compassionate heart of the beautiful Antoinette
Stirred and rose within her breast.
Her weeping spilled waves of tears on that most beautiful chest.
When the ladies of the court joined the queen in this tender pain,
Good King Louis, filled with noble candor, said to Franklin:
"Mr. Ambassador, see how the crimes of Albion
Affect the people of my empire,
Judging by the sentiments of the women of my court.
That is enough for tonight,

But as soon as Cynthia's rays shine again upon this place,
Come and complete the story of what your country
Has suffered at the hands of the barbarous English
And of the brilliant accomplishments of the proud Americans."
End of Canto VI

RC (DLC); above postscript: "His Excellency T. Jefferson Esqr President of the U. States"; ellipses in original; endorsed by TJ as received 16 May and so recorded in SJL.

GORDON IS MY GUIDE: possibly a reference to William Gordon's *The History of the Rise, Progress, and Establishment, of the Independence of the United States of America* (London, 1788; Sowerby, No. 487).

In Greek mythology, Taenarum (TENARE), the southernmost point on the European continent, was believed to have an opening to the realm of Hades (William Smith, ed., *Dictionary of Greek and Roman Geography*, 2 vols. [London, 1854-57], 2:1083-4).

[1] MS: "Your excellency's your Excellency's."

[2] Preceding word written above next word, indicating author's uncertainty which to use.

From Henry Dearborn, with Jefferson's Approval

SIR — War Department May 14th 1805

I have the honor of proposing for your approbation William Lyman Junr. Alexander John Williams and Henry Jonathan Williams as Cadets in the Corps of Artillerists

With high respect and consideration I am Sir Your Obedt. Servant

H. DEARBORN

[*Approval by TJ*:]
May 14. 1805.

Approved

TH: JEFFERSON

RC (PHi: Daniel Parker Papers); in a clerk's hand, signed by Dearborn; at foot of text: "President of the United States"; endorsed by a clerk. FC (Lb in DNA: RG 107, LSP).

YOUR APPROBATION: William Lyman, Jr., was likely the son of William Lyman, the recently appointed consul to London. On 1 Jan., Dearborn wrote to Lyman, informing him that his son would likely receive a cadet appointment in the near future. However, by the time of the appointment, Lyman and his family had already left for London (FC in Lb in DNA: RG 107, MLS; Franklin Bowditch Dexter, *Biographical Sketches of the Graduates of Yale College with Annals of the College History*, 6 vols. [New York, 1885-1912], 3:619; Madison, *Papers, Sec. of State Ser.*, 9:449-50). Alexander John Williams and Henry Jonathan Williams were the sons of Jonathan Williams. On 17 May, Dearborn wrote to their father, informing him of their appointments (ANB, s.v. "Williams, Jonathan"; FC in Lb in DNA: RG 107, LSMA; Heitman, *Dictionary*, 1:1039; biographical information in PPAmP).

From Josiah Wyatt

Dear Sir Newbury Port May 14th. 1805

Whith Respect; As i Am; i think; in duty bound; to write to you Sir; As you Sir; Are Made Choice Of; by the Majority Of the People; Of the United States; Of America; therefore Seek Peace & Persue it; for that Man; that knoweth his Masters Will; & doth it Not; Shall be beatton; Whith Many Stripes; therefor Seek first the kingdom Of God & his Righteousness; & All things Shall be Aded Unto You: As it is Unto me A Servant Of the lord; for: the Promise is; that No good thing Will he Whith hold; from them that Walk uprightly; therfore; dear Sir; Please to buy the truth; & Sell it Not; for in it; Are the Words Of eternal life; Perhaps; you Sir; May buy it; At A Cheaper Rate; than i did: for i have been in irons; for the truths Sake; four years; Whith Out bed Or frire: & All that Men & devills; Was Permitted; to inflict upon me; Never the less: i held to Mine in tegrity; that is; to Conquer Or die in battle; for that Man; Or Woman; that looketh back; After Puting their hand unto the Plough; is Not fit; for the king dom Of heaven; therefore; if you Sir; Are A friend; unto Religon; Please to be Still Pressing forward; for by the Jentlemen Select Men; Of the towns Of Newbury Port; Portsmouth; &; exeter; the Metroplus; Of the State; Of New Hamshire; in My Absence; Judge Smith Gave Orders; to the Select men; to Open My house: unlawfully: Contrary; to the law Of God: Or man; A White Rope; Seems to be to Good for them: for Judges; Or; Our Rulers; to Up hold burgaloary; & high way Robery; What Can be expected Of the Ruled: but; to follow their example; As the Answer; is very Plain; What will be the fatal Consequenceses; it appears to Me; that both Rullers: & Ruled: Are Pulling down; the Judgements Of God: On Our Own heads; As it Were Whith A Cart Rope: thereforore; i See that we as A People; Muist Repent; Or Perish Saith the lord Of hosts: if wee be willing & Obiedent; we Shall eat the good Of the land; but; if we Refuse; & Rebel: We Shall be devour'd Whith the Sword; for the mouth Of the lord; hath Spoken it:

Your Most Obiedent very humble Servant: a friend to Rulers & Ruled:

Josiah Wyatt
of Newbur Port Shipwright

All th'o i had Concluded As your honor will See by My Closing the fore Mentioned lines: As A Wise Man Alters his Mind: So i Continue in writing A few lines in Addition there fore As Justice Must & will take Place in the united States Of America: for the earth is the lords & the fullness thereof; he has A Sovrign Right to do Whith it As Seemeth him Just & Right & None Can Stay his hand Or Say Whith Any Propriety: What dost thou Or Why dost thou So for God has All Power: Nevertheless we are the Means in his hand Of Providence: Of doing good Or evil & Shall Receive Accordingly: therefore let us Rulers & Ruled give God; All the Glory for it is his Just due therefore i Request Restitution: According to the holy law Of Our God; Of the three mentioned towns: this is my Requet that i have Justice done me Whither for Or against Me; yours

JOSIAH WYATT of Newbury Port

in the Name & in the Strength of the lord Of hosts do i Write

PS—if it Should be Agreeable Please to Write me A line Or two

RC (MoSHi: Jefferson Papers); postscript written in margin of first page; addressed: "to thomas Jefferson first Majestrate Of the United States Of America"; postmarked 18 May; endorsed by TJ as received 24 May and "insane" and so recorded in SJL.

Josiah Wyatt (ca. 1777-1823), an alumnus of Phillips Exeter Academy, had been publicly declared non compos mentis in 1801 and placed under a guardianship (*General Catalogue of the Officers and Students of The Phillips Exeter Academy, 1783-1903* [Exeter, N.H., 1903], 4; Portsmouth *New Hampshire Gazette*, 22 Dec. 1801; *Newburyport Herald*, 3 June 1823).

SEEK PEACE & PERSUE IT: Psalms 34:14.

MAN; THAT KNOWETH HIS MASTERS WILL: Luke 12:47.

SEEK FIRST THE KINGDOM OF GOD & HIS RIGHTEOUSNESS: Matthew 6:33.

NO GOOD THING WILL HE WHITH HOLD: Psalms 84:11.

BUY THE TRUTH; & SELL IT NOT: Proverbs 23:23.

LOOKETH BACK; AFTER PUTING THEIR HAND UNTO THE PLOUGH: Luke 9:62.

JUDGE SMITH: possibly Jeremiah Smith, chief justice of New Hampshire and a former probate judge for Rockingham County (ANB).

AS IT WERE WHITH A CART ROPE: Isaiah 5:18.

IF WEE BE WILLING & OBIEDENT: Isaiah 1:19-20.

THE EARTH IS THE LORDS & THE FULLNESS THEREOF: Psalms 24:1 and 1 Corinthians 10:26.

NONE CAN STAY HIS HAND: Daniel 4:35.

From Thomas Carnes

Philadelphia May 15th 58005

from a farther a Brother a Sun honard and Dear Sir that is flatary Tom you Maryed in a Eirish famly War you Cot this o No the Nuse Paper Said Eaighteen Monts a Goe that a yanky Gantlman that had Bin a Riteng in a Eirish Brockers office had Mis Carided and tacken from a B and C Cash from Peter to Pay Pall £95.75896 all So a Brindal Bull hue had a Number of horns on his had No Dout this Brindal Bull Will Be found to your Sorow and you Said I Want to a franch

Scul fifteen year to Se Blind folded I Shall Bring out the a Compleshed Lady Marster of Barsteel hid from the God of thunder thease is the Ladyes that youst to in Ploy a Lowr to Black Ball his one Brother and Slip a Bill of a a thousand Starling in his hand Said Jeses Christ one of you twelve that Dips in this Dish Be trayed Me Said the all Mity God the hiden Seckrit that I Promest to the Juws Before the World Was Shall Cum to Parst for Not a Jot or a tital of My Word But Shall Be fulld fild

Not a Sparow fall to the Ground With out they Noledge for the hars in your had and the Sands in the Sease is Numberid this Can Not Be it is as true as the hare is on your hare is on your had you Can Not Se Me Wan I a Pear to the World With out you are a free Masson from the Resation of the Dad and at Prasant you are Not that or you Wood Not a Put this in the Nuse Paper one God or twenty Wood Not Brack your Lag or Pick your Pocket No God for Bid if it Lays in My Powr to you Nite the younited States I Shall Do it But if I Was to to trie to in Ger you With out Cors I Should Hirt My Salf But in Puting you in your Proper Place I Shall Put Bony Part in his and Every king and I Shall Stand War I orluered Did that No Ware that Ware you all Goe after Dath Can you Look at the Glob and Se the Diffrint Enamals and Say I Master of all and Can you Mack one Sais you My Mony Will Bie tham and Wot Cairs I So My Bad Manars Will Bie Me a Nother Wife and So We Can Go on for Ever No Said I I Stop hear and tack Care of your Childrin Said you you I Can Do My own Work you Do Not Now how Wall it Never two Late to Larn to Do Good thar Was three Man after Me to kill Me I Wars fore Worned By a Star and Stayed in a Chirch tul after one oclok in the State of Conatet and Laft the Chirch a Bout one in the Nite and Cot in a By Place opeset a tavan Dowr and a Bout two a Long theas three Gantlman Came and Raped to the Dowr and Want in and I Returned Back and the Naxt Day Bean Sundy I Drue up a Paper from the Bibal and Gave it to a Biship and he Reseved Me in to the Chirch With the Sants But Pardn Me Dear Sir I Do Not Mean to Be Made a Pope of in Site and Never out of Site My Sun and on ly Sun as the Woman Cald him that I Marid for My Wife Rachal Powrs of Boston thar is Not a Man on Earth that Suffred Wot I have to Save the World and I Shall Do it Dad or a Live for the free Massons in Boston is Cot My Ritans But Wan thea Rote in Books that all Mity God Parst Me Parfict thrue Prisen By thear Rufens Wie Did thea Lat the Docter Pisen Me Be Caus you Nocke the old Lady Down With the Hamar Did I Not Swar to the Lodge of free Massons to Be Jost and true [. . .]ou Did and So I Will I Was Very hapy to hear that Nuse from halafax and Pray to all Mity God that the Blacks Me Be Relased from thar Kruleal and that Bony Part May tack all tham armed Vasels and Sall tham But God for Bid that he Should kill a Man But he is a Man of two Mutch Sanse to Put tham to Dath you had Bater Sand a Vasal for the Man and that Will Larn theas Muny Chtehess

a frand to all Nashans tul Dath THOMAS CARNES

Moro

king of the Juws

Silince  John the Pap[. . .]test

o I had like to for Got Please to Sand Me two hundred Dollars on a Count of Seventy five had of Catly that My farther tuck from the Brutich army With a Party of Man With out orders from Janaral Woshantion and he Sad he Should Be Pade for tham

RC (MHi); torn; possibly misdated; addressed: "Mr Thomas Jafferson Prasadant of the unitedstats of a Maracky"; franked and postmarked; endorsed by TJ as received 14 May and "insane" and so recorded in SJL.

When Thomas Carnes wrote to TJ again, it was from Richmond (4 July and 28 Aug.).

58005: that is, 5805, using the Anno Lucis ("Year of Light") calendar employed by Freemasons, which adds 4,000 to the Anno Domini year (Bernard E. Jones, *Freemasons' Guide and Compendium*, rev. ed. [London, 1956], 373-4).

From James Cheetham

SIR New-york May 15. 1805.

Your letter of the 11th Inst. came duly to hand. The Condescending explanation which it Contains in respect to Mr. Alexander Richards, to whom Mr. Barnes, your agent, had written on the Subject of it, was altogether unnecessary to Convince me of your readiness to do in this, as in all other Cases, what is right. It is my duty, however, to state to you that Mr Richards has not paid to me the $19. which you mention. I am personally acquainted with that Gentleman. He is one of my Subscribers. He left this City on the 6th. Inst. with his family, to Settle in the County of St. Lawrence, in this State. He discharged the trifle which he owed to me the day before he went, but said not a word in relation to any Commands from Mr. Barnes. Excuse, Sir, the trouble which I have given you, and believe me

With perfect esteem, your Sincere friend,

James Cheetham

RC (DLC); at foot of text: "His Excellency Thomas Jefferson President of the U. States"; endorsed by TJ as received 17 May and so recorded in SJL.

From George E. Clymer

Sir — Philada. May 15 1805.

As my favorite method of attacking the Tripolitans has been in part communicated to you by Mr Evans, I think incumbent on me more, more fully, to explain my ideas on that subject.

To capture or destroy their Vessels is the thing we desire: and I think an attack in the following way, if rightly ordered & well conducted would infallibly enable us to attain that end. Let suitable Vessels be furnished with good *fire Engines* which would inable us to throw the water in such torrents on them and into their Port-holes as to prevent them from firing a gun after we get from 60 to 30 yards of their Vessels. Precautions, however ought to be used to prevent them from boarding our Vessels; as that would be their only means of resisting us. The Engines must be placed *below*, to prevent their being injured by the Enemy's shot, before we get near enough to play them and stop their fire. The Engines may have a constant supply of water without any trouble; and as flight would be their only means of escaping, our Vessels ought to be such fast sailers as to enable us to prevent it. As the Vessels proper to put this theory into practice would be light, active and in continual motion I presume that not much danger is to be apprehended from the enemy's Forts, especialy, after our Vessels got intermixed with the enemy; as they would be as likely to injure their own Vessels as ours.

If this mode of Attack should be adopted, I had contemplated to recommend my Patent Pumps for throwing the water, in place of the common fire Engines: but although they have been so much applauded, after long and effectual tryal where all other Pumps on different constructions had failed; Yet as I have not had leisure to try how far they would excel the common Engines in throwing water, (they would nevertheless have the advantage of not occupying above one fourth of the Space on board,) I should recommend those Engines that use has rendered more familiar; as the water can be thrown far enough with them to produce the desired effect.

What I have here said in favour of my Pumps can be so well attested by Judge Peters, and a number of other respectable Gentlemen, that it may possibly be the means of their commanding so much notice at some future period as to be tried and compared with those now in use; for, I conceive, that a knowledge of their superiority is all the recommendation they want, not only to justify those that have it in their power to adopt them in our Navy, but to make it their duty so to do.

If it should however be the Opinion of those Gentlemen, whom you may think proper to consult, and who must be better acquainted with the harbour of Tripoli than I am, that no advantages could be derived from such a mode of Attack, I hope Sir that you will have the goodness to pardon me for thus troubling you; whose mind has been much more excercised in conceiving Ideas than his pen has been in describing them; which will in some measure explain why it is so imperfectly done

I am Sir yr. Obedt Servt GEOE. CLYMER.

RC (DLC); at foot of text: "To Thoms Jefferson Prest. U.S."; endorsed by TJ as received 18 May and so recorded in SJL.

Born in Bucks County, Pennsylvania, George E. Clymer (ca. 1754-1834) received a U.S. patent in 1801 for a ship's pump and patents from Great Britain in 1817 and 1827 for his Columbian printing press. During the War of 1812, Clymer approached President Madison with a similar plan for using pumps to disable enemy warships (DAB; *List of Patents*, 26; Bennet Woodcroft, *Patents for Inventions: Abridgements of Specifications Relating to Printing* [London, 1859], 136-7, 176-7; Madison, *Papers, Pres. Ser.*, 6:324-7; Jacob Kainen, *George Clymer and the Columbian Press* [San Francisco, 1950], 9-22; Vol. 35:610-11).

COMMUNICATED TO YOU: see Oliver Evans to TJ, 8 May.

WHAT I HAVE HERE SAID: on the same day, Clymer wrote another letter, not found, which TJ forwarded to the State Department (Appendix IV; TJ to Clymer, 23 May).

From Henry Dearborn, with Jefferson's Approval

SIR, War Department May 15, 1805

I have the honor of proposing, for your approbation Satterlee Clark & Eleazer D Wood as Cadets in the Corps of Artillerists.

With high respect and consideration I am Sir, Your Obedt. Servt.

H. DEARBORN

[*Approval by TJ*:]

May 15. 1805.

Approved TH: JEFFERSON

RC (PHi: Daniel Parker Papers); in a clerk's hand, signed by Dearborn; at foot of text: "President of the U States"; endorsed by a clerk. FC (Lb in DNA: RG 107, LSP).

Satterlee CLARK served in the army as an artillerist and as a paymaster until his discharge in 1824. Eleazer WOOD received brevet promotions for gallantry during the War of 1812 and died during the siege of Fort Erie (Heitman, *Dictionary*, 1:305, 1054).

From David Gelston

SIR, New York May 15th. 1805

Enclosed is Capt. Grennelds bill of lading for two cases of wine, I also enclose an account of the expenses I have paid on the several parcels I have received,—and have the honor to be,

with much sincerity and respect, Sir, your obedient servant

DAVID GELSTON

RC (MHi); at foot of text: "Thomas Jefferson President United States"; endorsed by TJ as received 19 May and so recorded in SJL; also endorsed by TJ: "June 6. 05. pd. by draft on the US. at N.Y. 111 D 82." Enclosures not found.

From Samuel Harrison

MOST REVERED SIR Chittenden Vermont May 15th. 1805

When an unknown individual shall attempt to arise from obscurity, and address the greatest Character in the Nation, the natural enquiry will be: From whence comes this Audacity?

If I may be permitted to answer. It is from different motives, concentrating to one Focus: the Prosperity of the United States. The Motives are, To ameliorate the condition & civilize some of the aboriginal Inhabitants, Together with the extinction of the native right of soil within the limits of the Union, And the emolument of myself & connections.—

Another interrogatory will certainly follow. How can these desideratoes be accomplished?

I acknowledge Sir, I feel inadequate to the task of accomplishment; but with your Excellency's approbation & patronage I will contribute my Mite: And beg leave to state some preliminary incidents connected with what are premised.

And First I would inform your Excellency. That my native country is England: but my adopted one the United States. My Father with his Family migrated from Derbyshire in 1771 to Masachusetts and I resided there untill 1776: when in the beginning of January I engaged in the revolutionary War & marched to assist in the Blockade of Quebec I returned in June but soon engaged again and was mostly in the service of the country for nearly three years, though I never belonged to the regular line of the Army. I was in Bennington Battle & assisted in the reduction & capture of Genl. Burgoyne &c. After my return from the Army I married a young Woman in 1780 by the name of Keeler—And in 1783, accompanied with my wife's Brother, I again migrated from Massachusetts to Vermont & have been mostly immured in Chittenden almost ever since. My Wife's Brother Capt. Seth Keeler Died in 1790 & left a number of children, amongst whom he had a son named Seth Keeler, who several years ago married a daughter of Rufus Carver, the third child, and, first Son of Capt. Jonathan Carver, a descendant of John Carver once Governor of the then Colony of Massachusetts. This Capt. Jona. Carver bore a conspicuous share of the French War, before the American revolution: And after the Peace of Paris in 1763, He went a Journey to the Westward, explored the regions then unknown, or but partially known, to the Anglo Americans.

From Michillimakinac, I think, he proceeded to Green Bay, then to Winnebaga, then ascended Fox river, thence crossed to the Onisconsing, which he descended to the Missisippi; then ascended the Missisippi and wintered amongst the Naudowessaw Indians; and forming a reconciliation between the Naudowessian & Chippewaw Tribes; who had been long at enmity. As a compensation for his conciliatory services, He received from the Indians a DEED of a large Tract of Land within the present Limits of the now United States—Beginning at St. Anthony's Falls on the Missisippi then down the Missisippi to Lake Pepin where the Chippeway river enters the Lake. Then up the Chippeway a considerable distance, which I have forgotten. but I think, about 100 miles to a certain Boundary therein specified, which, I cannot at present ascertain, thence to another; And from that to St. Anthony's Falls—

Capt Carver returned to his Family in Massachusetts informed them of what had transpired and embarked for England to get from the authority of the Nation a ratification of his Indian DEED. But deceasing while in England; and the revolution commencing his Family & Friends have, untill lately, remained almost entirely ignorant of what had transpired—Since that it has been reported that hearing of the death of his wife he married again while there and had for[. . .] one Daughter in that Country. He left in America Two Sons & five daughters, who have since married and had Children & some of them,

Grandchildren, which now amount to between thirty and forty, some of whom have ventured to sell their Title to said Land—
His Children & friends have Used Various efforts to obtain his Papers from England, but in vain—a book of his Travels has been published & his transactions with the Indians made known but his children despaired off arriving at the knowledge of any thing more satisfactory respecting his transatlantic affairs untill an* extract from a London paper certified, "That a daughter off Capt Carver had been discovered, in obscurity in England, who was sole heiress of a Large tract of Land Situated on the Missisippi" &c.—After this Publication Mr Rufus Carver, son of the Capt., knowing I had kept a correspondence with my Friends in England, desired my assistance to help once more to discover what had transpired in that Country and get confirmed, if possible the Grant from the Indians, to Capt Carvers Heirs & their Assigns that right their progenitor had, with so much Labour acquired—
I Engaged to exert my feeble Abilities. And in pursuance of my task I have written to a Gentleman there of Talents sufficient to explore if possible the mystery of concealment. I am in daily expectation of an answer from him; when I promise myself and employers some sort of developement.
Since my engament with Mr. Carver I have been revolving in my own mind what method to pursue, to get if possible a confirmation from the authority of the United States. and being deficient in knowlege, I have asked the advice of my friends which way to proceed. but I find that different Persons devise different means, some advise me to Petition Congress and to make an Interest in that body—&c. But considering many circumstances I have ventured into the Ocean rather than to attempt to navigate the streams—I have ventured to address your Excellency rather than others, To whom I must make an introduction to introduce me to yourself for advice.
I have been emboldened to this by conversing with sundry Gentlemen who have had acquaintance with Gentlemen, acquainted with your Excellency—Particularly with a Col. Mitchell of Easton who has been a member of the Legislature of Massachusetts for about twenty years. In conversation with him I asked his advice what method I had best to pursue. he advised me "to write to your Excellency and state facts without any reserve. For though he had not the honour of a Personal Acquaintance he had been informed by some who had that honour (particularly Mr. Otis his former Colleague) That your Excellency was possessed of the most extensive knowledge of any Gentle-

*The report alluded to as above

man in the Union and would be free to Communicate upon a Subject of such magnitude."—

Thus Sir have I attempted to extenuate myself from Audacity and have laid aside that reserve I might have otherwise felt.

I have stated some trifling incidents which though insignificant in themselves may prove to be pregnant with mighty consequences not only to Individuals but, to the future Inhabitants of the United States.

May not these be some means Sir by which some of, "The aboriginal inhabitants of these countries" may be "regarded with the commisseration their history inspires"—That their condition may be ameliorated "By teaching them agriculture and the domestic Arts" And while your Excellency has employed a remaing revenue "To extinguish the native right of soil" with the Kasskasskians may not this purchase of Capt Carvers be applied to extinguish the claims of the Chipeway or Naudowessy Natives? And thus the Missisippi would *only* be embarrassed by the Native Claim from Lake Pepin to Kaskaskia River. The head of Navigation will by these means be clear & the remainder will be the more easily extinguished—

But I would not presume to dictate a Gentleman, or give information upon a subject on which I desire advice—Yet I pray your Excellency would investigate the same, and condescend to communicate to me the best method of securing to the Heirs of Capt. Jona. Carver and their Assigns—"That portion of Property which results to every man from his own Industry or that of his Fathers"—

I hope Your Excellency will forgive my rusticity and egotisms in this unpolished address & be pleased to grant my request, and give me your advice, & Direct to Saml. Harrison, Chittenden county of Rutland Vermont—Which will confer the greatest obligation on your

most obedient, though unknown yet humble servant

SAML. HARRISON

RC (DLC); torn; addressed: "His Excellency Thomas Jefferson President of the United States Washington Monticello or elsewhere"; franked; endorsed by TJ as received 11 June and so recorded in SJL.

Samuel Harrison (1756-1813) served in militia units during the American Revolution, sometimes as an officer. An early settler of Chittenden, Vermont, he served as clerk for the town proprietors and as a tax collector. In 1791, he represented the town at the state convention held to ratify the U.S. Constitution (Windsor *Spooner's Vermont Journal*, 15 July 1794; Abby Maria Hemenway, *The Vermont Historical Gazetteer: A Magazine, Embracing a History of Each Town, Civil, Ecclesiastical, Biographical and Military*, 3 [1877], 549-52; *Book of Biographies: This Volume Contains Biographical Sketches of Leading Citizens of Rutland County, Vermont* [Buffalo, 1899], 387; E. P. Walton, ed., *Records of the Governor and Council of the State of Vermont*, 8 vols. [Montpelier, 1873-80], 3:466, 480).

NAUDOWESSAW INDIANS: Harrison's terminology was derived from the Ottawa name for the eastern band of the Dakota Sioux, who fought intermittently with the Southwestern Chippewa, or Ojibwa, during the eighteenth century and with increased intensity during the nineteenth (Sturtevant, *Handbook*, 13, pt. 2:749; 15:744-5).

The GENTLEMAN with whom Harrison corresponded was Samuel Peters, an American-born Anglican minister then in London, who would ultimately become the principal claimant to the purported grant to Jonathan Carver (Milo M. Quaife, "Jonathan Carver and the Carver Grant," *Mississippi Valley Historical Review*, 7 [1920], 3-25; correspondence in MnHi; Gallatin to TJ, 13 Dec. 1804).

ABORIGINAL INHABITANTS: here and subsequently, Harrison quoted from TJ's second inaugural address.

CHITTENDEN COUNTY: properly, Chittenden, a town in Rutland County.

From Daniel L. Hylton

DEAR SIR Richmond Virginia May 15th. 1805

Having engag'd a Mill Wright to build me a Mill on McCombs patent plan, of which I presume a Model is lodg'd in the Archives of the general Government, & being apprehensive the undertaker is not thoroughly acquainted with the principles of it obliges me to lay myself under the disagreeable necessity of making application to a friend to endeavour to procure the plan for me. I have no acquaintance at the federal City I can venture to take that liberty with of doing me such a favour, indeed it is painful to me to ask this of you, as I well know your time is so much occupied with governmental business to render any personal attention, but if there is any mechanic with you, that can draw an accurate plan, I shall consider it an obligation confer'd on me if you will be so good as to have it done, for which I will with pleasure reimburse any expenses attending it, on knowing the amot., the favour will be thankfully acknowledgd by

Your Friend & Servt DANL L HYLTON

PS will you be good enough to give me your private opinion of its operation, & whether it takes much more Water than an Overshot Mill—

RC (DLC); endorsed by TJ as received 19 May and so recorded in SJL; endorsed by William Thornton: "Mr. Macomb's Patent is dated on the 26th: Augst. 1791. and expires in 14 yrs."

James Macomb's PATENT was for a horizontal hollow water wheel (ASP, *Miscellaneous*, 1:423).

From William Jarvis

Sir Lisbon 15th. May 1805

I had the honor to address you the 6 Octr. and the 14th. & 25 Novr. past, the latter accompanied by a pipe of Arruda Wine (the name of an estate within the termo of Lisbon) which I shall be happy to learn was to your satisfaction. As the amount was small I have omitted drawing for it in hopes to be favoured with your commands for another when Sir I will include both in a Bill—

I should oftener Sir take the liberty to address you did I not fear to obtrude upon that time which is so usefully employed in your Country's service: but what at all times would be a gratification to me, had I any thought of sufficient moment to interest or was it in my power to afford you profit or amusement, at this time becomes a duty. A Mr. Lewis Pontin of New York was some time ago at Montpellier when Monsr. Chretien a Physician of eminence of that place charged him with the accompanying treatise on administering of external remedies in different disorders, which this Gentleman has confided to my care to forward, as he is not going to the United States. A reflection naturally arising out of this present is, that it appears astonishing how any thinking man, whose mind is not warped by early prejudice, can be the advocate of an Hereditary System; when the honor a Nation confers on itself by the choice of a first Magistrate who is looked up to by the learned as the criterion of literary merit, is compared to the unmeaning homage that is paid to a Crown by its subjects.

Your elegant inaugural speech must afford much pleasure to every American who has not the interest of his party more at heart than the welfare of his Country. Your wit Sir may be compared to a new smooth razor, which cuts to the heart before the subject is aware that the wound is inflicted. But sir as there are few of our actions or expressions that misrepresentation cannot give an unfavourable turn to here possibly you may be accused of not discovering your wonted humanity; for to destroy those little ephemerous Gentlemen, your enemies, with two & forty pounders, because they have been pelting you with pellets of mud for several years, may by some, of an overstrained nicety & tenderness of feelings, be considered as taking too great an advantage of your superior powers. The view given of our finances, the objects pointed out for Legislative & public attention, and which by a system of wise oeconomy there is a prospect of being carried into execution at no very remote period, does as much honor Sir to your heart as it does to your head. If, as I think history somewhere relates, a few hours sufferings of an obscure individual, and the benefits implied from the general benevolence of his temper that he was desirous of conferring on mankind, have been considered by millions as merits worthy of adoration, what is due to a man who has for a length of time successfully employed pre-eminent abilities & profound knowledge to promote & perpetuate the welfare of his Countrymen and I may add the human race, notwithstanding his system, his plans & himself have been attacked with all the rage & virulence of disappointed malice? As the world has become too sensible, well-informed & enlightened to admit the most distant idea of adoration, the gratitude of posterity will no doubt confer the humbler but more durable honor, of ranking him among those Legislators & Philosophers who have contributed most to the happiness of their fellow Man.

Assuring you Sir of my most perfect Veneration I have the honor to be Sir Yr Mo: Ob: Servt. William Jarvis

RC (DLC); at foot of text: "Thomas Jefferson Esquire"; endorsed by TJ as received 1 July and so recorded in SJL. Enclosure: Jean André Chrestien to TJ, 20 Aug. 1804.

From Pendleton District, South Carolina, Sixteenth Regiment

We the people of the 16th. Regt. Commanded by Leut. Coln Eliab Moore, Assembled on public Occasion, & Again Address you and repeat our unshaken Confidence in your Administration after your first Election it was suggested by some that we was premature but sufficient specimen had been given of the rectitude of your mind and purity of Intention to convince us the Portrait was not Improperly drawn; as we were Among the first that did Publicly avow and testify our hearty approbation of your Measures in Goverment, so we should be Among the last that would fall under the Temptation of Illicit power we revere men in Office for their good dispositions only and who manifestly labour to distribute Justice and promote equality

Witness for the Regiment respectfully I am E. Brown

South Carolina
Pendleton District
15th May 1805

RC (DLC); at head of text: "To Thomas Jefferson President of the United States of America"; endorsed by TJ as received 26 May and so recorded in SJL.

For the 16th Regiment's previous address to the president and TJ's reply, see Vol. 34:27-8, 268-9.

From Philippe Reibelt

MONSIEUR LE PRESIDENT! Baltimore le 15 Mai 1805.

Permettez—qu'en Qualitè d'amateurs practiques de l'Agriculture—je Vous presente la Question, si Vous n'avez jamais cultivè le *petit Maïs d'Italie*, nommè: *Quarantino* (Zea Mays I. var. præcox, humïlis) qui donne sur 40,000 pieds □ depuis le Mois de Mars 4 recoltes, chaque à 8000 ℔—mes. francaise—qui'on a—il y a 5 Ans, commencé de Cultiver *en Suisse* avec *le même Succes*—excepté la 4me. recolte &c. — Et dans le Cas negatif, s'il Vous feroit plaisir, d'en avoir quelques grains avec les Observations necessaires?

J'ai l'honneur, de Vous saluer avec le plus profond, et le plus sincere respect.

REIBELT

EDITORS' TRANSLATION

MISTER PRESIDENT! Baltimore, 15 May 1805

Given our shared interest in agriculture, permit me to ask you a question. Have you ever grown the small Italian corn known as Zea Mays I, *quarantino*, *praecox*, *humilis*? Since March it has produced four harvests on a 40,000-square-foot field, each harvest yielding 8,000 pounds in French weight. Five years ago the corn was first planted in Switzerland with the same success, except for the fourth harvest, etc. If you have not planted it, would you like to have some seeds with the necessary instructions?

I have the honor of sending you my deepest and most sincere respect.

REIBELT

RC (DLC); endorsed by TJ as received 16 May and so recorded in SJL.

MAÏS D'ITALIE: TJ maintained an interest in propagating this variety of corn, which he most often rendered as "quarentine." By 1806 it made up a portion of the corn planted at Monticello (Betts, *Garden Book*, 336, 446; TJ to Thomas Mann Randolph, 2 June 1805; TJ to Christian Mayer, 20 June 1806; TJ to John Mason, 20 June 1806; Thomas Digges to TJ, 30 June 1806; William Hamilton to TJ, 7 July 1806; Bernard McMahon to TJ, 12 July 1806; McMahon to TJ, 26 Dec. 1806; TJ to Edmund Bacon, 21 Nov. 1806; memorandum to Bacon, 13 May 1807).

From William Short

May 15 [1805]

Jeffn. P.—ansr. his of May 4. & inclose note annulled—being supplied by that he inclosed for $7910.84—Vin du Cahusac—will write again—expect my sister hre—if not embarked. the pleasure of seeing him at Monti. will have great weight in deciding my route

FC (DLC: Short Papers); partially dated; entirely in Short's hand, consisting of an entry in his epistolary record. Recorded in SJL as received from Philadelphia on 17 May.

From Elisha Avery

SIR, Boston. May 16. 1805.

On my arrival in this place from Washington, I thought proper, in consequence of the favour which you deigned to confer on me while there, to apply to Genl Hull for the Office of Marshal of the Territory of Michigan.—Among the papers which I presented to Genl Hull, I took the liberty of laying before him the *note* which you did me the honour to write me, concerning the same appointment.—Genl Hull appeared *then* much disposed & *still* manifests a strong disposition to encourage my wishes: but not having had any communication from Your Excellency with regard to one which, I gave him cause to expect he would recieve, he hesitates giving me a definitive answer on the subject, hoping still to be indulged with some communication from you with respect to this affair.—Calculating with a degree of certainty on being favoured by the Government, I had resolved on going to Detroit; and though I have not as yet any positive assurance of an Office there I shall pursue my determination, trusting to the hopes that Genl Hull is pleased to afford me, that I shall not be disappointed should he not derive from You Sir some reasons, contravening his & my expectations.—I am aware Sir that the Proofs which I have already given you of my character & merits cannot authorise me to expect any considerable interest from you in my behalf.

I relied however on being able to make good my Pretensions to Genl Hull & hoped Sir that you would have so far attested my wishes, as to have enabled him to understand, that his conduct in Prefering me would be sanctioned by your approbation, in case he found in me those qualifications recommendatory to encouragement & confidence.—I have thought it probable Sir that Genl Hull would make mention of me to You in some of his communications, & that you would reply to his enquiries.—The object of this letter Sir is solely to request that you will condescend to trust to the evidence which I shall produce *him* instead of weighing my character & principles wholly by the testimony which I have hitherto furnished you, as I never considered those certificates as sufficient to give me full title to Notice & credit.

I hope for pardon Sir of my importunities, when I assure you that my Sole aim in seeking a Publick employment, is to secure me an independant existance, by proving my attachment to my Country & my Zeal for the continuance & promotion of the present wise & happy administration: believing that were I to be granted a share of publick confidence, I might be enabled to evince some claim to Patronage, & gain to myself such friends & such support as would tend to further my desire of arriving at usefulness & respectability.—

I have the honor to be with the Most Profound respect Your Excellency's Most Obdt huml Servt E. AVERY

RC (DNA: RG 59, LAR); addressed: "His Excellency Thomas Jefferson Esqe President of the United States"; endorsed by TJ as received 22 May and so recorded in SJL.

NOTE: TJ to Avery, 17 Feb.

From Henry Dearborn

SIR May 16th. 1805

Alth'o the sentence of the Court Martial upon Lt. Harper is an unusual one, I presume it will be safe, & not improper for you to approve it.

Yours, H. DEARBORN

RC (DLC); addressed: "The President of the United States"; endorsed by TJ as received from the War Department on 16 May with notation "Sentence on Harper."

In 1803, Lieutenant William A. HARPER of the Washington militia was charged with pocketing funds meant for the purchase of troop refreshments. At his initial hearing in 1804, he accused his commanders of incompetence. He followed that with a disparaging letter published in the *Alexandria Daily Advertiser*. In May 1805, Harper was formally acquitted of the initial charge, but found guilty of behavior unbecoming of an officer, in particular, the "disorderly, indecorous and disrespectful manner" in which he treated members of the court and his superior officers. He was sentenced to a five-year suspension of his command (*Alexandria Daily Advertiser*, 20 Sep. 1804; *National Intelligencer*, 31 May 1805).

To George Dyson

SIR Washington May 16. 05.

I wrote by the John Adams to mr Woodhouse of Marsalla, desiring him to send me a pipe of Marsalla wine. by an arrangement with mr Smith the Secretary of the Navy, I was authorised to desire mr Woodhouse to draw on you for paiment, with an assurance that your draught on the Navy department should be placed to the credit of your account with the US. this was done, and I inclosed to mr Woodhouse a letter of advice to be forwarded to you. another opportunity now offering of writing to you directly, I avail myself of it to inclose a duplicate for mr Woodhouse, which I ask the favor of you to forward, with such information as to the paiment of his bill as you may deem proper. Accept my salutations & respects. TH: JEFFERSON

PoC (DLC); at foot of text: "Mr. Thomas Dyson, Navy agent of the US. at Syracuse," with notation "shd be George"; endorsed by TJ. PoC of Dupl (same); with postscript: "June 28. 1805. the original of this by the Huntress, having been intercepted by a belligerent privateer, this Duplicate is now forwarded, covering a triplicate for mr Woodhouse"; endorsed by TJ. Enclosure: TJ to John Woodhouse, 5 May.

Notes on Appointments

[on or before 16 May 1805]

War.	Nominations	
Consuls.	Havanna.[1]	Cross. capt. George. S.C. late of the navy. Pierce Butler. Hill Henry junr.
rejected	Sto. Domingo.	Wm. Walton. Maryland. mercht. S. Sterett. Bp. Carroll
Vienna.[2]	✓ the port &[3] district of. Collector & Inspector of the revenue. Algernon Sidney Stanford of Maryld v. Francis removd	
Slade's creek	✓ Surveyor & Inspector of the revenue[4] for the port of. Ormond Tuley of N.C. v. Henry Tuley resd.	
E. Tennissee	✓ Atty. Edward Scott v. Thos. Gray. qu?	
	✓ Marshll.[5] Charles Tenant Porter to be contd.	
Orleans.	2d. Judges. ^✓Thruston. <*Abr. Baldwin not appble*>	
	Atty.[6] James Brown	
	✓ Surveyor. Porter	
Natchez.	Reciever. John Henderson. Sheilds[7]	
	✓ Register. Thomas Hill Williams	
	✓ Governor. <*Wilkinson. Rodney. Claiborne.*> Hammond.[8] Williams J. Brown	
	✓ Judge. Obediah Jones of Georgia v. Kerr decd.	
Ft. Stoddart.	Receiver. <*Rodomonic H. Gilmer of Tombigb. settlemt. Winston*> Smith	

Michigan. ✓ Governor. Hull <*Granger*>
Huntington Saml. Ohio

✓ Secretary Griswold Stanley. Conn.
<*Solomon Sibley of Michigan*>

Judges. Huntington speaks French <*Arthur Lee speaks French*> Woodward <*Root*> Jouett

Atty

Marshall.[9] Avery. speaks French.

Louisiana. Commandt. John B. Scott Virga v. Kennon.[10] Jackson of Ten. [. . .]

Govr. <*Hammond*>. Wilkinson

Judges. Meigs. Lucas. <*Root*>

Secretary

land titles. Woodward. Hunt

Atty. [. . .].[11] Andrew Epple. Mc.Kean. John Kennedy. Ten. legislators

Marshal. James Mc.Kay. see Louisa list. Gratiot

Naples Judge Admiralty. Jonathan. Russell. Christopher Ellery

New York Judge of the District ct. of N.Y. v. Hobart decd. Brockholst Livingston

MS (DLC: TJ Papers, 155:27137); undated; entirely in TJ's hand; in ink and pencil, with portions in pencil noted below; faint; on verso of sheet addressed in an unidentified hand: "The President of the United States."

This list comprises potential appointments that TJ considered from January to May 1805. He almost certainly compiled it in several sittings, sometimes entering names shortly after receiving recommendations and other times recurring to information that had come to him long before the making of the list. Many of the names show up in TJ's nominations to the Senate of 28 Jan., 26 Feb., 1 Mch., and 2 Mch., while others became recess appointments or ultimately were not nominated.

Although most names on the list were candidates for appointment, some were those of individuals who put forward the candidates. PIERCE BUTLER, for example, had recommended George Cross for the consulship at Havana in October 1803. The commission ended up going to Henry Hill, Jr. (TJ to Madison, 11 Mch.). The administration received a recommendation for William Walton, Jr., from Samuel STERETT and possibly from Bishop John Carroll, although no such communication from Carroll has been found (Madison, *Papers, Sec. of State Ser.*, 8:82).

The nominees for positions in ORLEANS Territory reflect information TJ obtained early in January, when he received a recommendation for Andrew Porter and learned that James Brown would prefer to be U.S. attorney (see enclosure to William C. C. Claiborne to TJ, 25 Nov. 1804; TJ to Claiborne, 7 Jan. 1805). Porter and Buckner Thruston were nominated to the Senate on 26 Feb., but TJ waited until receiving Brown's rejection of his previously issued judicial commission before giving him a recess appointment as U.S. attorney (see TJ to Madison, 11 Mch.).

The large number of emendations, many of them in pencil, indicate the unsettled status of TJ's choices for Mississippi Territory and the newly created territories of Michigan and Louisiana. JOHN HENDERSON was first recommended to become the receiver of the land office at Natchez in December (William Turnbull and Thomas Ewing to John Smith of Ohio, 7 Dec. 1804, in DNA: RG 59, LAR; endorsed by TJ: "Henderson John to be Reciever Natchez"). Next to Henderson's name, TJ added in pencil the candidate William B. Shields, who had been recommended for the position by Caesar A. Rodney in a letter of 6 July 1804, not found (see Vol. 44: Appendix IV). For the receiver of the land office at Fort Stoddert (STODDART) on the Mobile River, TJ may have chosen to replace his initial choice of Rodominick Gilmer with Joseph Winston before canceling that selection in favor of someone named Smith, possibly Thomas Smyth, Jr., who had been recommended to TJ as a customs officer several times, most recently in a letter of 8 Dec. 1804 from Gallatin that has not been found (Vol. 45: Appendix IV; see also Vol. 43:684).

For the judgeship of the federal DISTRICT court of New York, TJ nominated Daniel Tompkins on 1 Mch. After learning that Tompkins had turned down the appointment, however, TJ determined by 16 May that a commission should go to BROCKHOLST LIVINGSTON, who had been previously recommended for the position (William Keteltas to TJ, 16 Feb.; TJ to the Senate, 1 Mch.; Madison to TJ, 1 Apr.; TJ to the State Department, 16 May).

[1] Before preceding word, TJ added a square bracket in pencil.

[2] TJ numbered in pencil the four subsequent check marks, 3, 4, 2, and 1, respectively, the numbers corresponding with the order in which he submitted the nominations to the Senate on 28 Jan.

[3] Preceding word and ampersand interlined.

[4] Preceding ampersand and four words interlined.

[5] Before preceding word, TJ added a square bracket in pencil.

[6] Before preceding word, TJ added a square bracket in pencil.

[7] Preceding name in pencil.

[8] Preceding four names in pencil.

[9] Remainder of entry in pencil.

[10] Positions and names from this point to "Gratiot," with the exception of "Root," written in pencil.

[11] Several words illegible.

To James Oldham

SIR Washington May 16. 05.

As judge Gantt's first letter gave me reason to expect a 2d immediately, I have waited to recieve that. it came to hand last night and I now inclose you both. as your action at Common law is dismissed, and you are not one of the Suitors in the Chancery proceeding I do not understand how you are to share with those who are. but of this mr Gantt is a better judge. if I can at any time see mr Hewitt I will enquire of him what your prospects are, & at all times hand on to you any information from him. I surmise that little is to be hoped. Accept my best wishes.

TH: JEFFERSON

PoC (DLC); at foot of text: "Mr. Oldham"; endorsed by TJ. Enclosures: (1) John Mackell Gantt to TJ, 8 May, not found (see Appendix IV). (2) Gantt to TJ, 15 May, not found (see Appendix IV).

To the State Department

A Commission to Brockhurst Livingston of New York to be District judge of New York.

Thomas Fenwick of Washington county in the district of Columbia to be a justice of the peace for the sd county Th: Jefferson

May 16. 05.

PoC (DLC). Notation in SJL: "Nomns. Brock. Livingston. Thos. Fenwick."

From William Lee

Sir United States Consulate Bordeaux May 17th 1805

When the reputation of an officer of the United States is unjustly attacked, it is a duty he owes the Government and himself to vindicate his character. How far I have succeeded in this particular the annexed correspondence will shew. I beg leave Sir with great deference to lay it before you reposing the utmost confidence in that justice which so eminently distinguishes your administration.—

With the highest Veneration I have the honor to remain Your devoted humble Servant. Wm. Lee

RC (DLC); at head of text: "To the President of the United States"; endorsed by TJ as received 8 July and so recorded in SJL. Enclosures not identified.

To Philippe Reibelt

Washington May. 17. 05.

Th: Jefferson presents his salutations to mr Reibelt, and his thanks for the Communication of the Catalogues, which he now returns except 1. the Notice de la galerie des Antiques, & the Catalogues des estampes. the 1st. of these appearing to be a *complete* catalogue of the new acquisitions of the Museum, and the other comprehending matter new to him altogether, he begs leave to detain them a little longer for further examination. the species of corn mentioned by mr Reibelt, yielding 4. crops a year is entirely unknown to Th: Jefferson to whom a few grains will be very acceptable, and shall be immediately planted here.

PoC (DLC); endorsed by TJ.

CATALOGUES: see Reibelt to TJ, 12 May.

From Philippe Reibelt

MONSIEUR LE PRESIDENT! Baltimore le 17 Mai 1805

J'ai l'honneur, de Vous avertir, que j'ai pris la Libertè, de Vous adresser par le Schooner Polly & Sally d'Alexandrie une petite Caisse contenant les Livres specifiès, cijoint—dans la supposition, que leur examen Vous fera passer quelques moments agreablement, et que—peût etre—Quelques uns Vous Conviendroient—pour Vous, pour votre famille, et pour la bibliotheque des Departemens d'etat.

C'est le dernier extrait de mon premier transport, qui merite d'etre presentè a Vous.

Je Vous prie d'accepter mes profonds homages. REIBELT

EDITORS' TRANSLATION

MISTER PRESIDENT! Baltimore, 17 May 1805

I have the honor of informing you that I took the liberty of sending a small box on the schooner *Polly & Sally* from Alexandria containing the attached list of books, assuming that you would enjoy looking at them and would perhaps wish to acquire some for your family and the libraries of government bureaus.

It is the final part of my first shipment to warrant your consideration.

Please accept my deep regards. REIBELT

RC (DLC); above signature: "Le Depot de Levr. Schoell et Comp. a Paris"; endorsed by TJ as received 17 May and so recorded in SJL. Enclosure not found, but see below.

UNE PETITE CAISSE: TJ purchased a portion of the works Reibelt sent in this box, returning the remainder on 24 June (TJ to Reibelt, 29 May, 21 June, 24 June; List of Books Purchased from Philippe Reibelt, at 26 June).

To P. & C. Roche

Washington May 17. 05.

By a catalogue of yours published in Philadelphia, I percieve that you have the following books which I will ask the favor of you to send me, to wit

Connaissance des tems pour l'année 1806. avec les additions.

Leçons d'histoire par Volney. 2. v. 8vo.
Voyage d'Antenor en Grece. 3. v. 8vo.
Diccionario portatil Español-Ingles & Ingles-Español. por Gattel, 2. v. 16o.
should you also have the Connaissance des tems for the present year 1805. it will be acceptable. I observe you have Montucla complete. should you have the additional part by de la Lande to dispose of separately, I shall be glad of it. I already possess the original work of Montucla in 2. vols 4to. & want only the Additions.

If these books are well wrapped in strong paper, fortified by bits of paste-board on the exterior, and delivered at the Stage office addressed to me at this place, they will come safely. the cost shall be remitted as soon as made known to me. Accept my salutations & respects.

TH: JEFFERSON

PoC (MHi); at foot of text: "Messrs. P. & C. Roche"; endorsed by TJ.

Brothers and partners Peter (Pierre) and Christian Roche were French booksellers, with a shop and circulating library at 53 Walnut Street and later at 40 South Fourth Street in Philadelphia. TJ became a regular customer from 1805 to 1807. By 17 May 1809, the Roches frères had settled in New Orleans and opened a store selling foreign-language books (*Aurora*, 21 May 1805; *Relfs Philadelphia Gazette*, 26 July 1806; John M. Goudeau, "Booksellers and Printers in New Orleans, 1764-1885," *Journal of Library History*, 5 [1970], 9; MB, 2:1155, 1177, 1206, 1214; RS, 4:72n, 80).

VOYAGE D'ANTENOR EN GRECE: *Voyages d'Antenor en Grèce et en Asie, avec des notions sur l'Égypte* was translated by Étienne François de Lantier (Sowerby, No. 4331).

DICCIONARIO: Claude Marie Gattel published the pocket dictionary, *Nuevo diccionario portatil, Español é Ingles*, in Paris in 1803 (same, No. 4813).

Jean Étienne MONTUCLA died in 1799 during the printing of the third volume of his *Histoire des mathématiques*. His friend Joseph Jérôme Le Français de Lalande edited and completed the third and fourth volumes, which were published in Paris in 1802 (same, No. 3694).

From John Taggart

SIR

Philada. May 17th. 1805

I recd. your esteemed favor of the 2nd. Inst., and according to your instructions have Shipped the White Lead, on board the Schooner Liberty Captn. Fisher, bound for Richmond, to the care of Messrs. Gibson & Jefferson, She is to sail to morrow—Enclosed is a Bill of the same, and will at all times be happy to fill any Orders you may please to honor me with, with care & fidelity—

I am Your Obt. Servt

JOHN TAGGART

N.B. You have Bill of Lading enclosed likewise.

RC (MHi); at head of text: "Thomas Jefferson President of the UStates"; endorsed by TJ as received 19 May and so recorded in SJL; also endorsed by TJ: "June 6. 05. inclosd. draft on bk US. at Philada for 86.42." Enclosures not found.

From William Tatham

SIR/ Jefferson Street George Town, 17th. May 1805,

During several Years absence, & a month since my arrival here, I have felt myself precluded from paying the respects of a sincere friend to you, in person, on account of information communicated to me by Genl. Henry Lee, (while Governor of Virginia) accompanied by the return of a letter of mine unanswered, that, "I had so intruded on you, the last time we met at Richmond in Virginia, that you were obliged to leave town without doing the business you came from Monticello to transact."—

I design to set out for New York by Mondays stage, and am not certain when I shall return: I have therefore to request your information if this communication is founded in truth, or otherwise?

I have the honor to be Sir Yr. H Servt WM TATHAM

RC (DLC); at foot of text: "The President of The United States, (in his private capacity) Mr. Jefferson"; endorsed by TJ as received 19 May and so recorded in SJL.

From Thomas West

SIR Lancaster Ct House Virga. 17th. May 1805

Some time in the Year Eighteen hundred & two a Brother of Mine Edward West of Lexington Kentucky, obtained a patent for an improvement on Gun Locks, the Model of which is deposited in your patent office.—My object is to inquire of you whether or not you have ever seen and examined the improvement, and to Obtain your Opinion respecting the utility of the invention,—he has impowered me to dispose of the Patent right, and for that purpose I went to Richmond last winter at the Setting of our Legislature, and exhibited a pair of Pistols with this improvement to Captn. Clarke the Superintendent, and to the Master workmen of the Armory, each of those Gentlemen considered it, as one of the greatest improvements as yet invented, and worthy of being introduced into our Armory—It was near the close of the Session consequently too late to lay the business before the House for that purpose—I also presented the Pistols to a Number of the Members who were highly pleased with the contrivance.—I need say nothing more on the Subject, satisfied as I am that your general knowledge of Mechanics will readily point out to you the great Security and utility to be derived by an introduction of this improvement into general use—And if in your Opinion it is worthy of recommendation I trust that you will not hesitate to do so, as I propose to attend at the Setting of our Next Assembly to Make an offer of the Patent Right for the use of the Armory.—Your attention will very Much oblige

Sir Your Mo. obd Servant THOMAS WEST

RC (DLC); endorsed by TJ as received 24 May and so recorded in SJL.

Thomas West served as a jailor and owned a tavern in Lancaster County, Virginia (Richmond *Virginia Patriot*, 5 June 1812; biographical information in Vi: Thomas West Tavern Daybooks and Ledgers, 1809-1815).

EDWARD WEST: see Vol. 37:490n.

From Robert Williams

Washington M.T. May 17th 1805

By the last mail from New Orleans I had the honor of receiving a commission as Governor of this Territory—which I have accepted, but under a full persuasion that I may be admitted to return to North-Carolina as soon as the land business shall have been finished or will admit of my absence from the Board of Commissioners—and I hope to have permission to that effect from the President of the United States as soon as may be convenient to himself—I trust the propriety of this request will be duly considered and properly appreciated when it is known that my arrangements to come to this Country were merely temporary and with a view of returning again to my family in all this month—

I am now about to address you on a subject which from my present situation is almost too delicate for me to do Justice to—however the notoriety in this quarter of the facts it embraces aided by a sense of Publick duty emboldens me in the undertaking—when I arrived in this Country in the fall of 1803 I found the present Secretary Colo. West and his connexons with but a few others very enimical to the then Governor—It required no great foresight to know that this enmity was predicated on motives short of principle or the Publick good, but with a view to their own promotion this being fully understood by the federal side of the community here—they and very prudently too soon turned it to their own advantage by exposing the ambitious views of the one without the least regard or charity to the virtuous forbearance of the other and benefiting by the jarings among the Republicans.

When I returned last fall I found it no better and the dismissal of Edward Turner—West's son in law from the Office of Register roused all their resentment—In order to mortify if possible the Executive of the United States every exertion was made during the setting of the Legislature to appoint Turner the delegate to Congress this failing the Secretary became a Candidate himself in order to prevent any appointment knowing that he could not be elected but that a certain number of the Members would vote for him and it is notorious that some of those were influenced by promises of appointments to Office in this Territory—The fact is that Colo West is too hostile to the present administration and too unpopular here to answer any good purpose as Secretary to any Character that could be sent for it should seem that the strictest confidence and good understanding ought to exist between the Governor and Secretary—which cannot be expected between Colo. West and any man from the declarations of his family for some time past "that if he was not appointed the Governor he would not act as Secretary—In the present situation of things it is impossible for me to perform but partially the duties of the Office of Governor having none of the papers of that department nor the Seal or a Secretary I shall be obliged to make use of privates ones a call of the Legislature which must be before the annual meeting in order to appoint a delegate to Congress and to do some other business which their discordant dispositions at their last sessions prevented them from doing might in some measure remedy this they would pass a Law compeling the Officer to come to this place but they could not make the Secretary do his duty

Should the Executive think proper to appoint a Secretary in the place of Mr West I will take the liberty of mentioning Mr Thomas Hill Williams the Register of the land office here should there be no incompatibility.

The salaries of officers here are so inadequate to the expense of living that it would be but Justice and perhaps is the only way a Character could be got qualified to fill that office—Mr Williams is well qualified and is very popular in this Country it is a pitty the Government should loose his services and influence especially in this quarter—his delicacy has always kept him back in publick life and will continue to do so I am obliged not to let him have the least idea of what I now write but I am in hopes should he be appointed he would then accept—with such a Character as Mr Williams as Secretary I think I could administer this Government with ease to myself, satisfaction to the people and Consonant to the views of the General Government—

I trust the liberties I have taken in this letter will not be considered intrusive but it is because I believe the Republican cause has suffered much in this quarter for the want of proper information with the Executive of the United States as to this Territory and by that which was not correct

Accept assurances of my Very great respect

Robert Williams

P.S.

I here with enclose some of the Blanks the Secretary sent me

RC (DNA: RG 59, TP, Mississippi); at head of text: "private"; above postscript: "Thomas Jefferson Esq President of U States"; endorsed by TJ as received 25 June and so recorded in SJL. Enclosures: blank forms of militia commissions for Mississippi Territory (MSS in same, in a clerk's hand, seals affixed).

From Isaac Briggs

My dear Friend, Washington M.T. 18th. of the 5th. mo 1805.

By last mail, on the 11th. instant, I wrote to thee acknowledging the receipt of thy acceptable favour of March 14. '05.

During my short stay with Colonel Hawkins, on my way through the Creek Nation, I endeavoured to discover his sentiments respecting a removal of the Indians to the West of the Mississippi. I soon found that with a man of his talents and accuteness of penetration, I had undertaken a task of extreme delicacy—that, with my small portion of address, I should be in danger of being considered as a spy upon him, and of becoming a dupe, instead of making discoveries of any importance. I drew, however, from the whole of our conversation, this general inference:—That he will aid, with all his influence, any plan which, in his belief, will forward, but oppose any which will contravene, his benevolent views of *Civilizing* the Indians. This is his hobby-horse—his passion. He incessantly labors to impress the minds of these people with a high idea of the justice and friendship of the United States towards them—that he is the *paternal* guardian of their rights, and on this he founds his influence, which is indeed great.

In addition to my last I will now say a few words respecting this Territory. Just after the mail, containing that letter, was closed, the *Southern* mail brought a packet from the department of State, inclosing the Governor's Commission—*without any post-mark.*

Governor Williams's induction into office on the 13th. instant has produced the expression, as far as the opportunity has extended, of an uncommon degree of enthusiasm in the people. Party distinctions seem to be lost in the general joy—with one small exception. A *very small* junto, consisting of Cato West and others, is hostile to him—not personally so—it would be hostile to any man, *out of the clan.*

I am strongly persuaded that in few Sections of the Union could the elegant sentiment—"We are all Republicans, we are all Federalists"—be applied with more propriety than here, at this moment. Many perhaps would not utter the *phrase*, but their feelings are in unison with the *sentiment.*

An apprehension of the unreasonable expectations likely to originate from this enthusiasm, is cause of much diffidence in Governor Williams, which is increased by the reflection that many improper and unpopular measures of the late acting Governor cannot be reversed without perhaps erecting a dangerous precedent.

The Secretary, West, during his administration, removed the Seal and Executive records from this place, which has long been established as the seat of Government, to his own house about eighteen miles from hence; and refuses to return them or to come himself upon the Governor's application; but as I understand the Governor sends a detailed account of these proceedings, it will not be necessary for me to enter far into the Subject. Of one thing I am clearly convinced from the decided stand which these two Gentlemen have taken, that it is impossible for them to harmonize or act together, and that the public good will require an *instant* removal of *one* of them. Should the President think me correct in this opinion, I take the liberty of forwarding the name of Thomas Hill Williams Esquire Register of the land-office as a Gentleman happily qualified to fill the office of Secretary. With perfect confidence, I can recommend him as a Gentleman of talents and handsome acquirements—of correct discriminating Judgment—of great promptitude and system in business—and of a foresight and prudence uncommon in a young man. His political principles are purely republican. He has besides become very popular here. He possesses an unusual share of genuine modesty, which, it appears to me, will ever prevent his rising to those stations for which he is eminently fitted, unless his friends push him forward. We dare not let him know a tittle of our recommending him—but should his Commission arrive, we hope we can prevail on him to accept.

Perhaps it is not a good general principle to unite different offices in the same individual—but, as Salaries are pressed down in this expensive Country, I see no other way of availing ourselves of those qualifications which will ensure a faithful and dignified discharge of public duty.

Accept assurances of my esteem and affectionate wishes for thy happiness. ISAAC BRIGGS.

RC (DLC); at foot of text: "Thomas Jefferson, President of the United States"; endorsed by TJ as received 25 June and so recorded in SJL. FC (MdHi).

ENCLOSURE

Notes on Publications

Notes on the enclosed publications.

No 1. Cato—G. Poindexter

No 2. Anti-Cato, in his first attempt, failing to moderate the glowing zeal of Cato, has availed himself of the imprudent temper of his antagonist, and by a few squibs (too trifling to send) has fretted him quite from the field.

No. 3. Its authors are exposed in

No. 4. Castigator—Gener, E. Turner, the ex-Register, the son-in-law of Cato West;

Pugil, D.W. Brazeale, an unprincipled coward.

Poëtaster, John Shaw, Post master at Greenville who sometimes writes bad verses.

These three form the Secretary's privy-council.

Castigator has stated facts.

MS (DLC: TJ Papers, 149:26089); in Briggs's hand; undated. Enclosures not found.

In his 11 May letter to TJ, Briggs observed that an "ebullition of turbulent spirits" had commenced in the local press and promised, by the next mail, to "send thee all the pieces, to that time, with explanatory notes." The two newspapers in the territory during this period were the *Mississippi Herald*, edited by Andrew Marschalk, and the *Mississippi Messenger*, established in September 1804 by Timothy and Samuel Terrell (Brigham, *American Newspapers*, 1:426-7; Vol. 42:91n).

From George E. Clymer

SIR Philada May 18th 1805

Just after I wrote what you will have perused before this reaches you your favour of the 13th to Mr. Evans was Shewn to me—

I conceive the most effectual method of preventing an enemy from *boarding* our Vessels would be by throwing *boiling* water on them when nearly at close quarters which may be done with the same Engines with which the cold water was thrown at a distance by stopping the supply of cold and opening a communication with a cauldron of hot water, provided for the purpose; as a small jet of that or any other hot liquid in the face or on any part of the body would render it impossible for any man to continue the contest—for the hot water may be thrown, without any manual labour, as Mr Evans has intimated; for we know that it issues with a tremendous force and noise from a strong boiler in which it has been previously confined, and heated to a proper degree. The project is new and on that account may probably be turned to ridicule; but this does not appear to me a sufficient reason for witholding a communication on the Subject—

I am Sir yr obt. Servt GEOE CLYMER

PS An Experiment might be made upon a small scale to ascertain the practicability of this mode of attack, which, if successfull would lead to further attempts of the same kind—I should however be happy to hear the objections of proffessional men— G. C.

RC (DLC); endorsed by TJ as received 19 May and so recorded in SJL.

I WROTE: see Clymer to TJ, 15 May.

From Charles W. Goldsborough

Saturday, 18 May '05

C W Goldsborough, for the secretary of the navy, respectfully requests the President's signature to the enclosed instructions to the commanders of the bomb vessels, Spitfire & Vengeance, which vessels will probably be ready to sail on the 1st of the ensuing month.

RC (DLC); endorsed by TJ as received from the Navy Department on 19 May and "instructions to Captns" and so recorded in SJL, but as received 18 May. Enclosure: Robert Smith to Lieutenant Daniel McNeill, Jr., commanding the *Spitfire*, and Midshipman William Lewis, commanding the *Vengeance*, 18 May; instructing each officer to sail his vessel to the Mediterranean and join the naval squadron blockading Tripoli (FC in Lb in DNA: RG 45, LSO; NDBW, *Register*, 31, 34).

From Alexander McClean

DEAR SIR, Union Town 18th May 1805

Some two or three years ago I received through your direction "enclosed" a letter from Lady Sopheona Hartman of the Dutchy of Brunswick—requesting you (as well as my memory serves me) to make enquiry for her Brothers Widow and Children, or himself—if alive, alledging the existance of an estate in their favour, which she was disposed to apply to their Advantage if found—On receipt of the

Letter I searched, and found the Widow and offspring—I gave as full an account of them and their connections, as I could asscertain, and transmited the same with the Lady's letter enclosed to you,—the name of the Brother was George Frederick Charles Hartman a Serjeant in the Brunswick troops "vs" America.—We have reason to believe that the Brother was cast away on his return home—the family yet resides in Fayette County—the Widow is present while I write and is anxious to hear intelligence if any has arived—from the multiplicity of your business We cannot expect much of your time to be spent in business of this nature—If you can steal a moment to communicate (If any arival has taken place) it will oblige a needy Widow and Orphans.

I have the honor to be with unfeigned regard Your Excellencies most Obt. Servant. ALEXANDER MCLEAN

RC (MHi); at foot of text: "Thomas Jefferson Esquire"; endorsed by TJ as received 1 June and so recorded in SJL.

Alexander McClean (1746-1834), originally of York County, Pennsylvania, was a surveyor by trade. He and his older brothers laid the boundary between Pennsylvania and Delaware in 1761, after which McLean assisted surveyors Charles Mason and Jeremiah Dixon. Following his service in the American Revolution, McClean continued to serve on several commissions in charge of laying out state roads and county lines. He was also, at various times, a judge of the court of common pleas and a member of the Pennsylvania General Assembly. In 1783, McClean became Fayette County's first register and recorder, a position he held until his death (James Hadden, *A History of Uniontown: The County Seat of Fayette County, Pennsylvania* [Akron, Ohio, 1913], 778-85, 788).

Sophia Hartman's LETTER to TJ of 18 July 1803 was recorded in SJL, but has not been found. See Vol. 43:112n.

TRANSMITED THE SAME: no earlier letter from McClean has been found or is recorded in SJL.

From Philippe Reibelt

MONSIEUR LE PRESIDENT! Baltimore le 18 Mai 1805

C'est sur votre billet de hier, que j'ose Vous prier, de vouloir bien garder la Notice de la Gallerie des Antiques, et le Catalogue des estampes du Museum—et que j'ai en même tems l'honneur de Vous envoÿer çijoint tout ce, qui me reste des Grains du Quarantino avec les Observations necessaires.

Daignez accepter mes bien profonds et bien sincere respects

REIBELT

EDITORS' TRANSLATION

Mister President! Baltimore, 18 May 1805

I take the liberty of writing about your note from yesterday to ask that you keep the announcement from the antique gallery and the catalog of museum prints. I also have the honor of enclosing all my remaining Quarantino corn seeds with the necessary instructions.

Please accept my very profound and sincere regards. Reibelt

RC (DLC); endorsed by TJ as received 19 May and so recorded in SJL. Enclosure: excerpt of an article on a strain of Italian maize, published in a German-language Swiss journal at the request of the economic society of Bern by its representative, Mr. Morell; the variety must be kept separate from larger strains to prevent crossbreeding; it normally grows two and a half to four feet high and typically produces three or four ears, though sometimes only two; ears are usually two and a half to three inches (French measure) and rarely more than five inches; the seeds are always golden yellow, never reddish; it is planted and harvested within 40 days and is sowed three times on the same land, in March, May, and July; a warm summer followed by a mild autumn always results in a successful last harvest; the corn thrives in hot, humid weather; in dry conditions, seeds should be planted close together; even with irrigation, seeds should grow no more than eight to ten inches apart; the seeds need only be planted one to one and a half inches deep; this corn does not deplete the land like larger varieties; the masculine seeds do not require cutting; the plants can produce lycopodium; the ears can be thrashed by putting them in bags and stomping on them; the kernels come off easily; a first planting near Bern, using three-quarters of a pound of seeds on an open 800-square-foot plot at a density of one seed per foot, produced 16 pounds of seed in unfavorable weather conditions; the second planting, on an open, unfertilized field that was hand sown and tilled, and pruned twice, produced 86 pounds of kernels; the third planting was on a 40,000-square-foot field and produced 8,266 pounds of kernels, despite cool and wet conditions and the ravages of curious visitors, children, birds, and a hail storm; when mixed with rye or wheat, the corn flour produces delicious bread and porridges; Italians use it for dishes such as macaroni and polenta; its most lucrative product is alcohol (MS in same; undated; in Reibelt's hand, in French).

OBSERVATIONS NECESSAIRES: Reibelt appears to have composed his excerpt from an account by the Bern-based chemist and botanist Karl Friedrich Morell, who conducted experiments with the quarantino variety of corn in 1802 and 1803. His account was subsequently cited as an 1804 article entitled "Erfahrungen über das kleine Mais" (Georg Christoph Hamberger and Johann Georg Meusel, *Das gelehrte Teutschland: oder, Lexikon der jetzt lebenden teutschen Schriftsteller* [Lemgo, Germany, 1810], 591; François Ledermann, ed., *Festschrift zum 150jährigen Bestehen des Schweizerischen Apothekervereins* [Bern, 1993], 248).

From P. & C. Roche

Monsieur, Philadelphie, ce 18 May 1805—

La Langue française faisant tous les jours de nouveaux progrès aux Etats Unis, et étant même cultivée avec succès par beaucoup d'Américains, nous avons jugé à propos d'apporter de paris un assortiment considérable de Livres, & avons établi à Philadelphie une

Librairie française qui ne laissera rien à desirer pour la beauté des éditions, l'élégance et la Solidité des réliûres.

Connoissant votre amour pour les sciences et combien vous êtes jaloux d'encourager tout ce qui Sert à propager L'instruction publique, nous osons vous prier de regarder d'un oeil favorable notre établissement naissant; et nous Serons infiniment flattés de mériter votre approbation.

Nous avons l'honneur de vous adresser nôtre catalogue, Si parmi les ouvrages qui le composent, vous en trouvez quelquesuns qui soient dignes de fixer vôtre choix, en nous honorant d'une réponse, nous nous empresserons de vous les expédier.

En attendant, nous Sommes avec la plus haute considération & le plus profond respect, vos très humbles et très obéissants Serviteurs

Roche frères
Booksellers No. 53 Walnut Street

EDITORS' TRANSLATION

Sir, Philadelphia, 18 May 1805

Every day the French language is gaining new ground in the United States. Since many Americans are studying French, we thought it fitting to import a wide assortment of books from Paris. We have established a French bookstore in Philadelphia that will gratify readers with the beauty of the editions as well as the elegance and durability of the bindings.

Knowing your love of knowledge and your fervent encouragement of anything that can foster public education, we dare ask you to look favorably upon our fledgling business. We would be infinitely gratified to merit your approval.

We have the honor of sending you our catalog. If you find works that warrant selecting and honor us with a reply, we will send them promptly.

In the meantime, with the highest consideration and deepest respect, we are your very humble and obedient servants.

Roche frères
Booksellers No. 53 Walnut Street

RC (MHi); at head of text: "A Monsieur Jefferson, Président du Congrès des Etats Unis D'Amérique"; endorsed by TJ as received 20 May and so recorded in SJL. Enclosure not found.

From Mathieû René Rufini

Tres Nobles Tres Hauts et puisances Seigneurs

a Brunn en Moravie le 18 May 1805.

Le sousigner ci-devant Receveur dans les Douannes en Belgique de Sa Majeste L'Empereur Romaine et Autriche Roi d'Hongrie et de Boheme prend la respectuess liberté de suplier leurs hauts et puisances de vouloir avoir egard a ma tres humble Representation:

Comme le nomes Jean baptiste baron de Rufini mon legitime frere, qui est partis pour l'amerique l'an 1732 ou 33. et voila plusieurs anne, que je n'ai eu de ces nouvelles, j'ai suplier, il y a un et demi vos tres hauts et puisances vouloir m'en faire parvenir quelque Conoissance, il doit etre etablis a Montreal Quebec, Boston nouvelle Angletre etc selon les letres que j'en aie recue, et quil y avoit fait un brillant fortune, en y epousant un Dame Americaine.

Sil est mort, suplier tres humblement Votres tres Hauts et Puisances y faire parvenir la letre c'incluse a ces Descendent, et vouloir m'en donner un gratieuss avis. je suis

Tres Nobles Tres Hauts et Puisances Seigneurs Votre Tres humble et tres obeissant Serviteur

Mathieû René Rufini

EDITORS' TRANSLATION

Very great, noble, and powerful lords,

Brno, Moravia, 18 May 1805

The undersigned, receiver of duties in Belgium for His Majesty, the Holy Roman Emperor, Emperor of Austria, and King of Hungary and Bohemia, respectfully takes the liberty of begging your great and powerful eminences to consider my humble request. My legitimate brother, Jean Baptiste, baron of Rufini, left for America in 1732 or 1733. I have not had any news from him in several years. A year and a half ago I asked your great and powerful eminences to send me some news of him. Based on the letters I received, he must be living in Montreal, Quebec; Boston, New England; or some similar place, and have made a fortune there by marrying an American woman.

If he is deceased, I humbly ask your great and powerful eminences to forward the enclosed letter to his descendants and to be kind enough to notify me.

Very great, noble, and powerful lords, I am your very humble and obedient servant.

Mathieû René Rufini

RC (ViW: Tucker-Coleman Collection); in a clerk's hand, including first name of signature; endorsed by TJ as received 1 May 1806 and so recorded in SJL. Also recorded in SJL as received 21 Sep. 1805. Enclosure not found.

quelque conoissance: Rufini's earlier request may have been a subject for TJ and the State Department in August 1804. On 26 Sep. 1805, the department issued a public request for information on "John Baptist Baron of Rufini" (*Alexandria Expositor*, 8 Nov.; TJ to Madison, 23 Aug. 1804).

From J. P. P. Derieux

MONSIEUR Greenbriar C.H. May 19. 1805.

Me croyant toujours honoré de votre bienveillance, J'ose prendre la liberté de vous reiterer l'expression de mes sentiments de respect, et de vous faire part de l'evenement qui a detourné la résolution que j'avois prise d'aller vivre dans le KusKusKy. Prèsqu'ausitot mon retour de France, mon fils ainé S'est marié a la fille d'un fermier du voisinage, et n'ayant pu le determiner, n'y son frere a m'y accompagner, j'ai eté contraint de renoncer a un Etablisement qui dèpendoit principalement de leur assistance. Jusqu'a present nous sommes restés reunis sur la même ferme, mais comme ils vont travailler pour eux mêmes, et que, dèstitué de leur aide, mes Efforts a ce genre de travail, deviendroient insuffisants, nous avons mutuelement pris la résolution Mde Derieux et moi de laisser notre fils ainé avec ses trois soeurs ainées, sur la ferme dont les Bestiaux et les ustencilles m'appartiennent, et aprés avoir donné a notre Second fils un Mètier qu'il desire, nous nous proposons daller vivre dans une grande ville, a L'effet de nous procurer quelque Situation qui tel qu'elle puisse etre nous fournira mieux qu'ici les moyens et les occasions de travailler au sort des trois jeunes Enfants que nous prendrons avec nous, dont l'un un garçon de Cinq ans et deux filles de Sept et neuf. Jai dailleurs d'autant plus de raisons de me rapprocher d'un lieu de Commerce, que mon Cousin Plumard Derieux de Nantes, ma ecrit qu'il m'expediroit des marchandises En Commission, aussitot qu'il auroit appris que j'avois quitté les montagnes.

Oserois-je me flatter d'être assés heureux, Monsieur, pour pouvoir obtenir de vos bontés quelqu'emploi ou vous jugerés que mes foibles talents peuvent me rendre propre, ils ne me permettent pas, je le sais, d'aspirer a une Capacité publique, mais je mestimerois heureux et honoré de toutte Espece d'occupation a la qu'elle vous voudriés bien m'admettre, et si c'etoit auprés auprés de votre personne, j'en serois d'autant plus flatté que j'y trouverois d'avantage les occasions de vous donner des preuves continuelles de mon Zèle et du plus respectueux dèvouement avec le quel j'ay L'honneur d'être, Monsieur Votre trés humble et trés obeissant Serviteur P. DERIEUX

P.S. Mde. Derieux prend la liberté de vous prèsenter son respect.

EDITORS' TRANSLATION

SIR, Greenbriar Court House, 19 May 1805

In hopes that you still honor me with your goodwill, I dare take the liberty of renewing my respectful sentiments and informing you of the event that thwarted my resolution to settle in Kaskaskia. Almost as soon as I returned from France, my eldest son married the daughter of a neighboring farmer. Unable to persuade him or his brother to accompany me, I was obliged to forsake a project that depended largely on their help. Until now, we have remained together on one farm, but since they are going off to work independently and my own labor in this occupation would be insufficient without their help, we have all decided that Madame Derieux and I will leave our eldest son with his three older sisters on the farm whose animals and equipment I own. After setting up our second son in his chosen occupation, we plan to live in a big city in order to find employment that can provide the ways and means to support the three young children we are taking with us, a five-year old boy and two girls, seven and nine. I have all the more reason to be near a commercial center, since my cousin Plumard Derieux of Nantes says he will send me merchandise to sell as soon as he knows I have left the mountains.

Might I flatter myself, Sir, to be fortunate enough for your bounty to offer me some employment where you feel my modest talents could be useful? I know they do not allow me to aspire to public office, but I would consider myself happy and honored by any kind of occupation in which you would be willing to accept me. If that meant working with you, I would be so flattered that I would find innumerable opportunities to prove my zeal and the most respectful devotion with which I have the honor, Sir, of being your very humble and obedient servant. P. DERIEUX

P.S. Madame Derieux takes the liberty of sending her regards.

RC (DLC); endorsed by TJ as received 28 May and so recorded in SJL.

From David Ramsay

DEAR SIR, Charleston May 19th 1805

The bearer Mr Calhoun is a near relation of our late Senator of the same name & accompanies his widow on a tour to the Northern States. He has finished his education at Yale College with great reputation & is high in the esteem of his friends for virtue & talents. Unwilling to pass through Washington without being known to the President of the United:States he has requested a letter to you. Any notice you may take of him will be well bestowed & gratefully received. I have the honor to be with great respect & esteem your most obedient humble Servant DAVID RAMSAY

RC (ViW: Tucker-Coleman Collection); at foot of text: "President Jefferson"; endorsed by TJ as received 20 June and so recorded in SJL with notation "by mr Calhoun."

John C. CALHOUN met TJ at Washington in June. According to Calhoun they conversed on the subject of the French Toulon fleet, with TJ expressing his opinion that its destination would be Trinidad rather than Jamaica as commonly asserted (Robert L. Meriwether and others, eds., *The Papers of John C. Calhoun*, 28 vols. [Columbia, S.C., 1959-2003], 1:14). On 20 May, Ramsay wrote a similar letter to Madison introducing Calhoun. Although Calhoun was currently a "stranger" in Washington, Ramsay was confident that the "promising" young man would "ere long be well known there" (Madison, *Papers, Sec. of State Ser.*, 9:374).

OUR LATE SENATOR: John Ewing Colhoun, a cousin of Calhoun, died in 1802 (*Biog. Dir. Cong.*; Vol. 32:281n).

To William Tatham

SIR Washington May 19. 05

I do not remember that I ever returned a letter unopened to any mortal living, and had still less supposed I had done it to you, of whom I had seen much to approve, and always wished you well. I had heard of your being in town, and was conscious of nothing which should have prevented your calling on me. you would have met a reception dictated by antient & friendly recollections, and I now, in the same spirit present you my salutations and good wishes.

TH: JEFFERSON

PoC (DLC); at foot of text: "Colo. Tatham"; endorsed by TJ.

RETURNED A LETTER UNOPENED: see Tatham to TJ, 17 May.

To William Tunnicliff

Washington May 19. 1805.

Th: Jefferson presents his compliments to mr Tunnicliff and asks permission to add one other article to the list he formerly sent him to be procured in London, to wit, a Protracting parallel rule, which may be had where the other mathematical articles are procured.

RC (MoSHi: Jefferson Papers).

THE LIST: see enclosure at TJ to Tunnicliff, 25 Apr.

Statement of Account with Richard Gaines

Cr—Jefferson Esqr. to Richard Gaines	Dr.
May 20 1805	$
To 6 pair Black Morocco Slippers a/$1.75 ea	10.50
To 4 pair Calf Skin do—a/$1.50 ea	6.00
To 2 pair Calf Skin Ran Shoes a/1.75 ea	3.50
	$20.00

RC (MHi); endorsed by TJ with notation "June 6. 05. pd. by check on bk. US."

Richard Gaines owned a manufactory on Bridge Street in Georgetown where he sold men's and women's boots and shoes "made to order with promptitude and fashion." He moved to Cincinnati around 1811, set up a shoe store, and purchased a tanyard and property (*Washington Federalist*, 12 Mch. 1808; Cincinnati *Liberty Hall*, 4 Sep. 1811, 9 June 1812, 19 Oct. 1813, 12 July 1814).

SLIPPERS: on 8 Mch., Gaines provided TJ with a receipt for "Ten Dollars in full for Six pair of Ladies Slippers" (MS in MHi; endorsed by TJ; MB, 2:1147).

RAN: the rand was a thin leather strip featured in women's heeled shoes fashionable from the mid-seventeenth century onward to make it easier for the shoemaker to attach a delicate upper to the shoe (OED; Rebecca Shawcross, *Shoes: An Illustrated History* [London, 2014], 64; Connecticut *Norwich Courier*, 14 Feb. 1810).

According to his financial memoranda, on 6 June TJ drew $20 on the Bank of the United States to pay Gaines (MB, 2:1155; Notes on Personal Finance, [ca. 6 June]).

From Obadiah Jones

RESPECTED SIR, Lexington (Geo.) 20th. May 1805.

I lately received official information of my appointment as Judge of the Mississippi Territory. With due acknowledgments to those who conferred the honor on me, it is with regret I have to inform you that circumstances forbid my acceptance.

I am, Sir, with sentiments of highest esteem, Your obedient, humble Servt.

OBADIAH JONES

RC (DNA: RG 59, LAR); at foot of text: "His excellency, Thomas Jefferson"; endorsed by TJ as a letter of 22 May received 14 July and "declines judge Misipi" and so recorded in SJL.

TJ had nominated Obadiah Jones (d. 1825) of Georgia for a judgeship in Mississippi Territory in March. Jones received judicial appointments for Illinois Territory in 1809 and Mississippi Territory in 1810 and became receiver of the land office at Huntsville, Alabama, in 1820 (JEP, 2:119, 139-40; 3:178, 205-6; Madison, *Papers, Pres. Ser.*, 1:13-14, 22; 2:257-8, 266; *Terr. Papers*, 5:701-2; *Salem Gazette*, 5 July 1825; TJ to the Senate, 2 Mch. 1805).

From P. & C. Roche

MONSIEUR, Philadelphie, ce 20 May 1805

Nous Sommes honorés par la vôtre du 17 du Courant & conformément à vos desirs nous avons remis au Stage office en un paquet à votre adresse les divers ouvrages que vous avez choisi Sur notre catalogue;

en voici la facture:	$	Ct
1. Connoissance des temps pour L'année 1806 avec les additions un volume in 8o. Broché	2.	.—

1. Leçons d'histoire par Volney 1 volume 8o. Broché (c'est par erreur que l'on a porté sur notre Catalogue cet ouvrage en 2 vols.) } 1.25.—
1. Voyage d'Antenor en Grèce, jolie édition ornée de figures 3 vols. in 8o. réliés en basane filets 7. —.—
1. Diccionario portatil Español-Ingles par Gattel 2 vols in 16 réliés en basane filets 4. —.—
1. Les Tomes 3 & 4 histoire des Mathématiques de Montucla revue par La Lande 2 vols. in 4o. réliés 12. —.—

$26.25.—

L'histoire des mathématiques de Montucla formant un corps complet en 4 volumes in 4o. ne Se vend pas Séparément; cependant jaloux de pouvoir faire quelque chose qui puisse vous être agréable nous nous Sommes empressés de les joindre à l'envoy et avons écrit à paris pour demander ces deux dernieres volumes.

nous n'avons pas pour le moment dans notre magasin la Connoissance des Temps pour l'année 1805; mais Si vous desirez vous procurer cet ouvrage, de même que d'autres que vous ne trouvierez pas Sur notre catalogue, en nous en faisant passer la note nous nous chargerons de les demander à notre correspondant de paris qui mettra la plus grande célérité dans ses expéditions.

Vous aurez Sans doute reçu la lettre que nous avons pris la Liberté de vous écrire le 18 du Courant nous nous en référons à Son contenu & nous réitérons par celle ci l'assurance du plus profond Respect et de la plus haute estime.

Vos très dévoués Serviteurs P & C. Roche

EDITORS' TRANSLATION

Sir, Philadelphia, 20 May 1805

We are honored by your letter of the 17th. Following up on your wishes, we have entrusted to the stage a package containing the various works you chose from our catalog:

Here is the invoice: $ Ct

1. *Connaissance des temps* for the year 1806, with additions. One paperbound volume in octavo. 2. .—
1. *Leçons d'histoire* by Volney. one papberbound volume in octavo. (This work was erroneously listed as two volumes in our catalog.) } 1.25.—
1. *Voyage d'Antenor en Grèce*, an attractive illustrated edition of three octavo volumes bound in sheepskin. 7. —.—
1. *Diccionario portatil Español-Ingles* by Gattel. Two sextodecimo volumes bound in sheepskin. 4. —.—
1. Volumes 3 & 4 of *Histoire des mathématiques* by Montucla revised by La Lande. Two bound volumes in quarto. 12. —.—

$26.25.—

Montucla's *Histoire des mathématiques*, a complete set of four volumes in quarto, is not sold separately, but since we are eager to please you, we gladly included those two volumes in the shipment and requested the two remaining ones from Paris.

We do not have the *Connaissance des temps* for 1805 in stock, but if you wish to obtain this work, along with others you might not find in our catalog, let us know. We will request them from our Paris representative who will send them promptly.

You have undoubtedly received the letter we took the liberty of sending on the 18th. We renew its contents and reiterate the assurance of our deep respect and highest esteem.

Your very devoted servants, P & C. Roche

RC (MHi); at head of text: "Mr. Th. Jefferson président des Etas unis D'Amérique"; note by TJ below signature: "June 6. 05. inclosd. draft on bk US. for 36.75"; endorsed by TJ as received 22 May and so recorded in SJL.

From Caspar Wistar

Dear Sir Philadelphia May 20. 1805.

I presented your letter respecting the Roman Coin to the Society, & was requested to assure you in the name of the members of that Institution, that they accept with particular Satisfaction this new proof of your regard, & shall allways consider it as entitled to particular care, not only on account of its intrinsic merit, but of the liberal and enlarged views with which it was originally transmitted to you, & with which you have thus deposited it for the public advantage.—They also intend to offer their thanks to Mr Weinwich as soon as the Coin arrives.—In my individual capacity I must beg you to accept of my sincere thanks for the loan of the Valuable Book of Faujas, & to beg you to excuse my very long detention of it. I wished to keep it until I had received Campers account of the Elephant, or until a Sceleton of that Animal arrived here, but I have been greatly disappointed in both respects—Camper's Work, printed only for distribution among naturalists, & not for Sale, was sent me by his Son & lost in the West Indies where the Ship which carried it was driven by Stress of Weather—The Sceleton was procured at the request of the A.P.S. by Dr Roxborough of Madrass, but owing to Some mistake was not put on Ship board, & therefore will not come this year I am very desirous of ascertaining all the points of difference between the Mammoth *of America* & the Elephant—there seems to be a considerable resemblance, but the immense difference in the Teeth, as well as in the Countries which those Animals probably inhabited, prepare me to expect some difference in the Sceleton—I have heard of a Mammoths Head which was packed up in the Western Country to send to this place, but it has not yet arrived, & the report is so circuitous (from a British Officer to a Gentleman of the Genessee Country) that I cannot well investigate it—There is still stronger reason to hope that we shall have some more bones of the Megalonix—There is a person in the State of Ohio who has sent to Pittsburgh the bones of an immense unguiculated paw or foot, on their way to Philada. I do know why they have not arrived, but have heard that the Owners ideas of their Value are very extravagant indeed—As my hopes of Comparing the Sceletons of the Elephant & Mammoth are done away for the present, I will deliver Faujas to Dr Barton, & request him to finish the perusal as early as possible, & hope my Old friend Mr Randolph will forgive the Delay—

There are two Gentlemen who have requested me, to state to you what I know respecting them—Mr Clemt. Penrose a nephew of Mr Wilkinson is desirous of removing with the Genl. to the Western Country & has requested a place in the Land Office—I do not know any thing respecting his Talents for business, having never had any opportunity of forming an opinion, if I had been capable—but he is a Gentleman of good Character, & very amiable disposition, & I believe is well acquainted with the German & French languages—Mr Chas. Biddle of this City, the Father of Mr Nicholas Biddle who is private Secretary to Mr Armstrong the Minister to France, wishes his Son to study some branches of the Military Art in France, & has learned that he can do it with great advantage if he has a Military Commission—A request on this subject has been made to Genl. Dearborne—I have long known him & consider him as an uncommonly promising Youth—he acquitted himself with the greatest credit at the Commencement at Princeton two years ago—& I believe that every body who knows him has the same opinion respecting him—One of his Brothers, supposed to be the greatest proficient in Mathematics of his age in our City—died with Yellow Fever on board of Captn. Truxton—another is in the Prison at Tripoli—I ought not to conclude this long letter without begging you to forgive for writing it.

Your affectionate friend C WISTAR JR.

RC (DLC); endorsed by TJ as received 22 May and so recorded in SJL.

YOUR LETTER: TJ to Wistar, 30 Apr.

CAMPERS ACCOUNT OF THE ELEPHANT: a reference to the Dutch physician and anatomist Petrus Camper. Having dissected an Indian elephant and researched some African elephants, he contributed letters to collaborators in France and developed engraved plates that were intended for publication. Camper's death, however, prevented publication until 1802, when his son Adriaan Gilles Camper completed the work as *Description anatomique d'un éléphant mâle*. The younger Camper was elected a member of the American Philosophical Society and was presumably Wistar's contact (Robert Paul Willem Visser, *The Zoological Work of Petrus Camper [1722-1789]* [Amsterdam, 1985], 52-7; APS, *Proceedings*, 22, pt. 3 [1884-85], 390).

William Roxburgh (ROXBOROUGH), a prominent botanist, was likely acting on behalf of the Asiatic Society of Calcutta, which sent a skeleton of an elephant to the American Philosophical Society later in the year (DNB; APS, *Proceedings*, 22, pt. 3 [1884-85], 380).

TJ had previously received information from Charles Willson Peale on the large fossilized PAW OR FOOT, which had been obtained by a man named Jeremiah Reeder (Vol. 43:645-6, 663-4).

From Phebe Baldwin

SIR— Newjersey Paterson May the 21t 1805

My Letters to you have been written in the Language of truth—the inconveniens of Capt. Baldwins Situation, has been often repeated to you, by me, who feels tenderly affected for his Sufferings—

There are Several gentlemen in Congress, who Sincerely wish him to have an employment in his Countries Servise—it would be needless to trouble you with his different Marches from the walls of Quebec, to the Close of the War—

Now Sir, it only wants your approbation to establish him in Some business of a Public nature, that he may Spend the Evening of life, more free from disquietude

He has been requested, by all the Members from this State, to apply to the President without delay—for a Post in the Navy yard at longisland—Command of Some Garrison, or inspector of Some Arsenal—either of which he is Calculated to fill—

I am Sir, with the greatest Respect PHEBE BALDWIN

RC (DNA: RG 59, LAR); endorsed by TJ as received 24 May and "emploimt for her husbd" and so recorded in SJL.

To Benjamin Smith Barton

Washington May 21. 05.

Th: Jefferson presents his friendly salutations to Doctr. Barton: when sending him the dried specimens of plants from mr Dunbar he omitted to send some moss which he had taken out of the hotsprings of the Washeta, in a temperature of 150.° in which he says are some of the animalculae, inhabitants of the moss. Th:J. having no microscope here has been unable to see them: but he commits them now to the better hands of Doctr. Barton.

RC (PHi); addressed: "Doctr. Barton." PoC (DLC); endorsed by TJ.

SPECIMENS OF PLANTS: see TJ to Barton, 2 May.

SOME MOSS: see William Dunbar to TJ, 2 and 15 Feb.

From John A. Chevallié

Union tavern George town 21t. may 1805.

J. A. Chevallié Present his respectful compliments to his Excellency the President & take the liberty of Enclosing an abstract of James McKay's travels up the Missoury which he received last Evening from St. Louis des Illinois. if the President has not seen it before, he will be Very Wellcome to Direct a Copy to be taken, previous to its being returned to J.A.C.

RC (DLC); endorsed by TJ as received 21 May and so recorded in SJL. Enclosure not found, but see below.

RECEIVED LAST EVENING: Chevallié was in communication with Antoine Soulard, surveyor general for upper Louisiana. Chevallié shared Soulard's account of the Missouri River, dated March 1805, with Samuel Latham Mitchill, who published a translation in his journal, *The Medical Repository*. It is likely that Chevallié sent Mitchill the document he enclosed to TJ at the same time he sent Soulard's account. Immediately following the Soulard narrative, Mitchill published an excerpt from the journal of another Missouri explorer, Jean Baptiste Truteau, which he compared to "Mr. M'Kay's narrative." The *Repository* had yet to publish that narrative, so Mitchill was possibly confusing it with Soulard's, but in the following number of the periodical he published "Extract from the Manuscript Journal" of James Mackay. Mackay's account was not so much a journal as an overview of his trading and exploring experiences on behalf of the Spanish, with attention to the major Native American nations he had encountered. It also included an extract from the journal of his associate John Evans (*Medical Repository*, 2d hexade, 3 [1806], 308-15; 2d hexade, 4 [1807], 27-36; A. P. Nasatir, ed., *Before Lewis and Clark: Documents Illustrating the History of the Missouri, 1785-1804*, 2 vols. [St. Louis, 1952], 2:490-9; Vol. 42:194n).

From Edward Johnston

SIR Norfolk, May 21st. 1805

Under cover hereof you will please receive Bill Lading for three hhds of Bacon Hams, which I now forward to you at the request of Mr. George Jefferson of Richmond.—Wishing them safe to hand, I remain Sir with sincere respect Your Obed. Servt.

EDWD. JOHNSTON

RC (DLC); at head of text: "Thomas Jefferson Esqr."; endorsed by TJ as received 29 May but recorded in SJL as received 30 May. Enclosure: bill of lading, Norfolk, 21 May, being a printed form, with blanks filled by a clerk and signed by Job Palmer, master of the sloop *Montezuma*, describing a shipment consisting of "Three hogsheads containing Bacon Hams" with freight costs of "eleven Shillings per Hhd," addressed to TJ in Washington (MS in same).

To Samuel Latham Mitchill

Washington May 21. 05.

Th: Jefferson presents his friendly salutations to Dr. Mitchell & sends him the extract of a letter he has recieved from mr T. M. Randolph with a small bag containing, as he supposes the specimen of salt mentioned by mr Randolph. he received but one, tho' two are mentioned.

Extract of a letter from TMR. to Th:J. dated Edgehill May 11. 05

'A person from Greenbriar county of this state, the owner of a very large cave near the Courthouse from which great quantities of salt petere have been made, has, a day or two since, lodged with me a specimen of a kind of salt produced in an attempt to make salt petre from the earth of a newly discovered chamber of the cave. this specimen seems to consist of at least two distinct neutral salts, one of which is to my tongue Glauber's salts exactly. I suspect a third to exist also, but I have no means of ascertaining, nor even of determining the form of the chrystals which are so small they require a glass to magnify them. I send by the stage a specimen to you and one for Doctr. Mitchell which I must trouble you to forward to him. a promise which I could not avoid making the proprietor of the cave, to have the product of it analysed, & it's value determined for him, forces me to give you this trouble.'

PoC (DLC); endorsed by TJ.

LETTER FROM TMR: recorded in SJL as received 14 May, but not found.

To Ellen Wayles Randolph

Miss Eleanor W. Randolph to Th: Jefferson Dr.

1805. May 21.	To a letter which ought to be written once in every 3. weeks, while I am here, to wit from Jan. 1. 1805. to this day,[1] 15. weeks	5.
	Cr.	
Feb. 23.	By one single letter of this day's date	1
	Balance due from E. W. Randolph to Th:J. letters	4
		5

So stands the account for this year, my dear Ellen, between you and me. unless it be soon paid off, I shall send the sheriff after you. I inclose you an abundant supply of poetry, among which you will find Goody Blake, which I think you wanted. I will thank you if you will put on your boots & spurs & ride to Monticello and inform me how my thorns live. this part of the country is beautifying with them so fast that every ride I take makes me anxious for those at Monticello. your Papa in his last letter informs me the mumps have got into the family. let me know who have it & how all do. kiss your dear Mama for me & shake hands with all the little ones. present me affectionately to your Papa & accept mes baise-mains yourself.

TH: JEFFERSON

PoC (MHi); at foot of text: "Miss Ellen W. Randolph"; endorsed by TJ. Enclosure: "Goody Blake and Harry Gill, a True Story," by William Wordsworth (William Wordsworth and Samuel Taylor Coleridge, *Lyrical Ballads: With a Few Other Poems* [London, 1798], 85-93). Other enclosures not identified.

HIS LAST LETTER: Thomas Mann Randolph to TJ, 11 May, not found.

MES BAISE-MAINS: "my kissing your hand."

[1] TJ here canceled "to wit."

To James Sullivan

DEAR SIR Washington May 21. 1805.

An accumulation of business which I found on my return here from a short visit to Monticello, has prevented till now my acknolegement of your favor of the 14th. Ult. this delay has given time to see the result of the contest in your state, and I cannot but congratulate you on the advance it manifests, & the certain prospect it offers that another year restores Massachusets to the general body of the nation. you have indeed recieved the federal unction of lying & slandering. but who has not? who will ever again come into eminent office unanointed with this chrism? it seems to be fixed that falsehood & calumny are to be the ordinary engines of opposition: engines which will not be entirely without effect. the circle of characters equal to the first stations is not too large, & will be lessened by the voluntary retreat of those whose sensibilities are stronger than their confidence in the justice of public opinion I certainly have known, & still know, characters eminently qualified for the most exalted trusts, who could not bear up against the brutal beatings & hewings of these heroes of Billingsgate. I may say, from intimate knolege, that we should have lost the services of the greatest character of our country had he been assailed with the degree of abandoned licentiousness now practised. the torture he felt under rare & slight attacks proved that under those of which the federal bands have shewn themselves capable he would have thrown up the helm in a burst of indignation. yet this effect of sensibility must not be yielded to. if we suffer ourselves to be frightened from our post by mere lying, surely the enemy will use that weapon: for what one so cheap to those of whose system of politics morality makes no part? the patriot, like the Christian, must learn that to bear revilings & persecutions is a part of his duty: and in proportion as the trial is severe, firmness under it becomes more requisite & praiseworthy. it requires indeed self-command. but that will be fortified in proportion as the calls for it's exercise are repeated. in this I am persuaded we shall have the benefit of your good example. to the other falsehoods they have brought forward should they add, as you expect, insinuations of any want of confidence in you from the administration generally, or myself particularly, it will, like their other falsehoods, produce in the public mind a contrary inference. no evidence however of that confidence, which I could furnish should be wanting. an appointment to office would be such but at present there is no opening for it. no vacancy exists in your own state, and the only office here unfilled, has been otherwise tendered, & indeed would be incompatible with the views of your state, which destines you for the most distinguished mark of their affection & confidence, requiring your residence there. to the nation in general your election will be as gratifying as to that particular state: for never can we consider our union as solid while so important a member as Massachusets is disaffected. that we may not fail to obtain this accession to our harmony & prosperity, nor you so honorable a testimony of the esteem & approbation of a respectable state, no one prays more sincerely than I do: and with this assurance I tender you my friendly & respectful salutations.

Th: Jefferson

PoC (DLC); at foot of first page: "Judge Sullivan."

Sullivan's favor of 14 Apr., received 22 Apr. from Boston, has not been found. In 1807, Sullivan asked that TJ burn the letter, but TJ returned it to him instead (Sullivan to TJ, 3 June 1807; TJ to Sullivan, 20 June 1807).

result of the contest: Caleb Strong was re-elected as governor of Massachusetts, defeating his longtime Republican rival Sullivan, albeit with a "diminished federalist majority" over the previous year's contest (*National Intelligencer*, 3 May). After the election, Sullivan published in the *Independent Chronicle* a "Refutation of Calumny" in which he countered several electioneering charges against him, articulated his support of the federal Constitution, and asserted that TJ's administration had been "uniformly consistent with the spirit of that Constitution" (Boston *Repertory*, 1 and 5 Mch.; Boston *Independent Chronicle*, 8 Apr.).

heroes of billingsgate: an allusion to the vituperative language associated with the women from London's Billingsgate fish market, but used to describe vulgarity in speech more generally (oed).

GREATEST CHARACTER OF OUR COUNTRY: George Washington.

ONLY OFFICE HERE: between March and August 1805, TJ sought to fill the office of attorney general to which Robert Smith had been appointed before he returned exclusively to his former role as secretary of the navy (Jacob Crowninshield to TJ, 27 Mch.; TJ to John Julius Pringle, 15 June; TJ to John Breckinridge, 7 Aug.).

Notes on John Sibley's Account of Native American Tribes

[after 21 May 1805]

Sibley's acct of the Indians.

pa. 1. the French while possessing Louisiana had a fort & some souldiers 375 + 120 = 495. miles above Natchitoches on the Red river, at the antient settlement of the Caddos. their present settlemt 120. mi. N.W. from Natchitoches. the Caddos, Yattassees, Nandakoes, Nabedaches, Inies or Tachies, Nacogdoches, Keychias, Adais, & Natchitoches, all speak the Caddo language.[1] the Caddo country hilly, not rich. they raise corn, beans, pumpkins &c.

pa. 2. the Yattassees, live on Bayou Pierre, branch of Red river 50. mi. above Natchitoches. their village surrounded by a settlemt of French families, under the Spanish govmt, where there is a Spanish guard of a noncommd. officer & 8. souldiers. the rights to land of these French families were granted to them by the French govmt of Louisiana. the French had formerly a station & factory there, & another on Sabine river near 100. miles N.W. of the Bayou Pierre settlement. the original language of the Yattassees was not the Caddo but they have adopted that. 40. men. 25. women. Agricultural.[2]

pa. 3. Nandakoes on Sabine river 60. or 70. mi. W. of Yattassees where the former French station & factory were. 40. men.

Adaïs. 20. men. 40. mi. from Natchitoches & 20. mi. North[3] from where the Spanish Fort or mission[4] of Adaïs was. nobody now at the old post of Adaïs. it is grown up. Sibley's lre of Mar. 5. 05.

Aliche; pronounced Ayeish. 25. souls. near Nacogdoches. their native language different. but now speak Caddo.

4. Keyes or Keychies, 60. men. live on E. bank of Trinity river a little above where the road from Natchitoches to St. Antoine crosses it. have a peculiar native language, but speak Caddo. Agricultural

Inies or Tachies, from whom the province of Techas is called. 80. men. 25. mi. W. of Natchidoches, on a small branch of Sabine called Naches. their language is the Caddo. excellent land. agricultural.

Nabidaches on W. side of same river, 15 mi. above the Tachies. 80 men. same language. excellent land. agricultural.

Bedias on Trinity river 60. mi. S. of Nacogdoches. 100. men. language different from all others, but speak Caddo. they are hunters.

Accokesaws. on the W. side of the Colorado or Riv. Rouge 200 mi. S.W. of Nacogdoches. a fine country. have a language of their own, but communicate by the language of signs which they all understand. 80. men. the Spaniards 30. or 40. y. ago had a mission there, which they broke up and removed to Nacogdoches. they talk of resettling it. they are hunters.

pa. 5. Maies. on large creek St. Gabriel, on bay of St. Bernard, near the mouth of Guadaloupe river. 200. men. always at war with Spaniards, much attachd to French ever since La Salle landed in their neighborhood. Mattagordo is near them where the Spaniards talk of opening a new port & making a settlement, and where they say are the remains of a French block house. the cannon now at Labahie were brought from that place, & are known by the engravings now on them. have a language of their own, but speak Attacapa. converse by signs.

Carankouas. on an island or Peninsula in the bay of St. Bernard, 10. mi. long 5. mi. wide. very rich. a bluff adjacent is of coal which has been afire many years, affording light by night and smoke by day. coast continues shoaly out of sight of land. irreconcileable enemies to Spaniards, kind to French. 500. men. speak Attacapa.

pa. 6. Cances. a very numerous nation, consisting of a great many tribes, occupying from the bay of St. Bernard across the Rio Grande towards La vera cruz. hostile to Spaniards, friendly to French. are hunters and[5] use the bow chiefly. the Spaniards used to make slaves of them. many were sold to the Fr. inhab at Natchitoches @ 40. or 50. D. a number still there, but free. 20. y. ago the k. of Spain forbade making any more of them slaves, & emancipated those there. the women brought up there married natives & now have families. they have a peculiar language. speak by signs. in friendship with all other Indians except the Hietans.

Tankaways or Tanks. have no land nor fixed residence. they occupy alternately the country watered by the Trinity, Braces & Colorado, towards Sta. Fé. 200. men. hunters. have the best breed of horses.

7. Tawakenoes, or Three Canes. on W. side of the Braces 200. mi. W. of Nacogdoches towards Sta. Fé. 200. men. hunters. have guns, but hunt principally with the bow. they trade at Nacogdoches. they[6] speak the same language with the Panis or Towiaches.

Panis or Towiaches. the latter their proper name; the former their French appellation. they live on the South bank of the Red river 800. mi. above Natchitoches by the meanders of the river, but only 340. in by the nearest path.[7] they have 2. towns near together, the lower where their chief, called the great bear, lives is Witcheta town, & the other called Tawaahach. at war with Spaniards. friendly to French & Americans. at war with Osages. a rich country of prairies for many hundred miles round them. many horses & mules. they raise corn, pumpkins, beans, tobo. to spare, which they sell to the Hietans for rugs, horses & mules. have but few guns, little ammunition, which they keep for war, & hunt with the bow. they have some white hares & white bears. their language peculiar. 400. men.

8. Hietans or Comanches. wanderers. no villages, divided into numerous hordes unknown to one another. no estimate of their numbers. they have tents of dressed skins, conical, sfft. for a fa̦mily of 10. or 12. persons. they have 2. horses for every tent, besides which they travel on horseback. the horses never at large, but tethered. vast droves of wild horses among them. generally at war with the Spaniards, but friendly to French & Americans. they commit depredns on Sta. Fé & St. Antoine. cleanly & dressy. never remain long enough in any place to plant any thing. Cayenne pepper spontaneous among them. they wander over all the country from the Trinity & Braces, crossing Red river to the heads of Arcansa, Rio grande & Missouri & even to the waters of the Western Ocean, where they say they have seen ships. language peculiar. have that of signs.

pa. 10. Natchitoches. formerly lived at Natchitoches which took it's name from them, & was settled by the French 98. years ago [1707.] the remains of the Natchez nation, after their massacre of the French in 1728. fled and encamped on Red river 6. mi. below Natchitoches, & erected a mound now remaining. St. Deny, a Canadian, then Commandt. of Natchitoches with a few souldiers & militia & the Natchitoches attacked & exterminated the Natchez of this settlemt. the lake on which they encamped still called the Natchez lake. the Natchitoches now live 25. mi. by land, above the town of Natchitoches near lake de Muire. there remain of them but 12. men & 19. women. their original language the same as the Yattasee, but they speak Caddo, & French. they only claim the small part of land they live on, for which they have a title from the former govmt. agricultural.

11. Boluxas, emigrants from near Pensacola, about 42. years since. they live at the mouth of Rigolet de Bondieu, a division of Red river 50. mi. below Natchitoch. are catholics. 30. in number. peculiar language,

but speak Mobilian which is spoken by all the Indns. from the E. side of Misipi

Appalaches, emigrants from W. Florida from the river Apalachy. came over about the time the Beloxas did, & live on the river above Bayou Rapide. 14. men. have their own language, but speak Mobilian & French.

Alibamis, from the Alibama river in W. Florida about the same time with the Biloxas & Appalachies. live up Red R. near the Caddos. they speak Creek, Choctaw, Mobilian, French & some of them English. about 30. men. there is another party of them of 40 men on a small creek in Appelousa district 30. mi. N.W. from the church of Appelousa. agricultural.

12. Conchattas. are almost the same people as the Alibamas, but came over only 10. y. ago. on E. bank of Sabine river 80. mi. nearly S. from Natchitoches. 160. men. hunters, particularly of bears. a bear generally yields from 8. to 12. galls. oil, worth 1. D. a gallon, & the skin sells for 1. D. they say the Carankouas are 80. mi. S. of them, on the bay, which is the nearest point of the sea from Natchitoch. a few families of Chactoos have lately settled near the Conchattas. these last speak Creek, which is their native language.

Pacanas. 30 men. on the Qulquechose river which falls into the bay between Attacapa & Sabine, about 40. mi. S.W. of Natchitoch. they emigrated from W. Florida 40. y. ago. their village 50. S.E. of the Conchattas. have peculiar language, but speak Mobilian.

---

13. Attacapas [means Man-eaters] 20. mi. W. of Attacapa church towards Quelqueshoe. with some Tunicas & Humas married among them they are about 80. men. agricultural, & aboriginal of the part they live in. their language & the Carankouas the same.

Appelousas. [means Black head] aboriginal of their place which is 15. mi. W. from Appelousa church. 40. men. language peculiar, but understand Attacapa & French. agricultural.

Tunicas. formerly lived on the Bayou Tunica above point Coupé on the E. side of Misipi. now at Avoyall. 25. men. language peculiar, but speak Mobilian. agricultural.

Pascagoulas, emigrants from Pascagoula river. now on Red R. 60. mi. below Natchitoches. 25 men. language peculiar, but speak Mobilian & French. agricultl.

14. Tenisaws, emigrants from Tensaw R. which falls into the bay of Mobile, 40. y. ago. now removing to Bayou Boeuf, 25. mi. S. from Pascagoulas. speak Mobilian and French. agricultural.

Chactoos Aboriginal of their canton on Bayou boeuf 2. mi. S. of Bayou Rapide on Red R. towards Appelousa. 30. men. language peculiar but speak Mobilian. delightful lands. Bayou boeuf falls into the Chaffaleya & discharges thro' Appelousa & Attacapa into Vermilion bay.

Washas. they were inhab. of Barrataria when the French first came. only 2 men & 3. women living in French families, extinct as a nation & their language lost.

Chactaws. there is one village of about 30. men 12. mi. above the post on Washita, & on that river who have not been home for several years: & another village of 50 men on Bayou chico, in the Northern part of the district of Apelousa, who have been there about 9. years, having as they say the permission of the Govr. of Louisiana to settle there. they are liked neither by the red nor white people.

15. Arkensaws on the S. side the Arkansa, in 3. villages, about 12. mi. above the post or station. the 1st. village called Tawanima, 2d. Ousotu. 3d. Ocapa. 100. men. Aboriginal proprietors of the country on that river which they claim for about 300. miles above them to the junction[8] of the river Cadron with Arkansa. above that fork the Osages claim. they are at war with the Osages, but peace with all other people white & red. their language is Osage.

The preceding is a list of all the Indians South of Arkansa between the rivers Misipi & Grande. the Avoyals and Humas are extinct.

The following should have been at the head of the list, page 1st.

Caddoquis. 35. mi. W. of the main branch of Red R. on Bayou Sodo, navigable in rainy seasons within 6. mi. of their village. 120. mi. N.W. from Natchitoches. they have lived there but 5. years. their Aboriginal settlemt. was 375. mi. higher up the Red R. 100. men. very brave. boast that they never shed white man's blood. have great influence over the other Indian tribes. hostile to Choctaws, & Osages. most of them have guns.

MS (DLC: TJ Papers, 234:41890-1); undated, but not before receipt of Sibley's 5 Mch. letter to the War Department (see below); entirely in TJ's hand, including brackets.

SIBLEY'S ACCT: on 21 May, the War Department recorded receiving a letter of 5 Mch. from John Sibley enclosing "an Acct. of several Indian tribes." TJ commented on the account in a letter of 27 May to Sibley, and his notes closely follow Sibley's description of Native American groups then living in the areas of present-day Louisiana, Arkansas, Oklahoma, and Texas. TJ enclosed transcripts of Sibley's account, dated 5 Apr., in a message to Congress on 19 Feb. 1806 (DNA: RG 107, RLRMS; DNA: RG 46, LPPM, 9th Cong., 1st sess.; DNA: RG 233, PM, 9th Cong., 1st sess.; printed in ASP, *Indian Affairs*, 1:721-5).

As Sibley indicated in his account, many of the tribal groups—the Yatasi, Anadarkos (NANDAKOES), Nabedaches, Hainai (INIES), Nacadoches, Kitsai (KEYCHIAS), Adais, Natchitoches, and Eyeish (ALICHE)—could be considered part of the Caddoan linguistic group, which after removal to the Indian Territory coalesced as the Caddo tribe. The Bidais (BEDIAS) and Akokisas (ACCOKESAWS) were part of the Atakapa linguistic group and were culturally similar to the Karankawas (CARANKOUAS). The Mayes, or Malleyes, tribe, who were part of the Tonkawa linguistic group, were closely linked with the Karankawas at this time. The CANCES were the Lipan Apaches, who had fairly recently displaced coastal peoples in southern Texas and northern Mexico (Albert S. Gatschist, *The Karankawa Indians, the Coast People of Texas* [Cambridge, Mass., 1891], 35-6; Sturtevant, *Handbook*, 10:345-6, 390; 13, pt. 1:570-1; 14:616, 629-30, 659, 661, 663; Tyler, *New Handbook of Texas*, 4:586).

In 1787, Louisiana's Spanish governor Esteban Miró revived an earlier order that EMANCIPATED enslaved Native Americans, but the decree was not well enforced (Dayna Bowker Lee, "From Captives to Kin: Indian Slavery and Changing Social Identities on the Louisiana Colonial Frontier," in Max Carocci and Stephanie Pratt, eds., *Native American Adoption, Captivity, and Slavery in Changing Contexts* [New York, 2012], 93-4).

Of the Plains groups that Sibley discussed, the TANKAWAYS were the Tonkawa, while the TAWAKENOES, OR THREE CANES, were a band of the Wichitas, which Sibley referred to as the PANIS (Sturtevant, *Handbook*, 13, pt. 1:564-5, pt. 2:963).

The other groups were remnant populations of smaller tribes, most of whom—such as the Biloxis, Koasatis (CONCHATTAS), and Taensas (TENISAWS)—had relocated from the western Florida Gulf Coast region to areas west of the Mississippi (same, 14:183-5, 188-9, 413, 586, 593, 598, 668).

ARKENSAWS: that is, the Quapaws.

[1] Remainder of paragraph interlined.

[2] Word interlined.

[3] Word interlined.

[4] Preceding three words interlined in place of "post."

[5] Preceding three words interlined.

[6] MS: "the."

[7] TJ first wrote "in a strait line" before altering the text to read as above.

[8] Word interlined in place of "mouth."

From Thomas Claxton

HONORD SIR, Philada 22d May 1805

Inclosed you will find rough sketches of different lamps—Such of them as you may think proper to call for on your own account you will please to designate on the sheet of paper inclosed & send it back—The passage lanthorn marked out, is simple and easily mended—the size of the inferior priced ones is hardly to be discovered—please to say what shall be the price—the shades I have never seen before—if you wish a pair please to let me know it—The Steward has mentioned 4 table cloths for six or eight gentlemen—as different sizes vary the price very much, I shall be thankful Sir, if you will desire him to let you know the exact number of yards which will be most useful in length—of this article very elegant is to be had of various sizes—Inclosed you will find a pattern of India Matting—The width is yd and half price one dollar—I have thought that it will be a cheap covering for the passage upstairs, and have been informed that it will last several years—if you should approve of it, please to inform me—In the Steward's list I find four plated waiters of different sizes—the largest size of these is 22 inches long—price 55 dollars—I have thought that two of this size will be more proper in your house for tea and cake than such as one at present used—If you should be of that opinion Sir, please to signify it—Brussels Carpeting, when I last purchased here was from two dollars to two dollars 25 cents—it has now risen to two and 75—and I can get but $12\frac{1}{2}$ cents abated—it is exceedingly elegant—

I hope, Sir you will pardon me for troubling you with so many questions—nothing induces me to do so, but a desire to please you

I have the honor to be Sir With the most greatful respect Your Humble Servant THOS CLAXTON

PS The cost of this mat will not amount to more than canvass without paint

RC (MHi); endorsed by TJ as received 25 May and so recorded in SJL. Enclosures not found.

STEWARD: Étienne Lemaire.

To Jones & Howell

MESSRS. JONES & HOWELL Washington May 22. 1805.

Your favor of the 14th. has been duly recieved. the stoves bespoke by mr Latrobe, & mentioned to have been forwarded, were at my desire, of which I thought I had advised you at the time. be so good as, on the reciept of this, to ship for me to Gibson & Jefferson two tons of nail rod assorted from 6 d. to 20 d. Accept my friendly salutations and good wishes. TH: JEFFERSON

PoC (MHi); endorsed by TJ. Notation in SJL: "for 2. tons rod."

Jones & Howell's FAVOR of 14 May regarding mill irons and stoves has not been found (Appendix IV).

STOVES: see Jones & Howell to TJ, 9 May.

From Charles Pinckney

DEAR SIR, [February-22 May 1805]

I wrote you a few weeks since by Mr. Gorham, & finding another safe opportunity by Mr. Preble, I avail myself of it, to send you a Duplicate of what I wrote before, and to add that subsequent events have proved and confirmed beyond a doubt what I then told you, which was, that my conduct & the stand I made here, was the true reason of precipitating the rupture between England & Spain. At the time I wrote by Capt. Dulton to Mr. Madison, in July, England had then determined Spain should remain neutral, and Soler, her Minister of Finance, had but a short time before that, written Circular Letters to all the Sea Ports to that effect—It was only upon the stand they saw[1] I made here, and on the idea that our Government never would give way either on the Question of West Florida, or the Western limits of Louisiana[2] or the great pecuniary one of the French Condemnations and Spoliations, and the difficulty of amicably arranging them, that made England decide to alter her plan, and strike at Spain—nothing less than the decision of my conduct, & the tone I gave to my proceedings, at that time, could have produced, at so early a period, an event so fortunate for us. When I have the pleasure of seeing you, I shall be able to explain much more than I choose to trust to paper, even by this, as I consider it, very safe opportunity—We are still waiting Mr. Cevallos's answer to our third Letter, which is to be sent to you by this opportunity, and at present I can form no definitive opinion as to the result. I am extremely anxious about the conclusion as I wish so much to return, & also that we may be able to arrange every thing amicably, and annex Florida to our Republic—it is peculiarly valuable to us as a Nation, and in this light I wish it as a Citizen of the United States. as a Citizen of South Carolina, I am, if possible, still more anxious, because it will add great weight & security to that particular interest which Georgia South Carolina, Louisiana & Florida must compose, & which in the greatest part of its most valuable staples and productions, differ from the rest of the Union—these form, or will form when we obtain Florida, so great a proportion of the Territory of our Country, and particularly of its Sea-coast—its soil is so fertile & productions so extremely valuable, that there can be no doubt in a few years it will be so populous as to have great weight in the political scale, & enlightened, as I trust they will be, by their neighbours who, have the same local interests with themselves, it is to be hoped their weight will always be thrown into the republican one[3]—For these & many reasons, I am anxious now to annex Florida, and I confess I should not feel a little pleased in being one of the Instruments of doing it. I still have my fears we shall not get it at this time, as the French seem so anxious to make something out of it themselves—their expressing an opinion that West Florida is no part of the Cession of Louisiana, clearly proves this, & their wishing us to have no retrospect but in case of an agreement, only to date from the present time, is a clear proof that in case they find they are obliged to give way and can get no money from us, they wish all the monstrous grants of Land that have lately been made to Lauret & others, in which it is presumed Mr Talleyrand[4] is concerned, should be held valid, well-knowing how much they would increase in value when forming a part of the United States, and I should not be surprised if even he Talleyrand[5] & others should be anxious to have establishments and property there to which they may fly in case of new convulsions in Europe where every thing hangs by a thread, & they should escape with their lives—they are fully aware of this uncertainty & it is the conviction in my mind that it exists, which makes me (if France must have a Despot) prefer Bonaparte[6] to a Bourbon[7] while the one holds the reins all is uncertainty and force[8] and you may be assured that republicanism is gaining ground, while the return of the other would bring with it the sanction of ages & the support of all the Monarchies of Europe thereby making its continuance & transmission much more regular & secure than the other—I have no doubt the republicans are at this moment the majority in France, and that they will continue secretly & silently to increase while Bonaparte[9] holds the power, & that the moment he is no more, Liberty will have again a chance to do something—I am not one of those who suppose it is impossible for Frenchmen to be free—On the contrary, I think the french character, notwithstanding the unfortunate issue of their first attempt, is extremely improved even by the tempestuous Experiments they have made—I have therefore reason to believe their next essay will be made upon more moderate & rational principles, & succeed better—Our example will have an astonishing effect in removing the dangerous & false opinion that a people with an extensive Territory cannot be free and happy & continue united or protect themselves—it is now in the mouths of every well informed influential Frenchman, and this is so well known to Bonaparte[10] that be assured he hates our Government and detests its effects more, if possible, than he does England, and that nothing on Earth would give him so much pleasure as to injure, or if possible destroy it[11]—his conduct in getting

Louisiana & the navigation of the Missisipi into his hands when he did & his making the Spaniards stop the Deposit at New Orleans when he ordered it in 1802 are such unanswerable proofs of his Enmity to us as to leave no doubt of what would be his course if he had peace & the means to attend to it—As You must unquestionably hear it from another source I now inform you confidentially that the Deposit at New Orleans was stopped by the express Order & at the sole instance & application of the French Government & that I am now able to give you the highest most authentic & official proof of the fact & *that it was only done by their order.* but knowing You will recieve it from another & very respectable source I do not think it necessary now to give you my authority—there is nothing perhaps will astonish you & Mr Madison more than this fact & to You alone I now communicate it for the present in confidence: there is not a man in my office or about me who knows a word of the circumstances & therefore I put this in my own hand writing in this duplicate having *ordered a blank to be left here on purpose to be filled up by myself after the rest was copied.*

I well know the[12] sensation that such a development would make in the minds of the American people against the French, & that in their general detestation and abhorrence of this perfidious & unmanly act, (for it was certainly unmanly to do it & deny it in the manner they did) they would be apt to confound the Nation with their Government, whereas I still hope the french Nation will be not only always friendly to us when it is in their power to act from themselves, but that they will be one day much more like us in their situation & pursuits—for this reason I keep it a profound secret & leave it to you, when you hear it from the other source, to determine what use is to be made of it. I had proceeded thus far in writing you, when Mr. Cevallos's answer to our third note appeared. Our official letter to Mr. Madison will give a full account of it, & inclose a Copy by which you see fully that any further mildness & moderation are totally lost upon this Court, & that if we are to get what we have a right to, our Government must now look to a different course—in this, Mr. Cevallos has inserted a part of Mr. Talleyrand's note to the Spanish Ambassador, in July last, respecting our claims, evidently calculated to threaten us with the resentment of France, should we presume to persevere in our Claims for french spoliations within the Spanish Territory—these[13] remarks & particularly where he says "his Imperial Majesty would have expressed great displeasure at the Spanish Government had they entered into any arrangements with us respecting the french Condemnations & Spoliations *& would have had this displeasure expressed in a much stronger manner to the United States*" thereby treating us as Governments perfectly at his will & whom he could applaud or censure as he thought proper, will surprise you—this connected with the whole tenour of Mr Cevallos's Letter & the charge by both Governments (French & Spanish) on us of wishing to be paid twice for the same thing must convince You that all my opinions respecting the inutility of any attempts except those of force or fear are well founded—that my conduct to them in July last was the only one calculated to obtain our rights & that we must either come to something like that again or yield them which I am sure You will never do—this last letter of the Spanish Minister Cevallos & the inclosures must shew You the Difficulties I have had to encounter here in every important Question I had to discuss—such particularly as the French Claims the attempt to purchase Florida the stopping the Deposit at New Orleans, the act of the 24 February & the refusal to ratify the Convention in all of which there can be no doubt France interfered as much as possible against us & *that it is entirely owing to her Spain has been so extremely unfriendly to us* & still continues so as they would be afraid to push things so far if they were not backed by France: the present state of things promises nothing but a continued & positive refusal on the part of this Government to comply with our offers & Your directions as to the Claims—this being confirmed by Mr Cevallos in his last conference. We have determined to send Mr Preble with our dispatches whom I recommend strongly to your notice & protection & Mr Madisons—he has assisted greatly here in writing & translating—is extremely intelligent & will be able to explain much to You—I am preparing to return the moment the Special Mission is ended which being begun in Mr Monroes & my name, it was proper I should continue in it until the End—I expect it will now terminate soon & I fear not as we wish & as we have upon all occasions used the utmost mildness & moderation it will be a new proof to You that neither those or Justice can be depended upon as having the least influence here or with France—that my conduct has been zealous & most completely disinterested in endeavouring to first persuade & afterwards to compell them to a different course & this in the face of the most polite & friendly attentions personally in proof of which I enclose You a copy of one of the Prince of Peace's Letters to me dated only six days before Mr Cevalloss refusal to ratify the Convention & which will shew You the affectionate footing I was upon with him until then—in short there is no doubt they shewed me every kind of civility & particular personal attention in the hope it might make me recieve the refusal to ratify the Convention & to comply with our just demands as to the limits & french claims with less resentment than they well knew such treatment of our Government deserved, but they found they knew me very little to make such calculations—it was impossible for me who had at home so zealously & invariably opposed every attempt even from our own then Government & its Officers to injure the rights & insult the feelings of our citizens should suffer any foreign Government to do so merely from the ridiculous idea of being said to stand well with them—I would rather stand well with my own feelings & that our citizens should know that under no circumstances I can ever forget what belongs to their honour or rights & I am sure that my firm maintenance of them here has given me more respect in Europe than a contrary or more supple one would have done—

I have written you a long letter but the long & active & I trust steady & consistent part I have taken in the affairs of our own state & as far as I could in those of the United States make me feel an interest in them which is far more dear to me than any other consideration—I have been so much concerned in forming the constitutions of both & in doing all I could lately to bring them back to their original republican principles & place them in hands that I know will take care to keep them so that I own I am particularly anxious to explain to You my opinions & the motives of my conduct because I always wish to possess as I have hitherto done Your regard & good opinion & feeling as I do that my conduct in Europe is steadily & in the most disinterested manner maintaining the rights of our Citizens & the honour of our Government has invariably met the approbation of the European Governments I therefore consider it as giving me an additional claim[14] to Your friendship for me & in this opinion I have written You this long & confidential letter & which I send you by a very confidential opportunity I shall keep this letter open to see if any thing occurs before the opportunity goes but I have little or no hope that any thing will be done here now—Mr Monroe has some & I wish I may be mistaken & he right—he is very zealous & leaves no proper means untried to accomplish it—I am very glad he is come as I am sure & indeed know he will tell you that he highly approved my conduct here in July last now acts upon it himself[15] & sees by being present the necessity there was for it & that the stand I then made has been & will be productive of great public utility—being made on *truly independent & American Ground*, without considering the Views & opinions of any nation but our own it certainly attracted very much the attention of Europe & taught both France & Spain to know & feel the consequences of such conduct to us in future & should we ultimately succeed (which I still doubt) our firmness then & since the special mission begun will in the opinion of Mr   & myself have greatly contributed to it—

I keep this letter open until the return of Mr Dulton from Paris where we have sent to General Armstrong to see if any thing can be done there further or that it may yet be possible to get their influence to assist the negotiation here—

March 26: 1805

Captain Dulton returned last night with letters from General Armstrong stating that the French Answer is in the highest tone possible—that our claims as to West *Florida & French Spoliations are totally unfounded & must be abandoned & that at all events & hazards & without a moments doubt & hesitation France will support Spain against us even should things proceed* to extremities—thus it appears in the face of their most solemn promises they are determined to oppose us & to reduce our purchase of Louisiana to a mere nothing. however this may perhaps surprise You it does not me—When I recollect M Bs: conduct to us for the last 4 Years & particularly *the one to get back the ratification of the cession of Louisiana after it had been compleated & stop it entirely* & his earnest & irresistible desire to make peace with England that he & Spain together may pay more attention to us I see every moment new cause to wish the continuance of the War in Europe & for us to be on our guard the moment they think of peace—One would not suppose that England would be so lost to her own interest & safety as ever to join France & Spain against us but there is no knowing what misguided counsels stimulated by Revenge may prompt them to even against their own interest—When I recollect their former designs (in 1793) & see their present stupid & impolitic conduct in shutting us out of the West India Islands there is no knowing what even they may be tempted to do—

I enclose you an Extract which perhaps You have not seen & which gives us the View even Europe had of some of our former acts—every American must blush it had ever been possible for such remarks to be made & with truth—

April

It is now some weeks since we heard from Mr Cevallos & have written him a letter urging him to send us his answer to the Western Limits of Louisiana which he has promised & which closes the discussion of all the controverted points—after recieving this it must soon appear whether it is possible to do any thing here or now & as we have been now employed three months & very closely so indeed & the season advancing fast into summer I am hopeful we shall soon finish my anxiety being very great indeed To return with the greatest dispatch to Carolina & my little family—

April 26

We have just had another answer from Mr Armstrong stating that he had laid all our correspondence before Mr Talleyrand whose laconic & decisive answer was "that the more they considered the subject the more they (France) were convinced that Spain was right on every Question of the Controversy with us"—Some short time before this We had received Mr Cevalloss answer to the Western Limits confining them to the Natchitoches & thus abridging the once supposed extensive country of Louisiana to a mere nothing as to sea coast & proving what we scarcely ever doubted since the answer of France that she (France) wants to be paid Three times for this country—once as she was by us, secondly by Spain to save West Florida to her & place the Western Limit at the Natchitoches & if this succeeds then at some future period to sell the Floridas to us on something like the scheme already proposed through Mr —& for a price not unlike that given for Louisiana & she to recieve the money from us—

May 18

Finding it impossible notwithstanding all our attempts to get from this Government any propositions in return for those we had made & Mr Monroe seeing clearly that it was in vain to expect any thing like such an amicable adjustment as we could alone accede to, thought that it would be best for us to send in at this stage our ultimatum which was done in the manner our public letters announce to which on the 15th We recieved Mr: Cevallos's final rejection & refusal to do any one thing we expected or demanded—he refuses to pay a shilling for the french spoliations—to give up a foot of West Florida (as so called by the English) & scarcely a foot to the West of the Mississipi—in short he refuses every thing & has not even the decency to offer any thing or any mode of accommodation on the part of Spain—in return for great lenghth of time in attending on him, & for unexampled moderation & patience & every effort to conciliate he has displayed unwarrantable (in their situation at least) haughtiness of proceedure & a mode of rejecting *all our* claims which may be said to amount almost to defiance & contempt—Under these circumstances We have been inevitably compelled to put an end to the Special Mission & Mr: Monroe has this moment demanded his passports & audience of Leave to return to London & We are now waiting the answer

May 20: 1805

Mr Cevallos's answer is recieved appointing tomorrow for Mr Monroe's audience of Leave & the Passport will be immediately granted to him & this answer which is enclosed will convince You that every thing I have hitherto said & transmitted You is strictly true & that nothing is to be done with this Court but by fear & force & by removing the idea that we are not entirely to be directed by France in this or any other attempt to assert our rights either here or elsewhere & that We will not sacrifice every national claim to peace & Commerce—Our public letter is so full on this subject that I omit many observations that may be made but I now hope You will think & I am sure Mr Monroe will tell You so, that in the very arduous & difficult situations I have had here for nearly four Years, with the whole influence of France constantly opposed to our claims that I have never once forgot what was due to the rights or honour of our country, nor ever once suffered the idea to exist that she was either to be managed by or subject to the influence of any power on Earth—In finishing the Special Mission as We have done We give to Spain & France an Example of moderation they by no means deserved at least as to the manner in which we conducted the whole negotiation, & our offer & the terms in which We made & explained them—although for four months continually requested to do so they have obstinately refused to make us any propositions in return for those We made & in positively refusing to pay a shilling for the french spoliations—to yield an inch of West Florida—to insist on a line between the Adaes & Natchitoches to cut the Red River on the Westn limits & even to refuse to ratify the Convention of August 1802 except they had the right to annex a Declaration thereto destructive of the claims established by the 6th Article (which Mr Madison positively forbid us to accept) they have given us such a defiance as will call up all those feelings for which the freemen of our Country have hitherto been so peculiarly distinguished

For my own part I am at a loss what to do I am so extremely anxious to return home that every Day appears like a month to me & yet there being no one here I choose to leave to represent the United States or who is qualified for diplomatic discussion & not thinking myself authorised[16] to put an end to all diplomatic intercourse without your orders I am obliged to sacrifice my own interest & feelings & every personal consideration & remain sometime longer—Mr Monroe is decidely of opinion I ought to do so until I can get a proper person to take the place or until Mr Bowdoin or Mr Irvine arrives which I now find very uncertain & perhaps the honour of our Country makes it necessary they should not arrive until You know what has happened

& direct accordingly—I am completely tired of this situation in which I have acted, *as Consul, Agent for claims & Minister* & in short every thing for this last two Years & besides being obliged to stay so long & so dreadfully inconveniently from home have been saddled with the most enormous Expences that can be concieved—but in this as on every other occasion I have made my personal convenience & my interest give way to public considerations & the only Reward I wish is that my Country should think of me as they have always done & to believe that nothing can make me forget what belongs to their national honour & independence—I do not suppose it is necessary to add any thing to what our public letters & this & my private one to Mr Madison contains which he will shew You—I know great pains have been taken by interested men & my Enemies to weaken the place I once held in your Esteem as a friend to Liberty—I will hope You are too just to let any thing prejudice me with You until You see & hear me & give me an opportunity to detail what I know of men & things in Europe—I have not been an inattentive or unfeeling spectator nor an inactive one—Whatever You may for a moment have thought, I believe now I shall recieve from You, as I know I well deserve & will recieve from the American People at least the acknowledgement that I have refused to yield their rights in Europe with the same firmness I did at home & that although We have not been able to succeed yet that We have preserved our claims inviolate & have left to our Government & fellow Citizens the same opportunity to display their Zeal in asserting & defending, that We did in refusing to yield them—in your hands I am convinced they are always safe. the territory & pecuniary claims in Question are of great value, but much greater are the important & delicate points of national honour. in the refusal of Spain & the interference of France are involved not only in a high degree our national honour but little less than our independence, or at least our free agency as a nation & on the trying crisis I am to rejoice they are in hands so able & honest as they now are—

I am hopeful soon to see you in Washington & to assure You personally of the affectionate regard & respect with which I am always

Dear Sir Yours Truly CHARLES PINCKNEY

May 22: 1805

In Aranjuez

I must request You to correct a mistake in the long piece of 21 March 1803 to the Prince of Peace copy of which I sent You in my last as on looking over another copy made by the same clerk I find he omitted the word "*not*" which was in *the original sent to the Prince* & is also in my office Book—the original as sent to the Prince positively asserted that Florida did not include any part of the East Bank of the Mississipi on which assertion You will find We acted all through—

As my Expence at the Kings Sitio under the Special Mission has been totally extra I have by Colonel Monroe's desire & advice charged it as such, as there can be no doubt of Your allowing it—

I beg leave to present Captain Dulton to You as a most deserving Citizen—

RC (DLC); consisting of an undated Dupl of Pinckney's letter to TJ of February 1805 (see Vol. 45:594-600) with six additions dated 26 Mch. to 22 May; initial portion in a clerk's hand with emendations by Pinckney (see notes 1-11 below); remainder in Pinckney's hand (see note 13); at head of text in Pinckney's hand: "To serve as a duplicate to the last & with additions to which I request Your particular attention"; endorsed by TJ as received 2 Aug. and so recorded in SJL. Enclosure: Pedro Cevallos to James Monroe and Pinckney, Aranjuez, 20 May; Cevallos has presented the king and queen with an account of the Americans' 18 May letter requesting a passport and an audience of leave for Monroe; in response, "their Majesties have fixed to-morrow" for Monroe's audience and Cevallos will send the necessary passport (ASP, *Foreign Relations*, 2:667). Other enclosure printed below.

WE HAVE SENT TO GENERAL ARMSTRONG: Monroe to John Armstrong, 15 Feb., 26 Feb., and 1 Mch. (Madison, *Papers, Sec. of State Ser.*, 9:80, 82n; Monroe, *Papers*, 5:317-19, 327-9; ASP, *Foreign Relations*, 2:636).

LETTERS FROM GENERAL ARMSTRONG: Armstrong to Monroe, 12 Mch. and 18 Mch. (Daniel Preston, *A Comprehensive Catalogue of the Correspondence and Papers of James Monroe*, 2 vols. [Westport, Conn., 2001], 1:166; Monroe, *Papers*, 5:362; ASP, *Foreign Relations*, 2:636).

For an earlier report of Napoleon Bonaparte's desire to GET BACK THE RATIFICATION OF THE CESSION OF LOUISIANA, see Robert R. Livingston to TJ, 2 June 1803 (Vol. 40:470-4).

LETTER URGING HIM TO SEND US HIS ANSWER TO THE WESTERN LIMITS OF LOUISIANA: Monroe and Pinckney to Cevallos, 9 Apr. (Monroe, *Papers*, 5:367-9).

ANOTHER ANSWER FROM MR ARMSTRONG: Armstrong to Monroe, 5 Apr. (Madison, *Papers, Sec. of State Ser.*, 9:95, 98n, 205n; Preston, *Catalogue*, 1:166).

Cevallos gave Spain's ANSWER TO THE WESTERN LIMITS in a lengthy letter to Monroe and Pinckney dated 13 Apr., which dismissed American attempts to carry Louisiana's western boundary to the Rio Grande (Rio Bravo) as "illusory." Citing historical evidence dating to the late seventeenth century, Cevallos asserted that the boundary between Louisiana and the province of Texas should consist of a line commencing on the Gulf of Mexico between the Calcasieu and Mermentau Rivers and running north, passing between Los Adaes and Natchitoches, to the Red River. Since the limits north of this point "are doubtful and little known," they should be referred to the "prudent investigation" of a joint commission (Monroe, *Papers*, 5:373-7).

For Robert R. Livingston's recently proposed SCHEME for acquiring Florida, see Pinckney to TJ, 28 Jan.

OUR ULTIMATUM: Monroe and Pinckney to Cevallos, 12 May (Monroe, *Papers*, 5:389-91). CEVALLOS'S FINAL REJECTION: Cevallos to Monroe and Pinckney, 15 May (same, 393-4).

IRVINE: that is, George W. Erving, the recently appointed secretary of the U.S. legation to Spain (TJ to the Senate, 13 Nov. 1804).

OUR PUBLIC LETTERS: see Monroe and Pinckney to Madison, 1 Mch. and 23 May (Madison, *Papers, Sec. of State Ser.*, 9:79-82, 385-93). Pinckney's PRIVATE ONE to Madison, which largely duplicated the arrangement and content of his letter to TJ printed above, included a paraphrased copy of his 28 Feb. letter to Madison with additions dated from 18 Mch. to 22 May (same, 91-9).

[1] Preceding two words interlined in Pinckney's hand.

[2] Preceding six words interlined in Pinckney's hand.

[3] Word interlined by Pinckney in place of "scale."

[4] Name inserted by Pinckney into blank in text. In this and subsequent instances he may have originally intended to encipher the name.

[5] Name inserted by Pinckney into blank in text.

[6] Name inserted by Pinckney into blank in text.

[7] Preceding two words inserted by Pinckney into blank in text.

[8] Word inserted by Pinckney into blank in text.

[9] Name inserted by Pinckney into blank in text.

[10] Name inserted by Pinckney into blank in text.

[11] Remainder of paragraph in Pinckney's hand.

[12] The clerk here canceled "immeasurable."

[13] Remainder of text in Pinckney's hand.

[14] The remainder of the text of the February letter differs from the RC (see Vol. 45:599).

[15] Preceding five words interlined.

[16] Word interlined in place of "qualified."

ENCLOSURE

Extract from a European Gazette

Some taxes are, however, more partial in their first operation than others; and, in some cases, they totally ruin one part of the community in working their way into general diffusion. Others are particularly objectionable on account of the mode of their collection. When they employ too many hands in proportion to their produce, and thereby not only cause a serious deduction from the productive labour of the Country, but take the food from those who are employed in productive labour & put it into the mouths of those who do nothing that is profitable to the State, they are very injurious. The mode of collection may be odious & vexatious; as where it authorizes a set of Officers to call you before them; to keep you from day to day dancing attendance upon them; to treat you as a creature at their command; to schrutinize into the state of your concerns; to examine the depth of your purse; to overhaul your books & accounts; your deeds, leases, mortgages & bonds; to ascertain the state of your debts & credits; to remand you, and to call you up again at their pleasure. If, under such a system of taxation, a man can be said to be a *free-man*, I should be very glad to know, what it is that would make him *a slave. But, even all this is more congenial with my ideas of freedom, than the powers which*, in America for instance, are given by the excise laws. Count over the houses in the Streets of any City or Town, and you will find, that, into every fourth house, or thereabout, an *excise officer has*, (or at least had when I was in the Country) *at all times a right to enter, and range about in despite of the owner.* Many of them the Excise Officer never quits, without first putting his lock, or his seal, upon some part or other of the building; which lock or seal to break, or even to *touch*, the owner of the house trembles but to think of; and, if, by any accident, or by any temptation, he should have swerved from the limits prescribed to him; nay, even if suspicion fall upon him, he hastens to prostrate himself at the feet of him, whoever he may be, that happens, in the instance, to represent the dreadful ministers of Excise. If his supplications and all other means of mollifying fail, swift ruin awaits him. He is instantly shunned by his friends; the mask of destruction is set upon him; first a jail and last a poor-house are his lot. This terrible system it was against which the people of Pennsylvania so strongly remonstrated. It is said, that the excise Laws have been repealed, and that the system has been completely abolished, under the administration of Mr. Jefferson; if so, it is no wonder that he has been re-elected by the unanimous voice of the People. The Pennsylvania people, in one of their representations, said; "What is our situation? Our houses, regarded, in our law books, as our *castles*, are entered, at pleasure, by persons who come with an authority from our rulers to force their way into and about them, if we dare to resist. The quantity of our liquor, the dimensions of our vessels, are ascertained by these bold intruders, who may come & break in upon our repose at any hour of the night; who affix their locks and their seals to our doors & our utensils; who act the part of inquisitors, in the most odious manner; who set neighbour to watch neighbour, who make one defray the expence of keeping the other as a spy upon his actions; who, in short, seem intended for no other purpose than that of raising money upon us, in order to pay one for keeping another in subjection, & thus to render us in reality a Nation of slaves, suffering to retain the forms of freedom merely to disgrace it." Of the Excise laws in this Country, I know little or nothing; but, that they are, in their operation & effect, very far indeed from answering the above description given of the excise laws in America, I must, of course, be perfectly satisfied; because, were they not so, it is impossible that I should never have heard any thing said against them in parliament.

Tr (DLC: TJ Papers, 155:27161-2); undated; in a clerk's hand; endorsed by Pinckney: "This is an Extract from an European Gazette to shew you in what light some of our former acts which You have had repealed was viewed & how indispensable to our Character as freemen such repeal was—it was published in London." Printed in *Cobbett's Weekly Political Register*, 23 Feb. 1805.

WHEN I WAS IN THE COUNTRY: although Pinckney was evidently unaware of it, the author of the piece from which the extract was taken was William Cobbett, who was attacking taxation measures of the British government (John M. Cobbett and James P. Cobbett, *Selections from Cobbett's Political Works: Being a Complete Abridgment of the 100 Volumes Which Comprise the Writings of "Porcupine" and the "Weekly Political Register,"* 6 vols. [London, 1835-37], 1:530-44; DNB).

From John Reich

SIR Philada: May 22nd 1805

Observing, some time since a Resolution of Congress for preserving an evidence of National Respect and of perpetuating the Services of Commodore Preble, I trust that you will pardon the Liberty I have taken of addressing you on the subject.

Your being an admirer of the fine Arts, can justly appreciate and pardon the anxiety with which I Solicit the honor of executing the Medal, and did I not feel the most perfect confidence in my ability to give Satisfaction in executing the performance, I would not intrude myself on your notice. Well aware that an undertaking which shall at once express eminent services, national esteem, and the perfection of Art, is singularly arduous, and notwithstanding the high responsibility attached to the undertaking, and acutely feeling every insinuation that can be made or sentiment advanced by persons of various descriptions, when an artist Speaks of his Art or his execution, I cannot resist the inclination I have to be employed in these services.

I am fully sensible that this is not the Language generally used by applicants, but the very limited opportunities that this city affords for the exercise of my profession renders it improper for me to rely on particular recommendation or general celebrity.

I wish Sir, most sincerely that it was possible to convey to you my feeling on this subject and to convince you that in making the request, emolument is but a Secondary consideration—your attention will, believe me, confer a lasting obligation on

Sir Your very humble Servt. JN. REICH

RC (DNA: RG 45, MLR); at foot of text: "Thomas Jefferson Esqr Washington City"; below signature: "No 17h South Fourth St"; endorsed by TJ as received 24 May and so recorded in SJL with notation "N."

The RESOLUTION of 3 Mch. requested that the president "cause a gold medal to be struck, emblematical of the attacks on the town, batteries and naval force of Tripoli, by the squadron under Commodore Preble's command, and to present it to Commodore Preble" (U.S. Statutes at Large, 2:346-7).

From William Tatham

SIR/ Jefferson Street—Wednesday 22d. May 1805.

Trivial circumstances sometimes produce great ends:—You mentioned, yesterday after Dinner, your wish that some person would invent a means of facilitating the passage of your decanters round the table. I will engage to furnish you one, in a few days, which shall afford an useful lesson in the public Economy of our Country; and it can no where else be so happily introduced. It shall be cheap, simple, powerful, ornamental, and accommodating to yourself and Guests; and he must be a dull brain, indeed, who does not carry home more instruction than wine.

If you like my proposition, Sir, you will be so good as permit my Moddelor (who brings this note) to take the dimensions of Your Tables, and obtain a loan of one of your three Bottle Coasters.

If he does not completely please you I will bear the loss—If he does, The public shall pay a reasonable expence.

I have The honor to be, Sir, Yr. H St. WM TATHAM

P.S.—I am just about to deposit models in the Repository which explain the principles of my proposition, & its relative improvements. If you can either spare a few minutes now, or will permit me to leave the models with you for an examination at your greater leisure they shall be sent over to you immediately.—

Secretary of State's Office, Patent Right Repository. W. T.

RC (DLC); at foot of first page: "The President of the United States"; endorsed by TJ as received 22 May and so recorded in SJL.

TJ's guest list confirms that Tatham was at DINNER at the President's House on 21 May (Appendix II).

From Patrick Byrne

SIR 182 Market St philadelphia 23 May 1805

agreeable to my promise I now enclose alist of pamphlets, published whilst in Dublin—if you honour me with your Commands for one or more of them I will instantly attend to it

I am with the greatest respect Sir yr. obed & very hum Sevt

PAT. BYRNE

RC (MHi); written on a sheet with notation on verso in an unidentified hand: "Private, examd"; endorsed by TJ as received 25 May and so recorded in SJL.

Enclosure not found (see TJ to Byrne, 31 May).

MY PROMISE: see Byrne to TJ, 12 Mch.

To George E. Clymer

SIR Washington May 23. 05.

Your two letters of May 15. & that of May 18. have been duly recieved, & that of the two former which was in the nature of a Caveat is delivered to the Secretary of state for the Patent office.

With respect to the practicability & effect of the fire engine in naval actions, having no knolege of the subject myself, I am unable to give any opinion respecting it. but it shall be suggested to those who are in the way of making it useful to the public if it can be so. in the mean time my relations with the public render it not improper to assume on myself the giving you those thanks justly due to every one making communications on patriotic motives. I pray you to accept my salutations & good wishes & assurances of great respect

Th: Jefferson

PoC (DLC); at foot of text: "George Clymer esq."; endorsed by TJ.

To Daniel L. Hylton

Dear Sir Washington May 23. 05.

I called yesterday at the Patent office to enquire respecting Macomb's mill according to the request in your letter of the 15th. inst. there is a drawing of it, but no model; and no copy can be permitted to be taken from the office till the patent expires, which will be on the 28th. of August next. it is really nothing more than a bad edition of Barker's mill, which no mode hitherto devised has been able to make equal to the grinding of grain. the horizontal wheel, with vertical laddle-boards in the edge, & a horizontal spout striking them is better than Barkers but the same horizontal wheel of the size of a tub wheel, with laddle boards in the edge at the windmill angle ($54°\frac{3}{4}$) with a vertical spout is probably better; but whether either of them is equal to the tub wheel has not been sufficiently tried. none of them will do but where there is a waste of water. where that is scant, the breast or overshot wheel (according as the fall admits) is far preferable to all of them. should particular reasons continue your preference of Macomb's wheel, you can at present[1] only get the instructions from him, paying, I presume his patent price. but who or where he is, I know not. if you wait however till August I will have you furnished with a drawing. your application to me needs no apology. tho' not so much master of my time for the service of my[2] friends as formerly I am not entirely forbidden that privilege: and in availing myself of it for you, I am gratified by renewing antient recollections, and sentiments of unchanged esteem. present me in the spirit of early affections to mrs Hylton, and Accept yourself assurances of my constant friendship & respect. Th: Jefferson

PoC (DLC); at foot of text: "D. L. Hylton esq."; endorsed by TJ.

barker's mill: a type of breast-wheel mill that lessened the waste of water in the action of the wheel. An early description attributed the innovation to a Dr. Barker. The term has generally been applied to a different milling innovation that relied on a simple water turbine. TJ was familiar with an improvement on this latter approach patented by James Rumsey, who called it a Barker's mill (J. T. Desaguliers, *A Course of Experimental Philosophy*, 3d ed., 2 vols. [London, 1763], 2:453-4; David Brewster, ed., *The Edinburgh Encyclopedia*, 18 vols. [Edinburgh, 1808-30], 11:560-1; *The Franklin Journal and American Mechanics' Magazine*, 6 [1828], 273-5; Vol. 15:522-3; Vol. 18:146-50).

[1] Preceding two words interlined.
[2] TJ here canceled "present."

To Robert Smith

Dear Sir Washington May 23. 05

I have spoken with Genl. Dearborne on the subject of the Marines at N. Orleans, and he sais there is nothing in his department opposed to their discharge. it occurred however in conversation that as some of the gun-boats building on the Ohio are destined for N. Orleans, and two of them at least for immediate service, you might think it better to retain these marines to man them, as better subjects, and saving the expence of bringing them back & raising & sending others. instead therefore of sending the letter to Capt Carmick, I return it to you to forward it, or not as you shall think best. the moment we can have a gun-boat at N. Orleans we must order her to visit the bay of St. Bernard & Mattagordo. Accept affectionate & respectful salutations

Th: Jefferson

PoC (DLC); at foot of text: "The Secretary of the Navy." Notation in SJL: "marines." Enclosure not found, but see below.

letter to capt carmick: on 4 May, Smith wrote orders to Daniel Carmick, the commander of the marine detachment at New Orleans, to return with his officers and men on the first available vessel (FC in Lb in DNA: RG 45, MLS; NDBW, *Register*, 63).

bay of st. bernard & mattagordo: according to TJ's Notes on John Sibley's Account of Native American Tribes, [after 21 May 1805], the Spanish were considering the establishment of a settlement at Matagorda Bay.

From Thomas Claxton

Honored Sir Philada May 24, 1805

Accompanying this you will get a desert knife silver blade[1]—If you aprove of it, I can get two dozen at 36$ per dozen—If you should not approve, Sir you will please to return it—In the Steward's list are two casters[2]—a pair of elegant silver ones are to be had here price 140$ Plated ones are 70$ dollars per pair—please to say which you will prefer—a pair of elegant Sallad dishes[3] with blue glass Bowls—applicable to floating islands, fruit &c. price for the pair forty dollars—

If you should think proper, Sir, to order them, they will be very ornamental to your table—The size is 13 by 9 in. shape octagon—basket work—

I have the honor to be Sir Your most Humble Sert

THOS CLAXTON

RC (MHi); with notations by TJ in margin (see notes below); endorsed by TJ as received 26 May and so recorded in SJL.

[1] In margin in TJ's hand: "desert knives."

[2] In margin in TJ's hand: "Castors silver."

[3] In margin in TJ's hand: "Salad dishes."

From John Rhea

DEAR SIR, Sullivan Courthouse 24th. May. 1805

This day Your Letter of the thirtieth of April last past, being brought by the mail, via Jonesborough, from Knoxville was delivered to me. the sensations occasioned by reading it can be known to myself alone—towards You they are those of the highest esteem veneration and regard—as well for the kind intention there by manifested for a man, for whom I entertain a sincere disinterested friendship—as for the confidence and esteem evidenced towards me—

Some time past I had the pleasure of addressing a letter to You from this place—after the date of that letter, being at Greenville—Mr Duffield, expressing his sincere Gratitude to the President of the United States, informed me that the commission had arrived—whether he could accept, said he still had some doubts occasioned by information from Pensilvania respecting some of his friends, but that he would determine in a few days. I told him it was my opinion he ought to accept and go on as soon as possible.—On the week of the first monday of this month, he told me he had determined to accept—and would write to the secretary of state of the United States accordingly; and I believe he would have wrote to the President of the United States—had he not been prevented by his apprehensions, but it might be deemed an intrusion or improper—

A letter from Mr Duffield was delivered to me this day in which he writes, that on monday next he designs to go off—the following is an extract from the letter in his own words—"I view with anxious solicitude the present, as the most important epoch of my life, and I most solemnly assure You, if sertitude of intention, impartiality, temperance and perseverance will in any manner compensate for (what I am tremblingly conscious of) my own weakness and inability, they shall

shall to the utmost be my guide in official conduct. I feel a double solicitude on acct: of those whose friendship has so far overrated my very moderate acquirements and feeble talents." The foregoing extract is Genuine it evinces the determination, the high sense of honor and of duty with which he is inspired—

With Great pain and astonishment have I read the part of Your letter mentioning the information you have had respecting Mr Duffield. after reading it over and over, I have turned my attention to discover the source, but as Yet it evades me—it would indeed by very gratifying to me to discover it.

a candid and honest declaration was given by me at the time I had the pleasure of conversing with You respecting Mr Duffield. For several Years past Mr Duffield and myself have to gether, in the character of Lawyers, attended the same Courts in the District of Washington in the state of Tennessee, frequently lodging in the same house and in habits of intimacy—and I can safely state, that I never had reason to believe, from any observation of mine, that Mr Duffield has contracted a habit of drinking to a degree which renders him unfit for a Judge. had my knowledge been, that Mr Duffield had contracted such habit, my Esteem and respect for You and duty to myself would would forever have kept closed my lips respecting him. Jointly with Mr Anderson I signed my name to a writing recommendary of Mr Duffield to the President of the United States—My own knowledge of Mr Duffield induced me to sign it, and my motives were pure; and if the same writting was this moment before me, unsigned by me, I would, acting on my own knowledge, sign my name to it. The appointment of Mr Duffield was not spoken of by me to any person in Tennessee, except some talk with Mr Anderson & Mr Dickson on the way—and to himself at the time in my last letter mentioned—prior to the time he recived the commission, in this state—Since he received the commission several persons in my hearing have spoke of it—no one to my knowledge has disapproved of it in my hearing.

That you have received the information stated in your Letter I believe because You have wrote it, but as You Yourself have used the word—if—I hope You will excuse me for entertaining doubts respecting the authenticity of that information, and I do earnestly intreat You to suspend any unfavorable opinion of Mr Duffield, untill some more can be known of this, at present, to me misterious and unaccountable affair. pardon me for saying, that I have good hope, that the reputation of Mr Duffield will remain in the said particular, uninjured—and that he will have the happiness of being restored to your good opinion.

With heartfelt Gratitude the last part of Your Letter respecting Mr Tremble was read by me—Since my return to Tennessee he has not been seen by me—but I expect soon to meet him at Knoxville—

I have, this day, wrote to Mr Duffield to go if possible past Hawkins Courthouse and meet me there next monday or tuesday. but do not will know, how I shall be able, under existing circumstances, to communicate the information to him. I hope, however, he will meet me—

This letter might have been delayed untill after the expected interview with Mr Duffield—but a desire to acknowledge the receipt of Your Letter at the earliest moment prevailed—Should any Expression appear over warm, forgive it, and attribute it to an energy which is not in my power to restrain when writing or speaking of any character which is esteemed and dear to me.

Please to accept of my most sincere wishes for Your health and happiness and believe me to be with assured Esteem Your Obedient Servt

John Rhea

RC (DLC); at foot of text: "Thomas Jefferson the President of the United States"; endorsed by TJ as received 11 June and so recorded in SJL.

letter to you from this place: Rhea to TJ, 18 Apr.

write to the secretary of state: writing to Madison on 6 May, George Duffield acknowledged the receipt of his commission on 21 Apr. and conveyed his thanks to the president for the appointment. "An inevitable delay," however, would set back his departure for New Orleans by about three weeks (DNA: RG 217, MTA; endorsed by TJ: "accepts appmt as judge Orleans").

source: see Joseph Anderson to TJ, 25 Mch.

writing recommendary of mr duffield: Anderson and Rhea to TJ, 5 Mch.

From John D. Wyndham

Sir, May 24, 1805

In obedience to your Excellency's instructions, I attended at the Office of General Dearborn nearly the whole of the Time allotted to Business on Tuesday . . . and having again called yesterday—without seeing him; I am therefore induced once more to trouble your Excellency, relying on your usual goodness to pardon this liberty I have taken.—

Possibly I might long attend at the War Office before I was fortunate enough to see the General; and even then be unsuccessful, should there be no Vacancies—perhaps your Excellency would do me the Honor to say, whether or not *'tis possible* for my application to succeed?—

With the most profound respect I remain your Excellency's very obedient Servant

J. D. WYNDHAM

RC (DNA: RG 59, LAR); ellipses in original; at foot of text: "His Excellency Thomas Jefferson, &c. &c."; endorsed by TJ as received 24 May and "emploimt." and so recorded in SJL.

John D. Wyndham (ca. 1783-1813) had been an officer in the British army before becoming a cadet in the U.S. Military Academy from 27 May 1805 to 14 Nov. 1806, when he became an artillerist with the rank of second lieutenant. He was promoted to first lieutenant in January 1811, but was dismissed a year later for "drunkenness on duty" (George W. Cullum, *Biographical Register of the Officers and Graduates of the U.S. Military Academy at West Point, N.Y.*, 3d ed., 5 vols. [Boston, 1891], 1:76).

From Henry Dearborn, with Jefferson's Approval

SIR War Department May. 25. 1805

I have the honor of proposing for your approbation Nicholas Biddle as a Cadet in the Corps of Artillerists.

With high respect & consideration I am, Sir your Obedt. Servt.

H. DEARBORN

[*Approval by TJ*:]

May 25. 05.

Approved TH: JEFFERSON

RC (PHi); in a clerk's hand, signed by Dearborn; at foot of text: "President of the United States." FC (Lb in DNA: RG 107, LSP).

To William Dunbar

DEAR SIR Washington May 25. 1805.

Your several letters, with the portions of your journals forwarded at different times have been duly recieved; and I am now putting the journal into the hands of a person properly qualified, to extract the results of your observations, and the various interesting information contained among them, and bring them into such a compas as may be communicated to the legislature. not knowing whether you might not intend to make a map yourself of the course of the river; he will defer that to the last part of his work on the possibility that we may recieve it from yourself. Your observations on the difficulty of transporting baggage from the head of the Red river to that of the Arcansa, with the dangers from the seceding Osages residing on the last river have determined me to confine the ensuing mission to the ascent of the Red river to it's source, & to descend the same river again, which will give an opportunity of better ascertaining that; which in truth, next to the Missouri, is the most interesting water of the Missisipi. you will accordingly recieve instructions to this effect from the Secretary at War. Dr. Hunter does not propose to take a part in this mission, and we suppose that mr George Davis, a deputy of mr Briggs' will be the fittest person to take the direction of the expedition and Colo. Freeman as an assistant, & successor in case of accident to the principal. still these propositions are submitted to your controul, as being better acquainted with both characters. I write to Govr. Claiborne to endeavor to get a passport from the Marquis of Casa-Calvo for our party as a protection from any Spaniards who may be fallen in with on the route: and we offer to recieve one or two persons, to be named by him and *subsisted* by us[1] into the party, as a proof that the expedition is merely scientific, and without any views to which Spain could take exception. the best protection against the Indians will be the authority to confer with them on the subject of commerce. such conferences should be particularly held with the Arcansas and Panis residing on the Red river, and every thing possible be done to attach them to us affectionately. in the present state of things between Spain & us, we should spare nothing to secure the friendship of the Indians within reach of her. While Capt. Lewis's mission was preparing, as it was understood that his reliance for his longitudes must be on the Lunar observations taken, as at sea, with the aid of a timekeeper, and I knew that a thousand accidents might happen to that in such a journey as his, & thus deprive us of the principal object of the expedition, to wit, the ascertaining the geography of that river, I sat myself to consider whether in making observations at land, that furnishes no resource which may dispense with the timekeeper, so necessary at sea. it occurred to me that as we can always have a meridian at land, that would furnish what the want of it at sea obliges us to supply by the time keeper. supposing Capt Lewis then furnished with a meridian, & having the requisite tables & Nautical Almanac with him, 1. he might find the right ascension of the moon when on the meridian of Greenwich on any given day, then find by observation when the moon should attain that right ascension (by the aid of a known star) & measure her distance in that moment from his meridian. this distance would be the difference of longitude between Greenwich & the place of observation. Or 2dly. Observe the moon's passage over his meridian & her right ascencion at that moment. see by the tables the time at Greenwich when she had that right ascencion: that gives her distance from the meridian of Greenwich when she was on his meridian. Or 3dly. observe the moon's distance from his meridian at any moment, & her right ascension at that moment, & find from the tables her distance from the meridian of Greenwich when she had that right ascension, which will give the distance of the two meridians. this last process will be simplified by taking for the moment of observation that of an appulse of the moon and a known star, or when the moon & a known star are in the same vertical. I suggested this to mr Briggs, who considered it as correct & practicable and proposed communicating it to the Phil. society, but I observed that it was too obvious not to have been thought of before, and supposed it had not been adopted in practice because of no use at sea, where a meridian cannot be had, and where alone the nations of Europe had occasion for it. before his confirmation of the idea however, Capt Lewis was gone. in conversation afterwards with Baron Humboldt, he observed that the idea was correct, but not new, that I would find it in the 3d. vol. of Delalande; I recieved two days ago the 3d. & 4th. vols. of Montucla's hist. of Mathematics, finished & edited by Delalande; and find in fact that Morin & Vanlangren in the 17th. century proposed observations of the moon on the meridian, but it does not appear whether they meant to dispense with the time keeper: but a meridian at sea being too impracticable, their idea was not pursued. the purpose of troubling you with these details is to submit to your consideration and decision whether any use can be made of them advantageously in our future expeditions, & particularly that up the Red river.

Your letter on the current of the Missisipi, and paper on the same subject, corrected at once my doubts on your theory of the current of that river. constant emploiment in a very different line, permits me to turn to philosophical subjects only when some circumstance forces them on my attention. no occurrence had called my mind to this subject particularly since I had first been initiated into the original Torricellian doctrine of the velocities at different depths being in the sub-duplicate ratio of the depths. and tho' Buat had given me his book while at Paris, your letter was the first occasion of my turning to it, and getting my mind set to rights to a certain degree. there is a subsequent work by Bernard which is said to have furnished corrections and additions to Buat; but I have never seen it.

The work we are now doing, is, I trust, done for posterity, in such a way that they need not repeate it. for this we are much indebted to you not only for the labour & time you have devoted to it, but for the excellent method of which you have set the example, and which I hope will be the model to be followed by others. we shall delineate with correctness the great arteries of this great country: those who come after us will extend the ramifications as they become acquainted with them, and fill up the canvas we begin. with my acknolegements for your zealous aid in this business, accept my friendly salutations & assurances of great esteem & respect. TH: JEFFERSON

PoC (DLC); at foot of first page: "Mr. Dunbar."

The PERSON PROPERLY QUALIFIED with whom TJ placed Dunbar's journals has not been identified. Dunbar sent them to the president in installments throughout February and March 1805. TJ presented to Congress on 19 Feb. 1806 a condensed, narrative version, to which was appended a brief table of "Meteorological observations" consisting of daily thermometer readings and weather observations. This version, together with accounts by Meriwether Lewis and William Clark and John Sibley, were subsequently published as *Message from the President of the United States, Communicating Discoveries Made in Exploring the Missouri, Red River and Washita, by Captains Lewis and Clark, Doctor Sibley, and Mr. Dunbar* (Washington, D.C., 1806). Using the astronomical observations made by Dunbar and George Hunter, Nicholas King published a MAP of the Ouachita River, a copy of which TJ sent to Dunbar in early 1806. Dunbar sent his own "sketch of the Washita river" to TJ the previous November (Dunbar to TJ, 10 Nov. 1805; TJ to Dunbar, 12 Jan. 1806). For the disposition and publication of Dunbar's and Hunter's journals, see Trey Berry, Pam Beasley, and Jeanne Clements, eds., *The Forgotten Expedition, 1804-1805: The Louisiana Purchase Journals of Dunbar and Hunter* (Baton Rouge, 2006), 219-22.

SECEDING OSAGES: see Pierre Chouteau's letters to TJ of 12 Feb., 2 Mch., and 20 Apr.

COLO. FREEMAN: TJ's use of the title "Colo." led Dunbar to mistakenly assume he was referring to Lieutenant Colonel Constant Freeman, the U.S. army commander at New Orleans. Dunbar later learned that surveyor Thomas Freeman would lead the Red River expedition of 1806 (Dunbar to TJ, 18 Aug. 1804; Dearborn to Dunbar, 8 Nov. 1805, FC in Lb in DNA: RG 107, MLS; Dunbar to TJ, 8 Oct., 17 Dec. 1805; TJ to Dunbar, 12 Jan. 1806).

I WRITE TO GOVR. CLAIBORNE: TJ to William C. C. Claiborne, 26 May.

SUGGESTED THIS TO MR BRIGGS: see Isaac Briggs to TJ, 1 Mch. 1803.

CURRENT OF THE MISSISIPI: see Dunbar to TJ, 28 Jan. 1804, and TJ's reply on 13 Mch. 1804.

Pierre Louis Georges Du BUAT, a French military engineer, published a revised and enlarged edition of his *Principes d'hydraulique* in 1786. In addition to presenting the work to TJ, the author sent it to George Washington in 1788 (Sowerby, No. 3743; Washington, *Papers, Pres. Ser.*, 1:34-5, 93-4).

[1] Preceding four words interlined.

From John Gaillard

SIR, Charleston May 25th. 1805.

Mr Lehré a Resident of Charleston & one of its members in the State Legislature having expressed an Intention of passing through Virginia I beg leave to be permitted to introduce him to your acquaintance.—

This Gentleman is well acquainted with the political state of things in this Country & has contributed much by his exertions to the success of the republican Interest.

I am, Sir, very respectfully, yr. obt. Servt. JOHN GAILLARD.

RC (DLC); endorsed by TJ as received 24 Sep. and so recorded in SJL, where TJ connected it by a brace and notation "recd. by mr Lehré" with entries for letters received the same day from William Johnson of 25 May, William Butler of 30 May, Peter Freneau of 2 June, Thomas Moore of 28 June, and an undated letter from Paul Hamilton.

John Gaillard (1765-1826) served in the South Carolina legislature from 1794 until 1804, when he was chosen to succeed Pierce Butler in the U.S. Senate. Taking his seat in January 1805, Gaillard remained in the Senate until the end of his life. His tenure included several terms as president pro tempore (*Biog. Dir. Cong.*; N. Louise Bailey and others, eds., *Biographical Directory of the South Carolina Senate, 1776-1985*, 3 vols. [Columbia, S.C., 1986], 1:539-40).

From William Johnson

SIR Charleston May 25. 1805.

Mr. Lehrè the Gentleman who will have the honor of delivering this having undertaken a Tour to the Northward and proposing to pay his Respects to you at Montecello I have taken the Liberty to furnish him with this introductory Letter. I have the Pleasure Sir to assure you that this Gentleman has been an active and useful promoter of the Republican Interest in our Country from its earliest Revival; and on this Account as well as his other public services possesses a respectable Rank in the Confidence of his Fellow Citizens.

With the most profound Respect: Sir I remain your very hle Sert.

WLLM. JOHNSON JR

RC (DLC); endorsed by TJ as received 24 Sep. and so recorded in SJL, where TJ connected it by a brace and notation "recd. by mr Lehré" with entries for letters received the same day from John Gaillard of 25 May, William Butler of 30 May, Peter Freneau of 2 June, Thomas Moore of 28 June, and an undated letter from Paul Hamilton.

TJ appointed William Johnson (1771-1834) to the U.S. Supreme Court in 1804. Before his elevation to the federal bench, Johnson had been a prominent legislator and jurist in South Carolina. A Republican in politics and often independent in his legal views, Johnson is best remembered for his dissenting opinions from the Marshall court, as well as for the nationalism he espoused in response to the states' rights and nullification arguments of his native state. He remained on friendly, if not intimate, terms with TJ during both his presidency and his retirement, and the two men infrequently exchanged opinions on agriculture, politics, and Johnson's various writing endeavors (ANB; Ruth L. Woodward and Wesley Frank Craven, *Princetonians, 1784-1790: A Biographical Dictionary* [Princeton, 1991], 494-507; Vol. 42:497-8; Vol. 43:71; RS, 1:555n).

From J. P. G. Muhlenberg

SIR Philadelphia May 25th. 1805

Enclos'd I have the Honor to transmit a Letter I have just recievd from Mr. Appelton, the American Consul at Leghorn, who has consignd to my care for the President, one box Vine Cuttings, & four small ones, containing Strawberry Plants—Captn. Williams, to whose care They were comitted by the Consul, informs that altho' he strictly follow'd his instructions, and did every thing he could to preserve them, but is afraid, the strawberry Plants are beyond recovery—As there are still some hopes of preserving them—I have this day Shipped them for Richmond, addressd to the care of Messrs. Gibson, & Jefferson.

with Perfect Respect, I have the Honor to be The Presidents Obedt Servt P MUHLENBERG

RC (MHi); at foot of text: "The President of The U States"; endorsed by TJ as received 27 May and so recorded in SJL. Enclosure: Thomas Appleton to TJ, 16 Mch.

From Joseph Yznardi, Sr.

EXMO SEÑOR Madrid y Mayo 25. de 1805.

Despues de saludar á V.E. y manifestar el reconocimiento de mí Alegria por la feliz reéleccion en V.E. de la Presidencia de ese vasto Gobierno me veo en la obligacion de manifestarle el Sentimiento que me ha causado la noticia de haberse roto las negociaciones con esta Corte segun me acaban de informar, y hé confirmado con la Buelta de Mr. Monroe de Aranjuez a quien me hé ofrecido por si pudiese concurrir en algo qe. alterase su despedida pero este Caballero me há respondido prudentemente qe. su mision habia terminado y dado cuenta, con lo qe. concluyó mi deber en esta parte, pero no el tomar sobre mi mediante el favor qe. V.E. me dispensa creyendo mi honradez y confiando mis desinteresados oficios qe. en todo tiempo concilié á favor de ese Gobierno.

Tenga V.E. la bondad de recordar la complaciencia que tube quando le aseguré que el Cabo. de Yrujo se quedaria en ese Pais, como qe. al no haber sido por la insinuacion de V.E. Jamas lo habria logrado, ni sufrido yo las persecuciones qe. me há hecho en las comisiones prestas á mi cargo desempeñadas con tanta honradez y desinteres; ni tampoco dho Caballero habria variado sus Sentimientos &ca.

Yo Significo á V.E. mi modo de pensar sobre los disgustos qe. ocurren al presente entre los dos Gobiernos: Primero el deslinde de limites del Territorio perteneciente á la compra del Nuevo Orleans, Segundo el de perjuicios sufridos en la Guerra Ultima por los daños de Corsarios y detenciones en las confiscaciones de los Puertos Españoles cuyos resultados deben mirarse imparcialmente con dos respectos, el primero, el de la detencion y condena Arbitraria por los Consules Franceses, y el otro de todos aquellos qe. hayan sido autorisados por los Tribunales de S.M.C. los qe. siempre hé comprendido hallarse dispuesto este Gobierno á compensarlos pero los otros á mi ver los resisten bajo el pretexto de no haber tenido la culpa ni contribuido á semejantes condenas ademas de que comprende el mismo Gobierno de qe. por resueltas de las negociaciones hechas en Paris quando la compra dho de Nuevo Orleans, fueron comprendidas todas las hostilidades cometidas bajo el Pavellon Frances sin explicarse circunstancias cuya obscuridad es la que há movido la question como asi mismo el limite de dho. Nuevo Orleans baxo el pretexto de que la cesion hecha por este Gobierno al Francés no es la misma que esta há vendido al de America, en cuyos puntos se detiene segun estoy informado la final transacion de lo mas esencial de lo qe. vendrá á resultar un disgusto irremediable entre las dos Naciones pero el perjuicio total será evidentemente contra los Estados Unidos sin esperanzas de un resarcimiento qe. no sea muy remoto pudiendo tener las consequencias que siguen.

Con mucha facilidad y sin mayor resistencia los Ests. unidos tomaran posecion del terreno qe. los Franceses le vendieron, y aun si quieren hasta las Floridas pero en recompensa de esto consideraria yo la extension tan dilatada del comercio de ese Pais en todo el mundo, las ningunas fuerzas navales para hacer frente á una Guerra, las leves Esperanzas de tomar ninguna propiedad Española por hallarse totalmente suspenso su comercio y qe. lo qe. fluctuaba está en Poder de los Britanicos y qe. de forzosa necesidad debe la España considerarse como unida à la Francia, y qe. esta por su proprio Interes Sostendra los dhos qe. le paresca convenirle considerando una inmediata Alianza de ese Gobierno con el Britanico, qe. las resueltas serán el Beneficio de su solo Interes y en perjuicio patente de la Neutralidad qe. Goza el Pavellon Americano qe. por todo el tiempo qe. permanesca la Guerra sería el conducto para aprovecharse el comercio Español cuyas ventajas Niveladas con el perjuicio qe. la vulgaridad aparenta Sufrir en no pocesionarse de lo qe. se Solicita no compensará con mucho la excesiva extraordinaria contribucion qe. tendrá qe. hacer en el caso de una declaracion de Guerra qe. veo como indispensable á menos qe. se suavizen las pretenciones, y qual seria el unico medio de permanecer en la Amistad qe. conviene á Ambas Naciones y lo qe. yo represento á V.E. movido de un deseo Sincero nacido de las pruevas cordiales de Pacificacion propias y consequentes á lo qe siempre Ohý de V.E. por quien pido á Dios Gue su importante vida dilatados Años.

Exmo. Señor BLM á V.E su mas Obte Sor. J. Yznardy

EDITORS' TRANSLATION

Most Excellent Sir, Madrid, 25 May 1805

After greeting your excellency and manifesting the recognition of my joy for your excellency's happy reelection to the presidency of that government, I see myself in the obligation of expressing the feeling that the news of the rupture of the negotiations with this court caused me, as I have just been informed and have confirmed with the return of Mr. Monroe from Aranjuez, to whom I have offered myself in case it can bring about something to alter his farewell. Yet this gentleman has answered me prudently that his mission had ended and is accounted for, with which I conclude my duty in this part, but not for myself, due to the favor that your excellency grants me believing in my honesty and trusting in my disinterested services, which at all times I have furthered in favor of that government.

Your excellency will have the kindness of remembering the satisfaction I had when I assured you that the Caballero Irujo would remain in that country, which, if it had not been for the suggestion of your excellency, I would have never accomplished. Nor would I have suffered the persecutions that have been made against me in the commissions that come with my position, which I have undertaken with much honesty and disinterest; nor would the said gentleman have changed his feelings, et cetera.

I will express to your excellency my opinion about the disagreements that occur at present between the two governments: first, the demarcation of the limits of the territory belonging to the purchase of New Orleans; second, the damages in the last war on account of corsairs and detentions in the confiscations in Spanish ports, the results of which should be looked at impartially in two respects—the first, that of the detention and arbitrary sentencing by French consuls, and the other, all those that have been authorized by the tribunals of His Catholic Majesty. I have always understood this government to be willing to compensate the latter, but, in my opinion, to resist the others on the pretext of this not having been their fault and they not having contributed to such condemnations. Additionally that same government comprehends that as a result of the negotiations made in Paris at the time of the said purchase of New Orleans, all the hostilities committed under the French flag were included without explaining circumstances. This obscurity has motivated the question, as similarily with the limits of the said New Orleans, under the pretext that the cession by this government to the French is not the same as has been sold to America. On these points, as I am informed, the final transaction of that which is most essential is delayed, from which will result an irreparable upset between these two nations; but the total damage will be evidently against the United States, without hopes for compensation, which might not be very remote, and this might possibly have the following consequences.

With great ease and without much resistance, the United States will take possession of the territory that the French have sold them, and even Florida if they so desire. Yet counter to this I would consider the great extension of the country's commerce with the whole world; the almost nonexistent naval forces to confront a war; the meager hopes of capturing any Spanish properties, given that its commerce is completely suspended, and that what does move is in the power of the British; and that due to forced necessity Spain must consider itself united with France, which out of its own interests will uphold what it considers most convenient considering an immediate alliance of your government with the British, which will result in the benefit of its sole interest and in obvious detriment to the neutrality that the American flag enjoys and which for the duration of the war could be the conduit to take advantage of Spanish trade. These advantages, balanced with the damage that the vulgarity appears to suffer by not taking control of what it claims, will not equate with the excessively extraordinary contribution that it will have to make in case of a declaration of war, which I see as inevitable unless the demands are softened, and which would be the only means of remaining in the friendship that benefits both nations and that I have represented to your excellency, moved by a sincere desire born out of the cordial proofs of appropriate pacification consequent to what I have always heard about your excellency, for whom I pray to God to preserve you life for many years.

Excellent Sir, your most obedient servant kisses the hand of your excellency.

J. YZNARDY

RC (DLC); in a clerk's hand, closing and signature by Yznardi; at foot of text: "Exmo. Sor. Dn. Tomas Jefferson"; endorsed by TJ as received 15 Aug. and so recorded in SJL.

Early in his presidency, TJ asked Yznardi to help convince the Spanish government not to recall its minister, Carlos Martínez de Irujo (YRUJO). Irujo later cast blame on Yznardi for the threat of recall, which had been requested by the Adams administration (Vol. 35:392-3; Vol. 36:4-6).

From John Daly Burk

SIR May 26. 1805 Battersea near Petersburg.

The file of newspapers and the collection of the old laws of this commonwealth, which under certain restrictions you politely stated were at my service I want urgently at this moment; and I pray you to instruct me where and In what manner I must apply for the temporary possession of the first and for the inspection of the last—

The copy of laws in particular will be of signal benefit in the obscure & dreary period embraced within the suppression of Bacon's rebellion and the year 1752. Here the materials for history are scanty indeed and little is known of the state of society, of arts & manners. Those laws if they go so far back as either of the periods abovementioned will enable me to supply these defects. In my opinion if all the other papers & documents belonging to a people should by any fatality be lost, a bare but correct list of their laws would fully preserve the character of the people & the progress of arts; beside furnishing no contemptible materials for their history

Would it be convenient Sir, to have those papers enclosed to Governor Page; or Doctor Shore of This town, Who are very much my friends and at whose houses I might peruse them. My book is on the eve of going to press and every hour of my time is employed in endeavoring to make it as useful and interesting as my talents & opportunities will permit. to engage a person to wait on you for the purpose of examining those papers & noting the most material circumstances would but ill agree with my Circumstances, if indeed one sufficiently qualified could be engaged on any terms—

My Second volume is allready written: but the use of those papers, if I am fortunate enough to have an opportunity of seeing them in Season, will yet enable me to mingle their contents either in my notes or narrative—

I pray you Sir to excuse this intrusion. I know how important every moment of your time is to your Country: but I believe also that you are eminently superior to the pedantry of wishing to be thought so wholly immersed in state concerns, as to leave no room for the exercize of private benevolence. I believe too Sir, that a request of this nature from a man, who is employed in writing the history of your Country, altho' he can claim little more than the merit of zeal and fidelity, will not be thought wholly beneath your consideration.

With great respect & attachment I am your fellow Citizen

John D Burk.

RC (DLC); at foot of text: "Thomas Jefferson President of the U. States"; endorsed by TJ as received 29 May but recorded in SJL as received 30 May.

you politely stated: TJ to Burk, 21 Feb. 1803.

my book: the first two volumes of *The History of Virginia, From Its First Settlement to the Present Day* were published in Petersburg in 1804 and 1805 (Sowerby, No. 464; Vol. 39:434).

To William C. C. Claiborne

Dear Sir Washington May 26. 05.

My last letter to you was of the 26th. of March. since that I have recieved yours of Feb. 17. and Mar. 25. with respect to Dr. Sibley who was the subject of the last, I observe two specific charges: 1. that he left his wife but it does not appear whether the separation was through the fault or the will of her or him. 2. that he attempted to marry again. this is a charge of weight, but no proof being adduced, it cannot weigh against the integrity of his character affirmed by others, and his unquestionable good sense and information. I see no ground therefore for wishing his appointments had not been made. on the contrary we have already recieved from him a valuable statement of the several tribes of Indians residing within the territory of Orleans, and believe from the industry & intelligence he has already shewn in that department that we shall find him a valuable officer. we before had under contemplation the surveying the country on the West side of the Missipi into townships by lines running North & South from the sea to the Northern boundary, 33.° and extending Westwardly from the river about the breadth of 8. or 10. townships. having now recieved the locations of the several Indian tribes, we shall be able to take up the subject, and to make such provisions for it's execution as may give no uneasiness to them, as not only their rights but their comfort will be sacredly cherished. but on this subject particular instructions will be sent to yourself & Dr. Sibley, for quieting them effectually so soon as we have come to any certain conclusions. no pains must be spared, neither, to satisfy the inhabitants on the West side of the river, that in surveying the adjacent lands their rights will be liberally confirmed according to the equity of their situation and not to rigorous law. You have before known of Capt Lewis's mission up the Missouri and mr Dunbar's up the Wachita. we are now about to send one up the Red river. the original idea was that the same party should come down the Arcansa: but this is changed, & they will return down the Red river. the object of these missions is in the first place to ascertain the geography of the country, and then to give us such other details respecting it as men naturally wish to know. as it is possible that in proceeding to the sources of the Red river, beyond which they are expressly instructed not to go, they may fall in with some Spanish subjects, and may meet with obstructions from them, I wish you to ask a passport from the Marquis of Casa-calvo for the party. you may assure him on the honour & good faith of the government that the object of the journey is merely geographical & scientific, having in view nothing unfriendly to Spain, and to satisfy him of that, if he thinks proper to send one or two persons of his own choice as witnesses of our proceedings, they shall be recieved into the party and subsisted at our expence through the journey, but their pay or reward to go from him. as we have to settle a boundary with Spain to the Westward they cannot expect that we will go blindfold into the business. both parties ought to be free to make surveys of experiment preparatory to settlement, and each having a certain claim to the country must have equal right to procure the information necessary for elucidating their right. should the Marquis refuse to send any one, or to give a passport, he should be made to understand that should any violence be offered the party by subjects of Spain, it will have serious consequences. this will require delicate intimation to avoid the appearance of meaning it as a threat. in fact the Passport is a measure of precaution on both sides, to warn against the committing an aggression for want of due information, which might endanger the harmony, perhaps the peace of the parties. the passport is to be sent to mr Dunbar the director of the mission.   In my letter of the 7th. of Jan. I desired you to obtain the acquiescence of the government of West Florida, either thro' the Governor or the Marquis, in the passage of our Postrider through a corner of the country claimed by both, that is to say from Fort Stoddert direct towards N. Orleans. it will pass about 100. miles through the country claimed by both; and the passage of a courier is so innocent as never to be denied by one friendly nation to another, even where there is no mutual claim. it will stand in this case precisely on the same footing as the passage of our post by Baton rouge. not having heard from you on this subject, but presuming it could have met with no difficulty, our rider set out about a fortnight ago, and is probably with you by this time. his contract is to perform the journey always in a fortnight. we hope in time to reduce it to 10. days. you mentioned in one of your letters, the expectation that your legislature would establish an academy. should this be done, I would recommend to you a president whose name would give it immediate celebrity, a person whom I have known intimately 20. years, who was admitted to be second to no man in France in genius & science, and to no man on earth in integrity, benevolence & zeal to be useful to mankind. it is M. Dupont de Nemours. he has been over here & established his family in New York & Delaware. he is now in France but returns this spring; he has turned his eye to N. Orleans as the place where alone his possession of the language can render him useful, and has entertained thoughts of going there to instruct youth, even should it be at his own expence, as the best means now in his power of doing good. he will certainly decide to go there if invited to an institution and I pronounce with confidence there is not a man in the world better qualified than him in information & virtuous zeal for such a post. it happens that Made. du Pont is equally remarkeable for her sound understanding, information & benevolent zeal.

Mr. Gallatin thinks no location can be made for La Fayette under 1000. as.[1] the location therefore adjacent to N. Orleans must include so much swamp, or water as to make up 1000. as. he has at length sent over a power of Attorney to mr Madison, who will in future direct what is to be done. M. de la Fayette having expressed a particular confidence in M. du Plantier, who is otherwise known to us as meriting entire confidence, mr Madison will probably authorise him to act in every thing for La fayette. I will still thank you however to go on with the location adjacent to the city until M. du Plantier is ready to take the burthen off your hands. Accept my friendly salutations and assurances of continued esteem & respect. TH: JEFFERSON

P.S. Supposing it probable Dr. Sibley may be at N. Orleans, & yet not certain, I inclose a letter for him under your address in hopes you will be so good as to deliver or forward it as the case may be. it covers some blank Vocabularies for the languages of the Indians in that quarter.

PoC (DLC); at foot of first page: "Govr. Claiborne." Enclosure: TJ to John Sibley, 27 May.

VALUABLE STATEMENT: see Notes on John Sibley's Account of Native American Tribes, [after 21 May 1805].

ONE OF YOUR LETTERS: Claiborne to TJ, 25 Mch.

Armand Duplantier (DU PLANTIER) served in the American Revolution and subsequently became a planter and merchant in Orleans Territory. Writing to Madison on 10 Oct. 1804, Lafayette described Duplantier as "the best Connaisseur" of land in Louisiana, whose judgment regarding the location of Lafayette's grant would be "of high importance" (Madison, *Papers, Sec. of State Ser.*, 8:145, 148n).

[1] TJ here canceled "instead of locating only 600."

To Thomas Claxton

SIR Washington May 26. 05.

Your letter of the 22d. was recieved last night. the notes written on the face of the paper now returned will answer several of your enquiries. the shades therein mentioned are what I formerly requested you to get under the name of Cylinders. those I have heretofore seen were made to rest either on the table, or on a kind of mahogany waiter or saucer holding both the candlestick & shade. those figured by you seem as if they would easily overset. however they are so necessary for summer use that we must take them in any form. the table cloths should be 12. quarters square. as you say they are handsome, I will thank you to get half a dozen for me also. tho' I had rather have diaper than damask. I join you in preferring India matting for the passage above stairs. I have desired mr Smilie (the person whom I was told you employed) to provide floor cloth for the hall & passage below only. I think with you that two 22. I. plated waiters should be got for the house. you will observe in the inclosed that a pair of lamps are wanting here. take whichever form you prefer. be so good as to have my articles packed in a box addressed & forwarded for me to Messrs. Gibson & Jefferson at Richmond. about the time you recieve this Messrs. Jones & Howell will be shipping off some nailrod for me to the same address & could avail you of the same conveyance. Accept my friendly salutations & respects. TH: JEFFERSON

PoC (MHi); at foot of text: "Mr. Claxton"; endorsed by TJ. Enclosure not found.

From Jeremiah Halstead

SUR. New York Haspetol May 26 1805

Theas fuew Lineas are to in form you that I have bin a prissnor to this Haspetol thirty two months and am Veary much in want of a freand. my Lands in Dutchus County is Valued at thirty thousands pounds I have Several Hundread Dollars Wages Due mea—may the peace of god which passs all understunding Keape you Hart and mind guyded and Governed in the Right way

Sur you most Huble Servant JERAMIAH HALSTEAD

RC (MHi); at head of text: "Thomas Jefferson Cheff Justes of peace in the Cort of Chancrey"; endorsed by TJ as received 28 May and "insane" and so recorded in SJL.

THIS HASPETOL: an important function of New York Hospital, which was chartered late in the eighteenth century, was the housing and cure of mentally ill patients. In 1805, the hospital reported treating 75 patients for insanity, 15 of whom had been confined there since at least the previous year. Out of the 75 patients, 20 remained at the end of the year (William Logie Russell, *The New York Hospital: A History of the Psychiatric Service, 1771-1936* [New York, 1945; repr., New York, 1973], 45-53).

From Thomas Newton

Dear Sir Norfolk 26. May 1805—

I received your favor of the 2d, no wine having yet arived I hardly beleive any will, but should any arive, you can have what you please of it, tho if you should want, I can procure at any time for you, what you shall order, of as good wine & same kind, shpped by the house in Madeira, that in London & those in Madeira, I have heard have disagreed. I am glad to hear of other wines being introduced, as we were often imposed on in prices at Madeira. I shall with pleasure execute any commands you may have here. with my best wishes for yr. health & the greatest respect

Yr. Obt. Thos Newton

RC (DLC); endorsed by TJ as received 4 June and so recorded in SJL.

TJ's favor of 2 May has not been found, but Newton's comments suggest that TJ had been seeking assistance in obtaining Marsala (Appendix iv; see TJ to John Woodhouse, 5 May).

From Charles Willson Peale

Dear Sir Museum May 26th. 1805.

The Polygraph made for your use at Monticella has not yet arrived here, finding it did not come I went to the Stores where goods are deposited that come from Richmond &c, under the Idea that it might have been stored and no notice further taken on it, but I cannot get any intelligence about it. That which Mr Beckley had and the Small one are received. we have machinery in readiness and as soon as the Polygraph arrives it shall be put into complete order and sent to you to Washington by the Stages or by Water as you may please to direct.

I do not find it possible to make a Machine that can write an 8vo. page in so small a size as your Model, and obtain space sufficient to shut it up within the Gallows—there is no difficulty in getting the width, but the length of Machinery necessary to reach even $\frac{2}{3}$ down will be too long to shut up: for space must be allowed for the Pen-arms & Pens. I have therefore put my Sons improved Pen-bar &c to as Small a Machine as can be convenient for use—With this Machine you may write to the extremities of Post paper with ease by placing the paper diagonally. the lines will shew how the paper is to be placed, having nearly half of one sheet on the other, the changing of the paper to write to the bottom is cause of some trouble therefore I much prefer a Machine one or two Inches longer, to save the trouble of mooving the Paper. But you express the desire of having a very small Machine, I therefore send you this for a tryal of it, it will give you full knowledge of the disadvantages of a small Machine, and, if on tryal should you prefer another size there is little difficulty of sending such small Machines by the Land Stages. Before I quit the subject I beg leave to remark that the tops & bottoms ought not to be made thinner, because room must be had to sink the Inkholders into the bottom, and substance in the top, to prevent it from warping. For a permanent fixture I very much prefer a Machine with *three Pens*, altho' I have sildom occasion to use more than two, you may readily conceive that the great width has a greater certainty of writing correctly, and holding the middle Pen makes an equal ballance of the Pen-bar, there is very little difference in the labour of mooving three Pens or two, a very little addition of weight of the Machinery, which a few additional spiral Springs supports, and the number of Joints being equal of course there is no more friction in one than there is in the other.

I am much obliged to you for the Minerals.

A few tryals will discover the particular use of the lines on the Cloath, was the Machine intended for any person but your self I should be obliged to detail each particular operation, I will only remark that when you intend to write to the bottom, the sheet you write on must pass through the crack or crevice between the Gallows and board to write on.

Mr. Smith has not yet wrote for a Polygraph. It is surprising that an Invention so important as this, that so few purchasers come forward, nay many of my acquaintance who seem to know all the advantages of making copies in this mode, yet they postpone the purchase—I will now soon put a stop to the manufactury—as soon as what I have on hand is finished I shall once more make a publication, in pretty strong terms of recommendation of them, and if that fails to bring purchasers, I will then discharge my workmen—This I am unwilling to do, because they are now expert at every part of the Work, and I would have not much trouble with the manufactory in future, having Tools made at considerable cost that ensure the[1] accuracy of every part of the Work.

The Marquis Uroyo has one of two Pens which he is delighted with. he speaks of it in the highest terms of approbation in every company.

In the Model you sent, no room was allowed for the Pens when shut up—And as I have not made your contrivance to hold down the Ink pots, you might perhaps think I was neglectful of your directions. In the Machine sent having thicker stuf, makes it perfectly secure without. but I repeated before, this machine is only sent for tryal—I will with pleasure make any alterations from it you may desire and am with high consideration your friend C W PEALE

RC (DLC); at foot of text: "His Excellency Thos: Jefferson, Esqr."; endorsed by TJ; recorded in SJL as received 29 May. PoC (Lb in PPAmP: Peale-Sellers Papers).

[1] Peale here canceled "workman."

From Robert Smith

SIR, Baltimore May 26. 1805

Not conceiving it good economy to suffer the Company of Marines to remain at New Orleans merely for the purpose of manning the gun boats we are building on the Ohio I have forwarded the letter to Capt. Carmack. It is quite uncertain when those gun boats will be finished. Our Western Undertakers, not having had any experience in the construction and equipment of such vessels, will meet many and very serious embarrassments. I have encountered the trouble at this time of leisure of teaching the Ship-builders on the Western waters the art of building gun boats, not for the convenience of the present moment, but with a view to the advantages which the government will probably hereafter enjoy from having them thus taught. The same boats we could have built in the Atlantic ports at the same—perhaps at a less—cost and in much less time and with much less trouble to myself.

The gun boats building on the Ohio will, when ready for service, be manned, not by Marines, but by a few able seamen and such ordinary Seamen as may be necessary All of whom can with ease be entered at New-Orleans.

The two gun boats building under the superintendency of Com. Preble can, when finished, with Convenience be sent to the bay of St. Bernard.

Respectfully—Y. H. S. RT SMITH

RC (DLC); endorsed by TJ as received from the Navy Department on 26 May and "Marines at N.O" and so recorded in SJL.

THE LETTER: see TJ to Smith, 23 May.

TEACHING THE SHIP-BUILDERS: in letters dated 14 and 27 June, Smith forwarded detailed information on the construction of gunboats to the contractors in Ohio and Kentucky (DNA: RG 45, LSG).

Gunboats 11 and 12, superintended by Edward PREBLE, were constructed at Portland and Newburyport, respectively (Spencer C. Tucker, *The Jeffersonian Gunboat Navy* [Columbia, S.C., 1993], 48, 184-5).

To Thomas Claxton

SIR Washington May 27. 05.

Your favor of the 24th. was recieved last night. the purchase of the 2. doz. desert knives with silver blades, the silver Castors in preference to plated, and the sallad dishes, is approved. the knife sent on for a model is therefore not returned. Accept my salutations & best wishes. TH: JEFFERSON

PoC (MHi); at foot of text: "Mr. Claxton"; endorsed by TJ.

From John C. Delacoste

SIR New York 27th May. 1805.

Informed that Your Excellency has the intention of forming a National Museum at the seat of Government, I am led to believe that the collections composing the cabinet of Natural History, which I have begun some time past in this city, may be deemed worthy to form a part thereof, and I take the liberty of informing him, that the want of sufficient support and patronage from the inhabitants of New York compels me to break up the said institution and to dispose of the collections on hand, whereof I have the honour of inclosing a concise catalogue.

All the subjects are in high preservation, in perfect order, and methodically classed and arranged: a more favourable opportunity for procuring at once a variety of all kinds of indigenous and exotic subjects belonging to Natural History, and specially to the feathered tribe, will seldom, or never offer again.

The wish to see my said collections preserved from dissolution, induces me to dispose thereof at the rate of four Thousand Dollars, to which sum, the engagements which I have contracted in this city, amount. It will be obvious to every one, who has some Knowledge in that line of business, that the collecting, stuffing and preparing of such a number of subjects, must have cost more than double that sum.

The grief of loosing a property obtained at great expense, and by four years steady labour and exertion, would be greatly alleviated, if my proposition proving acceptable to Your Excellency, he should be pleased to appoint a commissioner in this City, for the purpose of viewing and examining the collections, and if approved of, of seeing them packed up by me, under his inspection, to be transported and placed in the National Museum, where, according to their primitive destination, they would contribute in diffusing and promoting the Knowledge of Natural History.

My taste and inclination being exclusively devoted to business and undertakings relative to that pleasing science, and particularly to Zoology, I take the liberty of offering my most respectful services to Your Excellency, for the purpose of collecting, preparing and preserving subjects belonging thereto, and of discovering such as are very rare, or yet unknown, in this immense continent, or elsewhere.

I make bold to assure Your Excellency, that my courage in travelling in quest of subjects is indefatigable; that my eagerness, and alacrity in the performance of that pleasing task are rather increasing than abating, and that my disinterestedness about the terms on which I may be employed, is as great, as the wish to obtain that favour. Deprived, by the consequences of the revolution of france, of valuable property on the coast of Dutch Guyana, I am since several years used to privations, and reconciled to my situation.

The Honour and satisfaction of being employed by the august head of a great and free Nation, who amidst the important and weighty occupations of administration, devotes to the promotion of arts and sciences all the time not taken up by business relative to Government, would be the greatest compensation I should wish to obtain for my exertions and Labour.

I have the Honour to be with the most profound respect Your Excellency;s Most humble, obedt and Dutyful Servt

J. C. DELACOSTE

RC (DLC); below signature: "No 225 Pearl Street"; endorsed by TJ as received 30 May and so recorded in SJL.

ENCLOSURE

Contents of Natural History Collection

Contents of the Cabinet

Quadrupeds—

37. individuals from the coast of Guyana—among which a Patira. a Jaguar, Several monkeys. a three toed, and a two toed Sloth, a coendou, a Tatou, A Great Ant-eater or Tamanoir, a middle and a least ant eater &a

18 Individuals of the State of Newyork. Viz, foxes, racoon, Squirrels, Skunks, Muskrat, canada Marmot &a

Birds.

215. individuals from the coast of Guyana. among which a Vulture, Maccaws, Toucans, Momot, cassiques, Trumpetter bird, or Agamie, hummingbirds, cottingas, Tanagres, Manakins, Cock of the rock, male & female. Flamingo, Spoonbill, Boatbill, Kamichi, Ibis &c &c

208. individuals of the State of Newyork, Viz Birds of prey, orioles, cuckoos, all kind of small birds, and a great variety of water fowl.

1 black ostrich and 1 Uppoe from Africa.

Amphibious animals.

38 individuals, indigenous and exotic, Viz, Alligators, Iguanas, Lizards, Turtles &c

23 Serpents & Snakes—among which 1 boa constrictor 14 feet long.

74 Fishes, the greatest part of the State of Newyork.

20 cases of insects and Butterflies, chiefly exotic.

108 Jarrs and Vials containing exotic fruits preserved in Spirits, dry fruits and seeds.

a few nests of birds, Wasps and other insects: a small collection of shells, of minerals and fossils, and some botanical curiosities—

A large box containing the Botanical collection made in Africa by the late Dr Perrein, deceased in this city. This collection which is not yet classed nor arranged contains new plants discovered by him, which he intended to send to Paris

The quadrupeds and Birds are contained in Glass cases Six feet high and measure upwards of 50 feet in length: they belong to the collections.

MS (DLC).

For the CONTENTS OF THE CABINET, see *Catalogue of the Natural Productions and Curiosities, Which Compose the Collections of the Cabinet of Natural History, Opened for Public Exhibition, at No. 38, William-Street, New-York* (New York, 1804).

THE LATE DR PERREIN: Jean Perreïn was a noted botanist and naturalist who died on 31 Mch. (*New-York Commercial Advertiser*, 1, 2 Apr.).

To John Wayles Eppes

DEAR SIR Washington May 27. 05.

Not understanding the conveyance to you by post beyond Richmond, I have thought it safest to remit the 100. D. for you to Gibson & Jefferson, subject to your order, which is done this day. I was never better pleased with a riding horse than with Jacobin. it is now really a luxury to me to ride. The early prevalence of sickness here this season will probably drive us hence earlier than usual, perhaps by the middle of July. I shall proceed almost directly to Bedford, and will there take to my assistance Mr. Clay & mr Clark and lay off at the

East end of the tract so much as shall, taking quality & quantity into consideration, be equal to the average value of 1000. as. of the whole tract generally. the tenderest considerations ensure a conscientious performance of this duty, and to be governed by the judgment of those who knowing the tract well will have no motive but to do what is right. I shall hope on my return from Bedford to find you at Monticello with the beloved children, objects of my tenderest sollicitudes. I shall not be without a hope of seeing mr & mrs Eppes also at Monticello. tho I cannot now repay their visits, if they will trust me 4. years, I will overgo the measure. you will see in the papers an extra letter of Elliott's of extraordinary aspect. it contains some absolute untruths. but what is most remarkeable is that expressions are so put together as to be literally true when strictly[1] considered & analysed, & yet to convey to 99 readers out of 100. the most absolute & mischievous falsehoods. it is a most insidious attempt to cover his own opinions & passions under the mantle of the executive, and to fill with inquietude the republicans who have not the means of good information. present me to mr & mrs Eppes & family & accept my affectionate salutations.

TH: JEFFERSON

RC (ViU); at foot of text: "Mr. Eppes." PoC (DLC). Notation in SJL: "100. D."

A letter of 9 May from Eppes, recorded in SJL as received from Bermuda Hundred on 15 May, has not been found.

For laying out a tract of land at Poplar Forest for Eppes, TJ was probably expecting the assistance of Charles CLAY, a longtime friend who lived nearby, and Bowling CLARK, TJ's former overseer there (RS, 2:78n; TJ to Eppes, 25 Mch.).

EXTRA LETTER OF ELLIOTT'S: during the spring and summer, Vermont Republican congressman James Elliott published 11 letters addressed to his constituents explaining and defending the reasons he had split with his Republican colleagues on a number of issues during the Eighth Congress. The letters were reprinted widely, and by late May, TJ could have possibly read the first six. From his characterization, the president was most likely referring to the fourth letter, in which Elliot discussed passage of the Twelfth Amendment, which he claimed had been "carried through both Houses by the undue influence of a few individuals, and by the combined operations of intrigue and terror" (New York *Daily Advertiser*, 13 Apr., 14 and 23 May; *Poulson's American Daily Advertiser*, 30 Apr.; *Alexandria Daily Advertiser*, 10 May; Keene *New Hampshire Sentinel*, 13 July).

[1] Word interlined in place of "closely."

To Gibson & Jefferson

MESSRS. GIBSON & JEFFERSON Washington May 27. 05

Having to remit the sum of 100. D. to Mr. John W. Eppes, and not certain of the safety of the post between him and Richmond, I have thought it better to deposit the sum with you subject to his order.

I therefore inclose you a postnote of the Richmond bank in favor of W. A. Burwell & indorsed by him to yourselves, which be pleased to recieve & pay to the order of mr Eppes. Accept my friendly salutations.

TH: JEFFERSON

PoC (MHi); endorsed by TJ.

RICHMOND BANK: that is, the Bank of Virginia. In his financial memoranda, TJ recorded at this day borrowing $100 from William A. BURWELL "for J. W. Eppes in boot between horses" (MB, 2:1154; Vol. 42:610n).

To John Sibley

SIR

Washington May 27. 05.

I have been some time a debtor for your letters of Mar. 20. and Sep. 2. of the last year. a constant pressure of things which will not admit delay prevents my acknoling with punctuality the letters I recieve altho I am not insensible to the value of the communications & the favor done me in making them. to these acknolegements I propose to add a sollicitation of a literary kind, to which I am led by your position, favorable to this object, and by a persuasion that you are disposed to make to science those contributions which are within your convenience. the question whether the Indians of America have emigrated from another continent, is still undecided. their vague & imperfect traditions can satisfy no mind on that subject. I have long considered their languages as the only remaining monument of a connection with other nations or of the want of it, to which we can now have access. they will likewise shew their connections with one another. very early in life therefore I formed a vocabulary of such objects as, being present every where, would probably have a name in every language; and my course, of life having given me opportunities of obtaining vocabularies of many Indian tribes, I have done so on my original plan, which tho' far from being perfect, has the valuable advantage of identity, & of thus bringing the languages to the same points of comparison. a letter from you to Genl. Dearborne giving valuable information respecting the Indians West of the Missisipi & South of the Arcansa presents a much longer list of tribes than I had expected; and the relations in which you stand with them, and the means of intercourse these will furnish, induce me to hope you will avail us of your means of collecting their languages. for this purpose I inclose you a number of my blank vocabularies, to lessen your trouble as much as I can. I observe you mention several tribes which having an original language of their own, nevertheless have adopted some other common to other tribes. but it is their original languages I wish to obtain. I am in hopes you will find persons situated among or near most of the tribes who will take the trouble of filling up a vocabulary, no matter whether the orthography used be English, Spanish, French or any other, provided it is stated what the orthography is. to save unnecessary trouble I should observe that I already possess the vocabularies of the Attacapas & Chetimachas, and no others within the limits before mentioned. I have taken measures for obtaining those North of the Arcansa and allready possess most of the languages on this side the Missisipi. a similar work, but on a much greater scale, has been executed under the auspices of the late empress of Russia, as to the red nations of Asia; which however I have never seen. a comparison of our collection with that will probably decide the question of the sameness or difference of origin, altho it will not decide which is the mother country & which the colony. You will recieve from General Dearborne some important instructions with respect to the Indians. nothing must be spared to convince them of the justice and liberality we are determined to use towards them, and to attach them to us indissolubly. Accept my apologies for the trouble I am giving you, with my salutations and assurances of respect.

TH: JEFFERSON

PoC (DLC); at foot of first page: "Dr. Sibley." Enclosures not found, but see Vol. 30:81-2.

VALUABLE INFORMATION: see Notes on John Sibley's Account of Native American Tribes, [after 21 May].

TAKEN MEASURES: see Vol. 42:457-8.

SIMILAR WORK: Catherine II tasked naturalist Peter Simon Pallas with compiling a list of core Russian words and their equivalents in about 200 languages (Sowerby, No. 4736; Vol. 29:201-2).

In INSTRUCTIONS written on 25 May, Dearborn urged Sibley to convince Native Americans, particularly those near Matagorda Bay, to side with the United States in case of a conflict with Spain. He also encouraged Sibley to arrange for a visit by chiefs of the principal nations to Washington and asked him to get acceptance of a survey of areas near the lower Red River (*Terr. Papers*, 9:449-50).

From Albert Gallatin

DEAR SIR 28 May 1805

The last paragraph of the enclosed letter seems to confirm the hints that Great Britain had not succeeded in forming any efficient alliance on the Continent.

There is an act passed by the legislative council of Orleans for dividing the Territory into Counties; which, if it has been received either by you or by the Department of State would assist in dividing the two land districts. It will be necessary to establish it soon as Mr. Thomson has accepted & writes that he will be on the spot in July.

By a sketch of the revenue (impost) for 1804, I find that after deducting the drawbacks, debentures, bounties, expences of collection

it amounts to	13,180,000
That of 1803 was only (in which our estimates are founded)	11,310,000
making an increase of	1,870,000
which arises from the following items vizt.	
New Orleans revenue	270,000
light Money & specific duties for six months at most	100,000
Mediterranean fund for six months	470,000
natural & war increase	1,100,000
	1,940,000
deduct increased expences of collection	70,000
Increases as above	1,870,000

Our receipts have not, however, kept altogether pace this year with that apparent increase, owing principally to the great re-exportations this year of articles imported last season.

The gross revenue of N. Orleans has been for the three

last quarters of 1804—	232,576
add for another quarter	68,000
Makes for the whole year.	300,000

The first quarter of 1804 gave but 34,000 dollars under the Spanish duties & regulations. Our laws commenced on 1st April.

With great respect and attachment Your obed. Sert.

ALBERT GALLATIN

RC (DLC); at foot of text: "The President of the United States"; endorsed by TJ as received from the Treasury Department on 28 May and "Orleans counties. finance" and so recorded in SJL. Enclosure not identified, but see below.

ANY EFFICIENT ALLIANCE: in May 1805, a number of newspapers printed an account detailing the uncertain state of British negotiations with Sweden and Russia (*Aurora*, 3 May).

On 10 Apr., William C. C. Claiborne approved AN ACT that divided Orleans Territory into twelve counties (*Acts Passed at the First Session of the Legislative Council of the Territory of Orleans* [New Orleans, 1805], 144-209).

From William Keteltas

SIR — New York 28h May 1805

This Day I leave New York for St. Louis under a full Impression I shall Receive Your Patronage Knowing I Deserve it

WILLIAM KETELTAS

RC (DNA: RG 59, LAR); at foot of text: "Thomas Jefferson President of the United States"; endorsed by TJ as received 2 June and "Office" and so recorded in SJL.

Petition of Michael McMahon

[28 May 1805]

The Petittion of Micheal McMahon, of the City of New York, tavern Keeper

Humbly Sheweth

That your Petittioner, has a Sickly wife and Helpless Family, and that, on the month of August. 1803 Shiped, One of his Lodgers With Lietuenant, Blake of the United States Navy—

That your Petittioner Put said mand on On board, a Vessel, bound for Boston with Enlisted Men, and received, a, Cheque on the Mahattan Bank in this City. a Copy of which, is hereunto Annexed—and on Presenting the same was Informed by the Cashier—that, Lietuenant Blake, had, with drawn his funds and that the Same could not be Paid—

That, some time after he sent, a Statement. of this transaction, to the Secretary of the Navy, Verified under Oath, and haveing received No Satisfaction, his compelled to trouble Yr. Excellency, on the Subject, haveing no doubt you Will Order Such Steps, to be taken as will Reinstate, your Petittioner, and possibly preevent. Officers in future, serveing Others, as he, has been—

Your Excellency, takeing the premises in, to consideration, yr Petititior Shall pray

Michael McMahon

RC (DNA: RG 45, MLR); in a clerk's hand, signed by McMahon; at head of text: "To, his, Excellency Thomas Jefferson, President of the United States, &. &. &."; with subjoined copy of a check drawn on the Manhattan Company on 11 Aug. 1803 in the amount of $28 on Joshua Blake's account and attestation by McMahon before Alderman James Drake, dated New York, 28 May 1805, to the truth of the statement; endorsed by TJ; recorded in SJL as received 31 May with notation "N"; also endorsed by TJ: "refd to Secy. Navy Th:J."

Michael McMahon operated a tavern and grocery in New York City (*John Langdon and Son's New-York City Directory, from May 1, 1804, to May 1, 1805* [New York, 1804]).

LIETUENANT, BLAKE: on 26 May 1803, Robert Smith assigned Lieutenant Blake to the brig *Merrimack* under construction at Boston (DNA: RG 45, LSO).

From Robert Smith

SIR, Baltimore May 28. 1805

I take the liberty of sending to you the enclosed letter. It explains itself.

Respectfully Your Hmble Servt RT SMITH

RC (DLC); endorsed by TJ as received from the Navy Department on 29 May and "Preble" and so recorded in SJL with notation "dated Balt." Enclosure: Edward Preble to Smith, Boston, 18 May, informing Smith that when in Washington he "heard the President express a desire to obtain a sample of Marsalla wine," and so he has sent to Thomas Tingey for TJ "a hogshead from New York, which I brought from Sicily"; he asks if it would be "improper for me to request you to mention it to the President" (RC in DLC).

From Robert Smith

SIR, Baltimore May 28. 1805.

The enclosed is a private letter in answer to one of the same kind from me. In calling it private I mean that it is not to be filed among the publick letters. It is submitted to your Consideration.

If it should hereafter be deemed expedient to send to Europe Com. Preble, it would not be proper to accede to any proposition so vague and indefinite as that made by him in relation to his expences. Some reasonable sum ought to be precisely fixed.

Respectfully Your Ob. Servt RT SMITH

RC (DLC); endorsed by TJ as received from the Navy Department on 29 May and "Preble's mission" and so recorded in SJL. Enclosure not found.

DEEMED EXPEDIENT: beginning in April, Edward Preble had discussed with Smith the possibility of undertaking a tour, lasting 12-18 months, of various European naval establishments (Christopher McKee, *Edward Preble: A Naval Biography* [Annapolis, 1972], 343-4).

To James Madison

[before 29 May 1805]

I have made some small verbal changes on the following grounds 1. the law recognises the right of the sheriff to use his posse comitatus without consulting any body. it is only *on his opinion* that his posse is insufficient, that the act comes into his aid by authorising him to apply to a judge or justice for an order to an officer for a military force. the law allows him to make the application without consulting us, but then it submits him to *our direction* in the use of it: and we, taking advantage of that, say he shall not use it at all unless he has previously been advised by a governor or Mayor so to do. this is an additional precaution for preserving peace which the law permits us to prescribe when once the Govr. or Mayor has advised, the marshall is then[1] to proceed with his armed force as the law directs, that is to say by demanding a surrender of the offender &c

RC (DLC: Madison Papers); undated; written on verso of a sheet addressed: "The President of the UStates"; addressed: "The Secretary of State."

TJ was responding to Madison's draft, not found, of instructions directed to federal marshals regarding the enforcement of a LAW "for the more effectual preservation of peace in the ports and harbors of the United States, and in the waters under their jurisdiction," passed 3 Mch. TJ's changes reflected his belief that, in the event armed force became necessary during the execution of warrants on crew members of foreign vessels and timely consultation with the federal executive was impractical, local civil authorities should play a regulatory role. TJ subsequently received copies of Madison's "Circular to the Marshals," which was enclosed in a "Circular to the Governors of the Several States," both dated 29 May (printed copies in DLC, with governors' circular endorsed by TJ as received from the State Department on 7 June and "act preservn. peace in harbors" and so recorded in SJL; U.S. Statutes at Large, 2:339-42; Madison, *Papers, Sec. of State Ser.*, 9:413-15).

[1] Preceding three words interlined in place of "Mayor is."

Invoice from Isaac Cooper

HIS EXCELLENCY TH JEFFERSON Washington 29th May 1805

To Isaac Cooper	Dollr Cents
to framing & glazing two Pictures	500
to thirteen Circular frames	13
	$18—

RC (MHi); in Cooper's hand; endorsed by TJ: "June 6. 05. pd by check on bk US."

To Albert Gallatin

TH:J. TO MR GALLATIN May 29. 1805.

I have no information that the act dividing Orleans into counties is passed. by the papers which came yesterday it appeared to have been twice read and committed. would not the *waters of the Red river* form one proper district, & the *residuary* country another? or the waters of the Red-river & the country *above & between* that & the Misipi for one, and the *residuary* country the other?

The financial part of your letter is highly pleasing. there must be something more in this increase of revenue than the *natural & war* increase. *depreciation* to a small degree in other countries, a sensible one in this, and a great one in England must make a part of it, and is a lesson to us to prefer ad valorem to fixed duties. the latter require[1] often retouching, or they become delusive. as to the Orleans revenue, I presume we may consider it as the consumption of 60,000. people & their increase, added to that of 6,000,000 & their increase: for tho' the former will increase faster than the latter it will only be by drawing off numbers from them. but from whatever cause, the increase of revenue is a pleasing circumstance, as it hastens the moment of liberating our revenue, & of permitting us to begin upon canals, roads, colleges &c. I presume you will locate on your map the Indians from Sibley's statement. my maps being in the hands of the binder I cannot do it. but when you shall have done it, I shall be glad to have a consultation with you on the extent to which we may lay off townships, & of the assurances we may give to the Indians included within them. I inclose you a paper at mr Madison's request. Affectionate salutations.

RC (NHi: Gallatin Papers); endorsed by Gallatin. PoC (DLC). Notation in SJL: "Orleans dists. finance. townshps." Enclosure: likely John Armstrong to Madison, 14 Feb. from Paris, detailing the present state of Franco-American relations and the reluctance of the French government to redeem debt incurred during the 1802 expedition to Saint-Domingue (Madison, *Papers, Sec. of State Ser.*, 9:39-42; see Gallatin to TJ, 30 May).

YOUR LETTER: Gallatin to TJ, 28 May. SIBLEY'S STATEMENT: see Notes on John Sibley's Account of Native American Tribes, [after 21 May 1805].

[1] Word interlined in place of "need."

To Gibson & Jefferson

SIR Washington May 29. 05.

There were lately shipped for me from Philadelphia 1. box of grape vines, and 4. open boxes of Monthly strawberries from Italy. altho' from the account I recieve of the latter they seem irrecoverable yet if there be any hope of life I would ask the favor of you to give them to any careful gardener in Richmond,[1] who will hereafter furnish me with some roots from them, if they live. their value is great, as in our climate they would bear 9. months in the year. the other box to be forwarded to Monticello by the first boat.

You have before this recieved 2. boxes from Monticello one for this place & the other for Philadelphia to which I will pray your attention. I hear nothing yet of my hams from Norfolk. will you be so good as to inform me to whose care there they were consigned? as also whether you have any offers for my tobacco? Accept my friendly salutations TH: JEFFERSON

PoC (MHi); at foot of text: "Mr. Gibson"; endorsed by TJ.

ACCOUNT I RECIEVE: J. P. G. Muhlenberg to TJ, 25 May.

2. BOXES FROM MONTICELLO: for the polygraphs TJ sent from Monticello, see TJ to Charles Willson Peale, 5 and 20 Apr.

For TJ's HAMS FROM NORFOLK, see Edward Johnston to TJ, 21 May.

[1] Preceding two words interlined.

From Gibson & Jefferson

SIR Richmond 29th. May 1805

Your favor of the 27th. Inst. is duly received inclosing a post note of our bank for $100.—which shall be held subject to the order of Mr. John W. Eppes. With respect we are

Sir Your obt Servts. GIBSON & JEFFERSON

P:S: Your Tobacco is still unsold & we are apprehensive we shall not shortly be able to obtain your limits—

RC (MHi); in Patrick Gibson's hand; at head of text: "Thomas Jefferson Esqre:"; endorsed by TJ as received 1 June and so recorded in SJL.

To Philippe Reibelt

SIR Washington May 29. 05.

The box of books announced in your letter of the 17th. is recieved, and I will ask the favor of you to send the remaining volumes of the Botaniste Cultivateur, and of the Traité des Abeilles; these being among those which I shall keep. they may come by the stage.

In the catalogue of titles & prices you inclosed, I need some explanations. 'Portefeuille des Artistes 4. V. 14. D 40 c' European price. the work recieved announces itself to be 1. Vol. in 4. Cahiers. are there 3. other volumes of 4. Cahiers each? or by the expression '4. V.' do you mean 4. Cahiers? the same questions as to 'Plans d'Architecture par Beker 4. Vol. 17. D 00' and 'Idem par Meinert 4. V. 16. D 80' 4. Cahiers of each of these are recieved. do these constitute but one of four volumes? or are they the whole work? if the latter, they would seem to be very dear. Beker for instance, at 27. D 02 c would be 61.

cents for every plate, many of which are mere ichnographies. I doubt whether the German Repertories or Dictionnaries will be taken at any of the offices. there is not one among us who knows even the German Alphabet. Accept my salutations & respects.

TH JEFFERSON

PoC (DLC); at foot of text: "Mr. Reibelt"; endorsed by TJ.

PLANS D'ARCHITECTURE: TJ referred to two German works that included architectural plates: Wilhelm Gottlieb Becker, *Neue Garten- und Landschafts-Gebäude* (Leipzig, 1798-99), and Friedrich MEINERT, *Die schöne Landbaukunst, oder Neue Ideen und Vorschriften zu Landgebäuden, Landhäusern und Oekonomie-Gebäuden im gefälligen* (Leipzig, 1798-1804).

GERMAN REPERTORIES: Reibelt appears to have sent TJ a periodical published in Weimar, *Allgemeines Repertorium der Literatur*, which consisted of bibliographies of recently published works classified by subject matter, and a similar work that listed works alphabetically (see Reibelt to TJ, 31 May).

From John Rhea

DEAR SIR, Hawkins Courthouse 29th. May 1805

In my letter from Sullivan Courthouse was stated that I expected Mr Duffield would meet me at this place—He arrived here on monday evening accompanyed by some gentlemen—who would escort him so far—and yesterday morning—he sett off for Orleans a considerable number of respectable Citizens accompanyed him about five miles, who after taking an affectionate leave, saw him safe over Holstein River—and returned—His departure appears to be regretted—His appointment appears to give general satisfaction—no one in my hearing yet yet spoken to the contrary—

The reason of my requesting him to come this was by me, with distress, communicated to him, he was greatly affected, intimated it was the more necessary for him to progress, and spoke, on the subject, as a man ought to do, who was conscious of not having merited such an information against him, and gave the most solemn assurances that his conduct and behaviour would be such as stated in the extract of his letter, communicated in my last to you—I cannot avoid saying that my opinion of and confidence in him is unimpaired—

Inclosed I have the pleasure of transmitting to you a begining of the vindication of Mr Duffields reputation—

Sincerely wishing you the possession of every blessing—I am with the most Sincere Esteem Your Obet Servt JOHN RHEA

RC (DNA: RG 59, LAR); at foot of text: "Thomas Jefferson The President of the United States"; endorsed by TJ as received 17 June and so recorded in SJL; also endorsed by TJ: "Duffield George. Orleans. judge." Enclosure: statement by citizens of Hawkins County, Tennessee, 29 May 1805, declaring that they "for several years past have been personally acquainted with George Duffield Esqr. during the time he continued in the profession of the Law in the court of pleas in and for the same County—And, so far as is within our knowledge, we do believe him to be a man of integrity probity and good demeanor, whose character and reputation is fair and unblemished by any ill habit"; signed by Richard Mitchell, clerk of the county court; Joseph Alexander, lieutenant colonel of the 4th regiment of militia; Joseph McMinn, state senator; George Maxwell, chairman of the county court; A. Nelson, sheriff; W. Armstrong, justice; William Paine, justice of the county court; William Bradley, major of the 4th regiment of militia (MS in same; in Rhea's hand, signed by all).

LETTER FROM SULLIVAN COURTHOUSE: Rhea to TJ, 24 May.

From Lauren Barns

Southington (Conn.)
30th. May 1805

MAY IT PLEASE YOUR EXCELLENCY

The consideration of my impropriety in attempting to detach your Excellency's mind from the concerns of a great nation, to attend to those of an individual; & of my presumption, that, being an unfortunate young man, whose name is scarcely known beyond the small circle of his acquaintance, & a total Stranger to your Excellency, should solicit favors before it has been in his power to render Services; these, added to my youth and inexperience, which preclude the possibility of addressing Your Excellency with becoming respect, conspire to fill me with so great a degree of diffidence that I almost recoil from my undertaking. I am however Greatly releived by a Sense of Your Excellency's unbounded goodness & benevolence, which, together with the pleasing hope that your Excellency will commiserate my unfortunate situation & wipe with a lenient hand the tear from the brow of Sorrow, triumphs over every other consideration, and incites me to proceed without farther apology—

My Father (Daniel Barns, who was a Captain in the Continental army) was reduced to poverty by the depreciation of Continental money, in which not only his pay for Services in the army, but his little patrimony was vested. His family being large and expensive he was unable to give me any education, excepting only what might be acquired at our village Schools.

At the age of fourteen I was put an apprentice to the tinplate working business, which, though a very good & profitable trade, was very irksome to me. My extreme attachment to books & desire of acquiring information increased with my years, and I had no time to devote to reading, except the hours by nature allotted for rest. My friends lent me some books, & when my daily work was done, & my companions either at rest or their amusements, I usually spent two or three hours in reading[1] History or Geography, or in Studying Arithmetic or English Gramur. My progress was slow, as I had not the benefit of a teacher. In this situation I was extremely discontented and my health was daily impairing. My Constitution is far from the robust, and I found that my exercise both of body and mind was more than I could endure; it therfore became necessary to leave off reading.

At the age of nineteen I determin'd to purchase the remainder of my time, & to work as a Journeyman in the Southern States, where wages are greater, till I could be enabled to pay up the notes Which I must give for the two years I had then to serve, & then to go into the study of Law. To this measure I was advised by some of my friends who then promised to render me some assistance after I should pay for my time. About this time (AD 1800) after a Serious examination of the great political question I declared myself a Republican, & openly espoused the cause. This was esteemed a "damnable heresy," and I was immediately denominated, Atheist, Deist, Infidel, Disorganizer, Jacobin and every opprobrious epithet that malice could invent, or our Self-righteous Priest could furnish for the use of his his obsequious adherents. At this time there were not in that town (Bristol, Conn.) more than 3 or 4 Republicans, & these so Silent on the subject that I was forced to bear the united Curse of Priest and people.[2] I soon found that I must forsake my Political creed, or that my former friends would forsake me. I then declared, & have never been guilty of a departure from the declaration, that no consideration should move me, nor threats, nor flateries persuade me to disguise my sentiments or to act contrary to the dictates of conscience. Republicanism soon began to increase, when I went to the Southward and workd, at my trade at Elizabeth-Town, (N.J.) Wilmington (N.C.) & Lancaster (Penn.) Successively and after I returnd, workd, in this town a few months & commenced the Study of Law on the first of November 1803—

I commenced my studies under as many disadvantages, perhaps, as any young man in America would think of encountering. My little Stock did not amount to quite one hundred Dollars, & the aid I expected from those that formerly called themselves my friends was cut off on account of my political principles. My father poor & opposed to me in political opinion. With the exception of a few young men, every one of my relations are federal & will assist me only upon Condition of my Joining their party. Nor are these the only men that have attempted to bribe me; but I have been Repeatedly assured by federal men of some consequence that, If I would Join their party and assist them as faithfully as I have done the Republicans I shall not want for assistance to complete my Studies. Great God! Is it not Enough that fortune has been so parsimonious to me as scarcely to allow the necessaries of Life, but those very men that ought to be my friends, and still profess to be such, must attempt to take an undue advantage of my Situation & deprive me of, the little all I have, my honor. Thank heaven, I have been endowd. with a Spirit to spurn their base offers & with them the base animals in the shape of men that could descend to such despicable meanness; & am determin'd not to "bow my knee" to the unhallowed "Baal" of aristocracy, nor kiss the image of Moses and Aaron displayd, in Connecticut Church & State Union.—

By the assistance of some Republican friends I have been enabled to pay my Quarterly Bills to the 1st. Inst. (i.e.) Eighteen months, (one half of the time required by the bar of this state for those that have not a liberal education.) I find this to be a very critical Period of my life: I have no money, & know not how to procure any in order to pursue my Studies. If I should give up the idea of completing my studies, I should not be qualified for any kind of business, nor could I pursue any with the least degree of avidity after Suffering so severe a disappointment, but should be totally useless to myself & to the world. At the thoughts of this I cannot but Shudder, especially when I take a retrospective view the ardour with which I have pursued every honest means in my Power, to acquire the little legal knowledge that I now have, & which is of such a nature as to be useless, unless it is Completed.

To Sacrifice my principles at the Shrine of Ambition, is a measure that I cannot but detest.

In this unfortunate dilemma I have the Presumption to address your Excellency, under the Pleasing hope that your Excellency's well known benevolence would extend itself to an unhappy young man, whose greatest ambition is to complete his Studies, and thereby be enabled to obtain a livilehood by his industry & lay a foundation for future usefullness: To attain which desirable end, he humbly begs your Excellency to grant him a little pecuniary assistance; for without a benefactor & such assistance he finds it impossible to pursue his studies.

My poverty forbids me to promise any Pecuniary Return, I can only say, that if fortune Should smile on & enable me I would then Gladly cancel the weighty obligation, and at all events Shall never cease to offer the little all that lies in my power the tribute of unfiegnd thanks, flowing from a gratefull heart.—

I have given a Sketch of my history, not because I deemd, it interesting, but merely to Show your Excellency that I have not "Called upon Hercules before I applied my own Shoulder to the wheell"; I have told my simple story without attempting a gloss, because I deem it more honorable to state facts simply, than to lie, Rhetorically—

I could produce vouchers to every part of my story But I forbear to do it for two important reasons. In the first place, because I do not know of any of my acquaintance who are known to your Excellency, & therefore did not deem their Certificates any better than my simple statement of facts; well knowing that many vouchers to a falshood, cannot make it true, & that truth will stand of itself. But the weightier reason is, because [. . .] no person whatever knows of my applying to your Excellency, nor[3] do I, at Present, intend that it shall be known.

If I should be so unhappy as not so far to merit your Excellency's attention & compassion as to obtain my request, I should never repine, but conclude that your Excellency was actuated by some wise & worthy motives, & should set down my failure on the long list of misfortunes & strive to bear them all With fortitude & composure of mind. If such should be my unhappy lot, I pray your Excellency to forgive this act of Presumtive folly in me, an act that nothing but an imperious necessity, Occasiond by a Steady adherence to my Political integrity, could Have drove me to; & pass an act of oblivion in my favor.

But if on the contrary your Excellency should think my unhappy Situation deserved commiseration & Should grant my request, a life spent in faithfullness to your Excellency I should deem inadequate to so great an act of Benevolence, no less than raising me from lowest pit of despondency to the Highest pinacle of hope.—

In such case I hope your Excellency will be pleasd. to enclose a Bank-bill & send by the mail, as this is a post-town. His excellency will be pleased to regulate the sum by his opinion of my deserts; However trifling the sum might be, it would be received with the most unbounded thankfullness & it would give me highest possible satisfaction know the reception this letter will meet with from your Excellency.

That this Country may be long happy under your Excellency's wise & Just administration, that your Excellency's few & feeble enemies may forthwith lay down their poisond, Shafts of falshood & malice, their long tried & fruitless weapons of warfare, and render to your Excellency the homage of well deserved praises; & that your E[xcellency] may long enjoy life & health and a double portion of [. . .] Blessing is the fervent prayer of

Your Excellency's very humble Servant LAUREN BARNS

RC (MHi); torn at seal; at foot of text: "His Excellency Thomas Jefferson President of the U. States"; endorsed by TJ as received 4 June and so recorded in SJL.

Lauren Barns (1781-1811) was admitted to the Connecticut bar in 1807 (Lorraine Cook White and Nancy E. Schott, eds., *The Barbour Collection of Connecticut Town Vital Records: Fairfield 1639-1850, Farmington 1645-1850* [Baltimore, 1998], 164; Litchfield, Conn., *Witness*, 29 Apr. 1807; New Haven *Connecticut Herald*, 4 June 1811).

MY OWN SHOULDER TO THE WHEELL: from Aesop's fable of Hercules and the wagoner.

[1] MS: "redaing."
[2] MS: "poeple."
[3] MS: "no."

From John Brown

SIR Frankfort 30th. May 1805

I take the liberty to inclose for your inspection a letter recd. from Judge Cobourn who last Winter made application through me for an appointment to the Bench of some one of the Territories of the U States. At that time I did not know that he had any knowledge of the French Language. Mr Cobourn for several Years past has filled a seat on the Bench of the General Court of this State with great reputation. He read Law under Judge Wilson decd.—is Very Studious—of an independent mind, & of an excellent moral Character.

I have the honor to be Sir Yo Mo obt Sevt. J. BROWN

RC (DNA: RG 59, LAR); at foot of text: "Thomas Jefferson Eq. President US."; endorsed by TJ as received 20 June and "Coburn to be judge Orleans" and so recorded in SJL. Enclosure: probably John Coburn to Brown, Mason County, 19 Apr.; noting that a judgeship in Orleans Territory might still be open, Coburn requests Brown's aid; he adds that he has been "tolerable proficient" in French and although not currently conversant in the language, could readily gain speaking fluency (same; endorsed by TJ: "Coburn John. to be judge Orleans").

From William Butler

SIR Charleston May 30th. 1805

Coln Lehre Commissiary general of the miltia of this State, is on a tower to the northward with his family for the benefit of their health—I have Known him for many years, haveing Served with him in the Legiselature of this State, he is a gentleman of the Strictest integrety and honor, In the many public Stations he has from time to time filled, he has all ways discharged the duties of them in Such a manner as to place him high in the Confidence of his felow citizens He is now a Representative in our State Legislature from the City of Charleston, which place he has Represented for Many years, upon evry occation he has Manifested him Self a firm and decided Republican—In the great Strugle that took place in this State in 1800 when america was convulsed to her center, he took a very active and Decided part, and was very instrumental in bringing about the happy change that was then effected—Permit me there for Sir, to take the Liberty of introduceing him to you, being assured you will find in him a gentleman of information and veracity, and one as Strictly attached to your Intrustt as any person in the union—

I am with the highest Consideration Sir your obedient & Humble sert—

WM. BUTLER

RC (MHi); at foot of text: "Thos. Jefferson Esqr. Presidt. of the united States"; endorsed by TJ as received 24 Sep. and so recorded in SJL, where TJ connected it by a brace and notation "recd. by mr Lehré" with entries for letters received the same day from John Gaillard of 25 May, William Johnson of 25 May, Peter Freneau of 2 June, Thomas Moore of 28 June, and an undated letter from Paul Hamilton.

William Butler (1759-1821), a planter and Republican from the South Carolina backcountry, served in the U.S. House of Representatives from 1801 until his retirement in 1813. A native of Virginia, he moved to South Carolina as a youth and became patriarch of a prominent family of planters and politicians. He saw considerable action during the American Revolution and later served as a major general in the state militia during the War of 1812 (*Biog. Dir. Cong.*; J. S. R. Faunt, Walter B. Edgar, N. Louise Bailey, and others, eds., *Biographical Directory of the South Carolina House of Representatives*, 5 vols. [Columbia, S.C., 1974-92], 3:114-16).

Invoice from Caldcleugh & Thomas

Philaa. May 30th 1805

Mr. Thomas Claxton. for Thos. Jefferson Esqr.

Bal. of Caldcleugh & Thomas

an Entry Lamp	24.00
a pair of Mantle Lamps	28.00
a doz of extra Glasses	2.50
Cask & Box	50
Porterage	25
	$55.25

Recvd. payment For Caldcleugh & Thomas JNO. JONES

RC (MHi); in John Jones's hand; at foot of text in Thomas Claxton's hand: "Rec'd Thos Claxton"; endorsed by TJ: "Claxton Thos. July 12th. D 81.35."

On 12 July, TJ reimbursed Claxton $81.35. That amount covered Claxton's payment to Caldcleugh & Thomas and the payment he made to Sperry & Huffnagle for TJ's diaper cloth (MB, 2:1159; Claxton to TJ, 1 June).

From Albert Gallatin

DEAR SIR 30th May 1805

I have taken notes of the situation of the Indian tribes in lower Louisiana as given by Sibley, and having compared them with Humboldt's & Nolen's sketches, think that I can locate them all with sufficient correctness for present purposes. But the great desideratum is a map, not good but at least tolerable. The documents we have are not merely imperfect but altogether contradictory, principally for the Attacapa & part of the Opelousa districts. I am now preparing at leisure moments a rough sketch in which the ascertained points will be fixed, and an attempt made to reconcile the clashing authorities. This, till we have better information, will at least do better than any of our existing maps, and I will locate the Indian tribes in it. Most of those tribes within the tract we mean to have surveyed are within the existing settlements and appear to be cultivators. It is presumable that they have but very limited claims; and, exclusively of the communications to be made by the Indian agent or superintendent, great confidence may be placed on the discretion, and tenderness for Indian rights, of Mr Briggs. At present, I can only add that in one of Clarke's sketches I have discovered three indian villages not mentioned by Sibly, one of Chitamachas at the place where Bayou Plaquemine unites with the Chafalaya, and two of a Nation called Ouachas or Couchas (the writing in French not being very legible) on the branches or Bayous of the Chafalaya below the Chitimachas. The bayou Chico mentioned by Sibley as a branch of the Opelousa and the seat of two tribes I can find in no map or sketch whatever. I believe that on examination of the relative situation you will find that the Opelousa & Attackapa districts will be much more conveniently united, as a land office district, with the Red river settlements than with those on the Mississippi.

I had earnestly requested that expenditure might be as moderate as possible for a few months in order that our receipts might so accumulate as to enable us to meet the French bills without borrowing. As it seems, by Mr Armstrong's last letter, that they will not come for some time, it is probable that we will avoid that evil recourse. But it is proper that I should state that the War Department has assisted us in that respect much better than the Navy Department, as will appear from the enclosed account of expenditures for each during the first five months of this year. Yet, in relation to the Navy no fleet has been fitted this spring; and four months pay to the 5 or 6 hundred men sent by the John Adams & Gun boats, which was the only extraordinary expence, is an object of only 60, or, 70 thousand dollars. As I know that there was an equal wish in both departments to aid in this juncture, it must be concluded either that the War is better organised than the Navy dept., or that naval business cannot be conducted on reasonable terms. Whatever the cause may be, I dare predict that whilst that state of things continues we will have no Navy, nor shall progress towards having one. As a citizen of the U. States, it is an event that I will not deprecate: but I think it due to the credit of your administration that, after so much has been expended on that account, you should have an increase of, rather than an impaired fleet. On This subject, the expences of the navy greater than the object seemed to require, and a merely nominal accountability, I have, for the sake of preserving perfect harmony in your councils, however grating to my feelings, been almost uniformly silent; and I beg that you will ascribe what I now say to a sense of duty and to the grateful attachment I feel for you—

With great respect Your obedt. Servt. ALBERT GALLATIN

If you have no objection, I would wish to be absent next week—a short jaunt will be of service to me—

RC (DLC); at foot of text: "The President of the United States"; endorsed by TJ as received from the Treasury Department on 30 May and "Navy expenses" and so recorded in SJL.

AS GIVEN BY SIBLEY: see Notes on John Sibley's Account of Native American Tribes, [after 21 May 1805].

HUMBOLDT'S & NOLEN'S: that is, information from Alexander von Humboldt and Philip Nolan.

CLARKE'S SKETCHES: a manuscript map by Barthélemy Lafon sent by Daniel Clark in the summer of 1803 (Vol. 41:211-2).

A NATION CALLED OUACHAS OR COUCHAS: the Washa, Chawasha, and Yakni-Chito tribes were affiliated with the Chitimacha in the region between Atchafalaya Bay and the Mississippi River (Sturtevant, *Handbook*, 14:188-9).

ARMSTRONG'S LAST LETTER: see TJ to Gallatin, 29 May.

ENCLOSURE

Summary of Expenditures

Payments by the Treasury
for Navy Department in 1805

	Drs.
2 Feby. to 30 March	250,000
April & May	295,000

Credit given in London	
Stg. 18,000	80,000
Drs.	625,000
Payments for War & Indian Departments January to May 1805	291,781.28

MS (DLC); in Gallatin's hand.

From Theodore Peters

MONSIEUR Bordeaux 30 Mai 1805.

Permettez moi de rappeller a votre Souvenir quilqu'un pour qui vous avez eu des bontés dont le Souvenir lui est cher et ne s'effacera jamais de sa mémoire; oui Monsieur vous daignates me reçevoir en Ami, vous prites un vif Interet a ce qui me regarde et j'en aurais éprouvé une preuve eclatante si votre bonne volonté n'eut été limitée par des devoirs, je les respecte trop ces devoirs pour que je me serois permis de vous en parler, vos moments d'ailleurs sont trop précieux pour que je vous aurais importuné de mes sollicitations; mais Monsieur je suis Pere et Pere sensible et comme tel j'ose vous solliciter en faveur d'un de mes Enfants qui élevé a Boston y retourne et desire devenir Citoyen Américain, brave Garcon, ayant le coeur noble, L'ame Sensible, Intelligent et de bonne conduite il est digne de ce titre, accordés le Lui, qu'il puisse aussi éprouver le bonheur de votre sage administration et contribuer lui même a celui d'une famille nombreuse et honête: Vous eutes la bonté Monsieur a mon depart de L'Amerique de m'assurer que si jamais un de mes Enfants passat sur le Continent vous le recevriez avec bonté, c'est ce qui m'enhardit a cette démarche excusez la en faveur d'un Pere qui desire ardemment le bonheur de ses Enfants.

Agreez mes Voeux pour votre bonheur et l'assurance de mon profond respect Votre Tres humble et Tres Obeïssant Serviteur

THEÓDORE PETERS

EDITORS' TRANSLATION

SIR, Bordeaux, 30 May 1805

Allow me to refresh your memory about someone who fondly remembers your kindness and will never forget it. Yes, Sir, you deigned receive me as a friend. You took a lively interest in me. If your good will had not been limited by your responsibilities, I would have experienced striking proof of your kindness. I have too much respect for your responsibilities to allow myself to speak to you; your time is too precious for me to bother you with my request.

But I am a father, Sir, a caring father, and as such I dare approach you on behalf of one of my children who was raised in Boston and is returning there. He wishes to become an American citizen. A good boy, noble, humane, intelligent, and upright, he is worthy of this title. Grant him the opportunity to know the happiness of your wise administration and to contribute to a large, honest family. When I left America, Sir, you were good enough to assure me that if one of my children ever came to the continent you would receive him kindly. This is what emboldens me to make this request. Forgive it in the name of a father who ardently wishes his children's happiness.

Accept my wishes for your happiness and the assurance of my deep respect. Your very humble and obedient servant THEÓDORE PETERS

RC (ViW: Tucker-Coleman Collection); endorsed by TJ as received 1 Dec. 1806 and "by his son" and so recorded in SJL.

TJ appointed Theodore Peters the vice commercial agent at Bordeaux in 1801. At least one of Peters's children, John Peters, was educated in BOSTON prior to his father's appointment. By 1822, John Peters was employed as a clerk in the War Department (Judah Delano, *The Washington Directory: Showing the Name, Occupation, and Residence, of Each Head of a Family and Person in Business* [Washington, D.C., 1822], 64; *National Intelligencer*, 11 Oct. 1837; Vol. 33:129).

From Robert Brown of Washington

SIR, City Washing May 31th 1805

the onnrabole the presedent of United States I am sorey to trobele your Honner you promised me to Spake to Mr Lenthrobe to put me in a Birth in the publick Imploy But finding him Not Coming fored Mr Lanthorng his the Management of the Bisness there Was a shore from the Ware office that I Don Before and i waiting in hops to Get a birth In this publick imploy there is athers imployd at it allso there is four hundred Dollars Keep from me At the Bericks But I hope i have Don Nothing amise More than Mr McNance that Got paid Evrey Coper But Wood Never Say a word if your honner Wood Be Kind anuff to Spaek to Mr Lenthoring for Me to Do the Sellar's at you house or fire profe Houses as I rimaaked to your honner Before I need Not purtend to Spaek to aney one Else But your honner I hope your Good hart will Concether Me I am Waiting Now for an answar from your Honner you Most Obdt. Set. ROBT BROWN

RC (DLC); addressed: "Mr thomas Jaffersense Presedent of United States"; endorsed by TJ as received 31 May and so recorded in SJL.

SOREY TO TROBELE: see also Brown to TJ, 22 Apr.

Brown probably meant Benjamin Henry Latrobe (LENTHROBE) and John Lenthall (LANTHORNG).

To Patrick Byrne

Washington May 31. 05.

Th: Jefferson presents his compliments to mr Byrne & his thanks for the inclosed catalogue of pamphlets, which he now returns not finding any thing in it which he has occasion to call for. in truth political pamphlets are of so ephemeral an interest that their value passes almost with the moment which produces them.

PoC (MHi); endorsed by TJ. Enclosure not found.

HIS THANKS: TJ acknowledged Byrne's letter of 23 May.

To John C. Delacoste

Washington May 31. 05.

In answer to M. De la Coste's letter of the 27th Th: Jefferson is bound to observe to him that no authority has been given for the establishment of a Museum at this or any other place on account of the General government: indeed that this is not among the objects enumerated in the constitution to which Congress are authorised to apply the public monies. whenever the revenues of the Union shall be liberated from calls of the first urgency, it is probable that an amendment of the constitution may be proposed, to authorise institutions for the general instruction. in the mean time it is the duty of the public authorities to keep themselves within their legitimate powers. he prays M. de la Coste to accept his respectful salutations.

PoC (DLC); endorsed by TJ.

To J. P. P. Derieux

Dear Sir Washington May 31. 05.

Your favor of the 19th. is recieved, explaining the arrangements proposed to be made with your family. of the propriety of displacing yourself to accomodate those who are younger & abler to help themselves, I am neither competent nor authorised to judge. it is certainly a mark of those affectionate dispositions of which I have ever known you susceptible. but it is but justice, in answer to that part of your letter respecting an office, to observe to you, that none but the offices of primary grade are within my gift. all others are appointed by those to whom they are immediately subordinate, who being responsible for their conduct, ought not to be controuled in their appointment. accordingly I make it a sacred rule never to give even an intimation in favor of any one. it would be decieving yourself therefore injuriously to let this expectation enter at all into the views inducing you to remove to a city; and it is from a sincerity[1] of disposition that I give frank information on this subject. the solid stemmed wheat you were so kind as to give me some grains of, has failed. how has it answered with you, & what are it's advantages? present me respectfully to Madame Derieux, & accept my friendly salutations.

TH: JEFFERSON

PoC (DLC); at foot of text: "Mr. Derieux." RC (Mrs. Ernest E. Garrison, Tampa, Florida, 1948); incomplete, consisting of final portion of MS only (see note 1).

SOLID STEMMED WHEAT: see Derieux to TJ, 7 Sep. 1803.

[1] Fragment of RC begins here.

From Philippe Reibelt

MONSIEUR LE PRESIDENT! Balt. le 31 Mai 1805:

Je m'empresse de repondre a Votre Lettre du 29—

1) que j'ai fait mettre les 2 Vol. rest. du traitè sur les Abeilles au Stage.

2) que je n'ai pas ajoutè les Vol. rest. du Botan. Cultiv. parcequ'on ne peut pas trouver le 3me. Volume—et que je demanderais donc cet Ouvrage par la premiere occasion de Paris pour Vous.

3) Que du portefeuille des Artistes, et des Plans d'Architect. de Becker et de Meinert—*Çe que Vous avez en çe Moment chez Vous*—coute en Europe respectivè 1440, 1700, et 1680 Cents. et que çes Ouvrages sont—par des egards particuliers—a Votre disposition pour l'addition des fraix d'importation seulement, c'est a dire 40 pC., taux, au quel je Vous fournirois des a pressant tout ce, que Vous commanderez.

4) Que le Repertoire et Dictionaire (non pas Germanique mais) general de la Litterature de l'univers, dont le premier donne d'apres une Classification trés exacte, tous les titres dans les Langues respectives—et l'autre de la meme manière alphabetiquement—sont en Europe unaniment regardès comme des Ouvrages absolument necessaires a toute bibliotheque Complette; et que c'est par çe Motif, et parceque je sais, que Mr Wagner possede la Langue allemande &c que j'ai pris la Libertè de Vous les envoyer.

J'ai en même tems le plaisir, de Vous annoncer, que Mr. Du Catel (le francais le plus instruit, le plus estimable, et le plus aisè en çette

Ville), a qui j'avois donnè—il y a 15 jours—4 grains de Quarantino, en a deja des plantes— Je Vous prierais de m'informer aussi du succes de Votre essai.

Je Vous presente mes bien profonds et bien sincers respects.

REIBELT.

EDITORS' TRANSLATION

MISTER PRESIDENT! Baltimore, 31 May 1805

I hasten to answer your letter of the 29th.

1) I put the remaining two volumes of the treatise on bees on the stage.

2) I did not add the remaining volumes of the *Botaniste cultivateur* because we cannot find the third one. I will request it from Paris at the first possible opportunity.

3) In Europe the *Portefeuille des artistes* and the plans of architecture by Becker and Meinert—which you now have—cost, respectively, 1,440, 1,700, and 1,680 cents. By a special arrangement, these works are at your disposal with only the addition of import costs, namely 40 percent. I can now provide anything you order at that rate.

4) As for the general—not Germanic—repertoire and dictionary of the literature of the universe: the repertoire provides an exact classification of all the titles in the respective languages; the dictionary does the same alphabetically. In Europe they are universally considered absolutely necessary works for any complete library. For this reason, and knowing that Mr. Wagner speaks German, I have taken the liberty of sending them to you.

At the same time I have the pleasure of informing you that Mr. Ducatel, the most educated, eminent, and wealthy Frenchman in this city, to whom I gave four quarantino seeds two weeks ago, has already planted them. Please keep me informed about the progress of your planting.

I offer my deepest and most sincere regards. REIBELT.

RC (DLC); endorsed by TJ as received 1 June and so recorded in SJL.

MR. DU CATEL: likely Edme Ducatel, who advertised as an apothecary and chemist in Baltimore (Baltimore *Telegraphe and Daily Advertiser*, 4 Oct. 1804; Reibelt to TJ, 3 Feb. 1806).

To Robert Smith

DEAR SIR Washington May 31. 05.

I return you Commodore Preble's letter which gives us time enough to consider on his mission. he proposes a longer one than I had supposed necessary. the hogshead of wine was yesterday brought here. it is really a painful & embarrasing thing. to reject may be supposed to imply impure motives in the offer. to recieve leads to horrid abuse. the former however has been my rule, where the thing is of any value, as the lesser evil. yet there are characters with whom it cannot be practised. in Preble's case various considerations oppose it. I have therefore determined to send him a counter-present, of a kind which cannot be unacceptable. he is a man of business, travels much, writes much. I will send him therefore a portable secretary, that is to say a Polygraph. the invention is new, ingenious, useful, and of equal cost with the hogshead of wine; and if given without any squint at that, cannot be unacceptable. Another case has occurred of greater difficulty. mr Harris, our Consul at Petersburg has sent me as a present, a small marble bust of the emperor Alexander. I had concluded to reject it; but mr Madison advises it's being recieved for the President's house, as destined for the office & not the officer; and this because of the relation between the thing & the person of the emperor, whose unequivocal and marked manifestations of friendship to our country should privilege him against any thing which might seem to be a slight. his bust is in the warehouse of Smith & Buchanan, and has been since sometime last year. will you be so good as to direct it to be forwarded here. I am ordering the purchase of a marble one at Rome, of general Washington, taken from Ciracchi's, as a companion to the other to be set up in the President's house. Affectionate salutations.

TH: JEFFERSON

PoC (DLC); at foot of text: "The Secretary of the Navy." Notation in SJL: "Preble. Harris." Enclosure not found; see Smith to TJ, 28 May (second letter).

THE HOGSHEAD OF WINE: see Smith to TJ, 28 May (first letter).

BUST OF THE EMPEROR ALEXANDER: see Levett Harris to TJ, 7 Aug. 1804.

SOMETIME LAST YEAR: see S. Smith & Buchanan to TJ, 9 Nov. 1804.

For the availability of a marble copy of Giuseppe Ceracchi's bust of George WASHINGTON, see Thomas Appleton to TJ, 25 Feb.

From Samuel Smith

SIR/ Balte. 31. Decr. [i.e. May] 1805

Permit me to return my Sincere thanks for the Appointment Conferred on Mr. Donaldson, I am persuaded that he will afford no Cause of regreat—His Father Coll. William Lowrey has been regularly bred & Accustomed to the Selling of Goods of all kinds, is a Man of Integrity and conversant in Accounts—I take leave to mention those qualifications that (Should Such a Character be wanted) he may be Obtained, he will be on the Spot—He might be of Service "perhaps" when Indian Trading houses Shall be established among the Osages. Sacs, &c &c—Coll Lowrey is a most excellent Militia Officer & warmly

Attached to the present Administration—He has been unfortunate in Trade, but never Suffered in his Character—he knows not of the information I am now presenting—

Capn. Mann, in the Schooner Commerce Carries the Bust of the Emperor of Russia, when my house recieves the Amt. of Cost, they will transmit it to you—I am Sir your friend & servt.

S. SMITH

RC (PHi: Daniel Parker Papers); misdated; endorsed by TJ with "May" written above "Dec.," as received 1 June, and "Lowry Wm. to be factor &c." and so recorded in SJL with additional notation "W."; endorsed by Dearborn: "to be returned to the President of the U.S."

APPOINTMENT CONFERRED: see TJ to the State Department, 30 Apr.

From "A Native Citizen of the United States"

[before 1 June 1805]

A PATRIOT of 1776, and uniform friend to his country, to the federative system, and the navy, who has had false accusations heaped upon him in secret, by *inimical*, *undeserving*, *invidious* and *jealous* men of *intrigue*, as is believed by those of discernment, takes the liberty, notwithstanding, from pure amor patriæ principles (as a professional man) to lay before the President of the United States, a few facts and observations, which he hopes may be useful, without any retrospect of the person or persons directing the helm of the navy abroad.

The writer of this sheet does not think it expedient to give his name, *as that is of no moment at present*, but he pledges himself to the President, that a proper attention to the hints here thrown out, under judicious and scientific management in the Mediterranean, will cause a new and brilliant *constellation* to appear and adorn our naval history, by a speedy and glorious peace with Tripoli, which will terrify all the Barbary powers from the manner it is obtained.

MR. PRESIDENT,

It has appeared obvious to me for several years past, that, single-handed, or in other words without foreign aid, the expensive and as yet unsuccessful war with Tripoli, was only to be ended with honour and advantage to the United States, and at the same time, insure security to our commerce in the Mediterranean and its neighbourhood thereafter, by prompt and efficient measures taken solely on our own bottom; or arising entirely from our own resources, and carried into effect by our own enterprises.

To accomplish, then, this important object in a speedy manner, I would recommend a force to be prepared and employed, so constructed as to enter and go into the harbour of Tripoli every where—*where their flotilla can move or take shelter*; for it is well known that our frigates cannot go into that harbour on account of its shoalness, so as to approach the town sufficiently near to effectually bombard and destroy the city, although they may approach several military works and demolish them, without entering the harbour, which is formed by a long chain of rocks to the northward and eastward of it—but the destruction of these works will not reduce the Tripolitans to American terms (if they are a brave enemy,) which it is to be hoped are humiliating terms, and such as those pirates ought to be reduced to, for the unprovoked aggressions committed against the United States; and by such means give them and their Barbary neighbours a proper idea of the true American character, which, there is well-founded belief, has been depreciated within the walls of all their towns by interested and private enemies to our country and government.

Under this impression, Sir, made strongly on my mind, added to the opinion entertained by the governments and people of Barbary, as to our desire for peace and riches, and great aversion to war, a suspension of arms with Tripoli obtained for money cannot be lasting; for there is certainly reason to believe, when we judge of the character of this people, that their government, or one or more of the Barbary governments, will embrace the first favourable opportunity of breaking such peace, so soon as our forces are withdrawn from their seas, or principally withdrawn, and either commence immediately a predatory war on our commerce, or exact, in some shape or other, a farther tribute; and under this belief of a nation never bound by the strict principles of honour and good faith, but by calculation of what they may gain or lose by a war with a Christian power—I am of opinion, that we should do as France did in the seventeenth century, with a squadron of easy draught of water, that destroyed a large portion of Tripoli, compelled the Bashaw to sue for peace, under the mouths of her cannon, and obtained from that people 500,000 livres, besides all their wives' bracelets, jewels, &c. together with the French ships and prisoners they had pirated; and this peace, which the Tripolitans so dearly bought, has been held undisturbed ever since, and is it not reasonable to suppose that they would equally remember a peace exacted from them by us, on similar terms; whereas these pirates, and their neighbours, on the contrary, will laugh us to scorn, at having viewed our ships, been menaced by them, and thereafter receive from us thousands of dollars, whether the same be considered as the purchase of peace or ransom of prisoners. Under this view of the subject our best policy would surely be, to command from them submission to our terms, under the muzzle of our cannon arranged in a line within their harbour, before the city, and close to its walls—I say, close to the city; as distant firing from ships or other vessels afloat, have in most cases, every where proved ineffectual; and with the people in question, it must have a tendency to harden and familiarize them to the hazard of active military operations, wihout any good consequence to us; and my own experience has taught me, that the nearer ships engaged with ships the better, so that they preserve sufficient room for manœuvres on the true principles of naval tactics, and without getting on board each other, unintentionally, as accidentally falling foul in battle, renders the issue extremely uncertain, and retreat impractible in case of need.

It is also equally advantageous for ships to engage close when anchored with springs; for, the nearer to military works on shore which are assailable from ships, when they are intended to be attacked, the better. Ships closely anchored to a place with springs in a seaman-like and officer-like manner, can bring their broad-sides to bear on any one object desired, or that it may be found advantageous to direct their fire at, while they lie steadily in such position, until the commanding officer thinks proper to alter it, and take another; and then the alteration may be made in a moment, according to circumstances, by veering out the cable and heaving in the spring at the capstern, or veering out the spring and heaving in the cable, according to the new direction wished to be given to the cannon—but another great advantage, Sir, in anchoring when an attack is made against a fort or other military works, is this: a ship thus anchored, with her sails handed or closely hauled up for handing, is a smaller object for your enemy's aim in firing, and being a smaller object is not of course so much exposed in her rigging and sails to the enemy's operations; nor are the crew so much exposed, because the being at an anchor precludes the necessity of men being stationed at every point for working the ship during a bombardment; a ship too being compelled to cease continuing a bombardment, and to retire from before an enemy's works, will be in a better situation when got under way by slipping or cutting the cable, &c. to haul off, by preserving her sails, rigging, and men as much as possible, than by having had them exposed as much as possible by being under way.—But besides these advantages, which a knowledge of naval tactics gives, and reason and common sense will prove, wherever the experiment is properly tried by real sea officers of skill, there are other great and solid advantages to be gained by being at anchor in an attack, as I have stated, and a very important one is the preservation of a ship from the dangers of getting on shore, when under way in a narrow pass or between reefs, added to the difficulty of bringing her guns very often to bear as desired, which Captain Preble (for whom I have great esteem) found and acknowledges in his official letter—hence, attacks on military works should be always made by ships anchoring (where there is anchorage) with springs and worming chains, &c. to preserve the cables, unless sufficient chains for riding the ship or ships are prepared for the purpose.

GUN BOATS.

Gun boats properly constructed and equipped with furnaces and grates for heating red-hot shot—bomb-ketches, calculated to throw shells and carcasses—fire-ships, properly prepared to burn a certain time and then explode, with proper sally-ports for their crews escape, and boats to attend them, and all these of small draught of water, is the only force to enter the harbour of Tripoli with, destroy their marine, and reduce the city to proper terms; and such a force, managed with system and vigor, would, in one single day favourable to the enterprise, take, burn, and destroy entirely, the enemy's flotilla, and when thus destroyed in part, and taken in part, together with the ships of trade in the harbour, the remaining business would be simply to place our whole flotilla and the enemy's taken and preserved, against the town and works as near as might be necessary, when red-hot and cold shot, grape-shells, and carcasses, &c. &c. &c. should be well applied until the enemy become sick of the feast, or have their city reduced to ashes; observing, at the same time, that while this business is going on within the harbour under proper arrangements and management, the ships that may be employed on the service should perform their part against the works from without the harbour: and this plan I repeat, as I have often repeated in conversation, would insure us a peace, and a lasting peace, with Barbary, and immortalize the American name for ages to come.

It will be observed, that I have, in recommending this plan, mentioned more than once, *proper arrangements* and *good management*—for proper arrangements and good management are more than one-half towards gaining a victory. I do not, by any means, intend, however, to reflect on past proceedings; but I think we should be extremely circumspect and cautious in giving any of the Barbary powers an opportunity of feeling an advantage gained over us; and that, in sending into their harbours at any time, any infernal, or fire-ships, they should be so *guarded*, and so *covered*, by a proper force, until the match is put to, and the fire is lighted up, that the project in no event could be defeated, or the men endangered in making their escape, by any of the enemy's craft boarding; for the capture of a fire-vessel by an enemy, or the preventing her from getting amongst their shipping, and of doing all the mischief calculated by such contrivance, is a matter of primary importance, inasmuch as voluntееers from a fleet, and even from the shore, will run every hazard, where the smallest success is probable, to defeat such a project, as was proved in the case of *Somers*, who was a lad under my tuition and orders in an Indiaman.

That we have more ships in the Mediterranean than are necessary for carrying on the war with Tripoli, is certain: yet I will not pretend to say it is bad policy to have them there. Large ships, however, are not the sort of vessels calculated for this warfare, for such vessels (as I have mentioned already) cannot enter their harbour, and may be driven off from an attack on their works made without the harbour, by red-hot shot well directed at them, should the Tripolitans take advantage of the time that has been allowed them to prepare furnaces, &c. for such purpose; whereas the gun-boats being such small objects, especially when placed END ON before the city of Tripoli in an attack, they will scarcely be affected by such preparations, as not one shot in an hundred would touch them. In carrying on the war by blockade or cruising, large ships are not necessary; either, because the enemy have no large ships to combat with, and smaller vessels can keep in shore to prevent supplies entering the harbour, more effectually than large ones; and they can, in case of running vessels on shore bound in, cover their boats by approaching close to the shore, while the boats are in the act of burning or bringing them off: whereas large ships cannot, on many parts of the coast of Tripoli, approach it, and large ships must, in bad weather or in doubtful weather, on account of their heavy draught of water, keep a good offing to avoid the shoals and dangers hereabouts; and by thus being far off, the enemy's supply-vessels and others, by keeping close in with the coast, from having the best of pilots and drawing little water, evade the vigilance of large ships, while, on the contrary, they would be intercepted by small corsairs stationed for that purpose. Hence I am persuaded, that two frigates, with the brigs and schooners of war, now on the Mediterranean service, is an ample force to reduce, in a single campaign, Tripoli to any terms we please (without having any thing to do with the ex-bashaw's projects, which may or may not be good policy or advantageous to us, the government being much more competent to judge from their information on that subject than I am) when combined with ——— gun-boats ——— bomb-ketches and ——— fire-craft, all properly prepared and conducted.

The writer, though not averse to being known, is, at present, not desirous of being known, and has, therefore, caused several copies of this paper to be printed, at his own expense, for the use of government; and his best wishes attend the campaign in the Mediterranean, which ought to commence by the first of June, with great vigor, as it would then end with honour and glory to the United States, before the first of September.

From the most honourable and the best of motives, I at one time, wrote a couple of letters to two gentlemen then at Washington, expecting they would be communicated to the government, or at least my opinions contained therein; one of them was not communicated, as the gentleman wrote me, for *reasons* he gave; the other I do not know whether it was communicated or not; the one that I know was not communicated, was in substance the same as this, and as I did not approve of the reasons given, as useful to our country, for not exhibiting it, or the purport of it, to the President, or Secretary of the Navy, I have been induced to present this sheet; and am, Sir, Very respectfully,

A NATIVE CITIZEN OF THE UNITED STATES.

Broadside (DLC: TJ Papers, 143: 24907-8); undated, but probably prior to 1 June 1805 from internal evidence.

WRITER OF THIS SHEET: Thomas Truxtun was likely the author of this printed tract. He had previously offered advice to TJ on naval affairs, including in the form of printed letters, and would do so again. The broadside is with some other Truxtun-related items in TJ's papers at DLC, such as the mariner's 25 Sep. 1804 letter to TJ. Biographical references in the letter are consistent with Truxtun's career, including experience in the China and India trade (matching the assertion of "Native Citizen" that he had commanded "an Indiaman"). The allusion in the second paragraph to "a new and brilliant *constellation*" may have been a wink to Truxtun's success as the first commander of the U.S. frigate of that name (ANB; Eugene S. Ferguson, *Truxtun of the Constellation: The Life of Commodore Thomas Truxtun, U.S. Navy, 1755-1822* [Baltimore, 1956], 71-91; Vol. 44:63-7, 268-70, 436-7; Truxtun to TJ, 18 Jan. 1806). The letter of "Native Citizen of the United States" must have been written after the navy's actions against Tripoli in August and September became known in the United States in February 1805, and likely before reinforcements for the Mediterranean squadron were dispatched in early June (*National Intelligencer*, 25, 27 Feb.; Vol. 45:550-1; Smith to TJ, 19 Apr.; Charles W. Goldsborough to TJ, 18 May). Two letters from Truxtun recorded in SJL during this time have not been found: one of 25 May from Philadelphia that TJ recorded as "Anonymous [Truxton]" and "Tripoline war" and another dated 14 June that related to the navy (see Appendix IV).

AS FRANCE DID: in 1685 a French fleet bombarded Tripoli and was able to obtain an indemnity and the release of captives (John A. Lynn, *The Wars of Louis XIV, 1667-1714* [London, 1999], 173).

For Edward Preble's OFFICIAL LETTER detailing the naval campaign against Tripoli in the summer of 1804, see TJ to the Senate and the House of Representatives, 20 Feb. 1805.

CARCASSES were hollow shells filled with burning material intended to set fire to their targets (OED).

Richard SOMERS commanded the ketch *Intrepid*, which exploded killing all on board during the 4 Sep. 1804 attack on Tripoli (Vol. 44:500n).

COMMUNICATED TO THE GOVERNMENT: in a letter to Madison dated 16 June that Madison evidently passed on to TJ, Truxtun noted that he had previously written to Senator James Jackson detailing his plan for defeating Tripoli without having to resort to paying tribute or a ransom for prisoners from the frigate *Philadelphia*, with the hope that the information would be presented to Robert Smith and the president (RC in DLC).

To John Daly Burk

SIR Washington June 1. 1805.

Your favor of May 26. is recieved and I am perfectly disposed to communicate to you the collections I possess as far as their condition will admit. what this is will need explanation.

I have a collection, nearly compleat, of the laws from 1624. to 1662. where Pervis's printed collection begins. but some of the volumes are in such a state of decay, that the leaf falls to pieces on being turned over. consequently as they never can be examined but once, I reserve that to the moment when the legislature shall decide to have an authentic copy taken. in the mean time I have sewed them up in oil cloth & seared the joints to preserve them from the air. these being antecedent to Bacon's rebellion, are not within the period of your desires.

The printed collection of laws in my possession which comprehends the period you mention, to wit, from Bacon's rebellion to 1752. are

Vol. 1. Pervis's collection 1662-1682.
2. Revisal of 1733. 1662-1732.
3. Revisal of 1748. 1662-1748.
4. Revisal of 1768. 1662-1768.
5. Fugitive sheets published each session. 1734-1772
6th. 7th. & 8th. vols are of subsequent dates.

the 1st. 2d. 3d. & 4th. vols above mentioned are in every lawyer's hands, therefore you will easily obtain them in your neighborhood. the 5th. volume is the only one of which there exists probably no other collection. this fact being generally known, the courts in the different parts of the states are in the practice of resorting to this volume for copies of particular acts called for in the cases before them. for this reason I have always refused to let it go from Monticello, not only because it might be lost, but because while it was gone out in the service of one person, many might have occasion to recur to it. but as the depositing it with Governor Page at the seat of government, will keep it within the access of others, and you mention that that deposit will be perfectly convenient for you, it shall be deposited there. My collection of newspapers is from 1741. downwards. the vols preceding 1752. shall be sent with the other to Richmond to be used by you either there or at Petersburg according to your convenience. these also being the only collection probably in existence, I purchased & cherish it[1] with a view to public utility. it is answering one of it's principal objects when I put it into your hands, & the same public principles will ensure your care of it, and it's restoration to it's deposit when you shall have taken what you desire from it. I will immediately write to mr Randolph to take these books from the library at Monticello, of which he has the key, & to have them safely conveyed *by water* to Govr. Page at Richmond to whom also I will write on the subject. altho' I have not yet had time to peruse the volume you have published (for indeed my occupations permit me to read almost nothing) yet occasional recurrence to parts of it, & the opinions of others who have read it, occasion me to regret that I am not in a situation to give you the benefit of all my materials. were I residing at home I could do it, & would with pleasure: and should a 2d. edition be called for after my return to live at Monticello, I am persuaded it will be in my power, as it is certainly in my wish, to furnish you with some useful matter, not perhaps to be found elsewhere. I pray you to accept my salutations & assurances of great respect. TH: JEFFERSON

PoC (DLC); at foot of first page: "John D. Burk esq."

6TH. 7TH. & 8TH. VOLS: according to TJ's statement of the laws of Virginia in his possession as of 1796, the sixth volume consisted of "fugitive sheets" of the sessions from 1775 to 1783. The seventh volume was the revisal of the laws from 1783 "by the Chancellors" and the eighth was the revisal of the laws from 1794 (Vol. 28:586).

In January 1778, TJ purchased a COLLECTION OF NEWSPAPERS of the *Virginia Gazette* from 1741 to 1760 that had been part of the estate of William Willie (MB, 1:457; RS, 3:190).

[1] Word interlined in place of "the collection."

Statement of Account with Thomas Carpenter

1 June 1805

Thomas Jefferson, Esq. Dr.

1805		
June 1.	to Thomas Carpenter	
	To two pair of Nankeen Sheravaloes	$ 6.50
	To a Silk Nankeen Coat and Breeches	22.–
	To making 4 Coats & furnishing all materials @ 34/3	18.27

$1\frac{1}{2}$ Yd Scarlet Cassimere for facing @ 15/	3.–
1 Yard of lace, there not having been enough sent	.75
To 4 Toilinette Waistcoasts with plated Buttons @ $4\frac{75}{100}$	19.–
To 4 pr of Cotton Cassimere Pantaloons @ $4\frac{50}{100}$	18.–
	\$ 87.52

MS (MHi); in Carpenter's hand; endorsed by TJ.

TOILINETTE: a fine cloth used for fancy waistcoats (OED).

On 5 Feb. 1806, TJ gave an order on the Bank of the United States in favor of Carpenter for $87.52 (MB, 2:1173).

From Thomas Claxton

HONORD SIR Philada June 1, 1805

Agreeably to your request, I have shipped for Richmond a passage lanthorn, two brass lamps and some diaper for table linen—of the diaper there are three pieces—each piece will make a cloth 3 yds long and two and a half wide, or as many smaller ones as may be convenient—I did not get more, not knowing whether it was the article exactly which you wished for—however, it is of excellent quality, and will be extremely useful in your family for breakfast cloths, &c.

The vessel will sail on the 4th of June—Inclosed, Sir, you will find the bill of lading, which you will please to forward to Messrs Gibson & Jefferson, Richmond

The price of the diaper is about 26$ so that if it should be made into 3 cloths of the largest size, they will be very cheap—about 8.75 each

I have the honor to be, with the greatest respect Sir Your Hble Svt

THOS CLAXTON

RC (MHi); endorsed by TJ as received 3 June and so recorded in SJL. Enclosure not found.

YOUR REQUEST: TJ to Claxton, 26 May.

DIAPER: according to an invoice dated 28 May, Claxton paid the Philadelphia firm of Sperry & Huffnagle a total of $26.10 for "3 Pieces fine Broad Diaper" at $8.70 each (MS in MHi, signed by "Sperry & Huffnagle" acknowledging payment, signed by Claxton acknowledging payment from TJ; see Statement of Account with Caldcleugh & Thomas, 30 May).

From Gibson & Jefferson

SIR Richmond 1st. June 1805—

We received your favor of the 29th. Ulto:, and shall attend to your directions relative to the boxes shippd from Philadelphia, those you allude to from Monticello have been sent on, the one to Mr. Peale of Philada. and the other to Mr. Edwd. Johnston of Norfolk, to whom your hams were likewise sent, to be forwarded to you—We have at length made sale of your Tobacco to Messrs. Bohn & Hubner at 40/. by extending the credit to 90, 120 & 150 days one third each—With respect we are

Sir Your obt: Servts: GIBSON & JEFFERSON

RC (MHi); in Patrick Gibson's hand; at foot of text: "Thomas Jefferson Esquire"; endorsed by TJ as received 5 June and so recorded in SJL with notation "tobo. sold 40/ 3. 4. 5. mo."

BOHN & HUBNER: Christian Bohn and John C. Hubner, natives of Germany, were trade partners who frequently consigned German goods, including linens, from their store in Richmond (Richmond *Virginia Gazette*, 13 Nov. 1798, 23 Apr. 1806; William Munford, *Reports of Cases Argued and Determined in the Supreme Court of Appeals of Virginia*, 6 vols. [Philadelphia, 1810-20], 4:403, 407-8).

From Thomas Jones

SIR. City of Washington June 1st. 1805

I dare say you will be much surprised at receiving a letter from one you have not the least acquaintance with upon earth. And much more so when you hear the subject it is upon; necessity Sir compels me to write to you for the lone of a little money to carry me to Baltimore: when I get there I will remit what your kindness will please to inclose me, I hope Sir you will not deem this impertinent but remit me a small sum to carry me to Baltimore & then I will remit it to you again Your compliance with the above will confer on me a favour that shall never be blotted from my memory THOS: JONES

N B. Please to Direct to the care of Saml. Burch Capitol Hill—

RC (DLC); addressed: "Thomas Jefferson Esqr. President of the United States, City of Washington"; endorsed by TJ as received 1 June and so recorded in SJL.

Samuel BURCH was perhaps connected to Benjamin Burch, who operated a boardinghouse on Capitol Hill (*Daily National Intelligencer*, 29 Oct. 1833, 17 May 1839, 1 Feb. 1848).

From Thomas Moore

6th. mo 1st. 1805

Thos. Jefferson President of *the United States.* has permission to use one of my patent Refrigerators of any size and for any purpose he may think proper.

THOS. MOORE

RC (DLC); printed form, dated by Moore and with blanks filled by him reproduced in italics; endorsed by TJ.

On 18 July 1804, TJ paid Isaac Briggs $13 for one of Moore's refrigerators (MB, 2:1132; Vol. 37:650-1).

To P. & C. Roche

Washington June 1. 05.

Th: Jefferson presents his salutations to Messrs. Roche, freres, and acknoleges the reciept of the books they sent him with particular thanks for the Continuation of Montucla's work. he prays them to send by the same conveyance the books below mentioned with a note of their prices, & the amount of the two parcels shall be immediately remitted.

Dictionnaire Portatif et de prononciation Esp. Franc. et Fr. Espagnol par Cormon. 2. v. 8vo.

Mer libre et Mer fermee par Champagne. 8vo.

Nouvel Antenor, ou voyages et avantures de Thrasybulle en Grece par Lantier. 8vo.

PoC (MHi); endorsed by TJ.

ACKNOLEGES THE RECIEPT: P. & C. Roche to TJ, 20 May.

J. L. Barthelemi CORMON was the author of *Dictionnaire portatif et de prononciation Espagnol-Français et Français-Espagnol à l'usage des deux nations*, published in Lyon in 1800 (Sowerby, No. 4812).

Jean François CHAMPAGNE wrote *La mer libre, la mer fermé, ou Exposition et analyse du traité de Grotius*, published in Paris in 1803 (same, No. 2115).

NOUVEL ANTENOR: Louis Adrien Duperron de Castera translated *Le nouvel Anténor, ou Voyages et aventures de Trasybulle en Grece: Ouvrage pouvant faire suite aux Voyages d'Anténor, par Lantier*, which was published in Paris in 1803 (same, No. 4332).

From William Eustis

SIR, Dorchester near Boston June 2. 1805.

Having ever considered appointments to office among the most delicate and perplexing duties which attach to the chief magistracy, and feeling a personal responsibility for every word of commendation in favor of a candidate, I think it a duty to communicate some information which I have received respecting the Mr Avery who was in Washington the last winter and whom I may be considered as having in some degree recommended to your favorable opinion. It is in substance that during his residence in France, his conduct was such as to reflect no honor on himself or credit to his country. Percieving him to be well received by Governor Hull, I have given him this information derived from some Americans who were acquainted with the habits of Mr A in France and whose testimony is equally disinterested & unquestionable. Knowing at the same time that your recommendation will amount to a command with the Governor, and believing that seasonable information of the course pursued by Mr A while in France would have impressed on the mind of the President a very different opinion of his character, I could not resist an inclination so far to intrude on your valuable moments as to communicate the information. It is possible that misfortunes may in the present instance have led to habits & conduct which would have been unknown or avoided in better circumstances: but the man who enjoys the favor of a virtuous magistrate over a free & virtuous people ought to have his path marked with honor and integrity.

Our legislature with the aid of nineteen additional delegates from Boston will have a lank majority in all its branches—this new & extraordinary measure is considered by the reflecting men of the federal party as their *finishing stroke*—and I have no doubt but the next year will verify their apprehensions—there appears to me a pride of corps among them to act to the full & to the last—and in the last agony many among them would be willing to carey in their fall & bury in their ruin the stable institutions of the country—spero scio meliora—

The health of old General Lincoln the Collector has received a severe shock since my return—he has recovered sed non est qualis erat—he may wear the summer and the year thro'.

It has been repeatedly mentioned among our friends that a tour thro' the Eastern States by the President might at the same time prove healthful and agreeable to him and politically useful. I take the liberty to mention it because the present summer appears to me more eligible than any other. Among all the uncertainties of life that of life itself is not the least: and if in a disposition carpere diem the public concerns should permit and inclination point to this direction you would make happy many thousand Republicans in Masstts and among them your most respectful & obedt. servt. William Eustis.

RC (DLC); endorsed by TJ as received 8 June and so recorded in SJL.

RECOMMENDED TO YOUR FAVORABLE OPINION: Eustis to TJ, 16 Feb.

ADDITIONAL DELEGATES: prior to the May elections for the Massachusetts General Court, Federalists in Boston opted to augment the city's representation to the maximum authorized by the state constitution, thereby increasing their delegation from 7 to 26 members. The controversial maneuver enabled Federalists to retain a slim majority in the legislature (Boston *New-England Palladium*, 26 Apr., 3 May; Boston *Independent Chronicle*, 29 Apr.; Boston *Columbian Centinel*, 1, 11 May; *Newburyport Herald*, 24 May; Thomas C. Amory, *Life of James Sullivan: With Selections from His Writings*, 2 vols. [Boston, 1859], 2:152-3).

SPERO SCIO MELIORA: I hope, I know, for better things.

James Sullivan had written to Madison on 17 Feb. regarding the declining health of Benjamin LINCOLN and recommended Elbridge Gerry to be his successor (DNA: RG 59, LAR, endorsed by TJ: "Gerry, Elbridge to be Collector Boston").

SED NON EST QUALIS ERAT: but he is not the same as he was.

From Peter Freneau

DEAR SIR, Charleston, June 2d. 1805.

The Bearer of this Thomas Lehré Esquire, being about to set out, with his family, on a visit to the Springs in Virginia, informs me that it is probable he will take the City of Washington in his way on his return. I have therefore taken the liberty to give him this as an introduction to you.—He is a Gentleman who has filled several very important Offices in this State with reputation to himself and satisfaction to his constituents; He is now one of the Representatives from this City in our State Legislature and Commissary General of the Militia.—

When party ran high in this state and it was found necessary as early as the year 1796 by the Republicans that an opposition should be made to the measures of the Federalists Mr Lehre was one who exerted all his energies in the cause of the people and much was due to them during the years of terror and doubt for the favorable change which took place in 1801. With such pretensions I am sure he will meet a friendly reception from the Chief Magistrate of the Union.—

With the most perfect regard and respect, I have the honor to be, Sir, Your most obedient & Very humble Servant

PETER FRENEAU

RC (DLC); at foot of text: "The President of the United States"; endorsed by TJ as received 24 Sep. and so recorded in SJL, where TJ connected it by a brace and notation "recd. by mr Lehré" with entries for letters received the same day from John Gaillard of 25 May, William Johnson of 25 May, William Butler of 30 May, Thomas Moore of 28 June, and an undated letter from Paul Hamilton.

To Robert Kinnan

SIR Washington June 2. 05.

Your favor of May 22. was recieved in due time and has been considered, but I do not percieve that the proposition it contains is founded in justice. we stood ensurers of the principal and interest due on the bonds. if any thing had been lost on them, it would have been our loss. if any thing was gained then, by damages on appeals &c., it should be our gain by a principle acknoleged in all cases. it is proposed on the ground of extra trouble and expence. but neither was greater than if the money had been to be collected from myself. the great mass was due from two persons, Ronald & Taylor, in mr Hanson's neighborhood & whom he met at every public place. the other 10. or 12. obligors lived all in one neighborhood, within the reach of a single lawyer, & not farther off than I should have been had I been at home, but in truth much nearer than I have actually been. our losses have been such as to exonerate us from the obligation of extra allowances. the Representatives of F. & Jones will have lost nothing with us. they will have recieved their whole principal & interest, save only for the 8. years interest, which accrued neither to our profit, nor by our fault. for the justification of my case however, I can only refer to my former letters, and repeat again for your determination my proposition of May 6. as the only ground to which reason can accede: adding my salutations and assurances of respect TH: JEFFERSON

PoC (MHi); at foot of text: "Mr. Kinnan"; endorsed by TJ.

YOUR FAVOR: recorded in SJL as received from Petersburg on 26 May but not found. TJ recorded sending Kinnan LETTERS of 28 Jan., 6 Mch., 8 May, and 17 Sep. 1804, none of which has been found.

From Levi Lincoln

SIR Worcester June 2d 1805

We are now reposing from our electioneering conflict. The struggle has been, in general, severe & spirited, and on the part of the federalists, bitter in the extreme. Their frauds, falshoods, and *force* have secured to them a Governor, Senate, council, and house, in this State. By *force*, I mean an intolerant and oppressive violence towards labourers, tenants, mechanics, debtors, & other dependants; every species of influence, and on every description of persons, has been practised and with a shameless effrontry. Individuals have been threatened, with a deprivation of employment, and an instant exaction of debt, to the last farthing, as the consequence of withholding a federal vote, or rather of not giving one. Persons steeped in poverty, were enabled by federal art & management, not charity, to claim property on the occasion, sufficient to qualify for voting. The chambers, and even the beds of the sick & dying, were forced to part with their possessors in this struggle. In addition to the old, & some new invented calumnies, against the general Govt. and a torrent of personal general abuse of the republican candidate for Governor, he was accused of the specific crimes, of bribery, perjury, & forgery, and emissaries were dispatched, or dispatched themselves, through the county to spread these falshoods. It had an effect. But notwithstanding the agency of this baseness, and the return of more votes, from some towns, then there were voters, federalism counts but a pitiful majority in favor of its accommodating or insidious votary. Boston acted, [as u]sual, in this business. Cold, divided, & dissatisfied, in the conduct of some of her republican leaders. Our cause has often been more injured by its difficult, or pretended friends, then by its most active and avowed enemies. Such friends, if they must be called friends, profess great attachment to the general *object* of pursuit; and yet disappr[ove] every measure deemed necessary for its attainment, th[e] persons who are to lead in those measures, the time, [the] means, & the mode of prosecuting them. With such charac[ters] every thing, which is; is wrong; wrong in time, in principle or in fact; and so far from being right, without a statement of what is right, as to justify persons separating from those with whom they profess, & had engaged, to act. Thus Sullivan was represented in private companies as unworthy of support by some persons who in public engaged to give him their whole support. These third party men having failed of getting a man into office, by representing him as unfit to hold it, effect to think that some other character might have been chosen by a large majority of votes, and are proposing to run a different candidate the next year. I am of an opposite opinion and am convinced that the republican success, depends on a *steady* & faithfull adherence to their old men, principles & measures. Firmness, independence spirit & perseverence can & certainly will revolutionize Mass—

The accompanying letter, is on a subject which I never meant to have troubled you with. I too well know the trouble & solicitude, which impertenate applications for office has given you, than to increase the burdens of this painful part of your [duty] without reluctance. Altho the inclosed, is too much in the style of teasing for office, as it is not for myself, or any friend, for I know neither of the incumbents, or the mentioned candidates, you will have the goodness to find, in my attachment to the general Govt. and the writers intentions to serve it, under the most violent persecution, an appology, for the impatience which he has expressed, and the liberty I have taken in communicating. I know nothing of Mr. Morgan, believe he has his friends, & that there may be different opinions on the expediency, or necessity of removing him. Should this be determined upon, of which I can say nothing, I am satisfied from good information Prescot would be a proper successor. Did Mr Upham speak of Morgan from his own observation I should place intire dependence on his representation. For he is a gent. of high reputation in the County, is a lawyer has been a representative, & was one of the electors, & what is more, a most obnoxious character to the violent federalists. With respect to the post office, I can add nothing. I have repeatedly conversed with Mr Granger on the subject, and am satisfied, if he could make the proposed removal consistent with his general arrangements, & sense of propriety, he would render, not only a very acceptable service to his political friends but a very important service to his country—

I am Sir with the highest esteem & the most affectionate recollection your, LEVI LINCOLN

I have forwarded Mr Upham's letter without having had his consent, who may not like to have his name made use of—

RC (DLC); torn; addressed: "Thomas Jefferson Presdt US."; endorsed by TJ as received 8 June and so recorded in SJL. Enclosure: Edward Upham to Lincoln, Northampton, Massachusetts, 13 May; Upham reports the oppression suffered by Republicans in Hampshire County, where Federalists "press, oppress, and persecute us without mercy"; with state patronage in Federalist hands, Upham expresses the need for "some encouragement or patronage from the federal administration"; specifically, he recommends replacing the Federalist postmaster for Northampton, Simeon Butler, with Daniel Wright, who "ever was and ever will be a sound Republican"; Upham also calls for the removal of Joseph Morgan, superintendent of the Springfield Armory, whose "drunkenness" has been ridiculed in Federalist newspapers; in Morgan's place, Upham recommends Benjamin Prescott, a former Federalist who has undergone a "*thorough conversion*" to the Republican cause; Upham asks Lincoln to present these requests to the president (same).

Joseph MORGAN had been appointed superintendent of the armory in November 1802. After receiving complaints regarding his conduct, particularly accusations of intemperance, Dearborn replaced Morgan with Benjamin Prescott (PRESCOT) in October (Dearborn to Morgan, 5 Nov. 1804, 22 Oct. 1805, and Dearborn to Prescott, 22 Oct., all in DNA: RG 107, MLS; Vol. 39:59).

For earlier complaints regarding the POST OFFICE at Northampton, Massachusetts, see Levi Shepherd & Sons to TJ, [30 June 1804].

To John Page

Dear Sir Washington June 2. 05.

Mr. John D. Burke, who is engaged in writing the history of Virginia is sollicitous to have the means of consulting some volumes of laws & newspapers among my collection at Monticello, and has asked that I would deposit them with you where he might have the convenience of consulting them. presuming he had your approbation I have desired mr T. M. Randolph to have them securely packed, addressed & forwarded to you. they will consist of 1. volume of laws, and some volumes of newspapers from 1741. to 1752. the former being the only collection of the laws from 1734. to 1772. now in existence, the courts in the different parts of the state are in the practice of recurring to it for copies of laws respecting cases depending before them. on this account I have generally refused to let the volume go from Monticello. but you will be able to place it in careful hands at Richmond, where it may be used by mr Burke and still be accessible for judiciary purposes. I will only ask your personal attention that the party to whom you confide it may take care of it. as to the volumes of newspapers, I have informed mr Burke he shall be free to take them home with him. I will therefore give you no other trouble with them but to deliver them to him, & recieve them again. when he shall be done with any of these mr George Jefferson will see to their safe transportation back to Monticello. May we hope the pleasure of seeing yourself, mrs Page and family there this year. I shall be at home during the months of August and September as usual, and be very happy to recieve you. it is possibly the last time we shall be within visiting distance. Judge Tucker's plan for collecting & preserving historical materials is certainly a good one. my doubts arise only as to the practicability of procuring a perseverance in it: and these doubts arise from having seen in experience so many literary associations rendered abortive by indolence. no aid is to be expected from any but those whose ruling passion is the love of science, and these in this country are too sparse and too few even to encourage one another. but this shall occupy our consideration when we meet at Monticello, and shall occupy any efforts of mine at any time & all times as yourself & judge Tucker shall prescribe. Accept affectionate salutations and assurances of constant friendship & respect. Th: Jefferson

RC (NN); addressed: "Governor Page Richmond"; franked and postmarked; endorsed by Page as answered 7 June. PoC (DLC).

ASKED THAT I WOULD DEPOSIT THEM WITH YOU: see John Daly Burk to TJ, 26 May.

I HAVE DESIRED MR T. M. RANDOLPH: TJ to Thomas Mann Randolph, 2 June.

I HAVE INFORMED MR BURKE: TJ to Burk, 1 June.

To Thomas Mann Randolph

DEAR SIR Washington June 2. 05.

Mr. John D. Burke who is writing the history of Virginia, sollicits very strongly the opportunity of examining so much of the collection of laws and newspapers at Monticello as relates to the period between Bacon's rebellion & 1752. I must therefore get the favor of you to take from the library at Monticello the vols of newspapers from the beginning (1744) to 1752. also that volume of the collection of the laws (I believe it is the 5th.) which contains the acts of each session, as published at the end of the session. I think the volume contains from 1734. to 1772. have them packed close & solidly in a water tight box to be made on purpose, addressed to Govr. Page, and sent by water by one of the most trusty boatmen, who may deliver the box to mr Jefferson for the Governor. I now write to the Governor as to the communication of them to mr Burke. he says his volume is ready for the press and only waits the examination of these volumes.

In the political line we have nothing new, except unpromising appearances in Monroe's mission. France does not befriend us in it. I have lately recieved a few grains of corn, originally from Italy, yielding 4. crops a year, at 40. days interval each; a winter musk melon, eaten in Dec. Jan. Feb. pumpkins of 127 lb cauliflowers of 25. to 30. lb. all of which I have put into the hands of gardeners here. I have no letter from Edgehill since yours of May 14. I hope the season will prove favorable for the Mumps. my kisses to my dearest Martha & the young ones, and affectionate salutations to yourself.

TH: JEFFERSON

P.S. the money for mr T. E. Randolph will be remitted this present week with all Lilly's other debts. they amounted to 500. D. which required some time.

RC (DLC); at foot of text: "TMRandolph"; endorsed by Randolph. PoC (MHi); endorsed by TJ.

YOURS OF MAY 14: a letter from Randolph written on 11 May and received on the 14th has not been found (see Appendix IV).

MONEY FOR MR T. E. RANDOLPH: in his financial memoranda for 6 June, TJ recorded withdrawing funds for several obligations of Gabriel Lilly, including one of more than £49 due to Thomas Eston Randolph, Thomas Mann Randolph's brother-in-law, for hiring of enslaved workers' labor (MB, 2:1155-6).

From George Tod

SIR.— Youngstown, Trumbull County. Ohio. June 2d. AD 1805.

Herewith is sent you a letter from Samuel Huntington Esquire, the chief judge of this State. Should it make on your mind, an impression favorable to myself, it will give me pleasure; and should you think proper to confer on me the appointment, which he has found inconvenient to accept, I trust you will find your confidence not misplaced.—

With great sincerity and respect I am Sir your very humble Servant.

GEORGE TOD.

RC (DNA: RG 59, LAR); at foot of text: "The President of the United States"; endorsed by TJ as received 15 June, misreading the place as "Gannystown," and "to be judge Michigan" and so recorded in SJL. Enclosure: Samuel Huntington to TJ, Cleveland, 18 May, not found (see Appendix IV).

George Tod (1773-1841) was an Ohio state senator. An attorney originally from Connecticut, he moved to the Northwest Territory in 1800 and quickly attained prominence, along with his friend and fellow Connecticut émigré, Samuel Huntington. Although Tod had served as secretary to Federalist governor Arthur St. Clair, he gravitated toward the Republicans. He served in the state senate from 1804 until 1806, when he was appointed to the state supreme court. Legislators failed in an attempt to impeach Tod in 1808, but succeeded in removing him from the bench in 1810. He subsequently served again in the state senate and then as an officer during the War of 1812 before receiving another state judiciary appointment (DAB; Franklin Bowditch Dexter, *Biographical Sketches of the Graduates of Yale College with Annals of the College History*, 6 vols. [New York, 1885-1912], 5:170-2; Donald J. Ratcliffe, *Party Spirit in a Frontier Republic: Democratic Politics in Ohio, 1793-1821* [Columbus, Ohio, 1998], 36; Vol. 40:429n).

Samuel HUNTINGTON declined his recent appointment as a judge of Michigan Territory (TJ to the Senate, 26 Feb.; TJ to Robert Smith, 9 June). Writing to Madison on 22 Aug., Huntington, William Sprigg, and Daniel Symmes recommended Tod to the president for the vacancy, believing he would conduct the office "with capacity and integrity" (DNA: RG 59, LAR; endorsed by TJ: "Tod George to be judge Michigan").

From John Barnes

SIR Geo: Town, 3d. June, 1805.

It appears from Mr Cheethams letter 15th: Ulto. that Mr. Richards—to whom, on the 20th May 1804, I wrote, requesting of him to pay Mr Cheetham $19. & Mr Erwin $8. is $27, which from his letter 26th: same Month—herewith inclosed (with Mr Cheethams to the President) I presumed to suppose, was paid—Credited his a/c and of course JB. debited the Presidents a/c therefor—

Mr Radcliffe—as was *then* expected—did not see Mr Richards—nor have I since recd—from himself a line of advice, relative to this a/c

Colo. Colfax when here this Spring—was presented with Mr Richards a/c which—included this paymt. still unnoticed as Supposing them paid—

my late remittance to Mr Richards,

$33.80 . . . to pay Mr Cheetham 25.80,

and Mr Erwin . . . 8 . . . was recd by Mr Richards Clerk, and paid to those Gentn. as ℔ recpt. which will be handed the President—to Morrow—in his May. a/c for this omission—of Mr Richards. I shall in Course of a post or two, write my friend Mr Ludlow—who will pay Mr Cheetham as well Mr Erwin the Amount of said omitted a/c.

I am Sir, most respectfully your very Obed. Servant

John Barnes.

RC (ViU: Edgehill-Randolph Papers); ellipses in original; at foot of text: "The President, UStates"; endorsed by TJ: "Cheetham's 19. D." Enclosure: James Cheetham to TJ, 15 May. Other enclosure not found, but see below.

colfax: probably William Colfax of New Jersey, who had been an officer in the American Revolution. During the late 1790s, he and Alexander Richards worked together as supply contractors and they continued to have business connections through at least 1805 (Washington, *Papers, Rev. War Ser.*, 22:584n; Syrett, *Hamilton*, 24:428; New York (State) and George Caines, *New-York Term Reports of Cases Argued and Determined in the Supreme Court of that State*, 3 vols. [New York, 1813-14], 3:98).

Richards's nephew, Charles W. Goodrich, wrote to Barnes on 18 May acknowledging the remittance sent to Richards and including under his signature two receipts of payment, written in Goodrich's hand and dated 18 May, one for $25.80, signed by Cheetham, and the other for $8, signed by Peter Irving (RC in MHi; calculations on verso in Barnes's hand, endorsed by TJ: "Newspapers. Cheetham. Irvine 1805"; see also Cheetham to TJ, 15 May, and Notes on Personal Finance, 4 May).

From John Barnes

Sir George Town, 3d. June, 1805.

I have herewith the Honor: to inclose the President UStates. His last Mos particular a/c and Genl. a/c to the 31 Ulto. Balance EE. $2,328.87½ . . . as well, Copy of Genl: Koscuisk's a/c, including my late & Annual remittance of *f*2500—current Florins—at the favorable ex: of 38 cts. ℔ gilder—is 5 ℔ Ct under par, and equal to $950.—will I hope be found nearly Correct.—I also, took the Liberty of addressing a few lines to the good Genl:—while in Baltimore. via Messrs. Van Staphorst & Hubbart, annexing Copy, of his a/c, to said date the 15th Ulto. for his Goverment; all which, I flatter my self, will meet the Presidents Approbation: I likewise inclose Minute of my particular disbursemts. on the Presidents Note for $1600—disctd. 8th &

10th. Ulto. at Bank of Columbia—with proceeds; ℔ Statement $900. placed to the Crt. of the Presidents. a/c

I have the Honor, to be Sir, your very Obed: Hble Servt:

JOHN BARNES.

RC (ViU: Edgehill-Randolph Papers); ellipsis in original; at foot of text: "The President, of the UStates"; endorsed by TJ. Enclosure: Tadeusz Kosciuszko's account with Barnes, 15 May 1805, for the period from 5 July 1804 to 15 May 1805 (Tr in MHi; endorsed by TJ). Other enclosures not found, but see below.

PRESIDENTS NOTE: for the disbursement of funds, see MB, 2:1153, and Notes on Personal Finance, 4 May.

To James Lyle

DEAR SIR June 3. 1805

Messrs. Gibson & Jefferson having had my tobacco in their hands for sale a considerable time, I have been in the constant expectation of sending you an order on them for one thousand dollars to be recieved at the term stipulated for paiment, which I desired them not to make more than 60. days. by a late letter from them I find they have not yet been able to sell for a reasonable price. the object of the present is therefore merely to assure you that so soon as they shall have sold the tobacco I shall forward you such an order on them. Accept my friendly salutations and assurances of constant esteem & respect

TH: JEFFERSON

PoC (MHi); at foot of text: "James Lyle esq."; endorsed by TJ.

LATE LETTER: Gibson & Jefferson to TJ, 29 May.

From William Prentis

SIR, Petersburg, June, 3, 1805.

Some time ago [I] took the liberty of writing to you on the subject of a History [of] Virginia—I have no other interest in the work than that of a [wish] to see a faithful and well digested History published. Mr. Burke has long since published the first volume, and I am sorry he does not progress faster—it is not however for want of a liberal subscription.

Since then I have been employed in endeavors to effect a Map of Virginia, a work I well knew was much wanting, and which would not fail, if accomplished, of rewarding the undertaken. With some difficulty and solicitude I at length prevailed on Mr. Madison, of Wmsbg.

in the work—he is equally interested in its publication, and I am well persuaded has spared no pains to render it as complete as possible, considering the difficulties we had to encounter in procuring correct materials for such a work. The Map has been examined by several gentlemen in Richmond; and other places, and very generally approved. Some small errors, however, are some times pointed out, which are occasionally corrected.

The bearer, Mr. William Davis, sets off to-morrow for the purpose of passing through all the principal towns in this State, with the Map, and it will give me much pleasure, Sir, if you will devote a short time to examine its merits. I am well assured of your disposition to promote works of real utility, and I am not disposed to bring forward one, which does not merit that character.

A Mr. Bossler, from Switzerland, who I have understood came recommended to you, is engaged to engrave the Map, and [. . .] I can discover, [. . .][1] the work will do credit to the State.

[With] sentiments of the highest respect, I am your most obedt. Servt.

WILLIAM PRENTIS.

RC (ViW: Tucker-Coleman Collection); mutilated; endorsed by TJ. Recorded in SJL as a letter of 20 June received that day "by mr Davis."

WRITING TO YOU: see Prentis to TJ, 14 Nov. 1803.

To compile a MAP OF VIRGINIA Bishop James MADISON, in 1803, enlisted the aid of draftsman WILLIAM DAVIS. Madison also recruited Prentis, who collected materials and promoted the subscriptions, which sold for eight dollars including a one-dollar deposit. On 22 June 1805, TJ paid Davis two dollars for his own subscriptions. The final work, *A Map of Virginia Formed from the Actual Surveys and the Latest as Well as Most Accurate Observations*, measuring almost four feet by six feet and consisting of six sheets, included a map of Ohio and a plan of Richmond. Madison, Davis, and Prentis submitted a preliminary version to the Virginia General Assembly for approval and employed Frederick BOSSLER, a Richmond engraver from Bern, Switzerland. According to Bishop Madison, Bossler, who had taught drawing and painting in Norfolk in 1803, had been recommended to TJ by Tadeusz Kosciuszko. The final authoritative version of the map was later printed, copyrighted, and hand-colored in Richmond in 1807, with a corrected and revised edition produced in 1818 (Richmond *Enquirer*, 1 Mch. 1805; *Medical Repository*, 2d hexade, 5 [1808], 302; Walter Ristow, *American Maps and Mapmakers: Commercial Cartography in the Nineteenth Century* [Detroit, 1985], 121; R. Lewis Wright, *Artists in Virginia before 1900: An Annotated Checklist* [Charlottesville, 1983], 14; Earl G. Swem, comp., "Maps Relating to Virginia in the Virginia State Library and other Departments of the Commonwealth, with the 17th and 18th Century Atlas-Maps in the Library of Congress," *Virginia State Library Bulletin*, 7 [1914], 84-6, 88; L. Minerva Turnbull, "Private Schools in Norfolk, 1800-1860," WMQ, 2d ser., 11 [1931], 295; Madison, *Papers, Sec. of State Ser.*, 6:249, 468-9; MB, 2:1157; Bishop James Madison to TJ, 23 Sep. 1805).

[1] Several words lost.

From Caesar A. Rodney

HONORED & DEAR SIR, Wilmington june 3d. 1805.

The Circuit Court of the United States for this District sat yesterday at New Castle, or rather ought to have met there, but judge Chase, did not attend, nor was the cause of his non-attendance known. At the term before he did not attend, because he was preparing for his trial. At neither term however was there any business for him to do, notwithstanding all the noise & clamour on the subject of dispensing with certain useless & expensive judges. I am really afraid from what has past the judges will consider themselves not merely independent but irresponsible & inviolable & that they will annex to their judicial characters the political maxim "that they can do no wrong." We have felt the disease & it will increase. What is the remedy? I must confess it is difficult to determine.

In a few days I shall remove to the city of Philadelphia for the purpose of pursuing my profession. I do not consider Delaware as lost to the Republican cause, nor do I despair of seeing the cause of liberty & truth triumphant here. We have I entertain no doubt a fair majority of qualified voters & nothing but fraudulent practices prevented us from gaining a complete victory at the last election. We are about to give new life to our torpid Republican paper by obtaining a new editor, who tho' he cannot be of sounder principles than the present, will have more time to attend to it. A firm, prudent & spirited paper would produce a wonderful change in this State, which I shall leave with reluctance. A very unpleasant change in the situation of my family & that of my father in law has rendered it necessary that I should remove elsewhere. A change affected by Federal intrigue combined with personal importance. In every situation believe me to be Dr. Sir with great personal & political esteem

Yours Very Sincerely C. A. RODNEY

RC (DLC); endorsed by TJ as received 6 June and so recorded in SJL.

The Senate acquitted Judge Samuel CHASE the previous March (Memorandum of Votes in Chase Impeachment Trial, [on or after 1 Mch. 1805]).

OUR TORPID REPUBLICAN PAPER: Rodney likely referred to the semi-weekly Wilmington *Mirror of the Times, & General Advertiser*, published by James Wilson (Brigham, *American Newspapers*, 1:84-5).

Petition of George Cuningham, with Jefferson's Order

To the President of the
United States— [on or before 4 June 1805]

The Humble Petition of George Cuningham now confined in the Jail of Washington County in the District of Columbia,

Humbly Sheweth that your Petitioner is confined for his fine and fees, under a prosecution for keeping a disorderly house,[1] As it appeared from the testimony of George Gloyd at December term 1804. Upon submission to the Honl. the Judges of the Circuit Court: they fined him five dollars, Since his confinement all his goods and chattles was taken by distress and Sold, His Wife and family are without a home, only depending on the bounty of their Neighbours,

Your Petitioner farther state, he is subject to fits, which renders him incapable of doing any kind of hard labour for a living. Which has put it out of his power to pay the fine and fees, for which he is confined.

Wherefore your Petitioner prays that you will be pleased to grant him a pardon, Remiting him his fine and fees,

He is the more imboldened to make his application as the Honl. the Court have shewn by the smallness of the fine their since of the Offence.—

And your Petitioner as in duty bound will for ever pray &.c.—

George Cunigham

We the undersign'd Judges, being of opinion that the facts stated in the annexed petition are true, respectfully recommend the petitioner to the mercy of the President of the United States.

W. Cranch.
June 4th. 1805.
N; Fitzhugh

[*Order by TJ*:]
Let a pardon issue

Th: Jefferson
June 6. 1805.

RC (DNA: RG 59, GPR); undated; petition in a clerk's hand, signed by Cuningham; recommendation of the court in William Cranch's hand, signed by Cranch and Nicholas Fitzhugh; endorsed by a clerk.

On 6 June, TJ signed a pardon for Cuningham, remitting his fine and court costs (FC in Lb in same).

[1] Preceding four words interlined, likely by Cranch, in place of "selling liquor after his license had expired."

From Albert Gallatin

DEAR SIR 4 June 1805

The enclosed papers were transmitted as a ground of complaint against Mr Hollingsworth district attorney of Maryland. I see clearly enough that he kept for some months money received on account of revenue bonds, and which he ought to have paid immediately to the collector of Oxford: and the question arising from that fact is whether it be sufficient ground for removal or some other step. But what the parties principally complain of is an attempt to extort by demanding, in the first instance, costs to which they say he was not entitled, and afterwards by issuing new writs. This part of the subject I do not understand, and cannot say whether he acted legally or not. I beg leave to submit the whole to your consideration and decision.

With great respect Your obedt. Servt. ALBERT GALLATIN

RC (DLC); at foot of text: "The President of the United States"; endorsed by TJ as received from the Treasury Department on 4 June and "Hollingsworth" and so recorded in SJL. Enclosures not found.

Zebulon HOLLINGSWORTH had drawn the ire of the Smiths, possibly members of the Baltimore political family of that name, who appear to have generated the documents Gallatin was enclosing. They objected to Hollingsworth's retaining fees for collection on some bonds due them, the settlement of which Hollingsworth had lodged with John Willis, the COLLECTOR at Oxford, Maryland. In letters of 12 Sep. and 21 Oct. 1805 to Joseph H. Nicholson, who was likely representing the Smiths in the matter, Gallatin indicated that both Hollingsworth and Willis acted improperly, but that Hollingsworth may have had reason to believe that charging costs was an acceptable practice. Gallatin had written to Hollingsworth and informed him how to proceed in similar cases in the future (Gallatin, *Papers*, 11:510, 648-9; Vol. 42:620).

To Albert Gallatin

TH:J. TO MR GALLATIN June 4. 05.

I think mr Hollingsworth's conduct has been wrong in every point with the Smiths.

1. as to the large bond, when a plaintiff accepts paiment from a def. pending a suit, and does not secure costs he loses them. should he afterwards go on to judgment, it will be against him, the paiment defeating the ground of action. it is the stronger in this case, as not only the writ had not been served, but was unknown to the def. and countermanded by the plaintiff.

2. as to the 2d. bond, altho' the non-paiment of interest, because mr Hollingsworth could not tell the def. what it was does not excuse the def.[1] it being incumbent on him[2] to know that & to discharge it,

& the plaintiff not bound to tell him, yet the acceptance of the interest afterwards by the marshall, without securing the costs, exonerates the def.

These papers shew 1. a very loose & incorrect stile of doing business in mr Hollingsworth. 2. a willingness beyond law to recieve costs. 3. a very improper detention of the public money.

I think he should be called on for a statement & explanation of the transaction. perhaps he can produce facts not stated to us, and may place those we know in new lights. should it retain it's present aspect, our disapprobation of his conduct should be made known to him to guard him in future. as there appears to have been some passion to lead him astray, a removal would be a severity we have not practised in any similar[3] case. affectte salutns

RC (NHi: Gallatin Papers); endorsed by Gallatin. PoC (DLC). Notation in SJL: "Hollingsworth."

The Smiths, principals in the case under review, had apparently requested Zebulon Hollingsworth's REMOVAL as U.S. attorney in Maryland (Gallatin, *Papers*, 11:648-9).

[1] Preceding five words interlined.
[2] Word interlined in place of "the def."
[3] Word interlined.

From Lafayette

MY DEAR FRIEND La Grange 15h. *prairial* 4h June 1805

This Letter will Be presented By Mm. Armand de Lesser and Casimir Rham two Swiss Gentlemen, Near Relations to My Excellent friends Mm. de Lesser. permit me to Recommend them to You, and as they Will Be Long on their Way I only Add the Expression of My Grateful Affection and Respect LAFAYETTE

RC (DLC); endorsed by TJ as received 3 Feb. 1806 and so recorded in SJL.

GENTLEMEN: Armand Delessert belonged to a prominent family of French industrialists, which included his uncle, Paris banker Étienne Delessert (Séverine de Coninck, *Banquiers et philanthropes: La famille Delessert, [1735-1868], aux origines des caisses d'épargne françaises* [Paris, 2000], 4, 63). For Henry Casimir de Rham, see Madison, *Papers, Sec. of State Ser.*, 9:430n.

From J. Athanasius Le Blanc

Newyork 4. Juin 1805.

J'ai l'honneur de transmêttre à Votre Excellence cette lettre, avec prière de vouloir bien y porter toute votre attention.

Créol de la Martinique, j'arrivais à new york il y a quelques mois, afin de me rendre en france près de ma famille, (sieurs et dames de Lapagerie,) d'où je devois faire ma résidence perpétuèle. Au mois de novembre je me rendis a philadelphie afin de me rendre à Baltimore, et de là, me rendre à ma destination, arreté dans cette première ville, par une maladie que je fis; je me vis contraint de suspendre mon voyage, pour le printems. Mais, au mois de May de cette année, je fûs arrêté par une ordre du gouverneur de newyork, soupconné de Crime de faux par moi émané, je fûs donc traduit dans les prisons de cette ville, d'où j'ai l'honneur de vous adresser la présente.

Vous sentez, et votre Excellence juge qu'après six mois d'absence d'une ville, il est hodieux de se voir injurié de cette manière. Engagé à donner Connoissance à votre Excellence de cette affaire, j'ai hésité à le faire, parce que je croyois véritablement que lorsque l'on est innocent, l'on est de suite mis à l'abri des imprècations, et des outrages. Mais, présenté au tribunal, la tournure de la longueur que prend cette affaire, me force à reclamer de votre Excellence mes droits, comme fesant partie de la famille Impériale.

Mr. L'attorney Général sait très bien à qui j'appartient; puisqu'il la annoncé aux juges; mais, il paroit que Mr. L'attorney Général, ignore qu'il n'a aucuns droits sur moi, et que c'est à ma famille seule à me juger, si je suis coupable. Voila Vôtre Excellence, mes droits, voila je pense ce qu'elle sait mieux que tout autre. Le tort que j'ai eu, dit-on: est celui de ne m'êttre point fait connoitre dès l'instant de mon arrivée en cette ville; Qu'avai-je besoin de le faire, tout le monde qui me connoit sait à qui je suis; et au reste pour quoi le faire, lorsqu'en l'an 1798, venant de france en cette ville pour me rendre à la Martinique, j'ai vû dans le *Marcantyle advertiser*, ma Cousine (Madame Bonaparte) être traité de Mulatresse, et que même Mr. de Maret releva cette injure. Lorsque je vois tous les jours des imprècations Contre sa Majestée Napoléon, et toute ma famille remplir les feuilles des Gazetiers. Or j'ai l'honneur de demander à votre Excellence, s'il y a avantage en pareil Cas à s'annoncer, et à se dire être de la Branche, que l'on méprise; puisque ceux qui l'ont faits, s'en sont repentis par la suite.

Voila, Votre Excellence Je le repête mes droits, et c'est en elle seule que j'attends protection à leurs reclamations. Agréé donc Votre excellence, examiner si la juridiction de ce pays, peut prendre sur elle de me juger; ce dont je suis assuré du contraire; et donner vos ordres afin que Monsr. L'attorney Général, sache le point où commence ses droits, et ou finit son devoir.

J'ôse espérer de Votre Excellence qu'elle voudra bien, m'honorer de sa réponse. Et me Croire avec tout le respect, et la vénération qui lui est dûe. De sa bienveillance Le très Humble, et très Obéissant serviteur. J: Athanasius Le Blanc

EDITORS' TRANSLATION

New York, 4 June 1805

I have the honor of sending this letter to your excellency with a request that you give it your full attention.

A Creole from Martinique, I arrived in New York a few months ago en route to France, where I intended to live near my family (the la Pageries). In November I went to Philadelphia in order to reach Baltimore and, from there, my destination. Falling ill in Philadelphia, I had to postpone my trip until spring. But in May of this year, I was arrested on orders of the governor of New York, suspected of false identity. I was imprisoned in this city, where I have the honor of writing this letter.

You will understand and concur that after six months away from a city, it is terrible to be insulted in this manner. When I was encouraged to apprise your excellency of this affair, I hesitated because I truly believed that an innocent person is naturally shielded from insults and denunciation. Yet the length of this affair and the direction it is taking in court force me to appeal to your excellency for my rights as a member of the imperial family.

The attorney general knows full well to what family I belong, since he told the judge himself; but he does not seem to realize that he has no authority over me, and that if I am guilty, only my family can judge me. These are my rights, your excellency, as I think you know better than anyone. They say my offense is not having presented myself upon arrival in this city. Why would I need to do so, since everyone who knows me knows who I am? And why do so, since in 1798, when I came from France en route to Martinique, I saw my cousin (Madame Bonaparte) treated as a mulatto in the *Mercantile Advertiser*. Even Mr. Maret noted this insult. Every day I see his majesty Napoleon insulted and my whole family filling the pages of the gazettes. I have the honor of asking your excellency if, under such circumstances, there is any advantage in presenting oneself and claiming to be from a lineage everyone disdains. Those who presented themselves immediately regretted having done so.

I thus reiterate my rights, your excellency. You alone can protect me. Please, your excellency, determine whether this country can take it upon itself to judge me. I am sure it cannot. And give orders so the attorney general will know where his rights begin, or where his responsibility ends.

I dare hope that your excellency will honor me with a reply, and that he believes I am, with all the respect and admiration his kindness deserves, the very humble and obedient servant of his benevolence.

J: Athanasius Le Blanc

RC (DLC); at head of text: "A son Excellence Thomas Jefferson Président des États Unies &a. &a."; endorsed by TJ as received 22 June and so recorded in SJL.

J. Athanasius Le Blanc, also known as Louis Hardi Le Blanc, was initially wanted by New York authorities in the fall of 1804 for defrauding a Saint-Domingue refugee of $5,200. After his arrest, Le Blanc was convicted by a New York court of forgery and sentenced to life in prison. Le Blanc sent another letter to TJ, not found, dated 7 June (New York *Daily Advertiser*, 13 Nov. 1804; *New-York Commercial Advertiser*, 17 June 1805; Appendix IV; TJ to DeWitt Clinton, 12 June; Clinton to TJ, 6 July).

SIEURS ET DAMES DE LAPAGERIE: in the summer of 1803, American newspapers reported that cousins of Josephine Bonaparte, the Tascher de la Pagerie family, left Martinique for France but were captured by a British ship en route (New York *Chronicle Express*, 1 Sep. 1803).

MR. L'ATTORNEY GÉNÉRAL: John Woodworth was New York's attorney general from 1804 to 1808 (New York *Daily Advertiser*, 9 Feb. 1804; *New-York Evening Post*, 22 Mch. 1808; *New-York Daily Tribune*, 4 June 1858).

ÊTRE TRAITÉ DE MULATRESSE: on 16 Oct. 1798, the New York *Daily Advertiser* published a story that claimed that Josephine Bonaparte was a mulatto, that the Vicomte de Barras had her first husband executed so that he could begin an affair with her, and that Barras later promised Napoleon Bonaparte a promotion if he would marry her.

MR. DE MARET: Le Blanc mistook the name of the author of a letter, signed "Marlet," that appeared in the 22 Oct. 1798 New York *Gazette Française*, rebutting the story about Josephine Bonaparte.

Notes on Personal Finance

1805.	June 4.		
		in bank	56.69
		Salary for May	2083.33
		borrow bk US.	1979.
		borrow bk Columb.	1484.25
			5608.02

Draughts.

	Phila.	Short.	500.	
✓		Taggert	86.42	
✓		Roches abt	36.75	
✓	N. York.	Gelston	111.82	
✓	Baltim.	Spear	230.	
			959.24	964.99

Richmd. bills

	Gibs. & Jeff	200
	Smith	621.
	Wardlaw	46.12
✓	Higginbotham[1]	100
✓	Kelly	100.

	✓ Allen	238.42	
	✓ J. Peyton	103.16	
	✓ Rogers	67.42	
	✓ Lilly	291.185	
	✓ Perry	300.	
	✓ Hope 464.815		2326.12
			350
			2676.12
Checks.	Barnes abt	328.875	
	✓ Lemaire	700	
	✓ Daugherty abt	100	
	✓ McCormick	50.	
	✓ Carpenter	94.25	
	✓ Colston	400.	
	✓ Burwell	100.	
	Stewart	100.	
	✓ Gaines	20.	
	✓ Cooper	18.	
	Maine	12	
	Tingey	33.33	
	✓ Webb	50.50	2006.955[2]
			5648.065[3]

MS (CSmH); in TJ's hand, including check marks; several figures overwritten or altered.

JUNE 4: see also Notes on Personal Finance, [ca. 4 June 1805].

BORROW BK US.: on 5 June, TJ discounted a $2,000 note on the Bank of the United States, receiving $1,979 in proceeds (MB, 2:1155).

BORROW BK COLUMB.: on 12 June, TJ discounted a $1,500 note on the Bank of Columbia. After a discount of $15.75, TJ received $1,484.25 in proceeds, which he miscalculated as $1,485.25 in his financial memoranda (MB, 2:1156).

TJ sent letters to David HIGGINBOTHAM and John KELLY on 6 June. Neither has been found, but notations in SJL indicate they enclosed $185 and $100, respectively (see Appendix IV). According to TJ's financial memoranda, the payment to Higginbotham included $83.33 for Michael Hope, with the remainder to be credited to TJ's account. The money sent to Kelly included $50 in charity for Bartholomew Kindred, with the remainder to be credited to TJ's account (MB, 2:1155).

A 6 June letter from TJ to Gabriel LILLY has not been found, but a notation in SJL indicates it enclosed $1,465 (see Appendix IV). According to TJ's financial memoranda, the amount was applied as follows: $238.42 to Hancock Allen for sawing; $103.16 to John Peyton for "sadlery, hauling &c."; $67.42 to John Rogers to settle an outstanding debt for hay, wagonage, and beef; $300 to John Perry; and $464.815 to Michael Hope. The remaining $291.185 was applied toward sundry smaller Monticello accounts for hauling, fodder, lime, corn, and hiring of enslaved labor (MB, 2:1149, 1155-6; TJ to Thomas Mann Randolph, 2 June).

TJ paid $328.875 to John BARNES on 14 June (MB, 2:1156).

On 6 June, TJ paid Étienne LEMAIRE $700 in partial settlement of his President's House accounts for 28 Apr. to 1 June. On the same date, he paid $51.845 to Joseph Dougherty (DAUGHERTY) for his stable account (MB, 2:1154-5).

On 3 June, TJ paid the Reverend Andrew T. MCCORMICK $50 for "one year's subscription," presumably for his membership at Christ Church, the Episcopal parish in Washington where McCormick was rector (MB, 2:1154; Vol. 36:225n; Vol. 44:734; Vol. 45:159-60; TJ to McCormick, 6 Nov. 1807).

CARPENTER: see Statement of Account with Thomas Carpenter at 24 Jan. 1805.

COLSTON: on 6 May, TJ agreed to purchase "2. Negro men," Isaac and Charles, from William T. Colston of Alexandria, payable in installments of $400 at 30 days and 60 days sight, respectively. TJ paid the first $400 note on 6 June and the second on 5 July. Isaac (b. 1768) and Charles (b. 1785) remained in TJ's possession for many years, although little is known about either. Both appeared on slave rolls TJ compiled during his retirement, with Isaac affiliated with Monticello while Charles, who was married to Aggy Hern (1789-1815), labored at Lego (MB, 2:1153, 1155, 1157; Betts, *Farm Book*, pt. 1, 128-31; RS, 4:386-7; 12:303).

For the $100 borrowed from William A. BURWELL, see TJ to Gibson & Jefferson, 27 May. TJ repaid Burwell on 6 June (MB, 2:1155).

For TJ's payment to Gilbert Stuart (STEWART), see TJ to Stuart, 18 June.

[1] Entry interlined.

[2] Figure interlined above four canceled sums.

[3] Figure written below three canceled sums.

Notes on Personal Finance

[ca. 4 June 1805]

	Checks.	
✓	Lemaire.	700
✓	Daugherty.	51.845
✓	Carpenter	94.25
✓	Burwell	100.
✓	Gaines	20.
✓	Cooper	18.
	Cash. Maine 12. pocket	
✓	Webb	50.50
✓	Colston	400
		1434.595

	Draughts.				lres	
Phila.	Taggert.	\	86.42		Taggert	
	Roches	\	36.75		Roches	
N.Y.	Gelston	\	111.82		Gelston	
Baltim.	Killer &				Killer &	
	Faremans[1]	\	230.		Faremans	
			464.99	\	Higginbotham.	
					100. self +	
					83.33. Hope	say 185
				\	Kelly. 50. self.	
					50. Kendred.	
				\	Hope.	

\ Lilly. for Hope

for	Thos. Whitlock.	83.33	
	Richard Price	76.67	
	David Anderson	60.	
	John Peyton	62.90	
	himself	181.915	464.815
for	Hancock Allen	238.42	
	John Peyton	103.16	
	John Rogers[2]	67.42	
	John Perry	300.	
	his list of debts	289.17	998.17
			1462.985
		say	1465

Richmond bills	183.33	185.
	100.	100.
	1462.985	1465
	1746.315	1750
<say 1760.>		

Richmd.	100.	3	300
	50.	2.	100
	20.	29	580
	10.	19	190
	5.	16	80
			1250
US.	50.	6	300
	20.	7	140
	10	6	60
			500.

1434.595
464.99
1750.
3649.585

MS (CSmH); undated, but see below; in TJ's hand, including check marks; several figures overwritten or altered; on verso of an address sheet directed to TJ as president at Washington.

CHECKS: TJ probably made these notes in conjunction with the Notes on Personal Finance, 4 June. He made the associated payments on 6 June (MB, 2:1155-6).

LRES: TJ noted payments in letters of 6 June, several of which have not been found (Appendix IV).

[1] Name of firm interlined in place of "Spear."

[2] Entry interlined.

From James Oldham

Sir. Richmond 4th. June 05.

your letter of the 16th. May inclosing Two Letters from Mr. Gantt was receivd in due Time; I am rady to beleive there never will be any thing recoverd on my Acct.: but no doubt judge Gantt and mr. Hewitt will conduct the business To the best advantage: I am about erecting my self a worke-shop and if it is convenient shall be very thankful for the sum of 100 Dollars; Your Dores are now in Hand and shal proceed to finish them as fast as possable. Adieu & may Heaven

Bless You Your moast Hmb. & Obt. Servent

Jams. Oldham

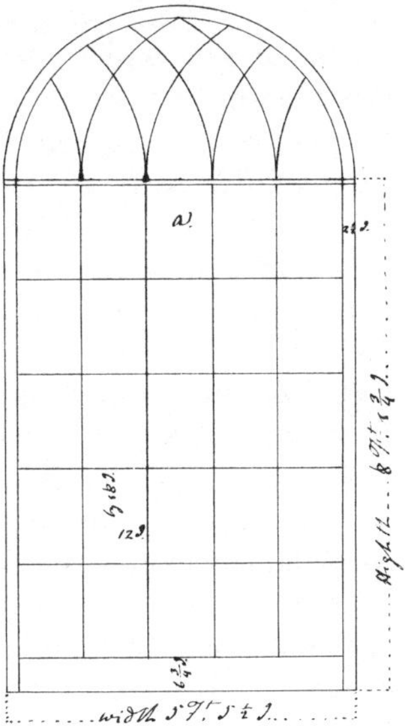

P.S. The two scetches markd a. & b. are for your consideration whether ether form will sute to make the sashes for the S.E. Piaza: each of them are drawn on scales of $\frac{1}{2}$ I. to the foot, and to sute the exact size of the arches. That of b. is to be maid in in Dores and placed in a fraim which will project $2\frac{3}{4}$ I. from the peears. The stiles of Dores $2\frac{1}{2}$ I. size of glass 12. by 18 I. If the dores are maid to Hinge to the edges of the fraims when Turnd in they will project but a small distance past the iner edges of the Brick peears & would be secour from Danger.

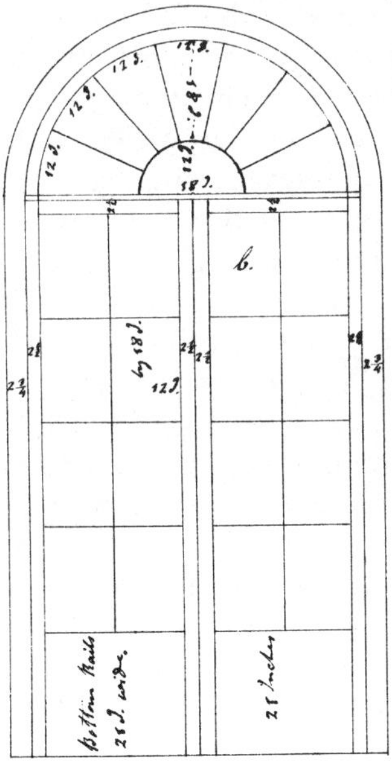

I do not recolect how many arches there are. but I think there are 5.

RC (MHi); endorsed by TJ as received 7 June and so recorded in SJL.

ERECTING MY SELF A WORKE-SHOP: on 14 June, TJ recorded a payment of $100 to Oldham (MB, 2:1156; TJ to Gibson & Jefferson, 14 June).

From Charles Pinckney

DEAR SIR Madrid June 4: 1805

Anxious that yourself & Mr Madison should be fully informed of every Event both officially & confidentially Colonel Monroe & myself have written you very much at large by Captain Dulton—lest however any accident should happen to him I send to Mr Madison by this which I consider a very safe opportunity a duplicate of a summary of Facts &c: &c: which I sent yourself & him before, which I have requested him to shew You—these will give you full information of every thing that has happened here up to the present time—in order to form a full & correct opinion on the whole of this Business & in order to do me the Justice, (if not the honour) which in the opinion of all the diplomatic corps here, of every impartial Government in Europe that dare express an opinion & of my inestimable friend Colonel Monroe himself, my firm & faithful conduct in July 1804 under the unprovoked & unexampled ill treatment to our government both verbally & by their acts then merited, I am to request you, not merely as my friend, but in justice to me, to recur to & read over the Documents I sent by Captain Dulton at that time—particularly my long Letter to Mr Madison explanatory of the Reasons which urged me to take a line of conduct then & adopt a Language nothing less than which could have been properly replied to the insulting conduct & Language then used—I can readily suppose Mr Madison & yourself could scarcely believe that Mr Cevallos could have used the Language I stated as coming from him in his conferences—I, to whom it was addressed, could scarcely then believe my own Ears, but you both will now I trust give full credit to every thing I then said & be ready to do Justice to those warm feelings & that inflexible & steady attachment not only to the rights & honour but to the republican modes of thinking acting & speaking which no American Minister ought ever to lose sight of—he ought never to do, say or write a thing that is not strictly consistent with the principles & opinions of the Government & People he represents—I trust I never have—nor do I know that in any of the great & trying Questions with which I have been constantly *afflicted for* three Years & a half here that I have once erred, but if I have, I am now sure & so must you be, that it was on the right side, & on that which is always the safest—You see if we had yielded then, we should now have had to yield more & have verified all Mr Yrujo has told them—"that our Government dare not assert any national claim or right but upon paper."—at present all your claims are inviolate, & your honour unimpeached—We have not yielded an iota & we (Colonel Monroe & myself) have already given You an opinion that we ought 244. 1597. 1127. 1343. 1651. 141. 1507. 374. 71. 290. 1590. 38 & this is also *General Armstrong's opinion & advice decidedly from Paris*—

I am preparing as fast as I can to return to Washington & if You should not be there & it is agreeable to You, I will visit you at Monticello, but if it should not be convenient *to you* to see me there be so good as to leave a Line for me at Washington with Mr Madison, or Mr Gallatin or in the Office of State to be delivered to me when I arrive there, for my Government—Mr Erving writes me he expects to be here in August, & if you ordered Mr Bowdoin on he will be here sooner—I am extremely anxious myself to be off—every day appears like a month until I can set out—

Until You see & hear me neither Mr Madison or yourself can form any opinion of what I have had to encounter here since the suppression of the Deposit at New Orleans up to the present time, with the irresistible influence of France constantly exerted against every claim we had of every description—I wrote you the other day & I now repeat from the highest & most unquestionable Authority that the Deposit at New Orleans was stopped by the Spaniards, *not only at the instance & request but by the positive command of the French Government in order that they might possess it at the time we were not in possession of the right* & that nothing, & I repeat *be assured that nothing*, but the then determined conduct of the United States made both give way & nothing can now extricate us properly from the present difficulties, but *the same decisive mode*

I mentioned to You in the copy sent You of a long office to the Prince of Peace of the 21st: March 1803 the essential Word "not" was omitted in the part asserting that the Floridas did not include the Eastern Bank of the Missisipi—it ought to read "which we always considered as not including the Eastern Bank of the Mississippi" &c so in the original & Office Book—I have had all my letters on subjects of consequence with Mr Cevallos copied into a Book to shew You & You will then see the Business I have had & the Difficulties I have contended with—I am very unwilling to trouble You much on any subject but in order to bring to your recollection the unexampled conduct of this

Government to us & my unwearied efforts & attempts to conciliate & get justice, I take the liberty of inclosing You copies of my two letters of June 1 & June 22—1804 to Mr Cevallos which I request you to be so good as to reperuse with care & they will enable you to recollect things that may perhaps have escaped you—

By Captain Dulton & this opportunity I sent accounts of my sitio extraordinary Expences with such explanations to Mr Madison as evinced the propriety of their being allowed to me—the totally extra expences I had at Aranjuez with Colonel Monroe admit of no doubt, but he was decidedly of opinion from what he saw & knew that they were all extra & ought all to be allowed to me & that it was proper I should apply for them—it is by his advice therefore I do, for as living at Madrid is much dearer than even at London, & twice dearer than Paris, You may easily guess the Money I have unavoidably spent here—by my inevitable Expences in Europe for the prices here, & the great losses I have encountered at home in consequence of my absence & the bad management there of my affairs, I am You may be assured a very great sufferer—I am always Dear Sir with grateful & affectionate respect & best wishes for Your happiness & health Yours Truly

CHARLES PINCKNEY

RC (DLC); at head of text: "(Private)"; endorsed by TJ as received 5 Sep. and so recorded in SJL. Enclosures: (1) Pinckney to Pedro Cevallos, 1 June 1804, replying to Spanish protests over passage of the Mobile act by Congress; Pinckney worries that Spain may use the act as an excuse to delay ratification of the claims convention with the United States and asks Cevallos if jeopardizing peace and friendship between the two nations is worth "a slip of Territory nearly barren; or the refusal of the Ratification of the Convention" (Tr in same). (2) Pinckney to Cevallos, 22 June 1804, in which Pinckney again impresses on Cevallos the "policy & propriety" of ratifying the claims convention; Pinckney reviews the "accumulated injuries & suffering" experienced by American vessels in Spanish ports during the past several years and presses for a "definitive avowal whether His Majesty will ratify the Convention as it was made or not"; the opposition to the transfer of Louisiana has led Pinckney to conclude that Spain no longer desires friendship with the United States and threatens to close "all further amicable discussion" between the two nations (Tr in same).

BY CAPTAIN DULTON: see Pinckney to TJ, February 1805 and [February-22 May 1805], and Madison, *Papers, Sec. of State Ser.*, 7:538-42.

GIVEN YOU AN OPINION: in their private dispatch to Madison of 25 May, Pinckney and James Monroe expressed their opinion that the United States should take possession of both Floridas and the whole country west of the Mississippi River to either the Rio Grande or the Colorado River (Madison, *Papers, Sec. of State Ser.*, 9:399-401). The key for Pinckney's cipher has not been found. In previous letters from Pinckney containing text in cipher that were decoded by Madison and Jacob Wagner, "244" was "to," "1127" was "Florida" or "Floridas," "1343" was "and," "1651" was "the," "71" was "im," and "38" was "ly" (Pinckney to TJ, 24 May 1802, RC in DLC, printed with Madison's decipherment of coded text in Vol. 37:494-502; Pinckney to Madison, 24 Jan. 1804, RC in DNA: RG 59, DD, Spain, printed with Wagner's decipherment of coded text in Madison, *Papers, Sec. of State Ser.*, 6:379-85; see also Ralph E. Weber, *United States Diplomatic Codes and Ciphers, 1775-1938* [Chicago, 1979], 152-3).

WROTE YOU THE OTHER DAY: Pinckney to TJ, [February-22 May 1805].

From P. & C. Roche

MONSIEUR Philadelphie Le 4e. Juin 1805.

Nous avons Reçus L'honneur de la Votre En date du 1er, du courant, Nous Nous conformons à Son Contenu, En Vous Expédiant Les articles que vous demandés.

Nous avons Mis ce matin le paquet au Stage office; nous Esperons qu'il Vous parviendra Bien Conditioné, Et Selon Vos desirs.

Recevés L'assurance de notre dévouement Sincere, Et Croyès nous. Monsieur: Vs. Tres humbles, & Trés obeissants Serviteurs.

P. C. ROCHE FRERES

1. dictionaire, Espagnol, & français de prononciation, par Cormon 2. vol. a 8o. rel.	$7.
1. La Mer Libre, la mer fermeé à 8o. 1 vol. Bro	50 c.
1. Le nouvel Anténor 1. vol. à 8o. rel. filets d'or. figres.	3.–
	$10.50 c.

EDITORS' TRANSLATION

SIR, Philadelphia, 4 June 1805

We had the honor of receiving your letter of the first of this month and are following up on its contents by sending the items you requested.

This morning we entrusted the package to the stage office, hoping it will arrive in good condition and according to your wishes.

Accept the assurance of our sincere respect and believe us, Sir, your very humble and obedient servants. P. C. ROCHE FRERES

1. Spanish and French pronunciation dictionary by Cormon, 2 bound volumes in octavo	$7.
1. *La mer libre, la mer fermée*, 1 soft-covered volume in octavo	50 c.
1. *Le nouvel Anténor*, 1 octavo volume, illustrated and bound with gold threads	3.–
	$10.50 c.

RC (MHi); at head of text: "Mr. Jefferson, president des Etats unis d'amerique"; endorsed by TJ as received 5 June and so recorded in SJL.

From William Roscoe

SIR— Allerton near Liverpool 4th. June 1805.

It is with particular pleasure that I avail myself of the opportunity afforded me by the publication of my history of *The Life & Pontificate of Leo X.* of requesting you will do me the honour of accepting a Copy, as a humble but very sincere token of the respectful esteem & attachment of the author. In thus venturing to introduce my own productions to your notice, I am sensible I may be accused of presumption; but from such a charge I find some shelter in the reflection that History is the peculiar study of those in high station, whose opinions & conduct have an important influence on the destiny of mankind; & I also flatter myself with the hope that the principles avowed in this work will be found in unison with those sentiments of enlightened toleration, liberal policy, & universal benevolence, which have been no less strikingly evinced in your practice, than energetically recommended & enforced in your public addresses to the great & increasing Nation over which you so deservedly preside.

I have the honour to be, with the most sincere respect, Sir, Your very faithful & obedt. Servt.

W: ROSCOE.

RC (DLC); endorsed by TJ as received 13 June 1806 and so recorded in SJL. Dft (Liverpool Central Library, England, 1955). Enclosure: William Roscoe, *The Life and Pontificate of Leo the Tenth*, 4 vols. (Liverpool, 1805; Sowerby, No. 171).

William Roscoe (1753-1831) was a lawyer and banker in Liverpool and a patron of the arts there. He wrote poetry and became a collector of books and paintings, with a particular focus on Italian works. In 1795, he published the first English-language biography of Lorenzo de Medici, a work that had occupied his spare time for some ten years and that gained him a wide audience. His biography of Leo X, who was Lorenzo's son, was something of a sequel to the former work, and although it drew criticism from Catholics and Protestants, it too went through multiple editions. Roscoe was elected to Parliament in 1806, but his advocacy for abolition of the slave trade was a dangerous position in Liverpool and his political career quickly ended. The 1816 bankruptcy of his bank marred the last period of Roscoe's life and forced him to sell most of his collection, but he remained active in civic affairs, helping to found the Liverpool Royal Institution, a learned society. He continued to write works of poetry, biography, and botany and remained one of the best-known men of letters in the English-speaking world (Philadelphia *National Gazette and Literary Register*, 11 Aug. 1831; DNB; RS, 1:164n).

From Edmund Searcy

SIR Kentucky, Woodford County June 4th. 1805

I see from an Act of Congress passed the last Session that you are Authorized to divide the District of new Orleans and Appoint Registers therefor as well as a recorder of Land Titles for Louisianie, either of thoses Offices, with your Approbation I should be glad to fill or that of Commissioner for Ascertaining and adjusting the titles and claims to Land within the Territory of new Orleans or the District of Louisianie; Disagreeable as it is to solicit An Office yet from my early aid and support to Frontier Settlements of Kentucky, I consider myself as much entitled to be gratified with any Office I am Qualified to fill as any other Citizen of the United States; And not having the Honour of personal acquaintance with you cannot expect an Appointment with out Asking it and have prefered applying myself; should I be so fortunate as to meet your approbation, I dont hesitate to say that I will Justify your giving me either of the above appointments by furnishing you Such certificates of recommendation as you may require from the Citizens of Kentucky. I am anxious to go into Louisianie and did last Summer solicit your appointment to explore the Red and Arkansas Rivers inclosing a Recommendatory certificate from Genl. Charles Scott Governor Greenup and Peyton Short Esqr. I suppose my Letter never reached you as I received no answer Those appointments were made before my application.

If Written recommendations will Secure me either of the Offices I have now requested or even that of a Surveyor a few lines on that Subject directed to Versailles, Woodford County will be very thankfully received by, And lay under great Obligations Sir your Most Obedt Humbl Sert.

EDMOND SEARCY

RC (DNA: RG 59, LAR); endorsed by TJ as received 22 June and so recorded in SJL with notation "Orleans or Louisa"; also endorsed by TJ: "Register of Orleans or Recorder of Louisiana."

MY LETTER: Searcy to TJ, 2 July 1804.

From DeWitt Clinton

SIR New York 5 June 1805

I have seen a project of a Bridge over the Navy Dam at the Walabocht on L Island. From my knowledge of the situation of the Navy Yard and the Country generally I can confidently assure you, that this erection will not in the least injure the public property & that it will greatly aid the general convenience. I beg leave therefore to solicit your prompt & favorable interposition. I have the honor to be Yours respectfully DeWitt Clinton

An early decision is important to the progress of the Work.

RC (DLC); at foot of text: "President of the U.S."; endorsed by TJ as received 8 June and so recorded in SJL.

PROJECT OF A BRIDGE: on the same day that TJ received the letter printed above, he received one dated 4 June, not found, from the Walleboght and Brooklyn Toll-Bridge Company, a firm recently incorporated by the state of New York to build a road between Bushwick and Brooklyn by way of a bridge over the mill pond at the U.S. navy yard. On 10 June, the company began advertising for a contractor to complete a 1,400-foot-long wooden bridge. The previous March, Congress had authorized the president to grant permission to the corporation approved by the New York legislature to build such improvements (U.S. Statutes at Large, 2:330; *Laws of the State of New-York, Passed at the Twenty-Eighth Session of the Legislature* [Albany, 1805], 378-93; New York *American Citizen*, 10 June; TJ to Robert Smith, 9 June).

To Wilson Cary Nicholas

Dear Sir Washington June 5. 1805

Retired to your farm and family I venture as a farmer and friend to ask your aid & counsel, in the helpless situation in which I am as to my own affairs. mr Lilly, my manager at Monticello has hitherto been on wages of £50. a year, & £10. additional for the nailery. he now writes me he cannot stay after the present year for less than £100. certainly I never can have a manager who better fulfills all my objects, altho' he can neither write nor read. yet from £60. to £100. is such a jump as I am unwilling to take if I can find another, equal to such trusts during my absence. the providing every thing for a family of about 40. negroes resident at Monticello; every thing for my family on my occasional visits, hiring and overlooking 10. or 12. laboring men employed in a little farming, but mainly in such other works as I have, superintending 10. or 12. nailers, providing their coal, selling the nails &c and some attention hereafter to a grist mill kept for myself. these are the charges. do you know any body equal to them, who could be had for Lilly's present wages? you will render me a service of the first order if you can help me to such a man, & oblige me particularly by as speedy an answer as possible, as I shall endeavor in the mean while to put off answering Lilly. the impossibility of looking out for myself here will I hope excuse my troubling you thus. Accept affectionate salutations and assurances of great respect.

Th: Jefferson

RC (William H. Scheide, Titusville, Pennsylvania, 1944); at foot of text: "W. C. Nicholas." PoC (MHi); endorsed by TJ.

HE NOW WRITES ME: Gabriel Lilly to TJ, 30 May, received 4 June but not found (Appendix IV).

To Thomas Paine

DEAR SIR Washington June 5. 05

Your letters No. 1. 2. 3. the last of them dated Apr. 20. were recieved April 26. I congratulate you on your retirement to your farm, and still more that it is of a character so worthy of your attention. I much doubt whether the open room on your 2d story will answer your expectations. there will be a few days in the year in which it will be delightful, but not many. nothing but trees, or Venetian blinds can protect it from the sun. the semicylindrical roof you propose will have advantages. you know it has been practised on the cloth market at Paris. De Lorme the inventor, shews many forms of roofs in his book to which it is applicable. I have used it at home for a dome, being 126.° of an oblong octagon, and in the Capitol we unite two quadrants of a Sphere by a semi-cylinder, all framed in De Lorme's manner. how has your planing machine answered? has it been tried & persevered in by any workman? France has become so jealous of our conduct as to St. Domingo (which in truth is only the conduct of our merchants) that the offer to become a mediator would only confirm her suspicions. Bonaparte however expressed satisfaction at the paragraph in my message to Congress on the subject of that commerce. with respect to the German redemptioners, you know I can do nothing unless authorised by law. it would be made a question in Congress whether any of the enumerated objects to which the Constitution authorises the money of the Union to be applied, would cover an expenditure for importing settlers to Orleans. the letter of the revolutionary serjeant which you inclosed to me was attended to by Genl. Dearborne, who wrote to him informing him how to proceed to obtain his land.

Doctr. Eustis's observation to you that 'certain paragraphs in the National Intelligencer' respecting my letter to you, 'supposed to be under mr Jefferson's direction, had embarrassed mr Jefferson's friends in Massachusets: that they appeared like a half denial of the letter, or as if there was something in it not proper to be owned, or that needed an apology' is one of those mysterious half-confidences difficult to be understood. that tory-printers should think it advantageous to identify me with that paper, the Aurora &c in order to obtain ground for abusing me, is perhaps fair warfare. but that any one who knows me personally should listen one moment to such an insinuation is what I did not expect. I neither have nor ever had any more connection with those papers than our antipodes have, nor know what is to be in them until I see it in them, except proclamations & other documents sent for publication. the friends in Massachusets who could be embarrassed by so weak a weapon as this, must be feeble friends indeed. with respect to the letter I never hesitated to avow and to justify it in conversation. in no other way do I trouble myself to contradict any thing which is said. at that time however there were certain anomalies in the motions of some of our friends, which events have at length reduced to regularity.   It seems very difficult to find out what turn things are to take in Europe. I suppose it depends on Austria, which knowing it is to stand in the way of recieving the first hard blows, is cautious of entering into a coalition. as to France & England we can have but one wish that they may disable one another from injuring others. Accept my friendly salutations & assurances of esteem & respect.

TH: JEFFERSON

PoC (DLC); at foot of first page: "Mr. Paine."

Philibert Delorme (DE LORME) was an architect whose precepts informed the construction of the dome on the Halle aux Bleds in Paris (Philibert Delorme, *Nouvelles inventions pour bien bastir et a petits fraiz* [Paris, 1576]; Vol. 38:619-21).

In a dispatch from Paris dated 14 Feb. and received in Washington in mid-May, John Armstrong noted that Napoleon had EXPRESSED SATISFACTION with a portion of TJ's 1804 annual message to Congress: "That part of the President's speech which looks towards the St Domingo business, and his exposition of the law 'erecting the shores &c of the Mobile into a collection district &c' *were so well received by the Emperor* and gave *so much satisfaction to his ministers* that I was induced to *seise the moment of their impression to turn* the *views* of *the latter* to the *policy of opening their colonies to an unrestrained [trade] with us. The result of* several *free communications on this subject is that they* are themselves satisfied of the *soundness of the policy* and will *engage to present it in such way as shall be best calculated to obtain for it the sanction of the Emperor* but that as no nation *gives privileges without some equivalent their movements* will be taken on the supposition that the *United States will make arrangements to pay a sum* of *money annually* or in any other way by which both parties may be sufficiently secured; *we* in the *enjoyment* of the *trade, they* in the *receipt* of the *money. I communicate this fact to you confidentially*, because in its present *stage it is* altogether *ministerial*" (Madison, *Papers, Sec. of State Ser.*, 9:40; words in italics written in code, one word in brackets omitted in original, supplied by Madison).

ATTENDED TO BY GENL. DEARBORNE: see Paine to TJ, 25 Jan., and Dearborn to TJ, [5 Feb.].

To Thomas Mann Randolph

DEAR SIR Washington June 5. 05

I recieved a letter yesterday from Lilly which gives me great disquietude. he has hitherto been on wages of £50. and £10. additional for the nailery. he writes me that he cannot stay after the present year for less than £100. certainly I can never get a man who fulfills my purposes better than he does: and if a moderate advance, as from 60. to £75. would have sufficed, I would have given it. but to £100. is a larger jump than I am willing to take if I can find another who will answer my purposes. do you know, or can you recollect one who would, and who could be got on Lilly's present allowance? I do not wish the least intimation of this matter to any mortal; and shall withold answering Lilly till I hear from you. my tenderest affections to my dearest Martha & the family, and sincere attachment to yourself.

TH: JEFFERSON

RC (DLC); at foot of text: "TMRandolph"; endorsed by Randolph. PoC (NHi: Gilder Lehrman Collection at the Gilder Lehrman Institute of American History).

To John Strode

DEAR SIR Washington June 5. 05.

In a letter to me some years ago you recommended some person to me as a manager, should I want one at Monticello. not having the letter here I am not able to turn to it, nor to recollect the name. the person whom I have there at present is at the wages of £60. & the ordinary allowance of pork & corn for his family. he is as good a one as can be. but I yesterday recieved notice from him that unless I would raise his wages to £100. he could remain only this year. this is so great a jump, that if I can get another worthy of confidence, I think to do so. were I at home to have an eye to the manager myself, it would be less important. but obliged as I am to abandon every thing to him, it is all-important to have one who may be confided in. my manager there has to provide for the maintenance of a family of about 40 negroes at all times, and for my own family about 3. months in the year; to hire annually and overlook about 10. laboring men, employed in a little farming but mainly in other works about my mills, & grounds generally; to superintend the grist mill, and a nailery of 10. to 15. hands, provide their coal, sell the nails &c. I love industry & abhor severity. would the person whom you formerly recommended answer these purposes, is he to be had or do you know any other? it would render me the most essential service could I get one in whom I could repose myself entirely. indeed no event of this kind could have afflicted me more, as the conduct of the present man leaves me as perfectly satisfied absent as present. he has required an immediate answer from me, which however I shall endeavor to put off till I hear from you. I think I shall be with you about the middle of July & shall have the pleasure of calling. in the mean time be so good as to give me some comfort on the above subject with as little delay as possible. accept my friendly salutations & respects

TH: JEFFERSON

PoC (DLC); at foot of text: "Mr. Strode"; endorsed by TJ.

PERSON WHOM I HAVE THERE AT PRESENT: Gabriel Lilly.

From Abraham Baldwin, David Meriwether, and Peter Early

SIR— June 6th. 1805

The office of one of the Judges of the Mississippi Territory being still vacant by the refusal of Mr Obadiah Jones to accept an appointment thereto, We take the liberty to recommend Mr. George Mathews junior of our state as a gentleman qualified in our opinions to fill the same—

ABR BALDWIN
D. MERIWETHER
PETER EARLY

RC (DNA: RG 59, LAR); in Early's hand, signed by all; at foot of text: "The President of the United States"; endorsed by TJ as received 30 June and "Matthews George jr. to be judge Misipi v. Jones" and so recorded in SJL.

In a letter of 20 Sep. to Madison, GEORGE MATHEWS, Jr., reported receiving his commission, dated 1 July, "by which it appears I am appointed a Judge of the Mississippi Territory." Mathews thanked the president for the appointment and informed Madison that he hoped to arrive in Mississippi early in November, when he would commence his duties (RC in DNA: RG 59, LAR; endorsed by TJ: "Matthews George. accepts judge Misipi").

To David Gelston

DEAR SIR Washington June 6. 05

Your favor of May 15. has been duly recieved, and I now inclose you a draught of the US. bank here on that at New-York for 111. D 82 c the amount of the duties you have been so kind as to answer for me, with my thanks and respectful salutations.

TH: JEFFERSON

PoC (MHi); at foot of text: "David Gelston esq."; endorsed by TJ. Notation in SJL: "111.82." Enclosure not found.

To Gibson & Jefferson

MESSRS. GIBSON & JEFFERSON Washington June 6. 05.

Your favor of June 1. is recieved, and the sale of the tobacco as therein mentioned is approved. the terms of 3. 4. and 5. months being long, might they not be reduced to 1. 2 & 3. by taking notes from the purchasers negociable at the Richmond bank? this would of course make to us the difference of the discount, which would be of little consideration: but it must depend on the form of the notes taken or agreed for, whether they be negociable or not. will you be so good as to inform me on this question. Accept friendly salutations.

TH: JEFFERSON

PoC (MHi); endorsed by TJ as a letter to George Jefferson.

To P. & C. Roche

MESSRS ROCHES Washington June 6. 05

The second parcel of books which you have been so kind as to forward to me came safe to hand, and I now inclose you a draught of the bank of the US. here on that at Philadelphia for 36. D 75 c the amount of the two parcels. Accept my salutations TH: JEFFERSON

PoC (MHi); at foot of text: "Messrs. Roche freres"; endorsed by TJ.

To John Taggart

SIR Washington June 6. 1805.

I now inclose you a note of the US. bank of this place on that at Philadelphia for 86. D 42 c the amount of the paint you were so kind as to purchase and forward for me, with my thanks for your attention to it. having a great quantity of painting to do, I may hereafter take the liberty of troubling you with similar applications. Accept my respectful salutations TH: JEFFERSON

PoC (MHi); at foot of text: "Mr. John Taggert"; endorsed by TJ. Notation in SJL: "86.42."

PAINT: see Taggart to TJ, 17 May.

From Charles Burrall

Sir, Baltimore June 8th: 1805

I have the honor to acknowledge the receipt of your Note of the 6th Inst: The letter it enclosed was for Messrs Keller & Forman; merchants in this City; to whom I delivered it immediately on receipt of the same.—They inform'd me that your former letter was by them received and that they had omitted to answer it.—

I am Sir with great respect your humble servant

Chas: Burrall

RC (MHi); at foot of text: "The President of the United States"; endorsed by TJ as received 9 June and so recorded in SJL.

TJ's NOTE OF THE 6TH has not been found and is not recorded in SJL. Recorded in SJL but not found are TJ's letters to local grocers and flour merchants KELLER & FORMAN of 8 May and 6 June and their responses of 10 June received 11 June (Appendix IV). According to TJ's financial memoranda of 6 June, he drew on the Bank of the United States in Baltimore in favor of Keller & Forman for orders by John Speer from Michael Hope and Hugh Chisholm for $100 each and James Dinsmore for $30 (James Robinson, *Baltimore Directory for 1804* [Baltimore, 1804], 13; MB, 2:1155).

To James Dinsmore

Dear Sir Washington June 8. 05.

After writing to you yesterday, I was at the painting room of mr Stewart (the celebrated portrait painter) who had first suggested to me the painting a floor green, which he had himself tried with fine effect. he observed that care should be taken to hit the true *grass*-green, & as he had his pallet & colours in his hand, I asked him to give me a specimen of the colour, which he instantly mixed up to his mind, and I spread it with a knife on the inclosed paper. be so good therefore as to give it to mr Barry as the model of the colour I wish to have the hall floor painted of. The painters here talk of putting a japan varnish over the painted floor and floor-cloth after the paint is dry, which they say will prevent it's being sticky & will bear washing. as I have not seen it I cannot say what it is. mr Barry is probably the best judge of it. Accept my good wishes. Th: Jefferson

P.S. The floor should be painted the instant you have it ready, and all other work should give way to the getting that ready

RC (ICN); at foot of text above postscript: "Mr. Dinsmore." Enclosure not found.

WRITING TO YOU YESTERDAY: TJ to Dinsmore, 7 June, recorded in SJL but not found.

From Benjamin H. Latrobe

Ches: & Del. Canal office,
Dear Sir — Cecil County Maryland June 8th. 1805.—

The Board of Directors & Committee of Works of our Company broke up only last night. The Subscribers are in debt to the Company for arrears of Subscriptions 86.000$ & upwards,—a deficiency fatal to any active operations this season. I have therefore been directed to discharge all our hands (about 300) excepting 60, and in this distressing business I have been all day engaged,—& have not yet compleated it. I hope to set out for Washington on Monday, & have Made an arrangement which will permit my much more frequent attendance in the city.—

I am in haste, but with the most grateful respect Your obedt faithful Servt

B H Latrobe.

RC (DLC); endorsed by TJ as received 9 June and so recorded in SJL.

The Chesapeake and Delaware Canal company was to be capitalized at $200,000 from subscriptions. It raised and expended about half of that total. Although Latrobe had made significant progress on the feeder for the canal, the company's directors decided not to resort to the legal system to collect the remaining subscriptions, a decision that Latrobe discussed without bitterness despite his assessment that failure to collect was "almost fatal to us." For his part, he accepted seven shares in the company's stock in lieu of the remainder of his 1805 salary (Wilmington *Mirror of the Times & General Advertiser*, 5 June; Latrobe, *Correspondence*, 2:88).

From Robert Williams

Sir — Washington M.T. June 8th 1805

Since my last to you and the Secretary of State of the 17th ult. enclosing a correspondence between Cato West as Secretary and myself duplicates of which were sent on last mail I have had no kind of correspondence with him except to receive the seal of this Territory neither has he been here and I yet remain without any aid or information from the official documents of this Territory—The enclosed paper contains a Publication of that correspondence at the instance of Mr West in a very mutilated state as you may observe by comparison what his objects are you as well as myself are to conjecture

The Legislature of this Territory is to be in Session on the first Monday in next month

With Sentiments of great Respt I Remain Yrs.

Robert Williams

RC (DLC); in a clerk's hand, closing and signature by Williams; at foot of text: "Thomas Jefferson President of the U States"; endorsed by TJ as received 9 July. Enclosure: probably *Mississippi Messenger*, 7 June, containing an exchange of four letters between Williams and Cato West, dated 14 through 17 May, published at West's request; the letters detail Williams's efforts to secure the return of the territorial executive department's records in West's possession; West refused, stating that returning them was inconvenient and unnecessary and suggesting that the governor was attempting to exert "undue control" over the secretary's office; on the 17th, however, West returned the seal of the territory to Williams.

From Robert Brent

Saty June 9th. 1805

Robert Brent has recd and accepts with much pleasure to Invitation of Mr. Jefferson for Dinner on Tuesday Next—

RC (ViU); Notes on Henderson Family's Warehouse Shares, [9 June 1805 or after], on verso.

From Robert Brown of Washington

The Honrable the Presedent June 9th 1805

With Submeshon I must trubele your honner onst more I find By Mr Lanthorn he has Set the Work to two of the Working hands that works at the Capitol No Birth for Me I understand in the publick But Still I hope that I have Not Don so much amisse But that I should Be paid fore hundred Dollars that Still Remanes Unpaid the publick was Good anuff to pay Charels McNance his Contract and I trust in your honner that I will Be paid Mine I hope Mr Lenthorn is Not Mifed With Me for Not appling to him first for the work: should have thought that Men that was imployed at the Capitol all the fore part of the yeare that work Mite Be Divided with othears Be so Good as to Give me answar Either the one waye or other

I am your most obt, Set, Robt, Brown

RC (DLC); addressed: "Mr thomas Jefferson of the United States"; endorsed by TJ; recorded in SJL as received 10 June.

Lanthorn: John Lenthall; see Brown to TJ, 31 May.

From William C. C. Claiborne

DEAR SIR, New Orleans June 9th. 1805

I did not until a few days ago receive your Letter of the 26th of March, and I pray you to be assured that its contents shall receive my careful attention. Mr. Briggs is now in this City, and in the Course of a few days the Location and Survey on the Canal of Carondelet, will be made under his immediate direction; and the result shall be transmitted to you without delay. I do not know, that on investigation, the claims of the City to the commons will be found strictly Legal, but the use of them is so essential to the Public convenience, and to the health of the Inhabitants, that I should be sorry they should pass into the hands of Individuals. The Lands on the Canal of Carondelet are not *at present* very valuable, but cannot fail to become so. You may rely upon my best exertions to promote the Interest of General La Fayette, not only from my disposition to comply with your wishes, but from my friendship and Gratitude for a Character who rendered my Country such eminent services.

This City is already becoming unhealthy. Many Americans will retire into the Country, and among them Mr. Graham, whose early departure I have earnestly advised. For myself I am not under serious apprehensions, and shall therefore for the present remain in the City, where duty requires my presence. As yet the Fevers are only Billious—But it is feared in the course of the Summer we shall again be visited by that dreadful scourge, which communicated to many families (the last year) so much distress.

I am Dear Sir, with great respect your faithful friend.

WILLIAM C. C. CLAIBORNE

RC (DLC); in a clerk's hand, signed by Claiborne; at foot of text: "Thomas Jefferson President of the United States"; endorsed by TJ as received 20 July and so recorded in SJL. FC (Lb in DNA: RG 59, TP, Orleans).

John GRAHAM had recently been appointed secretary of Orleans Territory (TJ to the Senate, 11 Dec. 1804).

To Thomas Claxton

TH: JEFFERSON TO MR CLAXTON. Washington June 9. 05

As we shall move into the Mamoth room within 2. or 3. days we shall be in immediate want of chairs for it. if therefore you could send a couple of dozen round immediately it would be well. a decent lanthorn is wanting for the middle of the passage upstairs. such as those in the Hall below stairs would be best. also about half a dozen semi-vase lamps to hang against the walls in the passages & stairways. our painter took to drinking a day or two after you went away & never returned. Capt Tingey furnished some others two days ago & they are going on well. the floor cloth for the hall is prepared & will be painted immediately in the Capitol. Accept my best wishes.

PoC (MHi); endorsed by TJ.

MAMOTH ROOM: that is, the East Room of the President's House, where the "Mammoth Cheese" had resided. Presented to TJ on New Year's Day 1802, the cheese seems to have made its last appearance at the president's 1805 New Year's Day reception, when it was served with cake and punch (William Parker Cutler and Julia Perkins Cutler, *Life, Journals, and Correspondence of Rev. Manasseh Cutler, LL.D.*, 2 vols. [Cincinnati, 1888; repr., Athens, Ohio, 1987], 2:180; Vol. 36:246-9).

Notes on Henderson Family's Warehouse Shares

[9 June 1805 or after]

right in warehouses.

the Widow		
John		
Sarah Kerr		
James L.	to Woodson to Peyton	
Charles	to Bramham to Anderson to Peyton	166.67
Isham	to James L. H. to Peyton	
Bennet H	to J. Henderson. to Seabrook. to Peyton	166.67[1]
Eliza Bulloch	to Peyton. warehouse. lots built & unbuilt. Mill	{ 100. warehouse 400. residue
Frances Lucy Nancy C. }	warehouse & lot.	300. D

for 2. shares, I have assumed to pay G:J.
Aug. 1. 201.

Richd. Seabrook purchased $\frac{3}{10}$ & by Anderson sold to Peyton 500. D

one was Bennet H's. the other 2. I suppose 'must have' been John's & Sarah's

MS (ViU); entirely in TJ's hand; undated; on verso of Robert Brent to TJ, 9 June 1805.

RIGHT IN WAREHOUSES: see TJ to Craven Peyton, 13 June, and enclosure. For the involvement of Tucker M. WOODSON, James W. BRAMHAM, Richard ANDERSON, and Richard SEABROOK in conveyances of Milton tobacco warehouse shares inherited by Bennett Henderson's heirs, see RS, 1:459-60.

[1] TJ drew a box around this figure.

To Charles Willson Peale

DEAR SIR Washington June 9. 05

The 8vo. Polygraph arrived in good condition, and gives me entire satisfaction. your son's improvement of throwing the pen to the left gives me the command of the 4to. page, as you see by this letter written with the 8vo. machine, and when I have written down the page as far as it commands, by taking a reef in the top, that is, by giving the letter the first fold it is to have when folded up, it brings up the bottom of the letter within the command of the pens. the desk polygraph from Monticello was delayed by the way by an accident. it went from Richmond some time ago, so that you have recieved it before now. pray call on mr Claxton for paiment while in Philadelphia, which he is instructed to answer. send it by water if you please.

Having determined never while in office to accept presents beyond a book or things of mere trifling value, I am sometimes placed in an embarrassing dilemma by persons whom a rejection would offend. in these cases I resort to counter-presents. your Polygraph, from it's rarity & utility offers a handsome instrument of retribution to certain characters. I have now such a case on hand, and must therefore ask you to make me one immediately of the box (not desk) form but not larger than the desk-ones you made for me, as they gave full command of the 4to. page and all beyond that is useless. let it be of fine wood & completely finished and furnished, & send it by the stage, if you think it may come safely by that.

I omitted to observe above that the taking a reef in the paper is less troublesome than the diagonal process.—The next[1] is the line after which it becomes necessary. consequently it is necessary only when your letter extends to this part of the page. Accept friendly salutations.

TH: JEFFERSON

P.S. as long as the port of Havre is blockaded, I shall not send Volney's Polygraph, unless by a government vessel, & as this is the place from which they go, I will ask the favor of you to forward it here by water with the desk-polygraph.

RC (TxU); at foot of text: "Mr. Peale." PoC (DLC); endorsed by TJ.

SUCH A CASE: Edward Preble; see TJ to Robert Smith, 31 May.

[1]Word interlined in place of "present."

From Craven Peyton

DEAR SIR. June 9th. 05

The papars enclosed is for your perusal, if Any of them shoud. be defective, you will please point it Out, & I will endeavour, to have the necessary alterations made. I discovared this to be the only mode in which payment coud. be had for fire wood. as not one single pence have as yet been collected owing to the interference of Henderson, you will perceave my reason for not haveing deeds fully executed from Anderson, before, as I wished to leave nothing in the doubtefull, I have forwarded all the depositions which I thought of consequence to M. Hay with a request he woud. enform me the state of the suite which he has failed to do, I expect deeds will be executed for those othar two shares in the ware house before Next Court, in my last to you I made a request to you to make some advances of money through the hands of M Geo. Jefferson, from my not recieveing An Answer concluded my lettar miscarried or it was not convenient for you to meet the Amts, at the time, although paymt might of been enforced from me long ago. One of the men have extended the day untill the first Monday in August this Amt. is £160.0.0—the othar amt. is £47.0.0 to be pd on the first Monday in Next Month, If it woud. suite your convenience to meet those debts & name it to Mr. Geo. Jefferson, it woud. exceedingly Oblege me, & the ballance which woud be due me you might pay at Any quite distant period. Although I made payment in each instanc in Negroes at a fair Cash price, but I can declare to you with truth that I had much rathar make a sacrafice of proparty then for you to be pushed & to be put to great inconveniences & these debts which I am now pushed for are not of my Own contracting although I am bound for them will you be so good as to let me hear from you by the return mail

with respt Yr. Mst. Ob st. C PEYTON

RC (ViU); endorsed by TJ as received 12 June and so recorded in SJL. Enclosures not found.

MY LAST TO YOU: Peyton to TJ, 25 Apr.

To Robert Smith

Dear Sir Washington June 9. 1805

I recieved last night the inclosed petition from the Walleboght company to build a bridge across the pond of our navy yard at New York, to which they ask a prompt answer. will you be so good as to state to me your opinion to enable me to answer them. in general I think it just and useful for the General government to give all possible facilities to state accomodation. I would consider too the navy yard at N.Y. as a thing for occasional use only, and entirely secondary compared to the one here; & that therefore it should not stand in the way of any material public conveniency. Brock. Livingston of N.Y. and Huntington of Michigan decline their appointments. the former is distressing. Affectionate salutations. Th: Jefferson

PoC (DLC); at foot of text: "The Secretary of the Navy." Notation in SJL: "Walleboght." Enclosure not found, but see note at DeWitt Clinton to TJ, 5 June.

On 11 June, the New York *American Citizen* reported that Brockholst LIVINGSTON had informed the secretary of state that he was declining his appointment to the U.S. district judgeship.

From William Eustis

Sir, Boston June 10th. 1805.

I had the honor to address you a few days since on the subject of a Mr Avery. I now take the liberty of soliciting your attention to one of a different nature.

In the result of our late gubernatorial election it is very evident that some strong prejudices against the republican candidate have had an effect in defeating our well grounded expectations of success. nor is it probable that (under the constant efforts of the federal party to promote them) they will be removed in another year. A general opinion also prevails that with Mr Gerry for our candidate we should have succeeded. Having supported & been supported by Mr Sullivan a mutual obligation subsists from which (if so disposed) we are not at liberty to depart without the interposition of some extraneous & justifying circumstance.

As it is generally understood that Mr Smith is reappointed Secretary of the Navy and the office of Attorney General remains vacant, would not Mr S. fill this office with entire competency and with equal honor and satisfaction to the Administration? In this case we should resume Mr Gerry for our Candidate at the next election when there can remain no reasonable doubt of success. This event alone is wanting to break down an opposition whose seat, soul, strength hope & reliance are concentered in Boston, it is wanting to ensure the triumph of Republican principles in this State and the peace and comfort of those who have advocated them within the vortex of a vengeful party.

It has formerly been suggested to me that Mr S. would accept this appointment: but I neither have nor shall (unless further advised) communicate with him on the subject. if desired his disposition may be easily ascertained.

This communication will be received as it is intended entirely confidential: it bears along with it the motive which led to it—should it be unfavorably received no injury will be sustained—should it want a courtly formality to recommend or excuse, the writer will have to lament that he has mistaken the character of the addressed.

William Eustis.

RC (DLC); at foot of text: "The President of the United States"; endorsed by TJ as received 16 June and so recorded in SJL; also endorsed by TJ: "Sullivan to be Atty Genl."

address you: Eustis to TJ, 2 June.

From Gibson & Jefferson

Sir Richmond 10th. June 1805

In answer to your favor of the 6th. Inst. we have to inform you that the purchasers of your Tobacco, objected to giving notes (negotiable at the bank) that it might not interfere with their own accommodation there, which at present is very limited to the first houses, owing to a want of specie—It is not usual with us to take such notes, but not being aware that you would require the proceeds sooner, and apprehensive that we should not again meet with so good an offer, we were induced to accept of it—

Your strawberries & Vines have come to hand, the former are irrecoverable, and we fear the latter will suffer materialy before we can get a boat—

We are respectfully Sir Your ob. Servts.

Gibson & Jefferson

RC (MHi); in Patrick Gibson's hand; at foot of text: "Thomas Jefferson Esqr."; endorsed by TJ as received from George Jefferson on 12 June and so recorded in SJL.

From George Logan

RESPECTED FRIEND Stenton June 10th: 1805

I thank you for your late affectionate Letter; and as a Citizen of Pennsylvania thank you for the interested concern you express on account of the political dissentions existing in our State. Be assured the whole has arisen from official disappointment, & the personal resentment of a few factious individuals. These desperate Characters having associated together for the purpose of destroying our excellent Constitution; it became necessary for a number of Republicans to unite to oppose their visionary & mad projects. This society will in a few days publish an address to the Citizens, in which a very candid view of the subject is taken. I will do myself the pleasure of forwarding it to you as soon as it is published.

Agreeably to your desire I waited on Mr: Brannagan, & delivered your message to him. he is perfectly satisfied with your reasons for not answering his Letter: he appears to be a modest inoffensive poor Man.

Having a sincere regard for your happiness & reputation, I wish you seriously to consider the observations I made to you last winter respecting Duane: he is doing more injury to the just principles of Republican Government than any Man ever amongst us.

Mrs Logan presents her best respects to you. I am desirous she should accompany me next Winter to Washington: Should she hear of its being the intention of Mrs: Randolph to be there, I hope she will comply with my wishes—

I am Your real friend GEOE LOGAN

RC (DLC); at foot of text: "Thos Jefferson"; endorsed by TJ as received 14 June and so recorded in SJL.

LATE AFFECTIONATE LETTER: TJ to Logan, 11 May.

At a meeting of the Society of Constitutional Republicans held on 10 June, the assembled members endorsed AN ADDRESS that supported the reelection of Thomas McKean and blamed divisions within the party on malcontents (*The Address of the Society of Constitutional Republicans, Established in the City and County of Philadelphia, to the Republicans of Pennsylvania* [Philadelphia, 1805]).

HIS LETTER: Thomas Branagan to TJ, 7 May.

From Thomas Munroe

Monday 10 June 1805

T Munroe presents his best respects, and has the Honor of enclosing for the Presidents signature a Draft on the Treasury for a further sum of Ten thousand Dollars.—

It has occurr'd to TM that it might, perhaps, be satisfactory to the President if applications to him from time to time for Drafts on the Treasury were accompanied by Accounts of the disbursement of the Amt. previously drawn—If such Accounts, or any kind of sketches or statements of Expenditures should be directed by the President to be rendered to him it will occasion TM but little trouble to furnish them whenever they may be required.—

RC (DLC); addressed: "President U.S."; endorsed by TJ as received 10 June. Enclosure not found.

To Martha Jefferson Randolph

MY DEAREST MARTHA Washington June 10. 05

I have been a month now without hearing from Edgehill, mr Randolph's letter of May 11. being the last I have recieved. Anne then had the mumps which of course were expected to go thro' the family, and heightens my anxiety to hear from you. our post is now I believe permanently established at three times a week. the spring here continues sickly & cold, & poor prospects of crops. we had yesterday cauliflowers & artichokes at table. the 40. days corn I mentioned to mr Randolph to have recieved & had planted here has failed: but I learn that a few of the same seeds have succeeded with a gardener at Baltimore. he had however but 4. grains, & of course there is still much risk. I count about this day five weeks (July 15.) to set out for Monticello, & after a few days rest to proceed to Bedford. I hope in the mean time to hear from you frequently and to know how your own health is particularly & how the dear children get on with the mumps. kiss them all for me, accept yourself my tenderest love, and affectionate salutations to mr Randolph. TH: JEFFERSON

P.S. I send you some magazines for your amusement.

RC (NNPM). PoC (CSmH); endorsed by TJ. Enclosures not found.

Thomas Mann Randolph's LETTER of 11 May has not been found (Appendix IV).

MENTIONED TO MR RANDOLPH: TJ to Randolph, 2 June. GARDENER: Edme Ducatel (see Philippe Reibelt to TJ, 31 May).

To Robert Smith

Dear Sir Washington June 10. 05

Mr. Smith of Ohio, who has undertaken the building of two gunboats, having employed his hands & got into readiness to begin, but not being furnished with drawings, has come on to this place express to obtain them. learning from your letter that they still are expected from Commodore Preble, I have in consideration of the uncertainty when they may come on, & the urgency of the work, advised him to continue his journey to Baltimore to consult with you on the subject. as those we have built here are so excellent, would it not be adviseable to let him go on with one at least on this model reserving the other for Preble's? and indeed would it not be better that the other undertakers should do the same if they shall be ready to proceed before Preble's drafts arrive? I am afraid that, waiting indefinitely for Preble's drawings, we shall not get these boats this season, in which case we should incur blame, & the public service suffer. as there can be no doubt of the excellence of these models, I should think it better to follow them than lose the season. Preble's will be ready for the appropriation of the next season. you will be so good as to consider this & to put mr Smith into such a train as may ensure us the work done in due season. Accept affectionate salutations and assurances of respect.

Th: Jefferson

PoC (DLC); at foot of text: "The Secretary of the Navy." Notation in SJL: "gunboats."

mr. smith of ohio: on 4 Apr., the navy secretary awarded John Smith of Ohio a contract to build two gunboats for the New Orleans station (FC in Lb in DNA: RG 45, LSG).

your letter: see Robert Smith to TJ, 26 May.

this model: on 13 June, Smith ordered Thomas Tingey to produce drafts of the gunboats recently constructed at the Washington Navy Yard, which he forwarded to the western contractors the following day (FCs in Lb in DNA: RG 45, LSG).

Petition of Peter Colter, with Jefferson's Order

To the President of the United States;

The Petition of Peter Coulter Humbly sheweth.

That he is a poor man, with a Wife and four small Children to support,—that he has for sometime past followed the Occupation of a Huckster or shop-Keeper, for which he obtained a Licence from the Honourable the Circute Court of Washington County for the district of Columbia—that he was presented and summoned to appear before the same Honorable Court at their sitting in December last—for Keeping a disorderly House, & then adjudged by the said Court to pay a fine of Ten dollars with the Cost, together amounting to 31$\frac{30}{100}$\$ or thereabouts, as will by the Clerks bill herewith more fully shew—Your petitioner will not say whether it was from Pique or malice, that induced those who presented him, to do so—But Humbly begs leave to observe, that he is Ignorant of the Laws, and prays that he may further observe, that he has never Knowingly willingly or Intentionally violated any Law of this his adopted Country—and that if he is compelled to pay the above fine with the Cost, it will nearly or quite ruin him, and reduce his helpless family to almost beggary—He there fore and for these reasons, humbly hopes the President of the United States will take into Consideration his Situation, and remit the above fine with the Cost & his Petitioner as in duty bound will, ever pray.

PETER COLTER

We the Subscribers residents of George Town, have Known the above Petitioner, Peter Coulter, for three or four years—during which time, he has been a very Industrious man & so far as our Knowledge extends believe him to be Honest—He is Poor and has a large family to support, & think him an object for the Consideration of the President of the United States—

Geo. Town 11th June 1805 E. W. WILLIAMS

This Petition is intended for the Honble. the Judges in order to obtain their recommendation to the President for a remission of Peter Coulter's fine.

Believing the facts to be as alleged in the within petition, We respectfully recommend to the President of the United States a compliance therewith.

W KILTY
W. CRANCH

[*Order by TJ*:]
June 18. 05.
Let a pardon issue TH: JEFFERSON

RC (DNA: RG 59, GPR); petition in a clerk's hand, signed by Colter; subscribers' statement in same clerk's hand, signed by E. W. Williams and 28 others, with signature of Thomas Smyth, Jr., bearing the following notation: "Tho. Smyth Junr—wishes to aid the poor Man from a Confidence in the Gentlemen who have subscribed their names to this paper"; referral to judges in a clerk's hand; recommendation of the court in William Cranch's hand, signed by William Kilty and Cranch.

TJ pardoned Colter for his fine and costs on 18 June (FC in same).

From Henry Dearborn, with Jefferson's Approval

SIR/ War Department June 11. 1805

I have the honor to propose for your approbation the following promotions in the Corps of Engineers (viz)

Captain William A Barron to be promoted to the rank of Major				
Captain Jared Mansfield	"	ditto	"	of Major
1st Lieut James Wilson	"	"	"	of Captain
1st Lieut Alexander Macomb	"	"	"	of Captain
2d Lieut Joseph G. Swift	"	"	"	of 1st Lieutent.
2d Lieut Walker K. Armistead	"	"	"	of 1st Lieutenant

And that William McKee, a Cadet in the Regiment of Artillerists be transferred to the Corps of Engineers

Accept, Sir, the assurances of my high respect and consideration

H. DEARBORN

[*Approval by TJ:*]

Approved

TH: JEFFERSON
June 11. 05.

RC (PHi: Daniel Parker Papers); in a clerk's hand, signed by Dearborn; at foot of text: "President of the United States"; endorsed by a clerk. FC (Lb in DNA: RG 107, LSP).

To Albert Gallatin

June 11. 05.

Th: Jefferson asks the favor of mr Gallatin to come half an hour before dinner to-day (say at 3.) to consult on a judge for N. York vice Livingston.

RC (NHi: Gallatin Papers); addressed: "The Secretary of the Treasury." Not recorded in SJL.

From Robert Gamble

SIR, Richmond. June 11th. 1805

My son Robert intending a tour to Europe it was my intention through the auspicious of some respectable friends to have solicited some letters—from you to characters in the Mercantile line or otherwise—both in France & England—And as the Ship had only commenced loading with Tobacco for Cherbourg—part of Which will be under his Management When it arives there—I had counted on sufficient time to have made the application—But a Brigg which sails in a few days from Norfolk for Bordeaux—has induced him to take his passage therein—without waiting for the *Ship* originally contemplated believing his arival in France previous to the Tobacco getting there—may be useful.—I am in consequence impelled to intrude on you in this hasty Manner—and Venture on the obliging disposition it is beleived you possess—to request the goodness of a few letters in his favor, & behalf—to some Characters in France—introductory as a young man of the Mercantile proffession—wishing to Visit European ports & Manufactories in order to form acquaintances & probably corresponding connexions—that may be useful to the Commerce of this Country.—He is about 23 years of age—has commenced a partnership with my other son under the firm of *John & Robt. Gamble Junr.*—I trust—his *conduct & deportment* will Justify such sentiments as a youth emulous to deserve—the patronage & good opinion of the respectable part of Mankind—is generally indulged with—

Possibly too—as an american born citizen it might be well to have some Authenticated Voucher & protection with him—Should it also so happen that he might need any pecuniary aid—Confident that no injudicious use will be made of assistance in this way.—will you have the goodness to priviledge him to obtain four or five hundred Dollars—from our Minister—or some publick officers in France—Should it so happen that he May have occasion for it but such occasion will only arise from some accident or occurrence not calculated on—and his engagements will be punctually & thankfully complied with either by remuniration in Europe or America as may be stipulated—

At a convenient time in two or three weeks a letter or letters to Colo. Monroe or some characters in England—will be in time to Meet him in London or Liverpool—to one of Which places I can forward them will be gratefully acknowledged—

It is expected the Brigg in which he intends to go—will Sail in about ten days—And if it would not too much interferre with the Multiplicity of publick affairs which doubtless occupy your time & continually press on you—your obliging attention to matters generally herein requested—would be duly appreciated—and highly esteemed—by Dear sir your obliged—and obedt. servt— RO. GAMBLE

RC (MHi); addressed: "His Excellency—Thomas Jefferson Esqr. President of the United States City of Washington"; endorsed by TJ as received 14 June and so recorded in SJL.

Gamble, a prominent Richmond merchant of long acquaintance with TJ, sent a similar letter to Madison on the same date (Madison, *Papers, Sec. of State Ser.*, 9:455-6).

Memorandum from Thomas Munroe

Account of monies received from the Treasury of the United States by Thomas Munroe in virtue of Warrants from the President of U.S. in part of the $130,000 appropriated last session of Congress for the public buildings in the City of Washington

1805				
February 5th.	Received a Warrant for	$8,000		
March 4th.	Ditto	5,000		
" 13th.	Ditto	10,000		
May 25th.	Ditto	10,000		Ds. 33,000.00
Of which sum of $33,000 there has been expended on the So. Wing of Capitol,				
For wages of the Several Mechanics, Labourers and others employed about that building, of which $4000 was paid to George Blagden		11,687.66		
For Freestone		6,223.52		
For Bricks		2,865.70		
For rough or foundation Stone		2,281.90		
For Lime		1,800.85		
For Sand		613.91		
For Lumber		494.05		
For Ironmongery & Smiths Work		141.63		
For Miscellaneous articles		72.38	26,181.60	
Presidents House				
For Workman & Labourers wages including dumb Waiter		1872.70		
For Lime		514.50		
For Bricks used last fall in drain		506.88		
For rough Stone delivered lately		247.50		
For Lumber		269.39		
For Ironmongery & Smiths work		216.27		
For Miscellaneous articles		186.58	3,813.82	
High-Ways				
For Trees, and topping them		43.31		
For Boxes for ditto		66.50		
For Bricks used last Fall in drains		94.37		
For Nails to repair Boxes & Smith for Sharpening labourers tools		9.35		

For Labourers Wages ($146.16 being for the new road north of Treasury	177.16	390.71	30,386.13
		unexpended Balance	Ds. 2,613.87

Note.

The above balance of $2,613.87 has, within a few hundred dollars, been temporarily advanced for the work going on about the War Office, for the work done in the Senate Chamber preparatory to the Trial of Mr Chase, and in anticipation of the funds of the City—all of which will be repaid & properly adjusted in T. Munroes Accounts to be rendered to the Treasury at the end of the year.

Thomas Munroe
11 June 1805

MS (DLC); endorsed by TJ: "Washington. Munroe Thos. Acct. expenditures to end of May. 05."

Because of a miscalculation in tabulating the expenditures on roads, there was a two-cent underestimation of the BALANCE.

From Philippe Reibelt

Monsieur le President! Baltimore le 11 Juin 1805.

De la, que Vous m'avez renvoyè en hyver la grande Gravure de Berlin dans le Style Monarchique et Guerrier, de la je ne puis point conclure encore, que Vous n'aimez pas non plus celui Champêtre de l'aimable Gessner—j'ose même en tirer une Consequence Contraire—et c'est dans cette supposition, au moins pas impropre—que je prend la libertè, de Vous presenter cijoint en humble offrande un Exemple de ce dernier Genre (Le Chêne de Palémon) executè par un des princip. Artistes Germaniques (Kolb) en Vous priant, de vouloir bien accepter graçieusement, aussi bien que les affirmations reiterées de mon intime respect. Reibelt

EDITORS' TRANSLATION

Mister President! Baltimore, 11 June 1805

Although in the winter you returned the large print from Berlin done in a royal and militaristic style, I do not take that to mean you would not like the pastoral style of the charming Gessner. In fact, I dare conclude the opposite. Since this assumption is not inappropriate, I take the liberty of enclosing this humble offering, an example of the latter genre, *The Oak Tree of Palémon* by one of the leading German artists, Kolb. I beg you to accept it graciously, along with this renewed expression of my deep respect. Reibelt

RC (DLC); endorsed by TJ as received 12 June and so recorded in SJL.

LA GRANDE GRAVURE: in January, Reibelt sent an engraving of Frederick the

Great, which TJ returned (Reibelt to TJ, 3 Jan.; TJ to Reibelt, 9 Jan.).

The pastoral artist and poet Salomon GESSNER was a major influence on German artist Carl Wilhelm Kolbe (KOLB), who may have created a print based on one of Gessner's idylls, in which a narrator extolls a particular oak tree (Colin J. Bailey, "Kolbe," *Print Quarterly*, 27 [2010], 448-9; *Oeuvres complettes de Gessner*, 3 vols. [Orléans, 1783], 3:12).

To Robert Smith

DEAR SIR Washington June 11. 05.

You will recieve from Capt Tingey information of the capture of our late store ship by a Spanish privateer, which seems too probable to be neglected. I presume it will be necessary for you immediately to order a duplicate supply for the Mediterranean. but will it not be worth while to send a swift sailing pilot-boat with an officer on board in pursuit of the captor & captured vessel? I presume she will be carried into St. Augustine or some port of Cuba. an impudent capture by two Providence privateers which had taken the mouth of the Missipi for their cruising grounds, adds proofs to the necessity of our protecting our coasts from these pirates, & consequently of getting our 2. brigs to sea with all the dispatch possible. the taking of uncommissioned vessels whereever found, and the bringing in for the purpose of harassing, under the delay & expences of adjudication all privateers found cruising on our coast, will greatly relieve our commerce without at all endangering our peace. Accept affectionate & respectful salutations.

TH: JEFFERSON

PoC (DLC); at foot of text: "The Secretary of the Navy." Notation in SJL: "Huntress."

CAPTURE OF OUR LATE STORE SHIP: on 10 June the *Aurora General Advertiser* announced the capture of an American ship three days after its departure from Alexandria. The ship matched the description of the *Huntress*, a storeship laden with supplies for the navy's Mediterranean squadron. On the 11th, Thomas Tingey wrote to Smith regarding the capture and reported on a conversation with TJ regarding the immediate outfitting of a relief ship for the Mediterranean (NDBW, 6:72-4, 110; Madison, *Papers, Sec. of State Ser.*, 9:452-3, 460).

The SPANISH PRIVATEER *La Maria*, captained by Antonio Lobo, was based in Puerto Rico (NDBW, 6:72).

IMPUDENT CAPTURE: on 27 May the *New-York Evening Post* printed an extract from a letter written by an officer serving on board the New Orleans revenue cutter, who recounted the rescue of the schooner *Felicity* at the mouth of the Mississippi River from two British privateers from New Providence.

From Robert Smith

SIR, Balt. June 11. 1805.

This day I received your favour of the 9h. with the application of the Body Corporate for permission to erect a Bridge across the pond of our Navy Yard at New-York. With you I think it just & useful for the General Government to give all possible facilities to State accomodations. Indeed, I class that disposition among the distinguishing characteristicks of our System. The enclosed sketch is, according to my ideas, the form of the proper instrument of writing to be signed by you. After correcting it in such way as you may deem proper, you will be pleased to send it to Mr Goldsborough my chief clerk to be fairly copied for you to sign. I have by the mail written to him upon the Subject

With respect to Prebles Medal I have to inform you that Preble has been spoken to; but not being of a taste sufficiently correct to make a good drawing of the action off Tripoli, the Commodore has undertaken to furnish the Navy Agents at Philada with a good drawing—There is, it seems, a good artist at Boston who is to execute the drawing.

The Brig building at this place will be launched about the Middle of next Month.

According to the ideas communicated to me in your letter by Mr John Smith of Ohio I have put the building of the gun Boats on the Western waters in the train suggested by you.

I am really sorry, that you experience such difficulties in filling the Office of District judge of New York. The Salary, it is true, is very small. But our friends that can afford it ought to shew more zeal in the Cause.—Pray—have you yet heard from Breckinridge?

Respecty. Y. H. S. RT SMITH

RC (DLC); at foot of text: "The President"; endorsed by TJ as received from the Navy Department at Baltimore on 13 June and "Western gunboats. Wallaboght. Preble's medal. brig." and so recorded in SJL. Enclosure not found.

PROPER INSTRUMENT: the law of 2 Mch., which authorized the president to grant a corporation permission to construct a bridge at the navy yard in Brooklyn, required "a proper instrument in writing under his hand" (U.S. Statutes at Large, 2:330; DeWitt Clinton to TJ, 5 June).

The BRIG *Hornet* was launched on 28 July (NDBW, *Register*, 73).

YOUR LETTER: TJ to Smith, 10 June.

From Benjamin Smith Barton

SIR, Philadelphia, June 12th, 1805.

of the plants with which you have favoured me,

No. 1. is a species of Dactylis.
No. 2. Solidago glomerata of Bartram.
No. 3. Solidago, a new species.
No. 4. a species of Aster.
No. 5. Solidago suaveolens: the Sweet-scented, or anise-Seed, Golden-rod of New-Jersey.
No. 6. Ascyrum multicaule of Michaux.
No. 7. Liatris elegans of Michaux. Serratula speciosa of Aiton.
No. 8. No. 9. No. X. } Three new species of Aster.
No. 11. No. 12. } Two varieties of a species of Panicum; and I believe the same as those called, in some parts of the United-States, ox-grass. They make good hay, but are dried with some trouble, owing to their large and succulent culms (stems.) Annual.
No. 13. a species of Cyperus.

The specimens being small and imperfect, I have found it difficult to pronounce, with confidence, concerning some of the plants. But I still more regret my long delay in answering your letter. It came to town during my absence in Jersey; and for some time after my return, I was (as I am at this time) a good deal indisposed. I hope your goodness will lead you to excuse me. No inattention to *your* requests could have been intended.

With respect to the animalcula, I have not been able to discover any of them: but, independently of Mr. Dunbar's authority, I doubt not of their existence in the temperature which he mentions. Vegetables of different kinds, and even animals, have been discovered in certain Asiatic springs, the temperature of which is considerably above 150.

I am preparing for the press the first number of my Indian Geography. It is my object, in this work, for which I possess some valuable materials, to give the Indian appellations of the principal rivers, lakes, mountains, &c., of the United-States, with their precise import. Retaining, as we do, the names Ohio, Potomack, Natchez, &c., an inquiry of this kind cannot be deemed altogether uninteresting.

With the highest respect, I have the honour to be, Dear Sir, Your very obedient & obliged Servant, &c., B. S. BARTON.

RC (DLC); endorsed by TJ as received 15 June and so recorded in SJL.

PLANTS: see TJ to Barton, 2 May and 21 May, and William Dunbar to TJ, 9 Mch.

To John Daly Burk

SIR Washington June 12. 05.

According to promise in my former letter I wrote to mr Randolph to forward the volumes desired to Richmond, and to Govr. Page that I had at your request consigned them to him. I have just recieved his answer wherein he says 'mr Burke deserves in my opinion encouragement to proceed in his work, & has every reason to believe that I will contribute any thing in my power to enable him to go on with a work of which in my opinion he has given an excellent specimen. but I would propose to you mr G. Jefferson as a person infinitely better[1] suited to the care of your valuable volumes. indeed my dear Sir I think your collection of laws & newspapers too valuable to be entrusted to mr Burke & myself alone.'

I shall consequently write to mr Geo. Jefferson to place the vol. of laws in one of the judiciary offices, or wherever else you can have convenient access to them, & others at the same time who may want it for judicial purposes; and to deliver to you the vols of newspapers, under the safekeeping of your honor. for such a purpose all difficulties shall be got over as far as depends on me. Accept respectful salutations.

TH: JEFFERSON

PoC (DLC); at foot of text: "John D. Burke esq."

MY FORMER LETTER: TJ to Burk, 1 June. TJ wrote to Thomas Mann Randolph and John Page the following day.

HIS ANSWER: Page to TJ, 7 June, received on the 11th, has not been found. TJ's reply of 12 June also has not been found (Appendix IV).

[1] Canceled: "calculated."

To DeWitt Clinton

DEAR SIR Washington June 12. 05.

On reading the inclosed letters, the bouncing airs the writer gives himself induced me to suspect he was not what he called himself. I sent my Secretary to Genl. Turreau with the letter to enquire who the writer was. they knew nothing of him, & their suspicions were not very different from mine. I should have taken no farther notice of the case but that the writer says the Attorney Genl. of N. York has agreed to suspend proceedings till he (the writer Le Blanc) recieves an answer from me. certainly he will recieve none. having neither official relation, nor personal acquaintance with the Attorney Genl. will you be so kind as to intimate to him that no answer from me ought to be waited for. we know nothing of mr Leblanc but what he says of himself in this letter. at the same time it would be prudent to keep ourselves clear of embarrasment in any event, by not using my name at all in the case. my application through you is as a private friend, & merely to prevent an useless delay of justice. Accept my friendly salutations and assurances of great respect. TH: JEFFERSON

RC (NNC); at foot of text: "Dewitt Clinton esq."; endorsed by Clinton. PoC (DLC). Notation in SJL: "Le Blanc." Enclosures were probably: (1) J. Athanasius Le Blanc to TJ, 4 June. (2) Le Blanc to TJ, New York, 7 June, not found (see Appendix IV).

To George Jefferson

DEAR SIR Washington June 12. 05.

Mr. John D. Burke of Petersburg, engaged in writing the history of Virginia, has asked the use of a volume of laws & some volumes of antient newspapers from the library at Monticello. I have desired mr Randolph to send them to you, & will pray you to deliver the volumes of newspapers to mr Burke himself: but the volume of laws being the only copy of the laws of that period now existing, and being consequently often resorted to in judiciary cases, I wish it to remain in Richmond where others, who may have occasion, as well as mr Burke, may have such free access as is consistent with the safekeeping of the volume. this may be in the office of any careful clerk who will undertake it for mr Burke, or wherever else you may think proper to deposit them. I have directed these volumes to be sent you well packed in a water tight box, so that they may be safe from rubbing & wet, and will pray you to have them returned to me with like care when mr Burke is done with them. Accept affectionate salutations.

TH: JEFFERSON

PoC (MHi); at foot of text: "Mr. George Jefferson"; endorsed by TJ.

VOLUME OF LAWS: see TJ to John Daly Burk, 1 June.

To Martha Jefferson Randolph

MY DEAREST MARTHA Washington June 12. 05

I have barely time to tell you that mrs Madison has executed your desires & I dare say to your mind. the commission to me has given me the greatest pleasure, as it always would that you would say to me freely at all times what want you have which I could gratify. my wishes are always to do what would be pleasing to you; but knowing nothing of what would be proper or acceptable, I do nothing. I see nothing as yet to hinder my departure on Monday & my being with you to breakfast on Thursday. mrs Madison is very seriously confined by surgical case which disables her from walking, and which it is feared may disable her from visiting Orange this season. the danger to mr Madison of staying here, may induce them to undertake the journey by short stages. my tenderest love my dear to yourself & all about you.

TH: JEFFERSON

RC (NNPM); at foot of text: "Mrs. Randolph." PoC (MHi); endorsed by TJ. Not recorded in SJL.

YOUR DESIRES: most likely items needed in preparation for the August wedding of Martha Jefferson Randolph's sister-in-law Virginia Randolph to Wilson Jefferson Cary (Vol. 35:266; TJ to Martha Jefferson Randolph, 24 June; Randolph to TJ, 11 July).

Dolley Payne Madison was CONFINED with an ulcerated knee (David B. Mattern and Holly C. Shulman, eds., *The Selected Letters of Dolley Payne Madison* [Charlottesville, 2003], 47).

From Robert Smith

SIR, Balt. June 12. 1805

There is too much reason to fear that it is our Store-Ship that has been taken by the Spanish privateer. But when I consider the numerous documents on board of her all shewing the cargo to be the property of the U. States and destined for our Squadron in the Medn. I cannot allow myself to apprehend that she will be detained one Moment after she is carried into port & her papers examined by any person capable of understanding them. I have however ordered Capt Tingey immediately to freight a Vessel and send her out with stores to supply the place of those thus captured. It is proper to inform you that with respect to provisions the squadron will experience no inconvenience from the loss of the Cargo of the Huntress. They will have a sufficiency. It was in this Vessel that we put the powder we got from Dupont at Wilmington.

With respect to the sending of a fast sailing pilot Boat with an Officer in search of the Captor and Captured Vessel it appears to me if at all necessary that it ought to be postponed until we possess more information in the Case. But when fully informed ought not the Case to be stated to the Spanish Minister with a call upon him to dispatch a Pilot Boat for the restoration of the Ship without delay. If at the port, where this captured Ship may be, they do not respect the documents on board of her, what security have we that they will respect any papers we may give to the Officer on board the proposed pilot boat. But I repeat it—I do believe they will respect the papers of Huntress—

Respectfully RT SMITH

RC (DLC); endorsed by TJ as received from the Navy Department at Baltimore on 13 June and "the Huntress" and so recorded in SJL.

Among the NUMEROUS DOCUMENTS ON BOARD the *Huntress* was a pass dated 18 May, signed by TJ, countersigned by Madison, and bearing the seal of the United States, which identified the *Huntress* as bound for Malta and Syracuse with stores and provisions for the U.S. Mediterranean squadron and asked "all whom it may concern not to give or suffer to be given to her any hindrance or molestation, but on the contrary to afford her every aid & facility she may need in the prosecution of her voyage." The ship also carried passports signed by the British and French ministers (FC in DNA: RG 59, DL; NDBW, 6:18, 21).

On 11 June, Smith ORDERED Thomas Tingey to charter a new vessel to carry supplies to the navy's Mediterranean squadron (same, 109).

POWDER WE GOT: the previous March, Smith had ordered 200 barrels of cannon powder and 20 barrels of priming powder from E. I. du Pont de Nemours & Co. (Smith to Riddle & Bird, 18 Mch., DNA: RG 45, MLS).

To Benjamin Smith Barton

DEAR SIR Washington June 13. 05.

Having recieved information early last winter of mr Boudinot's intention to retire from the Direction of the mint, and, as was then supposed, immediately, it became a matter of consideration with the administration who should be appointed to succeed him. it was thought that the duties of that office call for the best Mathematical talents which could be procured, as well on account of mechanical execution as the difficulty of the problems constantly occurring on the mixture of the metals recieved and delivered out. on this ground Sr. Isaac Newton had been appointed in England, and your respectable uncle here: and altho' this seems not to have been the ruling consideration in all the appointments of Directors, yet we thought it our duty to follow the best examples. on these considerations it was the general opinion of the members that Robert Patterson should be appointed to the office. the grounds of this appointment being so entirely distinct from your particular line of pursuit, it can of course give you no uneasiness. yet my sentiments of esteem for you could not be satisfied without mentioning it to you, who I am sure will feel it less than I have done. in truth this is far the most painful of my functions, which can be alleviated by no consideration but that of my being in it a mere machine, bound to act according to certain laws laid down for me by the Constitution & my oath of office. accept my respectful salutations & assurances of constant friendship. TH: JEFFERSON

RC (PHi); addressed: "Doctr. Benjamin S. Barton Philadelphia"; franked and postmarked; endorsed by Barton. PoC (DLC).

BOUDINOT'S INTENTION TO RETIRE: see Barton to TJ, 24 Dec. 1804, and TJ to Robert Patterson, 27 Apr. 1805.

RESPECTABLE UNCLE: David Rittenhouse (Vol. 25:18).

To Elias Boudinot

SIR Washington June 13. 05.

Your letter announcing your intention to retire from the Direction of the mint at the close of the present month has been duly recieved. presuming that before coming to that decision you had considered all the circumstances which might influence your determination, and had determined accordingly, it is not for me to say any thing on the subject, but, in consequence of your determination, to consider of a successor. I have therefore directed a commission for mr Robert Patterson of Philada to take effect at the epoch you have fixed on; who will recieve from you any matters of charge, or communications which you may be pleased to deliver to him.

Your letter of Mar. 23. having come to my hands at Monticello, I deferred answering it till I should see Genl. Dearborne here. but before I could get through some other indispensable business he took a journey to New York, so that it is not till since his return I have been able to consult him on the subject of that letter. he observes that neither the practice of the War department nor the object of the Indian appropriations seem to authorise his confiding the administration of them to any but the regular agents of the department, and consequently that he cannot make use of the services of the Missionary society in the line contemplated in your letter. Accept my salutations & assurances of respect. TH: JEFFERSON

PoC (DLC); at foot of text: "Mr. Boudinot"; endorsed by TJ.

Boudinot's LETTER of resignation, dated 3 June, has not been found (see Appendix IV).

LETTER OF MAR. 23: his letter of 23 Mch. has also not been found. For Boudinot's earlier efforts to secure APPROPRIATIONS to support the work of Presbyterian missionary Gideon Blackburn among the Cherokees, see TJ to Boudinot, 3 Aug.; TJ to Dearborn, 3 Aug.; and Dearborn to TJ, 23 Aug. 1804.

From Albert Gallatin

SIR, Treasury Department, 13. January [i.e. June] 1805.

I have the honor to enclose the copy of a letter from the Collector of New-Orleans, giving an account of the rescue of the schooner Felicity from two New-Providence privateers.

The former circular letter of instructions, which the Collector has not yet received, related only to the services expected from the Cutters for the protection of the revenue. Neither the Masters of those vessels generally, nor Capt. Newcome particularly, were ever authorized or instructed to protect vessels against attacks committed by the belligerent Powers within the jurisdiction of the United States, much less to make re-captures. But they are authorized by law, to board & examine all vessels *bound for the United States* within four leagues of the coast, and, in case any Vessel liable to seizure or examination shall not bring to, to fire at or into such vessel. For a more detailed view of their duties, I beg leave to refer to the 98th, 99th, & 102nd. sections of the act to regulate the collection of duties on imports & tonnage, passed March 22nd. 1799. How far it may be necessary to animadvert on Capt. Newcome's conduct, or to frame some instructions on the subject generally, is respectfully submitted.

I have the honor to be, with the highest respect, Sir, Your most obedt. Sert.

ALBERT GALLATIN

RC (DLC); in a clerk's hand, signed by Gallatin; misdated; at foot of text: "The President of the United States"; endorsed by TJ as a letter of "January (for June) 13. 05." received from the Treasury Department on 14 June and "Newcome" and so recorded in SJL. Enclosure: probably William Brown to Gallatin, New Orleans, 27 Apr., enclosing a letter, not found, from Joseph Newcome, captain of the revenue cutter, detailing the rescue of the schooner *Felicity* and stating that he has not yet received copies of the 1791 instructions for captains of revenue cutters (Gallatin, *Papers*, 10:891).

CIRCULAR LETTER: in a letter to Brown dated 16 Dec. 1804, Gallatin stated that he would forward a copy of Alexander Hamilton's June 1791 instructions to the captains of revenue cutters (same, 372-3; Syrett, *Hamilton*, 8:406-7, 426-33).

THE ACT: Gallatin likely referred to "An Act to regulate the collection of duties on imports and tonnage" approved 2 Mch. 1799. The sections that Gallatin cited governed the number of officers and men for each cutter, set their jurisdiction within four leagues of the coast, and determined when it would be legal for a cutter to open fire on a vessel (U.S. Statutes at Large, 1:627, 699-701).

From Samuel Harrison

SIR Chittenden Vermont June 13th. 1805

Having the temerity to address your Excellency about four weeks ago—I again beg leave to solicit your attention to a yet unknown individual; upon the subject of Capt. Carvers Indian Claim. I then mentioned to Your Excellency; that I was employed by a Son of the late Capt. Carver, in behalf of his children to pursue such legal measures as would validate the claim to his Posterity, their Heirs and Assigns.—I besought your advice upon the same: But as yet have received no Answer—

And since "I have ventured to embark on the Ocean;" I have not attempted to "Navigate the supernumerary Streams."

I then informed your Excellency—I had written to a Gentleman in London—capable of dispelling the mysterious gloom which had involved in obscurity the affairs of Capt. Carver—and that I hourly & anxiously expected a return.

I wrote to Your Excellency on the 15th. of May: and on the 22nd. I received a Letter from my Correspondent, dated London Feb 12th. 1805. it gave me some information; and mentioned a Packet sent to me Six days before, containing, as he was pleased to express himself, all he yet knew upon the Subject—The Packet I have not yet received. His intelligence corroborated what I before surmised and hinted to your Excellency. That Capt Carver married again after he had heard of the Death of his Wife, and had one Daughter born while in England—Who is married and has one Child—That many imagined her to be an only child, not knowing Capt Carver had been married in America—Many had endeavoured to deceive and Marry her for the sake her Missisippi Property: thinking her to be sole heiress to the Captain's claim—That both Englishmen and Americans had practised Deception, and insinuated That Rufus Carver, his Brother and Sisters were impostors, trying to cheat, or rob her of her Legal Right &c. &c. And had not Sir Richard and Lady Pearson interfered and taken her under their Protection, would have doubtless prevailed—

The Lady's Name is now Martha Pope, and is convinced that her Father, Captain Jonathan Carver was married in America, and is likewise willing her trans-atlantic Brothers & Sisters should share with her—She has employed Samuel Peters L.L.D. to negotiate for her and assist me in obtaining from your Excellency, together with the present Sachems a confirmation of their Claim.

Dr. Peters has desired me to make no delay but give immediate information to Mr Smith—(a Vt. Senator) whom he calls "One of your members at Congress"—For fear, "Some sly Trick & Manoeuvre should give into the hands of Mr Cox and his party at Philadelphia some undue advantage."

As I had before made communications to your Excellency—I waited some time expecting the Packet; but my expectations are yet frustrated for I cannot gain intelligence of its Fate.

On the 4th Instant I wrote in answer to the Gentleman, that I had already addressed your Excellency, and though I respected Mr Smith, with our other Vermont members: Yet as I had not with any of them an intimate acquaintance; I did not choose to attempt to Introduce myself to them to make intercession for another Introduction: but had informed your Excellency of the Subject myself without the round of Formalities practised in Europe that I was emboldened to do it by the advice of an Old Legislator in Massachusetts and I esteemed it the most ready way of completion. However, had I received his Letter a week sooner I should have complied with his Instructions and not have vexed your Excellency with audacious Intrusion—

I find myself embarrassed for want of the Packet, that I cannot lay before you those Particulars I expect it contains: But I expect Capt. Carvers claim was not ratified by the British Government, by *this clause* in the Doctor's Letter. "That Mr & Mrs Pope are well disposed towards Capt. Carvers American children, and that they had rather have a ninth of the land than the whole if her Brothers & Sisters would meet her there when confirmed by the President of the United States, and the present Sachems"—

I now feel more importunate for advice than when I before addressed your Excellency—Though employed to negotiate for others, I find myself unequal to the Task—and implore your information—

I desire to be informed whether your Excellency has Constitutional Power as the Executive—to validate the claim of Capt Carver, admitting you have the Disposition—

Or whether it must come before the National Legislature before it can receive your Excellency's Sanction—

*If it must be a legislative question I hope your Excellency will indulge me with a form, That the subject may be laid before Congress as coming from yourself—For I know you must be ashamed to lay before them my present confidential unformal Intelligence.

Or whether it must be a Judiciary Question.
I have examined the Constitution but cannot, *there*, find a solution to the Problems—My Interrogatories are to me unanswered—
And I find none of my acquaintance who has sufficient ability to afford the desired information—I have exposed my Ignorance; and again implore your extensive advice, protection and assistance—Sensible it is an object of your Excellency's attention to extinguish the "Native right of Soil" over such a considerable portion of Territory, Would it not be expedient to appoint some suitable Persons to explore the Country and discover the disposition of the present natives? Whether they are willing to ratify the DEED of Capt Carver? And Would not the 16th day of next June 1806 be a proper time to have the Persons concerned in the Mission; upon the Premises? By predicting the darkness of that day; previous to the Solar Eclipse (then to happen) Their credulity might be wrought upon, and they would discover a much greater superiority in the Genius of the Whites, than those of their own Complexion.—
But I hope my crime will be extenuated—for attempting to hint any thing to give addition to your superior wisdom—My proper sphere is to negotiate for the Heirs of Capt Carver—I want superior advice and cannot help fostering a secret confidence that you will be pleased to write in answer to my request and confer perpetual obligations upon one of your Excellency's admiring and humble Servants

SAML. HARRISON

RC (DLC); addressed: "His Excellency, Thomas Jefferson President of the United States Washington or elsewhere"; postmarked Boston, 14 July; endorsed by TJ as received 25 July and so recorded in SJL. Dft (MnHi).

SIR RICHARD AND LADY PEARSON: that is, British naval officer Richard Pearson and his wife, Margaret Harrison Pearson, with whom Jonathan Carver's English-born daughter Martha had lived as a house servant (DNB; D. S. Durrie, "Jonathan Carver, and 'Carver's Grant,'" *Report and Collections of the State Historical Society of Wisconsin, for the Years 1869, 1870, 1871 and 1872*, 6 [1872], 240-1).

PRESENT SACHEMS: that is, members of the Dakota Sioux nation with the authority to confirm the 1760s-era grant of land to Carver (see Gallatin to TJ, 13 Dec. 1804).

MR COX: probably Matthew Cox, another interested party in the potential grant, who according to Harrison's informant Samuel Peters would ignore any claims by Carver's American descendants (Peters to Harrison, 5 Mch., in MnHi; ASP, *Public Lands*, 4:85-6).

Petition of Jane McGraw, with Jefferson's Order

To His Excellency Thomas Jefferson,
President of the United States of America,

The Petition of Jane McGraw of George Town in the County of Washington and District of Columbia, most respectfully showeth.

That at a Circuit Court begun and held in the City of Washington on the fourth Monday in July One Thousand Eight Hundred and four, your Petitioner was presented by the Grand Inquest for the body of the County of Washington, for having retailed liquors contrary to Law. In consequence of which process was served upon your Petitioner, returnable to December Court Eighteen Hundred and four, at which said Court your Petitioner appeared and by the advice of her friends submitted her Case to the discretion of the Court, and the Law having fixed the fine to be imposed upon Persons for violating it, the Court were unable to mitigate the punishment and your Petitioner was fined the sum of Sixteen Dollars. Your Petitioner further represents to your Excellency that She was presented for having sold a less quantity than one pint of spirituous Liquor, contrary to an Act of the General Assembly of the State of Maryland, that at the time of your Petitioners selling the same, She had a Licence granted from the Circuit Court for the County of Washington to retail Liquors, but that Licence did not authorise Her to sell less than one pint. Your Petitioner did believe that the Licence which was granted Her did authorise her to sell any quantity, and was totally ignorant that by disposing of a quantity than a Pint, she committed an infraction of the Laws of Her Country, but her Ignorance of the Law was no Plea in a Court of Justice, and Her only remedy is by an application to your Excellency for a remission of the Fine which has been imposed upon Her. Although Ignorance of the Law is no Excuse in the Eye of the Law, yet your Petitioner trusts that in this case, it will have considerable influence in her application for Mercy. The Constitution of the United States has wisely given to the President the Power of Pardoning Offences against the United States thereby declaring that there might be some cases in which the party violating the Laws ought to be forgiven. Your Petitioner most humbly conceives that if in any similar case, the Humanity of the Executive was extended to a transgressor of the Law, that the like humanity will be extended to Her. Independent of the circumstance of Her Ignorance of the Law, Your Petitioner, will offer some considerations to your Excellency which she trusts will have their due weight in Her favor. She is a Poor Widow and has a family of Four Helpless Children to support by her Industry, and although the fine imposed would be but trivial to a Person in Opulent Circumstances, yet it is considerable to One as Indigent as herself. Your Petitioner has resided for a considerable time in this Place and during the whole of her residence she trusts She has so demeaned Herself as not to incur the hatred or displeasure of any of Her Neighbors. For a proof of her Character She begs leave to refer your Excellency to a Certificate from a Number of Gentlemen of the first respectability, which will accompany this Petition. Your Petitioner further states that since the time of her being presented by the Grand Inquest before mentioned She has discontinued to retail Spiritous Liquors in any manner, fearing least She might again ignorantly violate the Laws of Her Country, so that a repetition of the offence is not likely to happen, and no evil consequences arise, from an extension of the humanity of the Executive in her favor. In tender consideration of these circumstances, your Petitioner most respectfully solicits Your Excellency to extend to Her the provisions of the Constitution, giving the President the Power of pardoning all offences against the United States, and grant her a remission of the Fine imposed upon her By the Circuit Court, as She apprehends that no evil can result to the United States or to any part thereof by such a measure and as the payment of the fine will be severely felt by a Person in such penurious circumstances as your Petitioner,

And your Petitioner as in duty bound will ever pray; and soforth.

JANE MCGRAW
June 13th 1805

We the undersigned, Neighbors of Mrs. Mcgraw, know her to be an industrious orderly Woman, & believe her to be worthy to receive from the President the Favor she solicits.

S. B. BALCH.
GEORGE THOMSON
JOHN BALTZER JUNR
HUGH BROWN
BENJA. LACEY—
J M BEATTY
CHAS A BEATTY
WM STEUART
JOHN THRELKELD

June 1805
On the Within Statement of facts and the recommendation annexed to it We respectfully recommend to the President the remission of the fine as prayed

W KILTY
W. CRANCH.
June 18. 1805

[*Order by TJ*:]
June 18. 1805.
Let a pardon issue

TH: JEFFERSON

RC (DNA: RG 59, GPR); petition in McGraw's hand; attestation in an unidentified hand, signed by all; recommendation of judges in William Kilty's hand, signed by Kilty and William Cranch.

TJ pardoned McGraw and remitted her fine and costs on 18 June (same).

To Robert Patterson

DEAR SIR Washington June 13. 05.

Having now recieved notice from mr Boudinot that he resigns his office as Director of the mint, on the last day of this month, you will recieve the commission to succeed him in due time to recieve from him whatever he may have occasion to deliver over in form. I write to him on the subject, so that you may now enter into communication with him thereon, and consider the matter henceforward as public. most of the emploiment of that establishment coming from the merchants, it is my duty to recommend to you in a particular manner their accomodation and satisfaction. Accept my friendly salutations.

TH: JEFFERSON

RC (PPAmP); addressed: "Mr. Robert Patterson College Philadelphia"; franked and postmarked. PoC (DLC); endorsed by TJ.

I WRITE TO HIM: TJ to Elias Boudinot, 13 June.

From Charles Willson Peale

DEAR SIR Museum June 13th. 1805.

The Polygraph intended for your secretary and that for Mr. Volney were shipp'd yesterday, and the other which you are pleased to order is now in hand; having one ready made of the same board of which your Polygraph top is made, with a black and white string on the edge, it has a neat look, but not so rich as those with a variety of strings of different colours—it is about $\frac{3}{4}$ of an Inch longer than your last Polygraph, therefore I hope to make it write to the bottom of 4to. Sheet with ease, otherwise we will make another a little larger with all possible dispatch consistant with care to give the best workmanship. It shall be packed up in such a manner that no injury can happen to it by the jolting of the Stage waggon.

some Gentlemen have meet a few times at my House and planed a design of an Academy for the incouragement of the fine arts in this City. a handsome subscription is already made by very respectable Characters. and we hope soon to begin a building for the reception of Casts of Statues, also for a display of Paintings, by the exhibition of which a revenue may be had to defray the expence of a keeper who shall be capable to give instruction to the Pupels—pictures offered for sale will be exhibited for certain periods, if such are deserving public notice, and when sold, a pr. Centum on the sale, to help the funds of the Academy. out of these funds with what shall be thought reasonable for Pupels to pay for the use of the School, the living Models school will be opened at proper seasons. Mr. West is very anxious to have all his designs, the originals of his historical paintings placed here, which, my son Rembrandt says is very valuable, he told Rembrandt, that he had long contemplated and indeed had preserved his works for this express purpose. but I believe he thinks our Legislature will make appropriations for an establishment for the encouragement of the fine arts—and might be induced to purchase paintings as models of colouring, composition &c. if he knew the constitutions of our Country better he would loose all hopes from that quarter—By subscriptions a good building, and Casts in Plaster (which may be had cheap) a beginning may be made, and with proper management, the Academy may afterwards support its self. more I do not look for in my time.

accept my best respects, with much esteem your friend

C W PEALE

RC (DLC); at foot of text: "His Excellency Thomas Jefferson Esqr."; endorsed by TJ as received 14 June and so recorded in SJL. PoC (Lb in PPAmP: Peale-Sellers Papers).

ACADEMY: Peale and his son Rembrandt were among the 71 founders of the Pennsylvania Academy of Fine Arts. On 21 June, the founders had more than $2,400 in subscriptions and met to elect officers. Modeled on the New York Academy of the Fine Arts and the Royal Academy in London, the Pennsylvania Academy intended to "promote the cultivation of the Fine Arts, in the United States of America" with a twofold purpose of educating artists and exhibiting artistic works for the general public. The directors invited Benjamin WEST to be their first honorary member. The Pennsylvania LEGISLATURE incorporated the academy on 28 Mch.

1806 (Peale, *Papers*, v. 2, pt. 2:853-4; Frank H. Goodyear, Jr., "A History of the Pennsylvania Academy of the Fine Arts, 1805-1976," in Pennsylvania Academy of the Fine Arts, *In This Academy: The Pennsylvania Academy of the Fine Arts, 1805-1976* [Philadelphia, 1976], 16-18; Stephen May, "An Enduring Legacy: The Pennsylvania Academy of the Fine Arts, 1805-2005," in Mark Hain and others, *Pennsylvania Academy of the Fine Arts, 1805-2005: 200 Years of Excellence* [Philadelphia, 2005], 11-13; *Relfs Philadelphia Gazette*, 2 July).

To Craven Peyton

DEAR SIR Washington June 13. 05

On the 27th. of April I recieved from mr Jefferson for acceptance your note for 201. D. paiable about the last of July, which I sent back accepted and shall pay at maturity. I did not write you on it because I thought he would do so. since that your favors of Apr. 25. & June 9. have been recieved. the former proposed that I should pay £200. in 60. days (say July 1.) and £60. in 90 days (Aug. 1.) this I believe would not have been possible, an accumulation of other demands for July 1. happening to me beyond what is usual. but if I understand your letter of June 9th. rightly it will suffice if I pay £47. the 1st. Monday of next month & £160. the 1st. Monday in August. these paiments I can accomplish only allowing to about the 10th. of each month, as it requires for me the first week or ten days of the month always to accomplish my pecuniary reckonings. if this will answer, be so good as to notify me by return of post and I will immediately inform mr Jefferson that paiments shall be made him accordingly. as I shall be at home about the 22d. of July we will then arrange the balance. in the mean time, that I may perfectly understand these transactions, I inclose you a paper with the name of every coparcener, to which I will ask you to add the names of the persons through whom each share comes to, you, the price of each, and the time of paiment. I have done this in part myself, that you may see in what manner I wish it compleated. will you also be so good as to explain what are the particular objects purchased of Eliza Bullock for the 500. D. I observe the warehouse was 100. D. of it. could you also send me a note of the quantity of tobo. recieved at the warehouse for some years back, & the sum paiable on each hogshead. I shall be glad to recieve this information as soon as convenient. Accept friendly salutations.

TH: JEFFERSON

PoC (ViU); at foot of text: "Mr. C. Peyton"; endorsed by TJ.

ENCLOSURE

Henderson Family Warehouse Shares

A statement of the rights &c. in Henderson's warehouses.

the Widow's dower.		conveyed to[1] *Peyton* price *£85. pd. sold by Charles Henderson Att.y. in fact for the widow* time of paiment.
John.		conveyed to[2] *Seabrook who by Anderson conveys to Peyton* price. *£50.*— time of paiment *Ninety days.*
Sarah Kerr		conveyed to *E. Moore by him to Matt Henderson who conveys to Anderson & by him to Peyton. not compleat* price *£50.* time of paiment
James L.	conveyed to	Woodson[3] who conveyed to Peyton price *£140 for all his interest as ⅌ Deed* time of paiment. *pd. some time past.*
Charles.	conveyed to	Bramham, who conveyed to Seabrook, who by D. Anderson conveys to Peyton[4] price. *£50.* time of paiment. *Ninety Days*
Isham.	conveyed to	*John*[5] Henderson, who conveyed to[6] *Seabrook who by his attorney Anderson to Peyton* price *£50.* time of paiment. *Ninety Days.*
Bennet H.	conveyed to	John Henderson, who to Seabrook, who, by Anderson his Atty, to C. Peyton price. £50. time of payment *Ninety days.*
Eliza Bullock.	conveyed to	Peyton 100. D. for warehouse. 400. D.[7] for *This deed is in complyance of James L. Hendersons sale to Peyton with the addition of the Warehouse at £30.0.0* time of paiment.
Frances / Lucy / Nancy C.	conveyed to	Peyton price 300. D. time of paiment. *Ninety Days.*

MS (ViU); undated; in TJ's hand with blanks subsequently filled by Craven Peyton shown in italics; endorsed by TJ "Warehouse rights"; also endorsed by TJ, subsequently canceled by diagonal strokes:

		"£
the widow		85
John	50 + 112 - 10 =	162 - 10
Sarah		50. 150

			58 - 1
	James L.	140.	140
	Charles	50.	102
	Isham	50	102
	Bennet H.	50	
q?	Eliza	150	
	Frances / Lucy / Nancy C."	90	

PoC (same); written on verso of PoC of cover letter with additions by TJ (see notes below).

[1] On PoC, TJ filled this blank with "to C.P. Sep. 18. 02. all her dower except mill, warehouse & improved lots in Milton" and "to C.P. July 19 04. the warehouse."

[2] On PoC, TJ filled this blank with "the 102. as (No. 1.) & $6\frac{1}{4}$ as (No. 9) to Cr. Peyton. Apr. 30. 03."; "his right to Warehous to Richd. Seabrook July 17. 1802. who by Rd Anderson to C.P. June 5. 05"; "all his other property to James Lewis who to C.P. Nov. 8. 08."

[3] On PoC, TJ here interlined "Dec. 28. 99" and after "Peyton" inserted "Apr. 25. 01. & Nov. 29. 01. all his rights."

[4] On PoC, TJ first altered the text to read "conveyed warehouse to Bramham Oct 19. 02 who conveyed to Seabrook, who by R. Anderson conveys to Peyton June 5. 05." before canceling that to substitute "conveyed mill site (No. 8.) to John Hend. who to James Lewis who to Cr. Peyt. Nov. 8. 08" and "all his other property to James L. H. Mar. 18. 01. who to C.P. Mar. 19. 01. confirmd by Charles Jan. 31. 04."

[5] Name interlined by Peyton in place of TJ's "James L."

[6] Peyton here canceled "Peyton."

[7] Above this figure Peyton interlined "pd."

From Philippe Reibelt

Monsieur! Baltimore le 13 Juin 1805.

Un Pharmacien et Medecin—generalement instruit, digne d'etre recû en bonne Societè, parlant les trois principales langues vivantes, qui a quittè la rive gauche du Rhin par le même Motif que Moi, c'est a dire, puisque Nous prevoions L'Empire se mettre a la place de la Republique—et que j'ai amenè avec Moi en çe pays, a le projet, de fonder a CharlottesVille (pres Monticello) une pharmacie montée sur le pied francais, Anglais et Allemand.

Personne ne sauroit prononcer plus decisivement sur la Question: si les proprietaires environantes (grands et petits) pourroient y desirer un tel etablissement, et s'il y a probabilitè, qu'il reussiroit—et certainement personne n'est mieux disposèe, de diriger et proteger un Litterateur Republicain expatriè, que Vous, le Seul Chef des principes liberaux sur le vaste Univers.

J'ose donc Vous demander en Graçe, de me dire, quelle en est Votre persuasion?

C'est dans cette même Supposition, que je prend la libertè, de Vous annonçer, qu'un autre Compatriote de Moi, Dtr. Konz de Trêves—un homme des mêmes Qualités Morales, scientifiques et politiques va s'etablir de la même manière a Richmond. — et de le recomander a Votre protection, comme un eléve du Vieux Franck au grand hopital a Viênne.

L'un et l'autre seront par mon entremise fournis de la pharmacie de Mr. Du Catel d'ici, qui est sous tous les rapports le pharmacien le plus distinguè de çeux, qui sont immigrè de la france, et particulierement de S. Domingue.

J'ai l honneur de Vous presenter mes bien profonds et Sinceres hommages. REIBELT.

EDITORS' TRANSLATION

SIR! Baltimore, 13 June 1805

A physician and pharmacist—broadly educated, worthy of being welcomed into good society, speaking the three major living languages, who left the left bank of the Rhine for the same reason I did, anticipating that the empire would supplant the republic, and whom I brought with me to this country—seeks to found in Charlottesville near Monticello a pharmacy on French, English, and German practices.

No one can decide this question better than you. If the neighboring owners, large and small, wish such a business and it is likely to succeed, surely no one is more qualified to oversee and protect an expatriated republican man of letters than you, the one leader of liberal principles in this vast universe.

I therefore dare ask for your opinion.

In the same spirit, I take the liberty of informing you that another of my compatriots, Dr. Konz from Trier, a man with comparable moral, scientific, and political qualities, is going to found a similar establishment in Richmond. I recommend him to your protection. He is a student of the elder Frank at the great hospital in Vienna.

I will supply both of them from Mr. Ducatel's pharmacy here. He is by far the most distinguished of the pharmacists to have immigrated from France, especially from Saint-Domingue.

I have the honor of offering you my very deep and sincere regards.

REIBELT

RC (DLC); endorsed by TJ as received 14 June and so recorded in SJL.

VIEUX FRANCK: that is, Johann Peter Frank, a medical educator and innovator in the field of public health, whose son was also a prominent doctor (Erna Lesky, ed., *A System of Complete Medical Police: Selections from Johann Peter Frank* [Baltimore, 1976], ix-xiv; Otto M. Marx, "Descriptions of Psychiatric Care in Some Hospitals during the First Half of the 19th Century," *Bulletin of the History of Medicine*, 41 [1967], 208-9).

To John Rhea

DEAR SIR Washington June 13. 05.

Your letter of May 24. came to hand on the 11th. inst. exactly as I was signing renewed commissions for the renewed government of Orleans. in consequence of the hope held up in that that the information I had recieved respecting mr Duffield might not be correct, I have renewed his commission, and it is gone on by duplicates to New Orleans. still I must intreat you minutely to enquire into the fact of the improper habit imputed to him, as on the truth or falsehood of that will depend his confirmation by the Senate. Accept my friendly salutations and assurances of respect. TH: JEFFERSON

PoC (DLC); endorsed by TJ.

To Benjamin Rush

DEAR SIR Washington June 13. 05.

A considerable time before the reciept of your letter of Apr. 29. it was known here that mr Boudinot intended to retire from the Direction of the mint, & as was expected, immediately. it had therefore been made a question to the members of the administration who should be his successor. it was supposed that the duties of that office required the best mathematical talents which could be found, as well on account of the mechanical execution, as the difficulty of the problems constantly occurring on the mixture of metals. the appointment of Sr. Isaac Newton in England & of mr Rittenhouse here with the universal satisfaction these appointments had given seemed to give the sanction of the world to this principle of appointment, and therefore it was the general opinion of the members that mr Patterson should be placed at the head of the mint which was notified to him. it is true that this had not always been observed as the principle of appointment, but it was thought best to follow the best examples. altho the ground of this appointment is so distinct from your line of pursuit that it can give you no uneasiness, yet I could not deny to myself the satisfaction of explaining it. it is indeed far the most painful part of my duty, under which nothing could support me but the consideration that I am but a machine erected by the constitution for the performance of certain acts according to laws of action laid down for me, one of which is that I must anatomise the living man as the Surgeon does his dead subject, view him also as a machine & employ him for what he is fit for, unblinded by the mist of friendship. Accept affectionate salutations & assurances of constant esteem & respect.

TH: JEFFERSON

RC (PPRF); addressed: "Doctr. Benjamin Rush Philadelphia"; franked and postmarked. PoC (DLC).

To Gibson & Jefferson

MESSRS. GIBSON & JEFFERSON Washington June 14. 05.

I now inclose you in Richmond bank bills 970. Dollars, and have this day drawn on you in favor of

Charles Smith of Louisa for	621. D.
James Oldham	100.
William Wardlaw	46.12
balance to the credit of my account with you	202.88
	970

which you will be pleased to honour. Accept my friendly salutations

TH: JEFFERSON

4. bills of	100.	400.
1.	50.	50
14.	20	280
12	5.	60
		970.

PoC (MHi); endorsed by TJ as a letter to George Jefferson. Notation in SJL: "970."

On this day, TJ wrote letters to CHARLES SMITH, from whom he hired slaves, and WILLIAM WARDLAW, a doctor based in Charlottesville, neither of which has been found (MB, 2:930, 1156; Appendix IV).

From Richmond on 17 June, Gibson & Jefferson acknowledged receiving TJ's "favor of the 14th. inclosing Nine hundred & seventy dollars, which shall be applied as you direct" (RC in MHi; in Patrick Gibson's hand; at foot of text: "Thomas Jefferson Esqr."; endorsed by TJ as received from George Jefferson on 20 June and so recorded in SJL).

To James Oldham

SIR Washington June 14. 05.

Your favor of the 4th. inst. came to hand some days ago; but as the question about the sashes for the S.E. portico required attention & a recurrence to my papers, I have not had time to take it up till this moment. there are 5. arches to the Piazza, the measures of which you have taken. besides the sashes, they are to have Venetian blinds of a particular construction, now in hand here, under my own eye. according to the plan on which I have proceeded, each arch must have 2. square sashes, to slide up with leads in the common way. each sash 3. panes high & 5 panes wide, the panes $11\frac{1}{2}$ I. by 15. I. the semicircular sash above these must have it's base divided into 5. parts corresponding with the upright bars in the lower sashes, in the manner

represented in the margin. because each semicircular bar should appear to spring from the upright one below it, & be only a continuation of that upright one bending round & meeting it's corresponding upright on the other side. the 2. lower sashes will be 8. f. high when put together & lapped on one another in the middle, and they will be 5. f. 2 I. wide from out to out, including the depth of the 2. grooves in which they run on each side. I took these measures with great accuracy, and as the rest of the work is doing on the same measures, I wish your sashes to conform to them. if your sashes lap 1. I. at the middle, then each will be 4. f. $\frac{1}{2}$ I. high and 5. f. 2. I. wide, out to out.

I now inclose you an order on messrs. Gibson & Jefferson for 100. D. according to your desire. Accept my best wishes.

TH: JEFFERSON

P.S. will these thing be done in time to send up by the boats before the river gets too low to be boatable. I think it would be better to divide the semicircular sash into 5. panes instead of 7.

PoC (MHi); at foot of text: "Mr. Oldham"; endorsed by TJ. Enclosure not found.

From Thomas Mann Randolph

DEAR SIR, June 14. 1805.

Lillie communicated to me, a few days after he had written to you, his intention of leaving Monto. this Autumn. I had never heard a word from him before on the subject although I had learned from others sometime before that he had thoughts of the kind. He says that he finds he is doing nothing for his family which consumes necessarily in the groceries and cloathing he is obliged to buy allmost the whole of his wages; change, of course, is necessary for him; and it must be admitted it is his interest to risk it as that is the case. He speaks of going to Kentucke to settle on rented land, but I cannot help thinking that certain expressions with respect to him which were made use of by some gentlemen who will be directors of the company for clearing Rivanna if the subscriptions are made up, (which I think rather doubtfull,) were the cause of his inclination to leave your service. Those gentlemen said they would give him more than any other man in the State to superintend the laborers to be employed in that work. If they give him 100. £. he will lose by the change in the maintenance of his family and they will scarcely go beyond that. He has too much judgement to prefer that to his present situation and of course will most probably meet with disappointment. I will make myself acquainted with the character and qualities of all such as stand a chance to serve you well throughout the neighbourhood by the time you return in order to give all the aid I can in your choice. I cannot refrain from suggesting one idea which may retain Lillie I suspect without any sacrifice at all: even, I am strongly inclined to believe myself, with an advantage. The bare suggestion cannot be amiss. Supposing the whole work on the mill to be finished this year there will be hands enough to cultivate a good farm, I suppose, after returning its full force to the nailery. Lillie has so much understanding activity and perseverance that he could superintend the culture of one in the best manner with the aid of his Wifes son who lives with him and at the same time manage the nailery and direct any hired force you might chuse to employ for jobs to as much advantage as at present. So doing he would earn his present wages and deserve a liberal share of what he made besides. He would I think take pleasure in following precisely the mode of husbandry prescribed by you beforehand and I am certain would with 10. hands, one half men, save all your purchases of Corn, oats Hay and Butcher meat Butter &c without damage to the Land, which I am quite clear in opinion had better be cultivated well even in Corn frequently than be suffered to get covered with broom-straw. I have no doubt, though I cannot say I have any certainty, that he would be satisfied with this arrangement and gladly take his hopes from a share of the crop for increase of Salary. I have not heard a word from him on this subject but I know his inclinations and confidence in his agricultural skill and unless the ravages of the Hessian fly should have altered them would venture to pronounce the proposal would delight him. This insect has ruined my crop this year but has respected Cravens, thereby shewing that it ought not to influence in new agricultural projects. Shadwell is full convenient to Lillies House.

Martha is recovering her health with perfect certainty. Her appetite is good, her digestion, with prudence, not amiss and her recruit of strength such as to have induced her to resume her housekeeping in person. Ann, Ellen, Cornelia and Virginia have had the Mumps, Jefferson has them now very slightly. All are as well as need be. Mrs. Carr and Mrs Lewis have recovered thoroughly.

I am with sincere attachment yr &c. TH: M. RANDOLPH

RC (ViU); endorsed by TJ as received 17 June and so recorded in SJL.

From Ledyard Seymour

HONOR'D & RESPECTED SIR Hartford June 14th 1805

In the absence of Mr Granger the Friend of my Father, and who has for ought I Know, been soliciting on my behalf, permit me to approach your respected asylum of the chief-Magistracy of this our happy Country; convinced as I am of the apparent impropriety of addressing you on any subject, incapable as I am, and fearing that either the diffidence of my mind, or the inexperience of youth may delineate sentiments, imperfect, or erroneous—

Having had the good fortune of visiting the Capital of the Union, & the honor of an introduction, to your person thro' the politeness of Mr Granger it has emboldened me (tho perhaps too much) to proceed, & apply to the Father of our Country, freely confessing, that tho my Fathers property is ample to support his children in the decent, walks of Connect—I am however the youngest, & can never be habituated to a System like the present, of Legitimate proscription, & monopoly, My destinies, then are to myself unknown—In the year 1792, my Education was in a way completed at Yale College, an ill state of Health arising from sedentary Habits, determined me by my Fathers consent, to pursue Mercantile buisness, in 1794 removed to New York, with the wife of my Youth—my Capital nearly 2000 Dollars, made shipments under the patronage of Messrs David Gelston & Nathl G Ingraham the latter my brother by marriage, Buisness was very good & successfull untill the close of 1796—the capture by the British cruizers, of five Merchant Vessells, mostly large, for no transgression, of even a then existing Maritime Law, of their own, without a pretext, or even a colorable paper, or suspected goods, to a port of the So. part of St Domingo, where a British Ship had never been, seen, or soldier landed—combined to first Mutilate, & so absorb, my little all in the two years succeeding the first loss of 1795 my Bankruptcy was consequent to these events, in 1797. Ebeneser Stevens, Esqr. my uncle by marriage then a Friend to the interests of the Community, was my sole Creditor to my very alarming, or distressing amount, and notwithstanding the misfortune of the loss of the wife of my youth, contributed all in his power, to drive me to a Compromise, by involving a Father, in the Burthen of paying for Debts occasioned, wholly, (I most solemnly aver in the face of Heaven) by British Spoliation, in lieu for which He as Assigner, & by Bonds in Jugement, agreeable to the Tenor of the Laws of N York, has never recd. by the Appeals to the Admiralty of G. Britain a farthing—[. . .] me in a County Prison for Two years & six Months. a partial act of Insolvency as relating to him only relieved me from his cruelty, I wrote him I would never shelter myself behind a Bankrupt Law—went immediately to the Havana, where I resided three years from August 1800.—

acquired the idiom of the language, & Cultivated the affections of the Inhabitants with my whole heart, was successfull & returned & paid Two Thousand Dollars, of old debts. nor will I cease, paying them as long as life & Buisness enables me—remain single & tho not avaricious, shall, from a Compromise with My Uncle, whom I shall yet esteem, for his once disinterested assistance? apply without too great injury, a portion to the final discharge of all my Balances—No new Embarrassments, having been in any way that of—Thus having narrated every material occurrence for thirteen years of the most trying Scenes, that are incident to humanity & still believe myself unimpaired by an unsocial habit. The loss of the utility of a Language that I have acquired, I submit [with] cheerfullness to your decision, should Death or accident, [. . .] any room for me in any one of the Spanish Colonies, & my poor abilities, when exerted, not too deficient, for some port, certain that no action unless partaking deeply of human infirmity will ever tarnish the honor of my Country—Your Excelly. may rest assured that no Subject of a foreign power, or his property, could possibly induce me to a Violation of the Laws of Nations, or Spain—Alas Sir I shall submit with out a Murmur, & permit the stability of my principles to be analysed, from their perpetuity the attachment to your Administration, surpassed only by the belief that it has increased our respectability abroad, & the happiness of every individual, who rejoices in the prosperity of our Nation—With the utmost Respect. Your dutiful & respectful, Servant. & God preserve you many Years—

LEDYARD SEYMOUR

RC (DNA: RG 59, LAR); torn, illegible; addressed: "Thomas Jefferson Esqr. President of the United States"; endorsed by TJ as received 19 June and "to be Consul in some of the Spanish colonies"; recorded in SJL as received 20 June with notation "to be Consul."

To William Short

DEAR SIR — Washington June 14. 05.

Your favor of May 15. was recieved in due time. you will now recieve inclosed a draught of the US. bank here on that at Philadelphia for 500. D. if I rightly estimate the calls which will come on me the beginning of July I am afraid they will disable me from making the remittance for that month. an unexpected one from Albemarle has deranged the calculations I had made for that epoch. after that I hope interruptions will be less frequent.

By your letter to mr Barnes I percieve you were undetermined in what direction you would go to pass the hot & bilious season. this gives a hope still that we may have you at Monticello, for which place I shall set out about the middle of July: but having to proceed without delay to Bedford, I shall probably not be back to Monticello till the 1st. of August, where I should be very happy to meet you. we have lately recieved letters from Madrid, where our negociation was still going on, but evidently with such a disinclination on the part of Spain to come to a definition of boundary, that Monroe will be obliged to return to London & leave the matter unsettled. perhaps a stipulation that the parties shall leave the disputed country in statu quo, unsettled by both will answer our purpose quite as well as a present ascertainment as time is liberating our finances & increasing our strength, in that quarter particularly. Accept affectionate salutations & assurances of constant attachment & respect. TH: JEFFERSON

RC (DLC: Short Papers); at foot of text: "Mr. Short"; endorsed by Short as received at Philadelphia on 18 June. Enclosure not found.

To Robert Gamble

SIR Washington June 15. 05.

I recieved last night your favor of the 11th. requesting letters of introduction to England & France for your son, & a passport. the passport is now inclosed. early applications after I came into the administration for letters of introduction to foreign parts rendered it necessary to take into consideration the propriety of my furnishing such letters on any occasion. it was decided to be unadviseable & improper, & I have adhered rigorously to the rule then laid down. I have on one or two special occasions undertaken to mention gentlemen in my private letters to our foreign ministers; and being shortly to write to Genl. Armstrong in Paris & Colo. Monro in London I will with pleasure ask their attentions to your son. altho Colo Monroe's residence in Richmond made him probably acquainted with him personally, yet it will be a gratification to myself to contribute what I can to the desires of your son at those places. these letters will go in the official dispatches of the Secretary of state by the first conveyance. with respect to the pecuniary aid desired in the contingency of his wanting it, this could not possibly be taken from any public funds, and having myself not a single money connection in Europe, no circumstance would authorise me to ask it of Genl. Armstrong or Colo. Monroe. I say this the more frankly as I am satisfied the prudent precautions taken by your son would prevent his having occasion for this recurrence, & his experiencing any inconvenience from the want of it. Accept my salutations & assurances of respect. TH: JEFFERSON

PoC (DLC); at foot of text: "Mr. Robert Gamble"; endorsed by TJ. Enclosure not found.

To Samuel Harrison

SIR Washington June 15. 1805.

I have duly recieved your letter of May 15. respecting a claim of the respresentatives of Capt. Carver to an Indian grant of lands at St. Anthony's falls, & wishing to know what steps can be taken to give it effect. it will probably be long before any thing can be done. whenever Congress shall think proper to have that country surveyed & extend their land office to it, they will appoint a proper mode of deciding on the validity of any private claims to any portions of it before they begin to sell. in the mean time no recognition of the title can be had, nor any settlement permitted. if any exemption from these general principles of law be sought, it can only be from the legislature of the US. Accept my salutations & respects. TH: JEFFERSON

PoC (DLC); at foot of text: "Mr. Samuel Harrison"; endorsed by TJ.

To James Monroe

DEAR SIR Washington June 15. 05

Colo. Gamble of Richmond has desired me to introduce to your notice his son Robert who is gone to Europe on commercial concerns. the circumstances are known to you which render this application as unexpected as indelicate to be refused. his two daughters have married two good republicans. whether this is giving the pendulum another vibration, and he has made this an occasion of making an halfway advance, I cannot tell. I gave him a civil answer & promised to mention his son to you, altho it was certain you knew him, whereas I did not. I shall be glad the son should know I have complied with my promise.

When John Carey was collecting Genl. Washington's letters to Congress for publication, he proposed to proceed afterwards to publish the correspondence of Commanders in separate departments and of governors with him and with one another. I furnished him with my correspondence while governor of Virginia, reserving no copies, as I expected his publication would replace them. he has declined proceeding in the work, and it is extremely interesting to me to recover my letters, & those to me. mr Carey resides in London. his address is to the care of mr Taylor, cutler, Middle row Holborn. will you have the goodness to apply to mr Carey for these papers and return them to me by a safe conveyance. mr Carey is a man of learning, abilities, and of great worth.

Not knowing how this letter is to go I shall only add assurances of great affection to mrs Monroe & yourself & friendly salutations

TH: JEFFERSON

RC (DLC: Monroe Papers); addressed: "James Monroe Minister Plenipotentiary of the US. of America London"; endorsed by Monroe. PoC (DLC); endorsed by TJ. Notation in SJL: "Gamble."

TWO GOOD REPUBLICANS: William Wirt, who married Elizabeth Gamble in 1802, and William H. Cabell, who wed Agnes Gamble in 1805 (Philadelphia *United States' Gazette*, 28 Mch. 1805; Vol. 29:358-9n).

For TJ's efforts to locate JOHN CAREY, see TJ to Mathew Carey, 2 Apr. 1798 and 6 Jan. 1805. For his involvement with Carey's publishing endeavors, see Vol. 24:140, 151, 642; Vol. 25:105-6, 236, 581-2, 595, 630, 690; Vol. 28:324-5.

From Charles Willson Peale

DEAR SIR Museum June 15th. 1805.

The small Polygraph mentioned in my letter of the 13th. has now the Machinery to it and will write to the bottom with ease—but at the same time, that I put this machinery in the hands of the workman, my Cabenet Maker began one which I am certain is of a better size, yet it is my wish that you should make your choise which may be done by the time that the several boxes for paper, Pens, Wafers &c are compleated and a little time allowed for practicing with it.

The size of this Machine is 16 I. by 11 Inches, and the other in the hands of the Cabenet Maker is $17\frac{5}{8}$ long by $11\frac{5}{8}$. which gives a size of Cloath that two sheets of Post paper exactly covers, without laying one sheet on the Margin of the other. The Machine in hand shall have more ribband work to inrich it than the other, and will require about 5 or 6 days longer before it can be completely finished & sent, than the smaller one. While I wait for your orders my Workmen will proceed with diligence to complete both Polygraphs.

I have now published Mr. Latrobe's commendations of the Polygraph and if it does not bring a number of Purchasers, I shall then made no more of them, having now on hand about 20 of them all nearly finished. while I am waiting to know the result of this business, My Workmen shall be imployed in making such articles of curiosity as I can contrive to enrich the Museum, or be of use in my family as furniture.

Except my friendly salutations C W PEALE

RC (DLC); at foot of text: "His excelency Thomas Jefferson Esqr. president of U.S."; endorsed by TJ as received 18 June and so recorded in SJL. PoC (Lb in PPAmP: Peale-Sellers Papers).

MY WORKMEN: Samuel Jenkins and David Jones worked on the polygraphs for TJ and Latrobe (Peale, *Papers*, v. 2, pt. 2:853).

LATROBE'S COMMENDATIONS: Latrobe wrote to Peale on 8 June, enclosing endorsements of 14 Mch. and 4 June, which touted the polygraph's cost-saving measures and concluded that "no man of letters or property should be without it." William Duane published both of Latrobe's endorsements together in the *Aurora* for several days in mid-June (same, 847-9; *Aurora*, 15-26 June).

To John Julius Pringle

SIR Washington June 15. 05.

The office of Attorney General of the US. being vacant, it would be extremely pleasing to me if I could avail the public of your services in that station. I therefore take the liberty of proposing the Commission to you. tho' the circumstances which may principally influence your decision are unknown to me, it may not be improper to state some which lie more immediately under my view than your own. the practice in the Supreme court of the US. held here, & the district courts of Columbia held here & at Alexandria is said to be easy & profitable. the higher courts of Maryland & of the US. within that state are within half a day's ride, to wit, at Annapolis & Baltimore. the recess which the administration is in the practice of taking in the months of August & September, would enable them to dispense with your attendance till October or November, altho' it will be acceptable at any earlier moment convenient to yourself. so soon as you shall signify to me your acceptance, a commission shall be forwarded to you, & should we not be so fortunate as to obtain your aid, an early notice of that is desireable. Accept my salutations and assurances of great respect.

TH: JEFFERSON

RC (Margaret W. Smith, South Kent, Connecticut, 1977); at foot of text: "John Julius Pringle esq." PoC (DLC).

John Julius Pringle (1753-1843) of Charleston studied law with John Rutledge, became a member of the Middle Temple in London in 1773, and was admitted to the South Carolina bar in 1781. He was active in South Carolina politics, serving as speaker of its House of Representatives in 1787 and 1788 and as the state's attorney general from 1792 to 1808. Pringle married Susannah Reid, with whom he had 10 children, and lived at Runnymede, an estate on the Ashley River. A successful practicing attorney, he was also a trustee of the College of Charleston and president of the Charleston Library Society (DAB; J. S. R. Faunt, Walter B. Edgar, N. Louise Bailey, and others, eds., *Biographical Directory of the South Carolina House of Representatives*, 5 vols. [Columbia, S.C., 1974-92], 3:586-8; *Charleston Courier*, 20 Mch. 1843; Vol. 42:497).

From Benjamin Rush

DEAR SIR, June 15. 1805

I have just now recd your friendly letter, and take the earliest opportunity to express my entire satisfaction with the Contents of it. No man could have been nomd. as Mr B Successor that wd. be more agreeable to me than Mr Patter, & had I known before that he was a Candidate for the appt I should not have requested it. He will likewise I have no doubt be equally agreeable to all the officers of the mint all of whom are worthy men & very much yr friends.

I have only to beg that my appn to you may remain a Secret in yr own bosom.

The yellow fever the scourge of our Country begins to engage the Attention of the Courts in Europe. I have lately recd a number of Queries upon the Subject of its nature & Origin from the Governments of Etrutria & Prussia—the one thro the hands of a Dr Palloni—the other from the Prussian minister at the Court of London. My Answers to those Queries were calculated to impress in the strongest terms the domestic origin of the disease & that it never did & never can spread from importn or Contagion, I mend these facts in order to submit to yr Judgment whether measures similar to those taken by the Above Courts, might not be taken by our Natl. Government?—(Would a recomn. of such an inquiry be foreign to a message to Congress?)—Our State legislatures have erred egregy. & chiefly thro' ignorance in their laws for prevg the importn of the fever, & thereby embarrassed injured our commerce both at home and Abroad.—

Excuse the liberty I have taken in commg this hint, & believe me to be as usual your sincere Old friend of 1775 B RUSH

Dft (NcD-MC: Trent Collection); endorsed by Rush: "Copy of a letter to Mr Jefferson June 15. 1805." Recorded in SJL as a letter of 17 June received from Philadelphia on 19 June.

YOUR FRIENDLY LETTER: TJ to Rush, 13 June, in which he explained the selection of Robert Patterson to succeed Elias Boudinot (MR B) as director of the Mint.

PRUSSIAN MINISTER: the Baron von Jacobi-Kloest (Lyman H. Butterfield, ed., *Letters of Benjamin Rush*, 2 vols. [Princeton, 1951], 2:897n; Antoine-Chretien Wedekind, *Almanac des ambassades* [Braunschweig, 1803], 87).

From William Tatham

15th. June 1805.

W. Tatham's compts. to the President—He has written to Messrs. Learmonth's & Berry, (the House he is concerned for) Merchts. in London, for a Camera Obscura for the President's use, to be made as elegantly *Plain* as possible, by the best Workmen, with spare Glasses of several focuses, Diagonal Head, &c, compleat.—It will be paid for out of W.Ts, own private Monies in the Companies hands; but he can not say what the Price will be. He will, however, look for the Bill of the One he has, by which any importer will be able to settle an approximate Price; & the Acct. can be ultimately adjusted when it arrives.

W.T. will thank the President to spare the One he has, a day or two, as Mrs. Merry has expressed a desire to see it before she leaves Town for the Hot Season. It shall be sent back again immediately, after he has gratified the Curiosity of his Amiable friend.—

RC (DLC); addressed: "The President of the U. States," with notation "Private Note"; endorsed by TJ as received 15 June and so recorded in SJL.

Tatham dined at the President's House on 5 June (Appendix II). TJ previously purchased a CAMERA OBSCURA in 1794 (Vol. 27:47n).

From J. P. P. Derieux

MONSIEUR Greenbriar Court house ce 16. Juin 1805.

La reponse dont vous avés bien voulu m'honorer m'est parvenue par le dernier courier, et je m'empresse de vous donner les details que vous desirés sur l'espece de Bled blanc solide que j'apportai de France, qui doit se planter a un pied de distance, sa paille est trés grosse et remplie d'une Substance trés nourissante pour les Bestiaux, Ses Epis Sont Larges et d'une forme qui diffère beaucoup de celle des notres. j'en ay cette année quelques pieds dans mon jardin dont j'aurai L'honneur de vous faire part aussitot leur maturité, ainsi que de plusieurs autres especes de Bleds que j'attends dans une caisse de graines de jardinage qui doit incessament m'arriver de France. J'eleve aussi un Bled rouge superieur a la grosseur et a la force ordinaire du notre. Sa forme est oblongue et approchant un peu de celle du Seigle. J'ai une petitte fêve marbrée qui brulée et reduite en poudre a beaucoup L'odeur et le gout du Caffé. Sa plante qui S'eléve a un pied est trés branchée et garnie de feuilles concaves d'un beau vert pomme. je la crois d'autant plus Succeptible d'etre elevée en pots pour Servir d'ornement dans les appartements, quelle paroit conserver son eclat et sa même fraicheur dans les differentes Saisons, elle a resisté a nos fortes gelées du Printemps, je vous en envoie la feuille et prendrai la liberté de vous en remettre la graine Si vous n'en avés pas vous même. J'avois L'année derniere des Choux de fleurs qui ont produit têtes et graines dans la même saison ce qui ne m'etoit jamais arrivé depuis Vingt ans que je les cultive, et est d autant plus Surprenant que dans ce climat trés froid, il est presque juin avant que nos plantes commencent a prendre de la force. et que Souvent dés les premiers jours de Septembre La Végétation se trouve interrompue par les gelées. Je me donne beaucoup a la partie du jardinage, ne pouvant resister a la fatigue des autres travaux de la Campagne, par rapport a mes anciens rumatismes de Charlotteville qui me reviennent touttes les fois que j'essaye de m'y livrer. C'est principalement cette raison qui manque de fortune pour remplacer l'aide de mes Enfants, m oblige de chercher une Situation plus analogue a mes circonstances et m'avoit fait prendre la liberté d'esperer qu'honoré de votre protection et connaissant mon integrité j'aurois pu etre assés heureux pour obtenir de vos bontés quelqu'emploi de Confiance auprés de vous. Lorsque j'arriverai a Washington on m'avoit conseillé de Solliciter celui de votre Steward qu'on Supposoit devoir sous peu etre Vacant; mais L'esprit d'entousiasme pour le ohio avoit tellement gagné ma femme, que je negligeai cette occasion de vous offrir mes Services dans une Capacité dont j'ai toujours eu une parfaitte connaissance.

Le desir de vous apprendre, Monsieur, que pendant mon Sejour en France j'ai eu la Satisfaction d'avoir favorablement disposé mes plus proches parents, me fait prendre la liberté de vous communiquer une lettre de ma tente de Nantes et quelques pages de celle de son fils, qui a la mort d'une pere très agé jouira de beaucoup de Biens. Je juge par la Suite de sa lettre que je nai pas osé vous envoyer vu son volume, qu'on n'est pas generalement Satisfait de L'administration du nouvel Empire, et que c'est toujours la force militaire qui fait indistinctement tout respecter.

Je l'avois invité L'année derniere a venir visitter nos Etats ou il verroit que par les soins dun Chef aussi eclairé mais plus aimé que le sien. La douceur et L'equité de nos loix ne promettoit a ses habitants qu une continuation de bonheur et de prosperité. je crois que le commerce quil a en vue L'y amenera avant Longtems.

J'ai l'honneur d etre dans les Sentiments du plus profond respect; Monsieur, Votre trés humble et trés obeissant Serviteur

P. Derieux

EDITORS' TRANSLATION

Sir, Greenbrier Court House, 16 June 1805

The reply with which you honored me has just arrived and I hasten to provide the details you requested about the species of hardy white wheat I brought from France. Seeds must be planted one foot apart. The straw is thick and filled with a substance that can feed animals. The ears are wide and shaped differently from ours. This year I have a few plants in my garden which I shall be honored to share with you as soon as they are mature, along with seeds from several other types of wheat I am expecting in a package due to arrive soon from France. I am also growing a variety of red wheat that is greater in size and usual strength than ours. It is oblong and looks a little like rye. I have a small, marbled bean that roasted and ground smells and tastes a lot like coffee. The plant grows to a height of one foot and its many branches are lined with lovely apple-green concave leaves. I think it can grow just as well in pots as an ornamental plant for apartments, since it seems to stay bright and fresh in all seasons. It weathered the severe spring frosts. I will send you the leaf and take the liberty of giving you a seed if you do not have it. Last year my cauliflowers produced heads and seeds in the same season, which had never happened in the 20 years I have been growing them. It is all the more surprising in this cold climate where plants do not begin to bloom before June and vegetation is often interrupted by frost in early September. I spend a lot of time gardening since I can no longer do the more exhausting agricultural tasks. When I try, my old Charlottesville rheumatism recurs. The lack of resources to replace my children's labor is my principal reason for seeking a position more consonant with my circumstances, and taking the liberty of hoping that, favored by your protection and through your kindness, I might be fortunate enough to obtain some position of confidence in your employ, since you know I am a man of integrity. When I arrived in Washington I was advised to apply to be your steward, a position expected to become available soon thereafter. But my wife was so enthusiastic about Ohio that I missed this opportunity to offer my services in a role for which I was eminently qualified.

I wish to inform you, Sir, that during my stay in France I had the pleasure of making satisfactory arrangements for my closest family members. I take the liberty of sharing a letter from my aunt in Nantes and a few pages of a letter from her son who, at the death of his elderly father, will inherit significant wealth. From the rest of his letter, which I dare not send you because of its length, I gather that people are generally satisfied with the administration of the new empire and that military force still commands indiscriminate respect.

Last year I invited my cousin to come visit our states where he could see that, guided by a leader as enlightened but more beloved than his, the justice and benevolence of our laws promised only prolonged happiness and prosperity to inhabitants. I think the business he has in mind will bring him here before long.

With deepest respect, Sir, I have the honor of being your very humble and obedient servant.

P. Derieux

RC (DLC); endorsed by TJ as received 25 June and so recorded in SJL. Enclosures not found.

la reponse: TJ to Derieux, 31 May.

From William C. C. Claiborne

Dear Sir, New Orleans June 17th. 1805

A Mr. Lafon is now engaged in surveying the Land on the Canal of Carondalet;—He supposes that about eight or nine Hundred acres may be had, nearly half of which he says is excellent Land, and not subject to be overflowed. Mr. Briggs has been very unwell, and could not in person attend the surveying—

I am Dear Sir with great Respect Your faithful friend

William C. C. Claiborne

RC (DLC); at foot of text: "Thomas Jefferson President of the United States"; endorsed by TJ as received 2 Aug. and so recorded in SJL, but as a letter of 17 July. FC (Lb in DNA: RG 59, TP, Orleans). Enclosed in Gideon Granger to TJ, 23 July.

To Albert Gallatin

Th: Jefferson to mr Gallatin June 17. 05.

In the case of the rescue of the Felicity by Capt Newcome of the revenue cutter he certainly could not act as a revenue officer. but taking for granted the fact that the Felicity was taken within our jurisdiction, it was the duty of any citizen who had the means of vindicating our jurisdiction to do so. Capt Newcome, with the arms of the US. in his hands, for whatever other purpose they might have been put there, has done no more than the duty of a good citizen in using them to prevent the commission of a crime within our limits. whenever we shall be prepared to enforce respect to our jurisdiction, it may not be amiss to associate the cutters in that duty, by proper instructions, where the occasion shall fall in their way. for the present the only question is whether we should express our approbation of the act to Capt Newcome. I suppose it should be deferred till we have other information besides his. affectionate salutations.

PoC (DLC). Notation in SJL: "capt. Newcome."

From Albert Gallatin

Dear Sir 17 June 1805

It is necessary, according to usage, that you should add the word "Approved" with your signature to the enclosed requisition from the Dept. of State for certain payments to be charged to the contingent fund.

That fund has always been held to be solely at the President's disposal; and accordingly his signature to be essential to authorize the Treasury to pay.

Respectfully Your obedt: Servant ALBERT GALLATIN

RC (DLC); at foot of text: "The President of the United States"; endorsed by TJ as received from the Treasury Department on 17 June and "Louisa. expences" and so recorded in SJL. Enclosure not found.

In a letter of 25 May, Gallatin alerted Madison that Congress had failed to appropriate money for salaries for the governors, secretaries, and judges of the recently created Michigan and Louisiana Territories, the governments of which would be operating as of 1 July. Unless the president approved paying the territorial officers out of the CONTINGENT FUND, they would need to be informed of the circumstance (RC in DLC; endorsed by TJ: "Departmt Treasy. to mr Madison. May 25. 05. no approprn for Michigan govmt."). Madison replied on 4 June that TJ had decided to permit "an advance to each of" the officers "of a sum equal to a quarters salary to be reimbursed by retaining the 1st. quarters salary accruing to the person to whom the advance may be made" (Madison, *Papers, Sec. of State Ser.*, 9:402).

From Thomas McKean

SIR, Philadelphia. June 17th. 1805.

At the request of divers Gentlemen, I take the liberty of inclosing herewith to Your Excellency a recommendation of Mr. Hugh Lennox, for many years a reputable Merchant in this city, as successor to William Savage of the Island of Jamaica Esquire.—About seven or more years ago he was induced to proceed to that Island for the purpose of personally attending to a suit in Chancery there against the executors of a Merchant, who had died in the Island more than sixty thousand dollars in his debt, and after eight years litigation obtained a Decree in his favor; when he returned to his family here, but has lately been informed, that he will loose the fruits of all his assiduity & great sacrifices in the affair by the insolvency of the parties. However this circumstance, from his long residence in Jamaica, has afforded him the opportunity of acquiring a considerable knowledge of men & measures there.—Permit me, therefore, to add my name in favor of his application, and to subscribe myself, with particular attachment & regard,

Your Excellency's Most obedient humble servant

THOS M'KEAN

FC (PHi); in McKean's hand; at foot of text: "His Excellency President Jefferson"; endorsed in part by McKean: "Rough draft of a Letter to Presidt. Jefferson." Recorded in SJL as received 20 June with notation "Lenox to be agent Jamaica."

ENCLOSURE

Recommendation for Hugh Lennox

Being informed from unquestionable authority that William Savage Esquire, Agent for the United States, in the Island of Jamaica has resigned his appointment, and from the Great Mercantile intercourse between the United States and that Island, the residence of a Consul or Agent there is highly necessary, We therefore beg leave, from the knowledge we have, of the abilities & Integrity of Hugh Lennox of Philadelphia Merchant to recommend him, as a trust worthy person and one well qualified to fill the station of Consul or Agent for the United States of America, in the Island of Jamaica, to which place he will immediately repair on his appointment.—
Philadelphia 15th. June 1805

David Jackson	P. Muhlenberg
Wm. Turnbull	Edward Fox
Blair McClenachan	John Sergeant
J. B. Mc.Kean	Geo: Taylor Jr:
John Stillé	Andw. Pettit
Benjn Stillé	Chs. Biddle
Thomas English	John Barker
William Bell	Robt. Ralston
Robert Smith	Saml. Yorke
Thos. Ewing	Ralph Peacock
Francs. Gurney	Andw. Bayard
Danl Smith	Joseph Ball

RC (DNA: RG 59, LAR); in a clerk's hand, signed by all; at foot of text: "His Excellency Thomas Jefferson Esquire, President of the United States of America"; endorsed by TJ: "Lenox Hugh to be agent Jamaica v. Savage."

In a letter of 9 July to Gallatin, David Jackson, Jr., repeated his recommendation of LENNOX, who had "suffered in his property considerably by British depredations" and whose "commerce and accquaintance with Jamaica has been more extensive than any other" Philadelphia merchant (same; endorsed by TJ: "Lenox Hugh to be agt. Jamaica v. Savage").

Notes on William Sprigg

Sprigg Wm. of Cincinnati, an excellent man a lawyer brot up under J. T. Mason, now a principal judge of Ohio, would go to Michigan, because less laborious than his present duties which are beyond his force.
he is very much valued in Ohio.
whether he speaks French, not known.
from Colo. Worthington.

Mr. Smith also named him as the best appointment we could make, but at the same time regretting his loss to their state.

June 17. 05.
Mr. Sprigg of Geo. T. tells me that Wm. Sprigg is an accomplished Lat. & Greek scholar, reads French, but does not speak it, but has a remakable[1] aptness at learning languages. of a very weakly bodily habit. he has often heard J. T. Mason say he was the best lawyer that ever left his office.

MS (DNA: RG 59, LAR); in TJ's hand; written on verso of part of an address sheet by Charles Willson Peale, postmarked Philadelphia, 13 June, that probably covered his letter to TJ of that day; endorsed by TJ: "Sprigg Wm. to be judge Michigan v. Huntington."

TJ appointed William Sprigg a judge of MICHIGAN Territory on 30 June (Appendix I). Like Samuel Huntington, however, Sprigg declined the appointment (Thomas Worthington to TJ, 22 Sep.).

MR. SPRIGG OF GEO. T.: William O. Sprigg.

[1] Thus in MS.

From William Fuqua

SIR Crews Vill June 18th. 1805

In runing som lines betwen my land and a tract of land you sold mr. Thos. Warren in Fluvanas County I find the linds Rether interfer with Each other—and in looking in The Land office I Cannot find—whoues name the land was Pattorned in you sold warren—allso a Plat that I have seene apears that the Land of warrens was Survaied at the Request of you for Thos Warren—information as to the Patton or other wis will be thakfully Red.—and a few Linns to me at this Plase will Come to hand and the favor Acknowledged by your friend and

M. Obdt Hbl. servt. WILLIAM FUQUA

RC (DLC); endorsed by TJ as received 27 June and so recorded in SJL.

From William Henry Harrison

DEAR SIR Vincennes 18th. June 1805.

I have the honor to enclose herewith a list containing the names of the five persons whom I have selected for the Legislative Council of this Territory agreeably to the directions contained in your letter of the 28th. of April—In making this selection I have conformed as far as possible to the restrictions laid down in your letter. Four out of the five are I believe Staunch Republicans but both of the persons nominated from this County (Knox) were Federallists & as it is the largest in the Territory it was necessary to take one of them—I have chosen the one that was best informed & who appeared to be the choice of the Republicans of the County—Local policy was altogether the cause of the nomination of two persons whose politics as to the affairs of the Union were so essentially varient from those of nine tenths of the people—in all our elections the Contest lay between those who were in favor of adopting the second grade of Government & the admission of Negroes & those who were opposed to these measures.

I am satisfied that no Combinations exist amongst the Indians in this part of the Country to effect any purpose that would prove injurious to the United States I believe that the Delawares who reside on the West side of the Mississippi have made an other attempt to induce those of their Nation who live on White River to join them in a war against the Osages, but I hope that the measures I have taken to Counteract them will be effectual.

The Turtle is certainly doing us all the mischief he can, & altho' he has little or no influence with his own Tribe he has contrived to get the chiefs of the Putawatimies of St Josephs altogether under his controle—they could however be easily detached from him & he himself brought to a proper sense of his duty & his entire dependance on us if they were not encouraged & supported not only by the Traders but as I really believe by the Agent of the United States at Fort Wayne—

I have lately sent Colo. Vigo to the Miamis & Putawatimies to enquire into the causes of their uneasiness & to discover the Authors of the bad Advice which has been given them—I expect him to return in a few days & have no doubt of receiving very satisfactory information.

The Piankeshaws the Weas the Eel River Miamis the Putawatimies of the Wabash & the Kickapoos of the Vermilion River have lately been with me & I am persuaded that they are more warmly attached to us than they have ever been.—

It gives me great satisfaction to find that the management of the Indian Department has received from the people the same approbation which has been so justly bestowed upon the other measures of your administration. If my humble exertions have had the smallest tendency to produce this desireable result I shall always consider it as the most fortunate circumstance of my life—I have indeed exerted myself to execute your orders & to conduct the Government you have entrusted to me upon principles that you would approve—

Relying upon your indulgence & forgivness (if there should be any thing improper in what I am about to say) I must beg you to take into consideration the propriety of making a small addition to my salary as Superintendant of Indian Affairs I receive for my services in that Department 800 Dolls. per Annum which is Considerably less than any of the Agents or Sub Agents are allowed—& my duties & expenses are more than double—I have never received a single Six pence either directly or indirectly for issuing of licenses to Trade with the Indians—a practice which gave to my predecessor at least 1000 Dollrs. per Annum & from which it is said my Deputy at Detroit has received equal advantage—Exacting fees of this kind was one of the Charges brought against Govr. Sargent in the year 1800 & Congress admitted its propriety by declaring that his conduct had been Correct. As there was no law however which Authorised the receipt of such fees I condemned the practice upon my first entrance into the Territory & have never departed from the Resolution I then made of never taking a fee for the discharge of my official duties—The situation of the District of Louisiana was handled different from this Territory. A fee of 25 Dollars was by an act of the Government allowed to the Spanish Lieut. Governor for every Indian license & as the law was not repealed by us I should have been authorised & it was my intention to have taken the fee but upon my arrival at St Louis I was induced to give up the Idea for the following reason—It appeared to me to be a matter of importance to keep out of Louisiana that band of unprincipled Traders who have done so much Mischief in this Territory—& my Construction of the Treaty with Great Britain did not allow to the Subjects of that power the right of Trading there at all

An investigation was necessary to determine who came within the description that were to be permitted to trade & had I received the fees I should have been a Judge in my own case & it might have been supposed that the examination was not made with sufficient Strictness.—I mention these circumstances not for the purpose of blazoning forth my own disinterestedness but that the whole circumstances of the case may be before you—& I conceived it to be the more necessary as the Secretary of War has been informed by Captn Stoddard & Major Bruff who were my immediate predecessors in the Executive duties of Louisiana that they had received the Customary fee for issuing Indian licenses—Whether my application is or is not successful I must beg you my dear Sir to believe that it will not diminish my zeal & industry in the performance of my duties—Our legislature will meet on the 29th of July. One of their first acts will be a declaration of their political Creed in an address of thanks for the attention you have ever manifested for their interests—

I Have the Honor to be With the greatest Regard & attachment Dr Sir your Huml Servt. WILLM. H. HARRISON

RC (DLC); at foot of text: "Thomas Jefferson President of the United States"; endorsed by TJ as received 25 July and so recorded in SJL. Enclosure not found, but see below.

FIVE PERSONS: in addition to John Rice Jones of KNOX County, Harrison selected Benjamin Chambers, Samuel Gwathmey, Pierre Menard, and John Hay (Logan Esarey, ed., *Messages and Letters of William Henry Harrison*, 2 vols. [Indianapolis, 1922; repr., New York, 1975], 1:127; TJ to Madison, 29 Mch.).

The AGENT at Fort Wayne was William Wells, who during the previous year had alerted the administration to Little Turtle's discontent with recent developments (TJ to Dearborn, 16 Dec. 1804).

Harrison commissioned Francis VIGO on 26 May to meet with the Miamis, Potawatomis, and Eel River Indians. At a council held at Fort Wayne on 21 June between Vigo and representatives of the Miamis as well as a delegation of the Delawares, to whom Harrison had dispatched John Gibson, the tribes were invited to meet with Harrison at Vincennes so that Harrison could clarify the treaty signed between the United States and the Delawares and Piankashaws on 18 Aug. 1804 (Douglas E. Clanin and Ruth Dorrel, eds., *The Papers of William Henry Harrison, 1800-1815*, 3 microfilm reels [Indianapolis, 1993], 2:195; Esarey, *Messages and Letters*, 1:137-9; TJ to the Senate, 15 Nov. 1804).

MY PREDECESSOR: that is, Arthur St. Clair, governor of the Northwest Territory before its division. Charles Jouett was the U.S. Indian agent stationed at DETROIT (ANB; Vol. 42:488-9).

To Gilbert Stuart

June 18. 05.

Th: Jefferson pr[esents his compliments to Mr. Stewart,] and begs leave to send [him the inclosed for the trouble he gave him] in taking the head á [*la antique*. Mr. Stewart seemed to contemplate] having an engraving m[ade either from that or the first portrait;] he is free to use the one [or the other at his choice; the one not pro]posed to be used Th:J. [will be glad to receive at Mr. Stewart's con]venience; the other wh[en he shall be done with it.]

RC (NNMus); incomplete, consisting of left half of page only, including date, with text in brackets supplied from Charles Henry Hart, "Life Portraits of Thomas Jefferson," *McClure's Magazine*, 11 (1898), 48. Recorded in SJL at 17 June.

THE INCLOSED: according to TJ's financial records, on 18 June he paid Gilbert Stuart "for drawing my portrait 100. D." (MB, 2:1156).

TAKING THE HEAD: the "Medallion Portrait" (see illustration in this volume). TJ sat for the FIRST PORTRAIT by Stuart in May 1800 (Vol. 31:xliv-xlv).

From Jonathan Williams

SIR military academy U.S. West Point June 18. 1805.

among the Duties I felt myself bound to perform on resuming my Station at the Head of the Corps of Engineers, that of reviving the United States military Philosophical Society did not appear to be the least important.

The first, and most pleasing charge that devolves upon me, is to present the thanks of the Society for the honour you have done it, by becoming its Patron; and particularly for the very favourable sentiments expressed in your Letter of December 25. 1802.

To further the views of this Establishment, it became necessary and proper, to associate to it, the most distinguished Characters in our Country, & for this purpose, it was proposed to select some of the members of both Houses of Congress whose professional Walks have been best adapted to the objects of the Society; But apprehensive that offence might be taken in consequence of Omissions, which must be the result of Ignorance of individual Characters, it has been suggested, as the safer mode, to elect them all: This perhaps might seem presumptuous;—it has therefore been thought prudent to suspend the matter in hopes that you would obligingly intimate what in your Judgment would be the most proper.

I have the honour to inclose a model of an intended Circular to all new members, and we propose to have also printed, or engraved, a Certificate of admission as soon as the Seal shall be executed. These objects with postage, stationary, & other necessary expenditures, will require a small Fund, which we had thoughts of raising by an annual Tax on the members; but it occurred that, owing to their dispersed State, the Collection would be impossible even if there should be an uniform disposition to pay.

As this Institution is evidently for public Benefit, could not a small annual supply be appropriated from the contingencies of the War Department, without deviating from any established Rule? Of this we presume not to judge, but hope you will not think it indecorous to ask the Question.

A List of respectable Characters now stand nominated for the next Election, & you will oblige the Society by adding such names as you may think proper.

I have the honour to be with perfect Respect Sir Your most obedient servant

JONA WILLIAMS
President of the U.S. military Philosophical Society

RC (DLC); addressed: "Thomas Jefferson Esqe Patron of the United States military Philosophical Society"; endorsed by TJ as received 23 June and so recorded in SJL. Enclosure: circular to new members of the U.S. Military Philosophical Society, dated 18 June and written from the Military Academy at West Point, announcing that with TJ's consent the president of the United States may be considered to be the society's "perpetual Patron," soliciting the aid of members' "instructive communications," and setting the permanent meeting place at the academy (MS in same; in Alexander Macomb's hand with blanks to be filled in for the date of election of the member and the signature of the president of the society and signed by him as secretary to the society as "A true Copy from the minutes").

For the UNITED STATES MILITARY PHILOSOPHICAL SOCIETY, see Vol. 39: 145-6.

From George Blake

SIR Boston 19. June 1805

Your letter of 12th. march, with the petition of John Southack inclosed, I had the honor duely to receive;

The Judge who presided in the trial of this convict, having, since his return from the Southward, never been in town, until the late session of the Circuit court, I have had no opportunity of confering with him more seasonably on the subject concerning which his opinion was required.

I am now authorised to state, as the decided opinion of the court, with which my own is perfectly coincident, that the Culprit has not the least pretence of claim to a mitigation of his sentence. The fraud of which he is convict was in itself of a flagrant character; besides which it appeared on the trial, to have been but an item in a series of transactions of a similar nature in which the Defendant had long been concerned—

The strong belief which I entertained that the Judges cou'd not, under all the circumstances of the case, recommend this person as a proper object for Executive interference was the reason that I did not take extraordinary pains, to obtain more promptly the result of their deliberations—I have the honor to be with the highest respect & mo perfect Esteem—Yr. Obed St GEO: BLAKE

RC (DLC); endorsed by TJ as received 25 June and so recorded in SJL.

From Henry Dearborn, with Jefferson's Approval

SIR. War Department June 19. 1805

I have the honor of proposing for your approbation the following Promotions and appointments in the Militia of the District of Columbia

Major John McKinney to be promoted to the rank of Lieutenant Colonel Commandant of the 2d Legion, vice, Colo. Peyton resigned.

John Cohagan to be appointed Captain of a Rifle Company, vice Turner resigned.

Frederick Way to be appointed Lieutenant of Ditto, vice, William A Harper suspended by Sentence of a Court Martial, and

Ephraim Mills to be appointed Ensign of Ditto, vice, Smith resigned

Accept Sir, the assurances of my high respect and consideration

H. DEARBORN

[*Approval by TJ*:]

June 19. 05

Approved TH: JEFFERSON

RC (PHi); in a clerk's hand, signed by Dearborn; at foot of text: "President of the United States." FC (Lb in RG 107, LSP).

From Albert Gallatin

DEAR SIR Wednesday 19th June 1805

I enclose for your signature an Act making Cayahoga the port of entry of the district of Erie. It is dated as far back as 12th instt., in order that it may precede the commission already issued in favor of Mr Wallworth as collector.

With great respect Your obedt. Servt. ALBERT GALLATIN

RC (DLC); at foot of text: "The President of the United States"; endorsed by TJ as received from the Treasury Department on 19 June and "Cayahoga" and so recorded in SJL. Enclosure not found.

TJ issued a recess COMMISSION for John Walworth as collector of Erie District on 13 June (Appendix I).

To Charles Willson Peale

Dear Sir Washington June 19. 05

Your favors of the 13. & 15th. are recieved. if I rightly understand them, you have in hand one Polygraph $17\frac{5}{8}$ I. by $11\frac{5}{8}$ I. and another of 16. by 11. both of which will write to the bottom of a 4to. sheet. the larger one is that which will suit best as a present for my friend, and therefore I will ask you to send on that.

The smaller one of 16. by 11. I observe is only $1\frac{3}{8}$ longer than my 8vo. one & of the same width, for mine is $14\frac{5}{8}$ by 11. it's writing to the bottom of a 4to. page is an ample compensation for the $1\frac{3}{8}$ I. additional length. because the taking a reef in the sheet & having to replace the paper as must be done with mine in writing a quarto page, gives some trouble. if I had not been so humored by you already as to be ashamed, I should propose the recieving that in exchange for my small one, and paying any difference which might compensate the trouble. I placed a standing order at the stage office which they promised to observe, to charge to me the stage-postage, going & coming, on all these machines, which I hope they do, but which, as they chuse to bring in their bill but once a quarter may sometimes be unattended to by them, & escape my knolege. I pray you always to inform the office there that they will recieve their pay here. Accept affectionate salutations. Th: Jefferson

RC (TxU); at foot of text: "Mr. Peale." PoC (DLC); endorsed by TJ as a letter of 17 June and recorded in SJL under that date.

From Philippe Reibelt

Monsieur le President! Baltimore le 19 Juin 1805.

Encouragè par les Amateurs des Arts, qui ont concus l'ideè de la Lotterie cijointe, (et qui pretendent connaitre les Moeurs du pays) d'en presenter un Avertissement a Votre Excellence, (les francais se proposent d'y inviter aussi Mr. et Mme. Turreau)—je m'y prête quoique avec quelque repugnance—En Vous priant:

1) de ne pas le prendre en mauvaise Graçe, si çela ne seroit pas bien conforme au respect distinguè, qu'on Vous doit, et que je porte pour Vous sous tous les rapports;

2) Si cela n'est pas disconvenable, de le communiquer aussi a Messieurs les Secretaires d'Etat, Vos parens et Amis.

Daignez accepter mes hômages les plus purs et les plus sinceres.

Reibelt.

EDITORS' TRANSLATION

MISTER PRESIDENT! Baltimore, 19 June 1805

Patrons of the arts, who conceived the attached lottery and claim to understand the customs of this country, have asked me to present this announcement to your excellency (they are also seeking the support of Mr. and Madame Turreau). I do so reluctantly, asking you:

1) not to take umbrage if it does not correspond to the respect you deserve and in which I hold you, in all regards;

2) to share it with the cabinet heads, your family, and friends, if that is not inappropriate.

Please accept my most sincere and faithful regards. REIBELT

RC (DLC); endorsed by TJ as received 19 June and so recorded in SJL; with calculations by TJ, adding $55.75 to $33.45 (as 60 percent) for a total of $89.20 (see TJ to Reibelt, 21 June).

ENCLOSURE

List of Copies of Paintings and Other Works for a Lottery

having received from a celebrated Artist in Swizerland a few Copies from original paintings of the best Masters, executed in a new Manner of his own inventing, so true, that it is allmost impossible, to distinguish the one from the other—and wishing, to make them generally known to the Lovers of the Arts—It is proposed, as the best means of distribution, to dispose of them in a Lotterie, consisting of 4 pairs of these pictures—neatly framed—

1st. Lot	one pair, after originals of	Both & Dujardin	150 Doll.
2	ditto	Loutherbourg	140
3	ditto	Claude Lorrain	150
4	ditto	Van Berghem	80
	to which will be added:		
5	a Telescope, when drawn, measuring 16 feets—(from Swizerland)		100
6	one Set of the admired nat. history of Perroquets, vel. pap—in 4to.—with text		140
7	the Likewise admired (new) botanic-work by Duhamel, colored—vel. pap. 3 Vol. in folio		110
8 to 24	inclusive—Making 17 Chances of said Pictures of Perroquets		230
	in folio—viz: 2 of 10 peices each; 2 of 8; 4 of 6; 9. of 4	} 96 pieces.	
			1100
25	The Menagerie of Paris, 1 V. in fol. Engrav—with Text		20
26	one pair of Engrav. by a German Artist of acknowledged talents (Kolb)—the Bachanal, and the Dance, with an other Engrav, the Oack of Palemon by Gessner		16

27	the same 2 former Engrav—with 4 other Landscapes by Kolb, and the Children of Netscher, painted by Netscher, engr. by Geyser	15
28, 29 & 30—three Sets of 3 Engrav. by Kolb: the Going by Water, the Young Shepherd, and the Conversation—10 each		30
31, 32 & 33—three Sets of 2 Engrav. by the Same autor: the Baders, and the Shepherd resting near his flock—10 each		30
34, 35 & 36—three Sets of 3 Engrav. by the Same hand: the hunting of Stag, the hunting of Lion, and the fall of the damned—10 each		30.
		1241.

the whole will require 110 Subscribers at 10 Doll. each, so that there will be one pièce to every three tickets.

As soon as the Number shall be Compleated, the place and time of the execution of this Lotterie will be announced.

NB. Mr. Robert Gilmor d'ici a eu la Complaisance de diriger l'encadrement des tableaux d'apres le Gout d'ici et a pris 3 billets avant de partir au Niagara.

MS (DLC: TJ Papers, 150:26243); undated; in Reibelt's hand.

VAN BERGHEM: probably a reference to Nicolaes Berchem, a major Dutch painter of the seventeenth century (Jane Turner, ed., *Dictionary of Art*, 34 vols. [New York, 1996], 3:757-60).

BOTANIC-WORK: probably a recently published three-volume edition of *Traité des arbres et arbustes que l'on cultive en France en pleine terre*, by Henri Louis Duhamel de Monceau (William Fleischer, *Annuaire de la librairie* [Paris, 1802], 271).

The MENAGERIE OF PARIS was almost certainly the folio volume of prints of animals of France's natural history museum, published in 1801 as *La ménagerie du Muséum national d'histoire naturelle*, by Étienne de Lacépède and Georges Cuvier.

ROBERT GILMOR: that is, "of this place was kind enough to oversee the picture framing in accordance with local tastes and bought three tickets before leaving for Niagara."

To Robert Smith

DEAR SIR Washington June 19. 05

I have had under consideration the letter of Lieutt. Smith commander of Gun boat No. 1. from Charleston, respecting the capture of the Two friends, a registered ship, *at the bar* of Charleston. his idea, if that be his idea, of having a 16. gun brig with a regular officer to do the duty of the revenue cutter, is condemned by our own experience. the qualities which make a good officer of the navy, make a bad master of a cutter. until we get our harbours well provided with gunboats, and have some of our brigs & schooners free to cruize in their aid in time of war, we had better rub along as we have done, and not attempt regulations which we are not yet prepared to enforce. but I think Lt. Smith might be instructed, whenever it is understood that a *privateer* of any nation is cruising off the harbor of Charleston, to go out with his gun-boat from time to time, and to see that no violation takes place within the jurisdictional line of 3 miles from the shore. the bar of Charleston is compleatly within that. he should arrest any vessel & crew committing violation within that distance, bring them in & deliver them up to the justice of the country, taking care not to undertake this but where his force is superior to that of the privateer, and taking care also to keep strictly within the 3. miles, for which purpose he should go out at once and make himself acquainted with that line by marks or otherwise. I submit all this however to your consideration & pray you if you see reason to doubt of such instructions; you will explain it to me & in the mean time suspend them. Accept affectionate salutations. TH: JEFFERSON

PoC (DLC); at foot of text: "The Secretary of the Navy." Notation in SJL: "Two friends."

LETTER OF LIEUTT. SMITH: TJ likely referred to a letter written by William Smith, the navy agent at Charleston, to Robert Smith, dated 6 June (RC in DNA, RG 45, MLR). In this letter, Smith described the 5 June CAPTURE OF THE TWO FRIENDS, a U.S.-registered ship carrying a cargo of British dry goods and books for the Charleston Library Society, by the French privateer *L'Emerance*. The *Two Friends* was subsequently recaptured on 19 June by a British warship and carried to Jamaica, where the vessel was resold to its American owners and later completed its journey to Charleston in October (James Raven, *London Booksellers and American Customers: Transatlantic Literary Community and the Charleston Library Society, 1748-1811* [Columbia, S.C., 2002], 205-8; *Charleston Courier*, 6 and 7 June; Charleston *City Gazette and Daily Advertiser*, 7 June, 14 Oct.; *Alexandria Daily Advertiser*, 9 Aug.; Madison, *Papers, Sec. of State Ser.*, 9:456-9).

From William Jarvis

RESPECTED SIR Lisbon 20th. June 1805

Chance threw into my hands a present to you, from Monsr. Chretien, an ancient Physician of Montpellier, of a treatise on the method of applying external remedies in different disorders, & afforded me the pleasure to address you under date of the 15th Ultimo. I forwarded it by the Ship Frances Captn Nicholls for Boston, with a letter from the Author & that I took the liberty to write, in it.

A few days since I was at two large Wine Vaults upon the opposite Side of the River to look at some Wines; but altho' several good Wines were shewn me, I found in the technical Phraseology of the Wine Merchants, they had all been 'cut,' or in plain language, that the produce of five to six estates, the dry with the sweet, had been mixed to-gether to fit them for the English market, & in neither of those Vaults of 800 to a 1,000 pipes each, was there a single one of pure

Wine except Cacavallos. By this mixture the peculiar flavour of the several estates is lost. In a few days I shall make another excursion when I hope to be more successful. The Gentleman from whom I had the last Carasqueira & Arruda, having disposed of the whole of these Wines & not purchasing the Vintage the last two years, obliges me to take this method to obtain some of a flavour that I think will suit your taste. I shall ship a pipe by one of the first Vessels bound to the Southward, and agreeable to your wishes Sir, draw for the amount of both in the course of the summer or fall.

Before this will come to hand the dispatches from Messrs. Monroe & Pinckney forwarded by Mr Dalton will no doubt have informed you Sir of the event of the Negotiation with Spain; A determination on the part of that Court as impolitic as unjust. What may be the decision of Government I cannot say, but of this I feel certain, that it will be the most for the honor & interest of our Country which an enlarged & profound view of the subject shall dictate, and that our Citizens have such full confidence in the Wisdom, justice & moderation of your administration as heartily to join in such measures as you may deem the most advantageous. But I cannot help thinking that the Cabinet of the Tuilleries will never allow this difference to terminate in a rupture, & that such propositions will be made from this quarter to Mr Monroe as will enable government with honor to avoid the extremity; for the advantage We should derive in a contest with Spain from our local situation affording every facility We could wish for the invasion of their Colonies, from the similarity of climate fitting our Citizens for the contest without being exposed to the terrible mortality which so great a change commonly occasions in the Northern European troops sent to this quarter of the globe, from the at least doubtful attachment of the Spanish Continental Colonies to the mother Country & the disposition which it is natural to infer from the Political & Commercial disadvantages under which they labour, they must have to obtain their independence, from our great financial resources and the great assistance to be desired from the British Navy, (which Government would no doubt make a treaty with us on our own terms) must be as evident not to have much weight with that Cabinet. Should however Military Ambition have shut out all sense of justice from that Court, and force Government into a War, I am certain it will be undertaken & carried on with such spirit as to convince the world that our forbearance is owing to our moderation & that We are not inferior to either of those Nations in their boasted energy of character, courage & conduct. I must however truly say that I do not wish our Country to resort to Arms to prove points which have satisfactorily been proved in your excellent Notes on Virginia & practically established in our revolutionary War, but have a much greater ambition that the palm of political Wisdom should be conceded to us, by a continuance of Peace, enabling us to carry into execution the plans you have proposed for encreasing our prosperity & securing our happiness—

With the most perfect Veneration I am Sir Yr. Mo: Ob: & Hble servt
William Jarvis

RC (DLC); at foot of text: "Thomas Jefferson Esqr."; endorsed by TJ as received 16 Sep. and so recorded in SJL.

mr dalton: that is, Thomas Dulton (see Charles Pinckney to TJ, at 22 May and 4 June).

From James Sullivan

Sir
Boston 20th June 1805

I was exceedingly honoured by your condescention in your letter of the 21st. of may. The mail had scarcely gone from Boston with mine of the 14th. of april before I deeply regretted having troubled you with it. I then knew, on a moments reflection, that there was no vacancy, and that it would be ineligible for me to leave this State. The same friendly feelings which dictated your letter will consign that one to the flames.

The enemies of the present administration had suggested a report that you were adverse to the person whom the republicans here had agreed on for cheif magistrate. I had met an enemy where I never expected to have found one, assailing my moral character, but after having spent thirty seven years out of sixty from my birth, in public offices I did not expect now to have an attack on that ground which had ever been sacred before. Trying as this, and other slanders were, I did not loose the balance until the calumny of your having no confidence in me came into circulation; nor then, until it was traced to one who has pretended to be a republican. I am, however, now satisfied on this point.

there will never be an end to the malice and falshoods of this wicked combination who assume the appellations of federalists in order to deceive the people. those of them who hold the higher grade have become ashamed of low abuse in regard to the cheif national magistrate. They are now representing him as being in favour of a monarchy; but the people are too wise to listen to them. They want a civil war, but they have no way to introduce it; their prætorian guards are disbanded, and the militia will not make war on their own freedom. their hope from England declines as the misfortunes of that nation are multiplied.

Wishing you every felicity that patriotism, public and private virtues can claim I remain with the purest affection and duty your very humble Servant

JA SULLIVAN

RC (DLC); at foot of text: "President Jefferson"; endorsed by TJ as received 28 June and so recorded in SJL.

MINE OF THE 14TH. OF APRIL: letter not found, but see TJ to Sullivan, 21 May.

CALUMNY OF YOUR HAVING NO CONFIDENCE IN ME: Sullivan learned that Joseph Blake, the father of the Massachusetts district attorney, George Blake, spread the slander against him. Sullivan refuted the charges, including one that he accepted $3,000 in hush money, in his address "To the Publick" of 2 Apr. (*Newburyport Herald*, 12 Mch.; Boston *Columbian Centinel*, 13 Mch.; Boston *Repertory*, 12 Apr.; Sullivan to TJ, 7 Jan. 1806).

From Matthew Anderson

SIR

Exchange 21st. June 1805

Your favour of 15th. Feby last with a Small Box containg Eggs of the fine Italian Silk worm was duly recieved, and would have been immediately answered, but Mrs. Anderson wished first to try whether was any difference between them and her own stock. they both began to Hatch on the first day of may, and finished their work about the middle of the Present month—there is little or no difference except that the Cocouns from your Stock appear to be wound rather tighter & Mrs. Anderson has saved from them altogether. I really think it strange that more of our Country women does not raise them. the process is simple & might be profitable. the Eggs from which 25 or 30 yds of silk and the worms from which I suppose about 30 yds of silk may be manufactured, may be fed for a few days after hatching on a table 4. feet square and as they grow require more & more room—the room in which Mrs. Anderson feeds is 40. by 18. which she finds full small the last 2 or 3 weeks. the first fortnight a few two or 3 small girls are sufficient to feed them. the balance of the time they are Eating unless you have Mulbery trees very Convenient a Horse and tumbril will be necessary. I make however nothing less from my farm on Acct. of the worms & we wear little else but silk during the warm season. with us the Eggs are deposited on sheets of paper and when they hatch remain & feed on the paper for several days. I would give you the whole process, but that several authors have treated on the subject which I expect you have read. If you should ever have an inclination to Visit Gloucester it would give me Singular Pleasure to see you at my Cottage and if you could be here about the first of June you would see the worms some Eating & others working. Mrs.

Anderson unites in best wishes & respectful Complements to your Self & Household.

Yours Sincerely M ANDERSON

RC (DLC); endorsed by TJ as received 6 July and so recorded in SJL.

To John Armstrong of New York

DEAR SIR Washington June 21. 05.

Mr. Robert Gamble, son of Colo. Gamble a merchant of Richmond proposing to go to France & England on his commercial pursuits, the father asked from me a letter of introduction to you. I was the more surprised at this, as his federalism had distinguished itself by personal hostility to me, as also to mr Madison & Colo. Monroe. yet having made the request, I felt myself bound in delicacy to give him a civil answer. I informed him that it had been a rule with me in my present office never to give a letter of introduction, but that I should shortly have occasion to write to you & would mention his son to you. of the young man I know nothing, never before having heard of him. he has two sisters married to two most estimable republicans, for whom I have great friendship, & on whose account, as well as the peculiarity of my standing with the father, I will ask your notice of mr Gamble & even that you will let him know I had done so. the father even asked a letter of credit for his son: but this I declined. he the father has been twice bankrupt, tho' is now deemed in good circumstances: but has never been deemed delicate in his pecuniary dealings. not knowing how this is to go, I will only add my friendly salutations & assurances of great esteem & respect TH: JEFFERSON

PoC (DLC); at foot of text: "Genl. Armstrong"; endorsed by TJ.

LETTER OF INTRODUCTION: see Robert Gamble to TJ, 11 June, and TJ's reply on 15 June.

To Albert Gallatin

TH:J. TO MR GALLATIN June 21. 05.

the revival of antient slanders under pretext of new evidence, has induced Th:J. to do, what he never took the trouble of doing before, to revise some papers he happens to have here (for most of that date are at Monticello) and to make a statement of the transactions as they really took place, with a view that they shall be known to his friends at least. under this view he taxes mr Gallatin with reading the inclosed, altho' it extends to three sheets of paper. affectionate salutations.

RC (NHi: Gallatin Papers). Not recorded in SJL.

REVIVAL OF ANTIENT SLANDERS: under the heading "FACTS which will aid the future historian in delineating the true character of the present executive of the United States," the Boston *Repertory* of 31 May published a letter from Thomas Turner, a former member of the Virginia House of Delegates, who substantiated charges that had been aired in discussions of the Massachusetts legislature and appeared in the press during the winter. Turner started by elaborating on longstanding critiques of TJ's conduct as governor during the British invasion of Virginia. He also confirmed that TJ funded and approved of James Callender's *The Prospect Before Us*. He added to the record TJ's purported attempt to pay off a loan of specie from Gabriel Jones with depreciated paper money. In a lengthy discussion of TJ's attempted seduction of Elizabeth Moore Walker, Turner stressed that TJ's harassment had continued for 10 years, ceasing only due to "the inflexible virtue of the lady" and TJ's "heart wounding remorse." Turner claimed to have seen the correspondence between TJ and John Walker wherein TJ had acknowledged his guilt and completely exonerated Elizabeth Walker of any blame. The editor of the *Repertory* put a part of Turner's letter that concerned Sally Hemings into a separate note. Rumors of TJ's relationship with Hemings, Turner stated, were "unquestionably true," and their "eldest son (called Beverly)" was "well known to many." The letter was widely reprinted in Federalist newspapers (Leonard, *General Assembly*, 208, 212; Malone, *Jefferson*, 5:14-17; Isaac Story to TJ, 8 Feb.). For TJ's response to the charges in the *Repertory*, see also TJ to Robert Smith, 1 July.

ENCLOSURE

Chronology of Jefferson's Actions during the British Invasion of Virginia in 1780-1781

[on or before 21 June 1805]

Richmond. 1780. Dec. 31. at 8. A.M. the Governor recieves the first intelligence that 27. sail of ships had entered Chesapeak bay, & were in the morning of the 29th. just below Willoughby's point [the Southern cape of James river] their destination unknown.

Jan. 2. at 10. A.M. information recieved that they had entered James river, their advance being at Warrasqueak bay. orders were immediately given for calling in the militia, $\frac{1}{4}$ from some, & $\frac{1}{2}$ from other counties. the members of the legislature, which rises this day, are the bearers of the orders to their respective counties. the Governor directs the removal of the Records into the country, and the transportation of the military stores from Richmond to Westham [on the river 7. miles above] there to be carried across the river.

Jan. 3. at 8. P.M. the enemy are said to be a little below Jamestown; convenient for landing if Williamsburg is their object.

4. at 5. A.M. information is recieved that they had passed Kennon's & Hood's the evening before with a strong Easterly wind, which determines their object to be either Petersburg or Richmond. the Governor now calls in the whole militia from the adjacent counties.

At 5. P.M. information that at 2. P.M. they were landed & drawn up at Westover [on the North side of the river & 25. miles below Richmond] and consequently Richmond their destination. orders are now given to discontinue waggoning the military stores from Richmond to Westham, & to throw them across the river directly at Richmond.

The Governor having attended to this till an hour & a half in the night then rode up to the foundery [1. mile below Westham] ordered Capts. Boush & Irish, & mr Hylton to continue all night waggoning to Westham the arms & stores still at the Foundery, to be thrown across the river at Westham, then proceeded to Westham to urge the pressing the transportation there across the river, and thence went to Tuckahoe [8. miles above & on the same side of the river] to see after his family which he had sent that far in the course of the day. he arrived there at 1. aclock in the night.

Jan. 5. Early in the morning he carried his family across the river there, and sending them to Fine creek [8. miles higher up] went himself to Britton's on the S. side of the river. [opposite to Westham] finding the arms &c in a heap near the shore, & exposed to be destroyed by cannon from the North bank, he had them removed under cover of a point of land near by. he proceeded to Manchester [opposite to Richmond].[1] the enemy had arrived at Richmond at 1. P.M. having found that nearly the whole arms had been got there from Richmond, he set out for Chetwood's to meet with Baron Steuben, who had appointed that place as a rendezvous & Head quarters; but not finding him there, & understanding he would be at Colo. Fleming's [6. miles above Britton's] he proceeded thither. the enemy had now a detachment at Westham, and sent a deputation from the city of Richmond to the Governor, at Colo. Fleming's, to propose terms for ransoming the safety of the city, which terms he rejected.

Jan. 6. The Governor returned to Britton's, had measures taken, more effectually to secure the books & papers there. the enemy having burnt some houses & stores, left Richmond, after 24. hours stay there, & encamped at Four mile creek [8. or 10. miles below] & the Governor went to look to his family at Fine creek.

Jan. 7. He returned to Britton's to see further to the arms there, exposed on the ground to heavy rains which had fallen the night before, & then proceeded to Manchester, & lodged there. the enemy encamped at Westover.

Jan. 8. At half after 7. A.M. he crossed over to Richmond, & resumed his residence there. the enemy are still retained in their encampment at Westover by an Easterly wind. Colo. John Nicholas has now 300. militia at the Forest [6. miles off from Westover] Genl. Nelson 200. at Charles city, Courthouse [8. miles below Westover] Gibson 1000. and Baron Steuben 800. on the South side the river.

Jan. 9. The enemy are still encamped at Westover.

Jan. 10. At 1. P.M. they embark: & the wind having shifted a little to the North of the West, & pretty fresh, they fall down the river. Baron Steuben[2] marches for Hood's where their passage may be checked. he reaches Bland's mills in the evening, within 9. miles of Hood's.

Jan. 11. At 8. A.M. the wind due West & strong they make good their retreat.

During this period time & place have been minutely cited, in order that those who think there was any remissness in the movements of the Governor, may lay their finger on the point, and say when & where it was. hereafter less detail will suffice.

Soon after this, General Phillips having joined Arnold with a reinforcement of 2000. men, they advanced again up to Petersburg, & about the last of April to Manchester. the Governor had remained constantly in and about Richmond, exerting all his powers for collecting militia, and providing such means for the defence of the state as it's exhausted resources admitted. never assuming a guard, & with[3] only the river between him & the enemy, his lodgings were frequently within 4. 5. or 6. miles of them.

M. de la Fayette, about this time, arrived at Richmond with some continental troops, with which, & the militia collected, he continued to occupy that place, and the North bank of the river, while Phillips & Arnold held Manchester & the South bank. but Lord Cornwallis, about the middle of May joining them with the main Southern army, M. de la Fayette was obliged to retire. the enemy crossed the river, & advanced up into the country about 50. miles, & within 30. miles of Charlottesville, at which place the legislature being to meet in June, the Governor proceeded to his seat at Monticello, 2. or 3. miles from it. his office was now near expiring, the country under invasion by a powerful army, no services but military of any avail, unprepared by his line of life and education for the command of armies, he believed it right not to stand in the way of talents better fitted than his own to the cicumstances under which the country was placed. he therefore himself proposed to his friends in the legislature, that Genl. Nelson, who commanded the militia of the state, should be appointed Governor, as he was sensible that the union of the civil & military power in the same hands at this time, would greatly facilitate military measures.[4] this appointment accordingly took place on the 12th. of June 1801.

This was the state of things, when, his office having actually expired, & no successor not yet in place,[5] Colo. Tarleton, with his regiment of horse, was detached by Ld. Cornwallis to surprise mr Jefferson[6] (whom they thought still in office) & the legislature now sitting in Charlottesville. the Speakers of the two houses, & some other members of the legislature were lodging with
ıne 23 mr Jefferson at Monticello. Tarleton, early in the morning, when within 10. miles of that place, detached a company of horse to secure him & his guests, & proceeded himself rapidly with his main body to Charlottesville, where he hoped to find the legislature unapprised of his movement. notice of it however had been brought, both to Monticello & Charlottesville, about sunrise. the Speakers, with their Colleagues, returned to Charlottesville, and with the other members of the legislature, had barely time, to get out of his way. mr Jefferson sent off his family, to secure them from danger, and was himself still at Monticello making arrangements for his own departure, when a Lieutt. Hudson arrived there at half speed, & informed him the enemy were then ascending the hill of Monticello. he departed immediately, & knowing that he would be pursued if he took the high road, he plunged into the woods of the adjoining mountain, where being at once safe, he proceeded to overtake his family. this is the famous adventure of Carter's mountain which has been so often resounded through the slanderous chronicles of federalism. but they have taken care never to detail the facts, lest these should shew that this favorite charge amounted to nothing more than that he did not remain in his house, & there singly fight a whole troop of horse, or suffer himself to be taken prisoner. having accompanied his family one day's journey, he returned to Monticello. Tarleton had retired after 18. hours stay in Charlottesville. mr

Jefferson then rejoined his family, and proceeded with them to an estate he had in Bedford, about 80. miles S.W. where, riding in his farm sometime after, he was thrown from his horse, & disabled from riding on horse back for a considerable time. but mr Turner finds it more convenient to give him this fall in his retreat before Tarleton, which had happened some weeks before, as a proof that he withdrew from a troop of horse with a precipitancy which Don Quixot would not have practised.[7]

the facts here stated most particularly, with date of time & place, are taken from notes made by the writer hereof, for his own satisfaction[8] at the time: the others are from memory but so well recollected that he is satisfied there is no material fact mistated. should any person undertake to contradict any particular on evidence which may at all merit the public respect, the writer will take the trouble (tho' not at all in the best situation for it) to produce the proofs in support of it. he finds indeed that of the persons whom he recollects to have been present on these occasions, few have survived the intermediate lapse of four & twenty years. yet he trusts that some, as well as himself, are yet among the living; and he is positively certain that no man can falsify any material fact here stated. he well remembers indeed that there were then, as there are at all times, some who blamed every thing done contrary to their own opinion, altho' their opinions were formed on a very partial knowledge of facts. the censures which have been hazarded by such men as mr Turner, are nothing but revivals of these half informed opinions. mr George Nicholas, then a very young man, but always a very honest one, was prompted by these persons to bring specific charges against mr Jefferson. the heads of these in writing were communicated thro' a mutual friend to mr Jefferson, who committed to writing also the heads of justification on each of them. I well remember[9] this paper, & believe the original of it still exists, and tho' framed when every real fact was fresh in the knolege of every one, this fabricated flight from Richmond was not among the charges stated in this paper, nor any charge against mr Jefferson for not fighting singly the troop of horse. mr Nicholas candidly relinquished further proceeding. the House of Representatives of Virginia pronounced an honorable sentence of entire approbation of mr Jefferson's conduct, and so much the more honorable as themselves had been witnesses to it. And mr George Nicholas took a conspicuous occasion afterwards, of his own free will, & when the matter was entirely at rest, to retract publicly the erroneous opinions he had been led into on that occasion, & to make just reparations by a candid acknolegement of them.

MS (DLC: TJ Papers, 150:26239-41); undated; entirely in TJ's hand, including brackets in text. Described as MS (2) of Document I of Notes and Documents Relating to the British Invasions in 1781, [31 Dec. 1780 to 26 July 1816]; see Vol. 4:258-68.

12TH. OF JUNE 1801: that is, 1781.

NOTICE OF IT HOWEVER: up to this point, TJ's manuscript was substantively identical to one he prepared, probably in 1796, in response to the widely circulated first Federalist criticisms of his conduct as wartime governor. The remainder of the manuscript is more clearly a response to the account attributed to Thomas TURNER, who claimed that TJ's "*flight*" from Monticello "was effected with such hurried abruptness, as to produce a fall from his horse, and a dislocation of the shoulder." According to Turner, TJ proceeded despite the injury to Poplar Forest, where he resigned his office. Because part of the earlier manuscript was based on notes that TJ entered "on scraps of paper taken out of my pocket at the moment," the Editors printed it, along with a third version dating from 1816 and some supporting documents, at 31 Dec. 1780 (Boston *Repertory*, 31 May; Vol. 4:256-78).

TJ also expanded on a brief passage he added to his first account that incorporated some comments by GEORGE NICHOLAS in a 1798 pamphlet. Having been the politician who brought SPECIFIC CHARGES against TJ as part of the inquiry of the Virginia House of Delegates into his conduct as governor, Nicholas announced that he no longer held an "unfavourable opinion" of TJ's "political conduct" and considered him "one of the most virtuous, as well as one of the ablest, of the American patriots" (Nicholas, *A Letter from George Nicholas, of Kentucky, to His Friend, in Virginia* [Lexington, Ky., 1798], 28; Vol. 4:268n; Vol. 6:105-9).

[1] Preceding bracketed comment interlined.

[2] TJ here canceled "[arrives]."

[3] TJ here canceled "nothing."

[4] Following sentence interlined.

[5] Preceding four words interlined in place of "yet approved."

[6] Preceding two words interlined in place of "the Governor."

[7] TJ heavily canceled a sentence at the beginning of the next paragraph.

[8] Preceding seven words interlined in place of "himself."

[9] TJ here canceled three words.

From Benjamin H. Latrobe

DEAR SIR, Friday morning.— [21 June 1805]

We have now struck all the centers & I have employed Laborers to remove all the rubbish from the Ground story of the Capitol. If convenient to you to call when taking your ride at one o'clock, I shall be very happy to wait upon you to show You the Work, & will attend at the Building at that hour. The Men will then be at dinner & not return till two o'clock.

With true respect B H LATROBE.

RC (DLC); partially dated; addressed: "The President of the United States"; endorsed by TJ as received 21 June 1805.

From Thomas Munroe

Friday 21t. June 1805

T. Munroe presents his best respects to the President & has the honor of sending a Memdm. of the length and cost of the new road north & east of the Treasury—. T.M. thinking it had cost nearly a third more than it ought to have cost had some conversation with the Overseer on the subject—he said he had laboured under several disadvantages, and mentioned the digging up the gravel from the old road, and some other delays and difficulties at the gravel pit, which had caved in upon them unexpectedly, and covered with dirt large quantities of dug gravel; and he observed that the experience he had gained in making this piece of road would enable him, he was sure, to do more work for $100 less, and that he would be willing to enter into a Contract to do so, if there was any more such road to make—. T.M. has other reasons for believing that the present is not a fair or correct criterion by which the cost of making such road ought to be estimated, but that from a third to a fourth less would be nearer to the price at which it might be done.—

RC (DLC); endorsed by TJ as received 21 June and

"feet		D		f = 1. mile	D	
if 1130	:	cost 360	::	5280	will cost 1682.	
if it can be done for less by $\frac{1}{4}$					420	
it will cost about					1262	per mile"

(see note to Munroe to TJ, 3 July).

To Philippe Reibelt

SIR Washington June 21. 05

It has been out of my power sooner to acknolege the reciept of your favors of June 11. 13. & 19. of the box of books sent here, I retain Le Botaniste Cultivateur, in 1st & 2d. vol. in expectation of the 3d. and 4th.

Le parfait jardinier 4to	1.30		
Culture de la vigne. Rosier &c. 2. v 8vo.	2.50		
Des Abeilles. de la Rocca. 3. v. 8vo.	3.20		
Portefeuille des artistes 4. cahiers.	14.40		
Meteorologies des cultivateurs. 12mo.	.25		
Ton de la bonne compagnie petit format.	.30		
Plans d'Architecture par Becker 4. cahiers,	17.		
Landbaukunst von Meinert 4. cahiers.	16.80	55.75	
60. pr. cent		33.45	89.20

the box, with the residue is repacked, & I am on the look-out for a vessel by which to return it to Baltimore. in this is also returned the print of the oak of Palaemon, because it is a line in which I do not indulge myself except so far as respects fine things in architecture. I inclose your catalogue. the corn you were so kind as to send me, I put into the hands of a good gardener; but it has not succeeded. I therefore rejoice it has succeeded at Baltimore, as I think it very valuable. considering lotteries as a species of gambling I have never permitted myself to become an adventurer in them for any object. with respect to your friend who proposes to settle at Charlottesville in the line of Pharmacy & Medicine, it is my duty to say frankly that, however eminent, I do not believe he could succeed there. Charlottesville is itself a little village of about 20. families, scarcely at their ease. the country is very sparsely settled, & the business of a physician in it excessively laborious, as it can only be performed on horseback. it is one of the healthiest countries in the world, & already has, in itself & it's neighborhood, more physicians than it can maintain. these speak the language of the country, are natives, are in the midst of established friends & connections, possessed of the business of the individuals of the country, & could hardly be supplanted by any new competitor. with Richmond I am quite unacquainted, not having seen it the last 5. years, nor been there more than once or twice within the last 20. years. Accept my salutations & respects. TH: JEFFERSON

PoC (DLC); at foot of first page: "Reibelt"; endorsed by TJ.

TJ prepared an almost identical list of BOOKS, which included two sets of prices for each title, a full rate and a rate discounted by 37.5 percent. On that list TJ canceled LE BOTANISTE CULTIVATEUR and another work, which he identified as the six-volume "Modeles des portes, fenetres &c. Gothiques V meubles de Paris et Londres." The list printed above included only the discounted prices TJ compiled for the other list, to which he then added a 60 percent surcharge, which he subsequently explained as the "cost in Europe" (MS in same: TJ Papers, 155:27107, entirely in TJ's hand, on verso of sheet addressed "Mr. Jefferson"; List of Books Purchased from Philippe Reibelt, printed at 26 June).

PARFAIT JARDINIER: the author of this work appeared on TJ's other list as Mallet, probably Robert Xavier Mallet, who published several works on gardening and agriculture late in the eighteenth century (Sowerby, No. 811).

CULTURE DE LA VIGNE: *Traité théorique et pratique sur la culture de la vigne, avec l'art de faire le vin, les eaux-de-vie, esprit de vin, vinaigres simples et composés*, a collaboration of Jean Antoine Chaptal, François Rozier, Antoine Auguste Parmentier, and Louis d'Ussieux. TJ later characterized the work as "the best ever published on the vine, & on wines" (same, No. 787; RS, 2:82).

TON DE LA BONNE COMPAGNIE: probably *L'usage du monde, ou la Politesse, le ton et les manières de la bonne compagnie*, published in Paris in 1804.

To Robert Smith

DEAR SIR Washington June 21. 05.

Mr. Madison recieved from the Collector of the Customs at Philadelphia, yesterday, capt Kennedy's information respecting the capture of the Huntress, which substantially ascertains the vessel, the capture, & the port to which she is sent. I do not know what might be the expence of sending a small swift vessel to reclaim her, & to send her on her destination, with some respectable person from hence who knows her. the proportion this expence would bear to the value of the vessel must decide. but I presume that a private owner would in such a case hardly leave his vessel to the common chance of a trial. should you think to send after her, the person will be furnished with a letter from the Secretary of state to the Govr. of Porto Rico, & another from Yrujo. this last would require a week's notice

I recieved from the office yesterday drawings of the medal for Capt Preble. all is well but the size. custom has decided general points in these cases, & I happen to have acquired some knolege of them in the course of my superintending the making all the medals at Paris which were voted by the old Congress during the last war. that for Genl. Washington was 3. I. diameter, as those for crowned heads always are. those for Genl. Gates, Genl. Greene &c. were $2\frac{1}{2}$ Inches: those for Genl. Morgan, Wayne, Stewart &c were 2. I. the drawings sent me yesterday were 4. I. diameter. I understand it is to be engraved but still it should be understood to be made from a dye, which is impossible; no dye can by any force be made to impress so large a surface. I believe Indian medals have been engraved as large as this; but taste has never been consulted as to these. I submit these observations to your consideration & salute you affectionately.

Th: Jefferson

PoC (DLC); at foot of text: "The Secy. of the Navy." Notation in SJL: "Huntress. Preble's medal."

KENNEDY'S INFORMATION: on 12 June, Madison wrote to J. P. G. Muhlenberg requesting information from the merchant captain who had brought news of the capture of the *Huntress* (Madison, *Papers, Sec. of State Ser.*, 9:460).

On 11 June, Madison wrote A LETTER to the Marqués de Someruelos, the governor of Cuba, in which he enclosed a copy of his letter of the same date to Carlos Martínez de Irujo protesting the capture of the *Huntress* and asking for assistance in securing its release if the vessel was taken to a Spanish port (same, 452-3, 454).

ANOTHER FROM YRUJO: on 23 June, Irujo advised Madison that he had written to Someruelos regarding the *Huntress* (same, 492-3).

From Robert Smith

Sir, Balt. June 21. 1805

The letter of Mr[1] Smith alluded to in your favour of the 19th. I have not yet received—There is however some mistake in this—The Commanding Officer of Gun Boat No. 1 at Charleston is Mr Fanning a gentleman lately appointed by you in consequence of strong letters of recommendation from our friends in New-York. The Navy Agent at Charleston is Mr Smith and the letter is probably from him. I have desired my cheif Clerk to forward to me the letter. The idea of Mr Smith which you have quoted appears to me as it does to you and as to any additional instructions I beleive they are not necessary. The powers already given to the Commanding Officer of the Gun Boat on that Station are fully sufficient for every useful purpose.

If you should be of the Opinion that we ought to have a publick armed vessel out to scour our coast and that the pirates now infesting us will do us too much injury before the Brigs can be put to Sea, the[2] Adams of 32 guns a fast Sailer can be equipped for a Cruise in Three weeks.

I have this Moment received from Philada. information that Lord Nelson with his fleet has reached the West Indies—It is stated as a Certainty.

Our Merchants here from their own experience say that the pirates who took our Store Ship the Huntress have probably destroyed her papers and by money or stripes have procured from some of the Crew a written declaration of her being destined to St. Domingo—and that she will thus be Condemned in some little port—Some say there is a chance of her being re-captured by an Englishman—and in such case there will be great loss of time.

Surely it is the duty of Nations professing to be friendly to restrain their people from committing such Outrages upon this Government.

Respectfully, Sir Your Ob. Servt. RT SMITH

RC (DLC); endorsed by TJ as received from the Navy Department at Baltimore and "G.B. No. 1. the Adams. the Huntress" and so recorded in SJL, as received 22 June.

NELSON WITH HIS FLEET: the *Aurora* on 21 June published a confirmation that the Royal Navy had been sighted off St. Croix.

[1] Abbreviation interlined in place of "Lieut."

[2] Smith here canceled "John."

From Joseph Wheaton

EXCELLENT SIR Pickensville S. Carolina June 21st. 1805—

I trust in your goodness to excuse me for the liberty I take in my communication, if I err it is for want of better judgment; my zeal prompts me to every source which can benefit the public in the rout I am ordered to arange for the post road—I have returned thus far, and was hastening to Washington with all the Speed in the power of horses, to State to the President & to the P.M.G. the Situation of the road from the appalachy river to the chatahouchy river—your Excellency will See by the map its distance is about one hundred & forty miles on a direct line—but the tract or trail path pursued by the Mail is the one troden by the Indians—and is made so much meandering as to render it almost immesurable, and is so impeded by the fall of old trees & by others ocasioned by huricanes as renders it extreemly fatigueing to the horse and must disappoint the expectation of the government unless remedied—I waited to consult Colo Hawkins who approved of the rout I had chosen and agreed that it was the only one which could be used while Athens was one of the points to be passed through—I applyed to Colo Hawkins to obtain Consent of the Indians at the Convention of all the Chiefs of the four nations of Creeks at tucky batchy which took place on the 5th. Inst. for four or five families to settle on the road, at the fording places on the oakmulgee & flint rivers, and to have the road so marked, Straitened, & cleared of the fallen trees as to render the path pasable by neight and of which he had no doubt of obtaining—I have also sent off two respectable men from the frontiers of Georgia, Colo. Philips & Sylvanus Walker, who have many times been invited by the Chiefs of the Creeks, to Settle on those waters to obtain a general approbation of the Head men while at tucky batchy, and to be Supported in their Stations by Colo Hawkins—in this plan I have no doubt of intire Success—Last Evening at the House of the Honble. Jno. B. Earle I recd. letters from the appalachy unfriendly to the arrangement I had made, Obliges me to return immediately to that place to insure regularity in the departure of the mail—and will delay my coming to the Seat of government for 2, or 3, weeks—I therefore ask leave to Suggest to the President the expenditure of a Small Sum of money on this road through the wilderness to accomplish the objects I have named marking the trees for the path, & cuting of the logs which Lay across the path, and for fallen of Large trees across the narrow Streems to enable the post rider to lead his horse when he will be obliged to Swim in those rapid Streems of which there are about twenty on the whole road. between the two rivers mentioned, on the main Streems flats will be provided by those Settlers who have liberty to Settle there—with permition I will name the Sum of twenty five hundred Dollars—altho I have not been able to make an accurate estimate on this undertaking—I will hazzard an opinion that it will be amply Sufficient, and if it Should be indeed more than necessary—I feel as if I may be responsible for so necessary & valuable an expenditure—My whole attention and best endeavours may please your excellency shall be faithfully exerted to execute the object of my Journey. If I Shall be so fortunate as to meet your approbation it will be a grateful reward—

Please Sir accept the Homage of my heart and the assurance that I am your devoted Servant JOSEPH WHEATON

RC (DLC); addressed: "The President of the United States"; endorsed by TJ as received 12 July and so recorded in SJL. Enclosure not found.

On 3 Mch. Congress authorized the establishment of a POST ROAD between Washington and New Orleans by way of Athens, Georgia (U.S. Statutes at Large, 2:337-8). TJ's papers contain documents that relate to the portion of the route from northern Virginia to the western boundary of Georgia and may have been created about this time. An undated list, possibly in Wheaton's hand, recorded 28 places and distances from Fredericksburg, Virginia, to the "flat Shoals on the appalache R," calculating a total distance of 557 miles (MS in DLC: TJ Papers, 234:41885; undated; endorsed by TJ: "Road towards New Orleans direct"). Another undated document, in a different hand, listed 17 "Post Offices on the rout to Orleans Territory" from Virginia to High Shoals in Georgia (MS in same, 41849; undated; endorsed by TJ: "Post from Washington to New Orleans").

CONVENTION: a "National Council" of Creek leaders convened at Tuckabatchee on 5 June. Benjamin Hawkins communicated the government's desire that they send a delegation to Washington for the purpose of establishing an Ocmulgee River boundary with Georgia and authorizing a road through their territory. By the time the council adjourned on 13 June, the Creeks agreed to send a delegation but had not chosen its leader or date of departure (C. L. Grant, ed., *Letters, Journals and Writings of Benjamin Hawkins*, 2 vols. [Savannah, 1980], 2:490-3).

From Robert Williams

DEAR SIR, Washington MT. June 21st. 1805

Your letter of April the 28th. having been directed to Natchez I did not recieve til the return mail by which it was then too late to forward you an answer. inclosed was a blank Commission for the next Council which I shall fill up with the names best fitted, having due regard to your recommendation, but not til after the ensuing Session of the Legislature which commences on the first monday in next month. motives of policy suggest this delay, for I assure you it will continue to be pretty much as you express it, to substitute chance for choice—The Legislature was refractory enough last session and was a designation made and known now, as some on the nomination are of both houses it might render them more so, besides one of those nominated has since deceased in selecting another at this Session, perhaps some additional strength of character may be afforded.

Nothing in the way of political opinions could have afforded me more sattisfaction than the sentiments you have expressed indicative of the course you hint as proper to be pursued in my administration, not only because they accord with my own as already expressed in this quarter, but because I am convinced an administration on these principles will produce the desired effect, no portion of people are more disposed to support Republican measures and more attached to the present administration than those of this Territory, all they want is a chance; but he that affords it to them will and must expect to recieve all the vengence of a small party here, consisting principally of the Green family with the Secretary Cato West and his son in-law E Turner at their head, with a bellowing Pettifogger, and an unprincipled quack to write, and an apostate republican press to issue fourth their productions.

The news papers from this place I presume you see, I however enclose you the two last by which you will observe I am recieving the perquisites of office (abuse) the affair of the 1050 dollars is founded on my certifying that the atto. General was in office, and intitled to his pay as such for a certain time, as was customary on order to authorise the settlement of his account with the auditor and Treasurer who did settle the acct. accordingly and then aided this publication as tho the draft had been for myself or to my use but they are both of the Green and West families;—That of the Court a copy of the inclosed correspondance will inform you, except a few words that passed betwen the Judge and myself when he agreed to hold the Court at another house, but all in moderation as it was public, without any asperity but what the letters contain and no private intercourse or sociability between us is interrupted; Turner himself being present, who is one of the *squibers*.

You mention the cause of the distraction in our Legislative bodies is not well understood with you; So far as I have been enable to form an oppinion they took their origin from an intention to move the seat of Goverment and the site of Jefferson college from this place to a little town lately established about 18 miles off in Jefferson County by the name of Greenville in and about which Mr West and this party generally reside or are interested—this commenced in Governor Claiborne's time but the Executive check kept it from growing into much importance, but as soon as there appeared a probability of Mr West being at the head of a Legislature the project became formidable, tho conducted by intrigue, finding the election in Adams district would go against them for they were as hostile to Claiborne, the only reputed Republican as to the other three elected for that district—a plan was laid to have a return of the election from that part of Jefferson district composed of Claiborne County made so informal as to authorize the Sheriff of Jefferson to return the four members from that part of the district in which the Town of Greenville is, and some of them residing in it although two of them had but little more than half the number of votes, which those two Candidates from Claiborne had which were not returned, this measure being affected divided the house of Representatives equally as to number, except the Washington member who it was calculated could be brought over to their views but which failed—

this together with their views as to a delegate to Congress, and some objects of minor consideration produced a session of near 4 months, wrangling and bartering with and by the acting Executive for almost every thing they did, and at length rose without doing some of the ordinary business and the most important which was performed left in so crude a state as to be incapable of execution, perticularly a judicial system, all which has rendered a convention of the Legislature by me indispensible.

This in addition to sketches in some of my former letters to you and the Secretary of the Treasury, I have given you the outlines of the causes of the political confusion here which I am confident will soon cease to have any general affect, the body of the people, the wealth, respectibility and intelligence of this Country are well disposed to support the measures now so generally approved, except a few who are really hostile at heart to Republican principles, but they are disposed to be neutral—and Col. West and his small party, who will oppose the administration of this Government by any one but themselves

I am with very great Respt. yrs. ROBERT WILLIAMS

RC (DLC); in a clerk's hand, closing and signature by Williams; at foot of text in Williams's hand: "Thos. Jefferson Esq President of U. States"; endorsed by TJ as received 2 Aug. and so recorded in SJL. Enclosed in Gideon Granger to TJ, 23 July. Enclosures: (1) Williams to John Burnet, from Washington, Mississippi Territory, 27 May, asking Burnet to inform the judges of the supreme court that he has appropriated, for "indispensible public business," the house in Washington previously "used for Government purposes"; in its place, Williams has provided a "much more commodious" house for the court to hold its upcoming session (Tr in DLC; at head of text: "No. 1."). (2) Thomas Rodney to Williams, Washington, 27 May, stating that the law requires the court and the legislature to sit "at the same place"; Rodney therefore does not consider himself authorized "to hold the Court at any other Place, nor do I see any reason for doing so" (Tr in same; at head of text: "No 2"). (3) Williams to Rodney, 28 May, reiterating that the house claimed by Rodney for the court is currently being used by the board of commissioners and for other "public business"; Williams has tried to explain the situation "in as respectful a manner as I was capable," but disagrees with Rodney's interpretation of the law (Tr in same; at head of text: "No. 3"). (4) Rodney to Williams, 28 May, expressing regret over "any altercation" but declaring this affair to be "the first instance in America" in which a governor "has undertaken to dictate to a Court of Law and its Officers what they shall do or not do" (RC in same; at head of text: "No. 4"). (5) Williams to Rodney, 28 May, replying that the board of commissioners was previously displaced for the legislature by the executive, which now declines to displace the board for the court (Tr in same; at head of text: "No 5."). Other enclosures not found. Enclosed in Gideon Granger to TJ, 23 July.

The identity of the BELLOWING PETTIFOGGER is uncertain. Attorneys George Poindexter, William B. Shields, and Drury W. Breazeale were all critics of Williams (Robert V. Haynes, *The Mississippi Territory and the Southwest Frontier, 1795-1817* [Lexington, Ky., 2010], 76-7; Briggs to TJ, 18 May).

UNPRINCIPLED QUACK: John Shaw (Vol. 45:418-20).

APOSTATE REPUBLICAN PRESS: the Natchez *Mississippi Messenger*, whose editors were allied with the Green-West faction. Shaw was a frequent contributor (Haynes, *Mississippi Territory*, 77, 172-3; Vol. 45:420n).

From Sarah Amelia Bampfield

[on or before 22 June 1805]

With diffidence I attempt to address Mr Jefferson on a subject which nearly interests me—I beg to submit myself to your direction—Not doubting your care of me as circumstances renderd me incapable of Judging clearly

I wish to rectify any evil that May attend Judge Johnson his reputation or interest from the unfortunate circumstance which has taken place—and any assertions I may have made or wrote while under the torture and Malidiction of Mrs Lownds &c concieving I was suffering by his will—After she confined me—I see by an advertisment that my imprisonment ceased on the day after that was signed—I send you a note I wrote the 12 Mch bewildered in a strange place and insulted by every person indiscrimanately—I was in a temporary state of Madness

I inclose you the Aurora of the 28 Jany Many referances to the last letter I wrote Judg Johnson caught my eye particularly this—"To humble poor and obscure Mortals whose obscurity or fears prevent their obtaining redress but through the Medium of the *publick prints*"

This passage I pointed out to Mrs Lownds—the paper was taken out of my room and but lately I have procured

I hope not too late—My trunks & Desk was detained at Mr Hands and broke open several letters taken out some of which I did not imediately recollect this refer to one a rough coppy of the original wrote in pencil—There are many other papers In the same way. alluding to those letters—

Those Verses—I do not know who composed It was from those the Historical and Emblamatical engraving was taken—by *my* letter I find they were recvd as Mine Novr 1—I did not know it and have reason now to suppose I was persecuted to disgrace him—I know not who was the Author of the lilly of the Vally—who ever it is is the cause of all my Misfortunes—As the letter I have mentioned—was obtained by fraud I think it Necessary to observe to you (that it was a supprise to me—and am ignorant as to the person who turnd out against—Aristocresy and fraud—Nor have I ever shown one of his letters or Mine to any person whatever except one dated May 1801—To Mrs E H which I did after the 29 Feby as from the insulting usage of Mrs

Lownds & Mrs Nicholson I was obliged to do it—Mrs Lownds refused me the loan of $20 to take Me here and here they are against us both—My situation is truly distressing—every persons acts treacherously to me against him

May he live in Glory here and here after—I will use all my endeavors if you *will let me know what is Necessary*—to my own *disadvantage* to Clear him of any Aspersians—I must Mention this circumstance I borded at Mrs Fullerton Arch Street—They were talking Scandal of Many persons who lived in the House—and others who had calld on me—Miss Lowry her Neace and Myself went a shopping I told her that was just such a presant as I gave the last Lady I borded with in Charleston—Who was of all ∴ woman I ever met with the most adected to scandal—it had also *"Harmonie* on it—She had been talking ill of a person I was Interested for I gave it to her and told her I woud not leave her in an Error I had been playing *that part with her*—"*Americans 'Harmonies'—Duanes Book store date changed to 28 Jany*"

I sent to Mr H—n to sue Mrs Hand & to recover my letters but never saw him till the 7 Mch—I beg to submit our cause to you as a frend to both—And to use this as you think will lead to our advantage—I have sent to recall one my Sister wrote—"*as it by mistake*"

I have been blinded As to the real situation of this business and dont know who is friend or foe And am now as to the Evidance wether he sactiond it or not—but be it as it will call upon me if Necessary in his behalf—But let Me know the evidances—and take such measures as to prevent them imposing coppys of those letters as from me—they have every advantage I know no person at all—*Nor what is* [*doing*]

∴ my waiting woman—I *suspect*
pray forward this information to Charleston as soon as possible—and Also to write on to some persons in Philedelpha to enquire on what grounds they drew up there petition—If from letters—thus obtaind by force—let them be brought—to *Justice*

RC (DLC); undated; torn; written in the same hand as the promissory note enclosed in Elizabeth G. Tart and Sarah Amelia Bampfield to TJ, 30 June, and Bampfield's portion of their letter of 27 July; addressed: "Thomas Jefferson Esqr President of the *United States* District of *Columbia*"; endorsed by TJ as an anonymous letter received 22 June 1805 and "insane" and so recorded in SJL. Enclosures not identified, but see below.

Sarah Amelia Bampfield (b. 1774) was the daughter of Nathan Tart and Elizabeth Garden Tart of St. Thomas and St. Denis Parish near Charleston, South Carolina. Her 1794 marriage to merchant George Bampfield was cut short by his death two years later. Along with her sister, Elizabeth G. Tart, Bampfield wrote a dozen letters to TJ in 1805. According to SJL, TJ returned many of these letters to the post office unread. By 1809, Bampfield was legally under the care of her sister and brother-in-law (Robert F. Clute, *The Annals and Parish Register of St. Thomas and St. Denis Parish, in South Carolina, from 1680 to 1884* [Charleston, S.C., 1884], 26, 85; Charleston *City Gazette and Daily Advertiser*, 8 Oct. 1796, 23 Aug. 1809; TJ to Charles Burrall, 9 Aug. 1805).

THOSE VERSES: a manuscript in Bampfield's hand in TJ's papers headed "General Washington Lamentation" contains a transcription of a poem published as "The Separation" in the 25 Jan. 1804 edition of the *Augusta Herald* and a transcription of a newspaper advertisement for the poem, both enclosed by a hand-drawn six-sided border with other text running inside it (MS in DLC: TJ Papers, 147: 25677). Also in TJ's papers is a small scrap of paper in Bampfield's hand that reads "The Above refers to a Coppy of the original in pencil—Mr Hands 28 Jany 1805" and is signed "Constancy" (MS in same, 146:25528).

From Robert Brown of Washington

SIR

June 22th 1805

I met with Mr. Leathrobe he has not Let the Ballence of the work that is to Be Don Beside your house he all so told me if it was your Disire that I should Do the Remande part of the work I hope your honner will Be so good as to ferst Menthing it to him there has Been som one or two Ill Disposed pipele has spook to Mr Leanthall in andifrent Maner of Me, But I hope if I get the Werk to give Mr Lanthall Every Sattsfaction I am Sorey to Be trobling your Honner there is Not a days Work scence to Be had in the City and if it twas not for a dete I am in I should not incist for it

I am your mot Obt. st,

ROBT. BROWN

RC (DLC); addressed: "The Hounrable the Presedent of United States"; endorsed by TJ as received 22 June and so recorded in SJL.

LEATHROBE: Latrobe.

From Thomas Mann Randolph

DEAR SIR,

June 22d. :05

I am requested by Mr. Richard S. Hackley of New York to endeavor to procure for him information from Washington whether the Consulship at Bourdeaux has been lately vacated or not by the relinquishment or displacement of Mr. Lee. Certain connexions between him and myself forbid my refusing this request however disagreeable it is to comply with it. Being fully convinced that he cannot have an idea of being able by these means to gather any thing of the intentions or sentiments of the Government with respect to Mr. Lee, that such a thought never once struck him, I have found it more difficult to refuse. His intentions he has candidly made known to me. Having learned from his partner just returned from Bourdeaux of the dissatisfaction Mr. Lees conduct has given them he has conceived an idea that he might be removed and a hope of succeeding him himself if the place is not allready filled which he apprehends may have taken place. If it is not filled he means to come forward with the recommendations of respectable merchants of N[ew]-York, Norfolk and Bourdeaux, if there is time. His p[arti]cular acquaintance with Philip R. Thompson, and John Randolph enables him to add their favorable testimony of him besides. If no appointment has been made he intends to set about this immediately, having himself a full belief that one will be made. If I had any kind of correspondence with any other person who could say whether such an appointment had been made I should not trouble you with it: as I have not, I request a bare answer to that question; which is all Mr. R.H. contemplated when he applied to me, I am confident. He is here now & has been several days with us on a visit to T.E. Randolph and myself.

The family is well. Martha is at times much harrassed yet by Dyspeptic and Hypochondriac effects but has no complaint of a more serious nature. I have the greatest hope that the air and society at Monticello will restore her completely, in a short time. The cold weather in autumn will without fail do it if it is not sooner done.—The children, except Mary, have all had the mumps.[1]

With sincere attachment yours affecty: TH: M. RANDOLPH

RC (ViU: Coolidge Deposit); torn; endorsed by TJ as received 25 June and so recorded in SJL.

RICHARD S. HACKLEY, a New York merchant and lawyer who married Randolph's sister Harriet in December 1805, had previously sought the consulship at Nantes (Richmond *Enquirer*, 18 Jan. 1806; Vol. 38:418). MR. LEES CONDUCT: for William Lee's failed business ventures, see Vol. 44:515-16.

MARTHA Jefferson Randolph was in the first trimester of her pregnancy with James Madison Randolph, born on 17 Jan. 1806 (*Thomas Jefferson's Prayer Book*, ed. John Cook Wyllie [Charlottesville, 1952], plate 7).

[1] Sentence interlined.

From David Robinson

SIR, Kanawha County, Peters Creek June 22nd 1805

When I Recolect the acquisition of the Louisiana and the advantages we may Derive from it I wou'd with many Others Join in Blessing the happy Day with all the marks of Gratitude that Becoms Evry united American. It is Long Since I had a Desire to See that much talked of Country. But if it had not been for my Childeren I Should never have attempted it I have Labour'd thro many Dangers on the Kanawha and Ohio Rivers in the Last Indian war and with much Dificualty Give three of my Son's Education they all three are on the Mississippi One is at the Kaskaskia Town a Clerk and interpreter for the Bord of Commissiners he is an attorny One other is a Docter of Physic and the Other is pehaps in the Business of Surveying in the Indiana Teritory They all have the advantage of knowing the French Tongue from my Living at Gallipolis Some years During the Last ware. I have taken Some pains to keep a Journal of my travils thro' the Louisiana and think a Copie of it is my Duty to present you with I have it in Contemplation to pay an other visit to it Next Septemeber and perhaps will penitrate forth into the Country and bring an acurate account of the Salt Mountain and Volcano and make a Return of my Journals to your Honour you will please to actcept of the Notes and Remarks I have made if it merits notice. and if it is of any utility to the Commonwelth I wish it to Recive an impression of the Gramatical Correction if you think propper which will answer the Desired End of the author. I Live at a Great Distance from any Printing office and have it not in my Power to attend to it. I have procured a Small peice of the Rock Salt which Came from the Mountain and inclosed it to you though perhaps you have Seen Some of it before I have the honour Sir of Subscribing my Self your most Obsequious

David Robinson—

RC (MHi); addressed: "Hon. Thomas Jefferson Esqure Charlotts Ville Abemarle County"; endorsed by TJ as received 5 Aug. and so recorded in SJL. Enclosure not found.

David Robinson settled in the area that became Kanawha County, Virginia, sometime before 1789, when he was named one of the justices on the county's first court. He also served as a commissioner of revenue (George W. Atkinson, *History of Kanawha County, from Its Organization in 1789 until the Present Time* [Charleston, W.Va., 1876], 80).

Robert Robinson was awarded $500 by Congress for his work as clerk of the board of land commissioners at Kaskaskia (U.S. Statutes at Large, 6:94).

From William Taylor

Sir: Baltimore June. 22d. 1805

My friend Mr John Kelly of Charlottesville has forwarded me a memorandum of articles to be sent on to you for Mr. Randolph and I have this day sent a Trunk by The Stage to yr address to be forwarded to Monticello as soon as possible; with The enclosed letter of

Invoice &ca. Be pleased to direct some enquiry after The Trunk & let me be Informed if it is safely received.

I am, most respectfully Sir Yr mo. obt Ser WM. TAYLOR

RC (MHi): at foot of text: "Thomas Jefferson Esqr President of the United States"; endorsed by TJ as received 23 June and so recorded in SJL. Enclosures not found.

Massachusetts native William Taylor (ca. 1749-1829) was an established Baltimore merchant who conducted a large foreign business through the firm of Sylvanus Bourne, U.S. consul at Amsterdam. Financial difficulties during and after the War of 1812 forced Taylor into bankruptcy. In 1818 he moved to New Orleans, where for a short period he was with the firm of Taylor & Palfrey (William Allan and John Johnson, *Life and Work of John McDonogh* [Baltimore, 1886], 8-10, 34-5; Library of Congress, *Handbook of Manuscripts in the Library of Congress* [Washington, D.C., 1918], 404-5; *Baltimore Patriot & Mercantile Advertiser*, 4 Mch. 1829).

To James Currie

DEAR SIR Washington June 23. 1805.

Dr. Bruff a dentist the bearer of this, has resided some years in this place, and has justly acquired the character of a very excellent man. possessing talents of the very first order in mechanics he has applied them with great success to the invention & improvement of the instruments of his art & much to the advantage of those who have occasion to employ him. having been of that number myself, I speak from some experience of him. he pays a visit to Richmond, with some thoughts of a permanent settlement either there or at Petersburg. having a real wish he may meet with the success which his merit & skill deserve, any good offices you may be so good as to render him will give me pleasure & be gratefully felt by him. Accept my friendly salutations & assurances of great & constant esteem & respect.

TH: JEFFERSON

P.S. should your peregrinations in the months of Aug. or September lead you into the neighborhood of Monticello I shall be happy to see you there.

PoC (MHi); at foot of text: "Dr. Currie"; endorsed by TJ. Notation in SJL: "by Dr. Bruff."

For TJ's interactions with dentist and inventor Thomas BRUFF, see Vol. 36:125n and RS, 5:108n. Most recently, TJ had paid Bruff five dollars in January for drawing a tooth (MB, 2:1144).

To William Foushee

DEAR SIR Washington June 23. 05.

Dr. Bruff a dentist the bearer of this, has resided some years in this place, and has justly acquired the character of a very excellent man. possessing talents of the very first order in mechanics, he has applied them with great success to the invention and improvement of the instruments of his art, and much to the advantage of those who have occasion to employ him. having been of that number myself, I speak from some experience of him. he pays a visit to Richmond, with some thoughts of a permanent settlement either there or at Petersburg, having a real wish he may meet with the success which his merit & skill deserve, any good offices you may be in the way of rendering him, will give me pleasure, & be gratefully felt by him. Accept my friendly salutations & assurances of great esteem & respect.

TH: JEFFERSON

PoC (DLC); at foot of text: "Dr. Foushee"; endorsed by TJ. Notation in SJL: "by Dr. Bruff."

To Gibson & Jefferson

TH: JEFFERSON TO MESSRS.
GIBSON & JEFFERSON Washington June 23. 05.

Will you be so good as to procure & forward for me to Monticello two or three dozen bottles of Syrop of punch by the first boats?

PoC (MHi); endorsed by TJ as a letter to George Jefferson.

From William Short

[23 June 1805]

Jeffn. P.—June.—ansr. his of 14—balc. now due—after departure of sister, Niagara or Monticello—as to the Spa. negociation—& Mrs. Rands. ill health—

FC (DLC: Short Papers); partially dated; entirely in Short's hand, consisting of an entry in his epistolary record. Recorded in SJL as a letter of 23 June received from Philadelphia on 25 June.

From Robert Smith

SIR, Balt. June 23. 1805

Upon receiving your favor of the 21st. I immediately desired the Navy Agent of this place to inform me whether a fast sailing small Vessel could be procured for Porto Rico—upon what terms and where she could be put to sea. As soon as this information shall be Obtained it shall be communicated to you.

As you recommend the sending of a person, we shall, I fear, be obliged to send Capt Tingey unless he can find some person at the yard possessed of the information that may be necessary in reclaiming the Vessel and Cargo. But will such a person be necessary as the letter from the State Department will of course be accompanied with duplicates of all the Ships papers and other documents serving to identify the vessel and Cargo and to establish the fact that the Cargo is the property of the U. States destined for our Squadron in the Medn. Will the Statements made by this Government to the Governor of Porto Rico need the aid of any person to substantiate them? In my opinion this government should not only make a peremptory demand of the immediate release of the Vessel and Cargo; but should also insist upon the punishment of the Spanish Officer who thus dared to capture a Vessel manifestly employed in our public Service. Practices so injurious and at the same time so degrading to the U. States must be restrained.

Agreeably to your very correct ideas of the drawings of the Medal for Comr Preble I will give the necessary instructions.

Respecty. RT SMITH

RC (DLC); endorsed by TJ as received from the Navy Department at Baltimore on 24 June and "Huntress" and so recorded in SJL.

NAVY AGENT OF THIS PLACE: John Stricker.

On 29 June, Philadelphia navy agent George Harrison responded to Smith's INSTRUCTIONS by returning a sketch of Preble's medal and requesting authorization for the use of the machinery housed at the U.S. Mint (DNA: RG 45, MLR). On 3 July, Smith forwarded an authorization from the secretary of state to use the machines (Smith to Harrison, 3 July, DNA: RG 45, MLS; Madison, *Papers, Sec. of State Ser.*, 10:10-11).

From Albert Gallatin

[24 June 1805]

The enclosed communication from the collector of Philada., respecting the admission into port of foreign armed vessels, and sketch of an answer are respectfully submitted. All the other collectors, who have answered the circular, say that no provision is necessary—

A.G.

RC (DLC); undated; endorsed by TJ as received from the Treasury Department on 24 June 1805 and "peace in harbors" and so recorded in SJL. Enclosure: J. P. G. Muhlenberg to Gallatin, Philadelphia, 19 June, observing that no port regulation exists that designates a location in the harbor for foreign armed vessels; Muhlenberg suggests Marcus Hook, where the water is wide and deep and anchorage will not interfere with river traffic; Muhlenberg further recommends that pilots not carry foreign armed vessels beyond that place without authorization; such ships would still be liable to quarantine laws and could be ordered to the lazaretto if demanded by the board of health (FC in Lb in DNA: RG 56, Correspondence of the Secretary of the Treasury with Collectors of Customs, Philadelphia). Other enclosure not found, but see below.

Gallatin's ANSWER to Muhlenberg, dated 25 June, instructed him to consult with the board of health regarding enforcement of quarantine laws on foreign armed vessels, especially since they would likely arrive from the West Indies; in addition, "the President directs that no such armed Vessel shall be allowed, without special permission from this department, to pass above Fort Mifflin" (FC in same).

On 25 May the Treasury Department issued a CIRCULAR with instructions for carrying out the fourth section of the recently passed act "for the more effectual preservation of peace in the ports and harbors of the United States," which contained a new requirement that "commanders of public armed vessels" report to the collector on entering a port. This "provision being a new one," Treasury officers must "be careful, whilst you carry the same into effect, that the officers and flags of all nations shall be treated with respect." Collectors should also conform with existing state regulations and health and quarantine laws regarding the anchorage locations assigned to foreign warships. In the absence of such rules collectors could "make temporary regulations," but it was preferable that they report their recommendations to the Treasury Department "for the President's consideration and decision" (printed copy in DLC, endorsed by TJ: "Departmt. Treasury. May 25. 05. Armed vessels in harbor"; TJ to Madison, 29 May).

To Martha Jefferson Randolph

MY DEAREST MARTHA Washington June 24. 05.

I last night recieved a letter from mr Taylor of Baltimore informing me he had sent by the stage to this place the trunk of articles ordered by mr Kelly. I sent this morning to the Stage office; the trunk was arrived, & goes on this evening to Fredericksburg, where I shall desire mr Benson to forward it by the first stage to Milton. I had paiment made here for transportation as far as Fredericksbg that no delay might happen on that account. further could not be paid here, on account of it's being a different concern with which the stage-company here is unconnected. I hope you will get the trunk by the first stage. I have had here a considerable time ½ doz. pr of shoes for Virginia & ½ doz. pr for Anne, but am afraid to trust so small a parcel by the stage without a guardian. perhaps it will not come on till I go myself which will be this day three weeks. I take for granted that Virginia's marriage is to take place at Monticello, as we have so much more room there for our friends, & conveniencies of other kinds also. I will accomodate my trip to Bedford to the matrimonial arrangements. we have just heard from Capt Lewis, who wintered 1600. miles up the Missouri; all well. 45. chiefs of 6. different nations from that quarter are forwarded by him to St. Louis on their way to this place. our agent at St. Louis will endeavor to prevail on them to stay there till autumn & then come on. should they insist on coming immediately they will arrive in July, & may derange my departure. I am glad to find the family has got so easily thro' the mumps, & hope you will discover that you have had them, as I think you had when very young. my love to every body; to yourself unceasing affection. Greet mr Randolph also affectionately for me. TH: JEFFERSON

RC (NNPM); at foot of text: "Mrs. Randolph." PoC (MHi); endorsed by TJ.

LETTER FROM MR TAYLOR: William Taylor to TJ, 22 June.

VIRGINIA'S MARRIAGE: Virginia Randolph, who became an orphan at a young age and lived at Edgehill as the ward of her older brother Thomas Mann Randolph, married Wilson Jefferson Cary at Monticello on 28 Aug. (ViU: Carysbrook Memoir, 22, 32; Vol. 42:324n).

HEARD FROM CAPT LEWIS: TJ's information regarding Meriwether Lewis and William Clark and the western Indian deputation probably came from a letter from William Henry Harrison to Dearborn of 27 May, which the War Department received on 22 June. Harrison enclosed his correspondence with Pierre Chouteau at St. Louis regarding the arrival of representatives from the Arikara, Ponca, Sioux, Omaha, Otoe, and Missouri nations. Harrison also summarized a letter from Clark written on 2 Apr. from the expedition's winter camp on the upper Missouri River, where they "had met with no material accident" (DNA: RG 107, LRMS; Jackson, *Lewis and Clark*, 1:227-30, 242-4, 246-8).

To Philippe Reibelt

SIR Washington June 24. 05.

Hearing of no vessel bound from this neighborhood to Baltimore, I have this day sent your box of books to the stage-office, directing, as I have always done, the master of the stage office to put the costs of transportation into my account.

Having occasion for some book of tables, turning the present French measures & weights into the antient ones, to save one the trouble of calculation, I turned to your catalogue, & at pages 34-35 is one by Schweighauser in 12mo. one by Mallet Prevost in 4to. and Tables de reduction par Carondelet 8vo. will you be so good as to send me the one of the three which best answers the object abovementioned?

There are two works by Prony, viz Architecture Hydraulique, & Mechanique Philosophique which I should be glad to get if you have them.

I am one of the original subscribers to the Encyclopedie Methodique par Pancoucke, & have recieved as far as the 67th. livraison inclusive and compleat. but the trouble of remitting small sums of money to Paris[1] has been the reason of my recieving the Livraisons at very long intervals. would it be convenient for you to import the 68th. & subsequent livraisons for me[2] as they come out, or rather once a year, or so often as you have importations for your book-store. I shall be glad to allow your common advance to be relieved from the trouble of importing them for myself. Accept my salutations & respects.

TH: JEFFERSON

PoC (DLC); at foot of text: "Mr. Reibelt"; endorsed by TJ.

[1] Preceding two words interlined.

[2] TJ first wrote "import them for me" before altering the text to read as above.

From Robert Smith

SIR, Balt. June 24. 1805

I have the pleasure of informing you that a good & suitable Vessel can be procured at this place to proceed to Porto-Rico and thence to any other port or ports that may be found to be necessary. One Thousand Dollars must be paid for going to Porto-Rico and if necessary to go to any other port or ports then as much additional as in the opinion of two Respectable merchants ought to be paid. We may send in her any person. She will be ready to sail as soon as we please.

Mr. Madison may therefore prepare immediately[1] his letter to the governor of Porto-Rico. It is possible the Huntress may have been taken by some English armed vessel and in that case the person sent by us in this Vessel must be instructed to proceed in search of her. If it were certain that the Huntress had been taken to Porto Rico, the sending of a special agent as proposed by you would I believe not be necessary but as She may have been taken to some other port such an agent would be useful in instructing and causing the Captain of the

Pilot Boat (we are about employing) to proceed to such port. Possibly Capt Tingey could prevail upon the person from whom we freighted the Huntress to go in this Pilot Boat. He would answer our purpose and he has an interest in saving his Vessel.

I have by this mail directed my chief Clerk to procure and deliver to Mr. Madison copies of all the papers of the Huntress and her cargo. I have also instructed him as to the letter to be prepared for the government of the Special Agent; which letter will be submitted to you before it be sent to me for my Signature—But, Sir, would it not be more proper that the person sent in the pilot Boat should be the special Agent of the State Department acting under the instructions of Mr. Madison.

Respectfully RT SMITH

RC (DLC); endorsed by TJ as received from the Navy Department on 25 June and so recorded in SJL with notation "Huntress."

[1] Word interlined in place of "& send."

To William Taylor

Washington June 24. 05.

Th: Jefferson presents his compliments to mr Taylor & informs him the trunk of goods announced in his letter, arrived here last night, & goes on by the stage of this evening, as also his letter to mr Kelly.

PoC (MHi); endorsed by TJ.

HIS LETTER: Taylor to TJ, 22 June.

From Craven Peyton

DR. SIR. [before 25 June 1805]

I am very much pleased that it is convenient for you to meet those debts £47. the 10th July & £160. on the 10th of August as it will answer very well, you will be so good as to name it to Mr. Jefferson by the first mail, Bullocks deed is for the proportion of interest which James L. Henderson sold me with an addition of the warehouse & the store house Henderson & Connard formerly Occupied, at the time Henderson made the sale to me of the infant legatees shares, it was agreed on by him & his Mothar that he woud. give them land adjoining to theres where they then lived, which I suppose was satisfactory to Bullock, you will be astonished on seeing the warehouse list, at its decline but is easily remided by getting a Cash Commission establishd, which woud put it out of the power of the Merchants to treat the Planters with as much injustice as they do; for four or five years back Columbia warehouse I beleave have averaged 1500 Hhds. two thirds of which aught & woud of been braught to Milton if Justic coud. of been had, please enclose them othar papers to be recorded

with great respt C. PEYTON

RC (ViU); endorsed by TJ as received 25 June and so recorded in SJL.

CONVENIENT FOR YOU TO MEET THOSE DEBTS: see TJ to Peyton, 13 June.

From Charles Buxton

SIR New York June 25th. 1805—Greenwich St—

I feel a particular pleasure on enclosing herewith some designs & drawings (upon subjects that have engaged my attention) especially as I am of opinion, that they may be acceptable; judging from the slight opportunity I have enjoyed of conversing familiarly with you some years since—

To recall your recollection of me, I will only observe that on the 1st. of April 1793, (being married the preceding evening) I went on a jaunt to Philadelphia with Mrs B & a female friend; & according to previous arrangment lodged at Mrs House's; where during a stay of ten days I had frequently the gratification of being in your company—

I suggested to my friend Dr Mitchell my intention of writing to you, which meeting his approbation, shall hope the communication may be agreeable Being

Sir With every Sentiment of Respect & Esteem Your's

CHAS BUXTON

RC (DLC); at foot of text: "His Excellency Thomas Jefferson President of the American Philosophical Society"; endorsed by TJ as received 28 June and so recorded in SJL. Enclosure: five drawings illustrating Buxton's inventions, drawn by him, with a separate sheet of descriptions in his hand; drawings 1 and 2, each dated 1797, show details of a distilling furnace in which salt water is passed from a reservoir into a furnace chamber, where it is distilled at what Buxton describes as an anticipated rate of one "pint of fresh water per minute"; Buxton describes drawing 3, dated 1805, as a pipe for a fire engine, designed with an added "air vessel" to increase the distance at which water can be sprayed before losing pressure; drawing 4, dated 1802, he describes as an apparatus for "drawing the smoke of Segars or pipes of tobacco through water scented, to give tobacco fumes, any required flavour & render the smoke cool & mild"; and drawing 5, undated, illustrates "a method for arresting the progress of fire in buildings" by the addition of sheet iron firewalls placed in the grooves of supporting beams (MS in same: TJ Papers, 151:26405-9).

New York City physician Charles Buxton (1768-1833) was born in Radbourne, England, and studied at the University of Edinburgh before earning a medical degree from Queen's College (later Rutgers

University) in 1793. Buxton drew what became known as the "Bowling-Green Washington," which Cornelius Tiebout engraved and Buxton sent to George Washington in 1799 (John Howard Raven, *Catalogue of the Officers and Alumni of Rutgers College [Originally Queen's College] in New Brunswick, N.J., 1766-1916* (Trenton, 1916), 323; Washington, *Papers, Ret. Ser.*, 4:26; Vol. 16:xxxiii-xxxiv).

To William Eustis

DEAR SIR Washington June 25. 05.

Your two favors of the 2d. & 10th. inst. have been duly recieved. with respect to mr Avery, as he was to obtain the testimonies of his character in the Eastern states, & was himself in the same place with Genl. Hull in whose gift the office of Marshal for Michigan was, I left him to satisfy General Hull, himself on that point, & thought it best to add no bias by expressing any wish of mine to the General. I therefore did not write to him on the subject.—I believe, with you, that the Boston maneuvre, has secured the death of federalism at the end of the present year. the steady progression of public opinion, aided by the number of candid persons who had voted with them this year, but will be displeased with this measure, cannot fail to join Massachusets to her sister-states at the first election. the arrangement you suggested in your letter of the 10th. could not be adopted, because a prior one had been initiated. the person appointed is very distant & will not be here till Autumn. within a month from this time our annual recess will take place, for the months of Aug. & Sep. I have the pleasure to inform you that one of Capt. Lewis's barges, returned to St. Louis brings us certain information from him. he wintered with the Mandanes, 1609. miles up the Missouri, Lat. 47. Long. 101.° with some additional minutes to both numbers, as well, and peculiarly cherished by all the Indian nations. he has sent in his barge 45. deputies from 6. of the principal nations in that quarter, who will be joined at St. Louis by those of 3. or 4. nations between the Missouri & Missisipi, and will come on here. whether before our departure or after our return we do not yet know. we shall endeavor to get them to go on as far North as Boston, being desirous of impressing them correctly as to our strength & resources. this with kind usage, and a commerce advantageous to them, & not losing to us, will better secure their & our peace & friendship than an army of thousands.

I recieve with due sentiments of thankfulness the invitations of my Eastern friends to visit that portion of our country. the expected visit from the deputations of so many distant nations of Indians, provisional arrangements with Spain in lieu of the permanent ones proposed, in which we are not likely to concur, the presence of English & French fleets in the American seas, which will probably visit & perplex our harbors during the hurricane season will not permit me to be so far from the seat of government this summer. add to this that should I ever be able to make the visit it would probably be more generally agreeable, when there shall be less division of public sentiment than at present among you.

Accept my friendly salutations, & assurances of great esteem & respect TH: JEFFERSON

RC (Warner R. Howell, San Francisco, Calif., 1954); at foot of first page: "Dr. Eustis"; endorsed by Eustis. PoC (DLC).

PERSON APPOINTED: see TJ to John Julius Pringle, 15 June.

From Albert Gallatin

[25 June 1805]

Sketch of a letter to Isaac Briggs

Will the President be pleased to suggest whether any alterations or any thing to be added? A.G.

RC (DLC); undated; endorsed by TJ as received from the Treasury Department on 25 June 1805 and "survey of Orleans" and so recorded in SJL. Enclosure not found, but see below.

Gallatin wrote to ISAAC BRIGGS on 2 July, providing detailed instructions for superintending the survey of public lands in Orleans Territory. In conformity with the 2 Mch. act of Congress regarding land titles and claims in Orleans and Louisiana, and also "with the President's directions," the survey was to include the lands to be located for Lafayette, any existing land claims in need of survey or resurvey, the "alluvial or inundated country" between the Mississippi River and Bayou Lafourche on the east and the Atchafalaya River on the west, and lands west of the Atchafalaya deemed fit for cultivation. Briggs was also to lay out townships west of the Atchafalaya from the Red River "to the sea shore," but was not to survey "farther west than the Meridian of Natchitoches" (*Terr. Papers*, 9:459-62; U.S. Statutes at Large, 2:324-9).

From Charles Willson Peale

DEAR SIR Museum June 25th. 1805.

By tomorrows mail-stage I mean to send in one packing-case, two Polygraphs; one that you ordered for your friend, and the other in exchange for the 8vo. Size. If, on tryal, you should like the larger better than the other, be so obliging as to inform me, and I will have one made, send it to you & take the other back. I beg you not to be afraid of giving me trouble in the exchange of the Polygraphs, for I most anxiously wish you to possess such as will be perfectly to your liking, as you know how to use and appreciate the invention, this is not the case with all who have made tryal of them. The cost of carriage you tell me will be charged to you, and I beleive with the least care in shuting them up, no damage can happen to the Machinery.

I expect that those sent by Sea will have arrived about this time. it is matter of some wonder to me that you did not prefer for the use of your secretary, a machine of *three* pens, as I suppose you must frequently want more than two pieces of writing of the same subject. The additional weight of the Pen-bar is compensated by a great width of machinery, therefore greater accuracy of writing is obtained, provided the board to write on is well secured in a desk form. Altho' I seldom have occasion for more than one Copy of my letters, yet I commonly use the trible Polygraph & take away the 3d. Pen. I am with high reguard your friend C W PEALE

P.S. 27th. I have been disappointed in some parts of the Machinery of this new size, the moovements were not so correct as I could wish, therefore a delay of two days in sending it has been indispensible. I hope it will give intire satisfaction. a little more use will take off all the stifness of the Joints.

I am not certain whether it is so true as the smaller one—as I mentioned on the othir side, my desire, that you should make tryal of both these Machines, if one size pleases you better than the other, it is important that you should be satisfied, and if an Inch in length may not be thought too great an Incumbrance when you are jouneying, the chance is in favour of our doing better in one for your own use, as practice is necessary to obtain perfection. the fastening of the paper is certainly improved, and the longer the E. and W. Paralells, the better.

yours sincerely C W PEALE

RC (DLC); at foot of text: "His Excellency Thomas Jefferson Esqr."; endorsed by TJ as received 29 June and so recorded in SJL. PoC (Lb in PPAmP: Peale-Sellers Papers).

From Philippe Reibelt

MONSIEUR LE PRESIDENT! Baltimore le 25 Juin 1805.

J'ai eû l'honneur de recevoir çe Matin Vos 2 Lettres du 21 et 24—

1) Je suis penetrè de reconnaissance de l'obligeance extreme, avec la quelle Vous m'avez bien voulu a tous les points.

2) Je n'ai—malheureusement plus rien de çe, que Vous demandez—mais j'enverrais Copie de votre Lettre a Paris.

3) Je Vous enverrais sans faute les autres Volumes du Botan. Cultivateur, aussitot, que le manquant se retrouvera.

4) Peut être, que l'ouvrage Mechan.—çijoint Vous convient—le prix en est de 336 Cents.

Je Vous presente mes profonds respects. REIBELT.

EDITORS' TRANSLATION

MISTER PRESIDENT! Baltimore, 25 June 1805

This morning I had the honor of receiving your letters of the 21st and 24th.

1. I am deeply grateful for the great kindness you showed on all points.

2. Unfortunately, I do not have any more of those you requested, but will forward a copy of your letter to Paris.

3. I will send the other volumes of the *Botaniste cultivateur* without fail, as soon as the missing one is found.

4. The enclosed work on mechanics may suit you. The price is 336 cents.

I offer you my profound respect. REIBELT.

RC (DLC); endorsed by TJ as received 26 June and so recorded in SJL. Enclosure: Louis Claude Perŝon de Berainville, *Recueil de mécanique relatif à l'agriculture et aux arts, et description des machines économiques* (Paris, 1801 or 1802).

Notes on John Sibley's Accounts of the Southwest

[after 25 June 1805]

Sibley. on the country between Misipi & Rio Bravo.
on the Sabine are Salines.
rich low grounds about 3. miles wide
in dry weather but a creek
from Bayou Patron to Nacogdoches to a great extent is the handsomest country in the world. gentle hills with pleasant rich vallies & meadows.
continues to Trinity river. beyond tht more prairie.
from the river Nueces [Walnuts] to Rio bravo, poorer, abounds with Prickly pear 10. or 12. f. high. cochineal
on the Trinity many wild cattle, & millions of horses.
Nacogdoches. 100. families.
25. soldiers. all cavalry.

St. Antonio 250. houses mostly of stone.
the country round, rich prairie, gently hilly, beautiful clear gravelly streams of water. little timber
river heads 20 mi. above the city. used for irrigation.
sugar cane grows well here.
residence of the Govr. of Texas & a bishop.
60. or 70. souldiers.
from the river St. Antonio to Nueces very rich.
no settlements. silver ore
Labahie 100. below St. Antonio, on same river, 120 houses
60. or 70. souldiers.
Rio bravo or Grande.
on E. bank a town La Rado. 110. families
a company of souldiers.
here is the crossg. place frm. St. Antonio or Labahie to Mexico.
this is the only town on the E. bank of Rio Bravo below the settlemts of Sta. Fé which are 1000. mi. above
from La Rado to the mouth of Rio bravo 100. leagues
on the W. side of Rio Bravo, about 60. mi. above La Rado is a town Placido Riogrande, the more common crossg. place from St. Antonio to Mexico.
Ravillia, a handsome town a few leagues below LaRado, on W. bank.
no troops. much & fine cochineal.
West of Rio grande the country hilly, full of towns in the vallies amongst the mines of silver ore.
Valesillo is the 1st. mine worked, 50. mi. from river on the road to Mexico.
country full of sheep. some individuals 20, or 30,000
Montelrey, Montclova, Guawiela, Santander, are towns of 3. to 5000 inhab. buildgs. stone, streets pavd.
at Montelrey 100. coaches.
raise much chocolate.
150. mi. N. from St. Antonio towds. Red river, a mine of Platine not worked.
Santa fé half the size of N. Orleans. 5. or 6000. inhab. rich place. considble military. many small towns of 1. to 300 families in vicinity. Santa fé is a considble distance N.E. from river surrounded by high mountains, & rich silver mines the silver carried on mules to Mexico.
surrounded by Appaches, Hietans & Cances.
Rio grande near as large as Misipi. currt not stronger clear water, does not overflow

Nacogdoches, St. Antonio, Labahie, & La Rado are the only settlemts. in the province of Techas.
3. companies of souldiers among them all
their whole militia 7. or 800. most of them metifs, i.e. mixed Indian & Spanish.
Mattagordo, a small distance E. of the mouth of St. Antonio water for large vessels. settlemt proposed there.
the Accokesas near the mouth of Trinity. beautiful country. the Spaniards had a mission there 40. y. ago, which was broke up when Nacogdoches was established.

Distances.
Natchitoches to

	mi.
Fort Adaize	21.
Bayou Pedrie	9.
La Nanne	12.
Sea's ferry on Saline	15.
Bayou Patron	6.
Labinia	10.
Aiche Bayou	12.
Attoyaque Riv.	15
Amoledanes	3.
Bayou Attascosa	15.
Nacogdoches	10
	128

Nacogdoches to

	mi.
Angelina Riv.	21.
Naches Riv.	21
Trinity Riv.	35
Bayou Navasota	50.
R. Los Brazos dios	50
R. Colorado (red)	100.
R. St. Marcos	55.
R. Guadeloupe	25.
R. & city St. Antonio	30
Madina R.	15.
R. Nueses, a branch of Rio grande	85
Rio Grande	100.
	587

St. Antonio to

	mi.
Labahie	100[1]
St. Anto. to Rio Grande	200
Labahie to the Gulph	20
St. Antonio to Sta. Fé	600

Sibley's account of Red river.
the mouth of Red river, followg Misipi, 220. mi. from N. Orl.
water red, brackish. currt 2. mi. an hour.
Avoyelles, at high water, is an island abt 30. or 40. f abve high water.
the settlement is round a prairie 40. mi. circumference.
Hoomes's is on a bluff 120. above mouth of river
adjoining are low grounds 40. mi. sq. extendg to Appalousa. rich.
drained & watered by Bayou Robert & Bayou Boeuf, two streams of clear water, rising in the highlands between Red R. & Sabine, & falling into Chaffalya. well timbered.
Bayou rapids settlemt. handsome plantns
upper end of the Bayou choaked
this rapid is over a shoal of soft rock, easily cut.
from July to Dec. not water enough on it for loaded boats
River cane settlemt. wealthy inhabitants, on the Southern channel of an island 50. mi. long. 3. mi. broad.
40. families
Natchitoches. irregular village, meanly built, except half a dozen houses.
40. families, of which 12 or 15 are merchts. French.
Fort Claiborne 30. f. above river banks.
the lakes furnish plenty of shells for lime, also building stone, & stone coal.
Salines 12. miles N. of Natchitoches. water nearly saturated.
a Bayou from Spanish Lake. the lake 50. mi. circumf.
from this lake Bayou Dupont admits boats to within $1\frac{1}{2}$ mi. of Fort Adaize.
one mile above Grand ecore begins an isld 100. mi. long 30. mi. wide
on the S. branch is the Bayou Pierre stony creek[2] settlemt. settled by France before she ceded Louisa. to Spain, & was under the Comandt. of Natchitoches till 20. y. ago when by an agreemt between M. Vogene then Comdt. Natchitoches & M. Elibarbe Comdt. Natchitoches it was placed under the latter.
40. families. abound with provns.

Campti settlemt. a few families. 25. mi. in a streight line above Natchitoches. here begins the great raft. which choaking the river at the points of land prevents navign 100. mi. but boats pass up thro' lake Bistino.

Red river free of all obstructions from hence to Mountains

from the mouth of Little river Cane begins to abound and broad rich low grounds from 3. to mi. wide not subject to overflow.

at Long prairie there is a lake, antt. settlemt. of Caddos where the French had a settlement many years before they ceded Louisa. to Spain, they had here a fort, some soldiers, a factory, & a flour mill. a few years ago the mill irons & mill stones were brought down; about 25. years ago the French families moved down, & the Caddos 14. y. ago.

the river is forded here.

Riviere la Mine. silver mines 60. miles up it.

River Bahacheha, or Faux oacheta, or Missouri branch of Red river, heads near head of Arkansa so brackish cannot be drunk. on this & a branch of Arkansa the Panis find the Salt rock. from the mouth of this river to the main branch of the Arkansa 60. or 70. mi. the country between 33. & 34.° Lat.

Red river here & for 150. mi. up is a mile wide

About 40. y. ago Brevel went with party of Indians up Red river on a hunting voyage & to get horses. kept on S. side. the country generally a prairie. copses of cedar, button wood or Muskets, but not a stick 6. I. diam.

then mountainous country, & great deal of rock salt & silver ore. river now small & ramified.

after crossg. many mountains came to a stream running West.

went on to where streams became large & lands level, soil rich black loam. here many tribes of Hietans, Appaches, Cansas.

spotted tygers & white bears.

steered nearly South east for Sta. Fé. passed prairies, then hills, silver mines & arrived at a town of 100. houses in Sta. Fé settlemt.

many such towns for a great extent Southwardly towds. Mexico. inhabitants christian Indians & Metifs

rich mines. oar carrd on mules.

very high mountain between Sta. Fé & Red river.

from Sta. Fé settlemt reachd Panis towns in 18. days

he supposes a right line of 300. miles, all prairie.

Red river boatable a little above Pani old towns. above that for hundreds of miles not a tree large enough to make a canoe.

animals wild horses, buffalo, bears, wolves, elk deer, Foxes, Sangliers or wild hogs, antelope white hares, rabbits, spotted tyger, panther, wild cat

from mouth Red river to

		mi.
Black river		31
Avoyelles, lower end.		51.
La glaise, uppr end do.		15.
Rice's		6.
Hoome's		18.
Grubb's		21.
Bayou rapide		15.
Indian villages		22
Mt. Pleasant. Gillard's		7.
Rigolet Bondieu		6.
Monnet's		10.
Little River		24.
Bayou Brevell		20.
Natchitoches	266.	20
Grand ecore		10.
Campti		20.
Bayou Channo.		15.
Lake Bistino, thro' Channo		3.
thro' Bistino to uppr end		60.
thro' Bayou Daichet to the rivr		9.
late Caddo villages.		80.
Little river of the left.		80
Long prairie, right side		25
upper end of do.		25
Little prairie, left side		40.
upper end do.		5.
Pine bluff right side		12.
upper end do.		5.
Cedars		15.
upper end of do. at mouth of Little river of the right		40
round prairie right side first fording place	464.	20
lower end long prairie, left side		25
upper end do.		40
next prairie same side		12.
upper end do.		20
3 mile oak & pine bluff		30

Paccan grove	9.
upper end of the same	6.
carried forward	142
brought forward	142.
prairie next above Paccans	40.
upper end of the same	25.
pine bluff right side	45
white rock bluff	15
next prairie, right side	45
upper end do.	30
bayou Galle right side	6.
mouth of Mine river (Kiomichee)	25.
Pine bluff left side	25.
Bayou kick, or Bois d'arc creek	40.
the Pazzures, or Boggy R. rt side	8.
Blue river. right side	50.
Faux Oacheta, or Missouri branch	25.
Panis, or Towiache towns	70.
Panis, or Towiache old towns	150.
head bra. of Red R. or dividg. ridge	300
	1041
	266
	464
	1771
add gained by going thro' L. Bistino instead followg river	60
whole length of Red river	1831
then to the sea along the Misipi or Chafaleya 320.	

MS (DLC: TJ Papers, 234:41892-2a); undated; entirely in TJ's hand, including brackets.

On 25 June the War Department received a letter of 22 Apr. from John SIBLEY featuring a "Description of the Country" from Natchitoches to the Rio Grande, "noting the distance &c." TJ evidently drew on that communication for the first portion of the notes printed above (DNA: RG 107, RLRMS).

PLACIDO RIOGRANDE: the main road that connected Nacogdoches and San Antonio to Mexico passed through the presidio of San Juan Bautista, the site of Guerrero, Mexico (Tyler, *New Handbook of Texas*, 4:1139).

It is uncertain when the administration received SIBLEY'S ACCOUNT OF RED RIVER, but TJ's notes on it closely match a transcript dated 10 Apr. that he enclosed to Congress in a message of 19 Feb. 1806 (DNA: RG 46, LPPM, 9th Cong., 1st sess.; DNA: RG 233, PM, 9th Cong., 1st sess.; printed in ASP, *Indian Affairs*, 1:725-31).

During the 1780s, Etienne de Vaugine (VOGENE) served as commandant at Natchitoches, while Antonio Gil Ibarvo (ELIBARBE) commanded at Nacogdoches (Glenn R. Conrad, ed., *A Dictionary of Louisiana Biography*, 2 vols. [New Orleans, 1988], 2:808-9; Tyler, *New Handbook of Texas*, 3:812).

THE MOUTH OF LITTLE RIVER: Sibley was not referring to the Red River tributary of that name, the mouth of which is in present-day southwest Arkansas, but to the Sulphur River (ASP, *Indian Affairs*, 1:728-9; Dan L. Flores, ed., *Jefferson & Southwestern Exploration: The Freeman & Custis Accounts of the Red River Expedition of 1806* [Norman, Okla., 1984], 180).

RIVIERE LA MINE: the Kiamichi River.

FAUX OACHETA: the Washita River.

SPOTTED TYGERS: possibly a reference to jaguars.

A year later, Thomas Freeman and Peter Custis described INDIAN VILLAGES occupied by the Appalachees and Pascagoulas (same, 112-13).

Some of the stages Sibley included in his list of distances were branches of the Red River, such as the Rivière de Petit Bon Dieu (BONDIEU), now considered the main channel of the Red, and the first listing of Little River. The damming action of the Great Raft, an 80-mile long collection of driftwood in the Red, created distributaries, such as the one Sibley called BAYOU CHANNO, that no longer exist (same, 114-15; Jacques D. Bagur, *A History of Navigation on Cypress Bayou and the Lakes* [Denton, Tex., 2001], 61-5, 77-83).

[1] On line below, TJ canceled "Rio Grande 200."

[2] Preceding two words interlined.

Petition of David Briggs

TO THOMAS JEFFERSON, PRESIDENT OF THE UNITED STATES OF AMERICA.

Humbly sheweth,

The Petition of David Briggs, of Warwick in the County of Kent, in the State of Rhode Island and Providence Plantations, Mariner, That, at a District Court of the United States, holden at Newport, within and for the District of Rhode Island on the second Tuesday in May last, he was convicted of a breach of the fiftieth section of the Act of Congress, entitled, "An Act to regulate the Collection of Duties on Impost and Tonnage;" by which conviction your Petitioner's goods to the value of nearly two hundred and fifty Dollars, for having been illegally unladed and delivered from on board the Schooner Ann-Eliza, lately arrived within the District of Providence, from Surinam, were seized, condemned and sold, for the use of Government; and that your Petitioner was thereupon, by the Court aforesaid, further subjected to a penalty of four hundred Dollars, with Costs; for which penalty and Costs he is now confined, on Execution, in the County gaol in Providence: That in consequence of the aforesaid conviction he suffers all the disabilities prescribed by the Act of Congress aforesaid; that his name has been advertized by the Collector of the District of Providence aforesaid, in a public newspaper, pursuant to the directions of the Act aforesaid—

Your Petitioner would further represent, that according to the legal distribution of the aforesaid penalty of four hundred Dollars the one half thereof is payable to the Treasury of the United States; one fourth part to the Officers of the Customs, and the remaining fourth part to the original Informer: Which sums, together with the Costs of prosecution, yet remain wholly undischarged; and, as your Petitioner is totally destitute of property, and confined in prison, he is without the means and the hopes of ever discharging the same—

Your Petitioner would further represent, that his occupation for livelihood, from his early youth, has been that of an ordinary Seaman; and that in pursuit of his profession his industry and economy have alone, for many years, supported himself and his aged, indigent and helpless parents; and in the progress of his life he has struggled with all the embarrassments incident to friendless poverty, sickness and misfortune; and that the little property seized by Government on the present occasion was all the wealth the utmost industry and frugality have ever enabled him to collect and reserve from the immediate necessities of himself and his family—

Your Petitioner would further represent, that without the intervention of Executive mercy, by a remission of that part of the aforesaid penalty payable to the Treasury of the United States, he is without hopes of ever being released from his present confinement, or even of subsisting there, otherwise than at the public expense. In his present situation, borne down by the oppressions of poverty, bondage and infamy, his life is useless to himself, his family and his Country; but, restored to the exercise of his wonted Industry, and to his former habits of integrity, he fain would resume his duties to Society, and retrieve his forfeited reputation. For himself, however, he could with patience endure Imprisonment, or submit to any atonement that could again reconcile him to the offended laws of his Country; but when his destitue and helpless Parents, from the depth of grief and misery, implore in vain their only protector and supporter, every filial emotion urges him to the last effort for their relief. Impelled by motives thus powerful, your Petitioner appeals to the clemency of a mild and free Government, where he knows, that mercy is not deemed inconsistent with justice or policy.—

Therefore, your Petitioner respectfully submits his unfortunate Case to the consideration of the Executive, and humbly prays, that that part of the aforesaid penalty of four hundred Dollars, payable to the Treasury of the United States, be remitted to him; and that he may be restored to all the privileges and immunities, of which he has been deprived in consequence of his aforesaid conviction—Or that he otherwise be releived, as in the wisdom and clemency of the Executive shall be deemed proper.—And as in duty bound will ever pray, &c.—

Providence June 26. 1805— DAVID BRIGGS

RC (DNA: RG 59, GPR); in a clerk's hand, signed by Briggs; endorsed by TJ as received 20 July and so recorded in SJL. Enclosure: attestation, dated Warwick, 26 June, signed by Caleb Ladd and 27 others, stating that they have known Briggs "from his earliest youth" and that he has generally maintained "the character of an industrious and honest man"; his parents are indigent and completely reliant on him and Briggs has no means of making a living but by his own labor; Briggs's offence is his first known violation of the law and he has no resources to satisfy his fine; a postscript by Nehemiah Knight certifies that the subscribers are men of "good Character and standing in society," but adds that he has "not the least knowledge" of Briggs's character; a second postscript, by Arthur Fenner, concurs in Knight's opinion of the subscribers, but, like Knight, Fenner is "totally ignorant" of Briggs or his character (MS in same; attestation in an unidentified hand, signed by all; first postscript in Knight's hand and signed by him; second postscript in Fenner's hand and signed by him). Enclosed in TJ to David Howell, 21 July.

To James Dinsmore

Dear Sir Washington June 26. 05

Your's of the 22d. came to hand yesterday. I inclose you two specimens of cherry, one done with boiled linseed oil, the other with the newspaper composition you referred to. I think the former the best; but am inclined to believe that daily rubbing with wax will soon produce the same effect. I rather think therefore of leaving the floor to time to give it's proper colour. as you will but barely get the Hall floor down before my arrival, it must of course not be painted at all. I have another pound of terra di Siena for mr Barry, but suppose it, cannot go on till I go myself. I shall probably be at home on the 18th. of July. Accept my best wishes

Th: Jefferson

RC (facsimile in Goodspeed's *The Flying Quill*, June 1948). RC (Robert A. Siegel Auction Galleries, 11 Mch. 2019, lot 502); consisting of address sheet only; addressed: "Mr. James Dinsmore Monticello near Milton"; franked; postmarked Washington, 26 June.

Dinsmore's letter of the 22d was received 25 June but has not been found (Appendix iv).

From Albert Gallatin

Dear Sir June 26 1805

Donaldson, Penrose & Lucas appointed commissioners for upper Louisiana, and Thompson, Trimble & Vacher appointed for the western district of the Orleans territory have all accepted. Of the three appointed for New Orleans, we have received no answers from Gurley or Coburn, and Sebastian declines. His letter is now enclosed together with sundry recommendations received after the appointments had been made and which may assist in filling his place. Three agents must also be appointed; and I had contemplated James Brown for N. Orleans, Lewis for the western or red river district, and either Carr or Parke for upper Louisiana. When you shall have compared with the several recommendations already in your hands, I will wait on you in order to know the result.

Respectfully Your obedt Sert. ALBERT GALLATIN

RC (DLC); at foot of text: "The President of the United States"; endorsed by TJ as received from the Treasury Department on 26 June and "nominns" and so recorded in SJL. Enclosure: probably Benjamin Sebastian to an unidentified recipient, Frankfort, Kentucky, 3 June, declining his appointment as a land claims commissioner for the eastern district of Orleans Territory due to the temporary nature of the office; he asks the recipient "to communicate my determination to the President" (RC in DNA: RG 59, RD; endorsed by TJ: "Sebastian, Benj. declines as Comr. of E. district of Orleans"). Other enclosures not identified, but see below.

Writing to Madison from Pittsburgh on 19 May, John B. C. LUCAS expressed his determination to accept his appointments as both a land commissioner and a judge for Louisiana District (RC in DNA: RG 59, AOC; notation by TJ: "Lucas John B. C. accepts as Commr."). John COBURN wrote to Gallatin from Mason County, Kentucky, on 9 June to decline his appointment as commissioner. Although he had actively sought a federal office, the temporary appointment would not permit Coburn to provide for his family. If he could unite the office with some permanent appointment, such as register, then Coburn would "thankfully accept" (RC in DNA: RG 59, LAR; torn; endorsed by TJ: "Coburn John declines Comr. [. . .]").

SUNDRY RECOMMENDATIONS: in a letter to Dearborn dated 12 June from Washington, Kentucky, Daniel Vertner recommended local attorney Adam Beatty to fill the appointment that Sebastian declined (RC in DLC; endorsed by TJ: "Beatty Adam. to be Comr. East Orleans v. Sebastian"). Coburn wrote to Madison on 26 June to inform the president of General Henry Lee's desire to fill Sebastian's place as commissioner. Coburn described Lee as "among the most respectable of our Citizens" (RC in DNA: RG 59, LAR; endorsed by TJ: "Lee Genl. Henry of Kentucky to be Comr. of Orleans").

John Breckinridge recommended William C. CARR to Gallatin in a 25 Apr. letter. He believed that Carr, a young attorney who was raised in Kentucky but now resided at Ste. Genevieve, would "well discharge the duties of the agent or recorder" in upper Louisiana (*Terr. Papers*, 13:162n). William Henry Harrison, John Badollet, and Nathaniel Ewing recommended Benjamin PARKE of Indiana Territory to Gallatin for an appointment as agent for upper Louisiana (Badollet and Ewing to Gallatin, 30 May 1805, in NHi: Gallatin Papers).

To George Jefferson

MESSRS. GIBSON & JEFFERSON Washington June 26. 05

Mr. Craven Peyton has desired me to assume for him to you 156.67 D paiable the 10th. of July and 533.33 D paiable the 10th. of Aug. the first of these paiments will be a little too early for me. I will pay you 156.67 D on the 13th. of July (it will leave this place the

evening of the 11th.) and 533.33 D on the 10th. of Aug. (leaving this the evening of the 8th.) these being the precise days on which my reciepts will enable me to make these paiments for mr Peyton. Accept my friendly salutations
TH: JEFFERSON

PoC (MHi); at foot of text: "G. Jefferson"; endorsed by TJ.

PEYTON HAS DESIRED ME: Craven Peyton to TJ, [before 25 June].

To Thomas Mann Randolph

DEAR SIR
Washington June 26. 05.

Yours of the 22d. is at hand. there has been not only no new appointment of Consul at Bordeaux, but no idea that there will be a vacancy there. we know that mr Lee has given mortal offence to several of our merchants by refusing to cover foreign vessels under our flag, which he and all the other Consuls are instructed to be particularly vigilant in. he has been very meritoriously so, and his inflexibility has produced some accusations of a different nature which have been satisfactorily cleared up. indeed were he out of the way there is another person whose claims to the office are so equitable that they could not be passed over.

We are still uninformed whether the Indians from Capt Lewis will agree to stay at St. Louis till autumn. should they do so, I see nothing else which will prevent my leaving this on the 15th. of July. I shall defer giving Lilly a final answer till I get home. I am afraid the compromise you propose will not do because he will have no cropping hands separate from his jobbers. my tender love to my dearest Martha & the young ones, & affectionate salutations to yourself
TH: JEFFERSON

RC (DLC); at foot of text: "TMR"; endorsed by Randolph. PoC (MHi); endorsed by TJ.

ANOTHER PERSON: probably Isaac Cox Barnet (Barnet to TJ, 31 Dec. 1804).

Books Purchased from Philippe Reibelt

[24 Dec. 1804-26 June 1805]

1804.	Th: Jefferson in acct. with Reibelt.	
Dec. 24.	Plans des maisons de Paris	40.
	Histoire des Volcans	2.
	Vue de la colonie du Missipi.	2.
	2d. voyage a la Louisiane	4.

	Voyage a la Troade		8.	
	Annales du Museum des arts		10.	
	Voyage de Faujas en Angleterre		4.	
	Galrie des antiques		3.50	
	Voiage de Link en Portugal		2.25	
	De la richesse commerciale		2.875	
	Moyens de desinfecter l'air. Morveau		1.50	
	St. Venant des colonies modernes		2.50	
	Sentimental journey		1.10	83.725
	Cr. by note of bk US. on bk at Baltimore			83.725
1805.				
Jan. 23.	Correspondence de Rousseau		2.	
	Hist. nat. des Mineraux. Patrin		6.64	
	Hist. de Catherine II. Austera		6.78	
	Recueil sur les Salines. Struve		.75	
	Voiage de Terracine à Naples		.48	
	Voiage en Angleterre par Pictet		1.60	
	Soirées de Ferney		1.	
	Instn des droits maritimes. Boucher		4.85	
	do. commerciales. do.		4.85	
	Elemens de legislation. Perreau		1.60	
	Almanac des Ambassades Wedekind		1.35	
	Pour et Contre les E.U. Bridel		.72	
	Promenades au jardin des plantes. Pujoulx.		1.	
	[Annales du museum vol. IV. part of V.]			
	Piranesi.		13.80	
		47.42		
	Buffon de la jeunesse		1.20	
	Manuel d'hist. nat. de Blumenbach		4.20	
	Mineralogie de Haüy		11.52	
	Anatomie comparée de Cuvier		3.40	
	Flora bor. Americana. Michaux		8.64	
		28.96		
Feb.	Desodoart. Revolution de France		2.40	
	Bibliotheque geographique et instructive		10.	
	Elemens de zoographie		1.	
	Elemens physiques de la jeunesse		.40	
	Essai sur l'histoire general des mathematiques		4.	
	Lettres sur la botanique		2.80	
	voiage cosmographique[1]		1.	
	Cours de Morale de Demoustier		.80	
3.	Nouveau testament. 2. copies		1.60	
5.	respublicae diversae (10) Elzevir		4.90	

	respublica Hungariae		2.
3.	Dictionnaire Etymologique de Morin		2.80
	Dictionnaire de Poche par Catineau		1.90
13.	Romae Ichnographia.		.50
	Quator. partes orbit. vet. polyglott.		.10
	Leipsic		.10
	Annuaire de LaMarck		1.70
		38.	
	brought forward		114.38
Feb. 18.	Dictionn. de Poche de Catineau		3.80
	Pronouncing Dicty. by Tardy		1.95
	La Fontaine. fables		.64
	Contes		.64
	Resultats des guerres, traités &c Arnould		1.50
19.	Moliere		1.92
	Racine		1.39
	Corneille		2.74
	Anacharsis		9.28
			138.24
Mar. 7.	by draught of Washn. bank on Balt. do.		138.24
			0.

Apr. 18.	Plutarque de la jeunesse Blanchard		4.
May 4.	Vie de Guttenberg par Oberlin		
	Histoire du Polytypage &c par Camus. 8vo.		
6.	Manuel du Museum. 4. v. 8vo.		
June 21.	Le Botaniste Cultivateur par Dumont-Courset. 1st. & 2d. v. 8vo. 3d. & 4th wanting		
	Le parfait Jardinier par Mallet. 4to.	1.30	
	Traité sur la vigne par Chaptal, Rozier, Parmentier et Dussieux. 2. v. 8vo	2.50	
	Traité sur les abeilles par della Rocca. 3. v. 8vo.	3.20	
	Portefeuille des artistes. 4. cahiers.	14.40	
	Meteorologie des cultivateurs. 12mo.	.25	
	Ton de la bonne compagnie. p.f.	.30	
	Plans d'Architecture par Becker. 4. cahiers.	17.	
	Landbaukunst von Meinert. 4. cahiers.	16.80	
		55.75	
	60. p.c. on cost in Europe	33.45	89.20
25.	Recueil de mecanique par Person. 4to.		3.36

MS (DLC: TJ Papers, 155:27105); entirely in TJ's hand, including brackets in text; undated; on folded sheet addressed by Dearborn: "The President of the United States"; endorsed by TJ: "Reibelt."

TJ compiled this list in multiple sittings. It reflects information he had in hand as of 26 June, when he received Reibelt's letter of the preceding day, which enclosed the last item. For information on the acquired titles, see also Reibelt to TJ, 5 and 13 Nov. 1804, 4 Jan., 13, 16, and 17 Feb., 3 Mch., and 3 May 1805; TJ to Reibelt, 23 and 31 Jan., 29 May, and 21 June 1805.

[1] On next line, TJ canceled "voiage dans l'Amerique."

To Robert Smith

DEAR SIR Washington June 26. 05.

Your letter of the 24th. came to hand last night. Capt Tingey happening to come in this morning while mr Madison was here, we took into consideration the expediency of sending an express boat after the Huntress: & considering the letters which went off immediately from mr Madison & Yrujo to the Governors of Florida & Cuba, & since that, one from Yrujo to the Govr. of Porto Rico by a vessel sailing for Porto Rico the same day which may procure the liberation of the vessel; considering that if found by our express boat it will be too late for her to attain the object of her mission, and also weighing the uncertainty of the information of the capture & probability, if she was taken, we shall soon hear a confirmation, mr Madison seemed strongly against the expediency of the Express & capt Tingey concurred with him, so that on the whole we concluded to abandon the measure.

In a former letter you mentioned that the Adams could be ready for the sea in a short time. Capt Tingey says in 6. weeks; & that the Chesapeak will require a long time. would you think it adviseable for them to suspend their works on the Chesapeake, & get ready the Adams, so that if any circumstance should call for it, we might put a ship of force to sea? I suggest this merely as a matter for your consideration, without having myself formed an opinion on it.

I presume we shall have both the British & French fleets in our harbors during the Hurricane season. Affectionate salutations.

TH: JEFFERSON

PoC (DLC); at foot of text: "The Secretary of the Navy." Notation in SJL: "Huntress. Adams."

FORMER LETTER: Smith to TJ, 21 June.

From Ellen Wayles Randolph

DEAR GRAND PAPA [before 27 June 1805]

I now set down to write to you and hope you will answer my letter I have often tried to do it before but never could succeed, but now I am determined to do it I suppose you have heard that Cousin Eliza Pleasants is gone away. Uncle William and Mr. Hackley have been here and left us yesterday excuse the faults and bad writing of this letter since nothing but my anxiety to write to you and to show you I had not forgotten you could have made me do it your affectionate Grand Daughter

ELLEONORA W RANDOLPH

RC (MHi); undated; endorsed by TJ as received 27 June 1805 and so recorded in SJL.

COUSIN Elizabeth Randolph Pleasants was the daughter of Thomas Mann Randolph's sister of the same name (Melanie Randolph Miller, ed., *The Diaries of Gouverneur Morris: New York, 1799-1816* [Charlottesville, 2018], 707). WILLIAM Randolph was Thomas Mann Randolph's brother (William H. Gaines, Jr., *Thomas Mann Randolph: Jefferson's Son-in-Law* [Baton Rouge, 1966], 77).

For Richard S. HACKLEY, see Thomas Mann Randolph to TJ, 22 June.

From Samuel Overton

DR. SIR Franklin, Tennessee 27th June 1805

I have set out to the treaty to be held at the Chickasaw Nation. I still have doubts as to the safety of the person traveling from this towards Louisiania—I presume I shall be introducd to you as a man who act as an[1] agent to reside with some of the Indians Tribes, I should prefer the Cherokee, Chickasaw, Creeks, or Chacktaws—I would accept an appointment to act as an agent with any of the Indian Tribes in Louisiania—as I think I could do something of consequence for the Citizens of U. States if I was among the Indian Tribes at this time as it appears to be a perelious aera—this I presumed you will be informed of before this reaches you.

I am on my way to the treaty of the Chickasaw Nation—I am Dr. Sir with sentiments of Respect Yr. Obt. St.

SAML. OVERTON JR

NB excuse haste

S. O JR

RC (MoSHi: Jefferson Papers); endorsed by TJ as received 2 Aug. and so recorded in SJL.

[1] Preceding six words interlined in place of "an."

From Henry Sheaff

SIR Philada: 27 June 1805

You will Readily pardon me addressing this letter to you on so disagreeable Subject: being no Stranger to your Friendship for me, and mankind in General—my application originates being Security at the Custom House for Peter Kuhn; near Ten Thousand dollars; for which Judgement will be had against us both the 19 day of Augt. the officers in that department ever so lenient are not Cloathed with power to shew me much Indulgence. this Rest with the Secy of the Treasury—to whome I am an intire Stranger. I am fearfull Mr Kuhn Circumstances are such, the Havist burdon will fall on me, and who is least able to bare it—I want no delay on the part of the principal, as not much is to be had: Will you be so kind to intercede for me: that I may be Indulge'd from the day of Judgement: Say Three & Six month the Bonds shall be Regular discharg'd by me, I have been an unfortunate man with R Morris and others, I am now advanced in years with a numerous family—who look up to me for Bread Should this Request be Refus'd me I shall be a Ruined man at this period every thing dull and no Sales my Goods would be sacrefic'd. and I should become a beggar. the Indulgence of the Secy will enable me to sell off and Honorable discharge P Kuhn Debt—the attorney Genl. shall be Satisfied. from the Indulgence no loss will occure from the delay. I must once more intreat your Goodness in my behalf: this application may be improper but when you take my Sittuation: under your Consideration you will Readily pardon a distress'd person: May you long enjoy Good Health, has allways been the wish of

Sir Your obedient Humble Servt. HENRY SHEAFF

RC (NHi: Gallatin Papers); at foot of text: "His Excy Thomas Jefferson Esqr."; endorsed by TJ as received 29 June and so recorded in SJL. Enclosed in TJ to Gallatin, 30 June.

From Robert Smith

SIR, Balt. June 27. 1805

The reasons you have assigned for abanding[1] the Measure of sending out the Express-Boat are very satisfactory and I am greatly pleased with the determination. Be assured the Squadron shall not suffer on account of the Detention or the loss of the Huntress.

As in relation to economy on the general arrangements of the Navy Department it is unimportant whether the people of the Yard be employed upon the Chesapeak or the Adams. I have from the suggestions of your last favour, directed Capt Tingey to suspend the repairs of the Chesapeak and to attend to the equipment of the Adams so that she can be put in Commission whenever the President shall find it necessary. This can do no injury; and as a measure of precaution may be convenient.

As to the British & French fleets we want neither of them in our waters. Would that they were again both in their proper hemisphere.

Respectfully RT SMITH

Our farmers have already begun to send to this market wheat of the present year. It is very good and it is considered here a sample of what the wheat is generally. The price now is 1¾ Dols. ℔ Bushel and the *purchasers* are fearful it will soon be two Dollars. R S.

RC (DLC); addressed: "The President Washington"; franked and postmarked; endorsed by TJ as received from the Navy Department at Baltimore on 29 June and "Huntress. Adams" and so recorded in SJL.

YOUR LAST FAVOUR: TJ to Smith, 26 June. On the 27th, Smith instructed Thomas TINGEY to direct all repair work toward the *Adams* in order to get it ready as soon as possible (DNA: RG 45, LSO).

[1] Thus in MS.

From James Wilkinson

SIR Mississippi River, near St. Genevieve June 27th. 05.—

In a case which excites the sharpest self-reproach & exposes me to severe reprehension, I venture to address myself directly to you, with the hope that you may spare me the publick humiliation, which I have merited by an inexcusable (tho innocent) omission of Duty.

The precise injunctions of the Law, relatively to the Oath of Office I am to take, as Governor of the Territory of Louisiana, had escaped my observation until the last Evening, and the discovery has perplext, mortified & confounded me beyond expression: whatever may be your Judgment on the occasion, it cannot exceed my own self-condemnation, and unhappily for me, I have nothing to offer in extenuation of my fault, but the frank confession of it.

To remedy my delinquency & to prevent publick Injury & inconvenience, as far as may be possible, I propose this Day to take the Oath of Office, before John Edgar Esqr., of Kaskaskias, Judge of the Court of Common pleas, for, the County of   in the Territory of Indiana, (Evidence of which will accompany this Letter) and shall proceed to exercise my Civil functions, in all cases of exigency which may require prompt attention, relying on the recognition of the Government, (should it be found necessary) to confirm the Acts which may ensue.—

In the mean time, I intreat of you Sir, to pardon my presumption & to indulge me so far, as to authorize Mr. Edgar or some other Gentleman of Kaskaskias or St. Louis, to administer the oath agreably to the Letter of the Law; and you will thereby increase the Obligations already conferred on Sir

Your Zealous, faithful, obliged &, permit me to add, Affectionate Servant
JA: WILKINSON

RC (DLC); at foot of text: "Thos. Jefferson President"; endorsed by TJ. Recorded in SJL as received 8 Aug. Enclosure: Wilkinson's oath of office, declaring that he will uphold the Constitution and faithfully discharge his duties as governor of Louisiana Territory, sworn 27 June before John Edgar, judge of the court of common pleas of Randolph County, Indiana Territory (MS in same; oath in Wilkinson's hand and signed by him; attestation in Wilkinson's hand and signed by Edgar).

To Stephen Cathalan, Jr.

DEAR SIR Washington June 28. 1805

Since mine of May 5. your bill for 231 D. 09 c has been duly paid to Capt Hazard, whose acknolegement I have. since that too my loss of the wines & other articles shipped by the New Orleans has been confirmed, the vessel & cargo having been carried into Halifax, where the vessel was cleared, but the cargo condemned, on the supposition, I believe, of it's being French property. I must therefore repeat the request in mine of May 5. to send me a new supply of the Hermitage vierge de Jourdan, only instead of one hundred bottles, let it be two hundred; for when I wrote that, I thought it possible that some respect for justice in so palpable a case might have saved my wines in the New Orleans. be so good as to send also some boxes of the fine dry figs of Marseilles, & of Brignolles. these things may still be here in time for the meeting of Congress which is early in December. for their amount you will be pleased to draw on me at 30. days sight, which is a great convenience to me, there being too little commerce here to procure bills which would suit Marseilles. I learn from Capt. Hazard, & with sincere regret, the afflicting loss you have sustained in your family, and offer my friendly condolance. be so good as to present my best respects to the remaining members of your family, whom I always recollect with interest, & accept yourself my friendly salutations and assurances of respect & consideration.

TH: JEFFERSON

RC (Archives municipales, Marseilles, France); at foot of text: "Mr. Cathalan." PoC (MHi); endorsed by TJ. Notation in SJL: "200. b. Hermitage."

ACKNOLEGEMENT: probably William Hazard to TJ, 17 May, recorded in SJL as received 26 May but not found, which was likely in response to TJ to Hazard of 11 May, also not found, which confirmed payment of the $231.09 bill (see Appendix IV). AFFLICTING LOSS: see Cathalan to TJ, 8 Apr.

From Henry Dearborn, with Jefferson's Approval

SIR/ War Department June 28. 1805

I have the honor of proposing for your approbation Robert I. McKenny as a Cadet in the Regiment of Artillerists

Accept Sir, the assurances of my high respect and Consideration

H. DEARBORN

[*Approval by TJ*:]

June 29. 05.

Approved TH: JEFFERSON

RC (PHi: Daniel Parker Papers); in a clerk's hand, signed by Dearborn; at foot of text: "President of the United States"; endorsed by a clerk. FC (Lb in DNA: RG 107, LSP).

On 1 July, Dearborn forwarded a CADET warrant to Robert I. McKenny, with instructions to report to the military academy at West Point (DNA: RG 107, LSMA).

To William Fuqua

SIR Washington June 28. 1805.

Your favor of the 18th. was not recieved till last night. I do not think I retain any papers respecting the lands I sold to Thomas Warren, having delivered to him all the title papers; and the transaction is of so long standing that my memory has lost the traces of it. the lands were surveyed in the name of my father Peter Jefferson but whether patented in his name & lifetime or in my name after his death, I do not recollect. the records of the old Secretary's office will shew that. my deed to Warren very probably stated the title. that deed was recorded in Fluvanna I presume, tho' possibly it may have been recorded in the General court. the survey will be found on the surveyor's books in Albemarle. this is all the information I am able to give you from this place, nor do I suppose I could give you more from Monticello, where my papers are; because, as I before mentioned, I do not think I retained any papers respecting it. Accept my salutations & respects.

TH: JEFFERSON

PoC (DLC); at foot of text: "Mr. William Fuqua"; endorsed by TJ.

From Benjamin H. Latrobe

DEAR SIR, Stelles Hotel June 28th. 1805

I hoped yesterday morning to have personally answered the notes I had the pleasure to receive from you. But you were engaged when I did myself the favor to call, & I could not again wait upon you.—

The Method used, I believe most generally on the Wharves in London to raise Weights into & out of Vessels is by a *Walking wheel* as it is called. This Wheel brings your idea of the Wallower or Lanthern Wheel into use, but with this difference that the Man or horse walks within the Wheel, in the former & on it circumference in the latter. In

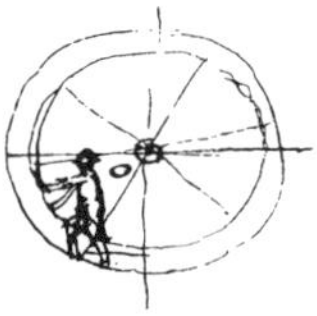

both cases his weight acts with a leverage equal to the cosine of the angle formed by a line drawn from the point of pressure on the circumference & the horizon. The wheels are used in the fortifications all over Europe & are worked by the prisoners. They are variously modified, & a thousand schemes have been tried to avoid their greatest defect the danger arising from an accidental disengagement of the Load,—by which circumstances many dreadful casualties have occurred. In large public works, these wheels, being only temporarily employed, & with less experience of danger, have been the cause of the loss of so many lives, that the hoisting machine, I have brought into use arose out of my extreme unwillingness to employ them, though otherwise undoubtedly the best means of employing the power of weight. I confess I am so pleased with your rope ladder that I shall give it a very fair trial, & have taken care to have one made, at the Navy Yard—

A few days ago (Monday) I received a most pressing letter from the president of our company to hasten my return, as our Clerk is again ill & has given notice of his resignation. Yesterday & today I have received two others, which have induced me to depend on your indulgence & to go immediately to the Northward for a short time, having first made all the arrangements for pushing the works with vigor. I shall return as soon as I can put my affairs in order at the Canal, where I must have another deputy.—

Your invitation for Monday next, Mrs. Latrobe as well as myself regret exceedingly that we cannot therefore have the honor of accepting.

I beg You to accept the assurances of the most grateful attachment & respect with which I am

Your faithful hble Servt B HENRY LATROBE.

RC (DLC); addressed: "The president of the United States"; endorsed by TJ as a letter of 28 June received 27 June and so recorded in SJL.

TJ evidently shared some NOTES, not found, related to the loading and unloading of heavy articles such as slabs of construction stone. For projects in Philadelphia, Latrobe introduced a HOISTING MACHINE that used hand cranks to raise stones. He employed the machine on his Washington projects as well (Darwin H. Stapleton, ed., *The Engineering Drawings of Benjamin Henry Latrobe* [New Haven, 1980], 240-1; Latrobe, *Correspondence*, 2:95-7).

From Daniel Ludlow

SIR New York 28th June 1805

I have the honor to enclose you William Hazards receipt for $\$231\frac{9}{100}$ paid him for your account. this I have been led to do in consequence of your letter to him (which you have enclosed) under date of the 11th. May, wherein you desire him to call on Mr. Ludlow to whom your agent Mr Barnes was to remit a draft on the Bank of the U.S. for the amount, on which Subject I have to observe that no such remittance has ever come to my hands and presume it has been omitted.

I have the honor to be Sir Your most obedt Servt.

DAN LUDLOW

RC (MHi); at foot of text: "His Excellency Thomas Jefferson President of the United States"; endorsed by TJ as received 30 June and so recorded in SJL. Enclosure: TJ to William Hazard, 11 May, not found (see Appendix IV). For other enclosure, see the following letter.

Daniel Ludlow (1750-1814) was a leading New York City merchant and president of the Manhattan Company. TJ had appointed him navy agent for the city in April 1801, based in part on a recommendation from Aaron Burr. The appointment drew criticism, however, due to Ludlow's Loyalist sympathies during the American Revolution. He resigned the office in November 1803. By 1808, financial reverses forced the dissolution of Ludlow's mercantile firm and his resignation from the Manhattan Company (ANB; New York *Public Advertiser*, 17 Feb. 1808; Vol. 33:308-9; Vol. 34:158n, 256, 522-3; Vol. 42:365n).

From Daniel Ludlow

SIR New York 28th June 1805

In the letter which I had the honor of writing you by this mornings post, I omitted enclosing you Capn William Hazards receipt, the same you have herewith—

I have the honor to remain Sir Your most obedt Servt.

DAN LUDLOW

RC (MHi); at foot of text: "His Excellency Thomas Jefferson"; endorsed by TJ as received 1 July and so recorded in SJL. Enclosure not found.

From Thomas Moore

SIR, So. Carolina, Spartanburgh District, June 28th, 1805—

Colonel Thomas Lehre of Charleston the Gentleman who will do me the honer to deliver this letter, intends making a tour to the springs in Virginia with Mrs. Lehre & his family, and returning to Carolina by Washington. It gives me great pleasure to have it in my power to introduce him to you, as one of our most respectable characters, & a firm Republican, who has long possessed the confidence of his fellow Citizens, he has held under our state government a number of important civil, & Military offices, all of which he has discharged with honer to himself, & advantage to the public. Republicanism in South Carolina is much indebted to the influence & indefatigable exertions of this gentleman.

I remain Sir, With the highest respect, your obd. servt.

THO. MOORE

RC (DLC); at foot of text: "Thomas Jefferson Esqr. President of the U. States"; endorsed by TJ as received 24 Sep. and so recorded in SJL, where TJ connected it by a brace and notation "recd. by mr Lehré" with entries for letters received the same day from John Gaillard of 25 May, William Johnson of 25 May, William Butler of 30 May, Peter Freneau of 2 June, and an undated letter from Paul Hamilton.

From J. Morey

MUCH HONOURED SIR, Doncaster Yorkshire June 28th, 1805

The difficulty I feel in addressing myself to you, elevated as you are by your Country, to the very summit of glory, may be more easily conceived than expressed.

If I be deemed impertinent in taking so great a Liberty, I would earnestly solicit your indulgence for my presumption; & beg you to attribute it, to my eagerness of becoming a Citizen of that Land, which time will hereafter recognize as one of the greatest in the Universe.—In matters of high importance, I have ever considered it the best, & the safest mode, to apply for information at the Fountain-Head, as being generally the most pure; for the turbid quality of a stream is more owing to its passing thro' different soils, than to any imperfection in the source.—The situation we fill here, is that of Mrs. Morey's keeping a limited Boarding School for Ladies; while I assist in some of the departments of it; & we have hitherto met with flattering encouragement.—It will naturally be enquired, why we wish to leave a Place where we are doing well. Here I beg leave to notice, that while I view the distorted & deranged affairs of this Country; the fear of horrible scenes taking place, awakens painful solicitude, for the future welfare of my Offspring.—Some time since, a ray of hope for the accomplishment of my wish to reach America, presented itself. I took the liberty of writing to Mr. Monro who kindly & liberally offered to assist us in establishing a School at Richmond, Virginia: but unfortunately he was called immediately after to Spain.

I address you Sir, as the present Father of a *small* Family, compared with the extent of your Country; & if it be not inconsistent with your high station, to honour me with your opinion, of the prospect of our meeting with success in any part of America, in Kentucky, or even as far as Louisiana; I should feel myself very highly obliged.—If your opinion be encouraging, we shall most gladly embrace the opportunity of being added to the number of your free & happy Family.—My eldest Son; nearly sixteen years of age, plays extremely well on the Piano, & will be able to teach very soon; & most of the other branches of Education are taught by ourselves. Still Sir, your distinguished sense must allow, that it would be rashness in the extreme, to encounter an uncertain Element, in order to transplant a wife & four Children, without a well grounded prospect of success.—You perceive Sir, I am taking that freedom with you, which a man would with his Friend; a Child with a Parent; & while I hear of your fulfilling the destinies of Providence; of your having been chosen, & rechosen, to the honourable situation you so ably fill; by a People enlightened, liberal & free; I look upon your virtues as being of that cast & complexion, to give me the hope of an indulgent reply.—Should your country be stocked with persons of our description, & it is your opinion that the chance would be against us, the obligation will be further enhanced by your kindly informing me, if Land, with a good Title, can be purchased in Kentucky upon eligible Terms; & near to some Town. It is true, the occupation would be novel to me, but man, with the use of his limbs, & a moderate understanding, united with Steadiness & Attention may overcome difficulties, which the indolent & pampered sons of wealth would shudder at the Idea of. I mention Kentucky merely on the supposition of its wanting Inhabitants, indeed I can easily suppose that there are few parts in the *Utd. States* which have not open arms ready to receive those who may be esteemed as benefactors to a country which they long to call their own. I would gladly transplant my family, into almost any part of that happy Soil, where the olive branch of Peace, has seemed to take so deep root, & should I be the object of fortune's favour, in receiving a flattering reply, gratitude will at all times oblige me to feel, what I now beg, with the highest consideration & respect, to subscribe myself your Excellency's most Humble & Obged Servt.

J MOREY

RC (DLC); addressed: "To his Excellency Thos. Jefferson Esqr. President of the United States of America"; franked; postmarked Baltimore; endorsed by TJ as received 12 Sep. and so recorded in SJL. Enclosure: undated newspaper announcement of Mrs. Morey's Doncaster "Boarding School, For Fourteen Young Ladies" with details on the cost of instruction and lodging.

J. Morey was teaching in Doncaster, England, by 1797. His wife's boarding school opened in 1799, and besides assisting her, he taught dance at another local academy. Mrs. Morey sold the boarding school in 1815 (*Leeds Intelligencer*, 3 July 1797, 23 Dec. 1799, 23 July 1804; *York Herald, and General Advertiser*, 30 Dec. 1815).

From James W. Muse

SIR, Powhatan C. June the 28th. 1805.

Being anxious to acquire a more perfect knowledge in science, and not having funds to execute so desirable a purpose, I have taken the liberty of writing to you to solicit your benevolence.

It has always been my wish to have a Classical and Scientifical education, but unfortunately my situation has never been such, as to enable me to carry it into execution. By the time I entered my eighteenth year, necessity compelled me to procure a subsistence from my own exertions. The only profession for which I was in the smallest degree qualified, was that of a teacher. I accordingly took a small school indulging the pleasing hope, that, I might, with frugality, save a sufficiency to give myself, at least one year's, schooling. But in that I am very much disappointed. Not having been in the habit of furnishing myself, I had no idea of the expences I must of necessity incur. With the most strict observance of economy, my salary is hardly sufficient to support me.

As I cannot defray the expences of an education, I wish to act as an assistant, in a public seminary, or to a private teacher. In such a situation I would be content with very moderate wages; provided I could have part of the day allotted me to study. My time should be devoted exclusively to study, and the duties that might be assigned me.

The object of this letter Sir, is to solicit you to procure me a place. I expect your surprise will be excited at such a request, from one, with whose character or person you are not acquainted. Should you think proper to assist me, you shall be furnished with sufficient evidence of my deportment.

I most earnestly Solicit you Sir, to use your interest[1] in endeavouring to procure me a situation. It is my[2] only hope; and should I fail in this attempt, I shall give up every idea of ever acquiring more knowledge than I now possess. If you comply with my request, I hope you will give me an immediate answer; as I shall enter into no engagement, until I hear from you.

A letter directed to Genito Bridge, will be thankfully received, and duly attended to.

Accept Sir, my wishes for your happiness and prosperity.

JAMES W. MUSE

RC (ViW: Tucker-Coleman Collection); endorsed by TJ as received 3 July and so recorded in SJL.

[1] Interlined in place of "influence."
[2] Muse here canceled "last and."

To Craven Peyton

DEAR SIR Washington June 28. 05.

Immediately on the reciept of your letter recieved on the 25th. I informed mr Jefferson that I would pay him for you 156.67 D on the 13th. of July and 533.33 D on the 10th. of August. on a rigorous attention to dates I found I was obliged to take three days more of July than you had desired. I now inclose you Bullock's deed, & that for the parts of the warehouse owned by the three girls, according to your request. I expect to be in Albemarle by the 18th. of July. Accept my salutations & respects. TH: JEFFERSON

PoC (ViU); at foot of text: "Mr. Craven Peyton"; endorsed by TJ. For enclosures, see Peyton to TJ, 25 Apr.

YOUR LETTER: Peyton to TJ, [before 25 June].

To Ellen Wayles Randolph

MY DEAREST ELLEN Washington June 28. 05

I recieved your letter (without date) with great pleasure, for it always gives me pleasure to hear from Edgehill. in return for your news from thence, I have none to give you from this place which would interest you, except that mrs Harrison Smith is well, dined with me the other day, & desired me to present her love in the first letter to you.

she is now in the country at a neat little box they have a few miles from the city. you do not inform me whether you have all read all the books I have given you; because till that is done you know I am not to give any more. I send you some pieces for your volume of poetry some of which have merit, and intend to catch you in bed in the morning of the 18th. of July; against which I know not how you are to guard yourself, but by not going to bed at all the over night. kiss your Mama for me, and tell her I write to her through you. Salute our dear Anne for me also, and all the little ones: and present my affections to your papa. tender salutations to yourself. to Virginia's meditations no interruption will be welcome. salute her for me however the moment of respite she has from reverie. TH: JEFFERSON

PoC (MHi); at foot of text: "Miss Eleanor W. Randolph"; endorsed by TJ. For enclosures, see Ellen Wayles Randolph to TJ, [before 18 July 1805].

YOUR LETTER: Ellen Wayles Randolph to TJ, [before 27 June 1805].

From Albert Gallatin, with Jefferson's Note

[29 June 1805]

Enclosed to the President for his signature
by his obed. Sevt. ALBERT GALLATIN

[*Note by TJ*:]
act dividing territory of Orleans into 2. districts for the land office, to wit by the Misipi & Cafaleya.
recd June 29. 05.

RC (DLC); undated; endorsed by TJ as a letter of 29 June 1805 received from the Treasury Department on that day and "land-districts Orleans" and so recorded in SJL. Enclosure: draft order, not found, for establishing districts in Orleans Territory (see below).

DISTRICTS FOR THE LAND OFFICE: the third section of the act of 2 Mch. "for ascertaining and adjusting the titles and claims to land, within the territory of Orleans, and the district of Louisiana" stated that "the territory of Orleans shall be laid off into two districts, in such manner as the President of the United States shall direct." Writing to John Thompson on 2 July, Gallatin enclosed "an extract of the act of the President establishing the boundaries of the Western & Eastern land districts" of the territory. On 8 July, Gallatin also sent copies to Allan B. Magruder, James Brown, Felix Grundy, James Trimble, and Francis Vacher. The office for the eastern district was to be located at New Orleans, the western district office in Opelousas County (U.S. Statutes at Large, 2:326; *Terr. Papers*, 9:463-4, 468-9; Gallatin, *Papers*, 11:278-9).

From General Washington Johnston

Honored Sir Vincennes June 29th. 1805.

In addition to a recommendation made in my favor by Governor Harrison (which I doubt not You'l find in the Honble. The Secretary of State's (Mr. Gallatin's) Office, having been inclosed by me, some time since—) I inclose you a Recommendatory Petition, signed by a number of Actual Settlers and farmers of Louissiana.

Excuse, if you Please, my intrusion! I am Honored Sir Your Hu'ble. Servt. Genl. W. Johnston.

RC (DNA: RG 59, LAR); at foot of text: "His Excy. Thos. Jefferson"; endorsed by TJ as received 2 Aug. and so recorded in SJL; also endorsed by TJ: "to be Comr. Louisiana." Enclosure: petition signed by 90 citizens of St. Louis district, recommending General Washington Johnston for appointment as recorder for the land office in Louisiana District authorized by Congress on 2 Mch.; the petitioners cite their familiarity with Johnston "and his knowledge of the French and English languages" (RC in same; at head of text: "To His Excellency Thomas Jefferson Esquire. President of the United States of America").

General Washington Johnston (1776-1833) was an attorney and postmaster at Vincennes. A native of Culpeper County, Virginia, Johnston settled in what became Indiana Territory while still in his teens. He served in the territorial and state legislatures and was speaker of the house of representatives (George R. Wilson, "General Washington Johnston," *Indiana Magazine of History*, 20 [1924], 123-53; Stets, *Postmasters*, 116).

Memorandum from Thomas Munroe

Received the Presidents Draft on Treasury of U.S. for		$10,000.
Paid out of it from 11 June to this day viz 29 June.		
Benjamin King, for Sundries, Presidents House	267.27	
John Philips, for Digging & removing earth, cellar East of the Presidents House	235.69	
Timothy Caldwell, for Bricks for the Capitol	508.24	
Josiah Riggin for Plank for—Ditto	215.39	
William S Gantt for Bricks for Capitol	279.	
John Lenthall on account of his Services	300.	

Robert Sutton for Hauling Stone to Prests. House	40.	
Jno. McCleland for Bricks for Gutters War Office to be repaid	123.25	
William Stewart for Lime for Capitol	753.75	
Ditto for Freestone—for Ditto	1100.	
William Nevitt On Acct. for rough Stone	100.	
William Foxton—plaisterer, work in Presidents Ho.	75.11	
Corns. Coningham—Lime for War Office to be repaid	42.21	
Sundry Waggoners from Fredk. Coty Md. for Lime, Capitol	57.90	
Saml N Smallwood for Plank—Capitol	30.06	
Ditto wharfage Sundries, Do.	4.14	
John Evans, balance of $1350, for Arching over the Office story of So wing of Capitol ℔ Contract	750.	
George Blagdin, On Acct. Contract for Cutting, Carving and fitting Freestone at Capitol	3,000.	
Seth Burke—for Lime—Capitol	600.60	
George St. Claire for Sand—Do.	209.52	
Benjamin King, for Materials & work—gin on Presidents Ho.	85.49	
Benjamin H Latrobe for a quarters Salary	425.	
Alexander Cockrane—Ironmongery for Presidents Ho	22.27	
Buller Cocke for Lime—Capitol	350.	
Waggoners Do Do	31.90	
Thomas G Howard—Hauling 231 barrells lime from wharf to Capl	23.10	
Sundries for work about War Office, to be reimbursed	284.79	
		9,914.68
	Ds.	85.32

N.B. $43,000 of the $130,000 appropriated last Session has been Drawn from the Treasury. 29 June 1805

THOMAS MUNROE

MS (DLC); at head of text: "11th. June 1805"; endorsed by TJ: "Washington. Munroe Thos. acct. to June 29. 05"; note by TJ at foot of text: "June 29. 05. gave warrt for 10,000."

From Robert Patterson

SIR, Philada. Saturday evening June 29h. 1805

On the receipt of your favour of the 13th. announcing the resignation of Mr. Boudinot, and your pleasure in appointing me as his successor, I entered into a free communication with him on the subject of the mint. He has shown me the most friendly attention, & has formally introduced me to the other Officers of the institution; from whom I doubt not to experience the most cordial co-operation.

But, Sir, the *commission*, which you were pleased to signify should be forwarded in due time, has not yet been received—I can therefore only take personal charge of the Mint, on Monday next, when Mr. Boudinot wishes to deliver it over to me; but will refrain from signing warrants, or doing any other official act, till fully authorized, or further instructed.

I am, Sir, with sentiments of the highest respect & esteem, Your Most obedt. Servt. RT. PATTERSON

RC (DLC); endorsed by TJ as received 1 July and so recorded in SJL.

From Robert Smith

SIR, Balt. June 29. 1805

The Enclosed I received this Moment. It is an Extract from the Coffee House Book of this place. It would thence seem that the Store Ship the Huntress has been recaptured by the English.

Respectfully RT SMITH

RC (DLC); endorsed by TJ as received 1 July and "Huntress" and so recorded in SJL.

ENCLOSURE

Extract from Coffee House Book

Extract fm. the Coffee House Book. June 29th.
Arrived the Schooner Baltimore 12 Days fm. Bermudas, The Cambrian & Driver have sent into Bermuda's the Spanish privateer Schooner Maria, Antonio LeBo Master, She had captured the Charles Carter[,] Tomkins, of Norfolk from Wilmington N.C. bound to Falmouth & the Ship Huntress of Boston from the City of Washington bound to Gibraltar loaded as the Captain Says for account of the government [of] the U.S. they were Recaptured in sight of the Westend of Bermuda by the British Letter of Marque's on the 9th Inst & supposed to have been ordered to Europe

MS (DLC); torn; in a clerk's hand.

The new captors of the HUNTRESS sent the ship to Liverpool, where in September 1805 a British admiralty court ordered that the ship and cargo should be restored to their owners (NDBW, 6:72-3, 278-9).

To Albert Gallatin

TH:J. TO MR GALLATIN June 30. 05.

I find by the inclosed letter from Henry Sheaff, that after having been once an immense sufferer as security for Robert Morris, he is now likely to be so again as security for Peter Kuhn. a man in distress may be pardoned the error of supposing that in a public transaction he can have a resource in the private regard of a public officer. but considering him as an innocent security, for a very large sum, as one sincerely meaning to discharge his engagements & asking time only that he may avoid useless sacrifice and make the most of his funds for the public benefit as well as his own, and indeed as a citizen entitled to be covered by the government from unnecessary loss, I presume he may expect such indulgence as these considerations & the course of business in the department justify. are these definite as to time, or indefinite & governed by circumstances?

When do you propose to leave town? I wish to know, because I must ask mr Smith's attendance previous to your departure, to consult on the depredations committed on our commerce.

RC (NHi: Gallatin Papers); addressed: "Mr. Gallatin"; endorsed by Gallatin. PoC (DLC). Notation in SJL: "Sheaff." Enclosure: Henry Sheaff to TJ, 27 June.

From James Oldham

SIR Richmond 30th. June 05.

I am exceding thankful for your favor of the 14 June. which has come safe to hand with its Inclosure: I have 14 Dores finish,d and Shall make the sashes for the S.E portico next. the Dores I shall send up by the first Boats that are from Milton: I finde I shall not have a sufficiency of Lumber to compleat the hole of the dores as early as I could wish owing to my calculating the quantity two scant, and it is very difficult to precoure seasond Lumber in this Plaice that will plain to $1\frac{1}{2}$ I. thick: Mr. Gallego is so well Pleasd with the ornements which Mr. Andrews has sent, has declind haveing any that are maid in this Plaice and desirs me to rite to Mr. Andrews for all that may be nesary for his House: I am perswaided his ornements will meet with a rady Sail in Richmond and hope he will send on an assortment immediatly:

Adue And may Heaven Bless You Your Obt. Hml. Sert.

JAMS. OLDHAM

P.S have Taken the Liberty to inclose the drawing of one of the frunts of the corinthian Modilions which must beg the faver of you ether to Solicet Mr. Andrews to have done or Please to order 115 of them Turnd and Sent with the composition: I cant get them Turnd in Richmond under 9d. each which is Two High.

RC (MHi); at foot of text: "Thoms. Jefferson Esqr:"; endorsed by TJ as received 4 July and so recorded in SJL. Enclosure not found.

From Elizabeth G. Tart and Sarah Amelia Bampfield

Bethlehem June 30th. 1805.

In our present unhappy situation we apply for assistance to Mr. Jefferson—, Mama is in a very ill state of health which is entirely owing to the present disagreeable Accomadation which she is obliged to submit to—. Captn. Kennedy her agent has failed in a remittance she expected—and the opinion here being against her wishes or inclination. we wish to go on to Baltimore to Mrs. Cave that she may be near a friend but have not the means—Inclosed she sends you her Note hoping you will render her that favor, which should it not be returned on demand she will as soon as the Season admits return home and be punctual in the payment of.

I enclose you one I have written to Governor M'Kean which Mama submits to your discretion fearing to cause any quarrels—& begs that some friend of Judge Johnsons may interfere but not himself. If 'tis necessary she begs you will call on her in Judge Johnsons favour—And the Letter need not be sent unless you think proper to do so—

You will I trust excuse our presumption as we are here friendless and unprotected—We are very respectfully yours.

ELIZABETH G. BAMPFIELD
and S A BAMPFIELD

RC (DLC); addressed: "Thomas Jefferson—Esqr. President of the United States District of Columbia Virginia"; franked and postmarked Bethlehem, Pennsylvania, 1 July; endorsed by TJ as received 3 July and so recorded in SJL with notation "[insane] same as Anon. Jun. 22." Enclosure: note dated Bethlehem, June 1805, which reads: "Captn Kenedy pay to the order of the Honble Thomas Jefferson—five hundred dollars and place the same to My account—Amelia Bampfield" (MS in same; in hand of Sarah Amelia Bampfield). Other enclosure not found.

Elizabeth G. Tart (1776-1817) was the sister of Sarah Amelia Bampfield. Together, the two women wrote a dozen letters to TJ in 1805. The following year, Elizabeth Tart married William S. Hasell of Charleston, South Carolina, who soon became the owner of the North Carolina *Wilmington Gazette*. In 1809, she and her husband were sued as the "Committees of Mrs. S. A. Bampfield." After her husband's death in 1815, it is possible that Elizabeth resumed using her premarital surname, and traveled to Liverpool, England, where she died in 1817 (Robert F. Clute, *The Annals and Parish Register of St. Thomas and St. Denis Parish, in South Carolina, from 1680 to 1884* [Charleston, S.C., 1884], 85; *Charleston Courier*, 11 July 1806; Charleston *City Gazette & Daily Advertiser*, 23 Aug. 1809; Raleigh, N.C., *Star*, 20 Oct. 1815; *New-York Daily Advertiser*, 16 Dec. 1817; Brigham, *American Newspapers*, 2:780-1).

Notes on Labor for Digging Cellars

June. 1805.

In digging for the Western offices of the President's H. the following assortment of labour, appeared well balanced.

3. diggers
3. loaders
3. carts (1. horse)
2. drivers

the earth was carried about 200. yds.

MS (CSmH); partially dated; entirely in TJ's hand.

Laborers dug the west side of the cellar wall at the PRESIDENT's House in the summer of 1804. In June 1805, John Philips was paid for digging the cellar to the east of the house (Thomas Munroe to TJ, 31 July 1804, 29 June 1805).

Recipe for Mahogany Varnish

[June 1805?]

A Varnish for mahogany furniture. from Gilbert Stuart

boiled linseed oil } in equal parts
spirits of turpentine }
add $\frac{1}{6}$ part of wax.
warm the whole in a gentle heat, to about the consistence of butter in hot weather.
rub it on the furniture with a woollen cloth.
it cannot be sat in the same day.
requires renewing, perhaps once a quarter.

MS (DLC); undated; entirely in TJ's hand, including endorsement: "Recipe. Varnish for furniture."

In 1803, GILBERT STUART set up a portrait studio in Washington. TJ invited the artist to dinner on a few occasions and sat for Stuart in 1805. The artist moved his studio to Boston in July 1805 (Carrie Rebora Barratt and Ellen G. Miles, *Gilbert Stuart* [New Haven, 2004], 239, 242, 285; Vol. 45:714, 720; Appendix II).

From Arthur Daly

Castlerea (a Post Town) Ireland
first July 1805

SIR

Nothing but the Justice and benevolence of your Character, could tempt an obscure Stranger, as I am, to intrude on your attention, but I trust, the anxiety of a Father for the fate of a Family of Eight individuals, however obscure, will plead my excuse—Not to take up your Excellency's time, which I know must be precious, I shall proceed to the Business which induces me thus to address you—

So long since as the Year 1792, I saw the heavy Clouds which were gathering over this, my Native Countrey (and which have since burst with such violence on it,) and wish'd, circumstanced as I was, with a numerous, young and helpless family, to avoid such distressful scenes—The only Countrey I thought safe to remove to, was America, and in order to secure as asylum there, I wrote to a friend in New York, towards the close of that year, to purchase a small tract of Ground for me in that Countrey, to which I might retire in case of need, if I could get my Family and Property safe from hence

Agreeable to my desire, he made a Purchase of One Thousand Acres (I fear unfortunately for me) in the State of Virginia, Monongalia County, and is, I believe, in the district call'd Indiana

In Spring 1797, I went to New York, and found my friend had removed his Family from that City to Lancingburg This disappointment, together with the heat of the place, brought on a Nervous Fever, and in the Month of August following, I was obliged to return to Ireland, without having seen the Lands, and finding it was very doubtfull, that as an Alien, I could ever obtain Possession of them

My friend is since dead, and the Title Deeds are in the hands of Mr. William Hill, Merchant in New York, one of his Execrs. As I plainly see our Political Storms are not yet over in this devoted Countrey, I would gladly make one effort more to avoid their fury, by removing my family to a place of safety—Born in the middle rank of Life and bred to the Linen Business, Practising Industry and Œconomy, and with a Property of Two to Four Thousand Pounds, as the case might be, I think my Family would not be useless members of such a State as yours, and tho' the loss or Possession of the above Lands, should not influence my resolution of going to America, yet I would be very glad to know, if, on my becoming a resident there, I should have a probable prospect of obtaining possession of what was Purchased and honestly paid for with my Money, and without the smallest intention or wish on my part to infringe the Laws of the State, and without my even knowing that any Law existed against such a Purchase

From your Excellency's goodness I would hope for this information, and also that you will not look upon the liberty I have taken, as quite unpardonable—

With the most respectfull Esteem for your Character, I am Sir your Excellency's Obedt. Humle. Servt. ARTHUR DALY

RC (DLC); endorsed by TJ as received 6 Oct. and so recorded in SJL.

WILLIAM HILL sold wine, tobacco, linen, and other sundries from his store at 80 Broad Street in New York (*New-York Commercial Advertiser*, 11 Apr. 1801).

From Henry Dearborn, with Jefferson's Approval

SIR. War Department July 1. 1805

I have the honor of proposing for your approbation George Bumford, Joseph G. Totten & William McRee Cadets, to be appointed Second Lieutenants in the Corps of Engineers

Accept Sir the assurances of my high respect & consideration

H. DEARBORN

[*Approval by TJ:*]
July 1. 05.
Approved TH:J

RC (PHi: Daniel Parker Papers); in a clerk's hand, signed by Dearborn; at foot of text: "President of the United States"; endorsed by a clerk. FC (Lb in DNA: RG 107, LSP).

On 1 July, Dearborn informed George Bomford (BUMFORD), Joseph G. TOTTEN, and William MCREE that the president had approved of their appointments (FC in Lb in DNA: RG 107, LSMA).

To Albert Gallatin

TH: JEFFERSON TO MR GALLATIN July 1. 05.

I return you Morris's letter, claiming for Kibber paiment of the bill to be drawn on us for monies due from France to Comfort Sands a bankrupt of whom Kibber is the assignee. the government is in this case merely the channel of paiment. as it is liable to no process from a court, it is bound to do voluntary justice, & precisely as a court would direct if it had authority. the money, claimed by two individuals, each for himself, should not be withdrawn from the ordinary tract of law, merely because it passes through the hands of the public. both parties being of New York we should direct our attorney there to bring a bill of interpleader, in the proper court, praying the court, as in Chancery, to call the parties before them, to interplead & shew their rights, & the court to decree to which we shall pay it; & to be informed that the money is placed in the bank or shall be brought into court under it's order. the parties will each immediately plead & prove their respective rights, and it may be brought on by motion, & decided at once. but should this be in the federal or state court? the parties being of New York, the state court has a right to decide claims between them, & we have no interest to change their natural forum. such a change might give an advantage to one over the other, by a change of the judge or of the rule of decision. I think therefore we should carry them before their own court to do justice between them in their own way. this proceeding may be instituted in the name of the District attorney. Affectionate salutations.

RC (NHi: Gallatin Papers); addressed: "The Secretary of the Treasury." PoC (DLC). Notation in SJL: "Morris, Kibber & Sands." Enclosure not found.

New York City merchant COMFORT SANDS declared bankruptcy in June 1801 and fellow city merchant Isaac Kibbe was named assignee of his vast estate. Sands had recently filed a claim in New York under the Louisiana treaty and conventions for the loss of a ship that had been taken by a French privateer and condemned at Bordeaux in 1797. Robert Morris, Jr., wrote to the State Department in the summer of 1805 regarding Sands's claim. Madison forwarded the letter to the Treasury Department as the proper arbiter of "questions which may be raised in whom the real interest of the claim resides" (DAB; Syrett, *Hamilton*, 26:55-6; Madison, *Papers, Sec. of State Ser.*, 10:220-1; Greg H. Williams, *The French Assault on American Shipping, 1793-1813* [Jefferson, N.C., 2009], 218; Vol. 42:402-3).

From Albert Gallatin

DEAR SIR [1 July 1805]

It appears from the enclosed letters of F. Baring, and Mr Merry that the last British instalmt. of 200,000 Stg. will be paid in London on 15th instt.—This is a great relief to us and still more to the Banks, as the exportation of that sum in specie would have distressed them at this moment beyond measure.—That being paid, the only extraordinary expence to be provided for is the 3,750,000 dollars claim assumed by the convention with France, payment of which may now be daily expected. On this day, after having paid the quarterly interest on the public debt, we have more than 4,200,000 dollars left in the Treasury; so that, instead of paying only 2 millions of those claims from the Treasury & borrowing the rest as we had stated in our estimates to Congress, we will be able to pay the whole without borrowing any thing. This will, if the bills come all at once & immediately, drain the treasury very low. But, as, if we overcome this difficulty, there is no probability, unless in case of war, that during your administration any other loan shall be wanted, it was an object to strain every nerve to meet this demand without recurring to that kind of resource. Within six weeks we will be at ease, and may then resume the suspended expenditures, particularly the payments on account of the sinking fund which are much in arrears.

I submit the draft of an answer to R. Morris, which I have purposedly made less explicit than your opinion seemed to purport, in order to be able to decide according to the circumstances of the case when they shall all be known.

I do not recollect any instance of a suit on a revenue bond in which I have interfered. The district attornies have on some occasions as I understand assumed the responsibility of giving some indulgence. But less is shown in that species of suits than in any other, not only because there must be a certainty in the collection of the revenue, but because the law directs in that case that the bond shall be put in suit on the day it becomes due if not paid. This subject, as to details, is under the immediate superintendence of the Comptroller as he has the direction both of the revenue and of all the suits in the United States, and, if Mr Sheaff had made an application to me, I would have referred it to him. If you have no objection to his letter to you being thus placed on the public files of that office, it may be referred in that manner; but if you have any, Mr Sheaff should write to the Comptrr. or to me and obtain from the district attorney a statement of the case with his opinion that the security of the United States will not be injured by the delay which may be granted—

Respectfully Your obedt. Servt. ALBERT GALLATIN

RC (DLC); undated; at foot of text: "The President of the United States"; endorsed by TJ as received from the Treasury Department on 1 July and "Morris v. Sands. Eng. instalmt Fr. bills" and so recorded in SJL. Enclosure: Francis Baring & Company to Gallatin, London, 21 May; they have learned that the British government "has formally acquiesced in the proposal to pay here on the 15th. July the third Instalment of £200,000" as required for the resolution of debt claims; although they have yet to receive a £50,000 remittance from Boston, they expect it daily and will pay the installment "on the Day presented" (Gallatin, *Papers*, 11:86). Other enclosures not found.

INSTALMT.: see Gallatin to TJ, 20 Feb.

DAILY EXPECTED: Gallatin had for some time been anticipating the arrival of bills for payment of American claims against French spoliations, which the United States assumed as part of the Louisiana Purchase. Due to the deliberation process of the French board of liquidation, U.S. minister John Armstrong was not able to start drawing up bills until 3 May. The Treasury Department received a list of the claims in September (Madison, *Papers, Sec. of State Ser.*, 9:203, 326; Gallatin, *Papers*, 11:489; Vol. 45:548-9).

From George Jefferson

DEAR SIR Richmond 1st. July 1805

Having but just returned home, after a longer absence than I had contemplated—and apprehending that you may be put to inconvenience from the long credit on which Mr. G. was induced to sell your Tobacco, in preference to reducing the price, I take the earliest opportunity of proposing, (as the notes he received I observe are not negociable at the Bank) that you send us your own notes made "negociable at the Bank of Virginia" at 60, 90, & 120 days, each for 1000$, to make even money. the first I have no doubt may be discounted the first discount day after its receipt; & the other two, so soon as they come within 60 days of being due—say in 30 & 60 days after the first.—payment will of course be received of Bohn & Hubner in time to retire them.

The acct. sales of your Tobacco, together with your account current, you will receive inclosed. From the balce. of \$:3143.$\frac{80}{100}$, which appears in your favor, is to be deducted \$:621.—the amount of your dft in favor of Mr. Smith, which has not yet appeared; this will leave $:2522.$\frac{80}{100}$, due you when we are in funds for the Tobacco.

I am Dear Sir Yr. Very humble servt. GEO. JEFFERSON

RC (MHi); at foot of text: "Thos. Jefferson esqr."; endorsed by TJ as received 4 July and so recorded in SJL. Enclosures not found.

For the payment to Charles SMITH, see TJ to Gibson & Jefferson, 14 June.

To Daniel Ludlow

SIR Washington July 1. 1805.

I recieved last night your favor of the 28th. and much regret that my omission to mention the Christian name of the mr Ludlow correspondent of mr Barnes, in my letter to Capt Hazard should have led him to present it to the wrong person. mr Charles C. Ludlow was the one meant, & to whom the remittance was made. I have seen a letter from him to mr Barnes acknoleging the reciept of it, & observing it had not been yet called for. I have therefore to ask you to have the goodness to call on him for it and I return you my letter to Capt Hazard, which with the present letter will explain the mistake committed, and authorise Mr. C. Ludlow's refunding the advance to you. I pray you to accept my thanks for this mark of your confidence in me, and for the advance you have so readily made to Capt Hazard on my account, with my salutations & assurances of respect.

TH: JEFFERSON

PoC (MHi); at foot of text: "Mr. Daniel Ludlow"; endorsed by TJ. Enclosure: TJ to William Hazard, 11 May, not found (Appendix IV).

From Samuel Latham Mitchill

Newyork, July 1, 1805

I beg you, Sir, to inform our friend T. M. Randolph that I have made a number of experiments upon the saline Substance which you forwarded to me. He is right in his judgment that the mass is a mixture of different salts. The trials I have made warrant the conclusion that there are three compound salts, to wit, Sulphate of Magnesia, Sulphate of Soda, and Muriate of Soda.

The first, which is the Epsom Salt of the English, or the bitter cathartic Salt of the shops, is the predominating Article. The second, which is the Sal mirabilis or Glauber's Salt is the next in quantity. The proportion of the third or common Kitchen salt seems to be very inconsiderable. The present hot Season being unfavourable to chrystallization, I have not made any attempt to determine the proportions of the several ingredients; tho there can be no doubt that the first is by a great difference the most abundant: and that the last is very trifling.

I do not find any more than the faintest Vestiges of Lime. Nor are the evidences any stronger in favour of the acid of Salt-petre.

It does not appear to me from the Sample that it contains any Salt-petre, And if the proprietor continues to work it, he must do so for the sake of the Epsom Salt.

I am sure to be pardoned for these details by him whose love of general Science, and whose labours to illustrate the History of Virginia, have rendered him famous not only in his own Country, but throughout the civilized world abroad.

I have seen Mr. R. R. Livingston since his arrival; and think he looks remarkably well.

Respectfully & truly yours SAML L MITCHILL

RC (DLC); at foot of text: "To Thomas Jefferson P.US."; endorsed by TJ as received 3 July and so recorded in SJL.

FORWARDED TO ME: TJ to Mitchill, 21 May.

Robert R. LIVINGSTON and his family arrived at New York from France on 29 June (Madison, *Papers*, *Sec. of State Ser.*, 9:501).

To Robert Smith

DEAR SIR Washington July 1. 05.

The inclosed copy of a letter to mr Lincoln will so fully explain it's own object, that I need say nothing in that way. I communicate it to particular friends because I wish to stand with them on the ground of truth, neither better nor worse than that makes me. you will percieve that I plead guilty to one of their charges, that when young & single I offered love to a handsome lady. I acknolege it's incorrectness; it is the only one, founded in truth among all their allegations against me. before I had sent the original to mr Lincoln I was advised to detach from it what related to transactions during the invasion in Virginia, a person in that state having undertaken to have that matter fully established, & communicated thro' one of the presses there. I will thank you for these papers when perused, & to consider their contents as communicated with the same latitude, as well as restriction, as to mr Lincoln, and that you will ascribe the trouble I give you in reading them to my counting you among those whose esteem I value too much to risk it by silence.

I shall leave this on the 15th. but mr Gallatin proposes a temporary absence about the 10th. before that time say the 7th I must pray you to visit us, in order to consult on two important questions. 1. what conduct shall we pursue as to naval spoliations & insults on our coast? and what as to the territorial contest with Spain? Accept affectionate salutations & assurances of constant esteem & respect.

TH: JEFFERSON

RC (CSmH); at foot of text: "The Secretary of the Navy." Enclosure: TJ to Levi Lincoln, 19 June, recorded in SJL but not found.

HANDSOME LADY: Elizabeth Moore Walker, the wife of John Walker. For the recent reappearance of the Walker affair in the press, see Isaac Story to TJ, 8 Feb., and TJ to Gallatin, 21 June.

PERSON IN THAT STATE: William A. Burwell had begun to collect testimony to refute allegations recently made by Thomas Turner in the Boston *Repertory*. A letter of 13 June from William Tatham to Burwell and a deposition by Christopher Hudson taken on 26 July are printed in Vol. 4:273-8. Additional testimonials gathered by Burwell included a letter of 28 June from John Beckley, who enclosed a second edition of his *Address to the People of the United States*, originally written during the election of 1800 to vindicate and extol TJ's "Public Life and Character" (RC in DLC, addressed: "Mr. Burwell at the Presidents House"; Vol. 4:273n; Vol. 32:125n). In a deposition of 12 July, Richard O'Brien testified that in 1781, after the brig he served on was lost to the British, he went to Richmond and remained there until British forces entered the city. Upon his arrival, he saw TJ there and recalled that the governor "continued upon the Spot during the whole scene" (MS in DLC; endorsed: "Signed in my Presence Wm A. Burwell"). An undated letter to Burwell from John Minor of Fredericksburg, postmarked 30 June, included Minor's recollection of a conversation with General Edward Stevens in 1796, in which Stevens called Charles Simms's charge that TJ abandoned his office in the face of the enemy "a D—d lie." Stevens claimed that he was in Richmond at the time as a member of the legislature. He asserted that TJ remained in the city "long after he thought it prudent that he should be gone" and did not leave "untill the Enemy entered the lower End of it" (RC in DLC; addressed: "William A Burwell Esqr. Washington Cty"; Vol. 29:193-6). Certificates by Robert Bradfute and James Steptoe, Sr., each dated 6 Aug., stated that both men lived near Poplar Forest in 1781 and that neither saw evidence that TJ had injured himself during his allegedly panicked retreat from Monticello. Burwell quoted liberally from these testimonials in his six-part "Vindication of Mr. Jefferson," which appeared in the Richmond *Enquirer* from late August to late September and was reprinted widely. Burwell devoted most of the series to rebutting Turner's assertions regarding TJ's conduct as governor. In the final installment, he cursorily dismissed the other attacks Turner made regarding TJ's support of James Callender, his payment to Gabriel Jones, his relationship with Sally Hemings, and his attempted seduction of Elizabeth Moore Walker. With regard to the last subject, Burwell challenged Turner to produce the "celebrated correspondence" between TJ and John Walker, which Turner claimed to have seen. Burwell asserted that without such evidence one must doubt the worst of the assertions, which could be easily disproven and about which "not even the slightest whisper" had circulated in Albemarle County (Richmond *Enquirer*, 23, 27, 30 Aug., 6, 13, 27 Sep.; Gerald W. Gawalt, "'Strict Truth': The Narrative of William Armistead Burwell," VMHB, 101 [1993], 118-20; Burwell to TJ, 15 Sep.).

Memorandum to Jacob Wagner

[on or after 1 July 1805]

Omissions in mr Wagner's list

dated March 1st	Mar. 7.	Daniel Coffin of Mass.[1] Collector & Inspector at Nantucket v. decd.	
not issued	11.	Edwd. Carrington of R.I. Consul at Canton	
no commn necessary		James M. Henry of Virga Agent[2] at Jamaica v. Savage. not to be renominated	
war office	13.	John B. Scott of Virga Colo. Commandant of Louisa.	
President alone appoints	May 3.	John B. C. Lucas of Pensva Clement B. Penrose of Pensva	Comrs. of land titles in the tery. of Louisa.
		Benjamin Sebastian of Kentucky. Comr. of land titles in E. distr. of Orleans	
		James Tremble of Tennissee Francis Vacher of N.J.	Comrs. of land titles in W. distr. Orleans
		Peter A. Schenck[3]	
is in the list	May 16.	Thomas Fenwick[4] of Washn. county Col. just. peace for sd county	
appointed by Presi	June 3.	Robert Brent[5] Mayor of Washn.	
do.	July 1.	Joshua Lewis of Kentucky a Comr. in E. distr. Orleans	

The above commissions appear by my list to have been signed, & they are not in mr Wagner's list. will he be so good as to examine & correct either his list or mine

RC (DNA: RG 59, MCL); undated; in TJ's hand, with notes added by Wagner rendered in italics; five names subsequently struck through by TJ (see notes below).

PETER A. SCHENCK was being considered for an appointment as marshal for New York (Gallatin to TJ, 9 May).

MY LIST: probably TJ's ongoing appointments list (see Appendix I). All the names above appear there, although sometimes with variant dates. Wagner's list has not been found, but it apparently consisted of individuals to whom the State Department had issued recess commissions. Thus Daniel Coffin, whose appointment gained Senate approval at the end of the preceding session, would not have been included in Wagner's list. Others did not appear because their appointments went through other departments or were solely at the president's discretion. TJ likely sent the list to Wagner and received it back with Wagner's explanations before his departure for Monticello on 15 July (TJ to the Senate, 26 Feb.; MB, 2:1160).

[1] Name subsequently canceled by TJ.
[2] Name subsequently canceled by TJ.
[3] Name subsequently canceled by TJ.
[4] Name subsequently canceled by TJ.
[5] Name subsequently canceled by TJ.

From John H. Anderson

THOMAS JEFFERSON
PRESIDENT OF THE
UNITED STATES

Maryland Somerset County,
Princess Anne. July 2nd. 1805

Altho'. I have not the Honor of an acquaintance with you personally, I am emboldened from my knowledge of your character, to assume the liberty of writing and soliciting your patronage. I am a young man of obsure parentage and without fortune consequently am compelled to have recourse to your goodness of heart for succour—I am willing to engage as clerk in any office, or in fact any thing, that I can make a decent support. Should you think me worth attending to you will do a poor young man a singular kindness—Any recommendations you may deem necessary I flatter myself I shall be able to procure—

I have the honor of being your Hble Servt.

JOHN H. ANDERSON

RC (MHi); addressed: "Thomas Jefferson President of the United States"; franked; endorsed by TJ. Recorded in SJL as received 7 July.

From Gabriel Duvall

DEAR SIR, Comptroller's Office, July 2. 1805.

The inclosed petition has been forwarded to me for the purpose of being laid before the President of the United States.—

I have no knowledge of the subject other than that obtained on a perusal of the petition & the letter from Mr. Hunter to me, which is also inclosed.

I am, with great respect & esteem, your obedt. Sert.

G. DUVALL

RC (DLC); at foot of text: "The president U. States"; endorsed by TJ as received 2 July and so recorded in SJL. Enclosures: (1) Petition of Philip M. Topham, 3 May. (2) William Hunter to Duvall, 21 June, asking Duvall to forward Topham's petition to TJ, explaining the merit in granting a pardon, and noting that the petition had been signed by Rhode Island's "highest officers of Government, and our most respectable Inhabitants" (RC in DLC).

To Albert Gallatin

DEAR SIR Washington July 2. 05.

The answer to Morris is perfectly well as it leaves the case open for decision as the fact or law shall be. I have dropt a line to Sheaff to address either yourself or the Comptroller on his case.—the prospect of avoiding a loan is really most pleasing. I observe mr Livingston is arrived, and the newspapers seem to suppose the call for the French money will soon take place. you have not told me when you propose to leave this place. I keep back my letter to mr Smith till you enable me to fix a day for his coming. Affectionate salutations.

TH: JEFFERSON

RC (NHi: Gallatin Papers); at foot of text: "The Secretary of the Treasury." PoC (DLC). Notation in SJL: "Morris &c."

LINE TO SHEAFF: TJ to Henry Sheaff, 2 July.

Several New York NEWSPAPERS reported that Robert R. Livingston returned carrying bills drawn by the U.S. minister to France on the Treasury under the Louisiana convention and that presumably "all the creditors under that treaty will receive their bills in the course of the summer" (*New-York Evening Post*, 29 June; *New-York Commercial Advertiser*, 29 June; New York *Morning Chronicle*, 1 July).

MY LETTER TO MR SMITH: TJ to Robert Smith, 1 July.

To Charles Ludlow

Washington July 2. 05

Capt Hazard, to whom a sum of 231. D 09 c remitted you on my account by mr Barnes, was to have been paid, and who was thereof advised by me, but with an omission of your Christian name, called by mistake on mr Daniel Ludlow, who was so kind as to pay it without particular advice. I wrote to mr D. Ludlow yesterday a request that he would call on you for the money, and having the last night recieved from him Capt Hazard's reciept, I now inclose it to you and pray you to consider mr D. Ludlow as authorised to recieve the money instead of Capt Hazard. Accept my salutations and respects

TH: JEFFERSON

PoC (MHi); at foot of text: "Mr. Charles C. Ludlow"; endorsed by TJ. Enclosure not found.

To Robert Patterson

DEAR SIR Washington July 2. 05

The failure to send your commission has been an act of forgetfulness of my own, or it should have been with you in time. I have directed it to be made out to-day & sent by this evening's post, under date of the 1st. inst. so that you will recieve it by the mail which carries this letter. Accept friendly salutations and assurances of great esteem & respect.

TH: JEFFERSON

RC (Cowan's Auctions, Cincinnati, Ohio, 2021); addressed: "Mr Robert Patterson Philadelphia"; franked and postmarked. PoC (DLC); endorsed by TJ.

From John Julius Pringle

SIR Charleston. S.C. 2d. July 1805

It is with much regret that I have to acquaint you that my professional and other avocations are such at present as to keep me indispensably engaged in this State and preclude my acceptance of the office of Attorney-General of the United-States.—The very polite manner in which you have done me the honor to propose to me the Commission would have superseded any other than the very cogent impediments above mentioned. Permit me to take this occasion of presenting you assurances of my most perfect esteem—

JOHN J. PRINGLE

RC (DNA: RG 59, RD); at foot of text: "The President of the United States"; endorsed by TJ as received 12 July and so recorded in SJL; also endorsed by TJ: "declines Atty Genl."

OFFICE: see TJ to Pringle, 15 June.

To Henry Sheaff

SIR Washington July 2. 05.

Your letter of June 27. was recieved in due time, and I referred it to mr Gallatin to know what indulgence could be granted in the case which was the subject of it. the following is an extract from his answer. 'I do not recollect any instance of a suit on a revenue bond in which I have interfered. the district attornies have on some occasions as I understand, assumed the responsibility of giving some indulgence. but less is shewn in that species of suit than in any other, not only because there must be a certainty in the collection of the revenue, but because the law directs in that case that the bond shall be put in suit on the day it becomes due, if not paid. this subject as to details is under the immediate superintendance of the Comptroller as he has the direction both of the revenue and of all the suits in the United states. mr Sheaff should write to the Comptroller or to myself, and obtain from the District attorney a statement of the case with his opinion that the security of the United states will not be injured by the delay which may be granted.'

You will percieve by the above the course you have to pursue, & altho the agents for the nation cannot, in any public transaction admit any influence from motives of private esteem, yet they will feel both a duty and pleasure in shielding a citizen from loss wherever it can be done without injury to those public interests which they are charged to take care of. Accept my friendly salutations & respects.

TH: JEFFERSON

PoC (DLC); at foot of text: "Mr. Sheaff."

From Volney

MONSIEUR LE PRESIDENT paris 2 juillet 1805

Il n'ya pas plus dun mois que j'ai reçu L'honneur de Votre Lettre en date du 18 fevrier; ce qui Vous prouvera la lenteur des communications, comme l'égarement de l'un de mes trois envois, prouve leur peu de sureté.

L'approbation que Vous donnez a ma theorie des Vents rehausse mon courage dans la guerre que font à mon champion le soleil les partisans de la froide Lune. Vous plaindriez Le pauvre lamark si Vous voyiez combien il prend la chose au serieux. *Cotte* parait être plus heureux en Nous donnant des tables de la periode Lunaire de 19 ans qui semblent indiquer quelque retour dans la serie des saisons; mais les Vents, pour le detail, restent en possession de leur inconstance. Cest un Ocean dont les flots subissent d'incalculables incidens.

je regrette que ma Geologie vous ait offert moins d'interêt: Sans doute y clarifier L'histoire et l'origine de Notre planete est une speculation de peu d'utilité: mais la connaissance du sol qui nous porte, qui Nous Nourit serat-elle moins importante que celle des mondes visibles et invisibles dont l'homme s'est si follement occupé? N'est ce pas ce sol qui fournit les remedes a la Medecine, les mineraux aux arts; de qui dependent les produits des Empires, L'industrie et le caractere de leurs habitans? N'est ce pas avec de bonnes Notions geologiques que l'on peut aquerir des Notions statistiques sur Letat passé et futur des Nations? &c &c

Vos remarques Monsieur le president, sur Notre climat de paris et sur sa constante *Nebulosite* sont d'une justesse dont je fais la triste Experience, etant devenu un Veritable hygrometre: Neanmoins je dois Vous observer que toute la France ne ressemble pas au bassin de la Seine: que ce ciel pur qui Vous plait en Virginie Existe dans tout le Midi de Nos Cevennes, dans plusieurs de Nos provinces interieures: Vous savez que Marseille compte 345 jours clairs et a peine onze pluvieux. au reste l'une de mes remarques de Voyageur qui m'a le plus frappé est la preference que chacun donne a son pays, a son local. en quittant Monticello dont vous celebrez le sommet *exempt* de rosées, je logeai chez le colonel Mathews qui me Vanta Les rosées abondantes de sa Vallée et qui plaignait de tout son coeur les lieux elevés et secs. Le highlander, Mr *Maclure* aime le Vent de N.O. qui frotte ses Oreilles; moi je crains tout bourdonnemt dans les miennes; et tout courant d'air dans mes yeux. je suis bien moins sensible au bourdonnement Moral des insectes-Noirs qui chez vous comme ici attaquent les Ruines et leur auteur. aprés les suffrages qua obtenû ce livre je dois dormir tranquile; il est naturel que Les charlatans qui Vivent de la fievre jaune crient contre les medecins qui cherchent a l'extirper—: Mais il faut Esperer que la Veritable Science Viendra a bout de l'un et de l'autre. Les progrés que Vous m'annoncez avoir été faits depuis mon depart dans la connaissance des fievres putrides et des fievres de climat me paraissent egalement interessans et satisfaisans; J'attends avec desir Le charmant cadeau que Vous m'annoncez, le *polygraphe* à deux plumes dont vous m'envoyez une epreuve très heureuse et tres convaincante. je n'en conçois point du tout Le méchanisme. Mr Cabanis Me charge de Vous temoigner toute sa gratitude de Votre souvenir. Sa santé est comme la Mienne, toujours faible et chancelante. Mr La Roche est retourné dans son gîte Original de Picardie, Vivre a la campagne prés de sa famille. Moi je fais Mon compte daller désormais passer les hyvers au Sud des Cevennes, les hyvers de paris me causant un etat continu de soufrance. j'ai contemplé avec satisfaction la Miniature jointe a Votre lettre, et mon plaisir a été dautant plus grand qu'en me retracant Vos traits, il m'a paru par leur embonpoint que Vous aviez aquis plus de santé—puissiez-vous ne jamais la perdre, et puissiez-vous vivre pour le Monde, et pour vous et pour vos amis aussi longtems que le desire celui qui Vous est le plus attaché.

VOLNEY

EDITORS' TRANSLATION

MISTER PRESIDENT, Paris, 2 July 1805

It is only within the last month that I had the honor of receiving your letter of 18 Feb., proving how slow mail is, just as losing one of my three mailings proves how unreliable it is.

Your approval of my theory of wind strengthens my courage in the war waged by the partisans of a cold moon against my hero, the sun. You would pity poor Lamarck if you could see how seriously he takes all this. Cotte seems happier, as he establishes tables for the 19-year lunar period, which suggest some resemblance to seasons. But wind remains unpredictable; it is an ocean whose currents undergo incalculable fluctuations.

I regret that you were less interested in my geology. Clarifying the history and origin of our planet may not be practical, but can knowledge of the land that bears and nourishes us be less important than the knowledge of visible and invisible worlds that men pursue so feverishly? Does the land not offer cures to medicine and minerals to the arts? Empires count on it for their production and for the labor and character of their inhabitants. Do we not need accurate information about geology to derive statistics about the past and future of nations, etc., etc.?

Your remarks are very true, Mister President, about Parisian skies being perpetually gray, as I am unfortunately learning, having become a true hygrometer. However I must point out that the Seine Valley does not reflect all of France: the clear sky you appreciate in Virginia exists everywhere south of our Cévennes Mountains and in several of our inland provinces. You know that Marseilles has 345 clear days a year and barely 11 days of rain. Moreover, one of the observations that has most struck me in my travels is how each person prefers his own country and region. After leaving Monticello, where you praised the hilltop for its dryness, I stayed with Colonel Mathews, who bragged about the abundant dew in his valley and his pity for high, dry places. Mr. Maclure, a highlander, likes the northwest wind that grazes his ears. I myself fear any whizzing in my ears or draft in my eyes. I am much less sensitive to the characteristic buzzing of black insects which attack ruins and their summits, here as in your country.

I am reassured by the approval my book has garnered. It is normal for the charlatans who make a living from yellow fever to decry doctors who try to eradicate it. But we must hope that true science will overcome them. The progress you describe since my departure in the understanding of bilious fevers and climate is both interesting and heartening. I await with eagerness the charming gift you announce: the two-penned polygraph. The sample you sent is handsome and convincing. I cannot visualize the mechanics of it at all.

Mr. Cabanis asked me to express his gratitude for your wishes. His health, like mine, is still poor and rocky. Mr. La Roche has returned to his native Picardy to live in the country near his family. I am content, going forward, to spend winters south of the Cevennes, since Paris winters cause me perpetual suffering.

I saw with pleasure the miniature portrait enclosed in your letter. My pleasure was all the greater because when I retraced your features they seemed fuller than before, suggesting that you had become healthier. May you never lose this good health, and may you live—for the world, yourself and your friends—as long I hope, who am the most devoted to you. VOLNEY

RC (DLC); endorsed by TJ as received 19 Dec. and so recorded in SJL. Enclosed in John Mercer to TJ, 13 Dec. 1805.

VOTRE LETTRE: that is, TJ to Volney, 8 Feb.

The MINIATURE was likely one of the 48 prints of Charles Balthazar Julien Févret de Saint-Mémin's profile that TJ purchased from the artist in November 1804 (Vol. 45:l-li, liii).

From John Barnes

SIR. George Town 3d July 1805,

Ever anxious to aid the Presidents wishes, I have hitherto, with, great & sincere pleasure, exerted my powers—while it answered the pressing excigences, and was commensurate with my little resources—in the fond Hope, it would ere this, have ceased to become necessary: but from the present, increasing difficulties (the President will please refer, himself to the inclosed several statemts.)—on the most mature consideration & reflection—I must, however reluctantly, confess my self, inadecate to the task, of Accomplishing—the responsibility. Attached to its, due performance—is far beyond, the powers & resources, I am possessed off—or, can command—

Two thousand dollars, at least, and that in Cash, will be required to preserve these four Mos Negociation from risque of demur!—to me: the Mortification would be extreme!—and even without a demur, the Redrawing & discounting—is of its self, a mortifying circumstance—I have ever wished the President to avoid—

moreover, another (tho less difficulty) await, the issue—my Absence to Philada. if not N York, in the course of this business—is almost—indispensable, for the safty of my *Credit*, as well, for a fall supply, of sundry Articles—which I cannot. Otherwise be—so well supplied with.—

—I would freely dispose of my public stock, but the general fall in price from 10-12½ & even 15 ℔ Ct. is too great a sacrifice.—

if it were possible, for the President, to loan this deficiency for six Mos. only.—I would risque every Other consequence—while without it. I fear some fatal Accident may, and will intervene—to effect—its failure—and humbly pray, the President will review—with his Usual Candor—these several particular & interesting circumstances—and if possible evert the threatening danger—with sentiments of high respect, and most sincere Esteem—

I have the Honor to be, sir, your very Obt Hble servant,

JOHN BARNES.

RC (ViU: Edgehill-Randolph Papers); addressed: "The President, UStates"; endorsed by TJ as received 4 July. Enclosures not found.

INADECATE TO THE TASK: on 2 July, TJ borrowed $1360 from Barnes and $640 from William A. Burwell to pay a $2000 note due to the Bank of the United States. The following day he discounted a new note with the Bank of the United States for $2000 and used a portion of that money to repay Barnes on 5 July. Burwell was repaid on 13 July (MB, 2:1157, 1159).

Statement of Account with Alexander Gordon

Mr Thomas Jefferson to Alx Gordon Dr.

1805			
July 3.	3	Dayes Board for servt @ 4/6	.13.6
	. 3	Dayes & nights—Hay for horse	.9.
	.12	Gallons Grain @ 1/	.12.
	. 1	Bridle 6/	.6.
			£2 .0.6

Please pay the above to Mr. Joseph Wheaton—

ALEXR. GORDON

RC (MHi); in Gordon's hand; TJ wrote "6.75" alongside the total; on verso in a clerk's hand: "Mr Thomas Jefferson To Alexander Gordon"; receipt by Joseph Wheaton on verso for payment on 24 Mch. 1806.

Alexander Gordon operated a tavern in Woodbridge, Virginia, near the Occoquan River toll bridge. In August 1805, he relocated to Occoquan Mills in order to accommodate those traveling by way of Nathaniel Ellicott's new road. Gordon was innkeeper at Alexandria's Washington Tavern in 1808 (John Davis, *Travels of Four Years and a Half in the United States of America; During 1798, 1799, 1800, 1801, and 1802* [New York, 1909], 251; *Alexandria Daily Advertiser*, 30 Aug. 1805, 11 Apr. 1808, 28 Aug. 1811).

PLEASE PAY: on 25 Mch. 1806, TJ recorded paying Wheaton for "Alexr. Gordon at Occoquan Jack's board 6.75." According to his financial memoranda, TJ stayed at Gordon's tavern on 15 July 1805 en route to Monticello. If his enslaved servant Jack was at Gordon's tavern awaiting his arrival, Jack's stay likely began on 13 July and not 3 July as stated in the statement printed above (MB, 2:1160, 1176).

To Edward Johnston

SIR Washington July 3. 05

Messrs Gibson & Jefferson of Richmond informed me some time ago that about the last of May, the[1] sent two boxes of mine to you, the one to be forwarded to mr Peale at Philadelphia, the other to myself here. I heard some time ago of the safe arrival of the one at Philadelphia; but hearing nothing of that which was to come to me here, I have feared some inattention of the master of the vessel might have occasioned a miscarriage to be looked after. will you be so good as to drop me a line of information whether it has been forwarded, & by what conveyance. Accept my salutations & respects

Th: Jefferson

PoC (DLC); at foot of text: "Mr. Edward Johnston"; endorsed by TJ.

INFORMED ME: Gibson & Jefferson to TJ, 1 June.

[1]Thus in MS.

From Thomas Munroe

3 July [1805]

T Munroe respectfully informs the President that there is another framed house building near Mr Pichons which evades or an attempt is made to evade[1] the proclamation by bringing down a hipp'd roof within twelve feet of the cill—The frame of[2] this House was put up today—the builder told TM some days since that it was to be a small brick house, but the brick work has stopp'd about two feet above the surface of the ground, and they seem to exult in the supposed or real[3] evasion—T.M. respectfully asks if any order can be taken concerning it—He should be much gratified by defeating this spirit of opposition—The area is less than 320 sq feet

RC (DLC); partially dated; subjoined to two memoranda, the first in the hand of Nicholas King and initialed by him on 22 June 1805: "The length of the new Road in the Presidents Square is, 1130 feet, or $68\frac{1}{2}$ perches nearly"; the second in Munroe's hand and signed by him: "The Cost of the above road ꝑ rolls returned by Overseer is $359.72" (see Munroe to TJ, 21 June); endorsed by TJ: "buildings evasive of proclamn T. Munroe's note."

NEAR MR PICHONS: that is, in the vicinity of the Seven Buildings on Pennsylvania Avenue between 19th and 20th Streets (Wilhelmus B. Bryan, *A History of the National Capital from Its Foundation through the Period of the Adoption of the Organic Act*, 2 vols. [New York, 1914-16], 1:414; Vol. 42:616n).

[1]Preceding seven words interlined.
[2]Preceding three words interlined.
[3]Preceding two words interlined.

From Thomas Carnes

July 4th in the year of owr Lord and Saver Jesus Christ Bean the fust Be Goten of the Dad hue is the Leving and all Mity God has Given to him the Charge of the fore Corners of the Earth Bean a Jast and Lafell M[an] and one that feard God an[d a]Surd Evel Bon in the ye[ar] of owr Lord July 4th 5805 all Mity God ReQuirs of Me to Rase the Dad and the World is Cot So Base that it is a hard thing to Do it By the Rule of Mascnary With out Pruving Murder and you Must Do this Sand for the Condemd Man that Was to Be hanged in Boston his Name is Daman and you Sand for him to Be Put in Philadelphia Gale and I Give you a Sat of Boston Davals and if all Mity God had Not Parst Me thrue Gale Purfect My Morals Bean in holanes in a furese year We Should a had france in a Maracky I Love a franck Man Wat I Mean is Bastel Cap By Eve a halat and Sand a Cum Mity to My Wife and in Daver to Mack hir Mack hir Con fashan [. . .] and Wan Daman Cats to [. . .] Prisen in Philadelphia I Cot a Book and the Master of the Grand Lodge Will tack this Book to him for I Mean all Mity God Shall be Pruved Be for I Cum Be Cos I Will Not Give My Salf oup to Man a Gane tul all Mity God is Pruved and if you Dont Pruve it By a Book that I Now a Riten and Daman and My Wife the on Visebal har Lat I Give the Marster of the Grand Lodge Six Dad Man and that is the art of a free Masson this is the Rady Way to find old Murder the onest Man No Need to fear this Later I ar the Master of the Devel in hall and you feer No one thing I Cot the Care of you and if My Wife Macks hir Con fashan I for Give hir alse I Sat hir on a Stage fifty feet high for I have tride to Purtack hir fifteen year and I oup Sat hir and [. . .] Culs and hir tan thousand [. . .] Dolars Bonds if I a had a [. . .] My one Brothers Wood a [. . .] Me She hid from all But all Mity God I not a Buly Sir I a Man of honar and if you Mind Me you tack Care of your Salf Please to Not Lat any Man Be Put to Dath tul you Se Me for a on Sartane I Will Not tack your farther Brother and Sun Dont you think that I Crazy think Sir if it Wes your Salf how you feel to Satle all Nashans Will this Do it yes Evary Body Must Se and the Bibal Will Stand france Can Not Stand With out the Bibal and the king of England is Rite and Boney Part is Rite Silince

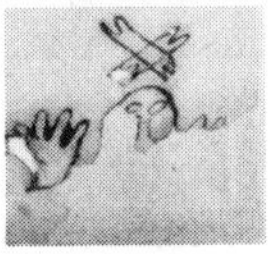

THOMAS CARNES

RC (DLC); torn; addressed: "Mr Thomas Jefferson Washanton Sity"; franked; postmarked Richmond, 8 July; endorsed by TJ as received 10 July and "insane" and so recorded in SJL.

From James Lovell

Sir Boston July 4 25 1805

When in August 1802 I first "spread myself with sincerity," before your official Chair, as we are taught to do, when we go for our daily bread, before an Altar; I hinted my odd yet serious intention of a *public* attempt to "rarify some of the clouds of our Religion and Polity." That intention has been hiterto artfully frustrated; which has driven me to the necessity of letting loose (after a few days) some Copies of what I now cover to You in print.

I meditate a repetition of this kind of freedom, whenever I shall have been informed by *any kind* of private communication that You are not offended at this present.

The People, of every grade, ought to be told, in the plainest language, that "the Liberty of the Press" was introduced into a "Bill of Rights" for the same reason and purpose *accurately* as an executive "Veto" was introduced into our "Constitutions," and for *no other* vizt. for individual & social *defence*: And, that both are prostituted alike when used for *offence*. When You nominated for the Land Office in Massachusetts a Person who is judged, by very many as well as by Myself, to have been long a vicious intriguing deceiver of the Populace, and an abuser of Federal-Officers, I was pleased with that strong proof of presidential Contempt of party-assaults from licentious-scriblers. It is really, Sir, an Extinguisher: Because the Creature is in fact an Accomplant, and of such Fortune as to make him trust-worthy in his place. This latter circumstance indeed gives Chagrin at his Luck, to several of the dirty junto of his old co-adjutors, who cannot avoid envious desires to occupy It themselves as often as they put their hands into their own lean pockets.

I was in hope of making that event subservient to my own designs, by sending a satyrical and justly-severe "Address to Honestus" (directed to Austin with my Name subscribed) to be printed by an high federal partizan Editor, then personally unknown to me. But, the "Managers" knew me so well as to smoke-me-out by the following last sentence of the address "and now, whilst you are contemplating your Patron and mine as the greatest Man upon earth, I will be preparing to inform him how little I think him, in more respects than One." The Rogues defeated me; and thereby postponed my display of a Veto which protects your Dignity & Emoluments from a vicious attack of a Legislative-*majority* as far up only as to *two thirds*, and then, leaves You to the *same* dernier resort as my humble self and my lawfull earnings vizt to the Opinion of "Independent

Judges" and the Sympathy of "Peers" The odds to be sure is much against me; because one single casting vote of the *meanest* number of an acting-legislature may, in the bold highway mode, rob me of $\frac{11}{12}$ths of my fees; or, in the sly pick-pocket *contingent* mode, *may* go to the *same* length.

I am with the courage of a man of Integrity and with the calmness of a conscious Protegé Sir your obliged Friend

JAMES LOVELL

P.S. I must mention a Chagrin which awaits You and every one who possesses a spirit of Tolleration like yours—pages 162/3 of Notes on Virginia and No. III of the appendix Editn. 1800—

The powerfull Author of "Discourses upon Davila" in his 93d page, leaving the rich materials of his own great magazine, borrows some Chips from the two conducting-Pillars of Moses, Chips capable of producing Smoke *or* Fire, alternately, *for party-purposes*, during the continuance of man upon earth. Alas! alas! Such is the lasting, too-potent effect of an Infant's exposure to the House-Maid's System of "Raw-head & Bloody-bones!"

I do not know what is the Hebrew of "Vulgus *vult* decipi," but Melchizedek must have *felt* the Idea.

RC (ViW: Tucker-Coleman Collection); at head of text: "Philosopher of Montecello"; endorsed by TJ as a letter of 4 July received 8 Aug. and so recorded in SJL. Enclosure: printed tract, framed as a letter from Lovell to the president of the United States, 4 July, from Boston; while ill, Lovell read with satisfaction John Adams's *Discourses on Davila*; he fears that Adams's "timeglass and mine also will be more than cracked" before they can apply their understanding, and he looks to TJ to accomplish "some changes for the better in our general Government"; TJ must be aware of the similarities between religious leaders and printers; a free press is a defense of liberty but also a tool of "*Offence* in the hand of Licentiousness"; the author objects to the distinction drawn between actions and words, which "*may* be as offensive as any of those other actions directed *plumply*" into one's face; although religious leaders are losing power, the "Bigotry of the Press demands the watchful eyes of Government, because it is rapidly gaining" the capacity to tyrannize; freedom of the mind lags in the United States because of partisan divisions; he hopes that the nation will support "one single Free Press, devoted to Truth," or else "truth itself" will be "regularly tortured, for the purpose of Dissention" (printed as *Copy of a Letter of July 4, 1805, to the President of the United States, Supposed by the Writer, to Be Fitted, Specially, for the Eye and Courage of the "Young Federal Republicans of Boston," and Also to Be Calculated, Generally, to Promote the Comfort of All Grey-Headed As Well As Green-Headed "Free Citizens," Every Where* [Boston, 1805]).

BEFORE YOUR OFFICIAL CHAIR: not found, but see Vol. 39:283-5.

LAND OFFICE IN MASSACHUSETTS: that is, the commissioner of loans, Benjamin Austin, Jr., who published pamphlets under the pseudonym HONESTUS (Vol. 40:621n).

CHAGRIN WHICH AWAITS YOU: Lovell was referring to TJ's warning in *Notes on the State of Virginia* that religious liberty through disestablishment needed to be accomplished before revolutionary ideals faded, and to the printing of Virginia's "Act for establishing Religious Freedom" as the third appendix (*Jefferson's Notes on the State of Virginia; with the Appendixes—Complete* [Baltimore, 1800]).

POWERFULL AUTHOR: John Adams, who in 1805 published an edition of *Discourses on Davila*, which originally appeared as a series of papers in 1790.

Children were frequently frightened with tales of the RAW-HEAD and Bloody Bones, two folk bogeymen (OED).

VULGUS VULT DECIPI: that is, the people want to be deceived. Melchizideck, king of Salem and "priest of the most high God," offered bread and wine to Abram and blessed him after the latter's victory in battle (Genesis 14:18-20).

From Ellen Wayles Randolph

July 4 1805

I have just recievd my Dear Grand Papa's letter, and am very much obliged to him for it, since I cannot have a greater pleasure than to recieve letters from him. I have a question to ask you that I did not put in my last letter, it is what is seventh fine art? I know six of them Painting, Sculpture, architecture, Music, Poetry, Oratory, but mama nor myself either cannot recollect the seventh. all the children have had the mumps except Mary who is the sweetest little creature in the world, always laughing talking and singing she has a great many ideas and is a very forward child for her age. Cornelia begins to read very well; we have none of us deserved new books we have not got half through those you gave us the last time you were at Monticello, but as far as I have got I am very much interested and we are going on with great spirit. Aunt Virginia Sister Ann and all the[1] children give their love to you. give mine to mrs H Smith. Mama's health is daily improving she has ridden out a good deal since you left us. Adieu my dear Grand papa, believe me to be your affectionate Grand Daughter

ELEONORA WAYLES RANDOLPH

RC (DLC: J. Henley Smith Papers); endorsed by TJ as received 9 July and so recorded in SJL.

LETTER: TJ to Ellen Wayles Randolph, 28 June.

[1] She here erased "other."

To Robert Smith

Washington July 4. 05.

Th: Jefferson incloses to mr Smith a rough sketch of his first undigested ideas of the matters to be considered at our meeting on Monday next, which he prays him to consider maturely before hand. affectionate salutations.

PoC (DLC).

OUR MEETING ON MONDAY NEXT: see Notes on a Cabinet Meeting, 8 July.

E N C L O S U R E

Notes for Instructions to Armed Vessels

Notes for consideration, & for instructions to any armed vessels which may be sent out to protect our commerce on our coasts.

Preliminary questions. Do the laws authorise the putting vessels in commission for the protection of our commerce? other than against Tripoli?
if they do not, should we not do it at our risk & ask an act of indemnity from Congress?[1]

What vessels? the Adams & Baltimore brig for the coast. 2. the for the Missisipi. 3. the for Cuba & the islands.[2]
Instructions.
Cruising grounds
The frigate & brig from St. Mary's to St. George's bank,[3] crossing each other always.[4]
The 3d (if to be had) from Florida point to Rio grande.[5]
The 4th. (if to be had) round Cuba & among the islands.[6]
To respect public ships of war, except when violating the 3. miles jurisdiction.[7]
To confine themselves to privateers.
If they find privateers without commissions, or with irregular or doubtful commissions, bring them in for examination.
If their commissions be regular, & they are found cruising within *sight of land* warn them to keep without that limit, & if found within it after warning bring them in as offenders against the law for preserving peace in our harbors & *waters*.[8]
If they have regularly siesed an American bottom, enquire if their conduct has been regular, viz.

have they plundered the vessel?
maltreated the crew?
separated the Master &c from his vessel?
forced the American to send his boat aboard?
do they refuse to exhibit their commission, to declare their names, vessel, flag or port?[9] in all these cases bring them in for examination.
If they have acted correctly, carry or send the prize & the privateer, if a Spaniard, to Havanna; if French to Sto. Domingo; if English to and deliver them up to the proper tribunal.[10]
If any American citizens are found engaged in the privateers, take them out, & keep them in safe custody to be brought home & delivered up to justice.[11]
You are not to extend your protection 1. to foreign vessels. 2. to American vessels engaged in the slave trade. 3. to American vessels engaged in any contraband commerce.

The Gunboats & Revenue cutters to be subsidiary.[12]

MS (DLC: TJ Papers, 163:28683); undated; entirely in TJ's hand. PoC (same, 151:26447). Dft (same, 128:22129); significant variations are recorded in notes below.

LAW FOR PRESERVING PEACE: under the first section of the 3 Mch. act for the preservation of peace in U.S. harbors and waters, anyone "on board of any foreign armed vessel" in waters within U.S. jurisdiction who committed "any treason, felony, misprision of treason, or of felony, misdemeanor, breach of the peace, or of the revenue laws of the United States" was subject to punishment (U.S. Statutes at Large, 2:339).

[1] In Dft TJ first wrote "If they do, what should be the instructions to such vessels" before altering the sentence to read: "If they do, what vessels shall we equip & what shall be the instructions to such vessels."

[2] Dft: "1. The Adams. 2. the Balt. brig. 3. the Chesapeake?"

[3] Preceding three words interlined in Dft in place of "Portland."

[4] Dft: "the two vessels always moving in opposite directions."

[5] Dft: "Rio Bravo," in place of canceled "Mata Gordo."

[6] This line is not in Dft.

[7] In Dft following this line TJ wrote: "the line of sight, the limit of their action. abt 20. to 30 mi."

[8] Dft: "law for maintg. ord. in our ports & seas."

[9] Dft: "do they refuse to shew their commn. decline themselves or do it falsely?"

[10] Dft: "and see them delivd to justice."

[11] Dft: "take them out & bring them home for trial."

[12] This line is not in Dft.

From Robert Smith

SIR, Balt. July 4. 1805.

Your favour of the 1st with its enclosure I have this moment received and be persuaded I well know how to appreciate such a Communication. As I shall leave this for Washington on the 7th (Sunday) I will bring the papers with me.—I would at this time only remark that as to the case of the lady there is not a *Gentleman* in the U. States of either party who does not hold in detestation the pitiful propagators of so pitiful a tale. Your Country by their approving voice at the last election have passed sentence on all the allegations that malice has exhibited against you. This decision being of the most honorable kind and being moreover of the last resort, ought to be and, I trust, is completely satisfactory to your own mind. Your numerous friends have long since formed their Opinions upon all those points of attack and the repetition of them at this time will only serve to excite their disgust. The feds here are really ashamed that such things should again be raked from the ashes. With the greatest personal regard I am Respecty Your Ob. Sert. RT SMITH

RC (MoSHi: Jefferson Papers); endorsed by TJ as received 5 July.

From the Inhabitants of Wakefield, Mississippi Territory

To his Excellency Thomas Jefferson, President of the United States of America, the humble petition of the undersigned inhabitants of Washington county in the Mississippi Territory, respectfully sheweth,

That your petitioners reside in a district of country entirely detatched from the rest of the territory, surrounded by the Indian tribes, and precluded by their situation from all immediate intercourse with any civilized people, but the Spanish subjects in West Florida,—that their interest and safety earnestly plead for the farther extinguishment of the Indian titles to lands in their neighbourhood, & for encouragement from the general government to extend the population of the district. During the existence of the Spanish government in this country, your petitioners were permitted under the faith of a treaty then supposed to have been concluded with the Indian nations, to make settlements on the lands lying between the Alabama and Tombeckbee rivers:—and although it is said that there is not to be found any evidence of the full ratification of such a treaty; yet no rent was demanded for the land occupied within the Indian boundary until the last year.

In consequence of the sterility of a large proportion of the land on the west side of the Tombeckbee, it is of high importance to the inhabitants of Washington county that the United States should possess the land lying between the two rivers:—and it is with much exultation that they behold at the present moment a more favourable opportunity, for obtaining a part of that tract of country, than has ever before offered itself to their view.

Your petitioners are informed that at a meeting held at Hobuckintoopa in June last with the Chacktaw nation, by the Honble. James Robertson and Silas Dinsmore commissioners of the United States, for the purpose of extinguishing their right to lands on the Mississippi, the said Indians absolutely refused to sell the quantity of land to be located as required by the said commissioners,—but that Hoomah Stubba the principal and authorized Mingoe of the lower Chacktaws proposed to the said commissioners to sell a certain tract of land to the United States on the east side of the Tombeckbee river. The acquisition of this territory, it is true, would not fully answer the wishes of your petitioners, nor afford to the United States so firm a footing in this country as their interest demands: since a tract of land lying between the Alabama & a ridge which divides its waters from those of the Tombeckbee, would still be claimed by the Creek nation of Indians. The acquisition would, notwithstanding, be of unspeakable importance, and would immediately open the door for increasing the strength of a settlement which would soon become a powerful barrier to the people of the Mississippi against the Creek nation, and to the people of South Carolina & Georgia against the Chickasaw & Chacktaw nations.

But the proposed purchase and consequent settlement of the country on the eastern bank of the Tombeckbee above the present settlements, is in another point of view still more interesting to the states of Tennessee and Kentucky. The difficulties and enormous expences under which the citizens of those states are labouring in the importation of foreign commodities, must induce them to avail themselves of the Mobille and Tombeckbee rivers,—and renders it of infinite importance to them, that civilized man should occupy the banks of a river unparalleled for the facility of its navigation, and which bountiful nature seems to have created in order to annihilate, as it were, the distance between those interior countries & the ocean.

Your petitioners feel happy when they reflect on the great and comprehensive views which have uniformly distinguished the present administration:—and how remote soever may be their situation from that of the rest of the United States, they rejoice in the persuasion that government regards their interests, and will provide for their protection and happiness.

They appeal to you as to the common father of confederated Americans, and they humbly pray that your Excellency would take the premises into your serious consideration, and would authorize the commissioners of the United States to extinguish the Indian title to as extensive a tract of land on the Tombeckbee river, as it may be in their power to obtain for the United States. HARRY TOULMIN

Wakefield in the Mississippi Territory 4th. July 1805.

RC (PHi: Daniel Parker Papers); in Toulmin's hand, also signed by 41 others; endorsed by TJ as received 23 Aug. Recorded in SJL as received 22 Aug. with notation "petn to buy lands on Tombigbee."

Harry Toulmin (1766-1823) was a native of England, where he became a Unitarian minister. He emigrated to the United States in 1793, and after securing a letter of recommendation from TJ, settled in Kentucky. He became president of Transylvania Seminary (later University) for a short time and then was appointed secretary of state, all while studying law. Asked to revise the state's criminal code, he collaborated on the three-volume *Review of the Criminal Law of the Commonwealth of Kentucky*. He subsequently published manuals for attorneys and magistrates, edited a collection of statutes passed in Mississippi Territory, and compiled *A Digest of the Territorial Laws of Alabama*. TJ appointed him judge for the part of Mississippi Territory east of Pearl River in 1804, and he remained an influential resident of the Tombigbee area for the rest of his life (DAB; Paul M. Pruitt, Jr., *Taming Alabama: Lawyers and Reformers, 1804-1929* [Tuscaloosa, Ala., 2010], 1-13; Vol. 27:270; Vol. 44:703).

For the negotiations conducted by JAMES ROBERTSON and Silas Dinsmoor, see Dearborn to TJ, 25 Mch.

Invoice from Thomas Davis

Thomas Jefferson Esqr Dr
To Thomas Davis

1805		
July 5th	To 1 Plaster Mashine 249℔ @ 14 cnt.	$34.86

RC (MHi); endorsed by TJ: "34.86 D July 5. 05 paid by ord. on bk US."

Thomas Davis was a Georgetown blacksmith. Although his machine was meant for grinding plaster into a suitable soil dressing, in 1815 TJ mentioned using it effectively for crushing corn cobs (MB, 2:1157; RS, 8:534-6).

From Nathaniel Ellicott

RESPECTED FRIEND THO. JEFFERSON Occoquan 5 July 1805

I have frequently Understood that you had an Idea of a Road from Washington Southwesterly to Cross Rappk. at or About Normond ford, that you had personlly Examined the Present different Crossing Places on Bull Run without being able to discover Any Very Eligible Situations for a great Public Road—(It is True I am much Interested in making; this my Situation as Public as Possible, it being a place of Considerable Trade Already) but I have I think a Very general Acquaintance with the ground All the Way up the Different branches of Occoquan And I Know of No Situation for Crossing that could be made Tollerable without Immence Labor, To and from this Place, the Roads are Already made Towards Washington to Within 3 miles of Alexa, and Towards Normonds Ford 12 Miles and there is a good bridge Across the River at this Place the hills on Each Side does not Exceed (in any Part 5.° Assent and for the most Part 3 to 4—Some few years back I had a Survey made of all the Principle Roads and Situations from Alexa. Southwesterly as far as Normonds ford and I find that a Strait line from the Capital in Washington to Normonds ford Crosses Occoquan but 1 Mile Above this Place, and to Speak Candidly and disinterestedly on the Subject I am of Opinion there is no way can Ever be got for Such a Road Nearer nor better than this

Rout, for from this Place (Which is but 15 miles (Measd) from Alexa. on a Strait line to Normonds ford, we Cross not the most Remote branch of Occoquan Nor Any other Water Course of Note the whole way, if Any other Information is wanted Such as the Course and distances or Even the Plott of the whole I can furnish it with pleasure—But a question Arises how could such a Road be made Even Supposing it to be of the most Immense Advantage and Convenience to the Union

—has the Executive any Power of this Kind

—has Congress and[1] Power of this Kind

—will our Virginia Legislature Pass a law to that Effect Unless to Incorporate a Company for the Purpose,

Our County Courts we Know will Never do Any thing of a Kind. In all this letter you will observe you are Addressed as a Private Citizen and if you See fit to Reply you will Please do it as Such, my freedom I am Sure you will Excuse

I am Respectfully Yrs N. Ellicott

RC (DLC); addressed: "Thos: Jefferson Esqr. President of the United States Washington"; franked; postmarked Colchester, Virginia, 6 July; endorsed by TJ as received 7 July and so recorded in SJL.

Nathaniel Ellicott (1763-1841) was the son of Andrew Ellicott. He acquired an interest in milling operations at Occoquan, Virginia, and in 1795 successfully led a petition drive to erect a toll bridge across the Occoquan River. After retiring, TJ asked Ellicott's advice on the manufacture of a powder mill for crushing plaster of paris, one of several Occoquan businesses that Ellicott and his partners advertised for sale in 1811 and 1812. Ellicott eventually moved to the Baltimore area (Charles W. Evans, *Biographical and Historical Accounts of the Fox, Ellicott, and Evans Families, and the Different Families Connected with Them* [Buffalo, 1882], 29, 149; *Alexandria Daily Gazette, Commercial & Political*, 11 Oct. 1811; *Federal Gazette & Baltimore Daily Advertiser*, 7 Dec. 1812; *Acts Passed at a General Assembly of the Commonwealth of Virginia* [Richmond, 1796], 53; RS, 3:500-1, 509-10).

[1] Thus in MS.

To George Jefferson

Dear Sir Washington July 5. 05.

I recieved yesterday your favor of the 1st. inst. I am now within 8. or 9 days of my departure for Monticello, & having to make arrangements for near three months absence. I find it will considerably facilitate them, if I can anticipate each of the paiments for my tobo by getting corresponding discounts in Richmd.[1] I therefore now inclose you my note for 1000. D. with a blank for the date which you will be so good as to fill up. and I will intreat you to inform me the moment you can know it is discounted, in which case I may draw on you for between 5. & 600. D. leaving the balance in your hands to the credit of my account. the remaining two notes shall be sent as soon as you will inform me what are the days of paiment for my tobo. and what date will be most convenient for the notes, to give time for the reciept of their amount from Bohn & H.

About 8. boxes &c will be sent from hence tomorrow to your address to be forwarded to Monticello by the first boats.[2] shall we have the pleasure of seeing you there in Aug. or September? Accept affectionate salutations

Th: Jefferson

PoC (MHi); at foot of text: "Mr. George Jefferson"; endorsed by TJ.

[1] Preceding two words interlined.
[2] TJ here partially blotted "Accept."

From Charles Ludlow

Sir— New York July 2nd: [i.e. 5] 1805.

On receipt of your Excellencys Letter of the 2nd: Inst: I waited on Mr: Daniel Ludlow and rectified the mistake by refunding him the $\$231\frac{9}{100}$ which he paid to Capt: Hazard and now return the paper with Mr: Ludlow's acknowledgment—

I remain most respecfully Your Excellencys hume Servt:

Chas: Ludlow

RC (MHi); at foot of text: "His Excellency Thomas Jefferson President of the United States"; endorsed by TJ as received 8 July and so recorded in SJL, but as a letter of 12 July. FC (NjMoHP); dated 5 July. Enclosure not found.

Notes on Personal Finance

1805

July 5. after taking up my 2 notes of May to bk US. & Col. = 3600. & payg Colston 400.

I have in bank US.	702.33
10. Disct. bk Col.	1583.20
	2285.53
✓ Lemaire	600
✓ Daugherty	127.83[1]
US ✓ King	115.42
US ✓ Davis	34.86
<*Maine*	*12*>
US ✓ Jones & Howell	253.33
US ✓ Peale	60.

US	✓	Stewart	40.
		<Maine	*12>*
	✓	Lenox	62.08
	✓	Claxton	81.35
	✓	Frithey	5.
		Maine	12
	✓	Maxwell	17.50
	✓	Barnes	164.675
		Lilly	280.
		Burwell[2]	70
	✓	Coxe	12.50
	✓	Pic	7.
	✓	Smith	36.
		Perry	50
		Monto.	240.
			2285.545

---

bk US	✓	Jones & Howell		253.33
	✓	Peale		60.
	✓	Stewart		40.
	✓	cash		150
				503.33
	✓	Lemaire	600	
	✓	Daugherty	127.83	
	✓	Lenox	62.08	
	✓	Claxton	81.35	
	✓	Maxwell	19.50	
	✓	Burnett & Rigden	35.	
	✓	Coxe	12.50	
	✓	Pic	7.	
	✓	Smith	36.	933.93
	✓	stage office	7.635	
		Maine	12	
	✓	Barnes	164.675	
	✓	Burwell	70.	246.675
		Lilly	280	
		Perry	50	} 402.595
		Monto.	72.595	
				1583.55
				1583.20
		Carpenter	87.52	

MS (CSmH); entirely in TJ's hand; on same sheet as notes of "Money operns," July-September, at 30 Sep.; with multiple emendations.

These two complementary lists record TJ's calculations of expenses that he expected to pay during July. After calculating the cash he would have on hand as of 10 July when he was to receive a discounted note from the Bank of Columbia, he drew up a list of expenses, the total of which almost matched his cash reserve. Properly added, the expenses in the top section would have totaled $2,269.545, but TJ's emendations make it impossible to determine which figures he used to arrive at his total. In the second section he appears to have compiled a list of payments as he made them, although as with the first list, alterations rendered some of his calculations inaccurate. Perhaps because he made the first payments, beginning with that to JONES & HOWELL, out of his account with the Bank of the United States, he did not add their total to the figure of $1,583.20 that he calculated at the foot of the document. TJ added the check marks next to payments he had arranged by 13 July. The payment to James MAXWELL was for footwear. That to BURNETT & RIGDEN was for earrings, part of a set of gift purchases. TJ did not make payments on two of the listed expenses, to Thomas Main for hedgethorns and to Thomas Carpenter for a tailor's bill, until October and February, respectively. He made all other payments in July. It is uncertain what expenses were included in the Monticello (MONTO.) line item (MB, 2:1157-60, 1165, 1173; TJ to Dolley Payne Todd Madison, 6 July).

[1] TJ first wrote "124.25" before altering the figure to read as above.

[2] TJ first wrote "Higginb." before altering the name to read as above.

From Mary Wallden

HONOURED THOMAS JEFFESON George town 5th July 1805

I have taken the privelege of pertisiononing to your benevolent hands hoping no offence I am a person that has a famyly to maintain And are a stranger in the place and have Workeed very hard to maintain them untill I have unfortunete Ly have had a spell of syckness Which have rendered me unabled to maintain them when bread are So dear I am in a state of Surfering at the present and shall Surfer unless I receive Some Reliefe from your benevolent hands Sur look in to my surferings of your humble pertischoner

MARY WALLDEN

RC (DLC); addressed: "Mr. thomas Jeffyson"; endorsed by TJ as received 8 July and so recorded in SJL.

SOME RELIEFE: on the day he received this letter TJ gave five dollars "in charity" to an unidentified recipient (MB, 2:1158).

Appendix I

EDITORIAL NOTE

Jefferson kept an ongoing list of appointments and removals through his two terms as president, with entries extending from 5 Mch. 1801 to 23 Feb. 1809. For the first installment of this list, ending at 14 May 1802, see Vol. 33, Appendix I, List 4. Beginning with Vol. 37, each volume's span of the list appears as Appendix I. The segment for the current volume continues at 11 Mch. 1805, with the president's recording of James Wilkinson's appointment as governor of Louisiana Territory. With Congress out of session, most of the names on the list were recess appointments and were formally nominated to the Senate when the Ninth Congress convened near the end of the year (TJ to the Senate, 20 Dec. 1805).

This was a working list, which Jefferson updated as he received information. He generally entered names when he signed commissions, but not always. The first five names on the list, for example, appear on a list that he sent to James Madison on 11 Mch. and that also included the names entered at 9 Mch. below. Possibly, the president had signed commissions on those days but neglected to enter the names on his running list until prompted by his message to Madison. Although several of the appointees for Orleans Territory, including William C. C. Claiborne, had already gained Senate approval, they received commissions a second time because of the passage of a new law regulating the territory's governance (U.S. Statutes at Large, 2:322-3; TJ to the Senate, 30 Nov. 1804).

List of Appointments

[11 Mch.-2 July 1805]

11. James Wilkinson of Maryld. Govr. of Louisa. from the 3d day of July next for 3. y.
Joseph Browne of N.Y. Secretary of do.
Return Jonathan Meigs of Louisana }
John B. C. Lucas of Pensva. } judges of do.
Rufus Easton of N.Y. }

9. George Duffield of Tennissee a judge of the Superr. court of the tery. of Orleans. resd.
James Brown late of Kentucky now of Orleans Atty of the distr. of Orleans.
John Thompson of Kentucky to be Register of the land office in the Western part of Orleans.
John W. Gurley of Orleans to be Register of the land office in the Eastern part of do.

<9. *James Tremble of Tennissee*> to be Recorder of the territory of Louisiana.

Henry Hill junr. of N.Y. Consul for the isld. of Cuba

Edward Carrington of R.I. Consul at Canton

James M. Henry of Virginia Agent at Jamaica. v. Savage

13. Scott John B. of Virginia Colo. Commandt. Louisiana.

James Robertson of Tenessee Silas Dinsmore	Comrs. to treat with Choctaws & Chickasaws.

Charles Jouett of Michigan. Comr. to treat with Wiandots, Ottaways, & Chippeways.

Joseph Wilkinson junr. of Michigan	Collector & Inspector of the district & port of Detroit.
Lewis Bond of Michigan	Collector & Inspector of the district & port of Miami.
Erastus Granger of New York	Collector & Inspector of the district & port of Buffalo creek
John Broadbent of	Consul at Messina
Abraham Gibbs of	Consul at Palermo
Frederic Degan of	Consul at Naples

Apr. 21. Thomas Newton of Virga Collector for the   of Norfolk v. W. C. Nicholas resd.

Michael Baldwin of Ohio Marshall of Ohio v.   Zeigler resd.

26. Gideon D. Cobbs of Tennissee Collector & Inspector of the district & port of Massac.

May 3. Christopher Ellery of R.I. Comr. of loans in the state of R.I. & Providence plantations

Augustus Sacket of N.Y. Collector & Inspector for the district & port of Sacket harbour.

James Lowry Donaldson of Maryld. Recorder of land titles for the territory of Louisiana.

John B. C. Lucas of Pensva Clement B. Penrose of Pensva	Comrs. of land titles in the territory of Louisiana.

Benjamin Sebastian } of Kentucky Comrs. of land titles in the Eastern district of Orleans
John Coburn }

James Tremble of Tennessee } Comrs. of land titles in the Western district of Orleans
Francis Vacher of N. Jersey }

12. John James Armstrong of to be Consul for the island of Teneriffe
Richard Parrott. of Washn. county Col. to be justice of peace for sd. county
14. Peter A Schenk. to be Marshal of N.Y. [I believe this was not carried into effect]
16. <*Brockhurst Livingston*> of N.Y. to be judge of the district court for the New York district.
Thomas Fenwick of Washington county Col. to be a justice of peace for sd county
June. 3. Robert Brent Mayor of Washington
10. Wm. C. C. Claiborne Govr. of the territory of Orleans.
John Graham of Kentucky Secy. of do.
John B. Prevost of Orleans one of the judges of do.
<*Buckner*> Thruston of Kentucky do.
12. George Duffield of Tennissee do.
13. Matthias B. Tallmadge. N.Y. judge of the District court of N.Y.
James Brown of Kentucky Atty } of the territory of Orleans.
Breton D'Orgenoy of Orleans, marshal }
John Wallworth of Ohio Collector of the district of Erie & Inspector of the revenue of the port of Cayuga.
30. William Sprigg of Ohio, one of the judges of the territory of Michigan.
July 1. Joshua Lewis of Kentuck a Comr. in the Eastern district of Orleans.
Thos. H. Williams of Misipi, Secretary for the Misipi tery. v. Cato West removd
George Mathews junr. of Georgia one of the judges of the Misipi tery. v. Obediah Jones declined
2. Robert Patterson of Pensva Director of Mint v. Elias Boudinot resigned.

MS (DLC: TJ Papers, 186:33099); entirely in TJ's hand, including brackets; being the continuation of a list that extends from 5 Mch. 1801 to 23 Feb. 1809; for the installment immediately preceding this one, see Vol. 45: Appendix I.

CHARLES JOUETT had been in Washington during the winter and likely recommended replacing the incumbent collector at Detroit with his brother-in-law, Joseph Wilkinson, Jr. After a letter in which Jouett claimed credit for the replacement gained notoriety, Gallatin received at least two letters advising him against the proposal (Gallatin, *Papers*, 11:141, 236; Vol. 45: Appendix II).

LEWIS BOND had previously been under consideration for a job in the land office in Detroit, and ERASTUS GRANGER was serving as inspector and surveyor at Buffalo (Vol. 42:96-7; Vol. 43:357; Vol. 44:169).

Writing to Samuel Smith from Baltimore on 2 May, George P. Keeports recommended his nephew-in-law, JOHN JAMES ARMSTRONG, a merchant, for the consulship on Tenerife in the Canary Islands. Although Keeports had never met him, he could vouch for Armstrong's character and reputation and was "willing to become responsible for his integrity and conduct." Enclosing the recommendation in a letter to an unidentified correspondent the next day, Smith lauded Keeports as "One of our Respectable Republican citizens" and argued that his assessment of Armstrong should be trusted (RCs in DNA: RG 59, LAR; letter from Smith endorsed by TJ: "Armstrong John James. to be Consul Teneriffe").

Appendix II

Dinner Guest Records

1. DINNER ATTENDANCE BY SUMMER GUESTS, [22 APR.-12 NOV. 1805]

2. DINNERS BY DATE, [22 APR.-1 JULY 1805]

EDITORIAL NOTE

Between 5 Nov. 1804 and 6 Mch. 1809, Jefferson kept an ongoing record of the guests he invited to dine at the President's House. The records had three components: a roster of the members of Congress recreated at the start of each congressional session and used as a checklist; a compilation of the congressional members he invited to dinner with the dates of those dinners noted after their names; and his dinner calendar (Dinners by Date). Although the first two lists confined themselves to Congress, the dinner guest calendar attempted to track every person, congressional or otherwise, whom Jefferson invited to his table. It was interrupted only by his absences from Washington. The first installment of the Dinner Guest Records is found in Volume 44, Appendix II. That appendix includes the Dinners by Date for 5-9 Nov. 1804 along with the two congressional lists, Members of Eighth Congress, Second Session, November 1804, and Dinner Attendance by Members of Congress, 5 Nov. 1804-27 Feb. 1805. The list of Dinners by Date for the congressional season of 1804-1805 continues in Volume 45, ending with a dinner on 7 Mch. 1805, the last one Jefferson recorded before he departed for Monticello on 14 Mch.

Jefferson was back in Washington on 17 Apr., and on 22 Apr. he began his annual round of dinners for the city's residential elite. Using the same practice he employed during the congressional season, Jefferson logged each dinner by date and then listed the surnames of those invited, marking guests who declined the invitation with a single stroke through their name (List 2 below). When invitations were extended to include companions or family, Jefferson recorded the surname of the head of the party along with a numeral, for example "Mad. 2" at 29 Apr., which in that case most likely denoted James Madison and Dolley Payne Todd Madison. Jefferson did not list houseguests and residents of the President's House on his dinner calendar except sometimes as "fam."

During the congressional recesses of 1805 and 1806, Jefferson also employed lists similar in style to his annual compilation of congressional guests. He called these "Summer" lists even though the 1805 one stretched from spring to fall (List 1 below). As with the congressional list, Jefferson appears to have written the names of his predicted summer guests early in the season and then added the dinner dates later, although he did so with less rigor on the off-season lists. A number next to a name indicated the number of persons in the household. For example, "3. Thornton" reminded Jefferson that William Thornton's family included his wife and his mother-in-law, who lived with the couple.

1. Dinner Attendance by Summer Guests

[22 Apr.-12 Nov. 1805]

Summer 1805.

2. Mad. Apr. 22. 25. 29. M.20. 27. Jun. 11. 22. Jul. 1. 8. O.27. 29. N.7
3. Gall. A.22. 25. 29. M.20. J.1. 11. 22. Jul. 8. 9. O.19. N.7.
3. Dearb. Ap. 22. M.15. M.20. J.1. 11. 22. Jul. 8. 9. O.14. 19. N.7.
2. Smith. Ap. 22. 25. 29. Jul. 8. 9. O.14. N.7.
4. Turreau. Ap. 29. Jun. 1. 22
2. Duval. May 27. Jun. 11. O.25.
3. Kelty. May 15. Jun. 17.
3. Beckly. May 27. Jul. 9
2. Harrison. May 15. Jun. 17. Jul. 1.
3. Nourse. May 15.
1. Tucker May 21. Jun. 11. 22. O.14.
2. Mason. May 9. June 1. 22. Jul. 9. O.14. 29.
3. Thornton May. 9. 27. Jun. 11. O.25.
3. S. H. Smith. May 9. Jun. 5. O.25
3. Hanson. May 3. Jun. 5. Jul. 1. O.19
2. Gantt. Jun. 11.
1. Mc.Cormic. May 3.
2. Cranch. May 15. Jun. 17.
3. Tingey. May 3. 21. Jun. 5. Jul. 9. O.19.
2. Wharton May 3. 27. Jun. 17. O.19. N.7.
2. Tomson May 3. Jun. 5. O.25
2. Vanness

D. C. Brent. May 15. 20. Jul. 1. O.31.
Rob. Brent. May. 21. Jun. 11. Jul. 1.

2. W. Brent. May 3. Jul. 9.

Oakley. Jun. 5.
Duncanson May 21. Jun. 5.
May. May 21. O.29.
Chandler. Jun. 5. N.12.
Coxe. June 17. N.12
Patterson. May 21. June 17.
Sprigg Wm. O. May 21.
<*Stewart*>. Ap. 25. May 9. Jun. 5. Jul. 1.
Templeman. Jun. 5.
<*Woodward. May*> 21.
Petrie June 1.
LeCabre Jun. 1.

2. Dr. Bullas. O.25
2. Rankin. O.25.
   Davidson N.12
   Ewell O.29.
2. Cathcart. O.25.

MS (MHi): entirely in TJ's hand; on same sheet as Dinners by Date from 28 Dec. 1804 to 30 Dec. 1805.

TJ struck through the names of Gilbert Stuart (STEWART) and Augustus Brevoort WOODWARD because both men left Washington before TJ ended his summer series of dinners (Carrie Rebora Barratt and Ellen G. Miles, *Gilbert Stuart* [New York, 2004], 287; Madison, *Papers*, *Sec. of State Ser.*, 10:160).

2. Dinners by Date

[22 Apr.-1 July 1805]

Apr. 22.
Mad.
Gall.
Dearb.
Smith.
fam. 2.
Apr. 25.
Nicholson
Mad.
Gall.
Smith.
Law.
Stewart
fam. 2.
Apr. 29.
Mad. 2
Gall. 3
Smith 1
Turreau 4
Rademaker 1
Cathcart. 2
<*Chevalier*>
<*Mason.*>
May. 3. Frid.
3. Tingey
2 Wharton
1 Thompson

3 Hanson
2 W. Brent
1 Mc.Cormic.
1 Obrien
<*Chevalier*>
May 9. Thursd.
<*Duval*>
<*Beckley*>
3. Thornton
<*Gantt*>
2 Mason
1 Stewart
3 S. H. Smith
Lewis[1]
May 15. Wed.
3 Dearborn
2 Kelty
1 Cranch
1 Harrison
1 Nourse
2 Carson
<*Vanness*>
1 D. C. Brent
May 20. Mond.
Mad.
Gall.
Dearb.
D. C. Brent
Richd Brent.
May 21. Tuesd.
Tucker
Rob. Brent
<*Chandler*>
<*Coxe*>
Fenwick
Duncanson
Sprigg.
May
Woodward
<*Oakley*>
Patterson

<*Templeman*>
Tingey
Chancey
Barnes.
Tathum
Freeman

May 27. Tuesd.
1 Mad.
2. Duval
3. Thornton
2. Beckley
2. Wharton
<*Cathcart*>
<*Bartlet*>

June 1. Sat.
1. Gall.
3 Dearb.
6 Turreau
2 Mason
1 Delisle
1 Chevalr

Wed. Jun. 5.
Tingey
Thompson
Chandler
Hanson
Oakley
Duncanson
Templeman
Stewart
Tatum
S. H. Smith
Bayard.

June 11. Tuesd.
Mad.
Gall.
Dearb.
Tucker
Thornton
Rob. Brent
Duvall

Gantt
Delile
Cathcart
Freeman
Findlay
<*Mason*>

June 17.

Kelty
Cranch
Harrison
Wharton
<*Fenwick*>
<*May*>
Coxe
Patterson
Bullas
Latrobe
Worthington
Peyroux

Sat. Jun. 22.

Mad.
Gall.
Dearb.
Tucker
Mason.
Turreau
<*Stewart*>

Mond. Jul. 1.

Mad. 3.
Young. 3.
Hanson 4.
Harrison 2.
Davy
D. C. Brent
Orr
Stewart.

MS (MHi); entirely in TJ's hand; being part of a list that extends from 5 Nov. 1804 to 6 Mch. 1809; cancellations made by a single stroke, which indicated that a guest declined, are rendered in italics within angle brackets.

CHEVALIER: John A. Chevallié.

CARSON: John Cassin of the navy yard.

JUNE 1. SAT.: TJ did not individually record Jean Baptiste Petry and Auguste de Cabre at this dinner, but he indicated 1 June next to each of their names on List 1 above. As first and second secretaries to the French legation, they were most likely among the six who accompanied French Minister Louis Marie Turreau to the president's dinner.

TATUM: William Tatham.

ORR: perhaps Benjamin Grayson Orr (Vol. 34:606n).

[1]TJ canceled "1" before this name.

Appendix III

Letters Not Printed in Full

EDITORIAL NOTE

In keeping with the editorial method established for this edition, the chronological series includes "in one form or another every available letter known to have been written by or to Thomas Jefferson" (Vol. 1:xv). Most letters are printed in full. In some cases, the letter is not printed but a detailed summary appears at the document's date. Other letters have been described in annotation, which, for the period covered by this volume, are listed in this appendix. Arranged in chronological order, this list includes for each letter the correspondent, date, and location in the volumes where it is described. Examples of letters not printed include brief letters of transmittal, multiple testimonials recommending a particular candidate for office, repetitive letters from a candidate seeking a post, and official correspondence that the president saw in only a cursory way. In other instances, documents are described in annotation due to the near illegibility of the surviving text. Using the list in this appendix, the table of contents, and Appendix IV (correspondence not found but recorded in Jefferson's Summary Journal of Letters), readers will be able to reconstruct Jefferson's chronological epistolary record from 9 Mch. to 5 July 1805.

From Thomas Appleton, 21 Mch. Noted at Appleton to TJ, 22 Mch.
From Gibson & Jefferson, 17 June. Noted at TJ to Gibson & Jefferson, 14 June.

Appendix IV

Letters Not Found

EDITORIAL NOTE

This appendix lists chronologically letters written by and to Jefferson during the period covered by this volume for which no text is known to survive. Jefferson's Summary Journal of Letters provides a record of the missing documents. For incoming letters, Jefferson typically recorded in SJL the date that the letter was sent and the date on which he received it. He sometimes included the location from which it was dispatched and an abbreviated notation indicating the government department to which it pertained: "N" for Navy, "S" for State, "T" for Treasury, and "W" for War.

From William B. Giles, 12 Mch.; received 21 Mch. from Richmond; notation: "John B. Scott to be Commdt."
To Morgan Lewis, 12 Mch.
From William D. Meriwether, 19 Mch.; received 19 Mch.
From [John S.] Jackson et al., 21 Mch.; received 16 June; notation: "on board the Amstdm." and "S." See Vol. 46:736.
From Bartholomew Kindred, 21 Mch.; received 21 Mch.
From George Clinton, 22 Mch.; received 1 Apr. from New York; notation: "Vacher."
From John Wayles Eppes, 22 Mch.; received 24 Mch. from Eppington.
From Elias Boudinot, 23 Mch.; received 30 Mch. from Philadelphia.
From John Meer, 23 Mch.; received 1 Apr. from Philadelphia.
To William Short, 23 Mch.
From William Dunbar, 24 Mch.; received 23 Apr. from Natchez.
From Thomas Lloyd, 26 Mch.; received 1 Apr. from Philadelphia.
To George Divers, 27 Mch.
From Brett Randolph, 28 Mch.; received 1 Apr. from Fredericksburg, Virginia; notation: "office."
From William Henry Harrison, 29 Mch.; received 26 Apr. from Vincennes; notation: "Dav. Coupland judge v. Griffin."
To George Hay, 30 Mch.
From Meriwether Lewis, 30 Mch.; received 13 July from Fort Mandan.
From John Hawkins; received 4 Apr.
From George Hay; received 4 Apr.
From Daniel Jerran, 4 Apr.; received 17 Apr. from New York; notation: "S."
From Thomas Newton, 6 Apr.; received 11 Apr. from Norfolk.
From Thomas McKean, 11 Apr.; received 17 Apr. from Lancaster, Pennsylvania; notation: "Penrose Comr. Rogers Consul."
To Burgess Griffin, 12 Apr.
From Samuel Coleman, 13 Apr.; received 18 Apr. from Richmond.
From Richard Cutts, 13 Apr.; received 20 Apr. from Boston.
To George Divers, 13 Apr.
From George Divers, 13 Apr.; received 13 Apr. from Farmington, Virginia.
From James Sullivan, 14 Apr.; received 22 Apr. from Boston.
From Elizabeth Connor; received 17 Apr.; notation: "petn. W."

From Richard Brent, 19 Apr.; received 22 Apr. from Dumfries, Virginia; notation: "Preslie Mitchell for navy. N."
From Dabney Carr, 20 Apr.; received 30 Apr. from Charlottesville.
To David Higginbotham, 21 Apr.
To Gabriel Lilly, 21 Apr.
From John Breckinridge, 24 Apr.; received 18 May from Lexington, Kentucky; notation: "Russel & Grundy Comr."
From Thomas McKean, 24 Apr.; received 26 Apr. from Philadelphia; notation: "Andrew Pettit Director of mint."
From Gabriel Lilly, 26 Apr.; received 30 Apr. from Monticello.
From John Perry, 27 Apr.; received 30 Apr. from Shadwell.
From Philippe Reibelt, 29 Apr.; received 30 Apr.
From Francis Forster, 1 May; received 1 May from Washington; notation: "emploimt in Navy."
To James Dinsmore, 2 May.
To Thomas Newton, 2 May.
From James Dinsmore, 3 May; received 7 May from Monticello.
From Michael Hope, 4 May; received 7 May.
From John Kelly, 4 May; received 7 May from Charlottesville.
To Gabriel Lilly, 4 May; notation: "265."
From Samuel L. Mitchill, 4 May; received 6 May from New York; notation: "Baron de Carrondeffer to explore."
From John Speer, 4 May; received 7 May from Charlottesville.
To James Dinsmore, 5 May.
From "Beatty et al.," 8 May; received 15 Aug. from Georgetown; notation: "Williams Waters, to be justice."
From John Mackall Gantt, 8 May; received 8 May from Bladensburg, Maryland.
From George Hay, 8 May; received 12 May from Richmond.
To Keller & Forman, 8 May.
To George Kelly, 8 May.
To John Speer, 8 May.
From William Walton, Jr., 8 May; received 31 May from Santo Domingo; notation: "S."
From John Wayles Eppes, 9 May; received 15 May from Bermuda Hundred, Virginia.
To James Dinsmore, 10 May.
To Gabriel Lilly, 10 May; notation: "175. D."
To William Hazard, 11 May; notation: "231.09 for Cathalan."
From Mary McDonald, 11 May; received 17 May from Winchester, Virginia.
From Thomas Mann Randolph, 11 May; received 14 May from Edgehill.
To Thomas Lomax, 13 May.
From Jones & Howell, 14 May; received 16 May from Philadelphia; notation: "mill irons. stoves. 125.74."
From George E. Clymer, 15 May; received 18 May from Philadelphia; notation: "S."
From John Mackall Gantt, 15 May; received 15 May from Bladensburg, Maryland.
From "Pittcarr & others"; received 16 May; notation: "on board the Carysfort St. Vincent. S."

From "Young & others"; received 16 May; notation: "on board the Carysfort St. Vincent. S."
From William Hazard, 17 May; received 26 May from Stonington, Connecticut.
From David Higginbotham, 17 May; received 21 May from Milton.
From John Kelly, 17 May; received 21 May from Charlottesville.
From Gabriel Lilly, 17 May; received 21 May from Monticello.
From Samuel Huntington, 18 May; received 15 June from Cleveland, Ohio; notation: "Geo. Tod. judge Michigan."
From John Perry, 18 May; received 21 May from Shadwell.
From Christopher Ellery, 20 May; received 24 May from Providence, Rhode Island.
From Robert Kinnan, 22 May; received 26 May from Petersburg, Virginia.
To Gabriel Lilly, 22 May.
From David Higginbotham, 23 May; received 28 May from Milton.
From Gabriel Lilly, 23 May; received 28 May from Monticello.
To Gabriel Lilly, 24 May.
From "Anonymous [Truxton]," 25 May; received 27 May from Philadelphia; notation: "Tripoline war."
To Burgess Griffin, 27 May.
From Jones & Howell, 28 May; received 31 May from Philadelphia; notation: "253.33."
From Joseph Wheaton, 28 May; received 27 June from Coweta.
To James Dinsmore, 29 May.
From Hezekiah Johnson, Jr., 30 May; received 20 July from Fort Massac.
From Gabriel Lilly, 30 May; received 4 June from Monticello.
From James Dinsmore, 1 June; received 4 June from Monticello.
To Gabriel Lilly, 1 June.
From Elias Boudinot, 3 June; received 5 June from Philadelphia; notation: "resigns Directr Mint."
From the Walleboght and Brooklyn Toll-Bridge Company, 4 June; received 8 June from Brooklyn.
To George Divers, 5 June.
To David Higginbotham, 6 June; notation: "185."
To Michael Hope, 6 June.
From John Hopkins et al., 6 June; received 2 Aug.; notation: "on bd. Mosambique" and "S."
To Keller & Forman, 6 June; notation: "230. D."
To John Kelly, 6 June; notation: "100. D."
To Gabriel Lilly, 6 June; notation: "1465. D."
From John Joseph Rey, 6 June; received 7 June from Georgetown.
From "Butler & others. (impressd.)," 7 June; received 5 Aug. from Port Royal, Jamaica; notation: "S."
To James Dinsmore, 7 June.
From James Gray, 7 June; received 26 Oct. from Plymouth; notation: "2 lres." and "S."
From J. Athanasius Le Blanc, 7 June; received 10 June from New York.
From John Page, 7 June; received 11 June from Richmond.
From William Stewart, 7 June; received 11 June from Monticello.
From Martha Jefferson Randolph, 8 June; received 11 June from Edgehill.

From David Higginbotham, 10 June; received 12 June from Milton.
From Keller & Forman, 10 June; received 11 June from Baltimore.
From John Strode, 10 June; received 15 June from Culpeper.
From John Taggart, 10 June; received 12 June from Philadelphia.
To John Page, 12 June.
To Charles Smith, 14 June.
From Thomas Truxtun, 14 June; received 15 June from Philadelphia; notation: "N."
To William Wardlaw, 14 June.
From Polly Logwood, 15 June; received 19 June.
From William Stewart, 15 June; received 17 June from Monticello.
From John H. Craven, 16 June; received 25 June from Monticello.
From Wilson Cary Nicholas, 17 June; received 25 June from Warren, Virginia.
From Marien Lamar, 18 June; received 15 Feb. 1806 from Madeira; joined by a brace in SJL with Asher Robbins to TJ, 13 Feb. 1806, and notation: "Wm. Riggs Consul Terceire."
From David Rumsey, 18 June; received 28 June from Ballston, New York; notation: "S."
To Levi Lincoln, 19 June.
From Lewis Deblois, 21 June; received 22 June from Alexandria.
From James Dinsmore, 22 June; received 25 June from Monticello.
From Albert Gallatin, 22 June; received 22 June.
From John Page, 23 June; received 27 June from Richmond.
To Reuben Lewis, 24 June.
From Gabriel Lilly, 25 June; received 2 July.
To John H. Craven, 26 June.
To John Strode, 27 June.
To Gabriel Lilly, 28 June.
From Abraham McKoy, 29 June; received 16 Aug. from New Orleans; notation: "N."
From James Graham, June; received 23 July from Lynchburg.
From John H. Craven, 4 July; received 20 July from Monticello.
From David Redick, 4 July; received 13 July from Washington, Pennsylvania; notation: "P.M.G."

Appendix V

Financial Documents

EDITORIAL NOTE

This appendix briefly describes, in chronological order, the orders and invoices pertaining to Jefferson's finances during the period covered by this volume that are not printed in full or accounted for elsewhere in this volume. The *Memorandum Books* are cited when they are relevant to a specific document and provide additional information.

Receipt for payment of $15 by Joseph Dougherty to Charles McLaughlin for TJ's dancing assembly subscription of December 1804, 2 May (MS in MHi; in McLaughlin's hand and signed by him; endorsed by TJ: "Mc. laughlin C. pd May 5. 05"). See MB, 2:1153.

Receipt for payment of $2.25 by Joseph Dougherty to Alexander Cochrane for "one pair of Boot,s Hooks including sundry Instruments," 4 May (MS in DLC; in Cochrane's hand and signed by him; endorsed by TJ: "Cochrane Alexr."). See MB, 2:1153.

INDEX

A comprehensive index of Volumes 1-20 of the
First Series has been issued as Volume 21.
Each subsequent volume has its own index,
as does each volume or set of volumes
in the Second Series.

THE PAPERS OF THOMAS JEFFERSON are composed in Monticello, a font based on the "Pica No. 1" created in the early 1800s by Binny & Ronaldson, the first successful typefounding company in America. The face is considered historically appropriate for The Papers of Thomas Jefferson because it was used extensively in American printing during the last quarter-century of Jefferson's life, and because Jefferson himself expressed cordial approval of Binny & Ronaldson types. It was revived and rechristened Monticello in the late 1940s by the Mergenthaler Linotype Company, under the direction of C. H. Griffith and in close consultation with P. J. Conkwright, specifically for the publication of the Jefferson Papers. The font suffered some losses in its first translation to digital format in the 1980s to accommodate computerized typesetting. Matthew Carter's reinterpretation in 2002 restores the spirit and style of Binny & Ronaldson's original design of two centuries earlier.

✧